WE THE

PRESIDENTS

How American Presidents Shaped the Last Century

Ronald Gruner

Cover and Interior: Chase Waterman/Greenleaf
White House Watercolor: Rostam Nour/NYart.com
Presidential Photographs: Library of Congress
Author Photograph: Hilda Champion

Published by libratum.press
Naples, Florida

Hardcover ISBN: 978-1-7378231-2-4
Softcover ISBN: 978-1-7378231-0-0
eBook ISBN: 978-1-7378231-1-7
Library of Congress Control Number: 2021922690

Second Edition: May 2022

Publisher's Cataloging-In-Publication Data

(Prepared by The Donohue Group, Inc.)

Names: Gruner, Ronald (Ronald H.), author.

Title: We the presidents : how American presidents shaped the last century / Ronald Gruner.

Description: First edition. | Naples, Florida : libratum.press, 2022. | Include bibliographical references and index.

Identifiers: ISBN 9781737823124 (hardcover) | ISBN 9781737823100 (softcover) | ISBN 9781737823117 (ebook)

Subjects: LCSH: Presidents--United States--History--20th century. | Presidents--United States--History--21st century. | United States--Politics and government--20th century. | United States--Politics and government--21st century. | Social problems--United States--History--20th century. | Social problems--United States--History--21st century.

Classification: LCC E176.1 .G78 2022 (print) | LCC E176.1 (ebook) | DDC 973.099--dc23

For
Emersyn, Lillian, Carter

Contents

Introduction

———— ⋆ ————

I never expected to write a presidential history. For nearly fifty years my life had been consumed by high-technology starting as a computer engineer in 1969 and ending as the CEO of a data analytics company in 2015. In between, I co-founded and served as the CEO of two pioneering technology firms in high-performance computing and the Internet. As a technologist, I needed to look forward, not backward as historians must. I had little time or interest for politics. Except for one New Hampshire town hall meeting in 1976 where Ronald Reagan spoke and a brief meet-and-greet for Barack Obama more than thirty years later, I had never attended a political event. Although I voted in every presidential election since 1968, "I voted for the man and not the party"—a sentiment heard more often in the past than today.

But my interest in political history and particularly, presidential history, was piqued in 2015, the year I retired. It was a period when American politics was transitioning from merely polarized to openly tribal. America had become deeply divided over economic, cultural, and ideological issues. Sadly, many Americans seemed to be shifting their loyalties from their country to their political party. The idea that there were two Americas, one Blue and one Red, had become, if not yet entrenched, a common theme. On the Blue side were socialists who hated America, and on the Red side, deplorables who clung to their guns and religion.

How had so many Americans come to despise each other? I had grown up and attended school in Oklahoma, a deeply Red State, and then followed my career to Massachusetts, one of the bluest of the Blue States, where I lived and worked for forty years. Great universities and hospitals largely defined Boston while oil, cattle, and farming dominated Ponca City, my birthplace. Sure, they were vastly different, but nothing, then or now, to justify the antipathy so many today feel against their fellow Americans. So, what was cleaving America apart?

President George Washington struggled with that question over 200 years ago. Two political parties had already emerged early in his presidency: Treasury Secretary Alexander Hamilton's Federalist Party, which supported a strong federal government, and Secretary of State Thomas Jefferson's Republican Party, which supported states' rights. The two men, and their embryonic parties, were bitterly divided. Distressed by the division, Washington, in nearly identical letters to Hamilton and Jefferson, pleaded:

> How unfortunate, and how much is it to be regretted. . .that whilst we are encompassed on all sides with avowed enemies and insidious friends, that internal dissentions should be harrowing and tearing our vitals.[1]

Washington's appeals for moderation were unsuccessful. Political parties had firmly established themselves as part of the political fabric of America. Washington reluctantly accepted their emergence and in his 1796 Farewell Address took care to warn future Americans of their destructive nature:

> The common and continual mischiefs of the spirit of [political parties] are sufficient to make it the interest and duty of a wise people to discourage and restrain it. . . . It agitates the community with ill-founded jealousies and false alarms; kindles the animosity of one part against another; foments occasionally riot and insurrection.[2]

President Washington could not have been more prescient. America in 2015 had become agitated by false claims, consumed by animosity, even hatred, of political opponents, and soon would be threatened by riots and insurrection.

The animosity between Hamilton and Jefferson, admittedly, was as much personal as political. But today, politics have metastasized far beyond two strong-willed individuals. Politics has become a multibillion-dollar industry composed of partisan news organizations, firebrand media pundits, subversive Internet sites, avaricious political action committees, and sponsored think tanks and universities.

It is the *American Political Industry* that has divided America. Like any profit-driven industry, its constituents have partitioned America into target markets that are then assiduously cultivated. As a result, much of the nation's news media, driven by profits and subdivided by political ideology, has become overtly politicized, forcing Americans to select their news sources based on their political views. But don't blame the viewer. It's human nature that most people are more comfortable with information that confirms, rather than challenges, their existing point of view. The unfortunate result is that two Americans could watch Fox News and MSNBC, for example, and form completely different judgments regarding the national news that day; accepting their preferred source as unadulterated truth and rejecting the other as biased misrepresentations. Then after the evening news, political commentators, rather than broaden perspectives, hammer home their own narrow ideological worldview. Contributing to this sorry mix are assorted foreign actors ranging from common grifters to the Russian Internet Research Agency spreading their own disinformation and dissension across America.

This politicization extends beyond the media into think tanks and universities where unabashed experts are paid to promote the economic and political ideology of their sponsors. Where once Americans had a reasonably unified view of their shared history, today's history is filtered through differing political lenses.

But no two Presidents have been more villainized, and more extolled, than Barack Obama and Donald Trump. So, not coincidentally, it was in 2017, the year the American Presidency transitioned from Obama to Trump, that I decided to write this book. It was also a notable year for me personally, that of my seventieth birthday, and a year of reflection.

Fortunately, researching and writing a book today, even on a complex subject, is not as difficult as might be expected. I found that particularly true writing a presidential history. Unlike even a few years ago, the historical archives held by presidential libraries, the White House, Department of State, and scores of other governmental agencies are online, and easily searchable. Research that formerly took days and often numerous trips to a distant library, today can be conducted comfortably in a few hours online. And certainly, my technical career, consumed with assembling and objectively interpreting facts, helped.

I've taken an unusual approach in writing a presidential history. *We the Presidents* is completely devoid of politics. Never discussed are the political battles and intrigue that occupy many presidential biographies. Nor will you find, except in a few quotations, the words *Democrat* or *Republican, liberal* or *conservative, left or right*. For many Americans, these labels have become divisive, even pejorative. Their mere mention tends to bias the discussion.

Another difference is that the book is more quantitative than most presidential biographies. The key criterion of a successful presidency is not political battles won, but rather the wellbeing and prosperity of ordinary citizens. For most Americans, that's closely related to their pocketbooks. So, throughout this book are discussions covering economic growth, personal income and income inequality, taxation, and other related topics. You'll also find numerous digressions discussing how disparate events from Shay's Rebellion in 1786 to the Financial Panic of 1907 to the Soviet invasion of Afghanistan in 1979 have altered history and shaped America in the process. Finally, with over 1,600 indexed references, I have striven to present verifiable facts rather than opinion, and then respected the reader to form their own judgments.

Of course, there are many outstanding presidential biographies written by professional historians, more than a few of which are Pulitzer Prize winners. This book, of course, does not approach their well-crafted work. But most professional biographies focus, in depth, on a single President over a relatively small span of time, typically a few years enveloping the President's lifetime. Rather, my contribution, if any, is that I've concentrated on how American Presidents over the last one-hundred years, from Warren G. Harding to Donald Trump, have shaped today's issues: immigration, healthcare, civil rights, tax and fiscal policies, income distribution, globalization, and the proper role of democratic government. Every generation, including ours, tends to believe they live in unique times. But these issues all had their roots in earlier presidencies, their branches extending into succeeding presidencies and, ultimately, to today.

Had President Warren G. Harding, for example, not selected Andrew Mellon as Treasury Secretary, Mellon likely would not have written his 1924 book, *Taxation: The People's Business*. A book that motivated Ronald Reagan's economic policies and today forms the basis of modern supply-side economics. Had President Jimmy Carter not put the nation on a path of energy conservation, American would not have reached energy independence forty years later. Had President Bill Clinton discouraged, rather than encouraged, NATO's expansion into Eastern Europe after the collapse of the Soviet Union, Russia today might be a close ally, as Germany and Japan are, rather than an adversary.

It's the intertwined threads of history, rippling upward to today, that have woven the intricate tableau that is America. This book tells a small part of that story.

Ronald Gruner
October 1, 2021

Prologue

———————✴———————

The years leading up to the Presidency of Warren G. Harding in 1921 were an era of political and social reform. A progressive period in which reformers sought to curtail unfair and corrupt business practices, provide protections for workers and consumers, and expand civil rights. It was also a period during which traditional white, Anglo-Saxon Americans renewed their resistance to the nation's growing racial diversity.

The Progressive Era had its roots after the Civil War with the rise of a new class of American entrepreneurs: men like Andrew Carnegie, John D. Rockefeller, Cornelius Vanderbilt, and J.P. Morgan. These ambitious and visionary business leaders built America's oil and steel industries, railroads and major banks. Carnegie's steel companies smelted the steel to build towering skyscrapers and lay rails across America; Rockefeller's Standard Oil refined kerosene to light the nation and later gasoline to power millions of automobiles; Vanderbilt's railroads interconnected the nation, from its great cities to its remote villages; Morgan's Wall Street empire financed much of America's expansion.

In less than half a century, laissez-faire capitalism had propelled the U.S. economy past every European country and made its adherents fabulously rich. But American workers were languishing. Working ten-hour days, six days a week, their average pay, adjusted for inflation, had stagnated from 1890 through 1920.[1] With labor so cheap, owners valued their workers little more than the machinery in their factories, mines, and mills. Working conditions were often horrendous, and dangerous. Not surprisingly, it was a period of great labor unrest.

In 1892, workers at Andrew Carnegie's Homestead, Pennsylvania steel mill went on strike protesting working conditions. Carnegie responded by calling in 300 Pinkerton agents. Sixteen men died in the ensuing confrontation. The violent Homestead Strike hardened the positions of both owners and workers. Over the next thirty years, armed battles between labor and management grew more frequent and more violent, culminating with the Battle of Blair Mountain in August 1921, five months after President Harding took office. The battle, the largest armed insurrection since the Civil War, pitted 10,000 West Virginia coal miners against 3,000 lawmen and strike-breakers. As many as one hundred men died in the fighting.

The poor working conditions in steel mills and mines weren't unique. On March 25, 1911, one of the nation's most tragic industrial disasters struck the Triangle Shirtwaist Factory in New York City. (A shirtwaist was a popular woman's dress with a seam at the waist and a bodice incorporating a collar and buttons similar to a man's shirt.) The factory was located on the upper floors of the ten-story Asch Building in Greenwich Village. Five-hundred workers, largely young immigrant women, were crowded together cutting and sewing garments. With no sprinkler system and surrounded by flammable cloth scraps, their workplace was a firetrap. The conflagration killed 146 workers, sixty-two of whom chose to jump to their deaths.

It wasn't just workers who were affected by lax and unsafe working conditions. Unwitting consumers were also victims. In 1906 Upton Sinclair published *The Jungle* describing the appalling meat packing plants in the Chicago stockyards:

> The meat would be shoveled into carts, and the man who did the shoveling would not trouble to lift out a rat even when he saw one—there were things that went into the sausage in comparison with which a poisoned rat was a tidbit. There was no place for the men to wash their hands before they ate their dinner, and so they made a practice of washing them in the water that was to be ladled into the sausage... cartload after cartload of it would be taken up and

dumped into the hoppers with fresh meat and sent out to the public's breakfast.[2]

Sinclair's graphic descriptions of the packing plants shocked Americans and caused many, no doubt, to push their breakfast sausage aside. Other writers, known as muck-rakers, exposed child labor, fraudulent medicines, price-fixing, rampant pollution, political corruption, and other abuses.

In 1901, Vice-President Teddy Roosevelt became President after President William McKinley was assassinated by an unemployed steel worker. For the next twelve years, Roosevelt and his hand-picked successor, President William Howard Taft, pursued a progressive agenda dismembering monopolies and regulating business practices.

In 1904 the Supreme Court ordered the break-up of the Northern Securities Company, a railroad trust which controlled three major railroads. In 1906 Congress passed the Pure Food and Drug Act to assure products met minimal purity and safety standards. In 1911 the Supreme Court found Standard Oil of New Jersey guilty of monopolizing the petroleum industry and ordered its break-up. That same year the Court ordered the American Tobacco Company to be split into four competing tobacco companies. In 1914 the Clayton Antitrust Act prohibited anticompetitive mergers, predatory pricing, while also legalizing lawsuits against companies and upholding the rights of labor to organize.

In 1913, Congress established the Federal Reserve as the nation's central bank. Six years earlier, the nation's banking system had nearly collapsed during the Panic of 1907. It would have, except for the private efforts by J.P. Morgan and his wealthy friends who provided hundreds of millions in personal funds to bail-out banks, the stock exchange, and even New York City.

The reforms reached even to the American Constitution; four Constitutional amendments were passed during the Progressive Era. To finance a growing federal government, the 16th Amendment established a federal income tax. The 17th Amendment replaced the legislative appointment of U.S. senators with public elections. The 18th Amendment prohibited the sale of alcoholic beverages (but not their consumption). The 19th Amendment gave women the right to vote.

The Progressive Era marked the beginning of today's activist federal government. As America transitioned from an agrarian to an industrial society, Americans became increasingly dependent on others for their food, clothing, housing, and livelihood. Progressive Era reforms helped assure American workers and consumers shared in America's growing prosperity—that they were given a "Square Deal," as President Teddy Roosevelt labeled his progressive agenda. Roosevelt's progressive Square Deal would be followed thirty years later by President Franklin Roosevelt's "New Deal" and then twenty years after that by President Harry Truman's "Fair Deal."

Understandably, America's oligarchs at the time weren't particularly pleased with Teddy Roosevelt's progressive politics. As the former President Teddy Roosevelt was leaving for an African safari, financier J.P. Morgan famously quipped: "America expects that every lion will do its duty."[3]

The years overlapping the Progressive Era had a dark side, the strong resurgence of what today is known as White Supremacy.

In 1902, Woodrow Wilson, then a professor at Princeton University, published his monumental *A History of the American People*. Southern white men, Wilson wrote, suffered under "the intolerable burden of governments sustained by the votes of ignorant negroes" and pronounced the Ku Klux Klan "an Invisible Empire of the South, bound together in loose organization to protect the southern country from some of the ugliest hazards of a time of revolution."[4]

A decade later, Wilson, now the nation's twenty-eighth President, was disturbed to find the federal government largely integrated. In 1913 the government was one of the few American institutions providing advancement opportunities for African-Americans. Wilson changed that. Shortly after taking office, Wilson ordered the segregation of federal facilities, basing his order on the need to reduce racial tensions. When Black journalist William Monroe Trotter, during an Oval Office meeting, argued that Black and white federal workers had worked together peacefully for fifty years, Wilson had Trotter escorted from the White House.

But it was a movie that most influenced America's race relations for a generation or more. The movie, *The Birth of a Nation*, was based on *The*

Clansman: a Historical Romance of the Ku Klux Klan, a book written by one of Wilson's former classmates. The 1915 film depicts two families, one Northern and one Southern, in the years surrounding the Civil War. Although a huge commercial success, the film is profoundly racist in its portrayal of African Americans "as brutish, lazy, morally degenerate, and dangerous."[5] The film helped inspire the rebirth of the Ku Klux Klan, a secretive racist organization founded in1865 by Confederate veterans but had gone dormant after a Supreme Court decision declared the Klan un-constitutional in 1882.

Racial discrimination, though, had spread beyond discrimination only against African-Americans. In 1906, San Francisco ordered all Asian children to be placed in separate, segregated schools. President Teddy Roosevelt persuaded the city's school board to rescind the order. In return, Roosevelt asked Japan to sign the "Gentlemen's Agreement" in which Japan promised to deny passports to its citizens wishing to work in the United States. A sullen Japan complied.

Immigrants from Southern and Eastern Europe, largely Catholics and Jews, were also declared a threat to American homogeneity. In 1911, a Congressional commission headed by Senator William P. Dillingham concluded, "The heavy southern and eastern European immigration of recent years had posed a serious danger to American society by bringing in large numbers of people who were dramatically different from the older stock of European Americans and who could not be assimilated."[6] The commission's conclusions contributed to the Immigration Act of 1917 which, among other restrictive provisions, created a "Barred Zone" from the Middle East to Southeast Asia from which no immigrants were allowed to enter.

In August 1914 Europe erupted into war after the assassination of Archduke Franz Ferdinand, the presumptive heir to the Austro-Hungarian throne. President Wilson was determined that the United States stay out of the distant European conflict.

On May 7, 1915, a German submarine sank the RMS *Lusitania,* killing 1,195 people including 128 Americans. Three months later, a German sub sank the SS *Arabic,* a British ocean liner bound for the United States.

Wilson still resisted calls for the United States to enter the war. In January 1917, British intelligence decoded an incredible telegram sent by German Foreign Minister Arthur Zimmerman to the German Ambassador in Mexico. The telegram proposed an alliance between Germany and Mexico, suggesting that the two countries "make war together, make peace together," while also offering "generous financial support and an understanding on our part that Mexico is to reconquer the lost territory in Texas, New Mexico, and Arizona."[7] Yet Wilson refused to declare war on Germany.

It was only after Germany instituted unlimited submarine warfare across the Atlantic Ocean that the United States, on April 6, 1917, declared war on Germany. Wilson promised the war would be "a war to end all wars" and would "make the world safe for democracy."[8] During the short eighteen months that America fought in Europe, 117,000 American soldiers died in brutal trench warfare.

In early 1918, Wilson presented his Fourteen Points plan to assure a peaceful transition after the war. One of his points led to the establishment of the League of Nations, "a general association of nations... to mediate international disputes."[9] But Americans wanted no involvement in a postwar Europe. The United States had resisted entering the European war until continuing to do so became impossible. Now, Britain and France, rather than building a lasting peace, demanded punitive concessions from a defeated and humiliated Germany, thus sowing the seeds for the Second World War.

Then, as the war was ending, a virulent new strain of influenza, the Spanish Flu, began to indiscriminately kill people at rates far higher than the war. Lacking vaccines and antibiotics, by 1920, an estimated fifty million people had died throughout the world, including 675,000 Americans.

Throughout the pandemic, health officials struggled to convince the public to practice good hygiene, limit social gatherings, and wear face masks. The public revolted over seemingly arbitrary public-gathering bans where theaters might be open, but churches closed. In much of America, though, face masks gained considerable popularity as an emblem of public spiritedness. Still, many resisted the masks even within the public health community. One notable critic was the Detroit health commissioner, Dr.

J.W. Inches, who declared: "These masks are worthless. . .a mosquito could jump through them."[10] A century later, during the 2020 COVID-19 pandemic, similar issues would divide Americans.

By summer 1919 the pandemic had run its course. In just two years, the nation had lost nearly 800,000 Americans to the First World War and Spanish Flu; nearly double the lives that would be lost during the forthcoming Second World War.

In 1920 Ohio Senator Warren G. Harding ran for President. Harding sensed the weariness wrought by the political activism of the Progressive Era and the suffering inflicted by the First World War and Spanish Flu. "America's present need," Harding declared, "is not heroics, but healing; not nostrums, but normalcy; not revolution, but restoration."[11]

Warren G. Harding

———————★———————

March 4, 1921 – August 2, 1923

> I can say to you people of the South, both white and Black, that the time
> has passed when you are entitled to assume that the problem of races is
> peculiarly and particularly your problem... Whether you like it or not,
> our democracy is a lie unless you stand for that equality.[1]

Warren G. Harding was lucky. When creditors took over the Marion, Ohio newspaper he owned, his father was sufficiently wealthy, and generous, to bail him out. A few years later, Harding married Florence Kling. Kling had divorced her first husband, a heavy drinker, after he had attempted to rob a train in 1885. Florence was as driven as Warren was easy-going. Intent on becoming a concert pianist, she practiced seven hours a day for years. Fortunately, as his future heir, her successful father had also trained her in business. Shrewd, smart, and focused, Florence quickly took control of her husband's floundering newspaper and turned it into the success that would allow Harding to pursue his political ambitions. Harding affectionately called her "the Duchess," and she called him "Sonny."[2]

Harding's luckiest break came one day in 1899 when he happened to need a shoeshine. Sitting next to him on the shoeshine stand was Harry Daugherty, a young Ohio lawyer who was already building a reputation as a political operator. Harding's distinguished bearing, good looks, and affability impressed Daugherty. Mark Sullivan, a respected journalist and political columnist, later wrote:

Harding was worth looking at. . . . His head, features, shoulders and torso had a size that attracted attention; their proportions to each other made an effect which in any male at any place would justify more than the term handsome. . . . His suppleness, combined with his bigness of frame, and his large, wide-set rather glowing eyes, heavy black hair, and markedly bronze complexion gave him some of the handsomeness of an Indian. . . . His voice was noticeably resonant, masculine, warm. . . . His courtesy as he surrendered his seat to the other customer suggested genuine friendliness toward all mankind.[3]

As Harding stepped down and cordially tipped the bootblack, Daugherty had a life-altering insight. Harding had the genuine affability, dignified bearing, and exceptionally good looks that could be molded into a President. At twenty-nine, Daugherty already knew he would never rise to high political office on his own merits; his real calling was as a king-maker. On that day, Daugherty found his future king. For the next twenty years, Daugherty would help propel Harding's political career from small-town newspaper publisher to President of the United States.

With Florence managing the newspaper, Harding turned to politics. Likable and non-controversial, Harding progressed rapidly, beginning with his election to the Ohio Senate in 1900, then to lieutenant governor, and finally to the U.S. Senate representing Ohio. By 1920, Harding, with Harry Daugherty's shrewd help, was running a longshot bid for President. These were the days, before party primaries, when political party bosses determined presidential candidates. After a night-long session in a smoke-filled room at Chicago's Blackstone Hotel, Daugherty convinced party bosses to support Harding as the party's compromise presidential candidate along with Massachusetts Governor Calvin Coolidge as Vice President.

Harding knew he would never win the presidency based on his policy insights. "An army of pompous phrases moving across the landscape in search of an idea," is how one pundit described Harding's speeches.[4] After twenty years in politics, the best praise *The New York Times* could muster was that Harding was "a very respectable Ohio politician of the second class," calling his Senate record "faint and colorless."[5]

Harding campaigned on an "America First" platform, later adopted by the Ku Klux Klan in the nineteen-twenties, followed by the isolationist America First Party in 1940 and Donald Trump in 2016.   OHIO HISTORY COLLECTION

Rather than campaign nationally, Harding borrowed William McKinley's campaign strategy and conducted a front porch campaign from his Marion, Ohio home. McKinley had won the 1896 presidential election after more than one million supporters traveled to McKinley's home to hear his carefully crafted speeches. By luck, Harding's front porch resembled McKinley's, with an expansive portico that served as a stage complemented by a large American flag fluttering in the front yard.

Harding campaigned on two platforms: "A Return to Normalcy" and "America First." Both departed from the tradition of campaigns based either on the character of the candidate, as in Abraham Lincoln's "Honest Old Abe," or on a specific policy initiative, such as Teddy Roosevelt's "A Square Deal for All."[6]

Harding's campaign slogans were well-timed. Americans were dispirited and exhausted. In the preceding three years, 117,000 American soldiers had died in the First World War, the Spanish Flu had killed 675,000 Americans, inflation had ballooned to 20 percent, unemployment was climbing towards 10 percent,[7] and hundreds of thousands of foreign refugees had flooded into the country. Harding attributed many of these problems to America's drift away from what he called *Americanism*. "Call it the selfishness of nationality if you will," Harding declared in a 1920 speech, "I think it's an inspiration to patriotic devotion to safeguard America first, to stabilize America first, to prosper America first, to think of America first, to exalt America first, to live for and revere America first. . . . In the spirit of the Republic, we proclaim Americanism and acclaim America."[8]

Decades later, Ronald Reagan merged Harding's nostalgia and Americanism into his 1980 campaign slogan, "Let's Make America Great Again." Thirty-six years after Reagan, Donald Trump successfully tapped into the festering resentment many Americans felt after being left behind economically when he adopted Reagan's slogan as simply, "Make America Great Again."[9]

Harding seldom discussed specifics beyond such impenetrable declarations as, "I would like the government to do all it can to mitigate, then, in understanding, in mutuality of interest, in concern for the common good, our tasks will be solved."[10] Unable to articulate a substantive platform, he told confidants, "I don't know much about Americanism, but it's a damn good word with which to carry an election."[11]

Short on substance, Harding's campaign compensated with showmanship. His campaign was the first to make use of celebrity endorsements when Al Jolson and seventy fellow performers visited Marion. Marching down the streets of Marion at the head of a brass band, Jolson and his fellow actors bellowed: "A man who'll make the White House shine out like a lighthouse. Warren Harding, you're the man for us!"

Caught up in the adulation, Harding gave a speech comparing himself to Shakespeare's Henry V rallying his troops in his "We Band of Brothers" speech before the Battle of Agincourt.[12] Harding's strong delivery "was like a blacksmith bringing down a hammer on an egg,"[13] the noted journalist H.L. Mencken observed. The crowd loved it.

After eight years of Woodrow Wilson, the cerebral former Princeton academic, voters liked Harding's down-to-earth style and awarded him 60 percent of the popular vote, outpacing his opponent James Cox by twenty-six points. The handsome and affable Harding was helped by women voters who three months earlier had attained the right to vote through the 19th Amendment.

Harding's landslide win remains the largest popular margin ever amassed by a President since the beginning of the modern two-party system in 1824. Lucky as always, Election Day was Harding's fifty-fifth birthday.[14]

A Productive First Year

President Harding's first year in office surprised his critics. It proved particularly productive with the passing of six major legislative acts, rivaling the legislative records of many of his predecessors.

To slow the influx of war refugees from Eastern and Southern Europe, Harding signed the Emergency Quota Act in May 1921, which established the first numerical limits on foreign immigration. The Act limited annual immigration from countries to three percent of that nationality's resident population in the United States based on the index year of 1910. The limits reduced immigration from countries that would, it was believed, dilute America's racial homogeneity.

During the early part of the twentieth century, for many Americans the concept of racial homogeneity wasn't controversial. America's discrimination against certain nationalities formally began in 1875 with the Page Act, which excluded Chinese women from immigration. By 1892, all Chinese laborers were banned and those already resident in the United States were required to carry identification attesting to their legal entry into the country, the precursor to today's Green Card. In 1907, President Teddy Roosevelt reached a "Gentlemen's Agreement" with Japan that voluntarily limited the immigration of Japanese laborers in return for the United States allowing Japanese students to attend American public schools. That same year, Roosevelt initiated a Congressional Commission headed by Senator Paul Dillingham to study the impact of immigration. In 1911, after three years of study, the Commission concluded that immigration from "Southern and Eastern Europe poses a grave threat to American culture and society and that Congress should take measures to restrict immigration."[15]

Decades earlier, the *Know Nothing Party* had promoted a platform to limit Catholic and Jewish emigration from Eastern and Southern Europe during the eighteen-fifties. The party claimed that the Pope intended to subjugate the United States by flooding the country with Catholics controlled by their bishops.[16] In 1887, the *American Protective Association* was formed with similar objectives, claiming the Catholic Church controlled Grover Cleveland and William McKinley.[17] Although both movements quickly failed due to weak leadership, their religious biases echoed well into the twentieth century. In 1890, the Immigration Restriction League lobbied Congress to restrict immigration. Prescott Hall, the League's co-founder, asked whether the United States, historically "peopled by British, German and Scandinavian stock, historically free, energetic, progressive," should allow itself to be overrun by "Slav, Latin and Asiatic races historically down-trodden, atavistic and stagnant?"[18]

Harding's 1921 Act was a precursor to the overtly racist National Origins Act of 1924 under President Coolidge. The 1924 act would set the tone for U.S. immigration policies over the next four decades,[19] a period during which America's foreign-born population would decline from 13.2 percent in 1920 to 4.7 percent in 1970.[20]

In June 1921, Harding signed the Budget and Accounting Act, which gave the President overall responsibility for the federal budget and consolidated overlapping federal budget functions into the Bureau of the Budget (later renamed the Office of Management and Budget in 1971). The Act allowed Congress to manage federal spending with a single, consolidated budget rather than deal with individual, often conflicting, budgets from multiple federal agencies.[21]

In August, Harding signed the Sweet Bill. The bill established the Veterans Bureau to provide medical services for war veterans through a specialized medical system dedicated to veteran care. The Bureau consolidated three previous veterans' agencies and formed the basis for today's U.S. Department of Veterans Affairs.[22]

In November, Secretary of State Charles Evans Hughes presided over the Washington Naval Conference during which the United States, Belgium, China, France, Italy, Japan, the Netherlands, Portugal and the United Kingdom, seeking to avoid another arms race like the one that preceded the First World War, agreed to a major reduction in warships. "Hughes sank in thirty-five minutes more ships," one journalist wrote, "than all of the admirals of the world have sunk in a cycle of centuries."[23]

Also, in November, Harding signed the first major federal social program, the Sheppard-Towner Maternity Act. The Act funded nearly 3,000 medical centers in which doctors treated pregnant women and their children. Many of the centers were in rural areas which provided women and children access to health care for the first time in their lives. Although the Act expired after eight years, it was a precursor to the social programs established during Roosevelt's New Deal.

Two days before Christmas, Harding defied public opinion when he commuted the prison sentence of Eugene V. Debs. "He is [in jail] where he belongs. He should stay there," *The New York Times* opined.[24] A fiery socialist labor leader, Debs was jailed for speaking out against America's entry into the First World War. "The master class has always declared the wars; the subject class has always fought the battles. . ." Debs thundered in a June 16, 1918 speech. "They have always taught and trained you to believe it to be your patriotic duty to go to war and to have yourselves slaughtered at their command. . . . No war by any nation in any age has ever been declared by the people."[25]

Debs was convicted under the Espionage and Sedition Acts, passed in 1917 and 1918, which made it a federal offense to use language "disloyal, profane, scurrilous, or abusive... about the form of government of the United States."[26] Although the Sedition Act was repealed in 1920, the Espionage Act remains in force. The Act was used in the nineteen-forties and fifties to prosecute alleged communists and, more recently, for prosecuting individuals alleged to have leaked classified information, including

Pentagon Papers leaker Daniel Ellsberg, WikiLeaks contributor Chelsea Manning, and NSA whistleblower Edward Snowden.[27]

Unlike today's politicians, Harding took little credit for the legislation passed during his presidency. A sincere Harding told confidants, "I am a man of limited talents from a small town. I don't seem to grasp that I am President.... I am not fit for the office and should never have been here."[28]

But Harding undersold himself. He was an out-spoken humanitarian at a time when America was deeply divided over race. On May 30, 1921, the nation's worst race riot erupted in Tulsa, Oklahoma. As many as 300 African-Americans were killed by marauding whites. An entire Black community, thirty-five square blocks of prosperous Black businesses known as "Black Wall Street," was destroyed. After deliberating how to respond, Harding chose to speak extemporaneously at Lincoln University in Pennsylvania, America's first degree-granting Black university. "Despite the demagogues, the idea of our oneness as Americans has risen superior to every appeal to mere class and group," Harding told the students. "And so, I wish it might be in this matter of our national problem of races." Referring to the Tulsa Massacre, Harding implored, "God grant that, in the soberness, the fairness, and the justice of this country, we never see another spectacle like it."[29] The university newspaper called the event "the high-water mark in the history of [this] institution."[30]

Harding did not receive a warm reception when he took his message of racial equality to the Deep South, the first sitting President to do so since Reconstruction. He spoke to a segregated crowd of 100,000 in Birmingham, Alabama on October 21, 1921. "I can say to you people of the South, both white and Black..." Harding declared as he pointed at the white section of the audience, "whether you like it or not, our democracy is a lie unless you stand for that equality.... I would say let the Black man vote when he is fit to vote; prohibit the white man voting when he is unfit to vote."[31] Half the crowd cheered, the other sat either in stony silence or booed and hissed. One Congressman denounced Harding's speech as "a blow to the white civilization of America." Harding further inflamed the crowd when he announced he supported the Dyer Anti-Lynching Bill that had been stalled in Congress since 1918.

A Ku Klux Klan parade in Binghamton, NY during the nineteen-twenties. President Harding popularized the America First slogan, but the Klan (which included women members during the decade) soon adopted it as their own.   BETTMANN/GETTY

A month after assuming the presidency, Harding had urged a joint session of Congress "to wipe the stain of barbaric lynching from the banners of a free and orderly, representative democracy."[32] It failed. Few Presidents other than Harding have had the courage to speak out against lynching. Even Franklin Roosevelt, fearing a backlash by Southern voters, refused to support anti-lynching legislation. By 2021, as President Trump was leaving office, nearly 200 anti-lynching bills had been submitted since the Civil War; none made it through both houses of Congress.[33] For over 150 years after the Civil War, federal law remained silent on the crime of lynching until signed into federal law by President Biden in 2022.

In September 1922, Harding again defied popular opinion when he vetoed a bonus bill for the five-million World War veterans declaring the bill would be a "disaster to the nation's finances."[34]

Harding supported Zionism, the Jewish effort to create a national home-land in Palestine, then under British Mandate. "I am very glad to express my approval and hearty sympathy for the effort of the Palestine Foundation fund on behalf of the restoration of Palestine as a homeland for the Jewish people," he declared in 1922.[35]

By 1923, nearly all of America had moved to an eight-hour workday ex-cept for the steel industry. When the chairman of US Steel recommended retaining the industry's twelve-hour workday, Harding wrote a public letter calling the practice barbaric. The public agreed, forcing the steel industry to reverse itself and adopt the eight-hour workday.[36]

Harding's most historic foreign policy decision was his refusal to join the League of Nations. His decision confounded Harding's political sup-porters, thirty-one of whom had signed a declaration during the presi-dential election stating that Harding supported the League. Nonetheless, Harding had gauged the temperament of the nation. Americanism and its attendant isolationism would remain popular until the Japanese attack on Pearl Harbor two decades later.

Four Exceptional Appointments

Perhaps Harding's greatest contribution as President was his appointment of four exceptional men to key positions in his administration: Andrew Mellon as Treasury Secretary, Herbert Hoover as Commerce Secretary, Charles Evans Hughes as Secretary of State and Charles Dawes as the first Director of the Budget. It was Harding's successor, Calvin Coolidge, who would most benefit from their contributions. Mellon would transform gov-ernment finance and remain in office until 1932. Hoover would serve eight years as one of the nation's most effective commerce secretaries before his own star-crossed presidency. Hughes would preside over the world's first disarmament conference and later become the eleventh Chief Justice of the Supreme Court. Dawes would win the Nobel Peace Prize in 1925 for the "Dawes Plan," which ended a European crisis resulting from crippling Ger-man reparation payments.

Charles Evans Hughes and Charles Dawes made significant contri-butions during their time in government, but it was Andrew Mellon and Herbert Hoover whose economic and political impact would ripple through America for the next century.

In 1873, Andrew Mellon joined his father's small bank and quickly took a leading role. The bank thrived under Mellon, financing Pittsburgh's expanding steel and petroleum industries. By 1914, Mellon had become one of America's richest men.

When Mellon took office in 1921 as Treasury Secretary, the country was in a deep economic slump. Unemployment was approaching 10 percent and industrial production had fallen 30 percent. Automobile production, a family car being a discretionary expense in those years, had dropped 60 percent. The nation also had a $26 billion ($350 billion in 2020 dollars) war debt from World War I. That may seem a small sum today, but in 1921 most of Washington D.C. still shared the Founders' fear of debt. In 1793, George Washington warned Congress, "No pecuniary consideration is more urgent than the regular redemption and discharge of the public debt."[37] "Nothing can more affect national prosperity," Alexander Hamilton, the nation's first Treasury Secretary, wrote, "than a constant and systematic attention to extinguish the present debt and to avoid as much as possible the incurring of any new debt."[38] Thomas Jefferson, often at odds with Hamilton, in this instance agreed, counseling future generations, "to preserve [our] independence, we must not let our rulers load us with perpetual debt."[39]

Mellon concurred with the nation's founders. The question was how to pay off the massive war debt. Some argued for the abolition of the income tax introduced eight years earlier in 1913 and its replacement with higher import tariffs, excise taxes, and a national sales tax. Mellon opposed these taxes as "regressive," as they would primarily impact poor and lower-income Americans. Taxes on clothing and food, for example, would be negligible to the wealthy but a real burden on the poor.

Instead, Mellon advocated a "progressive" income tax in which tax rates were based on the ability to pay; rates would be set low for low-income wage-earners then steadily rise as taxable income increased. But Mellon also believed it was counter-productive to overtax the wealthy. The wealthy, with their substantial discretionary income, financed the nation's economic growth by investing in stocks, bonds, and real estate. Mellon himself was a living example of that principle. After making a fortune in his namesake bank, Mellon plowed his new wealth back into America's fledgling industries, helping to finance the Aluminum Company of America (ALCOA), Carborundum, Gulf Oil, and Koppers.[40] The investments made Mellon even richer, but only after they built companies that employed thousands. Mellon well understood the issues surrounding over-taxing the rich.

Treasury Secretary Andrew Mellon's 1924 book, *Taxation: The People's Business*, described the theoretical basis for what today is known as supply-side economics.
LIBRARY OF CONGRESS

Mellon's answer to the taxation question resulted in a historical change to the tax system. Mellon argued that high tax rates caused the rich to avoid paying taxes by hiding income, employing tax shelters and even working less since much of their additional income would be taxed away. By lowering tax rates, Mellon claimed more taxes would be collected. He proposed cutting the top income tax rate from 73 to 25 percent. "It seems difficult for some to understand that high rates of taxation," Mellon later wrote, "do not necessarily mean large revenue to the Government, and that more revenue may often be obtained by lower rates."[41]

Congress was skeptical. Mellon responded by showing how Henry Ford increased his profits after reducing car prices from $3,000 to $380. Just as Henry Ford understood lower car prices led to more cars sold and thus higher profits, Mellon told Congress high tax rates resulted in widespread tax avoidance and that lower rates would generate more, not less, tax revenue.

Mellon, one of America's most respected capitalists, quickly sold Congress on his tax plan. Eight months after his appointment, Congress approved the Revenue Act of 1921 based on "Scientific Taxation," as Mellon called his tax theory. To encourage investment, Congress slashed taxes on capital gains to 12.5 percent, their lowest rate for the next one hundred years.[42] Those making $4,000 ($57,800 in 2020 dollars) and below received no cut. Higher-income brackets received larger cuts. Unwilling to slash taxes on the top bracket to 25 percent as Mellon proposed, Congress cut rates from 73 to 58 percent.[43]

The tax cuts quickly helped to reverse the nation's economic decline. Measured in 1918 dollars, real GDP had fallen from $76 billion in 1918 to a low of $62 billion in 1921. Within a year, a strong economic recovery was underway with GDP climbing to $66 billion in 1922 and $75 billion in 1923. After hitting 11.7 percent in 1921, unemployment plunged to 2.4 percent in 1923. The national debt, measured as a percentage of GDP, fell from 33 to 26 percent. It was a historic economic turn-around and Mellon was just getting started.

Like Andrew Mellon, Herbert Hoover was an American success story. Orphaned at the age of ten, Hoover graduated from the first class of Stanford University in 1895 as a geology major. By the age of forty, Hoover had retired with a four-million-dollar fortune (over $100 million in 2020 dollars) after shrewdly investing in international mining ventures.

After the outbreak of World War I, Herbert Hoover threw himself into international relief. When the Germans invaded Belgium, Hoover organized the Commission for Relief in Belgium, which, after Hoover personally negotiated with the Germans, delivered over two million tons of food to war victims. In 1917, as the United States entered the war, President

Wilson appointed Hoover the "Food Czar," responsible for delivering food to America's allies. Rather than rationing, Hoover implored Americans to cut back on meat and grains and "when in doubt, eat potatoes."[44] By the end of the war, Hoover was recognized as America's top efficiency expert, dubbing his frugal policies "Hooverizing."[45] The term became so popular it was even used in a 1918 Valentine's Day card:

> I can Hooverize on dinner,
> And on lights and fuel too,
> But I'll never learn to Hooverize,
> When it comes to loving you.[46]

Hoover's humanitarian efforts extended throughout his years in the Harding Administration. From 1921 through 1922, Hoover, now respected worldwide as "The Great Humanitarian," headed joint private and government efforts to distribute $60 million ($866 million in 2020 dollars) in food and supplies[47] to starving Russians after the Russian Revolution. Again, opposed by hard-liners for feeding communists, Hoover admonished his critics, "Twenty million people are starving. Whatever their politics, they shall be fed!"[48]

Most of Hoover's contributions as Commerce Secretary occurred after Harding's unexpected death during his five and a half years under President Coolidge. But Hoover's 1922 Annual Report of the Secretary of Commerce makes clear his intended direction. To minimize federal involvement, Hoover would encourage industrial collaboration rather than government oversight. In 1921, for example, faced with "the most difficult unemployment crisis that the country had ever faced," leading to "great agitation. . .for governmental doles and other fallacious remedies based upon the practices of European governments," Hoover called a conference of eighty-five industry and civic organizations "[to formulate plans] which would ameliorate the unemployment situation over the forthcoming winter. . . . The employers of the country cooperated in a vast extension of divided-time employment."[49]

In 1921, Hoover's collaboration coupled with Mellon's economic policies ended the postwar recession. But ten years later, both men would find their policies ineffective in dealing with the far more severe economic crisis of the Great Depression. Undaunted, Hoover and Mellon pursued their failed policies until driven from office.

The Ohio Gang

Unfortunately, Harding also appointed friends and political cronies, dubbed the "Ohio Gang," to key positions: Harry Daugherty as Attorney General, Albert Fall as Interior Secretary, and Charles Forbes as Director of the Veterans' Bureau, along with a motley collection of drinking buddies, golf partners, and general sycophants.

Harding was a keen poker player and twice a week played with the Ohio Gang. His late-night poker games, "the air heavy with tobacco smoke, trays with bottles containing every imaginable brand of whiskey,"[50] were infamous during Prohibition. One night, Harding lost an entire set of White House chinaware dating to the Benjamin Harrison administration on a single losing hand. But it wasn't all poker, cigars, and whiskey. Harding and his friends would occasionally sneak off to a burlesque show.[51]

The affable Harding had always found it hard to deny his friends. His father told him he was lucky not to have been born a girl, otherwise he would have been "in the family way" all the time.[52] Unable to hold the Ohio Gang in check, their corruption would ultimately destroy Harding's legacy.

Two years into his presidency, Harding learned that many of the Ohio Gang had betrayed his trust by using their government positions to enrich themselves. "I have no trouble with my enemies," Harding confided to newspaper editor William Alan White, "But my damn friends, my God-damned friends, White, they're the ones who keep me walking the floor nights!"[53] Seeking respite from Washington, Harding began an extended speaking tour throughout the American West and Alaska. Harding spent much of the trip pacing his private railroad car, dreading his return to Washington and the scandal he knew would soon erupt.

Harding never returned to Washington. Depleted by worry and weakened earlier by a virulent case of the flu, Harding died of a heart attack on August 2, 1923 while in San Francisco. Florence was reading to him from the *Saturday Evening Post* when Harding shuddered and quietly died.[54]

No President since Lincoln was more deeply mourned. An estimated nine million Americans came out to honor his funeral train as it made its way from California back to Washington. As the train passed, mourners sang Harding's favorite hymn, "Nearer My God to Thee."

After Harding's death, the widespread corruption of the Ohio Gang spilled out. In 1921, Harding had appointed Charles Forbes as Director of the Veteran's Bureau, the newly established agency to provide care to World War I veterans. With a budget of $500 million ($7.2 billion in 2020 dollars), 30,000 employees and contracts to build scores of facilities, the bureau was an embezzler's fantasy. Within two years, Forbes had stolen nearly $2.0 million through bribes, kick-back schemes, and selling pilfered hospital supplies. Harding quietly forced Forbes to resign, but not before one startled White House visitor caught Harding with his hands on Forbes neck shaking him "as a dog would a rat" while shouting "You yellow rat! You double-crossing bastard!"[55]

The Forbes scandal broke a few months after Harding's death. After a Senate investigation exposed the fraud, Forbes was convicted and sentenced to two years in prison. Forbes' conviction sullied Harding's reputation and shook Americans' trust in government. There was much more to come.[56]

The next scandal concerned an obscure piece of land in central Wyoming. Teapot Dome was an oil field set aside in 1909 as a strategic oil reserve for the U.S. Navy. Harding's Secretary of the Interior, Albert Fall, persuaded Harding to transfer the oil reserve to the Interior Department. Fall promptly leased the drilling rights to the Sinclair Oil Corporation and Pan American Petroleum and Transport Company, bypassing the normal competitive bidding process. In return, Fall received bribes totaling $404,000 ($6.2 million in 2020 dollars). In 1927, after years of civil and criminal litigation, Fall was convicted of bribery. He would be the first cabinet member ever sentenced to prison. Until Watergate, historians considered Teapot Dome the worst political scandal in the nation's history.[57]

But neither Charles Forbes nor Albert Fall quite compared with Harding's long-time friend and sponsor, Harry Daugherty, for brazen corruption. As Harding's campaign manager, Daugherty had brilliantly engineered Harding's nomination as a compromise candidate when party power brokers were deadlocked.[58] Grateful, Harding made Daugherty his

Attorney General. Daugherty quickly became an active extortionist. For starters, American Metal Company paid Jesse Smith, Daugherty's personal assistant, $200,000 to ensure a favorable legal decision regarding billions in German assets seized during the war. Another $40,000 went to his brother. Smith committed suicide and his brother was sentenced to prison. But Daugherty's true talent was shaking down bootleggers, collecting an estimated $7.0 million in protection money. Gangsters were invited to visit a secret hotel room where they dropped their payments in $1,000 bills into a large fishbowl.[59]

Daugherty was tried twice in federal court for defrauding the government but was acquitted both times and retired to Ohio to practice law.[60] In 1932 Daugherty published a self-serving memoir, *The Inside Story of the Harding Tragedy*. "Its title does not describe accurately Mr. Daugherty's book," *The New York Times* wrote, wryly commenting, "[It] being an account of the 'Harding tragedy' would only be accepted by those who believe the 'Harding tragedy' was Mr. Daugherty's connection with the administration."[61]

But the greatest damage to Harding's reputation came not from the Ohio Gang, but from a young woman. In 1927, Nan Britton published *The President's Daughter*, a 460-page book filled with details of her four-year affair with Harding. Britton, thirty years Harding's junior, claimed Harding fathered her daughter, Elizabeth Ann, in January 1919 during a tryst in Harding's Senate office. The Harding family refused to acknowledge the child, dismissing Britton as a liar and opportunist.[62]

Britton was left destitute, a single mother despised throughout her life as an amoral gold-digger. But technology vindicated her. In 2015, a DNA test on Britton's grandson confirmed that Elizabeth Ann Britton was, indeed, the daughter of Warren G. Harding.[63]

Beyond the Scandals

Historians generally place Harding near the bottom of rankings of American Presidents, typically sandwiched between John Tyler and Franklin Pierce.[64] Given Harding's short presidency stained by scandal, his low ranking isn't surprising. But Harding's presidency was hardly a failure. He signed bills that laid the foundation for today's Veteran's Administration, the Office of Management and Budget (OMB) and Medicaid. He staffed his administration with four brilliant, dedicated men who made major contributions for many years. Harding was the first sitting President to travel to the Deep South to condemn racial inequality. Against strong public opinion, he pardoned Eugene Debs who had been imprisoned merely for speaking out against America's entry into the First World War.

Eighty years after his death, Warren Harding entered the realm of pop psychology when Malcolm Gladwell, in his best-selling book *Blink*, wrote of the "Warren Harding Error." Gladwell described the human tendency to judge people by their appearance and personality rather than their real substance. "Many people who looked at Warren Harding," Gladwell wrote, "saw how extraordinarily handsome and distinguished-looking he was and jumped to the immediate, and entirely unwarranted, conclusion that he was a man of courage and intelligence and integrity."[65]

Warren and Florence Harding with Laddie Boy. Florence was smart, shrewd, and focused, managing the family newspaper while Harding pursued politics.   FPG/GETTY

However, Gladwell's indictment of Harding as a man lacking in courage, intelligence, and integrity is categorically wrong. Harding dared to tell a Deep South crowd of 100,000 that "I can say to you people of the South, both white and Black...whether you like it or not, our democracy is a lie unless you stand for that equality [of the races]." Harding had the intelligence to appoint Herbert Hoover and Andrew Mellon whose policies influenced American politics for the next century. And Harding had the integrity to never have enriched himself during his government service as his cronies so cynically had done.

Today, Harding's presidential star is rising. Historians are beginning to look beyond the scandals and appreciate Harding's considerable accomplishments during his short presidency. After the First World War, Spanish Flu pandemic, and a deep postwar recession, Americans wanted a return to normalcy. Harding provided it.

Calvin Coolidge

August 3, 1923 – March 4, 1929

> The people cannot look to legislation generally for success. Industry, thrift, character, are not conferred by act or resolve. Government cannot relieve from toil. It can provide no substitute for the rewards of service. It can, of course, care for the defective and recognize distinguished merit. The normal must care for themselves. Self-government means self-support.[1]

Shortly after midnight on August 3, 1923, Vice President Calvin Coolidge was awakened by his father climbing the stairs, calling his name. Coolidge and his wife, Grace, were on vacation at the family home in Plymouth Notch, Vermont. Given the late hour, Coolidge knew something was gravely wrong. President Harding had died of a heart attack three hours earlier in San Francisco. Coolidge and Grace quickly dressed. Before going downstairs, Coolidge said a prayer asking the Lord to give him the strength to lead the country.

A telegram soon arrived from the U.S. Attorney General urging Coolidge to take the presidential oath as quickly as possible. But who, at 2:00 am in a small Vermont village could administer the oath of office to the President of the United States? Coolidge suggested his father who held, perhaps, Vermont's humblest official position: a notary public. After finding a copy of the presidential oath in a book of Vermont statutes, his father retired to the kitchen to shave. Coolidge went across the street to the general store—now open due to its telephone being the sole link to the outside world—where he purchased a bottle of Moxie, his favorite soda.

At 2:47 am, his father administered the oath of office to Coolidge as the thirtieth President of the United States, the last President to take the oath under a kerosene lamp. Afterward, they all went back to bed.

Later that morning, Coolidge boarded the train for Washington. "I believe I can swing it," the new President was overheard to have said.[2]

Four years earlier, Calvin Coolidge was the Governor of Massachusetts. Starting in 1898, he had doggedly made his political ascent from Northampton, Massachusetts city councilman to mayor to state senator to lieutenant governor and finally, in 1919, to governor.

The First World War had ended in 1918, but the nation was hardly at peace. Inspired by the 1917 Russian Revolution, anarchists had started a terrorist campaign across the country. In late April 1919, thirty-six mail bombs were sent to prominent politicians and businessmen. Timed for delivery on May Day, the international holiday celebrating workers, few were delivered. The inept perpetrators had mailed the bombs in identical packages that were quickly identified. Only two people were injured, a Senator's wife and a housekeeper. In June, however, eight far more potent bombs were mailed that killed two people, one of whom was the bomber himself, whose parcel exploded prematurely as he was delivering it to the home of the U.S. Attorney General. Also, that summer severe race riots broke out across the country. Rioting in Washington, D.C. and Chicago left at least fifty dead, with unofficial estimates ranging far higher.

The Overman Committee, a five-person Senate Subcommittee, blamed the violence on the international communist movement. Birthed in 1848 with the publication of *The Communist Manifesto* by German philosophers Karl Marx and Friedrich Engels, the communist movement found its ultimate home in Russia following the Bolshevik victory in the 1917 October Revolution. The committee reported they had "found money coming into this country from Russia."[3] Other witnesses, including recent Russian emigrants, claimed a communist revolution, if spread to America, would overturn the government, close the newspapers, impose atheism and even make women property of the state.

It was in this heated political atmosphere that the Boston police force went on strike on September 9, 1919. With the streets unprotected, violence soon erupted as hoodlums overturned vendor carts, broke windows, and looted stores. Unable to maintain peace, the Boston mayor asked Governor Coolidge for help. Coolidge quickly sent 5,000 soldiers from the Massachusetts Militia to replace the striking police. Order was restored, but at the cost of nine lives, all but one shot by the peace-keeping militia. Coolidge fired the 1,100 striking policemen, replacing the officers with unemployed World War I veterans. Ironically, to assure their loyalty, the new police officers were given many of the benefits for which the police had originally gone on strike, including higher salaries, a pension program, more vacation days, and reimbursement for uniforms and equipment.

With fears of the Bolshevik menace running high, public sentiment ran strongly against the strikers. Senator Henry Cabot Lodge summarized what many Americans felt, claiming that "If the American Federation of Labor succeeds in getting hold of the police in Boston it will go all over the country, and we shall be in measurable distance of Soviet government by labor unions."[4]

Governor Coolidge's resolute leadership during the Boston police strike made him a national hero. The next year, Coolidge's fame earned him the position of Warren Harding's running mate. Three years later, Harding was dead and Coolidge the President.

When Ronald Reagan moved into the White House some sixty years after Coolidge broke the Boston police strike, he hung a portrait of Calvin Coolidge in the Cabinet Room, the only President to so honor the nation's thirtieth President. Reagan drew inspiration from Coolidge's portrait as he pondered whether to fire striking air-traffic controllers in August of 1981. Announcing his decision to fire the 11,000 controllers, Reagan quoted Coolidge: "There is no right to strike against the public anytime, anywhere."[5]

Weaned on a Pickle

Ask Americans today what they know about Calvin Coolidge, and most would be baffled. The few who could answer probably remember him as "Silent Cal," an enigma of a man famous for his taciturn comments and sour disposition. Alice Roosevelt Longworth (Teddy Roosevelt's out-spoken daughter banned from both the Taft and Wilson White House for ill behavior) described him as a man "weaned on a pickle." Others might more charitably comment that he had a wry New England wit.

Calvin Coolidge was described as having been weaned on a pickle; yet Coolidge possessed a wry humor matched by few presidents.   ARCHIVE PICS/ALAMY

Asked about a minister's sermon on sin, Coolidge replied, "He was against it." When asked how it felt to be President: "Well, you got to be mighty careful." And when a dinner companion commented, "My husband has bet me that I won't get more than two words out of you all evening," Coolidge famously replied, "You lose." Years later, when Coolidge died, one wag commented, "How can you tell?"[6]

The Immigration Act of 1924

A flinty New Englander, President Coolidge's approach to government reflected his speaking habits: anything more than the absolute minimum was wasteful. His forebears had emigrated from England in 1630, and for over two and a half centuries they made a hardscrabble living farming New England's rocky soil.

Coolidge carried their frugal habits to the White House. When farm prices collapsed, Coolidge twice vetoed bills to purchase surplus crops, declaring, "Well, farmers never have made much money."[7] When the Mississippi Flood of 1927 swept hundreds to their deaths, Coolidge initially resisted demands for federal flood relief, observing, "The Government is not the insurer of its citizens against the hazards of the elements."[8] When Congress passed a bonus package for war veterans, Coolidge vetoed it, declaring, "Patriotism...bought and paid for is not patriotism."[9] Congress overrode his veto.

Coolidge supported Harding's policies. Few were controversial at the time. By today's standards, however, the Immigration Act of 1924 was one of the most racist pieces of legislation signed in the last century. Its purpose was to preserve what Congress considered to be the ideal racial homogeneity of the American population, namely Western and Northern European. The Act replaced the Emergency Quota Act of 1921 passed during President Harding's first year to reduce the influx of Eastern and Southern Europeans—namely, Jews, Poles, and Italians—after the First World War and the Russian Revolution.

The 1924 Immigration Act had Coolidge's strong support. During his 1924 presidential nomination speech, Coolidge declared:

> Restricted immigration is not an offensive but purely a defensive action. It is not adopted in criticism of others in the slightest degree, but solely for the purpose of protecting ourselves. We cast no aspersions on any race or creed, but we must remember that every object of our institutions of society and government will fail unless America be kept American.[10]

Coolidge's views weren't unusual. The pursuit of racial homogeneity went back decades. In 1883, Francis Galton, a cousin of Charles Darwin, proposed that a human population's genetic composition could be improved by selective breeding. The selective breeding of plants and animals had been practiced for millennia. If plant and animal traits could be improved by selective breeding, why not humans? Galton suggested that controlling human procreation could be used to assure "that humanity shall be represented by the fittest races. . .one of the highest objects that can be reasonably attempted." Galton called his approach to improving the human race, *eugenics*.[11]

One of the first to support eugenics was Margaret Sanger, the founder of Planned Parenthood. In 1923, Sanger opined in *The New York Times* that:

> Birth Control is not contraception indiscriminately and thoughtlessly practiced. It means the release and cultivation of the better racial elements in our society, and the gradual suppression, elimination and eventual extirpation of defective stocks—those human weeds which threaten the blooming of the finest flowers of American civilization.[12]

In 1927, Sanger supported the Supreme Court decision written by Oliver Wendell Holmes that ruled forced sterilization of "human weeds" was allowed under the Constitution.[13] Today, Planned Parenthood acknowledges Sanger's flawed views while supporting the right of women to control their own bodies.

Similarly, Cold Spring Harbor Laboratory on Long Island has a racist heritage. Today, the renowned laboratory employs Nobel Prize-winning scientists to conduct research on cancer, neuroscience, and biology. But in 1924 Cold Spring Harbor was home to the Eugenics Record Office (ERO), founded in 1910 to research improving the human race through selective breeding. During the early nineteen-twenties, Harry H. Laughlin, the ERO's first director, testified before Congress to advocate forced sterilization and restrictive immigration laws that favored Caucasians. By 1931, thirty states had enacted forced sterilization laws and five years later at least 60,000 people had undergone the procedure.[14]

Laughlin and his work at the ERO were soon recognized by the German National Socialist (Nazi) Party. In 1936, Laughlin received an honorary degree from the Nazi-controlled University of Heidelberg as "a pioneer in the science of racial cleansing."[15] The ERO thrived for thirty years, sponsored by the Carnegie, Harriman, and Rockefeller Foundations, until Nazi racial persecution discredited eugenics as a racist deceit and the facility closed in 1940.

In 1924, however, eugenics and racial homogeneity were broadly accepted. So, it's hardly surprising that the Immigration Act of 1924 set immigration quotas based on the 1890 census, a period when the U.S. population was still largely British and Western European. (The 1890 census was also notable as it was the first census after six western states—North Dakota, South Dakota, Montana, Washington, Idaho and Wyoming—had been rushed to statehood arguably giving rural states disproportionate representation in Congress.)

The 1924 Act limited annual immigration to two percent of each nationality tabulated in the 1890 census with one major exception: all Asians, from China to India to Japan were excluded. The result was a quota system that overwhelmingly favored immigrants from the British Isles and Western Europe. Since Jews mainly resided in Eastern Europe and Russia, they were also largely excluded.[16] The Immigration Act passed on May 26, 1924 with strong Congressional support.

Two years later, in 1926, Adolf Hitler published the second volume of *Mein Kampf*, his manifesto outlining the ideology that the Nazis would adopt during their twelve-year reign. Although nearly 700 pages long, the book's thesis is based on just two propositions: an imperative to retain Germany's racial purity (*Herrenrasse*) and its destiny for eastward expansion (*Lebensraum*).

As Hitler wrote, America was admired throughout the world for its popular culture, innovation in science and engineering, economic success, and democratic institutions. But Hitler found something more sinister to admire about America, its immigration and naturalization policies. In a section discussing German citizenship, Hitler could find but one country practicing the immigration policies he considered essential to maintaining racial purity: the United States.[17] Hitler wrote:

> At present, there exists one State which manifests at least some modest attempts that show a better appreciation of how things ought to

be done in this [question of race]. It is not, however, in our model German Republic but in the U.S.A. that efforts are made to conform at least partly to the counsels of commonsense. By refusing immigrants to enter there if they are in a bad state of health, and by excluding certain races from the right to become naturalized as citizens, they have begun to introduce principles similar to those on which we wish to ground the People's State.[18]

Hitler's phrase, "by excluding certain races," referred to America's long-standing exclusion of nearly all foreign-born Asians from U.S. citizenship originating with the Naturalization Act of 1790. The Act limited U.S. citizenship to "free white persons." The restriction was lifted for Blacks in 1866 and in 1942 for Chinese who were American allies during World War II. But the restriction wasn't fully lifted until 1952 when the McCarran-Walter Act finally eliminated the "free white person" mandate first established in 1790.[19]

The immediate impact of the 1924 Immigration Act was to cut immigration from 358,000 in 1923 to 165,000 two years later. Immigration from Italy dropped by 90 percent. For many nationalities, including Czechs, Greeks, Poles, Spaniards, and Yugoslavs, the Act was so restrictive that more foreign nationals left the United States than emigrated to it. For the next forty-five years, the percentage of foreign-born workers in the U.S. labor force declined from 18.6 percent in 1920 to 5.2 percent in 1970, its lowest point over the last century.[20]

It wasn't until 1965 that the immigration formula under the National Origins Act was abolished in favor of a new quota system that gives preference to relatives of citizens and permanent residents—known today as chain migration—as well as specific professions and skills. But the 1965 law had unintended consequences. By 2017, as President Trump was taking office, foreign-born workers had increased to 17 percent of the labor force—nearly its level a century earlier. As happened a century earlier, many Americans viewed the foreign immigrants, millions of whom were undocumented, as a threat to their jobs, personal security, and national identity.[21]

Wonder Boy

Commerce Secretary Herbert Hoover got under Coolidge's skin. It was hardly surprising. Coolidge had lived most of his quiet life within 100 miles of Plymouth Notch, Vermont. Hoover had traveled the world, making his fortune managing and investing in mining operations. While Coolidge may have preferred that the Commerce Department stick to its traditional role managing lighthouses and fisheries, Hoover believed that new industries such as aviation, radio, and transportation needed government support.

Hoover was a hyper-active Commerce Secretary who drove initiatives in movies, radio, aviation, highway safety, product standardization, home ownership, and flood control. He was so involved across the federal government that some joked Hoover was "Secretary of Commerce and Under-Secretary of all other departments."[22]

Hoover's accomplishments included the Air Mail Act of 1925, which was the beginning of the airline industry. A year later the Air Commerce Act charged the Commerce Department with fostering air commerce, establishing regulations and operating aids to navigation. The Radio Act of 1927 established the precursor to the Federal Communications Commission (FCC) and charged the commission with regulating the radio waves and assuring radio stations operated in the public interest. That year, Hoover appeared on America's first television broadcast. "Today we have, in a sense, the transmission of sight for the first time in the world's history," Hoover told reporters 200 miles away. "Human genius has now destroyed the impediment of distance."[23]

During these years, Hoover's Commerce Department worked with industry to standardize tools, hardware, and packaging to make manufacturing and shipping more efficient. When the Mississippi River flooded in 1927, Hoover coordinated relief efforts across government and private agencies. And, when western states couldn't agree on how to distribute the waters of the Colorado River, it was Hoover who proposed the solution. When construction on the massive Colorado River dam began, the project was named after Hoover, not President Coolidge.

By 1928 Herbert Hoover was nearly as well-known to the public as Coolidge himself. The public loved him, but Coolidge had grown impatient with Hoover's tireless activism, calling him "Wonder Boy" and confiding to associates, "For six years that man has given me unsolicited advice, all of it bad."[24] Hoover's advice couldn't have been too bad. The economy boomed under Coolidge's presidency.

Coolidge inherited another remarkable cabinet member from the Harding administration, Treasury Secretary Andrew Mellon. Serving under Harding and Coolidge, Mellon led a modern tax revolution. Mellon, of course, was not the first American to rebel against high taxes.

Early Tax Rebellions

Most school children know the Revolutionary War began with a tax rebellion against the British in 1776. But few Americans realize that a second tax rebellion against their new government led to the drafting of the American Constitution in 1787.

It all started in 1754. For nine years the British fought the French and their Indian allies for control over North America. The British won the war, opening American expansion to the west. However, the war had cost England £70,000,000, doubling its national debt.[25] To help pay the debt, the British Parliament levied a series of taxes on the Colonies: the Sugar Act of 1763, the Stamp Act of 1765, the Townsend Revenue Act of 1767 and, lastly, the Tea Act of 1773, which led to the Boston Tea Party. Denied representation in the British Parliament, by 1776 Americans had had enough and declared their independence.[26]

During the ensuing Revolutionary War, the newly established Continental Congress had no taxation power yet was responsible for financing George Washington's army. Unable to tax, the fledging Congress relied on voluntary contributions from the thirteen states which, even when collected, were meager; so meager that General Washington protested "The Army, as usual, are without pay; and a great part of the soldiery without shirts; and though the patience of them is equally threadbare, the States seem perfectly indifferent to their cries."[27]

In desperation, the colonial government printed millions in bills of credit known as "Continentals." Despised everywhere as worthless, Washington wryly commented to John Jay, President of the Continental Congress, that "a wagon load of money will scarcely purchase a wagon load of provisions."[28]

After nearly eight years of war, the British were defeated, leaving America free, but deeply in debt.[29] With no ability to tax, Congress was unable to pay its soldiers and allies, primarily France and Holland. To raise funds, Congress twice proposed an amendment to the Articles of Confederation to allow Congress to charge a five percent tax on imports, but amendments to the Articles required the unanimous consent of all thirteen states, which New York, Rhode Island, and Virginia refused to grant.[30]

Unable to raise tax revenue, Congress and the states issued new debt certificates which were as worthless as the Continentals they had replaced. Many soldiers, impoverished and expecting never to be paid, sold their certificates to speculators for pennies on the dollar. Many of the more unscrupulous speculators were members of the Massachusetts Legislature, and former revolutionaries themselves. It wasn't long before the Legislature raised taxes to fund the redemption of the certificates at full face value, providing speculators with a huge profit.

Those profits fell on the backs of their fellow citizens. Farmers in western Massachusetts, unable to pay the new taxes, were faced with foreclosure and debtor prison. In August 1786, an open rebellion broke out led by Daniel Shays, a former colonial soldier, who raised an army of 1,500 men. The Massachusetts government quickly responded with a state militia privately funded by wealthy Boston bankers and merchants. By early 1787 the rebellion had been put down amid calls for the immediate execution of the rebels. Samuel Adams, known today for his namesake beer, was one of the most vociferous in calling for execution. "In monarchies the crime of treason and rebellion may admit of being pardoned or lightly punished," Adams maintained, "But the man who dares rebel against the laws of a republic ought to suffer death."[31]

Fortunately, tempers cooled and shortly after John Hancock was elected the new governor, he pardoned the rebels. But only after the rebellious farmers were marched to the gallows on June 21, 1787 and pardoned at the last minute.

Shays' Rebellion shocked America's Founders and clarified the impotence of the federal government under the Articles of Confederation. The Rebellion convinced George Washington to come out of retirement to attend the Constitutional Convention being held in Philadelphia that summer. Washington was quickly elected President of the Convention. Four months later, on September 17, 1787, the Convention finished its work when a new Constitution was signed and submitted to the thirteen states for ratification. Daniel Shays' Rebellion had been the catalyst that helped convince the Founders to replace the weak Articles of Confederation with a new Constitution providing broad federal powers over the states.

Four years later, the nation was again grappling with financial problems including a $77 million war debt. To help pay it, Congress imposed an excise tax on whiskey. Farmers in western Pennsylvania rebelled, refusing to pay the tax. Although Washington sought to resolve the dispute peacefully, by 1794 the Whiskey Rebellion turned violent when the insurgents tarred and feathered the local tax collector and set fire to his home near Pittsburgh. Washington, now President, organized a 12,000-soldier militia and marched west to quell the rebellion. Fortunately, word of Washington's imminent arrival was sufficient to disperse the rebels. Like Massachusetts Governor John Hancock seven years earlier, President Washington did not want to execute fellow Americans and pardoned the rebels.[32]

After two armed rebellions over taxation, Congress had learned its lesson. President Thomas Jefferson repealed the Whiskey Tax in 1802, and for the next 110 years the federal government relied almost exclusively on easy-to-collect import tariffs. It was not until the ratification of the 16th Amendment in 1913 that Congress imposed a permanent income tax.[33] Initially, the maximum tax rate was only seven percent, but by 1921 the top rate had climbed to 73 percent, including war taxes, for incomes over $1,000,000 ($14.5 million in 2020 dollars).[34]

The Birth of Supply-Side Economics

Andrew Mellon was one of the few Americans who fell into the top income tax bracket and well understood the impact of high taxes. After three years as Treasury Secretary, Mellon had developed a set of taxation principles that he published under the title *Taxation: The People's Business* in 1924.

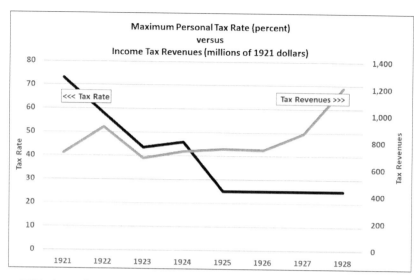

Maximum Personal Tax Rate (percent)
versus
Income Tax Revenues (millions of 1921 dollars)

From 1921 through 1928 Treasury Secretary Mellon cut the maximum personal tax rate from 73 to 25 percent. As he predicted, tax revenues increased.

IRS STATISTICS OF INCOME REPORTS

Mellon claimed high tax rates reduce both tax revenues and business investment. Although radical at the time, Mellon's reasoning was simple. If tax rates are very high, say 90 percent, taxpayers avoid paying taxes in any way possible. They might buy tax-free municipal bonds, invest overseas out of the government's reach, or simply not work as hard since taxes took 90 percent of their additional earnings. A small tax cut from 90 to 80 percent doubles the taxpayer's after-tax income. If the tax cut encourages taxpayers to reduce their tax avoidance and invest their new after-tax income, then both the government and economy benefit. Tax revenues increase as money comes off the sidelines and the taxpayer has more after-tax income to invest.

Mellon was not the first to advocate lower taxes to encourage business investment. In 1803, the French economist Jean-Baptiste Say proposed that the source of economic growth is the production of goods and services, not their consumption.

Say concluded the best way to stimulate an economy is through taxation policies that encourage investment in factories, innovation and training. These investments would result in the efficient production of goods and services, which attracts consumption.[35]

But, often forgotten today, is the obverse of Mellon's theory when tax rates are already low. A tax cut from 30 to 15 percent, for example, cuts revenues in half while only giving taxpayers a small increase in after-tax income. Such small cuts hardly motivate changes by the taxpayer. The result is that tax revenues fall with little offsetting economic benefit. Somewhere between these two extremes is a tax rate that maximizes tax revenues.

Today Mellon's principles are known as supply-side economics, or more pejoratively, "trickle-down" economics. Humorist Will Rogers popularized the descriptive phrase in 1932 when he mocked tax breaks for the rich telling his radio listeners, "The money was all appropriated to the top in the hopes that it would trickle down to the needy."[36]

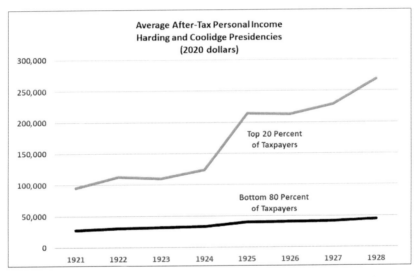

After-tax income increased broadly during the nineteen-twenties. But the wealthy benefited the most, helped after Treasury Secretary Andrew Mellon cut the maximum tax rate from 46 to 25 percent in 1925.   IRS STATISTICS OF INCOME REPORTS

Today, Mellon's taxation theory is named the "Laffer Curve" after economist Arthur Laffer, who revived Mellon's concept in the mid-nineteen-seventies, fifty years after Mellon first advocated it. In 2019, President Trump awarded Laffer the Presidential Medal of Freedom. During the ceremony, Trump lauded Laffer, commenting, "I've heard and studied the Laffer Curve for many years," calling the curve "a very important thing you did, Art. Few people in history have revolutionized economic theory like Arthur Laffer."[37]

Laffer made a career out of his eponymous curve which, given its origin, he perhaps should have insisted be renamed the Mellon Curve. Laffer did not revolutionize economic theory. Rather, he simply borrowed his ideas from Andrew Mellon, the father of modern supply-side economics.[38]

Population, Technology and Taxation

Coolidge, with Treasury Secretary Mellon's leadership, continued the deep tax cuts started by Harding. The top income tax rates fell from 73 percent in 1921 to 24 percent in 1929. During those years, tax rates for the lowest tax bracket dropped from four percent to 0.375 percent while the family deduction increased from $2,500 to $3,500 ($51,600 in 2020 dollars). In 1922, Harding slashed the long-term capital gains rate from 73 percent to 12.5 percent—a level never again achieved—where it remained until 1933.[39]

These were huge personal income tax cuts. No President since has come close. How effective were the tax cuts towards increasing tax revenues while also boosting the economy? Before answering that, let's consider two other factors: population growth and technology.

From 1921 through 1928 the United States experienced a baby boom that saw the population grow 1.6 percent annually, a rate only exceeded, and then only slightly, during the postwar baby boom from 1946 through 1964.[40] A growing population generates its own demand for products and services from baby clothes to college tuition. Recently, for example, a 2015 United States Department of Agriculture report estimated a middle-class family spends about $12,980 annually on their first child, which contributes directly to GDP growth.[41]

To finance the growing consumption, banks were evolving into "department stores of finance," providing consumer loans, mortgages, securities lending, and other services.

The emergence of new technologies also contributed to economic growth. During the nineteen-twenties, millions of homes were being electrified, thus increasing the demand for lighting fixtures, refrigerators, washing machines, and other appliances. National radio networks were springing up providing news, entertainment, and advertising, driving the sale of radios. Similarly, improved manufacturing processes drove car prices down driving demand up. By 1925, a new Ford Model T Runabout cost only $260, making car ownership affordable for millions of families. During the nineteen-twenties, Americans bought nearly twenty-six million cars.[42] And how better to use that new car than to take the family on a motor vacation consuming gasoline, staying in hotels, eating at restaurants, and enjoying various forms of entertainment?

It was the mix of expanding population, technological revolution and stimulatory economic policies that delivered spectacular economic growth from 1921 through 1929. Measured in 2020 dollars, real GDP grew from $521 billion to $709 billion, a healthy 3.9 percent annually. Unemployment plummeted from 11.7 to 3.2 percent.[43]

Mellon's earlier prediction that income tax revenues would rise as tax rates were reduced was spot on for the wealthy. Although their tax rates had been deeply cut, the top 20 percent paid significantly more total tax in 1929 than in 1921: $944 million versus $659 million. They could afford it: During those years, their aggregate pre-tax income had grown to $15.2 billion from $9.4 billion.

Where did this new money come from? Was it coming off the sidelines moving, say, from tax-exempt bonds to taxable stocks? Or was it a booming economy created by new businesses, increased productivity, and a growing population?

Credit the booming economy which was growing nearly four percent annually. Everyone benefited. From 1921 through 1929 the average taxpayer in the bottom 20 percent saw their real after-tax income, measured in 2020 dollars, increase from $17,200 to $22,600, a 32 percent increase; the middle 60 percent increased from $30,800 to $52,400, or 70 percent; while the top 20 percent went from $95,000 to $265,000, or 179 percent.

However, it was the top one percent who enjoyed the greatest income growth. The average taxpayer in this select group increased their after-tax income from $425,000 in 1921 to $1,964,000 in 1929, a year when a top-of-the-line Duesenberg sold for $379,000 (all in 2020 dollars). "You know, the rich are different from you and me," F. Scott Fitzgerald is said to have commented to Ernest Hemingway at the time. "Yes, they've got more money," Hemingway replied.

The wealthy did very well during the Roaring Twenties, but they also paid a large majority of income taxes. Mellon's tax plan was highly progressive, taxing the wealthy at much higher rates than average taxpayers. By 1929, the top one percent earned 25 percent of all pre-tax income but paid 82 percent of all federal personal income taxes.

As a former banker, one of Mellon's primary objectives as Treasury Secretary was to reduce the war debt incurred during the First World War—a task in which he excelled. From 1921 through 1928 federal surpluses totaled $6.6 billion, shrinking the federal debt from 33 to 18 percent of GDP.

But rising tax revenues were not solely responsible. Total federal tax revenues declined from $5.6 billion in 1921 to $3.9 billion by 1928. Personal income tax revenues increased, as Mellon predicted, but represented less than a third of federal tax revenues by 1928. The huge federal surpluses during the nineteen-twenties resulted almost entirely from spending cuts, from $5.1 billion in 1921 to $3.0 billion in 1928.

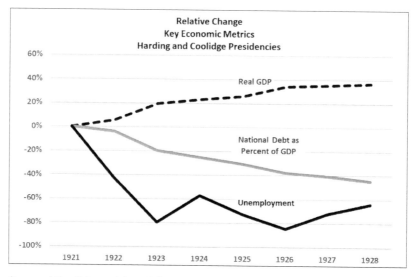

Harding and Coolidge achieved the rare economic trifecta of rising real GDP, decreasing national debt, and falling unemployment.

U.S. BUREAU OF ECONOMIC ANALYSIS | FEDERAL RESERVE | U.S. BUREAU OF LABOR STATISTICS

Coolidge and Mellon were a matched set. Coolidge cut government spending while Mellon cut taxes. Coolidge met weekly with his budget director, Herbert Lord, to find ways to shave expenses. No expense was too small. "Post office bags could be made of plain gray canvas," one biographer wrote, "not the traditional white with blue stripes, saving $50,000 a year."[44] Measured as a percentage of GDP, Coolidge shrank government spending 20 percent from 1923 through 1928. Many Presidents since have spoken of reducing the size of government. None has ever matched Coolidge.

Only the nineteen-sixties came close to the nineteen-twenties in achieving the economic trifecta of strong GDP growth, rising personal incomes for all taxpayers, and a reduction in the federal debt. Mellon's tax and spending cuts worked well in the nineteen-twenties, but successful economic policies during prosperous times often fail during economic downturns. Mellon would learn this painful lesson when his economic policies failed to counter the Great Depression. By 1932 he would be out as Treasury Secretary, shipped off to England as Ambassador to the United Kingdom.

Other Major Accomplishments

The booming economy, facilitated by Commerce Secretary Hoover and Treasury Secretary Mellon, were the hallmarks of President Coolidge's administration. But other accomplishments were noteworthy, and two led to Nobel Peace Prizes.

In 1924 Coolidge signed the Indian Citizenship Act which gave all Native Americans full U.S. citizenship. Although the 14th Amendment declared any person born in the United States to be a U.S. citizen, the amendment had historically been interpreted to exclude Native Americans.[45]

Also, in 1924, Coolidge appointed Charles Dawes, formerly President Harding's Director of the Bureau of the Budget, to head an international commission to find a solution to Europe's crippling war debt. Dawes proposed an innovative solution in which Wall Street loaned Germany $200 million that was used to rebuild German industry and pay off reparations to Britain and France. Germany's payment to Britain and France then allowed those countries, each with millions in war debt, to repay the United States. It was a brilliant plan, worthy of any modern financier, which used American capital to rebuild Germany, pay off Europe's war debts, and provide American investors an attractive return. In 1925, Dawes received the Nobel Peace Prize for his efforts in resolving the European debt crisis.[46]

Coolidge continued Harding's America First policy and kept the United States out of the League of Nations. Yet, his administration had a significant impact on international relations that continues to this day. In 1928, Coolidge's Secretary of State, Frank Kellogg, together with the French foreign minister Aristide Briand, signed the Kellogg-Briand Pact that renounced the use of war to settle international disputes. The pact was ultimately signed by over sixty countries and remains in effect today. Idealistic and unenforceable, the Pact stopped few wars, but it was nevertheless a small step towards the concept that war is a crime against peace. Much of the Pact's provisions were later incorporated into the United Nations Charter. In 1929 Kellogg was awarded the Nobel Peace Prize for his efforts on the Pact, the second member of Coolidge's administration to win the prize, an unbroken record.[47]

The Coolidge administration also played a significant role in repairing the relations between the United States and Latin America. In 1904 President Teddy Roosevelt extended the Monroe Doctrine to include the Roosevelt Corollary. The Monroe Doctrine had declared the United States would resist any effort by European powers to colonize or otherwise interfere in Latin America. Roosevelt's Corollary extended the doctrine by declaring the United States also had the right, as "an international police power," to intervene anywhere in Latin America to preserve order and protect lives and property.[48]

Roosevelt's Corollary essentially asserted that Latin American countries were more of a threat to their own security than any peril they faced from Europe. Between 1905 and 1934, the United States intervened militarily in Mexico, Nicaragua, the Dominican Republic, Haiti, and Honduras. The "Banana Wars" saw American troops intervene in 1907, 1911, 1912, 1919, 1924, and 1925 in Honduras, which was dominated by the United Fruit Company.[49]

In 1928, at the Sixth International Conference of American States held in Havana, Latin American countries introduced a resolution rejecting the Roosevelt Corollary. Coolidge, who had sailed to Havana on an American battleship, was sympathetic. Within months the State Department issued a memorandum rejecting the Roosevelt Corollary.[50] That memorandum was the first step towards reversing twenty-five years of American military intervention in Latin America, and in 1933 would lead to President Franklin D. Roosevelt's "Good Neighbor" Policy.[51]

"I do not choose to run."

On August 2, 1927, while vacationing at his "Summer White House" in South Dakota, President Coolidge held what was surely America's shortest press conference. Without speaking a word, Coolidge handed each reporter a strip of paper that stated: "I do not choose to run for President in 1928. There will be nothing more from this office today."[52]

Coolidge could easily have won reelection. He and First Lady Grace were loved by the American public. He had restored government integrity after the corruption under Harding. He cut taxes, slashed the national debt, and shrank the federal government. He kept the United States out of the League of Nations. His administration, unlike the progressive reformers two decades earlier, sought to assist business rather than regulate it. For six years, the American economy—except for farmers—boomed.

The Coolidge family on June 30, 1924. Within a week, Calvin, Jr. (far left) would be dead from blood poisoning.   LIBRARY OF CONGRESS

But, four years earlier, his son Calvin, Jr. had died of blood poisoning after a blister on his foot, contracted while playing tennis on the White House lawn, became infected. The best physicians of the day couldn't save the boy. For months, Coolidge was inconsolable, often sobbing at his desk. Grace remarked that after Calvin Jr. died, her husband "lost his zest for living."[53]

Coolidge claimed he was simply following George Washington's precedent when he chose not to run for a third term. But a brief paragraph in his 1930 autobiography likely provides the real reason:

> If I had not been President, [Calvin, Jr.] would not have raised a blister on his toe, which resulted in blood poisoning, playing lawn tennis in the South Grounds. In his suffering, he was asking me to make him well. I could not. When he went, the power and the glory of the Presidency went with him.[54]

Lyndon B. Johnson

November 22, 1963 – January 20, 1969

> I believe that the essence of government lies with unceasing concern for the welfare and dignity and decency and innate integrity of life for every individual. I don't like to say this and I wish I didn't have to add these words to make it clear, but I will: regardless of color, creed, ancestry, sex, or age.[1]

Today John Fitzgerald Kennedy lives on in the immortal words and works that he left behind. He lives on in the mind and memories of mankind. He lives on in the hearts of his countrymen.... No words are strong enough to express our determination to continue the forward thrust of America that he began.... Today, in this moment of new resolve, I would say to all my fellow Americans, let us continue."[2]

Let us continue. With these words, spoken on Thanksgiving Eve 1963, President Lyndon Johnson promised to secure the legacy of his predecessor, a promise on which he quickly delivered. Riding a wave of sympathy after Kennedy's assassination, Johnson pushed through Kennedy's proposed tax cuts, signed as the Tax Reduction Act on February 16, 1964. Five months later, Johnson signed the Civil Rights Act of 1964 outlawing discrimination based on race, color, religion, sex, or national origin. The Act was the most sweeping civil rights legislation since 1875. A year later, Johnson signed the Immigration Act of 1965, overturning forty years of prejudiced immigration policy. All were historic in their sweep.

Johnson had his own dreams. His first job had been as a schoolteacher in dirt-poor Cotulla, Texas. "I shall never forget the faces of the boys and the girls..." he recounted years later, "and I remember even yet the pain of realizing and knowing then that college was closed to practically every one of those children because they were too poor. And I think it was then that I made up my mind that this nation could never rest while the door to knowledge remained closed to any American."[3] That promise, made to himself four decades earlier, became the foundation of his presidency. He called it the Great Society.

Newly sworn-in President Lyndon Johnson and Lady Bird Johnson comforting Jackie Kennedy after her husband was assassinated in Dallas on November 22, 1963.
WHITE HOUSE PHOTO/ALAMY

President Johnson's legacy of elevating America's neglected and poor would be overshadowed. Johnson had inherited another, much darker legacy from Kennedy, a legacy that Kennedy had inherited from Eisenhower and Eisenhower from Truman: the conflict in Vietnam. Sucked slowly into that quagmire in Southeast Asia, Vietnam eventually took 58,000 American lives and left Lyndon Johnson a broken man.

The Kennedy Tax Cuts

Johnson knew he had a fight on his hands when he submitted Kennedy's tax plan to Congress. The plan cut income taxes for lower-income taxpayers from 20 to 14 percent and for upper-income taxpayers from 91 to 70 percent. These were deep tax cuts, second only to those under President Calvin Coolidge in 1925. Corporate tax rates were also reduced, but only slightly, from 52 to 48 percent—just enough to give Johnson bragging rights that Washington no longer taxed the majority of corporate profits.

It seems quaint today, but both parties of Congress were concerned the Kennedy tax cuts would increase deficits. Paying down the national debt was still a priority in 1964. For 168 years, Congress had followed the guidance George Washington offered in his 1796 Farewell Address:

> The accumulation of debt, not only by shunning occasions of expense but by vigorous exertion in time of peace to discharge the debts which unavoidable wars may have occasioned, not ungenerously throwing upon posterity the burden which we ourselves ought to bear. . . . It is essential that you should practically bear in mind that towards the payment of debts there must be revenue; that to have revenue there must be taxes.[4]

Johnson knew he would need to compromise to get the tax cut passed and agreed to cut spending. "[My budget] calls for a reduction from the preceding year in total administrative budget expenditures," he told Congress. "And it is only the second budget in nine years to do so. It calls for a substantial reduction in total civilian employment in the executive branch. . ."[5]

There were other skeptics. The Kennedy tax plan was based on demand-side economics, designed to give the most relief to consumers. Both Kennedy and Johnson believed the tax savings would be spent quickly, stimulating the economy. But Washington's venerable Tax Foundation disagreed. Founded in 1937, the Tax Foundation claimed its "engaged experts informed smarter tax policy at the federal, state, and global levels."[6]

The Tax Foundation believed a supply-side approach, giving the largest tax savings to corporations and the wealthy, would better stimulate economic growth. These savings would then be invested in new factories, equipment, and processes making the entire country more productive. "Most of the 'tax relief' goes to taxpayers in lower-income brackets," the

Foundation wrote in its February 11, 1963 report.[7] "Is this the kind of over-all reform of the tax structure that the economy needs?" the report asked.

Apparently, so. After the tax cuts, real GDP grew 4.9 percent annually from 1964 through 1969, versus 3.6 percent the prior six years. Employ-ment grew 2.3 percent versus 1.6 percent. The national debt, measured as a percentage of GDP, fell from 46 to 35 percent. From 1966 through 1969, unemployment averaged 3.7 percent, a four-year record never again matched. These were spectacular economic figures, together only exceeded over the last one hundred years during the Roaring Twenties under Presi-dents Harding and Coolidge.

Advocates for lower taxes argue the tax cuts were responsible for these strong economic results. They have a strong argument. During the four years preceding the tax cut, 1960 through 1963, the average personal fed-eral income tax rate was 12.7 percent. That rate dropped to 11.9 percent during the following four years, 1964 through 1967, saving the average middle-class taxpayer about $344 annually (in 2020 dollars). Overall, tax-payers saved an average of $31.4 billion each year after the tax cuts. Dur-ing those same years, the average corporate tax rate fell from 42.8 percent to 38.2 percent saving American companies $3.7 billion annually. These savings likely contributed to increases in consumption and business invest-ment whose growth increased to an average of 5.0 percent and 6.2 percent, respectively, during the four years after the tax cuts.

But other factors were at play also, particularly increased government spending. From 1964 through 1967 real government spending increased a blistering 6.5 percent annually, largely due to higher spending on so-cial programs. No period since has come close to this level of government spending growth.

There was something else fueling the economy during the nineteen-six-ties beyond government spending and lower taxes: optimism. Optimism is the fuel that powers consumer spending and business investment. Surpris-ingly, despite the Vietnam War, civil strife, and the assassinations of John and Robert Kennedy and Dr. Martin Luther King Jr., Americans were buoy-antly optimistic during the nineteen-sixties. The University of Michigan

Consumer Sentiment Index for the decade averaged 95.4, the highest of any decade since measurements began in the late nineteen-forties.[8]

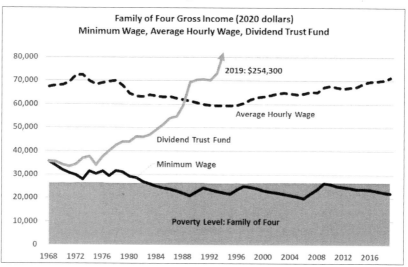

Over the last 50 years, hourly workers have had little increase in real wages. By 2020, a family of four working 3,000 hours a year at minimum wage made 37 percent less in inflation-adjusted dollars than in 1968, while a trust fund earning dividends increased seven-fold.

U.S. DEPARTMENT OF LABOR | U.S. CENSUS BUREAU | U.S. BUREAU OF ECONOMIC ANALYSIS

Contributing to that optimism was growing middle-class wealth. After tax-incomes for the middle 60 percent of taxpayers, adjusted for inflation, increased 23 percent during the nineteen-sixties. Unfortunately, the sixties were the last decade that America's middle-class prospered. After two decades of strong growth, middle-class incomes stopped growing as the sixties ended.

Most middle-class Americans understand they have been left behind economically. Few realize by how much. Tell a middle-class taxpayer their real income has hardly increased in fifty years and most would disagree. They might compare their paycheck today with their grandparents from fifty years ago. In 1970, for example, nominal middle-class income after federal taxes was $6,300; in 2018 it was $41,800. That's quite an increase but these figures ignore inflation. Measured in 2020 dollars, middle-class income after taxes increased only slightly from $42,100 in 1970 to $43,000 in 2018. During those same years, the after-tax income of the top 20 percent increased from $111,100 to $201,600. The very wealthiest Americans en-joyed the largest growth in after-tax income. The top one percent grew from $306,000 to $1,195,000.

After World War II, middle-class prosperity fueled the American Dream. But that prosperity was built in the nineteen-fifties and sixties. In the years since, most Americans have shared little in the nation's economic growth.

What the Hell's the Presidency for?

Three years after the Civil War, the 14th Amendment to the Constitu-tion granting American-born Blacks U.S. citizenship was ratified by every state (although Ohio's and New Jersey's ratifications weren't officially rec-ognized until 2003). Many states had little choice. Congress required the former Confederate states to ratify the amendment if they wished to rejoin the Union.[9]

The amendment forced Americans to reconsider who they were. A dec-ade earlier, in 1857, the Supreme Court had ruled in *Dred Scott v. Sanford* that no Black, whether free or slave, could claim U.S. citizenship. The Court declared members of the African race "are not included, and were not in-tended to be included, under the word 'citizens' in the Constitution.... The unhappy Black race were separated from the white by indelible marks, and laws long before established, and were never thought of or spoken of except as property."[10] Today, these are shameful words, but for much of America's history Blacks were, indeed, considered mere property.

The Supreme Court's *Dred Scott* ruling was based on 150 years of solid legal precedent extending back to the early colonial period. One of the first acts passed by Congress was the Naturalization Act of 1790, which declared, "that any Alien *being a free white person*, who shall have resided within the limits and under the jurisdiction of the United States for the term of two years, may be admitted to become a citizen."[11] For most early Americans, Blacks were considered property making it unthinkable that a member of the Black race could be a citizen.

That included Thomas Jefferson. The northeast portico of the Jefferson Memorial in Washington D.C. bears a famous inscription drawn from Jef-ferson's autobiography: "Nothing is more certainly written in the book of fate than that these people [America's slaves] are to be free." Stirring words, but the inscription omitted Jefferson's next sentence. "Nor is it less certain that the two races, equally free, cannot live in the same government. Nature, habit, opinion has drawn indelible lines of distinction between them."[12] Jefferson, a slave owner himself, supported freeing the slaves in principle but opposed their citizenship.

Jefferson's belief that Blacks should be free, but denied citizenship was widely accepted throughout the nineteenth century. During the Lincoln-Douglas debates in 1858, Stephen Douglas, the incumbent Senator from the free state of Illinois, argued:

> I hold that this Government was made on the white basis, by white men, for the benefit of white men and their posterity forever, and should be administered by white men and none others... We ought to extend to the negro every right, every privilege, every immunity which he is capable of enjoying, consistent with the good of society... but we have also decided that... he shall not vote, hold office, or exercise any political rights.[13]

The 14th Amendment passed after the Civil War was America's first step toward erasing the indelible lines of distinction Americans had drawn over the previous 150 years. In addition to giving Blacks the right to citizenship, the amendment's Equal Protection clause required that all individuals be treated the same by the law. Two years later, in 1870, the 15th Amendment prohibited federal, state, and local governments from denying a citizen the right to vote based on race, color, or "previous condition of servitude." For one hundred years the two amendments had little effect, circumvented by Jim Crow laws in the American South. The laws—named after a buffoonish, blackface minstrel show character who danced and spoke in an exaggerated African-American dialect—were meant to enforce racial segregation and limit the right of Blacks to vote, hold jobs, and obtain an education.

As a southern Congressman, Johnson understood how Jim Crow laws had subjugated African-Americans. During his first twenty years in Congress, Johnson fought efforts to overturn laws supporting segregation. But in 1956 Johnson had a change of heart and refused to sign the *Southern Manifesto*, a document that refuted the Supreme Court's *Brown v. Board of Education* decision to desegregate schools. The manifesto promised to use "all lawful means to bring about a reversal of this decision which is contrary to the Constitution and to prevent the use of force in its implementation."[14] It was signed by 101 senators and representatives, all from former Confederate states. The next year Johnson, now Senate Majority Leader, fought to assure the passage of the Civil Rights Act of 1957. The Act, likened by one Black leader to "soup made from the bones of an emaciated chicken,"[15] was a modest first step towards true equality.

Six years later, and only three days after assuming the presidency, President Johnson was determined that passing Kennedy's civil rights bill would be one of his top priorities.

But Johnson's political advisors counseled caution, knowing that supporting civil rights legislation would cost him southern votes in the upcoming presidential election. Johnson was resolute: "Well, what the hell's the presidency for? We have talked long enough in this country about equal rights. We have talked for 100 years or more. It is time now to write the next chapter, and to write it in the books of law."[16]

It took sympathy for a popular, martyred President and all of Johnson's legislative skills to pass Kennedy's civil rights act. The act, signed on July 2, 1964, ended a century of Jim Crow separate but equal doctrine by prohibiting discrimination based on race, color, religion, sex, or national origin. A year later, Congress passed the Voting Rights Act of 1965 that outlawed the barriers, such as literacy tests and poll taxes, which southern states had installed to limit the Black vote.

The civil rights laws were quickly challenged in court. On October 5, 1964, the Supreme Court heard oral arguments in *Heart of Atlanta Motel, Inc. v. United States*. The motel argued it had a right to refuse service to Blacks. The Court, in a unanimous decision, ruled against the motel, noting that most of its customers were out-of-state, and hence fell under the Constitution's commerce clause that gave Congress the power "to regulate Commerce... among the several States."[17]

The 1964 Civil Rights Act benefited not only Blacks but other groups who had historically suffered from discrimination, including women, the disabled, and gays. Before the Act, an employer could advertise for a white male under forty to fill a job or post a sign stating: "Help Wanted. No Coloreds Need Apply." The Civil Rights Act of 1964 ended those practices, at least overtly.

A huge backlash followed the passage of the 1964 Civil Rights Act. Angry white supremacists went on a murderous rampage throughout the South.

On June 21, 1964, three young civil rights workers, James Chaney, Andrew Goodman, and Michael Schwerner were arrested and then turned over to the Ku Klux Klan. Days later their bodies were found in an earthen dam. On July 11, Lt. Colonel Lemuel Penn was shot by Klansman as he was driving home from U.S. Army Reserve training. On February 26, 1965, Jimmie Lee Jackson was shot by state troopers while attempting to protect his mother and grandfather during a civil rights march. On March 11, the Reverend James Reeb was beaten to death while participating in the Selma Freedom Marches. On March 25, Viola Liuzzo was shot and killed by a Klansman in a passing car while she was ferrying Selma Marchers between Selma and Montgomery. On June 5, Oneal Moore, a newly hired Black deputy, was killed by a shotgun blast from a passing car. On July 18, Willie Brewster was killed coming home from work by members of the National States Rights Party. On August 20, Jonathan Daniels, an Episcopalian seminary student helping with Black voter registration, was killed by a deputy sheriff. On January 3, 1966, Samuel Younge, Jr. was killed by a gas station attendant when he objected to segregated restrooms. On January 10, the home of Vernon Dahmer, a wealthy Mississippi businessman, was firebombed the day after a radio station broadcast his promise to pay voter poll taxes for those unable to afford them. He died from severe burns.[18]

The murders continued through 1967 and 1968, culminating in the assassination of Dr. Martin Luther King Jr. on April 4, 1968. For years, King had encouraged patient, non-violent protest against racism, winning the Nobel Peace Prize in 1964.[19]

These murders were tragic, but race riots, fueled on both sides by decades of pent-up Black frustration and white resentment, killed even more.

In 1919, race riots erupted in nearly a dozen American cities as soldiers, home from the First World War, were unable to find jobs. That year a riot in Elaine, Arkansas resulted in the deaths of an estimated 237 Blacks and five whites. A 1921 race riot in Tulsa, Oklahoma was reported as officially killing thirty-six people; the Red Cross reported 300 deaths. "Despite being numerically at a disadvantage," an Oklahoma state study reported years later, "Black Tulsans fought valiantly to protect their homes, their businesses, and their community. But in the end, the city's African-American population was simply outnumbered by the white invaders."[20]

During the nineteen-sixties, hundreds of riots swept across American cities, killing scores, injuring thousands, and destroying urban centers.[21] Major riots occurred in Birmingham, Harlem in New York City, Watts in Los Angeles, Chicago, Tampa, Cincinnati, Atlanta, Newark, and Detroit. During the "Long, Hot Summer of 1967," over 150 race riots broke out that killed eighty-three people. The deadliest were in Detroit, where forty-three died, and in Newark, which cost twenty-six lives. The next year more than 110 cities erupted on the night of April 4, 1968 after King's assassination.[22]

America seemed to be tearing itself apart. President Johnson appointed a presidential commission to investigate the causes of the riots and propose solutions. Headed by Otto Kerner Jr., the governor of Illinois, the Kerner Commission was composed of nine white and two Black members drawn from government, industry, and civil associations. For months, the commission met in closed-door sessions listening to first responders, activists, local government officials, and social scientists. They then visited, usually incognito, twenty-three racially-charged cities to interview residents. In Milwaukee, for example, one commission member was shocked after he spent the day in a barbershop. Customers talked about segregation being far worse in Milwaukee than in the South. The city was so segregated that many Blacks had never interacted with white people.[23]

The commission issued its report on February 29, 1968.

Johnson was outraged. He had staffed the committee largely with moderate whites who he expected would conclude the riots were the fault of outside agitators or young Black "riff-raff," as an earlier study had concluded. Instead, as the *Washington Post* reported on March 1, "The Kerner commission points the finger of blame squarely on what it regards as one 'most fundamental' cause: white racism. It is the way white Americans act toward Black Americans. White racism, the commission found, has built up an explosive mixture of segregation, discrimination, and deprivation in the poor Black ghettos of the big cities."[24]

The Kerner Commission was unequivocal. "The Commission has found no evidence," their report stated, "that all or any of the disorders or the incidents that led to them were planned or directed by any organization or group, international, national or local." Instead, the commission members blamed the dreadful conditions in Black, urban ghettos—poor jobs, poor education, poor housing—for creating "a destructive environment totally unknown to most white Americans."

Addressing criticism that Blacks only needed to work harder to pull themselves out of poverty, as earlier immigrants had done, the report observed, "When the European immigrants arrived, they gained an economic foothold by providing the unskilled labor needed by industry. Unlike the immigrant, the Negro migrant found little opportunity in the city. The economy, by then matured, had little use for the unskilled labor he had to offer."

Regarding the role of the police in race relations, the commission declared: "To some Negroes, police have come to symbolize white power, white racism and white repression.... The atmosphere of hostility and cynicism is reinforced by a widespread belief among Negroes in the existence of police brutality and in a 'double standard' of justice and protection, one for Negroes and one for whites."[25]

Johnson had used every ounce of the political capital he had acquired after Kennedy's assassination fighting for civil rights. Now the Kerner Commission concluded that his civil rights legislation had only set high and unrealistic expectations. Without massive additional spending, America would evolve into "two societies, one Black, one white—separate and unequal."[26]

Johnson considered the report politically damning and attempted to have it embargoed. But major stories in *The New York Times*, *Washington Post* and *Newsweek* made that impossible. Johnson refused to discuss the report and when given thank-you letters that were to be sent to the committee members, refused to sign them. A few weeks later, Bantam published a paperback version of the report which quickly sold 740,000 copies.[27]

The report generated an immediate backlash that disputed its conclusions. William F. Buckley Jr., the publisher of the *National Review* and a respected political commentator, condemned the report and blamed the riots on "a psychological disorder which is tearing at the ethos of our society as a result of boredom, self-hatred, and the arrogant contention that all our shortcomings are the result of other people's aggressions upon us." Richard Nixon, running for President on a law-and-order platform, declared that the report "blames everybody for the riots except the perpetrators of the riots," and promised that as President, he would "meet force with force, if necessary, in the cities."[28]

Dr. King had preached change through patient, non-violent protest. King's "I Have a Dream Speech" during the 1963 March on Washington inspired millions, Black and white, and won support for civil rights legislation. But that support plunged after the violent race riots during 1967 and 1968. Instead, much of white America rejected the Kerner Commission's findings, and blamed Blacks instead.

The riots badly hurt the cause of American Blacks. Richard Nixon became President, in part, by promising to restore law and order to American cities. Long-term, expensive federal programs to train Black workers were replaced by welfare programs to address the symptoms rather than the causes of poverty. Plans to integrate and rebuild Black ghettos stalled. Some cities, like Detroit, never fully recovered. Police forces became militarized and police brutality would remain an issue for Black Americans through today.

King himself became the most prominent victim of the racial violence he had fought against when he was assassinated by a sniper on April 4, 1968 while standing on the balcony of a Memphis motel. King had, perhaps, foreseen his own death. "I've seen the promised land," he had told followers the prior evening. "I may not get there with you. But I want you to know tonight, that we, as a people, will get to the promised land. And I'm happy tonight." He was only thirty-seven when he was murdered.

America had not yet recovered from King's death when President Kennedy's brother, Senator Robert "Bobby" Kennedy, was killed two months later on June 6, 1968. Kennedy was shot while walking through a Los Angeles hotel kitchen on his way to deliver a victory speech after winning his party's South Dakota and California presidential primaries earlier that evening.

America seemed to have gone mad. President Kennedy, Martin Luther King Jr., and Robert Kennedy had been cut down by assassins. Three men who stood for tolerance, understanding and acceptance, killed by three who practiced the opposite. Their deaths inspired the bittersweet folk song, "Abraham, Martin and John," a poignant tribute to Abraham Lincoln, John Kennedy, Martin Luther King Jr., and Bobby Kennedy.[29] For those who lived through the nineteen-sixties, few protest anthems were more poignant, more evocative of that troubled time than "Abraham, Martin and John."

Immigration: Who and How Many?

On October 5, 1965 President Johnson stood at the base of the Statue of Liberty. He was there to announce the Immigration Act of 1965.

"Give me your tired, your poor, your huddled masses yearning to breathe free." These are the celebrated words at the base of the statue. But since 1921, those huddled masses had emigrated almost exclusively from Northern Europe. Immigration from Eastern and Southern Europe was tightly restricted and Asians were almost completely excluded.

Those exclusionary policies began in 1921 when President Warren G. Harding signed the Emergency Quota Act. The Act's impetus was to stop the influx of refugees, largely Jews and Slavs, flooding into the United States after the First World War and the Russian Revolution. But the Emergency Act went beyond that. The Act instituted a national quota system that strongly favored Western and Northern Europeans. Immigration from Eastern and Southern Europe and Asia was almost entirely halted.

It was not until 1952, when the Immigration and Nationality Act passed, that Asians became eligible for naturalized U.S. citizenship. (Chinese, American allies during World War II, were granted citizenship rights in 1943.).[30]

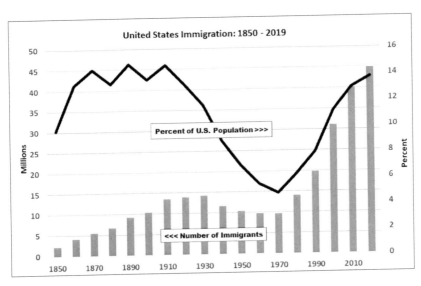

Earlier, federal immigration acts used national quotas to limit immigration largely to western Europe. The 1965 Immigration Act dropped national quotas. A surge in immigration, predominantly from non-European countries, followed.

MIGRATION POLICY INSTITUTE

The Immigration Act that President Johnson announced that day had its roots in the Kennedy administration. Kennedy had advocated immigration reform while a Senator. He wrote a short book, *A Nation of Immigrants*, in 1958 that proposed that national-origin quotas be replaced with a system that gave priority to relatives of U.S. citizens and permanent residents.[31] Kennedy had borrowed the idea from a 1953 study, *Whom We Shall Welcome*, initiated by President Truman.[32] Four months before his death, Kennedy sent his immigration reform proposal to Congress, but like much of the slain President's agenda, it would fall to President Johnson to pass it.

The Immigration Act of 1965 received strong Congressional support, passing the House 320 to 70. The Act replaced the discriminatory National Origins Formula, creating seven immigration categories and giving priority to the immediate relatives of U.S. citizens and permanent residents. For the first time, quotas were placed on immigration from Latin America, including Mexico.

Congress, however, as it had begun with the Chinese Exclusion Act in 1882, remained intent on maintaining America's racial homogeneity. The new Act, it was believed, would not dilute the nation's racial homogeneity since immigration was largely restricted to close relatives of U.S. citizens and permanent residents. Immigration from countries with few American citizens would naturally be limited.

Congress was wrong. The 1965 Act quickly changed immigration in the United States. After the 1921 and 1924 Immigration Acts, the foreign-born percentage of the American population declined from 14.7 percent in 1910 to 5.1 percent in 1965.[33] That trend reversed after the passage of the 1965 Immigration Act. The percentage of foreign-born hit 6.2 percent in 1980, 11.1 percent in 2000 and 13.7 percent in 2018, the highest level since 1910.[34] Few of the new immigrants came from Europe. In 1960, 84 percent of America's foreign-born population was either from Europe or Canada. By 2017, only 13 percent were Europeans. Twenty-seven percent were Asian and 50 percent Latin American.[35]

Immigration has been a contentious issue since America's founding. "In 1797 a member of Congress," Senator Kennedy wrote in *A Nation of Immigrants,* "argued that, while a liberal immigration policy was fine when the country was new and unsettled, now that America had reached its maturity and was fully populated, immigration should stop—an argument which has been repeated at regular intervals throughout American history."[36]

The debate over immigration—who and how many—remains with us today, as it has since America was founded.

The War on Poverty

Three months after taking office, President Johnson embarked on his "Poverty Tours," one of the most ambitious personal crusades ever undertaken by an American President.[37] Arriving in his gleaming Boeing 707 and greeted everywhere by brass bands and cheering crowds, Johnson met with impoverished citizens in cities from Pittsburgh, Pennsylvania, its mighty steel industry humbled by foreign competitors, to Rocky Mount, North Carolina, where tobacco sharecroppers struggled to eke out a living.

In the hard-scrabble Kentucky town of Inez, Johnson sat on Tom Fletcher's front porch to hear how Fletcher struggled to support his family on $400 a year. The local coal mine had closed and Fletcher, with just a grade school education, had been unemployed for two years. But President Johnson was encouraging. As Fletcher's eight children shyly shook the President's hand, Johnson's optimism assured them they would soon be back on their feet.[38]

President Johnson visiting with Tom Fletcher and his family during Johnson's 1964 Poverty Tour. With the coal mine closed, Fletcher had been unemployed for two years. Johnson promised to cure poverty, not just treat its symptoms.

EVERETT COLLECTION HISTORICAL/ALAMY

Johnson felt deep-rooted empathy for the poor. He had grown up surrounded by poverty in the Texas Hill Country. His first job was as an elementary school teacher to poor Mexican-Americans, children he knew had little hope for a better life. His first success as a junior Congressman had been to secure a hydroelectric dam to provide electricity to his former neighbors. For the rest of his life, Johnson considered helping those poor Texas farmers his proudest achievement.

Now, thrust into the presidency, Johnson vowed to end poverty in America. "Some people say if these Americans are poor, it's their own fault..." the President told a crowd in Rocky Mount, North Carolina. "I believe, the reason most people are poor is that they never got a decent break. They never had a fair chance when they were young, and they never got it later on."[39] Johnson was committed to giving them that chance. "This administration today, here and now, declares unconditional war on poverty in America..." he declared during his first State of the Union Address. "Our aim is not only to relieve the symptom of poverty, but to cure it and, above all, to prevent it."[40]

These were ambitious words. But in 1964, Americans were confident. And why shouldn't they be? The United States was the richest country in the world. America had won World War II, magnanimously rebuilt its former enemies, led the world with its industry and technology, and was on its way to the moon.

Johnson's social legislation, grandly named the "Great Society," was second only to Franklin Roosevelt's New Deal in its ambition to uplift the common man. His Economic Opportunity Act, signed in August 1964, provided job placement and training programs to help the poor bootstrap themselves into a better life, loans to help individuals start small businesses, the Job Corps, Volunteers in Service to America, adult education, and youth work-study programs. The Food Stamp Act of 1964 provided supplemental nutrition to families, especially children. The Elementary and Secondary Education Act of 1965 provided federal funding to poor school districts to help assure all Americans received a good education. Most sweeping of all, the Social Security Amendments of 1965 established Medicaid and Medicare to assure every American had access to healthcare.[41]

President Johnson's War on Poverty failed. After spending trillions of dollars over fifty years, Johnson's social programs never defeated poverty. At best, America has called a truce, its social programs today almost entirely focused on relieving the symptoms of poverty rather than finding a cure, as Johnson had promised.

During the first half of the nineteen-sixties, one in five Americans were living in poverty. But the booming economy during the second half of the decade helped drive poverty down to 14 percent. There it stopped. Since 1970 poverty rates have hardly changed, averaging 13 percent, falling to 11 percent during economic booms and rising to 15 percent during recessions.

In January 2020, an estimated 580,000 Americans were homeless,[42] with 225,000 living on the street, in abandoned buildings, or in their cars.

The failure to cure poverty has not lacked funding. From 1965 through 2019, Washington spent $22 trillion, adjusted for inflation, on job training and placement, health, income security, and nutritional supplements. But only three percent of that spending has been devoted to job training and related programs, efforts critical to reducing unemployment and poverty. The overwhelming balance was spent on health and welfare programs to counter the symptoms rather than the causes of poverty. That's an average of $11,900 (in 2020 dollars) annually for every man, woman, and child living in poverty.

Explanations abound for why poverty has remained so persistent for decades. A September 2019 White House report on homelessness, for example, largely blames overregulation of the housing market that "impedes home construction... reduces the supply of homes and thus increases homelessness." Other factors include drug addiction, mental health conditions, and the failure to integrate formerly incarcerated individuals back into society, the report concluded.[43]

A 2018 Heritage Foundation report places the blame squarely on what Heritage considers the self-defeating behaviors promoted by government welfare programs. "As the War on Poverty expanded benefits," the report cites, "welfare began to serve as a substitute for a husband in the home, and low-income marriage began to disappear.... Today, unwed childbearing, with its consequent growth of single-parent homes, is the single most important cause of child poverty.... If poor women who give birth outside of marriage were married to the fathers of their children, two-thirds would immediately be lifted out of poverty."[44] The Heritage report concludes with proposed policy initiatives designed to encourage individuals to pull themselves out of poverty, including: establish work requirements for welfare recipients; limit low-skilled immigration; improve administrative efficiency; and eliminate "waste, fraud, abuse, and excessive benefits in the welfare system."

But attributing today's poverty exclusively to misguided federal poverty programs fails to recognize a major reason so many Americans remain impoverished: the pay is terrible.

Over the last fifty years, America's lowest-paid workers have taken a 38 percent pay cut. The purchasing power of the federal minimum wage, $1.60 at the time, peaked in 1968 at $11.90 measured in 2020 dollars. In 2019 the minimum wage was $7.25. Yet, during those years, nominal GDP per capita increased by a factor of fourteen. Had the minimum wage increased at the same rate, the minimum wage would have grown to $22.25 by 2019. Unrealistic? Not at all. During those years the gross income for Americans in the top one percent income bracket increased from $69,000 to over $1.5 million—their income growing far faster than the nation's per capita GDP.

Rather than sharing in America's growing wealth, America's poorest workers have taken a huge pay cut. In 1968, a family of four working 3,000 hours (one parent working full-time and the other part-time) earned $35,700 (in 2020 dollars), well above the $26,100 poverty level. In 2019, our hard-working family only earned $21,750, placing them deeply in poverty. Similarly, a single mother with a child working full time at the minimum wage in 1968 earned $23,800, once again, comfortably above the $17,196 poverty level. In 2019, she would only earn $14,500 putting her firmly on the welfare rolls.

The nineteen-fifties and sixties were the golden age for working Americans. A hard-working family in 1968, earning the minimum wage, had a reasonably comfortable life. That same family working in 2019 would be dependent on over $4,000 in government programs to lift them out of poverty.

Ironically, some of America's richest companies benefited from President Johnson's War on Poverty. For decades, American taxpayers have paid for income supplements, food stamps, and healthcare for hard-working, but poorly-paid employees of many of America's largest companies. A 2013 Congressional report, for example, singled out Walmart for paying sales associates an average of $8.81 an hour, wages that placed many families near poverty levels and allowed them to qualify for supplemental income and food benefits. These people weren't deadbeats feeding off government largess, but workers with full-time jobs with one of America's richest corporations. The report estimated that federal and local governments paid an average of $904,542 per year in welfare benefits to Walmart employees for each Walmart Superstore, or over $3,000 per employee.[45]

That began to change in 2015 when Walmart announced that it would raise wages for entry-level employees to nine dollars an hour and then to ten dollars by early 2016. Walmart had come to realize that better pay was good business. "Customers need to be served," Walmart's CEO, Doug McMillan said at the time, "and associates need to be happy and love their job."[46] Walmart executives exceeded their promise when the company raised the hourly wage for 1.2 million Walmart workers to $13.38 in January 2016.[47]

Scores of other companies, from Amazon to Starbucks, have followed Walmart's example.[48] Nevertheless, according to the Bureau of Labor Statistics, in 2019 10 percent of full-time wage earners, nearly 12 million workers, earned less in their inflation-adjusted incomes than a minimum wage worker in 1968.[49] Simply raising the real income of these workers back to the 1968 level would significantly cut poverty, draw millions of disenfranchised workers back into the labor force, and reduce the cost of government welfare programs.

A long-held American maxim declares "You cannot help the poor by destroying the rich."[50] That's certainly true. But would raising today's poverty-level wages destroy the rich? No, few would even notice.

Since 1968, real GDP per employed worker nearly doubled from $71,000 to $137,700 (in 2020 dollars). Improved productivity was making America wealthier. But that new wealth flowed upward. Little wealth trickled down as Treasury Secretary Andrew Mellon had predicted one-hundred years ago. According to the IRS, the after-tax income for the middle 60 percent of all taxpayers, measured in 2020 dollars, barely increased from 1968 through 2018 growing from $42,100 to only $43,000. In contrast, the top 20 percent of taxpayers increased from $112,200 to $202,400 while the top one percent enjoyed an increase from $347,800 to $1.19 million. But even that's peanuts compared to those fortunate enough to live off stock dividends. A dividend trust fund earning $35,700 in 1968—the same income as our minimum wage family that year—would have received dividend income of $258,000 in 2020 while our working family's income fell to $22,300. Even the most fervent laissez-faire capitalist might find it difficult to argue that was equitable.

How would redirecting some of America's wealth to the working poor affect middle and upper-class Americans? Consider a simple example. In 2019, about 2.5 million two-parent families and four million single-parent families lived in poverty.[51] What would it cost American companies to raise these families back to 1968 income levels? About $70 billion annually. (The math: 2.5 million two-parent families working 3,000 hours a year and four million single-parent families working 2,000 hours per year at $11.75 an hour rather than today's $7.25 minimum wage would cost corporations $69.75 billion—4.5 percent of their 2019 pre-tax profits.) Seventy billion dollars is a lot of money, but a small percentage of the nation's $1.5 trillion pre-tax profits in 2019. Furthermore, today's corporations, and their shareholders, have benefited from far lower taxes than fifty years ago. In 1968, the effective corporate tax rate averaged 40.3 percent. In 2019, after decades of tax cuts, their effective tax rate averaged only 14.2 percent. In 2019, that saved American companies $400 billion.

Still, asking companies to shave $70 billion off their profits would hardly be popular with the American Chamber of Commerce and would set Milton Friedman spinning in his grave. Friedman, one of the twentieth century's most respected economists, bears considerable responsibility for today's income inequality. In 1970, Friedman famously declared, "There is one and only one social responsibility of business—to use its resources and engage in activities designed to increase its profits."[52] Friedman gave corporations the moral justification to focus on growing profits over all other considerations, the only limitation being to engage in "open and free competition without deception or fraud."

It likely wasn't mere coincidence that a few years after Friedman's proclamation, corporate dividends, began a steady climb from an average of 2.6 percent of GDP from 1950 through 1975 to an average of 6.0 percent from 2010 through 2020. While conversely, the average hourly wage, after rising for years, peaked in 1972 at $24.15 (in 2020 dollars) and then stagnated, averaging only $21.72 from 1973 through 2020.[53]

Henry Ford, the prototypical capitalist of the twentieth century, shocked the business world a hundred years ago when he raised his workers' pay to five dollars a day. Ford understood that if workers believe they are getting a good deal they're much more likely to show up for work, work diligently and not quit for a few cents extra pay. Paying workers well was good business. And Ford knew his workers would quickly spend their increased earnings, often on a new Ford.

Henry Ford's thinking holds true today. Paying America's poorest workers a living wage would result in money quickly flowing back into the economy as increased consumption. The government would spend less on programs to supplement incomes. And, given a chance to now earn a decent wage, millions more would return to the workforce.

That Bitch of a War

Shortly after declaring War on Poverty, America was fighting a very real war. For ten years, conflict in Vietnam had been at a low simmer after Hồ Chí Minh had driven the French from Indochina and the 1954 Geneva Accords partitioned the former French colony into North and South Vietnam. Both Eisenhower and Kennedy sent American military advisors to train the South Vietnamese to fight their northern countrymen. By the time Johnson ascended to the presidency, 200 Americans had been killed in skirmishes with the North and its allies within the National Liberation Front for South Vietnam, known as the Viet Cong.[54]

Three weeks before Kennedy's death, South Vietnam's President Ngô Đình Diệm was assassinated in a military coup covertly supported by the United States. Diệm, a fervent Catholic in a Buddhist country, had managed to maintain a stable regime for eight years. But in 1963, Buddhist monks, in the ultimate personal protest, were self-immolating themselves in the center of Saigon. Images of monks silently engulfed in flames spread around the world as symbols of protest against a detested government. After Diệm's death, a series of military juntas ruled South Vietnam until 1967 when Nguyễn Văn Thiệu, an accomplice in the Diệm coup, was elected president in a U.S. mandated election. North Vietnam promptly labeled Thiệu a U.S. puppet.

In contrast, Hồ Chí Minh was revered throughout North Vietnam as a selfless patriot and the country's liberator. From 1941 to 1945, Minh had fought a guerrilla war with American support against the Japanese occupation of Indochina. After the war, on September 2, 1945, Minh declared Vietnam a free country and drew inspiration from America's Declaration of Independence. Hồ Chí Minh pleaded with President Truman to support their independence against the returning French colonialists. Truman ignored him. Minh then fought a nine-year colonial war that eventually pushed the French out of Indochina after a crushing defeat in 1954.

Having fought the Japanese and the French, Minh was now committed to overthrowing the South Vietnamese government and uniting the country. In 1961, North Vietnam began surreptitiously moving troops into South Vietnam and, by 1963, an estimated 40,000 North Vietnamese troops had infiltrated South Vietnam. That year, 16,300 American military personnel, restricted to advising the South Vietnamese, were stationed in South Vietnam.

For Americans, the Vietnam War formally began on August 2, 1964 in the Gulf of Tonkin. For months, the South Vietnamese had been conducting covert commando raids along the North Vietnamese coast under the direction of the U.S. Department of Defense. In July, Lt. General William Westmoreland changed tactics and directed South Vietnamese patrol boats to begin shore bombardments of North Vietnamese facilities. North Vietnam responded by assigning torpedo boats to patrol their coast.

On August 2, three North Vietnamese torpedo boats approached the USS *Maddox*, an American destroyer gathering intelligence in international waters. The *Maddox* fired warning shots across the bow of the closest boat. The torpedo boats returned fire and launched torpedoes. The destroyer was unscathed. Minutes later, F8 Crusader jets called in by the *Maddox* heavily damaged two torpedo boats and left the third dead in the water, burning.

The next evening, the *Maddox,* now accompanied by the USS *Turner Joy,* was again on patrol, this time in stormy weather and high seas. Although more than one hundred miles offshore, both ships reported multiple radar targets coming from different directions. Targets would appear, disappear, and then reappear from different directions. Sonar operators reported torpedoes being launched. Over the next three hours the American ships fired nearly 400 rounds at the attacking vessels. Although believing themselves under attack, no torpedo wakes were sighted and the ship's radar-controlled guns were unable to lock onto a target.

As the battle wore on Captain Herrick, in command of the *Maddox*, began to suspect that the radar and sonar images were misinterpretations by anxious and inexperienced operators. Herrick sent a message to Honolulu stating: "Review of action makes many reported contacts and torpedoes fired appear doubtful. Freak weather effects on radar and overeager sonar men may have accounted for many reports. No actual visual sightings by *Maddox*. Suggest complete evaluation before any further action taken."[55]

Hours later, Herrick sent a second message contradicting his first: "Certain that original ambush was bona fide. Details of action following present a confusing picture. Have interviewed witnesses who made positive visual sightings of cockpit lights or similar passing near *Maddox*. Several reported torpedoes were probably boats themselves which were observed to make several close passes on *Maddox*. Own ship screw noises on rudders may have accounted for some. At present cannot even estimate number of boats involved. *Turner Joy* reports two torpedoes passed near her."[56]

Somehow lost in the confusion was the report of Commander James Stockdale. Stockdale had launched his F8 Crusader from the aircraft carrier USS *Ticonderoga* to search for the attacking ships. After flying for ninety minutes at a low altitude he found nothing. "I had the best seat in the house to watch that event," Stockdale, later promoted to rear admiral, commented years later, "and our destroyers were just shooting at phantom targets. There were no PT boats there... there was nothing there but black water and American firepower."[57]

After sorting through the conflicting reports, Secretary of Defense Robert McNamara declared the U.S. vessels had been attacked. President Johnson ordered retaliatory airstrikes, the first overt U.S. military action against North Vietnam. The next day eighteen *Ticonderoga*-based aircraft struck a major oil storage facility on the North Vietnamese coast. Although the attack was successful, the United States suffered its first combat losses. Two aircraft were shot down, one pilot was killed and the second, Everett Alvarez Jr., was captured, the first U.S. airmen to be taken prisoner by North Vietnam. Alvarez survived nine years in the infamous "Hanoi Hilton" prison. He returned home a hero.

On August 7, the Senate, with only two dissenting votes, approved the Gulf of Tonkin Resolution, stating: "Congress approves and supports the determination of the President, as Commander in Chief, to take all necessary measures to repel any armed attack against the forces of the United States and to prevent further aggression."[58] As with every military conflict since World War II, Congress never issued a formal declaration of war.

From the beginning, Americans were divided over the role the United States should play in a small country 10,000 miles from American shores. But President Johnson was reassuring. "We are not about to send American boys nine or ten thousand miles away from home to do what Asian boys ought to be doing for themselves,"[59] Johnson promised just days before the 1964 presidential election. That promise was short-lived. The next year 184,300 American troops had been deployed to Vietnam.

Some believed the war could be quickly won. During his 1965 campaign for California governor, Ronald Reagan commented in the *Fresno Bee* that, "It's silly talking about how many years we will have to spend in the jungles of Vietnam when we could pave the whole country and put parking stripes on it and still be home for Christmas."[60] Retired Air Force General Curtis LeMay wrote in his 1965 book, *Mission with LeMay*: "My solution to the problem would be to tell them frankly that they've got to draw in their horns and stop their aggression or we're going to bomb them back into the Stone Ages."[61] The cigar-chomping general had forgotten that strategic bombing doesn't win wars. During World War II, the American Army Air Force bombed every major city in Germany and Japan into smoldering ruins, yet it took troops entering Berlin to force a German surrender and two atomic bombs to end the war in Japan.

Many Americans objected outright to America's entry into what they considered an unjust war. Boxing Champion Muhammad Ali was both cheered and reviled when he declared: "My conscience won't let me go shoot my brother, or some darker people, or some poor hungry people in the mud for big powerful America. And shoot them for what? They never called me nigger, they never lynched me, they didn't put no dogs on me, they didn't rob me of my nationality, rape and kill my mother and father. . . . Shoot them for what? How can I shoot them poor people? Just take me to jail."[62] Ali lost his boxing license, his world championship, and nearly went to jail for his beliefs.

Although the Vietnam War was unpopular, the majority of military personnel serving in Vietnam had enlisted. Approximately 70 percent of those who died in the war were volunteers.   AMERICAN WAR LIBRARY | MILITARY FACTORY

Years later the Supreme Court confirmed his status as a conscientious objector. Ali eventually regained his championship title when he defeated George Foreman in the famous 1974 "Rumble in the Jungle" match fought in Kinshasa, Zaire.

President Johnson, like so many others, believed he could bomb North Vietnam into submission. In Operation Rolling Thunder, U.S. bombers attacked military and industrial targets throughout North Vietnam. But the North Vietnamese quickly rebuilt and with the aid of Soviet and Chinese weapons shot down 3,700 American aircraft and 5,600 helicopters over the course of the war.[63] American bombers eventually dropped 7.7 million tons of bombs on Southeast Asia, nearly four times the tonnage dropped over Europe in World War II.[64]

Yet the North Vietnamese refused to negotiate. In early 1968, the North Vietnamese Viet Cong launched the Tet Offensive, a coordinated attack on thirteen cities across South Vietnam. The surprise attack even breached the U.S. Embassy in Saigon. Americans were shocked by the boldness of the offensive. General Westmoreland, who had recently declared the war nearly over, requested 200,000 additional troops in desperation.[65]

Unable to drive the North Vietnamese into submission from 30,000 feet, Johnson was forced to commit increasing numbers of ground troops to Vietnam: 184,300 in 1965, 385,300 in 1966, 485,600 in 1967 and 536,100 in 1968.[66] Vietnam became a crushing, chaotic ground war with no clear front, an invisible enemy, and dwindling support back home. The stories of returning American soldiers capture the war's cost far better than statistics:

> Phil went into the hedge at the same spot that I did, took that left turn and took one more step. We heard a burst of gunfire and I yelled for Phil. There was no answer. I yelled a second time with no better result. I ran to the hedgerow and turned left. There lay Phil shot ten times from his stomach to his head. Phil, a hero in my eyes, died instantly. My closest friend and fellow Marine was a KIA (Killed in Action) from a simple daylight patrol. The incident changed me for the rest of my time in the war until I was wounded and Med Evac'ed to the states four months later. In reality, it changed me for the rest of my life. I never again got close to anyone in my squad or company. I fly the flag each November 25 in honor of Phil and will do so for the rest of my life.[67]

> As a mortar man, I was amazed at how the NVA (North Vietnamese Army) could hit us with their mortars by firing for effect with no adjustment round.... When the chopper landed, we received incoming rounds. The second round hit Charlie Company's tube on its yoke. The gunner and assistant gunner flipped slowly up in the air like rag dolls; both men were dead by the time they hit the ground. To set up near where a helicopter would land was clearly asking for trouble.[68]

Suddenly, one of the five American soldiers screamed, "Grenade!" Now I could see clearly that the old man, arms stretched above his head, had a grenade clutched between his hands, his finger grasping the pull ring. Two of the soldiers ran up and grabbed the old man. As one soldier wrapped his hands around the old man's hands and the grenade, the other pinned his arms. A third soldier ran up with a spare safety pin at the ready to insert into the grenade. I looked around the area for any other hostile action, but the old man appeared to be acting alone.[69]

When I returned from Vietnam it was March 1968 in the midst of the civil rights movement. I landed at Boston's Logan Airport in my Marine Corps Alpha Green uniform, with the medals and ribbons I had earned proudly displayed. I approached the sidewalk to catch a taxi, hoping that I wasn't dreaming and would not awaken back at Camp Carroll to another bombardment. Six taxicabs passed me by and drove off. I didn't realize what was happening until the state trooper stepped in and told the next driver, "You have got to take this soldier." The driver, who was white, looked up at us through the passenger side window and said, "I don't want to go to Roxbury." That was my initial welcome home.[70]

In October 1968, the CBS television reporter Walter Cronkite, "the most trusted man in America," made a fact-finding trip to Vietnam. "It seems now more certain than ever," Cronkite reported back to America, "that the bloody experience of Vietnam is to end in a stalemate. To say that we are closer to victory today is to believe in the face of the evidence, the optimists who have been wrong in the past."[71]

President Johnson chose not to run for reelection. He left the presidency a broken man. the Vietnam War had already taken nearly 37,000 American lives with little chance of victory. The Great Society was in shambles, its promise destroyed by the worst racial violence in decades. Three years later Johnson reflected in his memoirs:

> I knew from the start that I was bound to be crucified either way I moved. If I left the woman I really loved—the Great Society—in

order to get involved with that bitch of a war on the other side of the world, then I would lose everything at home. All my programs. All my hopes to feed the hungry and shelter the homeless. All my dreams to provide education and medical care to the browns and the Blacks and the lame and the poor. But if I left that war and let the communists take over South Vietnam, then I would be seen as a coward and my nation would be seen as an appeaser, and we would both find it impossible to accomplish anything for anybody anywhere on the entire globe.[72]

Richard M. Nixon

---*---

January 20, 1969 – August 9, 1974

> Above all else, the time has come for us to renew our faith in ourselves and in America. . . . Our children have been taught to be ashamed of their country, ashamed of their parents, ashamed of America's record at home and of its role in the world. At every turn, we have been beset by those who find everything wrong with America and little that is right. But I am confident that this will not be the judgment of history on these remarkable times in which we are privileged to live.[1]

On January 20, 1969, Richard Nixon was inaugurated as America's thirty-seventh President, ending eight years of political purgatory. After serving as Eisenhower's Vice President, Nixon lost his own presidential bid in 1960 to John Kennedy by only 112,827 votes, the smallest popular vote margin in American history.[2] Two years later, Nixon lost the California governorship to Pat Brown. Humiliated and embittered, Nixon swore off politics. "You won't have Nixon to kick around anymore," Nixon lashed out at reporters, "because, gentlemen, this is my last press conference."[3]

Hardly. By 1964, Nixon was actively campaigning for Barry Goldwater during the Arizona Senator's presidential bid, while also traveling the world as a private statesman to converse with world leaders. Four years later, America was wracked by riots protesting the Vietnam War and racial discrimination. With the nation in turmoil, Nixon ran for President on a law-and-order platform. This time, he won.

As President Nixon began his inaugural address, he faced a troubled nation. Eight years earlier, his former opponent John Kennedy, had addressed a nation at peace. As Nixon spoke, nearly 37,000 Americans had already died in Vietnam. Twenty-thousand more would follow over the next five years.[4] Kennedy took office during a period of relative racial tranquility. Nixon faced a nation wracked by racial discord. Over one hundred Americans had died during race riots across the nation.[5] Americans were inspired by Kennedy's appeal to serve their country. Nixon faced a rise in radical groups—Students for a Democratic Society, Weathermen, Black Panthers—in open revolt against America and its institutions. As Kennedy took office, political assassination seemed destined to America's remote past. As Nixon took office, John Kennedy, Martin Luther King, and Robert Kennedy had all died by the bullet. Kennedy inherited a healthy if sluggish economy primed for growth. Nixon inherited an economy suffering the highest inflation and budget deficits since World War II.

Facing a nation in political, military, and economic crisis, Nixon reached back to President Roosevelt's inaugural address during the Great Depression to find inspiration:

> Standing in this same place a third of a century ago, Franklin Delano Roosevelt addressed a nation ravaged by depression and gripped in fear. He could say in surveying the Nation's troubles: "They concern, thank God, only material things." Our crisis today is in reverse. We find ourselves rich in goods but ragged in spirit; reaching with magnificent precision for the moon but falling into raucous discord on earth.[6]

Nixon was one of America's most consequential Presidents—in the best and worst sense. His presidency confronted the Vietnam War, runaway inflation, stubborn unemployment, environmental reform, détente with China and Russia, and international monetary reform. It ended with the greatest constitutional crisis since the impeachment of President Andrew Johnson in 1867 and, for Nixon, another twenty years of political purgatory.

The End of the Vietnam War

On January 23, 1968, North Korean patrol boats captured and boarded the USS *Pueblo*, a U.S. Navy intelligence ship conducting electronic intelligence in international waters off North Korea. For the next eleven months the Pueblo's eighty-three-man crew endured degradation, torture, and threats of execution. Forced to praise their captors during a televised news conference, many prisoners defiantly extended their middle finger, an act they told their oblivious North Korean jailors was the Hawaiian good luck sign. Giving North Vietnam the finger would be America's only retaliation. President Johnson, already fighting a major war in Vietnam and not wishing to provoke the North Koreans, chose to do nothing in response.

Nixon, as would most politicians, seized on Johnson's inaction. "Respect for the United States," Nixon declared in a campaign speech, "has fallen all over the world. . . so that a fourth-rate military power will hijack an American naval vessel in international waters, then it is time for new leadership for the American people. . ."[7]

Three months after taking office, President Nixon learned the limits of presidential power. On April 15, 1969, a North Korean MiG-21 fighter, in an act nearly forgotten today, shot down an unarmed U.S. Navy EC-121 reconnaissance aircraft sixty miles off North Korea's coast. Thirty-one American servicemen were killed, the largest single loss ever suffered by American intelligence personnel. It was, undeniably, an act of war. But President Nixon came to the same conclusion President Johnson had just months earlier: a retaliatory attack on North Korea could easily trigger a resumption of the Korean Conflict. America, already entangled in an interminable war in Vietnam, simply could not risk igniting a second Asian conflict. Other than a stern condemnation, Nixon did nothing in response. North Korea had, again, tweaked America's nose and gotten away with it.[8]

More consequential than bolstering America's strongman image was Nixon's campaign promise to bring "an honorable end to the war in Vietnam," a war that had already killed nearly 40,000 Americans. Nobody knew how Nixon intended to end the war, and Nixon never said. Some conjectured he had a secret plan, a claim Nixon conveniently refused to deny.

In 1968, President Johnson suspended the bombing of North Vietnam in the hopes of reaching a peace agreement before the presidential election. The talks, held in Paris, failed. The North Vietnamese were stalling; months were spent just negotiating the shape of the conference table. North Vietnam believed the American public's growing impatience with the war would ultimately force the United States to capitulate on North Vietnam's terms. And they were right.

On July 25, 1969, after greeting the Apollo 11 astronauts a day after their return from their historic landing on the moon, Nixon gave a speech that fundamentally changed American foreign policy. "The United States would assist in the defense and developments of allies and friends," Nixon declared, "[but would not] undertake all the defense of the free nations of the world."[9] After fighting to a stalemate in Korea and Vietnam, the United States would no longer "pay any price, bear any burden," as President Kennedy had promised a decade earlier, to fight the spread of communism. For Vietnam, the new Nixon Doctrine meant the United States would train South Vietnamese troops to take over the war but would no longer fight it.

Nixon's approach, at first, seemed to be working. By the end of his first year in office, Nixon had reduced American troop levels from a 1968 peak of 536,100 to 475,200. Combat deaths declined from an average of forty-five deaths a day in 1968 to thirty-two deaths a day in 1969.[10] The trend continued for the next three years and by 1972, only 24,200 American troops remained in Vietnam.[11]

During these years, Nixon and his National Security Advisor, Henry Kissinger, attempted to honorably end the war. But the North Vietnamese never budged and the peace talks dragged on listlessly. The North Vietnamese knew the United States was disengaging and were patiently waiting for America's complete withdrawal.

In early 1972, an election year, the United States announced it would unilaterally withdraw American troops from South Vietnam without requiring North Vietnam to do the same. During America's slow withdrawal over the prior three years, North Vietnamese troops had infiltrated the south. With the Americans now departing, North Vietnam knew it had won the war. After years of desultory talks, a peace treaty was signed on

January 27, 1973 at the Hotel Majestic in Paris. The Majestic was an ironic choice. Twenty-eight years earlier, the German Army had surrendered at the same hotel after Allied troops had liberated Paris.[12]

North Vietnam soon began to flout the terms of the peace accord, moving troops inexorably towards Saigon. On April 30, 1975, Saigon fell. The last remnants of America's commitment to South Vietnam barely escaped as frightened American diplomats clambered aboard helicopters perched precariously on the U.S. Embassy's roof.[13]

After thirty years of colonial, civil, and geopolitical war, Vietnam was finally at peace.

The United States' rationale for intervening in Vietnam was based on Eisenhower's Domino Theory: the notion that if one Asian country fell to communism, many more would follow. But only two dominoes toppled after Vietnam: Cambodia and Laos, both long infiltrated by the North Vietnamese. Communism's advance stopped there. Burma, Thailand, Malaysia, and Indonesia never succumbed. Nor was nearby India tempted to abandon its British-acquired democracy. And certainly not Australia, New Zealand or Japan, as American hard-liners had feared during the height of the Red Scare in the nineteen-fifties.

Visitors to Hanoi today learn that the (former North) Vietnamese revere Hồ Chí Minh both as Vietnam's George Washington and Abraham Lincoln. In 1954, Minh, like Washington, fought a revolutionary war to liberate Indochina from French colonial rule. Twenty years later, like Lincoln, Minh fought a civil war to unite North and South Vietnam. (Minh, who died in 1969, did not live to see his final victory.)

But there was a difference. After the Revolutionary War, America's founders were magnanimous towards the former British loyalists, returning their confiscated property and even inviting them back into the government. Similarly, in 1865 President Lincoln promised to end the Civil War "with malice toward none, with charity for all."[14] After the war ended, Congress restored the rebellious states back into the Union; even the President of the Confederacy, Jefferson Davis, was pardoned after a brief imprisonment.

That did not happen in Vietnam. After the fall of Saigon, an estimated one million South Vietnamese were killed in retribution.[15]

Today, the former enemies have reconciled. The Vietnamese economy is booming, helped by the United States as Vietnam's largest export customer[16]. Over half a million American tourists stream into Vietnam annually. But American capitalists have little to teach Vietnam's wily entrepreneurs. After opening its first Vietnamese store in 2014, even McDonald's struggled against intense local competition.[17] Although Vietnam's government remains officially communist, its citizens have become shrewd capitalists.

American Disillusionment

The United States had never lost a major war before Vietnam, a war that took 58,000 American lives. It took years for America to heal. Johnson and Nixon struggled to end the war with honor, but after Saigon was ransacked by victorious North Vietnamese troops, America's humiliation was complete. Henry Kissinger, recipient of the Nobel Peace Prize after negotiating the 1972 Peace Accord, attempted to return his medal (the Nobel Committee refused to accept it) and gave his share of the $1.3 million prize to the families of service members killed or missing in action in Vietnam.[18]

The war disillusioned a generation of young Americans. As the first televised war, Americans saw the brutality of combat. There was no glory in it. The two most haunting images of the war were a badly burned nine-year-old Vietnamese girl fleeing the napalm bombing of her village[19] and a South Vietnamese general coldly executing a Viet Cong soldier with a pistol shot to the head.[20] Americans who saw these images never forgot them.

Americans learned that their soldiers, when pushed to the limit, could commit brutal atrocities. The worst happened in the village of My Lai on March 16, 1968. That morning, an exhausted and demoralized Charlie Company, after having been decimated during North Vietnam's Tet Offensive, was sent to the village on a search and destroy mission. No Viet Cong fighters or weapons caches were found. But the soldiers, led by Lieutenant William Calley, rounded up the villagers and methodically shot an estimated 500 women, children, and old men. PFC Dennis Konti later described the massacre's brutality: "A lot of women had thrown themselves on top of the children to protect them, and the children were alive at first. Then, the children who were old enough to walk got up and Calley began to shoot the children."[21] A cover-up immediately ensued. It was not until eighteen months later that the American public learned of the massacre.[22] For years Americans had been outraged by the atrocities committed by the Germans and Japanese during World War II. Before My Lai, Americans never believed their own soldiers capable of such war crimes.

Near the end of the war, during the summer of 1971, Americans were further shaken when Daniel Ellsberg, a military analyst at the RAND Corporation, a major government contractor, leaked a top-secret Department of Defense study. The 7,000-page document was a detailed history of America's clandestine involvement in Vietnam stretching back to 1945. After attempting to disclose the information to Senators William Fulbright and George McGovern and being rebuffed, Ellsberg leaked the papers to *The New York Times* and *Washington Post*. Dubbed the Pentagon Papers by the press, the confidential report revealed that for twenty years Washington, under Truman, Eisenhower, Kennedy, and Johnson, had conducted clandestine operations in Indochina. Presidents Truman and Eisenhower provided covert military aid to France in support of its colonial war with the communist-led nationalists. The Kennedy administration supported a CIA-directed coup against South Vietnam's President Diem in which he was assassinated. President Johnson was secretly bombing Laos and Cambodia while he pledged to the American people "we seek no wider war."[23]

Nixon attempted to block further publication of the Papers, but the Supreme Court ruled in favor of publication citing the First Amendment:

> In the absence of the governmental checks and balances present in other areas of our national life, the only effective restraint upon executive policy and power in the areas of national defense and international affairs may lie in an enlightened citizenry—in an informed and critical public opinion which alone can here protect the values of democratic government.[24]

The Supreme Court decision affirmed, if rather cautiously, the right of Americans to leak secret government information when necessary to "protect the values of democratic government." That decision reverberates to this day.

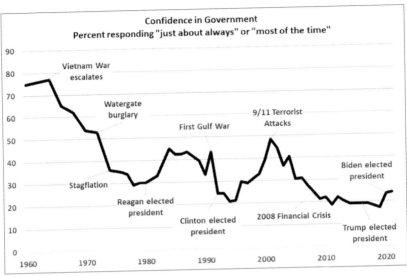

The Vietnam War, Watergate, Middle East wars, 2008 Financial Crisis, and 2020 election dispute have all contributed to a loss in Americans' confidence in their government.

PEW RESEARCH CENTER

Daniel Ellsberg's release of secret government information was unprecedented at the time. But today, leaks of disturbing government secrets have become common. In 2004, Joe Darby, an Army reservist, leaked shocking photos of American abuse of Iraqi prisoners at Abu Ghraib prison. In 2010, Chelsea Manning, an Army security analyst, leaked 750,000 classified or otherwise sensitive documents ranging from embarrassing diplomatic cables to videos of American gunships mistakenly firing on civilians. Edward Snowden, working for an NSA contractor, leaked up to a million documents, emails, and files regarding America's secret domestic surveillance and its military operations worldwide. In 2017, Reality Leigh Winner, a government contract employee, leaked NSA documents regarding Russia's attempts to intervene in American elections. That same year, Joshua Adam Schulte, working with a CIA contractor, stood accused of leaking highly secret software the United States uses to conduct cyber-warfare.[25]

Were Darby, Manning, Snowden and the other leakers traitors or patriots? Did the potential benefit of informing Americans of their government's questionable activities outweigh the harm of divulging American intelligence and military secrets?

Should the information even have been classified? Years after he leaked the Pentagon Papers, Daniel Ellsberg in a 2004 *New York Times* editorial observed: "All administrations classify far more information than is justifiable in a democracy.... Information should never be classified as secret merely because it is embarrassing or incriminating. But in practice... no information is guarded more closely."[26]

Triangular Diplomacy

President Nixon's greatest successes occurred near the end of his first term. From the beginning of his presidency, Nixon and his national security advisor, Henry Kissinger, saw an opportunity to seek détente with the Soviet Union and possibly even open diplomatic relations with the People's Republic of China (PRC).

After Stalin's death in 1953, the Soviet Union was slowly becoming less belligerent. In 1961, the United States and the Soviet Union signed the McCloy–Zorin Accords that established the foundation for negotiating future treaties with the objective that "disarmament is general and complete, and war is no longer an instrument for settling international problems."[27]

But China was uninterested in reducing Cold War tensions. China's hardline communist leaders considered their former Russian comrades "revisionist traitors" and claimed the Soviet Union had abandoned pure Marxist principles.[28] By 1969, the two communist nations were deeply divided and, after hostilities broke out along their 2,600-mile border, even fought a seven-month border war with dozens killed.

Nixon and Kissinger believed they could exploit the rivalry between the two former allies.

Since its founding in 1949, the United States had refused to recognize the PRC. American lobbying had denied the PRC, the world's most populous nation, membership in the United Nations. Instead, the United States recognized Taiwan, the small island nation formed when Chinese nationalists fled the mainland after the communist victory, as the lawful government of China. America's recognition of the PRC would bring it onto the world stage. Nixon and Kissinger reasoned this would then put pressure on the Soviet Union that could be exploited to America's advantage.

With Cold War sentiment near a peak, Nixon was perhaps the only American politician who could open high-level diplomacy between the United States and America's two communist foes. Nixon had been a dedicated Cold War warrior dating to his earliest days in Congress.

As a congressman during the late nineteen-forties, Nixon had proved himself a particularly effective member of the House Un-American Activities Committee (HUAC). HUAC's charter was to ferret out subversive activities by Americans with communist sympathies. As America entered the Cold War, there was concern that Soviet agents had infiltrated government, industry, and Hollywood. Nixon quickly became one of the Committee's most ardent members. His efforts helped to convict both the State Department's Alger Hiss who, as a Soviet spy, had passed information to the Soviets during the 1945 Yalta Conference, and Julius and Ethel Rosenberg, both of whom were sent to the electric chair after being convicted for stealing atomic bomb secrets for the Soviets.

With his outstanding HUAC record, no one—other than the fanatical John Birch Society—questioned Nixon's loyalty.

A ping pong match gave Nixon the opening he needed with China.

In 1971, the U.S. table tennis team was in Japan for the 31st World Table Tennis Championships. After missing the American team bus, an American player, Glenn Cowan, was invited to ride on the Chinese bus. Upon arriving, the sight of the Chinese team and a single American walking off the bus together caused a stir with the press. Photos were taken and when a journalist asked if Cowan would ever like to visit China, he didn't hesitate. Of course, he would. The Chinese chairman, Mao Zedong, read the news and immediately reached out to the United States, inviting the American table tennis team to visit China for a series of informal ping pong matches. With the championships ending in Japan, they were nearly next door. The Americans accepted and on April 10, 1971 the team and a small entourage became the first American delegation to visit the Chinese capital since 1949. After playing four matches they toured the Great Wall and other historic Chinese sites. The Americans returned home expressing warm feelings towards the Chinese. "The people are just like us," one team member commented. "They are real, they're genuine, they got feeling. I made friends, I made genuine friends, you see. The country is similar to America, but still very different. It's beautiful."[29]

Nixon entered politics during the "Red Scare" in the late nineteen-forties. After Soviet spies were uncovered in the Manhattan Project, many feared communists had infiltrated the government, academia and other American institutions.

Nixon recognized the opportunity and grasped it. That summer, Kissinger flew to Beijing on a secret mission to prepare a meeting between Nixon and the Chinese leadership. Kissinger's meetings went well. Shortly after his return, President Nixon, the long-time Cold War warrior and arch-enemy of communism, stunned the nation when he announced he would visit China the following year.

Later that year, in a major concession to the Chinese, the United States dropped its opposition to the PRC being admitted to the United Nations. On November 15, 1971, the PRC took its seat in the UN as the official China, booting out Taiwan, now an international orphan.

Three months later, from February 21–28, 1972, Nixon and Kissinger were in China. One of their first meetings was with Chairman Mao. Afterward, they were unsure what to make of him. Mao, clearly, had come from a peasant background, yet he had a tough, imposing physical presence. Rather than the formal, stilted style of most diplomatic discussions, Mao spoke in short, clipped sentences jumping from topic to topic in what appeared to be a rather haphazard manner. He also had a wry sense of humor, breaking the ice near the beginning of their conversation by joking about Kissinger's many "girls" with whom he secretly rendezvoused during his diplomatic trips. The divorced Kissinger had famously observed, "Power is the best aphrodisiac."

> Nixon: He doesn't look like a secret agent. He is the only man in captivity who could go to Paris twelve times and Peking once and no one knew it, except possibly a couple of pretty girls.
>
> Kissinger: They didn't know it; I used it as a cover.
>
> Mao: In Paris?
>
> Nixon: Anyone who uses pretty girls as a cover must be the greatest diplomat of all time.
>
> Mao: So, your girls are very often made use of?
>
> Nixon: His girls, not mine. It would get me into great trouble if I used girls as a cover.[30]

Reflecting on their conversation, Nixon and Kissinger concluded Mao was a far more skillful negotiator than they had initially thought. After establishing a relaxed atmosphere, Mao had subtly steered the conversation to cover all his agenda items. The critical issue was the status of Taiwan. Should it remain an independent country or be reintegrated into mainland China? The talks concluded with an agreement to leave the Taiwan issue open but to begin trade talks between the United States and the PRC as the first step to normalizing relations.

Nixon's mission to China was a major diplomatic and political success. Much of the trip had been broadcast to Americans on live television, showing Nixon to be a skillful statesman and a respected representative of the United States.

China was part of a larger plan. With relations between China and the United States warming, Nixon and Kissinger believed they were well positioned to negotiate with the Soviets. Moving remarkably quickly, Nixon traveled to Moscow three months after his China visit. Just four days after his arrival, Nixon and Soviet Premier Brezhnev signed the Strategic Arms Limitation Treaty (SALT I) on May 27, 1972 which limited each country's land and submarine-based ballistic missiles. Although talks had been ongoing since 1969, it took America's rapprochement with China to bring the negotiations to a successful close.[31] That same day, the two countries also signed the Anti-Ballistic Missile (ABM) Treaty that barred the two nations from employing defenses against strategic ballistic missiles, a pact intended as a deterrent to constructing additional offensive missiles.[32] During the trip, Nixon and Brezhnev also agreed to a trade deal for American wheat and a joint Apollo-Soyuz space mission planned for 1975, during which Astronaut Thomas Stafford and Cosmonaut Alexey Leonov made their historic handshake in space.

Over just a few short months in 1972, Nixon had reversed two decades of hostile relations between the United States and its two most dangerous adversaries, China and the Soviet Union. Nixon won reelection that year in a landslide, carrying every state but Massachusetts. With justified pride, Nixon proclaimed during his victory speech, "We are on the eve of what could be the greatest generation of peace, true peace for the whole world, that man has ever known."[33]

A Cemetery for Jobs

"Somebody has to tell the EPA," Texas Governor Rick Perry proclaimed in 2011, "that we don't need you monkeying around and fiddling around and getting in our business with every kind of regulation you can dream up. You're doing nothing more than killing jobs. It's a cemetery for jobs at the EPA."[34] Four years later, while campaigning for President, Donald Trump echoed Perry's sentiments, telling Fox News' Chris Wallace, "Environmental protection, what they do is a disgrace; every week they come out with new regulations." When Wallace asked who would protect the environment if the EPA was disbanded, Trump replied, "We'll be fine with the environment. We can leave a little bit, but you can't destroy businesses."[35]

Rick Perry's and Donald Trump's scorn for environmental regulations was not new. After the passage of America's first environmental legislation, the Rivers and Harbors Act of 1899, businesses and municipalities routinely flouted the law by continuing to dump industrial waste and raw sewage into the nation's waterways. As late as the nineteen-sixties, American companies, including such icons as General Electric and General Motors, continued to discharge huge quantities of industrial waste into America's waters. The borough of Manhattan alone dumped 150 million gallons of raw sewage daily into the Hudson River.

The human costs were high. Soot and acid rain from coal-fired power plants in the Midwest regularly drifted eastward into New England and killed fish and wildlife, covered cars with fine ash, eroded stone buildings and statues, and endangered those susceptible to respiratory diseases. During Thanksgiving 1966, "heat inversions trapped the chemicals and particulates from industrial smokestacks, chimneys, and vehicles" over New York City, killing an estimated 200 people. A 1969 oil spill off the Santa Barbara, California coast dumped three million gallons of crude oil into the ocean and killed thousands of birds and aquatic animals. That same year, the Cuyahoga River, engorged with industrial pollutants from the steel mills and factories that lined its shores, caught fire. In a cover story, *Time* magazine called America's rivers—the burning Cuyahoga, the filthy Mississippi, and the stinking Potomac Rivers—little more than "sewers."[36]

Yet, American industry was unmoved, and the public, believing pollution to be the cost of a modern industrial society, was largely apathetic.

Two best-selling books helped turn apathy into anger. In 1962, Rachel Carson's *Silent Spring* documented the harmful effects that the indiscriminate use of pesticides had wreaked upon the environment and, ultimately, on humans. Carson shrewdly used the Cold War hysteria to compare nuclear fallout to the unseen chemical threat of pesticides. "We are rightly appalled by the genetic effects of radiation," she wrote. "How then, can we be indifferent to the same effect in chemicals that we disseminate widely in our environment?"[37]

The chemical industry tried to paint Carson as a "bird and bunny lover," an overwrought spinster without a Ph.D., and a communist sympathizer. Their smear campaign failed. Her book flew off the shelves. No book since Thoreau's *Walden* did more to crystallize the importance of the environment for Americans, or to advance efforts for its future preservation.

Four years later, Ralph Nader's *Unsafe at Any Speed* again shocked Americans. Nader's book disclosed how General Motors routinely sacrificed safety, and the lives of their customers, for corporate profits. That year nearly 51,000 people suffered violent, often fiery deaths, in motor vehicle accidents.[38] In eight well-researched chapters, Nader detailed how the Chevy Corvair was prone to roll-overs that crushed its passengers, how passengers unnecessarily died in the "second collision" when their bodies ricocheted off the car's interior after a collision, and how sloping front grills pushed pedestrians under the car during a collision.

Unable to refute Nader's claims, General Motors tried to destroy Nader personally by using women to trap him in an illicit sexual relationship, interviewing acquaintances in search of incriminating information, and putting him under extended surveillance. When the smear campaign failed, GM's CEO was forced to publicly apologize to Nader during a Senate hearing. Nader sued General Motors for invasion of privacy and won $425,000 ($2.8 million in 2020 dollars), which he used to establish the Center for Auto Safety.[39]

Rachel Carson and Ralph Nader awakened America to the dangers of unbridled industry. As Nixon assumed the presidency in 1969, most

Americans were ready for Washington to play a larger role in protecting the nation's environment. After the divisiveness of Vietnam and civil rights, Nixon was anxious to support an issue popular with nearly all Americans. On January 1, 1970, Nixon signed the National Environmental Policy Act, which established a national environmental policy and required federal agencies to produce environmental impact statements for all new legislation. That year he also established the Environmental Protection Agency and the National Oceanic and Atmospheric Administration.

But President Nixon was just getting started. Over the next three years, Nixon signed the Clean Air Act, the Clean Water Act, the Endangered Species Act and even a Noise Pollution Act. These new regulations were wildly popular. Americans had become disgusted by American industry's abuse of the nation's environment and natural resources. With strong public support, environmental legislation sailed through Congress with huge margins: the National Policy Environmental Act passed the House 375–15, the Clean Water Act 366–11 and the Endangered Species Act 390–12.

Nixon did not stop with the environment. In 1970, he signed two bills enforcing workplace and automobile safety. The Occupational Safety and Health Administration (OSHA) was established to assure safe and healthy workplaces for American workers. It was needed. During the nineteen-sixties alone, workplace accidents killed far more Americans than the Vietnam War, over 125,000.[40] The OSHA Act passed the House 310–58 and the Senate 83–3. That year, Congress also established the National Highway Traffic Safety Administration (NHTSA).[41]

Today, the environment is far cleaner than it was fifty years ago: smog no longer chokes our major cities, sewage no longer pollutes our rivers, and industries no longer dump toxic waste wherever convenient. Industrial and consumer regulations have saved millions of lives. In 1970, thirty-eight workers died every day in workplace accidents. By 2017, workplace deaths had declined to fourteen a day, even though the workforce was nearly twice as large.[42] Safer cars and better roads have saved over a million lives since 1970. That year, 54,633 people died in traffic accidents. In 2018, 39,404 died despite there being twice as many drivers on the road. Had auto fatalities continued at their 1970 rate, nearly 50,000 more Americans would have died in 2018 alone.[43] Regulations mandating stern warnings on tobacco products and prohibiting advertising on radio and television reduced smoking and are estimated to have saved an estimated 167,000 premature deaths per year.[44]

But the thousands of regulations spawned by OSHA, EPA and many other federal agencies generated a backlash. Nixon's regulatory legislation has been criticized for leading to the greatest expansion of the government since Roosevelt's New Deal.[45] This expansion prompted Milton Friedman, the respected free-market economist, to employ his ultimate insult. "Nixon," Friedman declared, "was the most socialist of the Presidents of the United States in the twentieth century."[46]

For American workers, more consequential than economic ideology is the legitimate concern that regulations destroy jobs. Business leaders and politicians often speak of "job-killing regulations," and regulations have indeed curtailed, or even shut down, some industries. Tobacco, asbestos, and coal are prime examples. But lost jobs are often replaced by new industries. Many jobs lost in the dirty coal industry, for example, have been replaced by new jobs in clean natural gas, and more recently, in renewable energy.

But then, if regulations have cost jobs, so too has automation. Yet "job-killing automation" is a phrase seldom heard in corporate boardrooms. Automation benefits industry by increasing productivity, profitability, and rewarding shareholders while, at least in the short-term, reducing employment. Similarly, just as automation is ultimately beneficial to industry, well-managed regulations benefit society by giving every American a cleaner and safer world.

The Nixon Shock

Ask any competent economist the significance of August 15, 1971 and she'll tell you that was the day President Richard Nixon turned the world's monetary system upside-down. Two days prior, Nixon had convened a secret meeting of his economic team at Camp David. Notably attending the meeting were Federal Reserve Chairman Arthur Burns, Treasury Secretary John Connally, and future Fed Chairman Paul Volcker. After years of stable growth, the economy was slowing down. The timing was not good; Nixon was up for re-election the next year.

Nixon had seen this scenario before. While running for President in 1960, the nation fell into recession. President Eisenhower refused to use fiscal stimulus to spur the economy. Perhaps he believed the nation would soon recover and government intervention was not needed. Or perhaps Eisenhower wasn't anxious to support Nixon; the two men never had a close relationship. During the election, Eisenhower was asked about Vice President Nixon's major contributions. "If you give me a week," Eisenhower replied, "I might think of one."[47] As the election approached, unemployment was running six percent and climbing. Nixon lost the 1960 election by the closest popular vote margin of the twentieth century.[48] He blamed the poor economy for his defeat.

Nixon surprised the White House staff when he met unexpectedly with Elvis Presley on December 21, 1970. Elvis admired Nixon and volunteered to help fight the War on Drugs.   ALPHA HISTORICA/ALAMY

A decade later, Nixon again faced a sagging economy, except he was now President with, presumably, some control over it. But over the prior two years, after tinkering with the tax code, federal spending, and the money supply, economic growth remained sluggish. Something more drastic, a shock to the system, was needed.

President Nixon announced his "New Economic Plan" during a televised speech on August 15, 1971. Americans knew it would be a major speech. It was scheduled to preempt *Bonanza*, the popular western watched by much of America every Sunday evening.

Nixon's speech shocked the nation and angered America's allies. Today, economists remember it as the "Nixon Shock." The plan focused on increasing jobs, reducing inflation, and protecting the dollar. To increase job growth, Nixon proposed broad tax incentives to encourage both production and consumption. Manufacturers were given tax credits to incentivize upgrading their factories, and consumers were given a repeal of excise taxes to boost automobile purchases.

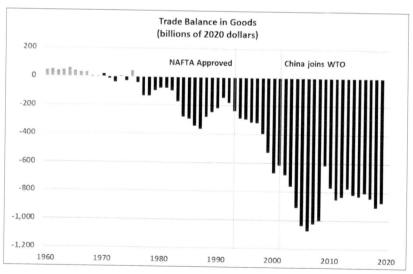

America's trade surplus turned into a seemingly permanent deficit around 1970 as Americans developed an appetite for foreign consumer goods and American manufacturers moved off-shore in search of cheap labor.   U.S. CENSUS BUREAU

To encourage domestic consumption and grow American jobs, Nixon proposed a 10 percent surcharge on all imports. America's trade balance had been deteriorating for years as American consumers developed a preference for many foreign goods. Nixon blamed the trade losses on "the unfair edge that some of our foreign competition has," declaring, "there is no longer any need for the United States to compete with one hand tied behind her back."[49] The claim of unfair treatment by America's trading partners would become a common rejoinder echoed by American Presidents for the next fifty years.

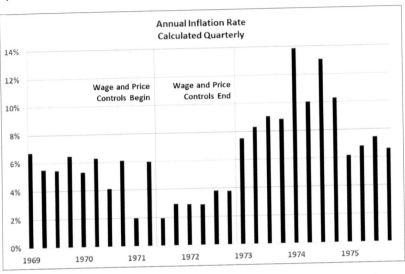

President Nixon's August 15, 1971 announcement of wage and price controls was politically motivated. The controls temporarily reduced inflation, which surged after the controls were lifted on January 15, 1973.   U.S. BUREAU OF LABOR STATISTICS

To reduce inflation, running near postwar highs, Nixon proposed a temporary freeze on all wages and prices, the first and last time these harsh controls have been imposed during peacetime.

Nixon's announcement of wage and price controls was a political, not an economic, decision. The move confounded economists, who almost universally despise wage and price controls. Earlier that year, Nixon told his staff, "The difficulty with wage-price controls and a wage board as you well know is that the God-damned things will not work. They didn't work even at the end of World War II. They will never work in peacetime."[50]

But Nixon soon accepted Treasury Secretary Connally's political advice. "To the average person in this country," Connally counseled, "this wage and price freeze—to him means you mean business. You're gonna stop this inflation. You're gonna try to get control of this economy. . . . If you take all of these actions... you're not going to have anybody... left out to be critical of you."[51]

Nixon saved the speech's bombshell for the end. "Speculators have been waging an all-out war on the American dollar. Accordingly, I have directed the Secretary of the Treasury to take the action necessary to defend the dollar against the speculators."[52]

Without informing, much less consulting, America's trading partners, Nixon announced he was pulling the United States out of the historic Bretton Woods Agreement. For nearly thirty years, Bretton Woods had been the monetary bedrock of international trade. In June 1944, as war still raged around the world, forty-four countries met at New Hampshire's majestic Bretton Woods Hotel and agreed to fix their currency exchange rates within a narrow range based on the American dollar. The United States guaranteed that those countries could, on-demand, exchange dollars for gold at $35.00 an ounce. It was a solid system that worked well for years. A foundation based on the American dollar, with the dollar secured by gold, and foreign currencies then linked to the dollar.

By the nineteen-sixties, the entire system was beginning to teeter. The booming American economy was injecting too many dollars into the international monetary system. With dollars flooding the international markets, the U.S. Treasury no longer held enough gold to redeem dollars at $35.00 an ounce. With dozens of foreign currencies tied to the dollar, their values, relative to the dollar, began to decline; and conversely, the dollar began to rise.

A strong dollar is a mixed blessing. It makes buying foreign goods or traveling abroad cheaper but hurts exports since, for foreign buyers, American goods and services become more expensive.

Nixon's speech that Sunday evening swept all that away. Over the next few months, the ten largest democratic industrial nations agreed to fix their currency exchange rates to the dollar. That interim system quickly fell apart as fixed rates became impossible to maintain. A year after Nixon's speech the dollar had weakened, declining relative to the nation's leading trading partners and making their imports more expensive and American exports more attractive. The German Mark fell from 3.4 to 3.2 per dollar and the

Japanese Yen from 360 to 300 per dollar.[53] Currencies were now free to float against each other based on supply and demand, a system that remains in place to this day.

Nixon's speech was political genius. The next day, *The New York Times* reported, "President Nixon has moved with startling decisiveness to stabilize the dollar and spur economic growth.... We unhesitatingly applaud the boldness with which the President has moved."[54] A CBS commentator compared Nixon's economic plan to his groundbreaking China initiative. The Dow Jones Average jumped 33 points; the largest single-day increase up to that time.

In the short term, Nixon's plan worked. In 1972, real GDP growth surged past five percent, inflation fell to 3.2 percent, and unemployment, after having climbed steeply for three years, began to fall. But those results were fleeting, as his successors would soon learn.

Nixon won the 1972 presidential election in a rout, securing 520 Electoral College votes versus Senator George McGovern's 17.[55] The Nixon presidency was at its peak with a growing economy, popular initiatives with China and the Soviet Union, and the end of the Vietnam War in sight.

News reports of a bungled burglary at the Democratic National Headquarters barely caused a ripple.

I am Not a Crook

Two weeks after President Nixon delivered his New Economic Plan speech, burglars broke into the office of Dr. Lewis Fielding, Daniel Ellsberg's psychiatrist. Ellsberg two months earlier had leaked the explosive Pentagon Papers, to *The New York Times* and *Washington Post*. The burglars hoped to find damaging information on Ellsberg.[56]

That day, September 3, 1971, marked the beginning of the end of the Nixon presidency.

Incredibly, the White House was behind the burglary. A group of White House staffers, glibly dubbed the "Plumbers," had been organized to stop information leaks deemed critical to national security—or damaging to the President. Their first job was to break into Dr. Fielding's office. Although the Plumbers failed to slow the leaks plaguing the White House, their mission soon evolved into an even more sinister calling: Dirty Tricks. Like the Plumbers, the Dirty Tricks operation was run out of the White House and assisted by the Committee for the Re-election of the President, or "CREEP" as the operation was soon dubbed.

The Dirty Tricksters were a hard-working group. Their tricks included forging letters under false letterheads, leaking false stories to the press, stealing confidential campaign files, and planting provocateurs to disrupt the political campaigns of Nixon's opponents.[57] One forged letter sabotaged Senator Edmund Muskie's presidential bid. As part of the operation, the White House submitted 490 names of political enemies to the IRS and ordered audits of their tax returns. The IRS refused.[58]

One of their dirty tricks would bring Nixon down.

On June 17, 1972, five burglars broke into the Democratic National Committee (DNC) headquarters located in the Watergate apartment complex. Their White House bosses had charged them to gather damaging information by stealing files and installing wire-tapping equipment. They nearly got away with it, but a security guard noticed that several door locks had been taped and called the police. Catching them red-handed, the police officers yelled, "Hold it! You're under arrest." Five pairs of hands shot up. "You got us," one burglar lamely replied. The officers immediately suspected something was unusual. All the burglars were older men, dressed in suits. Frisking them, a police officer found a small notebook with "White House" written on it.[59]

It has never been discovered precisely what the burglars were seeking. One theory was information as to whether the DNC knew about a $100,000 gift ($705,000 in 2020 dollars) made by the billionaire industrialist Howard Hughes to a Nixon friend that ultimately found its way to the President. Other theories suggested the burglars were seeking information about a Miami-based DNC kickback scheme, clandestine CIA operations in Chile to overthrow the government, or a call girl ring with ties to the White House.

Calling it nothing but "a third-rate burglary attempt," White House staffers were initially successful in stopping speculation that the White

House had been involved. And why not? The idea that the White House masterminded a common, ham-fisted burglary was too incredible for most Americans to believe.

What the public didn't know was that six days after the burglary, Nixon ordered his chief of staff H.R. Haldeman to shut down the FBI investigation. "Play it tough," Nixon instructed Haldeman. "That's the way they play it and that's the way we are going to play it... these people [the CIA] are plugging for, for keeps and that they should call the FBI in and say that we wish for the country, don't go any further into this case, period!"[60]

Nixon had forgotten that his Oval Office conversations were being recorded.

Slowly at first, but with growing momentum, the Watergate story rose to the level of a national obsession, propelled by two junior reporters with the *Washington Post*, Carl Bernstein and Bob Woodward. They soon had a confidential source who leaked damaging details about the case. Dubbed "Deep Throat" after the first mainstream pornographic film, the leaker's identity remained unknown for over thirty years.

Shortly before he died and encouraged by his daughter, in 2001 W. Mark Felt, the associate director of the FBI during the break-in, revealed he was Deep Throat. Nixon's former attorney accused Felt of being a traitor for leaking government secrets. To that charge, a *Los Angeles Times* editorial commented: "As if there's no difference between nuclear strategy and rounding up hush money to silence your hired burglars." Felt had acted out of mixed motives. He had been passed over to be head of the FBI after J. Edgar Hoover died. "So, the truth may be that Felt," the *Los Angeles Times* concluded, "was more an aggrieved FBI loyalist than a champion of truth. Still, he helped trigger a healthy skepticism of official secrecy. Sometimes less purity of motive does the body politic good."[61]

By January 1973, the five burglars and two accomplices had either pleaded guilty or been convicted of burglary, conspiracy, and violation of federal wiretapping laws. The presiding judge, John J. Sirica, was not satisfied. He believed the conspiracy was far broader than the seven convicted felons and promised severe prison sentences if they did not disclose their co-conspirators. The judge's threat worked. One of the burglars, James McCord, broke the code of silence in a letter to the judge:

> There was political pressure applied to the defendants to plead guilty and remain silent.... Perjury occurred during the trial in matters highly material to the very structure, orientation, and impact of the government's case.... Others involved in the Watergate operation were not identified during the trial when they could have been by those testifying.[62]

McCord's letter broke the case wide open. A month later, the White House announced that all previous statements denying White House involvement were "inoperative." Nixon fired four of his senior staff including John W. Dean, the White House legal counsel. Two months later, Dean testified to the Senate's Watergate Committee that he, Attorney General John Mitchell, and Nixon himself had been involved in the Watergate burglary, as well as the cover-up afterward. Nixon denied it, making it Dean's word against the President's. In a surreal exchange, when asked about Watergate, Nixon declared: "People have got to know whether or not their President is a crook. Well, I'm not a crook."[63] After months of investigation, the Senate Committee and the White House were at an impasse.

That changed on July 13, 1973. A deputy assistant to the President, Alexander Butterfield, was asked during the Senate investigation if White House conversations were ever taped. "I was wondering if someone would ask that," Butterfield dryly replied. "There is tape in the Oval Office.... Everything was taped... as long as the President was in attendance. There was not so much as a hint that something should not be taped."[64]

Butterfield's admission electrified the investigation. All efforts now focused on obtaining the tapes. For a year, the White House fought their release by claiming executive privilege, an innovative defense at the time. Desperate, Nixon ordered his Attorney General, Eliot Richardson, to fire the special prosecutor, Archibald Cox. Richardson, refusing Nixon's order, resigned, as did the Deputy Attorney General William D. Ruckelshaus. Finally, Robert Bork, Nixon's compliant Solicitor General, dismissed Cox. Rather than stopping the investigation, Nixon's firing of Archibald Cox, quickly dubbed "The Saturday Night Massacre," inflamed public opinion, and steeled the resolve of Nixon's pursuers.

While Americans remained mesmerized by Watergate, a quieter investigation was underway into Nixon's Vice President, Spiro Agnew.

Agnew was Nixon's pit bull, enthusiastically attacking the President's enemies. Agnew had a combative style that both drew from and fed the anger of many Nixon supporters, the so-called "Silent Majority." Regarding the press: "Some newspapers are fit only to line the bottom of bird cages." Regarding universities: "Education is being redefined at the demand of the uneducated to suit the ideas of the uneducated. The student now goes to college to proclaim, rather than to learn." For civil rights and war protesters, Agnew waxed especially poetic.

> As for those deserters, malcontents, radicals, incendiaries, the civil and uncivil disobedients among the young, SDS, PLP, Weathermen I and Weathermen II, the revolutionary action movement, the Black United Front, Yippies, Hippies, Yahoos, Black Panthers, Lions and Tigers alike—I would swap the whole damn zoo for a single platoon of the kind of young Americans I saw in Vietnam.[65]

In early 1973, an investigation by the United States Attorney General for Maryland quickly focused on Agnew, who had been that state's governor before assuming the vice presidency. The charges were tax evasion and accepting kick-backs for contractor work, including a $10,000 payment delivered in cash directly to the White House. Faced with incontrovertible evidence, Agnew pleaded no contest to the tax evasion charge and resigned as Vice President.

Nixon replaced Agnew with Gerald Ford, the well-liked House Minority Leader. Ford was a non-controversial choice, unlikely to cause problems for either Nixon or his opponents. He and Nixon, both Navy veterans, had been close friends since entering Congress in the late nineteen-forties. Nixon, having lost the 1960 presidential and 1962 California gubernatorial elections, once commented, "When you win, you hear from everyone—when you lose you hear from your friends." Ford had been that kind of friend.

Charges of tax evasion did not stop with Agnew. By late 1973, even as Nixon was fighting the Watergate charges, *The Wall Street Journal* reported that Nixon had paid less than $6,000 in federal income taxes while earning a total of nearly $800,000 in gross income ($5.1 million in 2020 dollars) during 1970, 1971, and 1972. The paper also reported that Nixon had failed to pay any state taxes either in California or the District of Columbia.

The *Journal's* reporting was relentless, forcing a Congressional investigation. In April 1974, the Congressional Joint Committee on Internal Revenue Taxation (JCT) found that Nixon owed $476,451 in back taxes and interest. In a settlement, Nixon agreed to pay $465,000. President Nixon was never charged with tax fraud. During his first term, he had asked the IRS to review his tax filings, which the IRS promptly approved. The JCT found that the IRS had been negligent in auditing the President's tax returns, prompting Donald Alexander, the IRS commissioner, to promise that "his agency would do a better job of auditing presidential tax returns in the future and that the President would be treated like any other taxpayer."[66]

Nixon resisted demands to hand over the White House tapes for nearly a year. On July 24, 1974, in a unanimous ruling, with one recusal, the Supreme Court ordered Nixon to turn over the tapes. On August 5, the White House released transcripts of the tapes that irrefutably implicated Nixon in the cover-up, and worse, efforts to bribe the burglars to keep quiet.

Congress was stunned when the tapes revealed the cover-up had begun just a week after the break-in when Nixon instructed Haldeman to order the CIA and FBI to shut down the investigation.[67]

The most incriminating comments occurred on March 21, 1973, nearly nine months into the White House cover-up. "We have a cancer, within, close to the Presidency, that's growing," White House Counsel John Dean told Nixon. "It's growing daily. It's compounding, it grows geometrically now because it compounds itself." Later in the conversation, Nixon and Dean discussed how to raise a million dollars of hush money for the burglars and their accomplices, to "keep the cap on the bottle," as Nixon drolly commented:

Nixon: How much money do you need?

Dean: I would say these people are going to cost, uh, a million dollars over the next, uh, two years.

Nixon: We could get that.... What I mean is, you could, you could get a million dollars. And you could get it in cash. I, I know where it could be gotten.... I mean it's not easy, but it could be done. But, uh, the question is who the hell would handle it?[68]

That brief conversation was the smoking gun. Two days after the transcripts were released, Senator Barry Goldwater, House Minority Leader John Rhodes, and Senate Minority Leader Hugh Scott met with Nixon to tell him he faced imminent impeachment, conviction, and removal.[69]

The next day, August 8, 1974, Nixon resigned from the presidency, effective noon the following day. Nixon remains the only U.S. President to resign from office.

Nothing was ever found on the tapes implicating Nixon in the actual break-in. It was the cover-up that brought him down.

For generations, Americans had trusted their President. They may have disagreed with his politics, but few questioned Teddy Roosevelt's sincerity of purpose during his trust-busting, or Franklin Roosevelt's motivation for putting people back to work during the Great Depression, or Eisenhower's reasons for building the Interstate Highway System, or Johnson' empathy for the disadvantaged when he established his Great Society programs.

Before Nixon, only the most cynical Americans believed a President would consistently lie to the American people. The Pentagon Papers and Watergate changed that. The Pentagon Papers revealed that for twenty years Washington had deceived the American public regarding its role in Vietnam, a deception that eventually led to 58,000 American soldiers and uncounted civilians dying in an ill-conceived war. Then, for two years, Americans watched non-stop media coverage of the growing Watergate scandal that culminated in the revelation that Nixon had not only lied about the cover-up, but actively participated in it.

After fighting the Watergate investigation for over two years, President Nixon resigned on August 8, 1974. Unbowed, Nixon departed flashing his iconic victory sign.

THE COLOR ARCHIVES/ALAMY

Shortly after the Pentagon Papers leaked, Nixon asked Haldeman what the implications were. "Out of the gobbledygook comes a very clear thing," Haldeman told Nixon. "You can't trust the government, you can't believe what they say, and you can't rely on their judgment.... It shows that people do things the President wants to do even though it's wrong, and the President can be wrong."[70]

Americans' trust in government peaked in 1965, not coincidentally, just before the United States fully committed to the Vietnam War. That year, 77 percent of Americans said they trusted the U.S. government all or most of the time.[71] What followed were years of political scandal, lost wars, financial crises, government gridlock, savage partisan politics, and in 2017, a President who routinely disparaged nearly every American institution. By 2019, less than one in five Americans, 17 percent, trusted Washington.[72]

When Nixon announced his resignation, drivers along Pennsylvania Avenue honked their car horns in celebration. Marchers outside the White House waved "No Amnesty for Nixon" signs. "My fellow Americans," President Ford declared as he took the oath of office, "our long national nightmare is over."[73]

For the remainder of his life, Nixon struggled to rehabilitate himself and establish a legacy. In 1978, Nixon published his memoirs, *RN*, which sold 300,000 copies despite being nearly 1,200 pages and boycotted by the aptly named Committee to Boycott Nixon's Memoirs.[74]

Nixon followed his memoirs with nine influential books on government, foreign affairs, and politics. By his death two decades after leaving the presidency, Nixon had become a respected, if flawed, senior statesman whose counsel was sought both by Presidents and foreign leaders.

Fifty-thousand mourners stood for hours in the rain during his funeral after his death on April 22, 1994. President Clinton and four former Presidents attended the funeral. During his oration honoring the deceased former President, President Clinton summarized Nixon's political career:

> As a public man, he always seemed to believe the greatest sin was remaining passive in the face of challenges. And he never stopped living by that creed. He gave of himself with intelligence and energy

and devotion to duty. And his entire country owes him a debt of gratitude for that service. Oh, yes, he knew great controversy amid defeat as well as victory. He made mistakes; and they, like his accomplishments, are part of his life and record.[75]

Gerald R. Ford Jr.

August 9, 1974 – January 20, 1977

> I have always believed that most people are mostly good, most of the time. I have never mistaken moderation for weakness, nor civility for surrender. As far as I'm concerned, there are no enemies in politics—just temporary opponents who might vote with you on the next Roll Call.[1]

Betty," Vice President Gerald Ford told his wife, "I don't think we're ever going to live in the Vice President's house."[2] Although Ford had been Vice President for nine months, the Fords were still living in the modest Virginia home they had built back in 1955. While Presidents lived expansively in the White House, Vice Presidents were on their own to find housing. The nation's second-highest officeholder had typically lived humbly in private homes, apartments, and hotels. But shortly after Ford succeeded disgraced Spiro Agnew as Vice President, Congress finally provided an official vice-presidential residence: the former residence of the Chief of Naval Operations on the grounds of the U.S. Naval Observatory. It perhaps helped that Ford had been a popular, affable member of Congress since 1949.

The Fords were awaiting the restoration of their new home when Alexander Haig, the White House Chief-of-Staff, drove out to their Virginia home to deliver explosive news. The White House would shortly release Oval Office audiotapes confirming that President Nixon, from the beginning, had been at the center of the Watergate cover-up. Not only had Nixon ordered the CIA to stop the investigation, he had personally volunteered to raise one million dollars in hush money. The tapes were the definitive proof the Watergate investigators had been pursuing for two years.

Haig told Ford that Nixon, faced with imminent impeachment and conviction, would likely resign and that he should prepare himself to assume the presidency. Surprisingly, had Haig's visit occurred a few years earlier, he would have been obliged to tell Ford to prepare for a constitutional crisis rather than the presidency. The Constitution failed to specify how to replace a President after his death, incapacitation, resignation, or removal. It wasn't until the 25th Amendment was ratified in 1967 that presidential succession was specified.

On August 9, 1974, Gerald Ford was sworn in as President, thus becoming the only man to serve as both Vice President and President without being elected to either office. Ford well understood this and acknowledged he lacked a popular mandate during his brief inaugural address. "I am acutely aware that you have not elected me as your President by your ballots. . . . I have not sought this enormous responsibility, but I will not shirk it. . . . My fellow Americans, our long national nightmare is over. Our Constitution works; our great Republic is a government of laws and not of men."[3]

After twenty-five years in Congress, Gerald Ford was respected as an honest and decent man. The House confirmed his nomination as Vice President 387 to 35, and the Senate, 92 to 3. Ford's basic humanity contributed to two charitable acts meant to heal a wounded nation but helped condemn him to a one-term presidency.[4]

Ten days into his presidency, President Ford told a large gathering at the annual Veterans of Foreign Wars (VFW) convention that he intended to grant conditional amnesty to Vietnam War dissenters. The amnesty allowed an estimated 210,000 draft dodgers and even deserters to be forgiven if they turned themselves in, reaffirmed their allegiance to the United States, and served two years in public service jobs. The veterans, many of whom had fought in Vietnam and lost close friends in the war, sat in startled silence. "How [is] granting amnesty of any kind," they asked themselves, "to a bunch of hippie, drop-out traitors. . . going to pull this country together?"[5]

Ford was undeterred and formally announced the plan on September 16, declaring:

> The primary purpose of this program is the reconciliation of all our people and the restoration of the essential unity of Americans within which honest differences of opinion do not descend to angry discord and mutual problems are not polarized by excessive passion. My sincere hope is that this is a constructive step toward a calmer and cooler appreciation of our individual rights and responsibilities and our common purpose as a nation whose future is always more important than its past.[6]

But the fury arising from Ford's amnesty for Vietnam War dissenters was lost in the firestorm that arose after Ford's next effort at national reconciliation.

Three weeks after his VFW speech, Ford issued an unconditional pardon to Richard Nixon. Ford knew his decision would be unpopular but justified Nixon's pardon on the grounds of saving the nation from years of "bitter controversy and divisive national debate" should Nixon be criminally prosecuted. Ford asserted that Nixon had already been prosecuted by suffering the indignity of being the first President forced to resign in disgrace. "I do believe that the buck stops here," Ford declared, "that I cannot rely upon public opinion polls to tell me what is right. I do believe that right makes might and that if I am wrong, ten angels swearing I was right would make no difference."[7]

Many in Congress fiercely condemned the pardon and suggested Ford had cut a deal promising to pardon Nixon in exchange for his resignation. A House committee hauled Ford in to testify, the first President ordered before a congressional committee of inquiry since Abraham Lincoln. Although the committee found no evidence of a pardon deal, Ford was damaged politically by the television images of an American President being interrogated by his former colleagues.[8] Ford's press secretary, Jerald ter-Horst, resigned over the pardon. Within months, Ford's approval rating was slashed in half, from 70 to 37 percent.[9]

Ford went to his grave confident he had been right to pardon Nixon. Unburdened of a potential prison sentence, Nixon went on to spend twenty productive years writing, lecturing, and advising Presidents.

Ford's pardon of the Vietnam War dissenters helped to remove the stigma of dodging military service. Most of America's Presidents after 1992 would have had a more difficult time getting elected if Ford had prosecuted the dissenters as traitors. After President George H.W. Bush, no President has served with distinction in the military. Clinton "went to great lengths to avoid the Vietnam-era draft... used political connections to obtain special favors, and... made promises and commitments which he later failed to honor."[10] George W. Bush "shirked his wartime duties, first finagling his way to a safe berth in Texas thanks to being the son of a congressman, and then barely bothering to turn up for drills at all."[11] Barack Obama was a Harvard law student during the First Gulf War and was too old for military service following the 9/11 Terrorist Attacks. Donald Trump "obtained a felicitous doctor's note testifying to his burden of debilitating bone spurs in his heel, though later he could not remember which foot was so afflicted."[12]

Whip Inflation Now

President Ford inherited more than a broken political system. Nixon also handed off the worst economy in over forty years. After the booming nineteen-sixties, inflation and unemployment had begun to rise. By 1973, the unprecedented combination of high unemployment together with high inflation was so dismal that economists coined a new term to describe the phenomenon: the Misery Index.[13]

From 1950 through 1969, unemployment had averaged 4.7 percent and inflation 2.2 percent. Added together, that's a tolerable index of 6.9 percent. Six percent was considered to be ideal, with four percent unemployment and two percent inflation. But after years of stability, the index rose steadily during Nixon's presidency and by 1974 hit a previously unimaginable 16.7 percent. Unemployment that year was high, but inflation was far worse at 11 percent, a level only exceeded in 1920 and 1947 as the nation recovered from two world wars.

★

Eleven percent inflation is ruinous, quickly reducing purchasing power. But a little inflation is beneficial to an economy. How can rising prices be beneficial? Human behavior. If prices are rising, consumers tend to accelerate their purchases hoping to save money. Falling prices have the opposite effect. Falling prices slow economic growth as consumers defer purchases. Governments understand this and historically have set their monetary policies to target an inflation rate of about two percent. Like the proverbial donkey and carrot on a stick, the expectation of rising prices (the carrot) keeps consumers (the donkey) plodding ahead.

There's another reason governments like moderate inflation. Inflation reduces the cost of borrowing money. With two percent inflation, a government that issues a bond maturing in ten years will repay the loan in money worth 18.3 percent less than the money it borrowed.

Economists didn't realize it at the time, but as Ford was assuming the presidency the nation was in the midst of the Great Inflation, a period from 1965 through 1985 when inflation averaged over six percent and at times flirted with 14 percent.[14] By 1985, the value of a 1965 dollar had fallen to $0.29. Economists consider the Great Inflation the third most damaging economic event in the last 100 years, behind only the Great Depression and the 2008 Financial Crisis.

A confluence of factors was responsible for the Great Inflation. The classic definition of inflation is too many dollars chasing too few goods. This can happen in several ways. The government, wishing to stimulate the economy, can print money to increase the money supply. Or consumers can pull money out of savings and spend it, increasing the money in circulation. Or the supply of goods can fall, increasing the value of those goods. All three scenarios contributed to the Great Inflation.

President Johnson, presiding over an unpopular war, chose not to move the country to a war-time economy. An old economic adage warns a nation can either afford guns or butter, but not both. As the Vietnam War escalated, Johnson, rather than cutting back consumer spending, pursued expensive Great Society programs. From 1965 through 1969, the money supply (M1) grew 5.1 percent annually, up from 2.2 percent the prior five years. All those new dollars flowing into the economy kicked off the first round of inflation which hit 5.5 percent in 1969, just as Nixon became President.

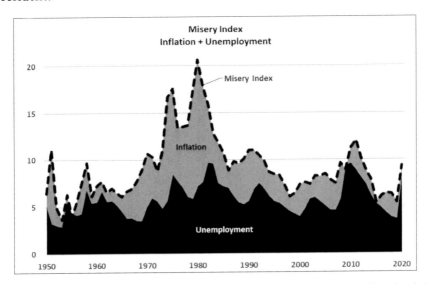

Economists dubbed the years 1965 through 1985 the Great Inflation. When both inflation and unemployment rose steeply in the nineteen-seventies, a new economic metric was born: the Misery Index.   U.S. BUREAU OF LABOR STATISTICS

This was shockingly high. Inflation averaged only 1.5 percent during the nineteen-fifties while Nixon was Vice President. In August 1971, worried about high inflation hurting his upcoming presidential election, Nixon installed limited wage and price controls.

The controls were primarily a political move urged on by Nixon's Treasury Secretary, John Connally. But the decision was also supported by Nixon's economic advisors, notably Federal Reserve Chairman Arthur Burns. Burns believed the nation was in a wage-price spiral. As prices increase, workers demand higher wages; to pay the higher wages, producers increase prices, which then creates demand for higher wages and starts the cycle over. A freeze on wages and prices presumably breaks the cycle. But during the freeze, companies, seeing their prices frozen, often cut back on new investment, thus reducing supply. Consumers, with flat paychecks, postpone making purchases, increasing pent-up demand. Once the freeze is removed, high demand and limited supply balloon inflation. This occurred after both World Wars when inflation hit 15 percent.

As the controls are phased out, managing the return to a free economy is difficult. During the nineteen-seventies two events, one natural and one man-made, made it far more difficult.

A severe drought began in Asia in the summer of 1972 and rapidly spread worldwide, principally affecting rice, wheat, and corn production. Concerned about feeding its own people, Thailand, the world's largest rice exporter, stopped rice exports in early 1973. For nearly a year, the world rice market collapsed which severely affected countries dependent on food imports. Total grain production during 1972 was nearly 10 percent short of that needed to meet worldwide consumption.[15] Food prices soared. In the United States, the consumer price index for food and beverages climbed 18 percent in 1973 and another 11 percent in 1974. By the end of 1975, food prices had climbed 48 percent above their early 1972 levels.[16] The high prices resulted in another new phrase coined during the Great Inflation: sticker shock.

No commodity has more impact on consumers than food. The food crisis of the early nineteen-seventies is largely forgotten today, but at the time, it was a major contributor to both inflation and the growing anxiety—coupled with the disillusionment of Vietnam and Watergate—that the country was coming apart.

Consumers soon got a second shock, this time at the filling station.

On October 6, 1973, Egypt and Syria attacked Israel on the Jewish holiday of Yom Kippur hoping to catch the Israeli army by surprise. The attack was in retaliation for the Six-Day War of 1967 in which Israel captured and then occupied territory four times its original size. As Egypt and Syria drove deep into Israeli territory, the United States, initially hesitant, began airlifting arms and equipment to Israel. With American support, the tide quickly turned and three weeks after the war began, Israel dealt Egypt and Syria another humiliating defeat.[17]

Furious that the United States intervened, the Arab members of the Organization of Petroleum Exporting Countries (OPEC) retaliated with an oil embargo against the United States and its allies. The impact was immediate. U.S. crude oil imports, after growing 35 percent annually from 1970 through 1973, slowed to seven percent in 1974. Foreign oil prices shot up four-fold from $2.70 a barrel in 1973 to $11.00 in 1974 ($58.80 in 2020 dollars).[18]

For the century since Edwin Drake drilled his first oil well in Titusville, Pennsylvania, domestic oil had met America's energy needs. But starting in the late nineteen-fifties, the nation's growing oil appetite made it necessary to import oil. By 1973, nearly 40 percent of America's oil was imported, largely from the Middle East.[19] Fortunately, Middle East oil was both plentiful and cheap. The tiny Middle Eastern countries, though sitting on enormous oil reserves, had little negotiating leverage over the mighty United States.

That ended with the 1973 oil embargo. The Middle Eastern oil producers, working together, had finally learned to flex their muscles, and flex them they did as when the Shah of Iran declared:

> Of course, [oil prices] are going to rise. Certainly! And how! However, it's a solution you of the West have wished on yourselves. . . . You've increased the price of the wheat you sell us by 300 percent, and the same for sugar and cement. . . . You buy our crude oil and sell it back to us, refined as petrochemicals, at a hundred times the price you've paid us. You make us pay more, scandalously more, for everything, and it's only fair that, from now on, you should pay more for oil. Let's say. . . ten times more.[20]

Nixon's price controls slowed the rise of gasoline prices, but gas still became more expensive and jumped from $0.39 a gallon in 1973 to $0.59 ($3.44 in 2020 dollars) the next year.[21] Worse, supplies soon dried up. With prices capped, American oil companies were slow to increase production to fill the gap. Drivers waited in block-long lines at filling stations only to find that once reaching the gas pump, the station was out of gas.

With oil scarce and profits squeezed by price controls, oil companies cut back on services. Before the oil embargo, three uniformed attendants often rushed out to fill your tank, clean the windshield, and check the oil and tires. Today, drivers pump their own gas and clean their own windshields. But before the embargo that was nearly unthinkable, especially for women, many of whom still wore white gloves to church.

The oil embargo drove America into a recession and pushed unemployment to 8.5 percent in 1975, the highest since World War II. With high unemployment, high inflation, and slow economic growth, yet another new economic term was coined: stagflation.[22]

Stagflation dumbfounded economists. The combination of high inflation and high unemployment wasn't supposed to happen. An economic principle, the "Phillips Curve," declared unemployment and inflation to be mutually exclusive; they could never both be simultaneously high.[23] High unemployment would force inflation down, and vice versa. But the Phillips Curve fell apart in the nineteen-seventies when both rose together.

Immediately after taking office, President Ford called a summit of his economic advisors to develop solutions for rebooting the economy. Two months later, Ford proposed a nine-point economic program, "only one point [on] which all advisers have agreed." No wonder. In past years, the Federal Reserve had either fought inflation by shrinking the money supply or combated unemployment by growing it.

In 1975, both inflation and unemployment were high, and rising. Economists were in uncharted territory. Which to fight first?

Ford's economic team chose inflation. Their inflation-fighting program included increasing domestic food and oil production while reducing exports, cutting oil imports by one million barrels a day, eliminating government waste, increasing penalties for anti-competitive activities, reducing lending rates to encourage investment, raising taxes to reduce deficits, and a public awareness program to encourage conservation.[24]

It is the last proposal that is remembered today. The conservation program encouraged citizens to plant gardens, spend less on groceries, carpool, and turn the heat down. The program even had a snappy slogan, "Whip Inflation Now," instantiated by a big red button with the letters, "WIN."

WIN was a public relations campaign right out of World War II. Ford and much of his staff had lived through the war and recalled the many slogans governments used to remind everyday citizens of the war effort, and how they could contribute to it: "V for Victory," "Loose Lips Sinks Ships," "Together We Can Do It," and the quintessentially British, "Keep Calm and Carry On."

But "Whip Inflation Now" simply didn't carry the same gravitas. The WIN button became an object of ridicule after Ford began using the slogan in political campaigns. Jokesters turned the buttons upside down suggesting the inverted letters stood for "No Immediate Miracles" or "Need Immediate Money." The popular television show, *Happy Days*, spoofed the button inscribing "Happy Days are Here Again" above a picture of President Ford.[25]

Still, President Ford's WIN button unintentionally lightened America's mood. It even may have helped reduce inflation, which fell briefly from 11 percent in 1974 to 5.8 percent in 1976. But inflation soon resumed its climb. This time, fear was the driver. Charles Schultz, soon to head President Carter's Council of Economic Advisors, cautioned that "[The current inflation] has nothing to do with shortages or an overheated economy," but rather is "a kind of inertia of past inflation in which prices chase wages and wages chase prices."[26] America was now in a wage-price spiral.

Americans also were beginning to face strong foreign competition costing millions of American jobs. From 1950 through 1969, America's manufacturing workforce grew an average of 1.8 percent annually. During the nineteen-seventies, annual manufacturing employment growth sank to one-half percent.

President Nixon, rather than challenge American industry to compete, had blamed foreign competitors for having an "unfair edge" that forced America "to compete with one hand tied behind her back."[27] Americans would hear similar condemnations fifty years later under President Trump.

But consumers just want the best product at the best price. Increasingly, that product was not American. Why buy a Chevrolet when Toyotas got better gas mileage, were more reliable and cheaper? Rather than a Zenith television, why not Sony with its much crisper colors? Why buy American machine tools when German and Swedish machines were considered the best in the world?

Remarkably, after dealing with historic inflation and unemployment, rising imports and an oil embargo, Ford managed to hand his successor, Jimmy Carter, a stronger economy than the one he had inherited from Nixon. As Ford was leaving office in 1976, the Misery Index was down four points and GDP was growing 5.4 percent annually. But it would be a short respite.

Hardliners Kill Détente

President Ford's first diplomatic effort began in November 1974 at a dilapidated Soviet health spa near Vladivostok, Russia. The spa resembled "an abandoned YMCA camp in the Catskills," Ford later recalled. The occasion was a meeting with Soviet General Secretary Leonid Brezhnev to discuss extending the first Strategic Arms Limitation Treaty (SALT I) signed by President Nixon and Brezhnev in 1972.

President Ford wearing the Alaskan Wolf fur coat he gave to Brezhnev departing Vladivostok. The two men developed a close personal relationship but were unable to capitalize on their friendship due to Cold War hard-liners opposing détente.
WHITE HOUSE PHOTO/ALAMY

A warm, personal chemistry quickly developed between Ford and Brezhnev. Both men had been sports stars in their youth: Ford in football and Brezhnev in soccer. Brezhnev particularly liked Ford's direct style after dealing with Nixon's cryptic approach to negotiating.[28] The meetings went well for the Americans. So well, that Secretary of State Henry Kissinger was "exuberant," declaring "the Soviets had made almost all the concessions."[29]

The Soviets badly wanted to make a deal and weren't ashamed to admit it. As the summit was ending, Brezhnev shocked Ford when he grasped the President's hand. "The Russian people had suffered horribly in World War II," Brezhnev told Ford. "I do not want to inflict that upon my people again. We have accomplished something very significant, and it's our responsibility, yours and mine, on behalf of our countries, to achieve the finalization of the document.... This is an opportunity to protect not only the people of our two countries but, really, all mankind. We have to do something."[30]

Ford was deeply moved by Brezhnev's sincerity. Climbing the stairs to Air Force One, Ford turned and impulsively gave Brezhnev his huge Alaskan Wolf coat given to Ford by a friend. Brezhnev, donning the coat, was visibly moved.[31]

Returning home, Ford found Washington far less cordial. Preparing for the summit, the Soviets had been concerned the Americans would toughen their stance "to compensate for the setbacks in Southeast Asia."[32] Their concerns were well-founded. Although Ford and Kissinger believed they had prevailed in the negotiations and that extending the Strategic Arms Limitation Treaty was to America's benefit, much of Washington disagreed. After losing in Vietnam, America was suffering an identity crisis. American hardliners, notably an outspoken Ronald Reagan, were pressing for an end to détente (French for relaxation), believing "agreement with the Soviets was more dangerous than stalemate..."[33]

Burdened with a weak economy, the lingering backlash over Nixon's pardon, and little political support, Ford was unable to capitalize on the goodwill established at Vladivostok. The pressure from hardliners to remain tough with the Soviets became so great that Ford eventually dropped the word détente from official documents and promoted "peace through strength."[34]

Kissinger called the unwinding of détente a lost opportunity. Anatoly Dobrynin, the Soviet Ambassador to the United States, was even more disappointed. He declared the Vladivostok Summit the high point of détente between the Soviet Union and the United States.[35]

The warm personal relationship between Ford and Brezhnev was a lost opportunity to reduce Cold War tensions. It would take more than a decade, after President Reagan and Soviet Premier Mikhail Gorbachev established their own special relationship, that American and Soviet relations would begin to thaw.

Five months after the Vladivostok Summit, President Ford presided over the last battle of the Vietnam War. Largely forgotten, it was fought on a small island off the coast of Cambodia, known today as Kampuchea.

On May 12, 1975, the Cambodian Coast Guard intercepted and boarded the SS *Mayaguez*, a U.S.-registered container ship making its routine run between Hong Kong and Singapore. A month earlier, Cambodia's U.S.-backed government had fallen to the communist Khmer Rouge. The Khmer Rouge claimed the *Mayaguez* was sailing in Cambodian waters and suspected the vessel was a CIA spy ship.[36]

Three days later, President Ford launched a rescue operation, encouraged by Kissinger who, humiliated by losses in Vietnam and Cambodia, "was determined to give the Khmer Rouge a bloody nose."[37]

The first wave of the rescue operation began at dawn on May 15 and consisted of eight CH-53 transport helicopters and nearly 200 Marines. The rescue attempt was a disaster.

The Marines attacked the wrong island. Believing that the *Mayaguez* crew was being held on the island of Koh Tang, the giant CH-53 helicopters attempted to land on the island's narrow beaches. Hundreds of Khmer Rouge soldiers were dug in and heavily fortified. Three American helicopters were immediately lost and four were damaged so severely they were forced to withdraw. Little more than half the Marines were able to land. Once on the ground, the fighting was fierce.

Unknown to the Marines, minutes before their attack on Koh Tang the Khmer Rouge had announced they were releasing the crew. "We only wanted to know the reason for its coming and to warn it against violating our waters again,"[38] the communique declared. By noon, all crew members of the *Mayaguez* were safely aboard the USS *Harold E Holt*. President Ford announced the crew had been released—but conveniently failed to mention that the Khmer Rouge had announced their release earlier that morning before the failed Marine assault.

Henry Kissinger greeting China's ailing Mao Zedong on December 2, 1975 with President Ford approvingly looking on. Mao died nine months later. In 1978, the United States and the People's Republic of China restored full diplomatic relations.

NIDAY PICTURE LIBRARY/ALAMY

Once the crew was aboard the *Harold E Holt*, the Marines were ordered to withdraw. In the confusion, three were left behind on the beach. The three unfortunate men were summarily executed by the Khmer Rouge—the last Americans to die in the Vietnam War.

In August 1975, the United States, Canada, the Soviet Union, and every European country (except Albania, which signed in 1991) signed the Helsinki Accord. The Accord was a devil's bargain, and a bad one at that. Years after the end of World War II, the Accord recognized the borders established by the Soviet Union after the war, including a divided Berlin, assuring Soviet hegemony over Eastern Europe indefinitely. In return, the signatories agreed to guarantee the human rights and other fundamental freedoms of their citizens as well as open communications and travel between Eastern and Western Europe.[39]

The Soviets quickly violated the Accord, persecuting their citizens for political dissent. The Soviet crackdowns continued until the mid-nineteen-eighties when Gorbachev's policy of *glasnost* began to loosen political discussion and dissent within the Soviet Union.

"We never wanted it," Kissinger told Ford, referencing an earlier conversation with Nixon. "But we went along with the Europeans.... It is meaningless. It is just a grandstand play to the left."[40]

More successful was Ford's visit to China. In December 1975, Ford and Kissinger met with the Chinese leadership as a continuation of the Triangular Diplomacy Kissinger and Nixon had initiated three years earlier. During their 1972 visit, Mao Zedong had broken the ice by joking about the "girls" Kissinger secretly met during his diplomatic trips. But with Kissinger now married, that subject was taboo. Yet once again, the Chinese broke the ice during the Americans' first meeting with China Vice Premier Teng Hsiao-ping:

> Teng: I hear that the foreign press has been commenting on my vice of chain-smoking, so I have taken out a cigarette for them. Our foreign minister has the same bad habit I have. I tried for ten years to fight this habit, but I have always failed.
>
> Ford: If you don't mind, I will smoke a pipe.
>
> Teng: I suppose people who don't smoke at all, like the Doctor [Kissinger], are the best people in the world. Those who smoke pipes are the second-best; and we who smoke cigarettes are the worst.
>
> Kissinger: My wife smokes. Her nurse tried to help her stop. The result was that the nurse stopped, but she didn't.[41]

Within minutes, the conversation took up a more serious topic. The Chinese were concerned by Soviet expansionism, even more so than the United States. Unlike the United States, China shared a 2,600-mile border with the Soviet Union:

Teng: Because now the issue that is confronting the people of the world is the international question, and especially the danger of war. And to speak frankly, the question we are mostly concerned with is Soviet expansionism. . . . As Chairman Mao once said to the Doctor, our common task that we face is how to deal with that SOB [the Soviets].

Kissinger: I thought he said "bastard." (laughter)

Teng: So, the question that we have been discussing is how we should deal with this bastard. . . . And as we discussed last night at the banquet, this is both the most important point in common, and also a point where our differences are not small.[42]

Ford assured Teng that "[the United States] will resist expansion in either the east or the west—any military expansion by the Soviet Union—and with our nuclear capability." But Teng remained concerned the United States was not taking the Soviet threat seriously:

Teng: As for the global strategic situation, we also feel that at present the United States is in a defensive position and the Soviet Union is in an aggressive position. We also feel the contemporary situation is very similar to the state-of-affairs prior to the outbreak of World War II. To put it plainly, we believe that to a very great degree the Soviet Union has taken the place of Hitler.[43]

In 1972, Nixon and Kissinger had suspected an ideological rivalry was developing between the Soviet Union and China. But by 1975, it was clear the relationship had gone far beyond disputes over communist ideology. The Chinese considered the Soviet Union's territorial ambitions comparable to Hitler's aspirations for territorial expansion into Eastern Europe and Russia. Gravely afraid of their Russian neighbors, the Chinese were imploring the United States to thwart Soviet aggression. Since Vladivostok, American hardliners had accused Ford of being soft on the Soviets, and now he was hearing it from the Chinese.

The talks continued for three days, with few tangible results. As the talks ended, the diplomats chose not to issue a joint communiqué. "So little seems to have happened here," one journalist complained.[44]

But progress was made. The two countries understood each other much better and confirmed that they shared a mutual interest in containing the Soviet Union. Although not yet ready to restore full diplomatic relations, Ford established a United States Liaison Office in Beijing as a precursor to an American Embassy. Ford appointed George H.W. Bush, America's former Ambassador to the United Nations, as its head.

Ford also played a critical role in establishing the Group of Seven (G7), an international forum composed of the heads-of-state of seven major countries.

During the 1973 Oil Crisis, finance ministers from United States, France, West Germany, and the United Kingdom began meeting to discuss the oil embargo and related international issues. Japan soon joined the group and then, in 1975, at President Ford's request, the five countries plus Italy met in France. The meeting resulted in the formation of the Group of Six, which agreed to meet annually with a rotating President hosting each meeting. In 1976, again at Ford's request, Canada joined, making it the Group of Seven (G7). The next year, the European Union was invited to join as a permanent guest. Russia joined in 1997, briefly making it the G8, but was ejected in 2014 after it annexed Crimea.

Today the G7 meets annually to discuss global issues including the environment, education, health, trade, and security. The group comprises about a third of the world's GDP based on purchasing power parity (PPP). PPP uses the actual price of goods and services within the country, rather than official exchange rates which can be manipulated, to calculate a more realistic GDP. If membership were based strictly on true GDP, in 2020 the G7 would have consisted of China, the United States, India, Japan, Russia, Germany and Indonesia.[45] Instead, the G7 remains an exclusive club of seven "advanced economies" that share similar values of democracy, human rights, and the rule of law.

Starting in 1999, the G7's role as an international forum has been complemented by the more inclusive G20, which includes Argentina, Australia, Brazil, Canada, China, France, Germany, India, Indonesia, Italy, Japan, Mexico, Russia, Saudi Arabia, South Africa, South Korea, Turkey, the United Kingdom, the United States, and the European Union.

In founding the G7, President Ford recognized the world was tightly interconnected; the 1973 Oil Crisis proved that. The G7, and later the G20, are but two of the many global organizations established since the end of World War II to foster international understanding, cooperation, and development, starting with the founding of the United Nations on October 24, 1945.

In 2019, the United States contributed $12.2 billion to 183 international organizations ranging from $3.3 billion to the United Nations down to $2,297 for the International Arctic Science Committee. The World Health Organization and the World Trade Organization received $421 million and $23 million, respectively. The World Food Organization received $2.6 billion.

The foreign contributions by the United States strike many as wasteful, money better spent at home. But the $12.2 billion the United States contributed to international organizations in 2019 represented only $37.00 per American, about ten cents a day.[46]

Over the past century, Americans have often resisted international entanglements. In 1915, President Woodrow Wilson's policy of "America First" attempted to keep the United States out of the First World War. In 1920, President Warren G. Harding again embraced America First to encapsulate his policy of distancing the United States from Europe after the First World War. Twenty years later, the slogan was revived by the America First Committee that promoted American Isolationism in the face of growing threats from Germany and Japan. (The America First Committee disbanded itself three days after the Japanese attack on Pearl Harbor on December 7, 1941.).

In 1971, Senator Barry Goldwater, furious that the United Nations had accepted "Red China" as a member (at the urging of President Nixon and

Secretary of State Kissinger), fumed on the Senate floor, "The time has come to recognize the United Nations for the anti-American, anti-freedom organization that it has become." Goldwater further urged his Senate colleagues, "The time has come for us to cut off all financial help, withdraw as a member, and ask the United Nations to find a headquarters location outside the United States. . ."[47]

Similarly, in 2018, President Trump scolded the United Nations Assembly. "We reject the ideology of globalism, and we embrace the doctrine of patriotism. . . . The United States is the world's largest giver in the world, by far, of foreign aid. But few give anything to us. . . . The United States will not be taken advantage of any longer."[48]

But today's advocates for American Isolationism have a limited view of history. During the early part of the twentieth century all the great foreign powers—Austria-Hungary, Britain, France, Germany, Japan, Russia—embraced rabid nationalism. By 1914, tensions had grown so high that a single assassination in Eastern Europe triggered the First World War. For three years the United States believed it could stay out of the European war. But by early 1917 America was forced into the conflict after German submarines sank ten American merchant ships delivering supplies to Britain.[49] Two decades later, the United States again believed it was isolated from foreign threats, protected from German and Japanese aggression by two oceans. But America was again thrust into war when the Japanese attacked Pearl Harbor on December 7, 1941 and, four days later, when Germany declared war on the United States.

After two World Wars costing an estimated eighty million military and civilian lives,[50] the United States moved from isolationism to internationalism. For seventy-five years, America led the world, starting with the United Nations, in the establishment of organizations promoting international cooperation in myriad areas. America promoted open trade over trade barriers, democracy over authoritarianism, and human rights over oppression. These policies have largely worked since the end of World War II contributing to relative peace and growing prosperity for much of the world. A return to American Isolationism, the idea that the world's nations are composed of winners and losers, would deny the lessons of history.

Heroes Walk Alone

America was at an emotional and economic nadir in August 1974 when Gerald Ford was elevated to the presidency. The United States had lost its first major war after committing billions of dollars and 58,000 American lives to Vietnam. Richard Nixon had resigned in disgrace. Unemployment and inflation were near historic highs. Drivers waited in gas lines a block long. Americans were dejected and disillusioned. The University of Michigan's consumer sentiment index had fallen to its lowest point since its record-keeping began.[51]

President Ford was denounced for his Nixon and Vietnam pardons, mocked for his WIN button, and even ridiculed as clumsy after he tripped descending the stairs of Air Force One. Chevy Chase played Ford on *Saturday Night Live* as the "Klutz in Chief." Ford took it all with good grace, never lashing back at his critics, and even invited Chevy Chase to perform at a White House dinner.

Under Ford, America slowly recovered. After two years of recession, real GDP grew 5.4 percent in 1976. Unemployment remained stubbornly high, but inflation fell from 11 to 5.8 percent. America celebrated its two-hundredth birthday in 1976 with parades, fireworks, and patriotic concerts. Consumer sentiment soared to 89.7. *Happy Days*, a nostalgic look at America in the nineteen-fifties, was America's favorite television program.[52]

Ford lost the 1976 presidential election to Jimmy Carter. Americans were still angry over Ford's two pardons, and after years of war, scandal and economic malaise wanted a change. Carter, a peanut farmer from Georgia who had never held national office, represented that change.

History remembers Gerald Ford well. Alan Greenspan, Ford's Chairman of the Council of Economic Advisers, declared: "Jerry Ford was the most decent man I ever encountered in public life."[53] In 1999 President Clinton presented Gerald Ford the Presidential Medal of Freedom, the nation's highest civilian award. "Steady, trustworthy, Gerald Ford ended a long national nightmare," Clinton said. "When he left the White House after 895 days, America was stronger, calmer, and more self-confident. America was, in other words, more like President Ford himself."[54] In 2001, Ford was honored with the Profiles in Courage award inspired by John Kennedy's book of the same name. "President Ford presided over this nation during one of its darkest hours, and in an effort to heal a divided nation, he made a very difficult decision that many believe may have cost him the presidency,"[55] Caroline Kennedy stated as she presented Ford the award.

Ford died the day after Christmas 2006. His obituary in *The New York Times* included a passage from Henry Kissinger's 1999 memoir in which Kissinger declared Ford a President in the heroic mold, a vanishing breed. Kissinger's description of the evolution of presidential politics was prescient:

> The modern politician is less interested in being a hero than a superstar. Heroes walk alone; stars derive their status from approbation. Heroes are defined by inner values, stars by consensus. When a candidate's views are forged in focus groups and ratified by television anchor-persons, insecurity and superficiality become congenital. Radicalism replaces liberalism, and populism masquerades as conservatism.[56]

James E. Carter Jr.

January 20, 1977 – January 20, 1981

> We must begin to scrutinize the overall effect of regulation in our economy. Through deregulation of the airline industry, we've increased profits, cut prices for all Americans, and begun—for one of the few times in the history of our Nation—to actually dismantle a major federal bureaucracy.[1]

A school principal shaped Jimmy Carter's lifelong moral philosophy. When he was twelve years old, Miss Julia Coleman suggested the young Carter read *War and Peace*, Tolstoy's chronicle of Napoléon's invasion of Russia in 1812. A dense 1,415 pages, the book must have taken the precocious student the entire summer to read. What struck the young Carter was that the book wasn't about Napoléon or the Russian Czar or their generals. Rather, Tolstoy told of the common people: the wives, students, peasants, and soldiers, whose love for their land led to Napoléon's defeat. Carter finished the book believing that "even the greatest historical events are controlled by the combined wisdom and courage and commitment and discernment and unselfishness and compassion and love and idealism of the common ordinary people."[2]

Years later, President Carter invoked Miss Coleman during his inaugural address. Recalling her classroom advice that, "We must adjust to changing times and still hold to unchanging principles," Carter urged Americans to "create together a new national spirit of unity and trust." Carter's address focused on the moral and spiritual obligations of Americans. Although millions of Americans were struggling economically, Carter scarcely mentioned inflation, unemployment, or the energy crisis, instead sprinkling references to the human spirit and spirituality throughout his address.[3] Like the common Russians who defeated Napoléon, Carter believed it would be ordinary Americans whose moral and spiritual values would conquer America's problems.

Although President Carter inherited a better economy than had his predecessor, Gerald Ford, the Misery Index—the combination of inflation and unemployment—was still near historical highs.

Learning from Ford's embarrassing WIN ("Whip Inflation Now") campaign, Carter chose not to engage economic issues head-on and certainly not in a high-profile publicity campaign. He was fortunate that during his first two years in office the nation slowly, and largely on its own, recovered from the food and oil shortages that had hit the nation in 1973. Real GDP grew a robust 4.6 percent in 1977 and then climbed to a booming 5.5 percent the next year. That year, corporate profits were up 20 percent from his election two years earlier. Industry was slowly becoming more bullish with gross private domestic investment rising to 20.3 percent of GDP in 1978, up 34 percent from 1975. And it wasn't big government spending boosting the economy; during those years, the federal government's share of the GDP decreased by 10 percent.

The fragile recovery didn't last. After years of simmering unrest under their despotic Shah, Iranians were on the verge of revolution. In late 1978, a massive strike by oil workers nearly shut down Iranian oil production, dropping daily production from six to 1.5 million barrels. In early 1979, the Shah of Iran fled into exile and, after a series of power struggles, the Iranian cleric Ayatollah Khomeini became the first leader of the newly formed Islamic Republic of Iran. As foreign oil imports fell, oil prices began a steep climb from $12.80 a barrel in 1978 to $35.50 a barrel ($112 in 2020 dollars) in 1980.[4] Consumers, companies, and governments began to hoard gasoline, exacerbating the shortages. Many states implemented rationing programs that allowed drivers to purchase gasoline only on specific days. The lines were even longer than those six years earlier during the Arab oil embargo.

During his single term, President Carter, a Georgia peanut farmer, deregulated oil and transportation, launched America towards energy independence, brokered peace between Egypt and Israel, and appointed Federal Reserve Chairman Paul Volcker.

RBM VINTAGE IMAGES/ALAMY

In 1979, the Misery Index, under 14 percent the prior three years, jumped to 17 percent in 1979 and real GDP growth straight-lined. On July 25, President Carter, in one of his most consequential acts as President, fired Arthur Burns and appointed Paul Volcker as chairman of the Federal Reserve. Earlier, as the governor of the New York Federal Reserve Bank, Volcker had argued that misguided monetary policy was the root cause of the nation's inflation. In the early nineteen-seventies, Fed Chairman Burns, directed by President Nixon that "We'll take inflation if necessary, but we can't take unemployment,"[5] focused on unemployment by keeping interest rates low to help assure Nixon's reelection. But low interest rates, by making money cheap, had increased the money supply fueling inflation throughout the decade.

Volker, though, believed inflation was the greater evil and formulated a painful plan to finally rein it in. There was simply too much money circulating in the economy. Volcker began raising the federal funds rate (the rate commercial banks charge each other for lending their excess funds overnight) from 11 percent in August 1979 to 14 percent by the end of the year, 17.6 percent in 1980, and then an astronomical 19 percent in 1981. Credit dried up, reducing the money supply. But after fifteen years of rising inflation, workers and companies were slow to change and continued to demand higher wages which, in turn, pushed prices up. That momentum drove inflation to 13.5 percent in 1980. But slowly, the Fed's tight money policy began to lower wage and price pressures. Inflation began to fall, and fall rapidly: down to 10.3 percent in 1981, 6.1 percent in 1982 and finally to 3.2 percent in 1983.

Volcker's cure worked, but like chemotherapy, the cure was nearly as painful as the disease. In 1982 real GDP declined 1.8 percent, the largest drop since 1946. Unemployment peaked at 9.7 percent, the highest since 1941. Unable to obtain credit, 25,000 businesses failed, also a postwar high. Home and car sales declined dramatically. Indebted farmers drove their tractors to Washington to protest high interest rates. It was the price to be paid after a decade of loose money.

After Volcker's intervention, inflation has never again come close to the levels suffered during the Great Inflation from 1965 through 1985. From 1983 through 2021, Federal Reserve policies limited average annual inflation to 2.7 percent, far below rates during the Great Inflation. Years later, the St. Louis Federal Reserve summarized Volcker's contribution:

> Without his bold change in monetary policy and his determination to stick with it through several painful years, the U.S. economy would have continued its downward spiral. By reversing the misguided policies of his predecessors, Volcker set the table for the long economic expansions of the nineteen-eighties and nineteen-nineties.[6]

Carter, though, received little recognition for hiring and then supporting Paul Volcker as he administered his bitter economic medicine. By 1980, Volcker's cure had pushed the nation into recession, just as Carter was running for reelection. An election he would lose.

The Moral Equivalent of War

The winter of 1976–1977 was brutally cold. Chicago temperatures hovered below freezing for a record forty-three straight days. Buffalo was buried by fifteen feet of snow, and for the only time in recorded history, it snowed in Miami. Temperatures across the eastern United States averaged nine degrees below normal. Natural gas consumption was nearly twice normal levels, creating shortages throughout the eastern United States and leaving families huddling around their fireplaces to keep warm. Schools were forced to close and nearly 1.8 million were out of work when businesses temporarily closed due to fuel shortages.[7]

For years, America's appetite for energy had been growing. In 1950, 228 million British Thermal Units (BTUs) of energy were consumed annually for every man, woman, and child in the United States. As President Carter took office, per capita energy consumption had increased to 353 million BTUs, the equivalent of nearly 3,000 gallons of gasoline for every man, woman and child in the country.[8]

During the nineteen-fifties, the United States was nearly self-sufficient in energy, importing less than two percent of its energy. But by 1977, America was importing 23 percent of its total energy. The nation had become acutely sensitive to energy stresses whether from supply interruptions or unusually high demand. In 1973, Americans had seen a handful of tiny countries concentrated in the Middle East wreak havoc on the American economy when they shut off oil exports. Now, four years later, fuel shortages resulting from an unusually cold winter disrupted much of the eastern United States. Something had to be done.

On April 18, 1977 President Carter spoke to Americans wearing a beige cardigan sweater and sitting in front of a crackling fire. The topic was energy. Carter's speech was one Miss Julia Coleman might have given herself had she held Carter's advanced engineering degree. Carter opened his speech as a principled teacher. "We must not be selfish or timid if we hope to have a decent world for our children and our grandchildren," Carter admonished.

Now the engineer, Carter presented a detailed energy program that focused point by point on reducing the nation's energy consumption. Setting specific goals for 1985, Carter challenged Americans to reduce growth in annual energy consumption to less than two percent, to cut oil imports in half, to alleviate the natural gas shortage by increasing coal production by two-thirds, and to use solar energy in more than 2.5 million houses.

Closing again as the principled teacher, Carter lectured, "I am sure each of you will find something you don't like about the specifics of our proposal. It will demand that we make sacrifices and changes in every life. To some degree, the sacrifices will be painful—but so is any meaningful sacrifice."

In a statement that likely cost him millions of voters, near the end of his speech Carter warned big car lovers: "Those citizens who insist on driving large, unnecessarily powerful cars must expect to pay more for that luxury."[9] Carter was seldom accused of pandering to voters.

Calling the need for energy conservation "the moral equivalent of war," Carter hoped to rally Americans to radically reduce their energy consumption. *The New York Times* was skeptical, reporting, "It is doubtful that the public will rally to Mr. Carter's trumpet.... [To] the ordinary householder the problem of how to pay last month's fuel oil bill looms much larger than whether there will be enough fuel, at any price, in the winter of 1985."[10] The august *New York Times* had misread Americans. True, many didn't support Carter's call for conservation. They refused to be inconvenienced, loved their big cars and trucks, or doubted that an energy shortage even existed. But other Americans, in their own self-interest, lowered their thermostats to sixty-five degrees, insulated their homes, and abandoned their gas-guzzlers for smaller, fuel-efficient cars—often from Japan.

President Carter's speech was the kick-off to his energy agenda. He quickly established the Department of Energy, forging together dozens of disparate energy-related agencies into a cabinet-level department. In 1978 he signed the National Energy Act, which began the deregulation of energy prices, promoted renewable energy, encouraged energy-efficient power plants, changed energy standards from voluntary to mandatory, liberalized the distribution of natural gas, and established tax policies to encourage conservation. Carter's 1980 Energy Security Act promoted renewable energy from windmills to synthetic fuels, including corn-based ethanol. The Act also increased the Strategic Petroleum Reserve to one billion barrels of oil for use in a national emergency. Symbolically, Carter installed solar panels on the White House and lowered temperatures to a chilly sixty-five degrees.

After attending the U.S. Naval Academy, Carter had served in the Navy for seven years. Having seen nuclear submarines cruise for years on a few pounds of enriched uranium, Carter might naturally have promoted nuclear energy as a major energy source. The United States has abundant uranium deposits. But Americans had developed a deep-seated fear of nuclear radiation. From 1951 through 1962 approximately one hundred above-the-ground nuclear weapons tests were conducted in Nevada spreading radiation throughout the western United States and as far as New England. Decades later, studies estimated anywhere from 11,000 to 145,000 people died from the resulting radiation-induced cancers.[11] Then in 1979, as Carter was developing his energy program, the highly publicized partial meltdown of the Three Mile Island nuclear reactor and the nuclear disaster film *The China Syndrome* cemented public opinion against nuclear energy. To this day, nuclear power only generates about 20 percent of the nation's electricity.[12]

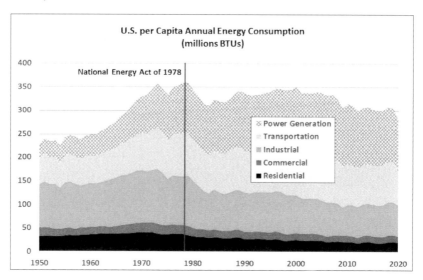

Carter's emphasis on energy conservation, including the National Energy Act of 1978, helped slow the rampant growth of U.S. energy consumption.
U.S. ENERGY INFORMATION ADMINISTRATION

Although mocked by partisan politicians, contested by energy companies, and resisted by automobile manufacturers, President Carter's efforts to change America's energy habits were successful. After climbing for decades, America's per capita energy consumption peaked in 1978 and then began to fall. By 1985 per capita energy consumption was down 10 percent, far lower than Carter's 1977 energy plan. America's per capita energy consumption would never again return to its 1978 high. Crude oil imports also declined steeply, from 6.6 million barrels a day in 1977 to 3.2 million in 1985.[13] During those same years, energy from renewable sources increased from five to eight percent of total U.S. energy consumption.[14]

Economists have described Carter's policies as the "most sweeping energy legislation in the nation's history."[15] Although President Carter permanently altered the arc of America's energy consumption, subsequent Presidents attempted to reverse Carter's energy initiatives, especially when renewable energy threatened fossil-fuel-based corporations.

President Reagan chose not to restore the solar panels after the White House roof was replaced. Today, one of the original White House panels resides in the Solar Science and Technology Museum in Dezhou, China.[16] When Reagan abandoned solar energy, China stepped in and today manufactures 80 percent of the world's solar panels while the United States produces one percent.[17]

Reagan would also later slash spending on renewable energy research, roll back fuel economy standards, and weaken clean energy initiatives. After a brief Carter-inspired growth spurt from 1977 through 1983, renewable energy would stagnate for twenty-five years until President Obama's policies grew renewable energy from seven to eleven percent of America's total energy production.

By 2019, the United States had become energy independent.[18] New hydraulic fracturing technologies ("fracking") get nearly all the credit. But that is wrong. Per capita crude oil production fell from 1978 through 2019. In 1978, the American oil industry produced 29.9 barrels of oil per American. By 2019, oil production, including the increased production due to fracking, had fallen to 19.6 barrels per American, well below its 1978 high. Coal production fell 37 percent. Coal production, measured on a per capita basis, peaked in 1951 and has been in decline ever since.[19]

America's total per capita energy production, driven by growth in natural gas, nuclear power, and renewable energy, only increased 8.5 percent from 1978 through 2019.

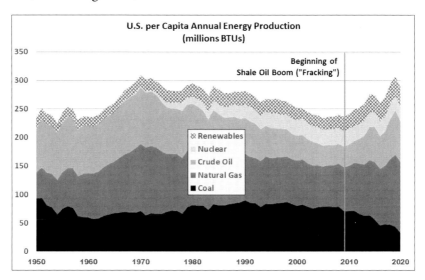

Energy conservation, led by President Carter, and a revolutionary oil extraction technology pioneered by Texas oil man George Mitchell, together, restored U.S. energy independence.　　　　　　　　　　U.S. ENERGY INFORMATION ADMINISTRATION

But consumption fell 15 percent. In 1978, per capita energy consumption peaked at 358 million BTUs, equivalent, as noted earlier, to every American that year consuming nearly 3,000 gallons of gasoline. By 2019, consumption had declined to 304 million BTUs, or about 2,500 gallons of gasoline per American. That decline continues to save American families several thousand dollars a year in energy costs.

It has been the decline in per capita energy consumption, not increased energy production, which has primarily made America energy independent. And that decline was spear-headed by President Carter.

Like Volcker's economic policies, President Carter has received little credit for America's energy transformation. But it was Carter who started that transformation on April 18, 1977, warning Americans that "[The energy crisis] is the greatest challenge that our country will face during our

lifetimes. The energy crisis has not yet overwhelmed us, but it will if we do not act quickly."[20]

Many scoffed, mocking Carter's cardigan sweater and refusing to turn down their thermostats. But Carter was right. For decades America's per capita energy consumption had been growing at an unsustainable rate of 1.6 percent annually. America had become addicted to cheap foreign oil. But a year after Carter's speech, America's energy appetite began a steady decline. Today, the average American consumes 15 percent less energy than she did on April 18, 1977, the day Carter started the energy revolution.

Jump-Starting Deregulation

Like his economic and energy initiatives, President Carter's deregulation efforts have also been largely forgotten. For nearly 100 years before Carter's administration, the federal government added layer upon layer of regulations to its law books. Carter changed that, starting with his 1978 State of the Union address. "We really need to realize that there is a limit to the role and the function of government," Carter told the nation. "Bit by bit we are chopping down the thicket of unnecessary federal regulations by which government too often interferes in our personal lives and our personal business."[21]

Unlike most Presidents who had spent their careers in politics, Carter had been a successful farmer and understood the burden that excessive regulation had on everyday Americans and small businesses.

It started with railroads. By the end of the nineteenth century, railroads had transformed transportation for both people and goods by providing, for example: the ability to make a day trip from a farming village to a large city for shopping; to ship cattle and goods to markets hundreds of miles distant; to travel a thousand miles from large eastern cities to visit the West. All this was as empowering for nineteenth-century Americans as international jet travel is today.

But there was a darker side. Railroad cartels controlled large parts of the country, locking out competition and keeping prices artificially high; pricing was often predatory. Farmers, connected to their markets by short-haul lines, were over-charged. Other shippers felt railroads were practicing dis-criminatory pricing even among similar customers in the same region. As criticism grew, the railroads had been able to forestall government inter-vention through largess, including free annual railroad passes to politicians, journalists, ministers, and other opinion leaders.

But the rapacious behavior of the railroad monopolies finally forced Congress to act. In 1887, the Interstate Commerce Act was passed, which required shipping rates to be non-discriminatory and "reasonable and just." The 1887 Act provided guidelines but did not regulate rates, that would follow in the 1906 Hepburn Act. The 1887 Act also created the Interstate Commerce Commission (ICC), the country's first regulatory commis-sion, for monitoring and enforcing provisions of the Act. Over the next fifty years, the ICC grew to regulate all forms of transportation: railroads, trucking, airlines, ocean shipping, even bus lines.

In 1970, the Penn Central Railroad filed for bankruptcy. It was the largest bankruptcy in the nation's history. As the new Interstate Highway System made trucking an attractive shipping option, passengers abandoned trains for their cars, and the northeast industrial base declined, Penn Central failed to adapt. Much of the blame was assigned to over-regulation by the ICC.[22]

To help the railroads compete, President Ford tip-toed into deregulation in 1976 with the passage of the Railroad Revitalization and Regulatory Re-form Act. But the Act was not the sweeping overhaul its grand name sug-gests. It primarily focused on finalizing plans for nationalizing portions of the U.S. railroad system as the freight-based Conrail and passenger-based Amtrak.[23]

It was under President Carter that the Staggers Act was passed in 1980. The Act revitalized American railroads and began the deregulation trend that continues to this day.[24] The Staggers Act liberated the railroads by al-lowing railroad companies to set their own rates. Its impact was immediate. In the thirty years before 1980, the railroad's share of the transportation market, squeezed by competition from trucking and airlines, sank from 56.1 to 37.5 percent. After 1980, rail's marketshare soon stabilized and then increased to 40 percent. Remarkably, rail shipping rates declined over four percent annually in the 15 years after the passage of the Act.[25] Today the railroads are a dynamic part of the American economy and sufficiently profitable to have enticed Warren Buffet to buy Burlington Northern Santa Fe (BNSF) for $44 billion in 2009.[26] Well run, railroads today are very profitable. In 2019, BNSF earned $8.1 billion in operating income.[27]

In 1980, Carter signed the Motor Carrier Act that deregulated the trucking industry. The Act largely removed federal regulations governing pricing, routes, and the types of commodities trucks could transport. Within ten years the number of licensed trucking companies doubled to 40,000. The combined deregulation of trucking and railroads facilitated intermodal shipping, in which sealed containers carrying goods move freely between trucks, trains, and ships, and which subsequently increased 70 percent from 1981 through 1987. Overall, a Department of Transportation analysis estimated that the total savings resulting from the combined Staggers and Motor Carrier Acts were between $38 and $56 billion.[28]

Carter was just getting started. The Airline Deregulation Act of 1978 changed Americans' travel habits. Before 1978, airline fares and routes had been closely regulated. With prices tightly controlled, the only means airlines had to compete was through their service, and that they did. Seats were spacious and the food was excellent, even in economy class. First-class enjoyed carved Chateaubriand and champagne served by attractive stewardesses in French-inspired uniforms. Boeing 747 jumbo jets featured an upstairs lounge reached by a spiral staircase where passengers, treated more like guests, could mingle over drinks. With three-person crews, the captain would often stroll back into the cabin to chat amiably with passengers. Passengers, for their part, dressed in suits, were polite and enjoyed conversations with their seatmates. For those of means, the nineteen-fifties, sixties, and seventies were the golden age of air travel.

But few could afford to fly. In 1974, the cheapest fare from New York to Los Angeles was $1,600 (in 2020 dollars). The 1978 Act changed that. Today a quick Internet search finds many transcontinental fares under $300, often well under.[29] Overall, average air travel prices have dropped by half since 1978, putting air travel within the reach of most Americans. In 1965, airlines flew 274 passenger-miles for each American. By 2016, per capita airline travel had increased nearly eight-fold to 2,075 miles per American.[30]

Although people are flying far more, no one would suggest that we are living in the golden age of air travel any longer. Hub and spoke routing has replaced many direct flights and often requires two or more flights to reach a destination only 500 miles away. Airplane seats are still spacious—for those twelve and under. Airline food has declined from delicious hot meals to plain hot meals to sandwiches to warm nuts to peanuts and, finally, to a small bag of pretzels. Attending to hundreds of passengers, flight attendants hardly have the time to comfort, cajole, or chat with passengers. And if you're frightened by flying, don't expect the captain to come back to offer a few comforting words. He's locked inside the cockpit to protect the crew from would-be terrorists.

Deregulation led to fierce competition. Since 1980, relentless price competition has bankrupted nearly every major American airline. Some recovered, many did not. American, Braniff, Continental, Delta, Eastern, Frontier, Northwest, PanAm, TWA, United, US Airways, and many more once proud names have filed bankruptcy in the years since deregulation.[31] To survive, cost-cutting must be relentless. One story has it that shortly after deregulation, Robert Crandall, American Airline's tough-minded CEO, ordered salads to be served with one rather than two olives. Most passengers didn't notice. The airline saved $40,000 annually. "A recession is when you have to tighten your belt," one airline executive declared. "Depression is when you have no belt to tighten. When you've lost your trousers, you're in the airline business."[32]

But the free market responded. Airlines that adapted to the new environment like Alaska, JetBlue, and Southwest have, if not thrived, survived. Airlines have learned that American flyers view airline travel as a commodity and will tolerate personal inconvenience and mediocre service in exchange for cheap tickets. The market has spoken, but it had a price. A 2019 survey of global airline passengers rated the world's top ten airlines. None were American.[33]

Carter understood that regulations had economic costs, and established procedures to minimize the growth of new regulations. In 1978, Executive Order 12044 established rules for evaluating the impact of proposed regulations. Two years later Carter signed the Paperwork Reduction Act to minimize burdensome federal reporting requirements. As a result, all new regulations today must undergo a rigorous, and public, cost versus benefit analysis before their approval.[34]

At the end of his term, Carter reminded Congress that, "The Nation must recognize that regulation to meet social goals competes for scarce resources with other national objectives."[35] Nearly every President since Carter has boasted about slashing regulations, but Carter was the first and, according to *The Wall Street Journal*, most consequential:

> In the greatest deregulatory effort of the twentieth century, President Jimmy Carter led the opening of competition in the railroad, airline and trucking industries. Peer-reviewed economic studies have consistently shown that the transportation deregulation of the Carter era produced significant price reductions and improvements in service.[36]

Carter's deregulation efforts even changed the drinking habits of millions of Americans. Before Prohibition in 1920, the United States had 1,500 breweries brewing thousands of beers for local markets. Thirteen years later, after Prohibition was repealed, Washington placed restrictive laws on the making of beer, resulting in the exclusion of small-scale brewers from the market. Over the decades, the market consolidated into a few giant brewers that provided Americans with a limited variety of largely similar, bland beers.[37]

For decades, an American tired of drinking Pabst, Miller, or Schlitz wasn't allowed to brew his own beer. That changed on October 14, 1978 when Carter signed legislation legalizing home brewing. Americans began to experiment brewing their own beers, some of which were so good that many amateur brewers went into business for themselves. This, along with the legalization of brewpubs in 1982, started the craft brewing industry which has made America the most innovative beer-producing country in the world. Today, over 8,000 American brewers[38] brew every kind of beer imaginable, from Mamma Mia Pizza Beer, best consumed with pepperoni pizza, to Samuel Adams Boston Lager, originally brewed in Jim Koch's kitchen and now considered one of the world's best beers.[39]

So, if you're a beer drinker, raise a toast to Jimmy Carter, not just for deregulating energy and transportation, but also for paving the way to better-tasting beer.

A Man, a Plan, a Canal, Panama

"A Man, a Plan, a Canal, Panama" is a famous English palindrome, a phrase that reads the same forwards and backwards. It also succinctly describes one of America's proudest accomplishments. The man was President Teddy Roosevelt. The plan was to build a canal regardless of the political, economic, and engineering challenges. The canal was the Panama Canal that connected the Atlantic and Pacific Oceans. Carter gave the canal back to Panama, an action invoking both admiration and condemnation.

In 1881, after finishing the Suez Canal, the French began the construction of a canal across the Isthmus of Panama, a province of Columbia at the time. The French were confident. The canal would be less than half the length of the Suez and be built using the latest technology, powerful steam excavators the size of a small house. But by 1894, the French had given up. The unfinished project had cost nearly $300 million and taken an incredible 22,000 lives. Torrential rains quickly rusted equipment; the tropical jungle swarmed with venomous snakes and spiders; and accidents and tropical disease killed as many as 200 workers a day.[40]

The project lay abandoned until 1903 when the United States attempted to sign a treaty with Columbia giving the United States rights to build and control the canal. Columbia refused. That hardly stopped the project. Rebels inside Panama, a province of Columbia at the time, were fomenting revolt, seeking freedom from Columbia. President Roosevelt quickly dispatched the USS *Nashville* to Panama to block Columbian troops from suppressing the revolt. On November 3, 1903, Panama declared its independence. Two weeks later, Panama and the United States signed the Hay-Bunau-Varilla Treaty, which gave the United States the rights, in perpetuity, to build and administer a canal within a ten-mile-wide canal zone that cuts through the middle of Panama.

The treaty was broadly condemned. Although American warships had secured Panama's independence, many Panamanians condemned the canal treaty as an infringement on their newly acquired national sovereignty. Columbia, and much of Latin America, considered the treaty nothing more than American gunboat diplomacy. *The New York Times* called the treaty "an act of sordid conquest." President Teddy Roosevelt was unapologetic. "I took the Isthmus," Roosevelt later boasted, "started the canal and then left Congress not to debate the canal, but to debate me."[41]

The canal opened for commerce in 1914, two years ahead of schedule. It remains one of history's greatest engineering accomplishments and for decades a source of American pride. "American pluck and luck conquered all," as a 1928 textbook put it. "The grand dream was realized. In 1913 the waters of the Atlantic and the Pacific were united."[42]

But from the beginning, Panamanians resented the Americans. Panamanian school children were taught that just days after Panama's independence that the United States coerced a sweetheart deal to permanently control the canal. The canal, bordered by five miles of land on each side, split Panama asunder from the Atlantic to the Pacific.

Pressure on the Americans to leave Panama crystallized in 1956 when Egypt nationalized the Suez Canal after nearly a century of joint British and French ownership. Eight years later, anti-American sentiment in Panama peaked on January 9, 1964 when a dispute over the right to fly the Panamanian flag in the Canal Zone led to mass rioting and looting. Twenty-one Panamanian civilians and four American soldiers died after U.S. troops were called in to stop the violence. International sentiment turned against the United States. The British and French, having recently shed their colonial empires, accused the United States of colonialism. Cuba, China, and the Soviet Union raged against American Imperialism. Egyptian President Nasser urged Panama to nationalize the canal as he had the Suez Canal in 1956.[43]

Serious negotiations for a settlement with Panama began under President Nixon but stalled under President Ford. The issues were simple: bending to international opinion versus preserving American control and pride. "If these [Canal] negotiations fail," Secretary of State Henry Kissinger warned, "we will be beaten to death in every international forum and there will be riots all over Latin America."[44] Ronald Reagan disagreed. "We bought it. We built it. We paid for it. And Panama should be told that we intend to keep it,"[45] Reagan asserted during his 1976 presidential campaign.

Initially hesitant, President Carter soon supported the transfer of the canal to Panama. In 1977, the Senate narrowly ratified two treaties that included provisions certifying the United States could use military force to guarantee Panama's neutrality and assuring perpetual use of the canal by the United States. After a transition period, the United States turned the canal over to Panama on December 31, 1999. Skeptics predicted the Panamanians would be poor managers. They were wrong. The canal's new owners have been good stewards. In 2019, 13,738 ships passed through the canal, far more than in 1999.[46]

Like the Marshall Plan after World War II, returning the canal to Panama was an act of American goodwill and generosity. "If Theodore Roosevelt were to endorse the treaties, as I'm quite sure he would," President Carter told Americans, "it would be mainly because he could see the decision as one by which we are demonstrating the kind of great power we wish to be."[47]

A Bridge to China

On January 1, 1979, the United States and the People's Republic of China (China) restored diplomatic relations. It had been seven years since President Nixon and Chinese Premier Zhou Enlai signed the Shanghai Communiqué that declared their intent to restore relations between the two countries. But there was a stumbling block: Taiwan, a small island nation off the coast of mainland China. In 1949, communist revolutionaries won the civil war that had been simmering across China for twenty years. The remnants of the former government fled to Taiwan. Although mainland China's population was 540 million[48] and Taiwan's only eight million[49], the United Nations recognized Taiwan as the legitimate government of China.

Two decades later, to curry favor with the Chinese during their "Triangular Diplomacy" between China and the Soviet Union, President Nixon and Secretary of State Kissinger encouraged the United Nations to accept "Red China" as a member while also retaining Taiwan's membership. But mainland China demanded the United Nations recognize but one China. The United Nations acquiesced, over the objection of the United States, and in 1971 accepted China as a member, ejecting Taiwan from the international organization.

Following the restoration of full diplomatic relations, Carter also announced the United States was abrogating the 1954 Sino-American Mutual Defense Treaty between the United State and Taiwan. The United States was no longer bound to come to Taiwan's defense if invaded by China.

Congress, led by Senator Barry Goldwater, challenged Carter's abrogation of the treaty. The issue eventually wound up on the front steps of the Supreme Court. But the Court considered the issue to be political and refused to rule.

Carter's abrogation of the treaty with Taiwan wasn't unusual. The United States often abandoned treaties considered no longer useful, starting with the hundreds of Native-American treaties signed in the nineteenth century.[50] More recently, the United States walked away from the Anti-Ballistic Missile Treaty in 2001, the Iran Nuclear Deal in 2017, and the Intermediate-Range Nuclear Forces Treaty in 2019.

One group though was delighted by the restoration of relations with China: American business. China, with a billion people, was the world's largest market. With four times the population of the United States, surely the United States would sell more goods to China than China would sell to the United States.

But that never happened. Rather than import goods from the United States, China demanded American companies establish joint ventures to manufacture their products in China, employing Chinese rather than American workers. Within a decade, scores of America's top companies were operating in China including AT&T, Eastman Kodak, Gillette, Heinz, Nabisco, and Reynolds Tobacco.[51] In 2000, the year before China joined the World Trade Organization (WTO), China exported six times more goods to the United States than it imported.[52]

President Trump blamed the WTO for granting China unfair trade advantages. Perhaps, but since China joined the WTO, the growth of America's trade deficit with China, adjusted for inflation, has slowed. From 1991 through 2001, America's trade deficit with China increased an average of 18 percent annually. After China joined the WTO, the rate decreased to 10 percent from 2001 through 2011, and then from 2011 through 2019 slowed to a mere 1.1 percent annually.

Politically, it's easier to blame the WTO than American industry for trade deficits. The China trade hurt American workers but has been a windfall for American companies. A 2019 survey of 200 American companies operating in China reports that 97 percent are profitable. Although trade tensions are rising, 87 percent reported that they intend to remain in China. Only three percent of the companies stated an intention to move their operations back to the United States.[53]

Enduring Peace and Unending War

Every President since Truman has sought peace in the Middle East. President Carter brokered an enduring peace between Egypt and Israel, but he also pursued Cold War policies in Afghanistan that contributed to decades of instability, war, and terrorism.

At the suggestion of First Lady Rosalynn Carter, the President invited Israeli Prime Minister Menachem Begin and Egyptian President Anwar el-Sādāt to participate in peace talks at Camp David, the presidential retreat. Carter had already laid the groundwork for the talks during trips to the Middle East where he met individually with both men. Carter found that both Begin and Sādāt were willing to talk. After thirteen days of off-and-on-again negotiations, in which Carter played a conciliatory role, the parties reached an agreement.

On September 17, 1978, the three leaders signed the "Framework for Peace in the Middle East" that provided a political structure for establishing Palestinian self-government and peace between Israel, Egypt, and the other Arab states. Six months later, Israel and Egypt signed a peace treaty that jointly earned Begin and Sādāt the 1978 Nobel Peace Prize. The other Arab countries, furious with Egypt for its unilateral negotiations with Israel, refused to consider the framework for peace and for the next decade suspended Egypt's membership in the Arab League.[54] Sādāt would pay a higher price. He was assassinated on October 6, 1981 by Islamic radicals angered by his agreement with Israel.[55]

Egypt's Anwar Sadat, President Jimmy Carter and Israel's Menachem Begin are pleased after signing the Camp David Accords on September 17, 1978. Six months later, the Accords led to the 1979 Egypt-Israel Peace Treaty.   WORLD POLITICS ARCHIVE/ALAMY

Carter must have felt tremendous satisfaction as he left the Camp David negotiations. More than forty years after its signing, the Egypt-Israel peace treaty continues to be honored and remains one of the few examples of reconciliation in the Middle East.

Carter's quiet contentment after Camp David was short-lived. Five events over the next two years would overwhelm his presidency and lead to decades of chaos in the Middle East: on January 16, 1979, growing discord forced the Shah of Iran to flee Iran in disgrace;[56] on July 16, 1979, Saddam Hussein became President of Iraq;[57] on November 4, 1979, Iranian college students stormed the American embassy in Tehran, taking 52 American hostages;[58] on December 24, 1979 the Soviet Union invaded Afghanistan;[59] and, finally, on September 22, 1980, Iraq invaded Iran.[60]

Fed by the combustible mixture of oil and religion, the Middle East was about to explode.

In 1953, President Eisenhower was under pressure to protect British oil interests threatened by Iran's legitimately elected populist government. Unwilling to send American troops, Eisenhower used the CIA to covertly overthrow Iran's democratically elected prime minister, Mohammad Mosaddegh, and replaced him with the more pliable Mohammad Reza, the eldest son of Reza Shah Pahlavi, an army officer who had become the ruler of Iran in 1925.

After assuming power, the new Shah moved Iran towards a modern, western society. By the early nineteen-seventies, Iranian women were wearing mini-skirts, high school bands were marching in American-style parades, and men and women were eating together in French restaurants. The American political establishment considered Iran's secularization a triumph for Western values. But the reforms were deeply resented by Iran's conservative Muslim clergy. Opposition to the Shah's government slowly grew and by 1978 the regime was bordering on collapse. Dissatisfaction with the Shah's extravagance, economic policies, and oppressive methods finally led to open revolt. On September 4, 1978, known today as Black Friday in Iran, the Shah's security forces killed sixty-four protesters.

Four months later, on January 16, 1979, the Shah fled the country, appointing Shapour Bakhtiar as Prime Minister. Two weeks later Ayatollah Khomeini, a revered Islamic cleric exiled for threatening to overthrow the Shah, triumphantly returned to Tehran to the cheers of millions. By December, Khomeini had replaced Bakhtiar's secular government with a theocracy, the Islamic Republic of Iran.

Six months after the Iranian Revolution, Saddam Hussein assumed power in neighboring Iraq. Sensing an opportunity now that Iran had lost its American patronage, and concerned that Iran's revolution might spread to Iraq, Saddam launched a massive attack against Iran on September 22, 1980. Although caught by surprise, Iran responded quickly with counterattacks using American F-4s and F-5s acquired under the Shah. The war soon devolved into a stalemate with neither side achieving significant military gains but each suffering tremendous human losses, including thousands of Iranians killed by Iraqi gas attacks.

Although Iraq launched an opportunistic attack on Iran, many countries supported Iraq, largely for religious reasons. Almost since its birth, Islam has been divided into two major factions: Shia and Sunni. The two sects differ in their belief as to Muhammad's true successor. Iran, a Shia country, had earlier declared that the monarchies of Sunni-based Saudi Arabia and Kuwait were illegitimate, un-Islamic forms of government and called for their overthrow. So, not surprisingly, Saudi Arabia and Kuwait supported Iraq with substantial financial aid. And with Iran, a former American ally, now an avowed enemy of the "Great Satan," the United States also provided military, financial, and intelligence support to Iraq.

By 1984, Iraq had suffered an estimated 80,000 combat fatalities. That year a desperate Saddam Hussein began to attack Iranian shipping in the hopes of provoking Iran into closing the Strait of Hormuz and thereby forcing the United States to enter the war. The Iranians didn't bite. Two years later, prompted by a request from Kuwait, the United States Navy began to provide protection to oil tankers traversing the Persian Gulf that were being harassed by Iranian gunboats.

By early 1988, the U.S. Navy was regularly engaging Iranian naval forces. On July 3, tragedy struck. That morning the USS *Vincennes*, the latest Ticonderoga-class guided-missile cruiser, exchanged fire with Iranian gunboats. In the heat of battle, the *Vincennes* mistakenly fired on an Iranian airliner, Iran Air Flight 655. All 290 people on board, including over sixty children, perished. Navigating in Iranian waters, the state-of-the-art *Vincennes* had somehow mistaken the lumbering Airbus A300 airliner for a much smaller and faster F-14 fighter jet.

President Reagan immediately called the incident "a terrible human tragedy," but the American government otherwise showed little remorse. During his presidential campaign, *Newsweek* reported that Vice President Bush only recognized the downing of Iran Air 655 by promising his supporters: "I will never apologize for the United States. I don't care what the facts are. . . . I'm not an apologize-for-America kind of guy."[61] Three months later the *Vincennes* returned to port in California greeted by cheering crowds, red, white, and blue balloons, and a Navy brass band. Captain Rogers was later awarded the Legion of Merit decoration "for exceptionally meritorious conduct in the performance of outstanding service as commanding officer...from April 1987 to May 1989." In America, Captain Rogers was a decorated hero, in Iran, a reviled war criminal.

In 1996, the United States finally acknowledged its role in the tragedy. While never specifically apologizing for shooting down Iran Air 655, the U.S. did express "deep regret" and paid a total of $61.8 million to the families of the victims as compensation.[62]

Today, the downing of Iran Air 655 carries an emotional weight for Iranians similar to the 9/11 terrorist attacks for Americans. Every year on July 3, Iranian children sail to the crash site in the Persian Gulf. There, they throw gladiolas into the sea to commemorate the 290 passengers and crew who died.

A month after the Iran Air 655 tragedy, Iraq and Iran had finally had enough of the carnage and signed a cease-fire on August 8, 1988. Iraq achieved none of its territorial goals. Most historians consider Iran the victor for having withstood Iraq's onslaught for eight years, the longest conventional war of the twentieth century.

The Seeds of September 11, 2001

While supporting Saddam Hussein in his war against Iran, the United States was also being drawn into another war. In April 1978, the communist People's Democratic Party of Afghanistan seized power. The new communist government met immediate opposition from traditional, devout Afghanis. Fighting erupted and quickly expanded into a bitter civil war.

On July 3, 1979, President Carter signed a directive authorizing Operation Cyclone, a covert CIA program to channel aid to the Mujahideen who opposed the communist regime in Afghanistan. (Mujahideen is Arabic for those who engage in Jihad or religious war against non-believers.) Zbigniew Brzezinski, Carter's national security advisor, encouraged the clandestine support, advising Carter that the directive would draw the Soviets into an Afghanistan war. Brzezinski hoped the war would prove unsustainable for the Soviets and ultimately hand the Soviet Union its own disastrous Vietnam.[63]

On December 24, 1979, 30,000 Soviet troops invaded Afghanistan. Two days later, Brzezinski wrote a memo to Carter: "We should not be too sanguine about Afghanistan becoming a Soviet Vietnam. . ." Brzezinski cautioned. "It is essential that Afghanistani resistance continues. This means more money and arms shipments to the rebels. . ."[64]

Years later in 1998, Brzezinski boasted in *Le Nouvel Observateur*, a French news magazine, how the United States had lured the Soviets into an unwinnable war: "The day that the Soviets officially crossed the border, I wrote to President Carter, essentially: 'We now have the opportunity of giving to the USSR its Vietnam War.' Indeed, for almost ten years, Moscow had to carry on a war that was unsustainable for the regime."[65]

Over the next ten years, the Soviets poured over 100,000 troops into Afghanistan but were never able to subdue the wily Mujahideen guerrilla fighters supported by American dollars and weapons. The proxy war between the United States and the Soviet Union ultimately cost a million Afghan lives. In 1989, the Soviets left Afghanistan, utterly defeated. The Russians had achieved nothing at the cost of 15,000 Soviet deaths. (For a Russian perspective on the war, see the movie, *The 9th Company* directed by Fedor Bondarchuk.)

The British paid a similar price in the nineteenth century when they fought two wars in Afghanistan in 1839–1842 and 1878–1880. Together, the wars cost 25,000 British and allied lives.[66] In one 1842 battle, 16,000 British soldiers and camp followers were massacred after being trapped in the Khyber Pass. We only know what happened as the Afghans allowed one man, Dr. William Brydon, to survive to tell of the massacre.[67] The hellish wars inspired Rudyard Kipling to write one of his most famous poems, *The Young British Soldier*, that immortalized the combat and deaths of British soldiers in Afghanistan. The poem ends tragically:

> When you're wounded and left on Afghanistan's plains,
> And the women come out to cut up what remains,
> Jest roll to your rifle and blow out your brains
> An' go to your Gawd like a soldier.[68]

The Soviet invasion attracted Islamic freedom fighters from across the Middle East who flocked to Afghanistan to help repel the invaders. One was the son of a wealthy Saudi family named Osama bin Laden. Bin Laden was deeply opposed to outside intervention in Afghanistan and believed the Afghan civil war was an internal Muslim affair. He used his family contacts to organize support around the Muslim world and sent money and weapons in addition to fighters to join the Mujahideen. In 1988, bin Laden formed Al Qaeda as a network to help channel resources into Afghanistan, efforts indirectly supported by the United States. Both bin Laden and the United States were virtual allies fighting against the Soviets. Bin Laden and the Afghan Mujahideen provided the fighters; the United States money and much of the weaponry.

The United States eventually supplied billions in weapons and financial support to the Afghan Mujahideen, largely through CIA channels in Pakistan.[69] Ironically, one of the most successful weapons provided by the United States were the thousands of Stinger anti-aircraft missiles. The simple, shoulder-launched missiles were highly effective against Soviet helicopters. Unfortunately, twenty years later, these same missiles, now in the hands of the Taliban, were a continual threat to American aircraft during America's own Afghan war that began in 2001.

American Malaise

During the first two years of Carter's presidency, Americans enjoyed solid economic growth. Real GDP grew over five percent annually. Inflation was flat and unemployment was falling. But by early 1979 the economy had turned downward. A second oil embargo triggered by the Iranian Revolution generated gas lines even longer than those during the first embargo six years earlier. Inflation was again on the rise. Fearful of another energy crisis, consumer sentiment fell sharply. After years of political and economic turmoil, Americans were tired and demoralized.

America had endured poverty and unemployment during the Great Depression, death and deprivation during World War II, and the threat of nuclear war during the nineteen-fifties but had remained a proud and confident nation that believed in itself and its government. That changed in the nineteen-seventies when the Pentagon Papers revealed how Washington had lied to Americans regarding its role in Southeast Asia; when the Watergate investigation revealed the President had obstructed justice and then lied about that as well; when chronic inflation and unemployment remained high for so long economists coined the new term "stagflation" to capture the misery; and, tragically, when the United States left Vietnam in defeat after the loss of 58,000 American lives.

What America needed at that moment was a pep talk. What it got was a sermon.

On July 15, 1979, Carter gave a televised speech, ostensibly to present his new energy program. But much of the speech dealt with what Carter described as a crisis of confidence:

> I want to speak to you first tonight about a subject even more serious than energy or inflation.... It is a crisis of confidence. It is a crisis that strikes at the very heart and soul and spirit of our national will. We can see this crisis in the growing doubt about the meaning of our own lives and in the loss of a unity of purpose for our Nation. The erosion of our confidence in the future is threatening to destroy the social and the political fabric of America.... Our people are losing that faith, not only in government itself but in the ability as citizens to serve as the ultimate rulers and shapers of our democracy.... Human identity is no longer defined by what one does, but by what one owns. But we've discovered that owning things and consuming things does not satisfy our longing for meaning. We've learned that piling up material goods cannot fill the emptiness of lives which have no confidence or purpose.[70]

No modern President had ever lectured Americans quite like this. Franklin Roosevelt at the depths of the Depression left Americans inspired and hopeful. Carter's speech demoralized, even shocked, many Americans. The President seemed to be blaming everyday citizens, and not their government, for America's problems. "The Malaise Speech," as it was soon labeled, largely defined Carter's presidency. It would not be until President Trump's "American Carnage" inaugural address some thirty-eight years later that a President painted a darker picture of America. Just months later, a singular event cast an even darker shadow across America, and Carter's presidency.

On November 4, 1979, a mob of Iranian students scaled the walls of the American embassy in Tehran, over-powering its Marine contingent, and taking fifty-two Americans hostage. The mob was angry. Iran had attempted to extradite the Shah back to Iran to stand trial for alleged crimes committed during his twenty-five-year reign. The United States refused.

After negotiations failed to free the hostages, the United States mounted two rescue attempts. The first, in January 1980, was a clever, and courageous covert operation in which CIA and Canadian operatives, posing as a movie production company, successfully rescued six Americans who had evaded capture during the embassy take-over. Disguised as members of a movie crew, the hostages were whisked out of the country under the noses of the unsuspecting Iranians.

The second attempt was a disaster. Three months after the successful CIA operation, eight helicopters departed the USS *Nimitz* in a daring attempt to rescue the hostages. The rescue was a complex two-day operation with an overnight stop in the middle of the Iranian desert to refuel. A combination of poor communications, aircraft failure, and a blinding sandstorm led to the mission's failure and the deaths of eight American servicemen and an Iranian civilian. With his rescue plan a debacle rivaling Kennedy's thwarted Bay of Pigs invasion, President Carter went on national television to accept the blame for the failure and loss of American lives.[71]

Iran held the hostages for fifteen months. America never felt more impotent. As the presidential election loomed in November 1980, consumer sentiment hit a postwar low[72] and Carter's job approval rating fell to the lowest level since Harry Truman fired General MacArthur.[73] Viewed as weak and ineffective, Carter lost the presidency to Ronald Reagan in a landslide.

After his loss, Carter intensified his efforts to secure the release of the hostages. Finally, after months of negotiations, the Carter administration reached an agreement with the Iranians on January 19, 1981, Carter's last full day in office. Implicitly acknowledging the United States' interference in Iran's affairs since 1953, the agreement included the pledge that "It is and from now on will be the policy of the United States not to intervene, directly or indirectly, politically or militarily, in Iran's internal affairs."[74] The

United States also transferred $8.0 billion into an Iranian escrow account—frozen Iranian assets that had been held in U.S. and European banks after the fall of the Shah.[75]

The Iranians waited until a few minutes after Reagan's inauguration the next day to announce the hostages had been released. Carter, not wishing to compromise their release, had said nothing of the completed negotiation the day before. When President Reagan proudly announced the release of the hostages shortly after his inauguration, Americans naturally believed that it was Reagan who was responsible for their release.

Carter's failure to free the American Embassy hostages during his term contributed to his 1980 reelection loss to Ronald Reagan.   BETTMANN/GETTY

Carter never corrected that misperception, nor did Reagan.

After leaving the presidency, Jimmy Carter let his accomplishments speak for themselves. Too often, they haven't. He and Rosalynn have quietly focused on human rights and disease prevention around the world. Beyond writing several memoirs, Carter has made little effort to burnish his presidential legacy.

That legacy is substantial. Carter fathered the deregulation movement. His sweeping deregulation of the transportation industry was, according to *The Wall Street Journal*, more consequential than any subsequent President's efforts. Mocked at the time for promoting conservation, Carter was right when he said that energy conservation, not energy production, would play the pivotal role in returning the United States to energy independence. Carter promoted a lasting peace between Egypt and Israel. After a decade of stagflation, Carter appointed Paul Volcker to head the Federal Reserve. By 1985, Volcker's tight-money policies had broken inflation's back, never to return to levels remotely close to those of the nineteen-seventies.

Carter has said his favorite President is Harry Truman.[76] Like Truman, Carter left office deeply unpopular. And like Truman, Carter's substantial contributions are slowly becoming better recognized.

Ronald Reagan

———※———

January 20, 1981 – January 20, 1989

I've spoken of the shining city all my political life... it was a tall, proud city built on rocks stronger than oceans, wind-swept, God-blessed, and teeming with people of all kinds living in harmony and peace; a city with free ports that hummed with commerce and creativity. And if there had to be city walls, the walls had doors and the doors were open to anyone with the will and the heart to get here.[1]

A s Ronald Reagan looked out across the National Mall during his inaugural address, he faced a troubled nation. Reagan was the fifth President to assume leadership over an America in turmoil. Johnson's presidency followed Kennedy's assassination. Nixon's came after deadly race riots, war protests and the assassinations of Martin Luther King and Robert Kennedy. Ford's presidency followed Nixon's resignation in disgrace. Carter inherited an economic crisis second only to the Great Depression. Reagan began his inaugural address by summarizing the nation's current plight:

> We suffer from the longest and one of the worst sustained inflations in our national history. . . . Idle industries have cast workers into unemployment, human misery, and personal indignity. . . . Those who do work are denied a fair return for their labor by a tax system which penalizes successful achievement and keeps us from maintaining full productivity. . . . For decades we have piled deficit upon deficit, mortgaging our future and our children's future for the temporary convenience of the present.[2]

Fifty years earlier Franklin Roosevelt began his presidency at the depth of the Great Depression. Americans were adrift and fearful. Roosevelt promised help in the form of "the Government itself, treating the task as we would treat the emergency of a war."[3] Roosevelt promised to employ all the resources of the federal government to fight a war on unemployment, poverty and the "practices of the unscrupulous money changers."

Forty years later, Americans still trusted their government. "In this past third of a century, government has passed more laws, spent more money, initiated more programs, than in all our previous history," Nixon boasted during his 1969 inaugural address. But there was still more to be done and Nixon promised to continue government efforts "in pursuing our goals of full employment, better housing, excellence in education; in rebuilding our cities and improving our rural areas; in protecting our environment and enhancing the quality of life—in all these and more, we will and must press urgently forward."[4]

But in the twelve years that separated Nixon from Reagan, confidence in the federal government had plummeted. The defeat in Vietnam, the scandal of the Pentagon Papers and Watergate, Washington's impotence dealing with runaway inflation and persistent unemployment, had all undermined confidence in the federal government.

As he spoke, Reagan knew many Americans were now asking themselves the question posed nearly twenty years earlier in his celebrated speech, "A Time for Choosing," delivered in October of 1964 in support of presidential candidate Barry Goldwater. Should Americans trust an "intellectual elite in a far-distant capital" or "make our own decisions and determine our own destiny."[5] During his inaugural speech, Reagan no longer considered the issue a question, but confidently declared:

> In this present crisis, government is not the solution to our problem; government is the problem. From time to time we've been tempted to believe that society has become too complex to be managed by self-rule, that government by an elite group is superior to government for, by, and of the people. Well, if no one among us is capable of governing himself, then who among us has the capacity to govern someone else?[6]

Reagan made shrinking government, cutting taxes, and reducing regulations the major themes of his administration. "It is time," Reagan said, "to reawaken this industrial giant, to get government back within its means, and to lighten our punitive tax burden."[7]

Reagan had campaigned on, "Let's Make America Great Again."[8] The slogan was the perfect antidote to the disillusionment and malaise many Americans felt after twelve years of political scandal, military defeat, and economic crises. Now Reagan needed to produce. He did, and quickly, with help from Jimmy Carter.

Two hours after his inauguration, President Reagan announced the release of the fifty-two American hostages Iran had held for 444 days. After months of tedious negotiations between the Carter administration and the Iranians, an agreement had been reached on January 19, the day before Reagan's inauguration. But Carter chose not to announce the agreement as the hostages wouldn't actually be free, airborne and out of Iranian airspace until the next day. That happened as Reagan delivered his inaugural address.

Americans, naturally, attributed the hostages' release to Reagan. For decades, disingenuous politicians have capitalized on this misconception. During the 2016 presidential election, for example, Senator Marco Rubio declared: "When I become President of the United States, our adversaries around the world will know that America is no longer under the command of someone weak like Barack Obama, and it will be like Ronald Reagan, where as soon as he took office, the hostages were released from Iran."[9]

Then, eight days after taking office, President Reagan signed Executive Order 12287, which removed the remaining price controls on gasoline, propane, and U.S. produced crude oil. What many Americans had forgotten was that Carter, the year before, had already announced the staged decontrol of oil prices. "Full decontrol," the Mises Institute later wrote, "was scheduled to take place in the spring of 1981, but Reagan upon taking office lifted controls almost immediately, thus receiving credit for what was mostly the action of his predecessor."[10] Reagan's executive order was a brilliant political move that allowed him to claim credit for deregulating oil.[11]

"President Abolishes Last Price Controls on U.S.-Produced Oil," *The New York Times* proclaimed the next day.[12]

Ronald Reagan, known as the "Great Communicator," developed his communication skills as a radio announcer, screen actor, television host and corporate spokesperson before entering politics.   AF ARCHIVE/ALAMY

Reagan's first few days in office demonstrated his unique communication skills in contrast to Carter's. Although Carter freed the Iran hostages and deregulated oil, Carter received no credit. Nor did he ask for it. Carter, a modest Christian, had taught Sunday school since serving as a midshipman at the Naval Academy. More a preacher than a politician, Carter thought in moral and spiritual terms,[13] beginning his inaugural address by asking Americans "to do justly, and to love mercy, and to walk humbly with thy

God," quoting the Prophet Micah.[14] While Carter had learned his communication skills teaching Bible class, Reagan had honed his as a radio announcer, actor, and television host.[15] Reagan left his audiences confident, inspired and often amused. Carter regularly left his reflecting on their moral and spiritual failings.

Ronald Reagan was a life-long optimist, proclaiming in his high school yearbook, "Life is one grand, sweet song, so start the music."[16] President Reagan's optimism, and skills as the Great Communicator, served him, and ultimately the nation, well.

Reagan's Greatest Foreign Policy Decision

From its founding in 1968, the Professional Air Traffic Controllers Organization (PATCO) had legitimate grievances regarding working conditions and outmoded equipment. PATCO's President Robert Poli claimed that 89 percent of PATCO controllers never made it to retirement. They burned out due to job stress. Since federal employees were prohibited by law from striking, PATCO conducted regular work slow-downs and sick-outs. After years of lobbying, little had been achieved to improve the controllers' working conditions.

PATCO had supported Reagan during the 1980 presidential campaign. Reagan had been a seven-term President of the Screen Actors Guild and even led the Guild's first strike during the nineteen-fifties after the studio chiefs refused to negotiate film and television residuals. In return for their endorsement, Reagan promised to support PATCO's drive for better working conditions. "I have been thoroughly briefed by members of my staff as to the deplorable state of our nation's air traffic control system..." Reagan wrote the PATCO president. "Too few people working unreasonable hours with obsolete equipment.... You can rest assured that if I am elected President, I will take whatever steps are necessary to provide our air traffic controllers with the most modern equipment available and to adjust staff levels and workdays that are commensurate with achieving a maximum degree of public safety."[17]

PATCO's contract expired two months after Reagan's inauguration. The union demanded an extraordinary 100 percent pay increase, claiming their work stress justified the huge increase. Reagan refused. Rather than negotiate, a confident PATCO declared a strike on August 3 to demand better working conditions, a thirty-two-hour week, and a substantial pay increase. PATCO believed Reagan, a former labor organizer, would be sympathetic. They were also confident he would never fire them—highly-trained specialists who controlled the nation's airways—if they went on strike. They were mistaken. Reagan ordered the controllers to return to work within forty-eight hours and declared that those who did not would be fired.

Since 1955, the President had the authority to fire federal employees who, against federal law, went on strike. No President ever had, considering it too disruptive.[18] In 1970, 200,000 postal workers went on strike to protest their pay. The postal workers, whose starting pay was about twice the minimum wage, were infuriated when Congress offered a mere 5.4 percent increase after having given themselves a generous 42 percent raise the year before, boosting Congressional pay to $42,500 ($299,700 in 2020 dollars).[19]

Nixon, after campaigning on law and order, vowed to break the postal strike. To replace the striking postal workers, Nixon brought in 23,000 Army, Navy, and Air Force personnel to deliver the mail. It didn't work. The servicemen left huge volumes of mail sitting in post offices, undelivered. Nixon was forced to negotiate.

Surely, PATCO believed, if the government couldn't replace mailmen, it could never replace air traffic controllers, one of the most skilled and critical jobs in the nation.

What the union bosses didn't know was that shortly after moving into the White House, Reagan had hung a portrait of President Calvin Coolidge in the Cabinet Room. Reagan looked to Calvin Coolidge, not Richard Nixon, for guidance. And that guidance was clear. In 1919, Coolidge, as Governor of Massachusetts, fired 1,100 striking Boston policemen and replaced them with World War I veterans. "There is no right," Coolidge had proclaimed, "to strike against the public anytime, anywhere."[20]

Forty-eight hours after Reagan's deadline, only 1,300 controllers had returned to work. Reagan promptly fired the 11,345 controllers who failed to return. In a remarkably well-executed contingency plan, Reagan replaced the controllers with FAA managers, military controllers, and recent-ly-trained new hires. Within months, air travel had largely been restored, although it would be several years before operations were totally returned to normal. The union was decertified and three union leaders were given ten day jail sentences for encouraging their members to stay off the job.[21]

The firing of the PATCO controllers defined the early years of Reagan's presidency. The world, including the Soviet Union, quickly learned that Reagan's tough rhetoric was backed up by tough actions. Here was a man to be taken seriously. Secretary of State George Schultz called the PATCO firings Reagan's most important foreign policy decision.[22]

Punitive Taxes and Burdensome Regulations

Two weeks after his inauguration, President Reagan gave his first televised address on February 5. Reagan, in the cordial and compelling manner that Americans would come to admire over the next eight years, described the nation's economic problems and their causes:

> [America was in] the worst economic mess since the Great Depression [caused by] government policies of the last few decades.... The federal budget is out of control, and we face runaway deficits of almost $80 billion... larger than the entire federal budget in 1957.... There are seven million Americans caught up in the personal indignity and human tragedy of unemployment.... Today this once great industrial giant of ours has the lowest rate of gain in productivity of virtually all the industrial nations with whom we must compete in the world market. We can't even hold our own market here in America against foreign automobiles, steel, and a number of other products.... Punitive tax policies and excessive and unnecessary regulations plus government borrowing have stifled our ability to update plant and equipment. When capital investment is made, it's too often for some unproductive alterations demanded by government to meet various of its regulations.[23]

Reagan blamed big government, federal deficits and burdensome regulations for the nation's economic problems. These were not new issues as they echoed the policies promoted by President Carter. "The principal elements of my economic strategy," Carter declared in his 1978 Economic Report to

Congress, "are managing federal budget expenditures carefully... gradually reducing the share of our national output devoted to federal spending; using tax reductions to ensure steady growth of the private economy; working to reduce the federal deficit and balance the budget; promoting greater business capital formation in order to enhance productivity gain..."[24]

Carter considered smaller government and lower taxes sound economics. Reagan turned them into an ideology. Its name was Reaganomics.

President Reagan's claim that the national debt was out of control was seriously misleading, and a good example of how statistics are easily manipulated. Measured in nominal dollars, Reagan was right. The national debt had increased enormously from $257 billion to $908 billion from 1950 through 1980. By that measure government spending was wildly out of control. But then, so was the cost of bread, which jumped from twelve cents a loaf in 1950 to fifty cents in 1980.[25] Measuring the national debt in 1980 dollars yields a different conclusion. The debt had only increased three percent since 1950, from $880 to $908 billion. But the best measure of debt is based on the ability to repay it. A $5,000 credit card debt is far easier for a family earning $100,000 to repay than for one earning $25,000. Measured as a percentage of GDP, and the nation's ability to repay, the national debt had steadily declined from 86 percent in 1950 to 32 percent in 1980.[26]

Had Reagan simply maintained the long downward trend that he inherited, the national debt would have fallen to its lowest level since 1931 as he left office in 1989. Instead, measured as a percent of GDP, the decline reversed itself and debt climbed to its highest level since 1961.

Starving the Beast

Reagan had a plan to reduce government spending: starve the beast. Americans might claim that they wanted smaller government and less wasteful government spending—unless it's for that new hospital wing, defense contract or infrastructure project in their backyard. So go ahead and cut spending, just don't cut mine. But cutting taxes, well that's something nearly everyone can get behind. Reagan understood this. He also knew that taxes fund government spending, so cutting taxes would force Congress to cut spending—starve the beast. "Over the past decades we've talked of curtailing spending," Reagan explained, "so that we can then lower the tax burden.

But there were always those who told us that taxes couldn't be cut until spending was reduced. Well, you know, we can lecture our children about extravagance until we run out of voice and breath. Or we can cure their extravagance by simply reducing their allowance."[27]

Reagan's analogy to cutting a child's allowance is appealing. But as Reagan was cutting Washington's allowance, he made a serious mistake. He forgot to take away the credit card.

Reagan moved quickly to cut taxes, signing his first tax cut seven months after taking office. The Economic Recovery Tax Act of 1981 cut tax rates from a range of 14–70 percent to 11–50 percent in addition to cutting estate taxes, capital gains taxes, and corporate taxes. The Act also indexed tax rates for inflation so taxpayers wouldn't be taxed at higher rates even though their inflation-adjusted income hadn't changed. Five years later, the Tax Reform Act of 1986 reduced the maximum tax rate to 38.5 percent in 1987 and then 28 percent in 1988, the lowest rate since 1931.

Tax revenues plummeted. By 1985, federal tax revenues (not including Social Security trust fund revenues), measured as a percentage of GDP, had fallen to their lowest level since 1943, 10.8 percent.

But the historically low tax revenues failed to reduce Congressional spending. Rather than declining, Congressional spending increased. By 1983, federal spending (not including Social Security) had climbed to 17.5 percent of GDP, the highest since the Korean Conflict decades earlier. With tax revenues down and spending up, by 1983 deficits had soared to their highest level since the end of World War II, nearly six percent of GDP.

Reagan soon realized his plan to starve the beast had failed. With deficits increasing, Reagan began to walk back his tax cuts, and even devise new taxes.

In 1982, the Tax Equity and Fiscal Responsibility Act repealed the 1981 Act's accelerated depreciation deduction, increased unemployment taxes, instituted withholding on dividends and interest, doubled cigarette taxes, and tripled telephone taxes. In 1983, Social Security taxes were increased. In 1984, the Deficit Reduction Act delayed scheduled tax cuts from the 1981 Act, extended taxes on liquor and telephone services, and reduced income averaging. In 1985, the cigarette tax increase was made permanent.

In 1986, the capital gains rate was returned to 28 percent, the level Reagan had inherited from Carter. In 1987, the Omnibus Budget Reconciliation Act extended telephone excise taxes and eliminated tax loopholes.

Reagan's tax walk-backs slowed but failed to stop ballooning deficits. The national debt exploded. After declining steadily for 34 years to 31.5 percent of GDP shortly before Reagan took office, the debt had swollen to 50.6 percent as he left. Other than World War II, only Herbert Hoover, struggling with the Great Depression, increased the national debt more.

Reagan's plan to cut taxes to force spending reductions was a failure. With its unlimited credit card, Congress simply borrowed more money when tax revenues fell. "We didn't starve the beast," one Reagan official said. "It's still eating quite well—by feeding off future generations."[28]

The Rebirth of Supply-Side Economics

President Reagan's efforts to reduce federal spending by starving the beast failed. How successful were his other economic policies? We'll consider four factors: gross domestic product, employment, personal income, and the national debt.

Reagan's economic policies were based on supply-side economics. One of the supply-side economics' core tenets, Say's Law, was originally proposed by the French economist Jean-Baptiste Say in 1803. Say's Law has been expressed as "supply creates its own demand."[29] Hence, economic growth is driven by the production of goods and services, not by their consumption. Say's perspective differed from the renowned Scottish economist, Adam Smith, who believed consumption drove economic growth. "Consumption is the sole end and purpose of all production," Smith wrote in his landmark *The Wealth of Nations*. "And the interest of the producer ought to be attended to, only so far as it may be necessary for promoting that of the consumer."[30]

Say's Law suggests that governments should promote policies to encourage investment in factories, innovation, and training. These investments would then increase the production of attractive goods and services which, in turn, would encourage consumption.[31]

Andrew Mellon, Treasury Secretary under Harding, Coolidge and Hoover, adopted Say's principles during the nineteen-twenties. Mellon's 1924 book, *Taxation: The People's Business*, turned Say's theory into practical economics, what Mellon called "scientific taxation." "Give tax breaks to large corporations," Mellon stated, "so that money can trickle down to the general public." Mellon's statement both concisely defined supply-side economics and coined the memorable term "trickle-down economics."[32]

Decades later, in 1974, the economist Arthur Laffer resurrected Mellon's economic theory at a lunch meeting with White House chief of staff Donald Rumsfeld, his assistant Dick Cheney and Jude Wanniski, a journalist for *The Wall Street Journal*. As the topic moved to taxes, Laffer described Mellon's tax theory by drawing a curve on a napkin illustrating Mellon's claim that, up to a point, lower tax rates increase tax revenues while higher taxes, after a point, decrease revenues. As the meeting broke up, Wanniski quietly pocketed the napkin. Four years later, Wanniski immortalized his earlier dinner discussion in a 1978 article[33] entitled, "Taxes, Revenues, and the Laffer Curve."[34]

The idea behind the Laffer Curve is simple. When tax rates are zero, no taxes are collected. Likewise, when rates are 100 percent, no taxes would be collected—who would work when all their earnings are taxed away by the government? Somewhere in between these two extremes, maximum tax revenues are generated. The trick is to know where.

If tax rates are very high, say 90 percent, taxpayers will try to avoid taxes in any way possible. They might buy tax-free municipal bonds, or invest overseas out of the government's reach, or simply not work as hard since taxes take 90 percent of everything they make anyway. A tax cut from 90 to 80 percent doubles the taxpayer's after-tax income, while only cutting tax revenues 12 percent. If that tax cut motivates taxpayers to reduce their tax avoidance, then the government is far ahead. Tax revenues will increase as money comes off the sidelines. It works just the opposite on the other end of the curve. A tax rate cut from 20 to 10 percent cuts tax revenues in half while only giving the taxpayer 12 percent more after-tax income. That's not going to motivate much change in taxpayers. The result is that tax revenues decline. Somewhere between these two extremes is a tax rate that maximizes tax revenues.

Arthur Laffer is considered the modern father of supply-side economics. His tax policies have been either embraced or scorned by every president since Ronald Reagan.

Say's Law and Mellon's scientific taxation were the basis for modern supply-side economics. Today, a version of Laffer's legendary napkin lies enshrined at the National Museum of American History.[35] Mellon's seminal book, largely forgotten, is available on Amazon for a few dollars.

Reagan embraced the Laffer Curve, believing lower taxes would not only increase tax revenues but also stimulate production. "These [tax cuts]," Reagan declared during his February 5 economic speech, "are essential to provide the new investment which is needed to create millions of new jobs between now and 1985."

It's a logical argument. A new car purchase, for example, spurs the economy just once; an investment in a new factory helps finance jobs for years. But the problem is this. Put $1,000 in the pocket of a struggling taxpayer and the money is quickly spent on consumption: clothes for the kids, home repairs, school tuition or maybe a new television. But put $1,000 in the bank account of a wealthy taxpayer and its disposition is much less certain. Yes, it may be invested in new factories and equipment as supply-side theory suggests, but it may just as likely be spent on imported luxury goods, self-indulgent personal services or just sit idly in a bank account.

By late March 1981, the Reagan administration had a detailed economic plan that projected strong economic growth capped by a billion-dollar budget surplus in 1984. The non-partisan Congressional Budget Office (CBO), though, wasn't nearly as enthusiastic, declaring "the budget would still be in deficit in fiscal year 1984—perhaps by nearly $50 billion."[36]

The CBO wasn't the only skeptic. That December, Reagan's budget director David A. Stockman gave a candid interview in *Atlantic* magazine in which Stockman confessed, "I've never believed that just cutting taxes alone will cause output and employment to expand.... [The] Kemp-Roth [tax cut] was always a Trojan horse to bring down the top rate.... It's kind of hard to sell 'trickle down,'" Stockman explained, "so the supply-side formula was the only way to get a tax policy that was really trickle down."[37] Stockman's candor nearly got him fired. Instead, he was "taken to the woodshed," as Stockman described his subsequent tongue-lashing by President Reagan.

But Stockman was right. In 1984, rather than a surplus, the federal government ran a $185 billion deficit, far higher than the CBO had projected. It soon got much worse. During Reagan's presidency, deficits totaled $1.3 trillion ($2.8 trillion in 2020 dollars)—more inflation-adjusted debt than had been accumulated in the prior thirty-five years. The huge deficits resulted from both low tax revenues and high spending.

Unfortunately, as Stockman feared, the tax cuts also failed to stimulate business investment. During the Reagan years, non-residential business investment fell from 14.7 percent of GDP in 1981 to 12.6 percent in 1988. (During those years, investment in residential construction increased. Much of the growth, though, resulted from the deregulation of the savings and loan industry. Six years later, the boom ended in a housing crash that ultimately cost taxpayers $130 billion.) Even more confounding for supply-side advocates was that business investment had grown more rapidly during the nineteen-seventies—a decade of "punitive" taxes as Reagan described them—growing from 11.6 to 14.2 percent between 1970 and 1980.

If the tax savings from Reagan's tax cuts didn't finance new factories and equipment, perhaps they were used to hire more manufacturing workers. That wasn't the case either. During the six years preceding the Reagan tax cuts, 1977 through 1982, manufacturing employment averaged 18.5 million. After the tax cuts, from 1983 through 1988, manufacturing employment fell to an average of 17.6 million, a loss of nearly a million workers.

Real GDP growth was very strong though, averaging a sizzling 4.5 percent from 1983 through 1988. If business investment wasn't fueling the economic growth, what was?

Consumer sentiment. After a decade of war, inflation, high unemployment, and political scandal, Americans were feeling buoyant under Reagan. After hitting bottom at 51.7 in 1980, consumer sentiment soared after Reagan took office, hitting 100.9 in 1984, its highest level since the go-go sixties. The same optimism also drove the stock market. The S&P 500 index climbed from 133 in 1980 to 436 in 1992, driven, not by growing profits, but by rising price-earnings ratios that skyrocketed from 7.4 to 25.9. Decades earlier, Franklin Roosevelt's sunny optimism and Winston Churchill's steely resolve energized their nations during difficult times. Reagan did the same for America.

As a result, consumption climbed under Reagan, hitting 63.4 percent of GDP as Reagan left the presidency in 1989, well above the 60.8 percent during the four Carter years.

Much of that increased consumption, though, was attributable to America's top income earners. During the Carter years, the top quintile (top 20 percent) of taxpayers took home an average of 46 percent of the nation's after-tax income (not including state and local taxes). As Reagan left the presidency in 1989, their share had climbed to 53 percent, its highest level since 1930. Other Americans fared poorly. America's great middle-class, the middle three income quintiles, saw their share of after-tax income fall from an average of 51 percent to 44 percent during those same years. The bottom quintile of taxpayers was left with an even smaller remnant of the economic pie. Their share dropped from 3.4 percent to 2.8 percent.

Aggregate statistics, like these, interest economists, but what did it mean for the average American taxpayer?

During Reagan's presidency, 1981 through 1988, a taxpayer in the bottom quintile suffered an income loss, measured in 2020 dollars, from $7,600 to $6,800, the middle three quintiles enjoyed a modest gain from $37,300 to $39,300 while the top quintile enjoyed a robust increase from $102,700 to $141,700. The top one percent fared, by far, the best. Their income increased from $284,000 to $681,000, a $397,000 increase.

Not considered in these income statistics, though, is the contribution federal social spending—including unemployment, food supplements, tax credits, healthcare, Social Security, and many other programs—had on personal income. That impact is substantial for lower-income taxpayers. But federal social spending, measured as a percent of GDP, declined from 9.5 percent to 8.7 percent during the Reagan years.

Fifty years before Reagan, the humorist Will Rogers joked about President Hoover's tax policies, commenting, "The money was all appropriated for the top in the hopes that it would trickle down to the needy."[38] But Hoover's trickle-down policies didn't work in 1932, and, unfortunately, failed again fifty years later under President Reagan.

Economic growth during the Reagan years was good, but is often exaggerated. Indeed, a small industry has developed promoting the idea of the "Reagan Expansion."

In October 2000, Senator Connie Mack's Joint Economic Committee issued a report entitled, *President Reagan's Economic Legacy: The Great Expansion*.[39] "Today, principally as a result of the supply-side policies pursued by the Reagan administration, the U.S. economy is healthy" the report confidently proclaimed.

The report bases its claims on the strong economic growth from 1983 through 2000 but provides few historical comparisons. Real GDP growth from 1983 through 2000 averaged 3.6 percent annually. That's impressive, but not historic. From 1963 through 1980, real GDP growth was the identical 3.6 percent. Senator Mack's report proudly boasts 36.1 million new jobs from 1983 through 2000, an average annual employment growth of 1.8 percent. Not mentioned was that employment growth from 1963 through 1980 was significantly stronger at 2.2 percent. Also, not mentioned were that real, after-tax corporate profits (measured in 1980 dollars) fell during the Reagan years: from an average of $160 billion during the nineteen-seventies to $129 billion during the years after the Reagan tax cuts, 1983 through 1988.

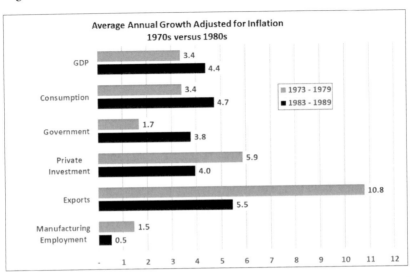

Economic growth during and after Reagan's presidency was excellent. But partisan claims that the "Reagan Expansion" was historic are exaggerated. Economic growth during the preceding years was often equal or better.

U.S. BUREAU OF ECONOMIC ANALYSIS | U.S. BUREAU OF LABOR STATISTICS

Similarly, Larry Kudlow, formerly President Trump's Director of the National Economic Council, in a March 4, 2014 *Wall Street Journal* editorial claimed, "We would hardly speak of an "American century" if not for the economic expansions that came with these three historic tax cuts [in the nineteen-twenties, nineteen-sixties and nineteen-eighties]."[40] Together, these decades averaged real GDP growth of 3.8 percent annually. That's impressive, but not mentioned were the years 1934–1940 when real GDP grew a historic 7.3 percent, 1950–1959 at 4.3 percent, and 1992–2000 at 3.8 percent. All were years of high taxes.

An August 12, 2021 *Wall Street Journal* editorial, authored by Arthur Laffer and Stephen Moore on the fortieth anniversary of the Reagan tax cuts, boasted that "[nominal] gross domestic product grew at an annual rate of 7.3 percent from 1981–89. . . . the equivalent of 'growing a new California.'"[41] But not mentioned, real GDP, after being adjusted for inflation, grew slightly faster from 1971 through 1979, 3.6 percent, versus Reagan's 3.5 percent. Also not mentioned, was that employment growth was far better during nineteen-seventies, an average of 2.6 percent annually, versus 1.9 percent under Reagan.

When economics and politics mix, *caveat publicae*—the public beware.

Although the Reagan economy was not as historic as often claimed, two events during Reagan's tenure were: a steep decline in inflation and increase in the federal debt.

Inflation climbed sharply from 1963 through 1980, averaging 5.8 percent annually and peaking at 13.5 percent in 1980. Inflation averaged only 3.3 percent from 1983 through 2000. Federal Reserve Chairman Paul Volcker was responsible.

On October 6, 1979, during a press conference known today as Volcker's Saturday Night Special, Volcker announced a drastic change in the Fed's monetary policy. Rather than the traditional fine-tuning of short-term interest rates, Volcker promised to put a rigid cap on the growth of the money supply to drive down inflationary expectations. The *Washington Post* summarized the ensuing battle in his December 9, 2019 obituary:

> The Saturday Night Special became a celebrated moment in Fed history. Over the following three years, the Fed drove inflation down from around 12 percent to around 6 percent. It was a grueling battle: At one point, Volcker's monetary straitjacket caused the short-term interest rate to rise to 20 percent, prompting a congressman to accuse him of "legalized usury beyond any kind of conscionable limit." The economy endured two recessions, and unemployment hit double digits; furious farmers drove their tractors to Washington and encircled the Fed's headquarters. But by dint of iron-willed persistence, Volcker turned the inflationary nineteen-seventies into the disinflationary nineteen-eighties.[42]

Although Volcker had been appointed by Carter, Reagan wisely supported Volcker even as Volcker's draconian monetary policies forced the nation into two recessions. It paid off. By 1983, inflation was dead.

The only regret President Reagan mentioned during his 1989 Farewell Address was his failure to control deficits.[43] After promising to reduce federal spending, spending increased during the Reagan years to an average of 21.4 percent of GDP—well above the Nixon, Ford, and Carter years which averaged 18.8 percent. With spending up substantially, and tax revenues down, the national debt jumped from 32 percent of GDP in 1980 to 51 percent in 1989, its greatest increase since World War II.

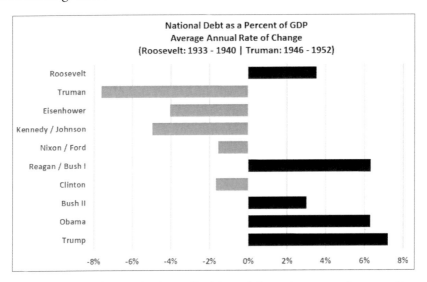

National Debt as a Percent of GDP
Average Annual Rate of Change
(Roosevelt: 1933 - 1940 | Truman: 1946 - 1952)

Reagan proposed to "starve the (spending) beast" through tax cuts. But spending accelerated, largely on defense, swelling the national debt. It was Reagan's greatest disappointment.   WHITE HOUSE OFFICE OF MANAGEMENT AND BUDGET

Years later, Treasury Secretary Paul O'Neill warned against high deficits during the second Bush administration. Vice President Dick Cheney chided O'Neill for his caution, "You know, Paul, Reagan proved deficits don't matter."[44] That was a stretch then, but recently huge deficits have been justified, even deemed healthy, by advocates of Modern Monetary Theory (MMT). The theory suggests that the United States can issue very large amounts of debt without kicking off an inflationary spiral so long as demand for the dollar, as the world's reserve currency, remains high. But if MMT turns out to be wrong, Cheney's quote will someday earn him an honorary place in the Pantheon of Discredited Economists. He'll have good company with Irving Fisher who just weeks before the 1929 market crash declared: "Stock prices have reached what looks like a permanently high plateau."[45]

Get the Government off My Back!

One of Ronald Reagan's major campaign promises was to "get the government off the backs of the people." Nearly a century earlier, the federal government had begun to establish regulations, and the government agencies to enforce them, to assure fair competition, the health of its citizens, and the protection of the environment. In 1887, the Interstate Commerce Commission was established to regulate transportation. In 1906, the Pure Food and Drug Act began the regulation of the food and drugs Americans consume. During the Great Depression, the Securities and Exchange Commission, the Federal Communications Commission, and many other agencies were established to regulate commerce. In 1970, the Environmental Protection Agency was established to protect the nation's air, water, and other natural resources.

But regulations had their costs. Regulation of the transportation and communication industries slowed competition and interfered with market forces. Environmental regulations made building a new highway or constructing a new building complex, time-consuming and expensive. Regulation of banking and finance slowed innovation and growth.

President Carter was the first to roll back major government regulations including those on the airlines, railroads, trucking, and oil. Reagan's emphasis was to cut red tape rather than restructure entire industries, as Carter's massive deregulation had done.[46] With the lone exception of the financial industry, Reagan's changes were evolutionary and largely completed the deregulation of the transportation industries begun by Carter.

Reagan's most significant contribution to deregulation was Executive Order 12291. The order required regulatory agencies to apply cost-benefit analysis to all new major regulations. *Time* magazine considered Reagan's executive order (EO) one of the nine most influential executive orders ever issued, alongside Franklin Roosevelt's EO 7035 to establish the Works Progress Administration, Harry Truman's EO 9981 to desegregate the military, and Dwight Eisenhower's EO 10730 to use the National Guard to protect African-American students entering Little Rock Central High School.[47]

Before Reagan's executive order, regulators focused on the benefits of a regulation, with little emphasis on its costs. No one questions that leaking, underground gasoline storage tanks, for example, are harmful to the water supply. But a regulation that simply mandates the tanks must be replaced would bankrupt thousands of small, family-owned gas stations. Reagan's EO 12291 required regulators to weigh the financial impact of the regulation against its benefits.

No presidential action has done more to reduce the regulatory burden than Reagan's EO 12291. The Code of Federal Regulations (CFR) documents all federal regulations. From 1960 through 1980, the CFR grew from 22,877 to 102,195 pages, an average annual increase of 7.8 percent. From 1981 through 2019, after Reagan signed EO 12291, the growth of the CFR slowed drastically, to 1.6 percent.

Reagan wasn't an anti-regulation ideologue, however. In 1985, scientists detected a massive hole in the atmosphere's ozone layer over Antarctica. Ozone, high in the atmosphere, shields the earth from cancer-causing ultraviolet radiation. The Reagan administration was initially skeptical. Earlier, the chairman of DuPont had called the ozone depletion theory "a science fiction tale... a load of rubbish... utter nonsense."[48]. But two years later, as a scientific consensus emerged, the United States and two dozen other nations signed the Montreal Protocol that banned chlorofluorocarbons (CFC), the chemicals attacking the ozone layer.

The Montreal Protocol was the world's first global climate-control treaty. In 2003, the Secretary-General of the United Nations, Kofi Annan, stated that "perhaps the single most successful international agreement to date has been the Montreal Protocol."[49]

Deregulation has its risks; presumably, there were valid reasons, originally, for instituting the regulation. The deregulation of the savings and loan industry by Presidents Carter and Reagan is an example of good intentions gone wrong.

In 1932, the passage of the Federal Home Loan Bank Act made it easier for people to purchase homes. The Act encouraged the growth of local savings and loan banks by allowing higher interest rates on savings accounts than commercial banks. The S&Ls were nevertheless limited with respect to the maximum interest rates payable on savings accounts, and they were prohibited from offering checking accounts. Typically owned and managed by local businessmen, S&Ls thrived after World War II, becoming an integral part of many small communities. By 1965, there were over 6,000 nationwide.[50]

But high inflation during the nineteen-seventies made it difficult for these small banks to attract depositors because their savings accounts, limited by law, were now paying well below the rate of inflation. Formidable competitors were also entering the industry: brokerage firms offering money market accounts that paid higher interest rates than banks, plus checking and credit card services. Merrill Lynch's Cash Management Account (CMA) pioneered these new services, which *The New York Times* touted as "the leading edge of the revolution in financial services that is transforming Wall Street."[51]

To help small banks survive, President Carter signed the Depository Institutions Deregulation and Monetary Control Act of 1980, which began the phase-out of interest-rate ceilings on savings accounts and allowed the S&Ls to offer interest-bearing checking accounts.[52] The Reagan administration expanded on Carter's deregulation in 1982 when the Garn–St Germain Depository Institutions Act largely eliminated the differences between S&Ls and commercial banks. Small, sleepy S&Ls could now make commercial and consumer loans, offer credit cards and even make speculative investments just like the big New York investment banks.

The savings and loans industry took off. Many small-town bankers quickly got in over their heads, making complex commercial loans to finance risky endeavors, even investing in the hot, new junk bonds that paid high yields due to their high risk. From 1982 through 1987, new home construction grew a blistering 14 percent annually.[53] But many of these homes were built on speculation. Texas bankers were particularly aggressive in financing a glut of speculative condominiums so massive that, after sitting unsold for years, many were plowed under by bulldozers.

As bank balance sheets weakened, federal regulators, in a practice euphemistically termed "forbearance," looked the other way in the hope the weak banks would eventually recover. Many didn't. S&Ls began to fail: 118 between 1986 and 1987, 205 in 1988 and then 327 in 1989 alone, representing $135 billion in assets ($282 billion in 2020 dollars).[54]

One of the most notorious bank failures was led by Charles Keating, a successful real-estate developer who got into banking after buying Lincoln Savings and Loan. Lincoln had been a typical small-town bank led by conservative, local management. Keating fired the management and put the bank on a fast track, making speculative investments rather than low-paying home loans. Land purchases, real estate equity, and junk bonds replaced mortgages in the bank's portfolio. The scheme initially worked well, driving the bank to even more frenzied investing. From 1984 through 1988, Lincoln's assets grew from $1.1 to $5.5 billion. During pep talks, Lincoln's salesmen were told to "always remember the weak, meek and ignorant are always good targets,"[55] a quote that could have been attributed to Gordon Gekko from the 1987 film, *Wall Street*.

By the end of 1986, federal regulators found that Lincoln was badly overextended with $135 million in unreported losses and significant breaches of the federal investment limits. Keating invoked the political help of five U.S. senators, the Keating Five, to whom he had made significant political donations: Alan Cranston, Dennis DeConcini, John Glenn, John McCain, and Donald Riegle. Keating also paid renowned economist Alan Greenspan $40,000 ($94,500 in 2020 dollars) to write a letter to the chairman of the Federal Home Loan Bank Board declaring Lincoln Savings and Loan was "a financially strong institution that presents no foreseeable risk to the Federal Savings and Loan Insurance Corporation."[56]

Keating's pressure campaign worked. In May 1988, in an unprecedented move, bank regulators forgave Lincoln's past violations and declared Lincoln solvent. Feeling vindicated rather than chastised, Keating renewed his risky investing by spending $300 million on The Phoenician resort in Phoenix. By April 1989, the Federal Home Loan Bank Board had finally had enough and seized Lincoln's assets. Keating was convicted on charges of conspiracy, racketeering, and fraud. He served four and a half years in prison before the convictions were overturned calling for a new trial. Keating then pleaded guilty to lesser charges and was sentenced to time already served. The federal government spent $3.4 billion cleaning up Lincoln's losses.

Keating's conviction was one of over 1,000 major cases successfully prosecuted by the Department of Justice for fraud and other abuses that sent dozens of bankers to jail.[57] Even Neil Bush, the son of President George H.W. Bush, was caught up in the scandals. As a director of Silverado Savings and Loan, Bush failed to inform the board that the bank had made $100 million in sweetheart loans to his business partners. The loans failed, helping to bring down Silverado and ultimately costing taxpayers $1.3 billion. Neil Bush managed to stay out of jail but was fined $50,000 and settled a federal lawsuit for $49.5 million along with his fellow bank directors.[58]

Similar debacles were repeated hundreds of times as nearly 800 S&Ls collapsed. The bank failures eventually cost taxpayers $130 billion as the federal government reimbursed twenty-five million depositors who lost money in federally insured accounts.[59]

Economists and politicians still debate the causes of the savings and loan crash. That should be unnecessary. The debate had been resolved in 1988. That year the United States League of Savings Institutions published a book entitled *Where Deregulation Went Wrong: a look at the causes behind savings and loan failures in the 1980s.*[60] The S&L trade association traced the failures to the elimination of regulations; regulatory relaxation; fraud and insider trading abuses; opportunistic, and occasionally fraudulent, savings and loan executives; dereliction of duty on the part of the boards of directors; examination and supervisory staffs insufficient in number; inexperience in savings and loan operations; and the inability or unwillingness of the Bank Board and its staff to deal with problem institutions promptly.

Rather than deflect, the trade association's analysis was a remarkably candid assessment of the issues which nearly destroyed their industry. It placed the blame squarely on deregulation and the resulting lax oversight of the newly empowered S&Ls.

After some 7,000 banks failed during the Great Depression in the nineteen-thirties, the banking industry became heavily regulated. Memories of that crisis had largely been forgotten fifty years later as the S&Ls lobbied for looser regulations. With good intentions, the Carter and Reagan administrations granted them their wishes. It was like giving candy to a baby.

The savings and loans collapse would be repeated twenty years later when continued deregulation of the financial industry coupled with easy money was a prime contributor to the 2008 Financial Crisis, the nation's worst economic crisis since the Great Depression.

Spunky Harley-Davidson

President Reagan was in a celebratory mood on May 16, 1987 preparing for his weekly Saturday morning radio address. He had a great American success story to tell.

Harley-Davidson Motorcycle was founded in 1903 in Milwaukee, and by 1920, the company was the largest motorcycle manufacturer in the world.[61] By the mid nineteen-fifties, after delivering 90,000 military motorcycles during World War II, Harley had vanquished all its American competitors.

Harley's big bikes got a boost in 1953 with the movie, *The Wild One*. "Nobody tells me what to do," gang-leader Marlon Brando threatened. "You keep needlin' me, and if I want to, I'm gonna take this joint apart. And you're not gonna know what hit ya."[62] Few motorcycle riders were as tough as Brando, but they sure felt like it when they roared off on their Harleys. (Brando rode a 1950 Triumph Thunderbird in the movie.)

But by 1983, after decades of poor management in the face of intense foreign competition, Harley was near bankruptcy and, in desperation, petitioned Washington for tariff protection. Reagan had mixed feelings. "One of the key factors behind our nation's great prosperity," Reagan had told Americans in an early speech, "is the open trade policy that allows the American people to freely exchange goods and services with free people around the world."[63] Yet Reagan was reluctant to let what was now the last remaining American motorcycle manufacturer go out of business. On April 2, 1983, Reagan signed a special tariff plan on imported heavyweight motorcycles extending over five years. Import tariffs were set the first year at 49.4 percent, declining steadily to 14.4 percent in the fifth year.[64]

The tariffs worked. Under their tariff umbrella, Harley introduced new models, improved reliability, cut manufacturing costs, and revamped its marketing. Soon the motorcycle maker began to thrive. Four years later, a year before the tariffs were scheduled to expire, Harley's management requested the tariffs be removed.

Reagan was proud of this iconic American company. "Today, Harley-Davidson is once again a leader in developing new motorcycle technology," Reagan told listeners. "They're now selling more and more bikes on virtually every continent of the earth. In fact, they are the only major motorcycle manufacturer in the world to have increased production last year. And, yes, they have also increased exports. These Americans, confident in themselves and their product, have asked that their special tariff be removed so that they can meet their competition head-on."[65]

Reagan's radio address that day had a larger purpose: to tell America his administration was returning to free trade. From the beginning of his presidency, he agreed to use quotas and tariffs to protect American companies only with great reluctance, and only over the short term whenever possible. Reagan justified his actions, believing they provided "companies like Harley-Davidson breathing room" and did not represent permanent protection against foreign competition.

Harley-Davidson was one of America's few success stories fighting off foreign competition during Reagan's presidency.

The Big Three auto makers—General Motors, Ford, and Chrysler—had kept the automobile and light truck market to themselves through the nineteen-fifties and sixties. After building cars on their own terms for sixty years the Big Three believed they owned the market. American cars were big and comfortable, built to cruise on the nation's new interstate highways. Americans had grown accustomed to Detroit's planned obsolescence, low gas mileage, and mediocre quality, even joking about it. FORD: Fix Or Repair Daily. CHEVY: Can Hear Every Valve Yell. DODGE: Drains Or Drops Grease Everywhere.

In 1965, Detroit commanded 91 percent of the American market. The largest foreign competitor, Volkswagen, had barely three percent. But Volkswagen's hip advertisements for their subversive "Beetle" urged Americans to "Think Small." A growing number of American drivers were. It was an early sign that Americans were beginning to change their view of their beloved cars. Two events in 1965 accelerated that transition.

Ralph Nader's landmark book, *Unsafe at Any Speed*, documented the poor safety of many American automobiles, particularly the Chevrolet Corvair. Nader's description of the "second collision" as the human body careens inside the car interior after an accident (the first collision) is chilling. That's especially true when the reader learns Detroit well knew seat belts would greatly reduce fatalities but resisted installing them due to their additional cost. The belief that "safety doesn't sell," as famously declared by Ford's Lee Iacocca, ran deep throughout Detroit.[66]

That same year, Toyota and Nissan entered the American automobile market. Five years later Honda followed. Foreign cars remained a niche market until the 1973 and 1979 oil embargoes brought the importance of superior gas mileage to the fore. Overnight, Americans began to demand smaller, fuel-efficient cars, cars the Japanese had been building for years. Japanese imports also had a significant price advantage. Even after shipment across the Pacific Ocean, a 1979 Honda Civic listed for only $3,649[67] versus a similarly-equipped Ford Fiesta at $4,493.[68] Much of the difference was due to high wages negotiated by the powerful United Auto Workers union. An American autoworker typically earned $13.43 an hour that year ($51.00 in 2020 dollars), 49 percent higher than the average manufacturing wage in the U.S.[69]

Detroit recognized these issues years before imports became a factor but resisted changing its business model. In 1966, when Washington issued its first automobile safety standards, Henry Ford II fumed: "Many of the temporary standards [seat belts, laminated windshields, safer door locks, collapsible steering wheels]... are unreasonable, arbitrary, and technically unfeasible. If we can't meet them when they are published, we'll have to close down."[70] Ten years later when Washington issued the first gasoline mileage standards in response to the 1973 Oil Embargo, General Motors President E.M. Estes claimed the new standards would reduce the automobile market in which "the largest car the industry will be selling in any volume at all will probably be smaller, lighter and less powerful than today's compact Chevy Nova."[71]

Estes' protests were on the mark when he lamented fuel economy would result in smaller cars like the Chevy Nova; that poor excuse for a car compared to the 3,600-pound Chevy Impala. Today, the world's best-selling car is the Toyota Corolla, as it has been for fifty years.[72] The Corolla weighs 2,885 pounds, far less than Estes' scorned Chevy Nova.[73]

But in the late nineteen-seventies, Detroit was optimistic. Car sales hit 11.3 million in 1978 after bottoming out at 8.6 million in 1975, giving Detroit hope the country was recovering from years of stagflation, scarce oil, and expensive gasoline. Still, there were troubling signs; one in five cars sold in the United States was now imported.[74]

By 1979, America was headed towards recession driven by Treasury Secretary Paul Volker's efforts to bring down inflation. Wracked by Islamic revolution, Iranian oil production had fallen by nearly five million barrels a day. Long lines formed at gas stations, many states instituted gas rationing and gas prices soared past a dollar ($3.60 in 2020 dollars), breaking a psychological barrier that few Americans ever expected to see. Car sales plummeted and by 1981, when Reagan took office, sales were down to 8.5 million cars.[75] Of that, 2.9 million were imported. Americans had initially bought Japanese cars for their better gas mileage, but millions soon came to prefer them for their higher quality and lower maintenance costs. And for being small, nimble, and fun to drive. Unfortunately for Detroit, the world had little interest in American cars. American car exports were a trickle compared to imports, only 545,164 cars—86 percent of which were shipped to America's big-car-loving Canadian neighbor.[76]

Something had to be done. With imports headed towards 30 percent of the American market and beyond, most Americans would soon be driving a foreign car if Washington didn't act to stop the invasion.

Faced with the loss of millions of American jobs, Reagan reluctantly agreed to limit Japanese car imports. Reagan chose to employ quotas rather than tariffs. Trade tariffs would have been a federal tax on each car, thus raising the sticker price. Quotas limited the number of Japanese cars imported each year without, in theory, raising their cost. However, with strong demand for their cars and imports capped, Japan quickly raised its prices. Two years after Reagan imposed the quotas, Japanese car prices were up an average of $1,500. Japanese car dealers also cashed in, often charging $1,000 to $2,000 over sticker price. Honda Accords were in such demand that dealerships were bribing Honda executives to provide them more cars, resulting in the nation's largest car dealer and Honda Motors being indicted on bribery and corruption charges.[77]

American car buyers collectively paid an estimated $9.0 billion more each year due to the price increases.[78] Had Reagan used tariffs instead of quotas, much of that new revenue would have flowed to the United States Treasury rather than the automobile manufacturers and their dealers.

The United States International Trade Commission estimated the quotas saved about 44,000 American jobs. That's about $200,000 ($481,000 in 2020 dollars) in additional costs every year for each job saved.[79]

Detroit, rather than using Reagan's protective quotas to grow their market share by building better, affordable cars, were more interested in profits and raised their prices. In 1984, the Big Three generated $10 billion in record profits, easily topping the previous $6.2 billion record set the year before.[80]

Unlike spunky little Harley-Davidson which asked that motorcycle tariffs be removed a year early, Detroit fought the resumption of head-to-head competition with foreign carmakers. "This is a sad day for America, for American workers, and American jobs," Chrysler's Chairman Lee Iacocca grumbled. Ford's chairman predicted: "[Reagan's decision] will create jobs in Japan at the expense of jobs for American workers." For once, management and the unions agreed. The United Auto Worker's President called Reagan's decision "a severe blow… especially to the 2.5 million Americans and their families whose livelihoods depend directly on a healthy [U.S.] auto sector." Only General Motors, having struck an import deal with Toyota, supported Reagan's decision.[81]

Unlike his speech praising little Harley-Davidson's pluck, Reagan had no praise for GM, Ford, and Chrysler.

The Japanese plowed their profits into building state-of-the-art American factories: Honda in Marysville, Ohio; Nissan in Smyrna, Tennessee; Toyota with a GM partnership in Fremont, California and Georgetown,

Kentucky; Mazda, Mitsubishi, and Fuji-Isuzu also built large plants. By 1990, their American factories were manufacturing 1.65 million automobiles to Japanese quality standards at costs below Detroit.[82]

Having captured the compact market, Toyota, Nissan, and Honda introduced the Lexus, Infiniti, and Acura luxury brands to compete with American luxury cars. And successfully so. In 2019, Lexus' North American car sales were 324,667[83], while Cadillac, once America's premier luxury car, sold less than half that, only 156,246.[84]

Whereas Japan was laser-focused on manufacturing automobiles, Detroit had a mixed record. Ford introduced the innovative Taurus in 1985, which became America's best-selling car from 1992 through 1997.[85] Chrysler acquired Jeep from American Motors in 1987, today one of America's strongest brands. Both proved strong moves. But General Motors chose to diversify by purchasing Electronic Data Systems and Hughes Aircraft for a combined $7.7 billion.[86] GM later spun off both companies.

GM did make a valiant attempt to compete with the Japanese when it established the Saturn Corporation in 1985 as a "new kind of car company." Largely independent of its parent, Saturn had its own factory, labor agreement, and dealer network. The new Saturn models were well received. Customers especially liked Saturn's "no-haggle pricing," which took much of the anxiety out of buying a car. GM even launched the brand in Japan in the early nineteen-nineties with right-hand drive. But GM's big-car culture soon seeped into Saturn, which began to upsize its cars and worse, relabel mediocre GM cars as Saturns. Saturn soon lost its unique identity. In 2004, Saturn was integrated into GM and after the 2008 Financial Crisis shut down entirely, ending GM's experiment to directly compete on Japan's terms.

Ten years after Reagan imposed quotas, Japan's share of the U.S. car market had climbed to 25 percent. Fortunately for American workers, millions of formerly imported cars were now made in Japanese factories located in the United States. The Japanese were beating Detroit at its own game using American workers.

By 2019, Detroit's market share in its home market had fallen to 44 percent,[87] a market share which would have been far smaller except for the

"Chicken Tax." The little-known tax is actually a tariff imposed on light truck imports since 1964. That year, to protect its farmers, the European Common Market blocked American chicken exports to Europe. In retaliation, the United States imposed a 25 percent tariff on light trucks and vans. The tax was primarily targeted at Volkswagen's mini-bus popular with America's counter-culture youth during the nineteen-sixties.

The tariff was never removed.[88] Today, the top-selling American vehicles are the Ford F-series, Dodge Ram, and Chevrolet Silverado pickups—all still protected from foreign competition by the 1964 Chicken Tax.[89]

Despite his efforts, during Reagan's two terms America's trade imbalance in goods increased from $23 billion in 1981 to $94 billion (1981 dollars). After nurturing the world economy back to health after World War II, America's former foes had become formidable trade competitors.

Unlike Nixon in 1969 and Trump in 2017, Reagan never blamed others for America's trade imbalance. "The way up and out of the trade deficit," Reagan explained during his May 1987 Harley-Davidson radio address, "is not protectionism, not bringing down the competition, but instead the answer lies in improving our products. . ."[90]

Saving Social Security

From its establishment in 1939, the Social Security Trust Fund (officially, the Federal Old-Age and Survivors Insurance Trust Fund) had been that rare government program that regularly generated budget surpluses. By 1974, the fund had accumulated $45.9 billion ($241 billion in 2020 dollars) in assets set aside for future beneficiaries.[91] But high unemployment and inflation over the next few years cut payroll tax revenues and raised benefit costs. By 1977, the fund had fallen to $35.9 billion. The program needed an update.

President Carter raised Social Security taxes and froze benefits. "This legislation," Carter promised, "will guarantee that from 1980 to the year 2030, the Social Security funds will be sound."[92]

Carter had been too cautious. Social Security continued to lose money. Rather than a fine-tuning, Social Security needed a major overhaul. As Carter left office, the trust fund had fallen to $24.5 billion. It was now President Reagan's problem.

Unwilling to raise taxes, Reagan proposed selective benefit cuts of nearly 30 percent. Millions of older Americans were enraged. Retirees, who had paid Social Security taxes for decades, didn't want their retirement benefits cut. Reagan, caught in the vice of reality and politics, commissioned a presidential commission to propose a solution. Heading it was the respected economist, Alan Greenspan.[93]

After a year of contentious deliberation, the Greenspan Commission released its report on January 20, 1983. The changes were extensive. To broaden Social Security's tax base, the commission proposed extending Social Security to newly hired civilian federal employees and employees of non-profit associations, the reduction of "windfall" benefits for those who contributed little in Social Security taxes, a delay in cost-of-living increases, an increase in the combined payroll tax to 12.4 percent, taxing a portion of Social Security benefits, reducing benefits and gradually increasing the retirement age.[94]

These were difficult changes, but the sacrifices were, as equitably as possible, spread across workers, employers, and beneficiaries. Under Reagan's leadership, the commission's recommendations were accepted with few changes, becoming law on April 20, 1983.[95]

Social Security quickly returned to solvency. As Reagan was leaving office in 1989, Social Security was generating a $50 billion annual surplus and climbing.[96]

Reagan was pragmatic. After building his presidential campaign around smaller government and lower taxes, he nevertheless raised taxes to save Social Security, a government program second only to defense in its size.

Although Reagan saved Social Security, he lost an opportunity to reduce government spending by stopping the annual raids on the Social Security trust funds administered by the federal government.

For years, Congress had borrowed from the Social Security trust funds to supplement the revenues from income and excise taxes. This redirection of funds set aside in trust allowed Congress to finance its deficits without needing to borrow from the public. Every year Social Security ran a surplus, rather than depositing the surplus in a trust fund for safekeeping, Congress redirected the funds to its general account to be spent as it pleased. In return, Congress issued promissory notes pledging to repay the fund in the future. Today, there are no funds in the Social Security trust funds (or most of the other 120 federal trust funds set aside for safe-keeping), only a government ledger holding "special non-marketable Treasury securities" promising to repay the borrowed money.[97]

For decades, the billions in Social Security surpluses flowing into the Treasury have been irresistible to Washington. In 1989, the surpluses were large enough to finance the entire Veterans Administration with $20 billion left over. By 2002, the surpluses had grown so large they were able to finance the Afghanistan and Iraq wars. Rather than raising taxes or selling war bonds as was done in the two world wars, over $1.6 trillion in Social Security surpluses from 2002 through 2016 financed the Middle East wars without asking Americans to pay a cent.[98] Had Americans been asked to finance the wars through higher taxes, they may well have refused. Instead, the wars were fought, and the cost was passed on to future generations. Fifty years earlier, Alf Landon, running against Franklin Roosevelt in the 1936 presidential election, had predicted this would happen:

> There is every probability that the cash [workers] pay [into Social Security] will be used for current deficits and new extravagances. We are going to have trouble enough to carry out an economy program without having the Treasury flush with money drawn from the workers."[99]

Landon had been right. For decades Congress raided the Social Security, and other, trust funds to finance "current deficits and new extravagances." With the Greenspan Commission, Reagan had an opportunity to stop that practice and hold Congress accountable for its spending. He failed to seize it.

Mr. Gorbachev, Tear Down this Wall!

Ronald Reagan's 1981 inaugural address hardly mentioned international affairs, America being so consumed with its domestic problems at the time. Yet President Reagan's contribution to ending the Cold War would prove to be one of his greatest legacies.

For three decades following World War II, the Soviet economy grew steadily at four percent annually.[100] In fifty years, Russia had transitioned from a backward, agrarian society into one of the world's largest industrial nations. But by the mid nineteen-seventies, Soviet economic growth had begun to slow. The Soviet Union was too large, too complex, and too bureaucratic to be centrally controlled. "Under Lenin," Zbigniew Brzezinski, President Carter's National Security Advisor, observed, "the Soviet Union was like a religious revival, under Stalin like a prison, under Khrushchev like a circus, and under Brezhnev like the U.S. Post Office."[101]

Soviet planners were attempting to make thousands of detailed decisions from how many apartments to build to the number of refrigerators to manufacture to what crops to grow. In capitalism, the market, driven by Adam Smith's Invisible Hand, makes these decisions as millions of producers and consumers act in their self-interest. Under communism, an army of central planners tried to anticipate the economy's needs years in advance. With a population of 250 million spread across eleven time zones and fifteen republics, the task had become overwhelming.

By the early nineteen-eighties, agriculture was beginning to fail and with oil prices in decline, Soviet foreign reserves were insufficient to purchase grain without external borrowing. That put further pressure on an economy that had already begun to stagnate. "The Soviet system," Russians quipped, "is not working because the workers are not working."

The Soviet invasion of Afghanistan in 1979 placed additional strain on the Soviets, both economically and militarily. President Carter retaliated for the incursion by placing a trade embargo on grain, ordering a boycott of the 1980 Moscow Summer Olympics, and providing support to the Mujahideen fighting the Soviets. Reagan broadened Carter's initiative into the Reagan Doctrine, a policy of confronting Soviet expansion wherever it was found, whether in the Middle East, Africa, Asia, or Latin America. Rather than simply containing the growth of communism, the Reagan Doctrine advocated rolling back Soviet advances both overtly and covertly. For the next six years, Reagan covertly countered Soviet influence throughout the world including in Chad, El Salvador, Ethiopia, Liberia, Libya, Mauritius, Nicaragua, and Suriname.[102]

Tensions peaked in 1983 when NATO installed nuclear-tipped Perishing II missiles in Europe that would "be able to fly 1,000 miles in six to eight minutes, and land with high accuracy and virtually no warning on targets deep inside the Soviet Union."[103] The Soviets, quite understandably, resented these new weapons as a major escalation of the Cold War. The European-based missiles could destroy Soviet cities and missile sites before a counter-attack could be launched. Old-guard Soviet leaders remembered Hitler's surprise attack on Russia in 1941 and feared Reagan was planning a pre-emptive nuclear attack on the Soviet Union.[104]

President Reagan meeting with Afghan Mujahedeen in 1983 to discuss U.S. support battling the Soviets. The Mujahedeen would later become fierce enemies of the United States.   RONALD REAGAN LIBRARY/AP

With tensions running high, on September 1, a Soviet Su-15 fighter shot down Korean Airlines Flight 007, killing 269 passengers and crew. The giant Boeing 747 airliner had, (allegedly) due to pilot error, wandered 200 miles off course into Soviet airspace. In 1991, formerly classified communication transcripts indicated the Soviets believed the airliner was a disguised American reconnaissance aircraft sent to track a Soviet missile test scheduled for that day. Yet the Soviet fighter pilot, contrary to long-standing international protocol, did not attempt to contact the airliner by radio before shooting it down.[105]

Weeks later, on October 25, American troops invaded the tiny Caribbean nation of Grenada, a former British colony of 91,000 citizens. Days earlier, a coup had overthrown Grenada's leftist-leaning government, executing Prime Minister Maurice Bishop and seven government officials. Since Bishop had come to power in 1979, the United States had been concerned about the impact that a Black-led socialist government would have on other Caribbean nations. In 1981, U.S. military forces staged a mock invasion of Grenada on a small island off Puerto Rico but stopped short of an actual invasion. A year later, the coup and its brutal executions, concerns over a Cuban military build-up, and the safety of 800 American students residing on the island contributed to Reagan's decision to invade. American troops, at the cost of nineteen American lives, quickly secured the island.[106]

The invasion had strong public support in the United States. After a stalemate in Korea, the Cuban Bay of Pigs fiasco, and defeat in Vietnam, Reagan proudly cited Grenada as the first successful roll-back of communist influence since the beginning of the Cold War.[107] Much of the Caribbean also supported the invasion. "It had to be done," read an editorial in a Bridgetown, Barbados newspaper. "There was no way that the small nations of the Eastern Caribbean, in particular, could rest comfortably after events took an unexpectedly brutal turn in Grenada over the past few days unless action was taken against the ruthless military regime there."[108]

The invasion, though, was criticized by the United Nations and many of America's allies. "The Americans," Margaret Thatcher fumed, "are worse than the Soviets, persuading the governor [of Grenada] to issue a retrospective invitation to invade after they had taken him aboard an American warship."[109]

Was America's invasion of the tiny island justified? Ask the Grenadians. Today, October 25 is celebrated in Grenada as Thanksgiving Day in remembrance of America's role in restoring democracy.

But not all American interventions were as principled. America's covert operations forced it, at times, to partner with sadistic murderers. One of the worst was Roberto D'Aubuisson Arrieta, a major in the Salvadoran

Army. Known as "Blowtorch Bob" for his interrogation techniques, Arrieta was said to have personally tortured and killed hundreds of civilians during the Salvadoran Civil War.[110] In total, an estimated 75,000 civilians were murdered by Salvadoran government forces covertly backed by the United States.

One covert operation, the Iran-Contra Affair, spanned from the Middle East to Central America and even threatened the Reagan presidency.

In 1979, after years of corruption, the Nicaraguan dictatorship of Anastasio Somoza fell, igniting a civil war between the American-backed Contras and the Soviet-backed Sandinistas. Much of the Contras' funding, though, came from its cocaine trade. Unwilling to support drug traffickers, Congress passed the Boland Amendment in 1982, which prohibited U.S. military support to the Contras.[111]

Deprived of Congressional funding, the Reagan administration found another source of funds to support the Contras. During the Iran-Iraq War, the United States had begun to secretly sell advanced missiles to Iran to be used against Iraq, an American ally at the time. In return, Iran agreed to assist in the release of seven American hostages being held in Lebanon by Iran-backed Hezbollah. The proceeds from the missile sales, in defiance of Congress, were secretly diverted to the Nicaraguan Contras fighting the Soviet-backed Sandinista government.

The Reagan administration was forced to stop the clandestine missile sales in 1986 when a Lebanese magazine exposed the arrangement. By then, the United States had sold Iran 1,500 missiles for $30 million ($71 million in 2020 dollars). Several members of Reagan's administration were convicted of conspiracy, perjury, and fraud, although only a government contractor (and former CIA agent), Thomas Clines, went to prison. Although Reagan was never implicated in the clandestine operation, his reputation was tarnished at the time, as was that of the United States.

Like the Pentagon Papers fifteen years earlier, the scandal exposed how duplicitously the American government sometimes operated: secretly selling powerful weapons to the enemy of an American ally then using the proceeds to covertly fund a civil war Congress had specifically prohibited.[112]

★

Beyond the Reagan Doctrine policy of countering Soviet moves at every turn, President Reagan employed three additional strategies to weaken the Soviet Union.

Knowing the Soviet economy was faltering, Reagan increased real defense spending 35 percent between 1981 and 1985 in an effort to "bankrupt the Soviet Union" as the Soviets tried to maintain military parity with the United States.[113] Major new weapons programs were either started or given renewed emphasis, including the B-1 bomber, the Trident nuclear submarine, and the MX multiple-warhead nuclear missile.

Reagan then raised the stakes with the Strategic Defense Initiative (SDI), announced in 1983. SDI was a defensive system that consisted of ground-based missiles and space-based lasers designed to shoot down incoming Soviet ICBMs before they struck their American targets. A fanciful idea, at least for nineteen-eighties technology, SDI was quickly labeled "Star Wars" by pundits. But the Soviets couldn't afford to be quite so blasé. America's nineteen-sixties space program had gone from hapless rocket failures to putting a man on the moon in eight years. If the Americans could make Star Wars work, it would fundamentally change the balance of power between the two nations. The Soviets would no longer be able to depend on Mutually Assured Destruction as a deterrent to a pre-emptive nuclear attack by the Americans. It was a brilliant strategic move on Reagan's part.

Reagan's strong communication and diplomatic skills contributed to the end of the Cold War. During the early years of his presidency, Reagan, abandoning normal diplomatic restraint, described the Cold War as a historic conflict between good and evil, labeling the Soviet Union an "evil empire" while likening the United States to a "shining city on a hill." In a June 1982 speech to the British Parliament, Reagan predicted, "freedom and democracy will leave Marxism and Leninism on the ash heap of history:"

> The decay of the Soviet experiment should come as no surprise to us. . . . One of the simple but overwhelming facts of our time is this: of all the millions of refugees we've seen in the modern world, their flight is always away from, not toward the communist world. Today on the NATO line, our military forces face east to prevent a possible

invasion. On the other side of the line, the Soviet forces also face east to prevent their people from leaving.[114]

As he often did, after a stinging condemnation of the Soviet Bloc, Reagan used humor to break the tension. "The Soviet Union," Reagan joked, "would remain a one-party nation even if an opposition party were permitted because everyone would join the opposition party," which drew considerable laughter. He then graciously complimented his British hosts by recognizing the plucky spirit of the British under adversity. The "reluctance to [promote our democratic ideals over those of totalitarianism] reminds me of the elderly lady whose home was bombed in the Blitz. As the rescuers moved about, they found a bottle of brandy she'd stored behind the staircase, which was all that was left standing. And since she was barely conscious, one of the workers pulled the cork to give her a taste of it. She came around immediately and said, 'Here now-there now, put it back. That's for emergencies.'"

Reagan enjoyed collecting anti-Communist jokes. Many of the jokes were supplied by the CIA office in Moscow where agents picked them up from locals commenting on their political system. One of Reagan's favorites described the plight of Soviet consumers:

> You know, there is a ten-year delay in the Soviet Union for the delivery of an automobile. You go through quite a process when you are ready to buy, and then you put up the money in advance. So, the customer laid down his money, and the fellow in charge told him: come back in ten years and get your car. The customer asked: Morning or afternoon? And the fellow behind the counter answered: Ten years from now, what difference does it make? And the customer said: Well, the plumber is coming that morning.[115]

Reagan often poked fun at himself. Accused of dozing off in cabinet meetings, Reagan quipped, "I have left orders to be awakened at any time during a national emergency, even if I'm in a cabinet meeting."[116]

No wonder so many Americans loved Ronald Reagan.

Reagan's strategy of challenging the Soviets on military and economic fronts bore little fruit in his first term: Soviet leaders kept dying. Leonid

Brezhnev slipped away in 1982, Yuri Andropov in 1984, and Konstantin Chernenko just a year later in 1985. Their average age was seventy-three when the Russian lifespan was sixty-two years.[117] Finally in March 1985, the Soviets chose a much younger man, Mikhail Gorbachev, fifty-four years old, as their leader.

Gorbachev had revolutionary ideas for reforming the Soviet Union. His efforts were based on two initiatives: *Perestroika* ("restructuring") and *Glasnost* ("openness").

Perestroika was a domestic initiative that loosened state control over industry, decentralized economic decision-making, allowed limited private ownership, and opened up foreign investment.

Glasnost was an international initiative to revitalize the Soviet Union's relationship with the eight Warsaw Pact nations of Albania, Bulgaria, Czechoslovakia, East Germany, Hungary, Poland, and Romania. Glasnost granted these nations, long tightly controlled by the Soviet Union as a buffer zone against the West, the right to manage their affairs without Soviet interference.

Gorbachev's appointment opened new opportunities for Reagan. The two leaders quickly held their first summit eight months later in Geneva. Reagan prepped extensively for the meeting, anticipating Gorbachev to be another hardline Soviet leader. Instead, Reagan found Gorbachev intent on liberalizing the Soviet system through his Perestroika and Glasnost initiatives. Reagan quickly saw that a more open Soviet Union would work to America's advantage. Although little concrete progress was accomplished during their two days in Geneva, both men left believing, as Margaret Thatcher had earlier said of Gorbachev, "We can do business together."[118]

As Reagan's relationship with Gorbachev warmed, Reagan stopped referring to the Soviet Union as the Evil Empire. Gorbachev didn't seem to mind the label though. "We are so critical of our own country," Gorbachev told reporters, "that even the President's criticisms are weak. We know what our problems are."[119]

Reagan and Gorbachev met again a year later in October 1986 in Reykjavik. Again, little apparent progress was made due to Reagan's insistence on continuing his SDI program. Yet both sides left the meeting believing a sweeping arms reduction agreement was in reach.

President Ronald Reagan, speaking before the Berlin Wall at the Brandenburg Gate in Berlin, famously implored: "Mr. Gorbachev, tear down this wall!"

DPA PICTURE ALLIANCE/ALAMY

They were right. Gorbachev later dropped his insistence that SDI be part of any arms control agreement (perhaps because the Soviets had concluded SDI was a paper tiger) and in December 1987, the two leaders met in Washington, D.C. to sign the Intermediate-Range Nuclear Forces (INF) Treaty. The treaty required both countries to destroy their missiles with intermediate ranges between 500 and 5,500 kilometers. It was the most sweeping arms reduction treaty signed to date.

That year, Reagan gave the most famous speech of his presidency. He did so over the objections of his State Department and National Security Council. "The [speech] was naïve," a top U.S. diplomat claimed. "It would raise false hopes. It was clumsy. It was needlessly provocative."[120] Even Secretary of State George Schultz urged Reagan to change the wording. Reagan was undeterred. "The boys at State are going to kill me," Reagan told a staff member, "but it's the right thing to do."

Reagan gave the speech on June 12, 1987 in Berlin on the occasion of Berlin's 750th anniversary. Standing on a high platform with the Berlin Wall as a dramatic backdrop, Reagan gestured to the wall and implored:

> General Secretary Gorbachev, if you seek peace, if you seek prosperity for the Soviet Union and Eastern Europe, if you seek liberalization: Come here to this gate! Mr. Gorbachev, open this gate! Mr. Gorbachev, tear down this wall![121]

Tear down this wall! Those four words fanned the hopes of millions in the Eastern Bloc. For forty years, the Iron Curtain had cleaved Europe apart, from Poland in the north to Albania in the south. To the west was freedom and prosperity, to the east subjugation and privation.

For Reagan, the timing was perfect. Perestroika, Gorbachev's plan to restructure the communist economy, was failing. Economic chaos followed as the Soviet Union struggled to move from a command to a mixed economy. Soviet industry couldn't adapt quickly enough. For sixty years, Soviet factories and farms had been told what to build, what to plant, and when to do it. Now they were being asked to let the market decide. From 1985 to 1989, real Soviet GDP sank nearly six percent annually.[122]

Glasnost, though, was working too well. Soviet citizens were learning about their brutal past under Stalin, the far better living standards enjoyed by the West and the discontent that their Soviet satellites felt towards Mother Russia. Throughout the Soviet Union and its Eastern Bloc allies, citizens were beginning to question the entire Soviet system.

By 1989, as President Reagan was leaving office, Perestroika had ruined the Soviet economy while Glasnost had empowered citizens throughout the Soviet Union and its Soviet satellites to question their governments. Revolutionary change was within sight, but still just out of reach. As Russians joked at the time, "We are still on the leash and the dog dish is far away, but now we can bark as loud as we want."[123]

The Reagan Legacy

Shortly before Reagan left office, Burton Yale Pines, a senior vice president at the Heritage Foundation, wrote *The Ten Legacies of Ronald Reagan*, a report predicting Reagan's top legacies.[124] Five of the report's legacies focused on countering the Soviet Union by rebuilding the military, taking a tough stance against Soviet aggression, and starting the Strategic Defense Initiative (SDI). Surprisingly, the Heritage report did not mention the inspiration Reagan's words spread behind the Iron Curtain. When he urged, "Mr. Gorbachev, tear down this wall"; when he spoke to the world of the American Revolution which enshrined three words, "We the people"; and when he likened America to "A beacon for all hurtling through darkness seeking freedom,"[125] Reagan inspired millions to seek freedom.

Ronald Reagan was beloved even by his political adversaries. In 1991, Mikhail and Raisa Gorbachev visited the Reagans at their California ranch where they were each given "ten gallon" cowboy hats.   MIKE NELSON/GETTY

Ronald Reagan left many legacies, but his greatest legacy was the optimism, vision, and goodwill he conveyed to Americans. The fifteen years preceding Reagan's presidency had been dreadful: the assassinations of John Kennedy, Martin Luther King Jr., and Robert Kennedy; the race riots; the Pentagon Papers; Watergate; the Vietnam War; stagflation; the oil embargoes; the Iran Embassy hostages; all capped by President Carter's Malaise Speech that blamed Americans' moral failings for the nation's problems. America was deeply depressed. Nine months before Reagan was inaugurated, Gallup's consumer sentiment index hit the lowest level ever recorded, 51.7.

Reagan's plain-spoken optimism and old-fashioned patriotism quickly lifted the country. "On you depend the fortunes of America," Reagan told Americans in his First Inaugural Address. "You are to decide the important questions upon which rests the happiness and the liberty of millions yet unborn. Act worthy of yourselves."

Reagan restored America's vision of itself. Americans thanked him for it, giving Reagan the highest job approval at the end of his term since Franklin Roosevelt.[126]

George H.W. Bush

> Great nations like great men must keep their word. When America says something, America means it, whether a treaty or an agreement or a vow made on marble steps.[1]

O n April 30, 1789, George Washington took the oath of office as America's first President. Washington was visibly nervous. Little wonder that the great general's voice was tremulous as he accepted responsibility for "the preservation of the sacred fire of liberty, and the destiny of the Republican model of Government."[2] It had taken the extraordinary skills of America's Founders to coax thirteen rebellious colonies into a single nation, a nation that could easily fling itself apart. The Founders knew democracy was the most fragile of all forms of government. The Athenian democracy lasted a mere 200 years, torn apart by war and despots. The Roman republic, after years of discord, abandoned democracy for a monarchy. Benjamin Franklin, when asked whether the Founders had created a monarchy or a republic, replied, "A republic, if you can keep it."[3]

Swearing on the same bible as Washington, George H.W. Bush, took the oath of office 200 years later on January 20, 1989. The great American experiment in democracy had exceeded beyond the dreams of any of its Founders. The United States had not only flourished but served as a beacon of freedom throughout the world. "I come before you," Bush proclaimed during his inaugural address, "and assume the Presidency at a moment rich with promise.... For a new breeze is blowing, and a world refreshed by freedom seems reborn. . . . The totalitarian era is passing, its old ideas blown away like leaves from an ancient, lifeless tree."[4]

Bush, of course, was speaking of the winds of change blowing through Eastern Europe and the Soviet Union. Even as he spoke, he could hardly have foreseen how quickly the world would be transformed.

The year 1989 is remembered throughout Europe as "annus mirabilis," the year of miracles. Plucky little Estonia led the way. On November 16, 1988, Estonians defied their Soviet overlords and declared Estonia a sovereign state and that Estonian, rather than Soviet, laws would rule the country. After Estonia's brave declaration, the freedom movement within the Soviet Bloc built quickly. In February 1989, Poland's Solidarity became the first independent trade union to be recognized within the Soviet Bloc. In March, mass demonstrations in Hungary demanded democracy and in April Hungary dismantled the barbed wire and electric fence bordering Austria, effectively opening its border to the West. In June, Poland held its first free elections since the communist takeover; the Solidarity party won in a landslide. In August, two million Estonians, Latvians, and Lithuanians joined hands in a 375-mile human chain linking their three countries in a heartfelt demand for an end to Soviet occupation. In September, Poland elected its first non-communist government in four decades. In October, Hungary replaced its communist government with the Hungarian Republic. On November 9, the Berlin Wall fell as two million East Berliners poured into West Berlin, joining in, "the greatest street party in the history of the world."[5] Events accelerated in December. Václav Havel, a Czech dissident, was elected the first post-communist President of Czechoslovakia—eleven months earlier Havel had been wasting away in jail as a political prisoner. The transition was so peaceful the Czechs called it their Velvet Revolution. Bulgaria announced the Communist Party would abandon its monopoly on power. Poland rejected communism by restoring a capitalist system. And Romanians overthrew their corrupt, communist government. Remarkably, after forty years of harsh Soviet suppression, Romania's revolution was the only transition to end in bloodshed when the new government summarily executed former President Nicolae Ceaușescu and his wife, Elena, on Christmas Day.

In December 1989, President Bush and Soviet General Secretary Mikhail Gorbachev met aboard warships off the coast of Malta. The location was symbolic. President Roosevelt and Prime Minister Churchill had met there in February 1945 to plan the postwar world. Decades later, Bush and Gorbachev declared the Cold War over. "The world is leaving one epoch and entering another," Gorbachev declared. "We are at the beginning of a long road to a lasting, peaceful era."[6]

President George H.W. Bush and Soviet General Secretary Mikhail Gorbachev announced the end of the Cold War at the Malta Summit, December 3, 1989. The summit followed a year of upheaval as Soviet Bloc countries declared their freedom.

AP PHOTO/DOUG MILLS

The road wasn't that long for Gorbachev and the Soviet Union. Within months, the Soviet Union began to unravel. In March 1991, Gorbachev, to quell growing internal rebellion, proposed the Soviet Union be replaced by the Union of Sovereign States, a confederation of equals. There was little interest. On July 1, 1990, the Warsaw Pact, the Soviet counterpart to NATO, disbanded. Stunned, Soviet hardliners in Moscow revolted and attempted a coup on August 18, placing Gorbachev under house arrest. Disorganized and with little support from the army, the coup quickly collapsed after Russia's President, Boris Yeltsin, announced his support for Gorbachev.

A little more than a year later, on December 8, 1991, the Soviet Union quietly expired when the leaders of Russia, Ukraine, and Belarus declared the Soviet Union disbanded. Replacing it was the Commonwealth of Independent States. On December 21, eleven additional Soviet countries joined the Commonwealth. Torn in every direction, on Christmas Day 1991, the Soviet Union declared itself disbanded. Gorbachev resigned as President. That evening the Hammer and Sickle was lowered for the last time over the Kremlin. The world watched, stunned, as the once mighty Union of Soviet Socialist Republics quietly exited the world stage.

How could the world's second most powerful nation simply dissolve? Theories abound, largely based on geography.

Americans believe that President Reagan's tough stance against the Soviets coupled with increased military spending pushed the Soviet Union to the brink of collapse. U.K. Prime Minister Margaret Thatcher asserted at Reagan's eulogy in 2004 that Ronald Reagan had won the Cold War without firing a shot.[7] The Russians scoff at this, claiming that Gorbachev's Glasnost (open government) and Perestroika (restructured government) policies unleashed internal forces that doomed the Soviet Union. The former Soviet Bloc countries believe that their steady drive for freedom, beginning with Poland's Solidarity labor movement in 1980, made the Soviet collapse inevitable.

The role of Pope John Paul II, the first Polish pope, is seldom mentioned; the Vatican hardly promotes its political activities. On June 2, 1979, Pope John Paul II celebrated Mass with three million Poles in Warsaw's Victory Square. "My pilgrimage to my motherland in the year in which the Church in Poland is celebrating the ninth centenary of the death of Saint Stanislaus," the Pope declared, "is surely a special sign of the pilgrimage that we Poles are making down through the history of the Church not only along the ways of our motherland but also along those of Europe and the world. . . . I must nonetheless with all of you ask myself why. . . after so many centuries. . . a son of the Polish Nation, of the land of Poland, was called to the chair of Saint Peter."[8]

The Pope, and millions of Poles, believed his historical papacy was ordained by God to free the Polish people from Soviet domination. The Pulitzer Prize-winning historian John Lewis Gaddis agrees, declaring the Pope's Victory Square Mass the "trigger that led to communism's collapse worldwide."[9]

Inspired by the Pope's message of faith mixed with Polish nationalism, Poles began a steady call for freedom, starting with the Solidarity labor movement in 1980. "Without the Polish Pope," historian Timothy Ash has written, "no Solidarity revolution in Poland in 1980; without Solidarity, no dramatic change in Soviet policy towards Eastern Europe under Gorbachev; without that change, no velvet revolutions in 1989."[10] Perhaps most definitively, Mikhail Gorbachev also agrees asserting, "The collapse of the Iron Curtain would have been impossible without John Paul II."[11]

Generally, though, it is Gorbachev who, outside the United States, has been credited for ending the Cold War. Critics of America's policies claim that Reagan, by "[presiding] over the biggest peacetime defense buildup in history,"[12] escalated the Cold War. In the years preceding Gorbachev, Cold War tensions had grown so high that the Soviets shot down an unarmed South Korean airliner in 1983 when it wandered into Soviet territory. Had the Soviets replaced Konstantin Chernenko, Gorbachev's predecessor, with another hardliner, the Cold War could easily have continued to escalate.

Gorbachev, instead, took the initiative to reduce tensions, both inside and outside the Soviet sphere.[13] In a December 1984 speech, four months before assuming the role of Soviet General Secretary, Gorbachev introduced Glasnost and Perestroika, polices aimed at making the Soviet Union more open and market-driven.[14] Then, shortly after taking office in 1985, Gorbachev proposed a ban on all nuclear weapons by 2000. Although dismissed by the United States, Gorbachev's audacious proposal finally opened fruitful discussions between the United States and the Soviets, starting with the Geneva Summit in November 1985.[15] Two years later, Gorbachev announced the unilateral withdrawal of 500,000 Soviet troops from Central and Eastern Europe. That same year, the Soviet Union stopped jamming the BBC and Voice of America radio broadcasts, opening communications with the democratic West. Finally, as Gorbachev's liberal policies began to unleash revolution throughout the Soviet Bloc, he refused to intervene militarily, allowing the former Soviet satellites to regain their freedom and dooming the Soviet Union.

In 1989, Gorbachev won Germany's Otto Hahn Peace Prize "for outstanding services to peace and international understanding, especially for his contributions to nuclear disarmament of the great powers and the creation of a fundamentally new political order in Europe."[16] The next year Gorbachev won the Nobel Peace Prize.

Reagan received few international honors other than an honorary Berlin citizenship and a few scattered statues throughout Europe.

History, though, has a flair for irony. While Reagan, snubbed internationally, is revered by millions in the United States for ending the Cold War, Gorbachev, honored internationally, is reviled by millions of Russians for the collapse of the Soviet Union.

The Forgotten Invasion

President Bush memorably presided over the end of the Cold War and the First Gulf War. Few today remember Bush ordered the invasion of Panama in December 1989. Eclipsed by the fall of the Berlin Wall, the collapse of the Soviet Union, and the First Gulf War, the Panama Invasion has largely been forgotten. But, at the time, it was the largest American military intervention since the Vietnam War, and far more successful.

One of the invasion's unstated objectives was to capture one man, Manuel Noriega. Since his student days in the nineteen-fifties, Noriega had been a CIA operative who provided the United States with intelligence regarding communist activities in Latin America, especially neighboring Nicaragua. Noriega steadily rose through the ranks of the Panamanian military and, after the death of strongman Omar Torrijos in 1983, became the military dictator of Panama.[17]

Unbridled power soon corrupted Noriega who began to support his lavish lifestyle through drug trafficking and other illicit operations including selling thousands of fake Panamanian passports to Fidel Castro for use by underground communist agents. In 1987 Congress cut off Noriega's military and economic aid and, a year later, indicted Noriega *in absentia* for aiding the importation of cocaine into the United States. In May 1989, during Panama's presidential election, Noriega's troops assured his reelection by seizing the nation's polling places. In October, a U.S.-backed coup to replace Noriega failed. In November, the United States blocked Panamanian registered ships from docking at American ports. Panama responded by declaring that the United States and Panama were "in a state of war."[18]

On December 20, 1989, the United States invaded Panama with 28,000 troops and 300 aircraft. American aircraft bombed the barrios (city districts) surrounding Noriega's residence. The Chorillo barrio was so devastated that locals called it "Little Hiroshima."[19] Noriega fled to the Vatican diplomatic mission in Panama City. After days of psychological warfare, including blaring rock-n-roll music continuously night and day, Noriega surrendered. Noriega, an erstwhile American ally, spent the rest of his life in an American prison.

Forty-two days after the invasion, American troops left Panama after installing a new government. The invasion killed an estimated 300 civilians plus 250 Panamanian and twenty-three American soldiers. In a national address, President Bush justified the invasion as necessary to protect Americans stationed in Panama, restore democracy, secure the safety of the Panama Canal, and combat drug trafficking. Tactically, the invasion was one of the most successful American military operations ever mounted.

The invasion was strongly supported in the United States and, if not supported, condoned by American allies.[20] Others condemned the attack as a throwback to America's gunboat diplomacy during the Banana Wars of the early twentieth century. The Organization of American States and the United Nations General Assembly both passed resolutions condemning the invasion. The Soviets declared the invasion "an act of open, international terrorism against a small and, in essence, a defenseless, state."[21]

Nonetheless, since America's intervention in 1989, Panama remains at peace. By 2020, Panamanians had elected six presidents from three different political parties in free and fair elections.[22]

Frankenstein's Monster

The End of History and the Last Man is American political scientist Francis Fukuyama's rather whimsically entitled book, written as the Soviet Union was in collapse. Fukuyama had concluded that the triumph of democracy over communism ended humankind's long search for the best form of government. The fall of the Soviet Union was not just a point on the timeline of political history, the author theorized, but the end of political history itself. With democracy's triumph over communism, humankind's struggle for the ultimate form of government had finally ended.[23]

Not everyone agreed with Professor Fukuyama. Even as the Soviet Union was quietly dying, a radical faction within Islam had been metastasizing in the Middle East for a decade. It began with the 1979 Soviet invasion of Afghanistan.

Like the Soviet invasions of Czechoslovakia and Hungary years earlier, the invasion of Afghanistan was the Soviet response to a tottering communist regime. But the Soviets were now fighting in the "Graveyard of Empires," a land whose tribal leaders had repelled outside invaders for centuries. The Soviets poured over 100,000 troops into Afghanistan, but never subdued the wily Afghan freedom fighters.

The Afghanis had help. The United States, through CIA channels in Pakistan, funneled an estimated $20 billion in military aid into Afghanistan. That aid helped defeat the Soviets, but also fueled abiding anger over western intervention in Islamic lands. Pakistani Prime Minister Benazir Bhutto recognized America's intervention in the Middle East was breeding a dangerous strain of militant Islam. During a June 1989 visit to Washington, Bhutto warned President Bush, "Mr. President, I am afraid we have created a Frankenstein's monster that could come back to haunt us in the future."[24]

Shortly after the Soviets invaded Afghanistan, Iraq launched an air and ground attack on Iran on September 22, 1980. Iraq's Saddam Hussein believed that Iran, destabilized after its Islamic revolution, would be an easy target. He misread the Iranians who had inherited the ancient empire of Persia. Persia, like Afghanistan, had been a target of foreign ambitions since Alexander the Great.

Caught by surprise, Iran responded swiftly with counterattacks using American fighter jets acquired earlier under the Shah. The war soon devolved into First World War-like trench warfare, with both sides suffering tremendous human losses for no military gain. Neither Iraq nor Iran ever gained the advantage. In 1988, the war-weary combatants signed a ceasefire. After a huge cost in blood and treasure, Iraq had achieved none of its territorial goals.

His territorial ambitions unfulfilled, Saddam Hussein remained restless. He soon found a new target in Kuwait. The small, oil-rich country had loaned Iraq $14 billion during its war with Iran. Kuwait was now insisting on being repaid. Hussein demanded the debt be forgiven. Iraq, Hussein claimed, had thwarted Iran's advance into Arab lands. Kuwait refused. Hussein countered, claiming Kuwait was pumping oil far above its OPEC quota, making it impossible for Iraq to generate the oil revenues needed to repay the debt. More dubiously, Iraq claimed Kuwait was stealing Iraqi oil by slant drilling beneath their border into Iraq's Ar-Rumaylah oil fields.

In weighing an attack on Kuwait, Hussein misjudged the United States. After receiving massive American support during his war with Iran, Hussein considered America a strong ally. The U.S. ambassador, April Glaspie, unintentionally reinforced Hussein's confidence. "We have no opinion on your Arab-Arab conflicts, such as your dispute with Kuwait," Glaspie told Hussein. "Secretary [James] Baker has directed me to emphasize the instruction, first given to Iraq in the nineteen-sixties, that the Kuwait issue is not associated with America."[25] Glaspie was advocating a peaceful solution through the Arab League. Hussein, however, interpreted her comments to mean the United States would not intervene in a war with Kuwait.

Iraq launched its attack on August 2, 1990, catching the Kuwaitis by surprise. By the end of the first day, the royal Al-Sabah family had fled into the desert. The overwhelmed Kuwaiti army put up a vigorous, but futile resistance. Six days after the invasion began, Saddam Hussein declared Kuwait the nineteenth province of Iraq.[26]

With Kuwait crushed, an Iraqi attack on Saudi Arabia appeared imminent. Iraq owed Saudi Arabia $16 billion which, like Kuwait earlier, the Saudis refused to forgive. Fearing an immediate invasion, Osama bin

Laden, the scion of a wealthy Saudi family, proposed using his Al Qaeda fighters—hardened fighters who had helped defeat the Soviet Army in Afghanistan—to defend Saudi Arabia. The Saudis refused and instead invited the United States to station troops inside Saudi Arabia. The United States quickly agreed. By late 1990, 500,000 American troops were deployed inside Saudi borders only a few hundred miles from Mecca and Medina, Islam's two holiest sites. The sight of western infidels inside his country enraged Osama bin Laden.[27]

The international reaction to Iraq's invasion of Kuwait was immediate. In contrast to Iran, Iraq had attacked a friend. After Iraq refused a United Nations resolution to withdraw, President Bush assembled a coalition of thirty-four countries to drive Iraq out of Kuwait. On November 29, 1990, the United Nations ordered Iraq to withdraw by January 15, 1991, authorizing the use of military force if Iraq failed to comply.

Hussein ignored the ultimatum declaring an American invasion would be "the mother of all battles." American pundits chuckled over the phrase but having been drawn from the Quran to describe Mecca as the mother of all holy sites, Muslims considered the expression sacred.[28]

On January 16, 1991, the United States and its allies began bombing Iraqi military targets. Iraq responded with Scud missile strikes against Israel, hoping to draw other Arab nations to its side. The ploy failed. America and its allies pounded Iraq from the air for over a month. On February 24, the ground war began when American and coalition troops entered Kuwait. A hundred hours later, Kuwait was declared liberated. Iraq suffered over 20,000 troops killed in action, while coalition troops, benefiting from superior American technology including laser-guided missiles and stealth fighters, suffered 190 combat deaths.[29]

Bush's Gulf War was the first major American military victory since World War II.

On March 7, President Bush made a victory speech before a joint session of Congress. "We went halfway around the world to do what is moral and just and right," Bush declared. "We lifted the yoke of aggression and tyranny from a small country that many Americans had never even heard of, and we ask nothing in return. We're coming home now proud, confident, heads high. There is much that we must do at home and abroad. And we will do it. We are Americans."[30]

Congress gave Bush a three-minute standing ovation accompanied by shouts of "Bush! Bush!" It was the pinnacle of Bush's presidency and, throughout much of the world, the highpoint of American prestige.

A decade of war had left the Middle East in shambles. Iraq's failed wars with Iran and Kuwait rendered it a devastated country.[31] Iran lay shattered. Afghanistan, abandoned after the Soviet defeat, was left to its tribal warlords. Saudi Arabia had become a hotbed of religious zealots, incensed by American infidels stationed within its borders.

Driven from his Saudi home after condemning the Saudi royal family as American puppets, bin Laden settled in Sudan in 1992. Outraged that Saudi King Fahd welcomed American troops onto Saudi soil bordering Islam's two most sacred sites,[32] bin Laden vowed to devote his life to fighting the United States and its presence in Islamic lands.

Bin Laden soon began his terrorist activities, using his construction company as a cover. Al Qaeda operatives trained and armed the Somali rebels who killed eighteen U.S. Army Rangers in the 1993 Black Hawk Down attack. Al Qaeda was linked to the attempted assassination of Egyptian President Hosni Mubarak, the bombing of a U.S. National Guard training center in Riyadh, and the bombing of an American military residence in Dharan, a major center of the Saudi oil industry.

In 1996, Sudan, under international pressure, expelled bin Laden and confiscated the assets of his construction company. Saudi Arabia revoked his citizenship. His wealthy family terminated his annual $7.0 million stipend. Shunned and homeless, bin Laden returned to Afghanistan, where his transformation from the privileged son of a prominent Saudi family to an international terrorist was complete.

Within months bin Laden issued a fatwa (an Islamic legal statement) on August 23, 1996, titled "Declaration of War against the Americans Occupying the Land of the Two Holy Places." The fatwa declared: "[American] aggression was the worst catastrophe that was inflicted upon the Moslems since the death of the Prophet. That is, the occupation of the land of the two holiest sites, Islam's own grounds, the cradle of Islam...launched by the Christian army of the Americans and their allies." Bin Laden's fatwa urged that Muslim "efforts should be concentrated on destroying, fighting and killing the enemy until, by the Grace of Allah, it is completely defeated."[33]

Throughout the nineteen-nineties, Bin Laden seemed a distant threat for most Americans even after his terrorist attacks killed hundreds in the bombings of U.S. embassies and the USS *Cole*. On September 11, 2001, bin Laden was the mastermind behind terrorist attacks that killed nearly 3,000 Americans.   *NEW YORK DAILY NEWS* ARCHIVE/GETTY

Few took bin Laden's fatwa seriously. How much damage could a handful of bedraggled zealots hiding in Afghani villages do to the mighty United States?

Bin Laden, though, quickly turned his proclamation into deadly assaults. On August 7, 1998, Al Qaeda attacks killed 224 people in the simultaneous bombings of U.S. embassies in Tanzania and Kenya. The attacks came eight years to the day after American troops entered Saudi Arabia. On October 12, 2000, seventeen sailors were killed off the coast of Yemen when a bomb-laden skiff rammed the USS *Cole*, a U.S. Navy destroyer. Then, on September 11, 2001, terrorist attacks killed nearly 3,000 innocent people in the World Trade Center, the Pentagon, and on four airliners. Fifteen of the nineteen terrorists were from Saudi Arabia.[34]

When Francis Fukuyama wrote *The End of History,* he presumed humankind's search for the perfect government to be a rational process, built on a shared intellectual heritage that ran from the Greeks through the Enlightenment and to the American Constitution. During the Cold War, although capitalists and communists disagreed, both shared a common intellectual heritage: Francis Bacon, John Locke, Adam Smith, and Karl Marx, among many others.

Radical Islam—like other extreme forms of religion—does not share that heritage. Its adherents reject the idea that humankind's destiny is a continual search for the betterment of all peoples. For Radical Islamists, history ended in the year 632 when the archangel Gabriel revealed the final words of God to Muhammad, later transcribed in the Quran. As bin Laden's fatwa wrote, "No other duty after Belief [in Allah] is more important than the duty of Jihad."[35] For those who reject Allah, the Quran's teachings are clear: "Slay or crucify or cut the hands and feet of the unbelievers, that they be expelled from the land with disgrace and that they shall have a great punishment..." (5:34)[36]

Read my Lips

George H.W. Bush was never quite able to make up his mind about taxes. While campaigning against Reagan in 1980, he disparaged Reagan's tax cut plan as "Voodoo Economics" declaring, "It just isn't gonna work."[37] Later, as Reagan's Vice President, Bush sheepishly claimed he had only been joking. In 1988, running for President himself and sticking to the Reagan line, Bush promised during his nomination speech, "Read my lips: no new taxes." But two years later, President Bush raised the maximum personal tax rate from 28 to 31 percent as part of the Omnibus Budget Reconciliation Act of 1990.[38] An uproar ensued. "Read my lips: I lied,"[39] was how the *New York Post* headlined the tax increase on its front page. House Representative Newt Gingrich, soon to become Speaker of the House, called the tax increase "an act of supreme stupidity."[40]

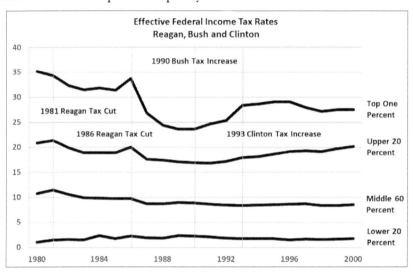

After Bush promised, "Read my lips: no new taxes," the 1990 Bush Tax Increase became a hot political issue. But few taxpayers, only those earning over $200,000, actually paid higher taxes.   IRS STATISTICS OF INCOME REPORTS

For all the political uproar over Bush's broken promise, most taxpayers received a small tax cut. Only the wealthiest taxpayers paid higher taxes and then, just barely. How was that possible? Because the tax brackets were raised as part of the tax increase. In 1989, the top bracket started at taxable income over $30,950. In 1992, after the tax increases, the top bracket was raised to $86,500. Although tax rates had been increased, fewer taxpayers fell into the upper brackets. As a result, only taxpayers with gross incomes of $200,000 or more paid higher taxes. From 1989 to 1992, their effective tax rate increased, from 23.7 to 25.3 percent. Taxpayers in the top income bracket, $1.0 million or more, paid an average of $71,000 in increased taxes. That's a lot, but most could probably afford it. Their average gross income was $2.6 million ($4.8 million in 2020 dollars) in 1992.

President Bush's tax increase was so timid that it decreased total income tax revenues, measured as a percentage of GDP, from an average of 7.7 percent between 1988 and 1990 down to 7.3 percent during 1991 and 1992. The political uproar over Bush's tax increase wasn't over higher taxes—99 percent of taxpayers effectively got tax cuts—but over his broken promise.

Why did Bush promise to never raise taxes? Because he accepted the advice of Roger Ailes, his media manager during the 1988 presidential election (and later the founder of Fox News). As Ailes later recounted: "At the time, the race was close, and Dukakis had given us an opening by talking about [raising] taxes as a last resort.... What you have to say to get on top of an issue like taxes is that you'd rather see your kids burned in the street than raise them."[41]

New Regulations

Bush's first assignment as Reagan's Vice President was to lead a task force chartered to reduce government regulations. One wonders if his heart had been in it. Eight years later, President Bush, rather than cutting regulations, increased them with two wide-sweeping regulatory acts: The Clean Air Act and the Americans with Disabilities Act (ADA). Both established new regulations that affected the American economy from mom-and-pop stores to its largest corporations.

The Clean Air Act of 1990 extended earlier clean air acts passed in 1963, 1970, and 1977. The 1990 Act focused on reducing four environmental threats: acid rain, urban air pollution, toxic air emissions, and stratospheric ozone depletion. Other than ozone depletion, these environmental threats have been well understood for 170 years.

In 1872, the *Glasgow Medical Journal* issued a ten-page review of *Air and Rain: The Beginnings of a Chemical Climatology*, a pioneering book written by chemist Robert Angus Smith. Twenty years earlier, Smith had coined the term "acid rain" to describe the acidic rain falling on northern British cities. "Headaches and languor," the medical journal's reviewers wrote, "which a few hours house-to-house visitation among the poor of Glasgow always produces.... The diminution of force and frequency of the pulse and quickening of the respiration... were the physiological effects of de-oxygenated air, the substituted carbonic acid being the principle lethal agent."[42] Even then, the source of the "lethal agent" was understood. "The source... is undoubtedly her coal combustion." Glasgow had one of the highest mortality rates in Britain, and Smith attributed the deaths to the city's polluted air. "A man may eat bad butter once or twice a day," the medical journal concluded, "but if the air is bad, he lives in it."[43]

The four Clean Air Acts beginning in 1963 have greatly improved the quality of America's air. A 2007 EPA report stated that since 1970, air pollutants from industrial sources have declined 70 percent even while America's economy has tripled in size.[44]

The Americans with Disabilities Act has had more mixed results. The ADA was modeled after the Civil Rights Act of 1964. It remains the most sweeping disability rights legislation ever signed. The ADA prohibits discrimination in employment and requires access to public facilities and transportation based on physical and mental disabilities. Before the ADA, a blind person, for example, could be denied employment in a telephone call center simply because it was inconvenient for the employer. A disabled veteran could effectively be barred from public transportation because he or she was unable to manage the steps onto a bus or train.

For years, industry and even religious groups lobbied against the legislation, concerned over compliance costs and the intrusion of the federal government into employment decisions. Much of that opposition dissipated on March 13, 1990 when dozens of disabled Americans cast aside their wheelchairs and laboriously pulled their broken bodies up the Capitol steps, an act remembered today as the "Capitol Crawl." "You can't watch that," one commentator observed, "without being well aware of the difficulties of people with disabilities when they confront obstacles like stairs."[45]

Today, America's infrastructure is much friendlier to the disabled. Curbs have cuts to allow street crossings in wheelchairs, public facilities have ramps, elevators have braille inscriptions, and public transportation has wheelchair lifts. Unfortunately, the ADA's impact on employment has been less successful. Nearly two decades after its passage, a 2008 employment report by the Bureau of Labor Statistics observed that "researchers cannot yet agree on the impact of the ADA or even how to measure the impact."[46] In

2019, 30.7 million Americans over the age of sixteen were disabled. Only 6.3 million, one in five, were employed.

During the nineteen-sixties and seventies, Washington imposed thousands of new environmental and safety regulations. In 1980, President Reagan promised to cut regulations to "get the government off the backs of our people." Reagan's staff were "true ideologues who campaigned on deregulation and did not care about public opinion," wrote Clarence Ditlow of the Center for Auto Safety.[47]

As President, Bush sought a middle ground, exemplified by his approach to the auto industry. "The White House under Bush," administration officials declared, "would herald a new balance for the auto industry, between a barrage of new safety and emissions standards during the nineteen-seventies and the deregulation and lack of government access by consumer and environmental activists during the Reagan years."[48]

The Clean Air Act and ADA resulted in many new federal regulations requiring expensive investments that ranged from upgraded bathroom stalls to million-dollar smokestack "scrubbers" to reduce harmful power plant emissions. But after Reagan's aggressive deregulation, the country seemed ready for a change. Both acts flew through Congress with large margins. The ADA passed the House with a unanimous voice vote[49], while the Clean Air Act passed 275–104.[50]

One of History's Great Transitions

George H.W. Bush was a true war hero. Accepted into Yale University, he instead enlisted in the Navy on his eighteenth birthday, June 12, 1942. A year after enlisting, Bush earned his wings as a Naval aviator, the Navy's youngest at the time. The Navy selected the nineteen-year-old Bush to fly the Grumman TBM Avenger torpedo bomber, the largest plane the Navy flew off its aircraft carriers. Naval aviation was one of the most dangerous assignments during World War II. Half of Bush's flight squadron were either killed or captured during the war. Bush flew fifty-eight combat missions, made 128 carrier landings and was shot down twice.

In 1944, Bush's Avenger was hit while attacking a Japanese radio transmitter. He nevertheless managed to complete the attack and then, reversing course, bail out over the ocean. One of his two crew members was able to bail out, but his parachute failed. The other never escaped the burning aircraft. Rescued by an American submarine, Bush was awarded the Distinguished Flying Cross for heroism. Undaunted, he quickly returned to his flight squadron to fight through the end of the war.

After the war, Bush graduated from Yale, Phi Beta Kappa. Two decades later, he had made his fortune in the West Texas oil fields. Like many true heroes, Bush was modest and soft-spoken. Those traits, though, didn't serve him well in politics, especially after following the eloquent and often tough-talking Ronald Reagan. When Bush announced his intention to run for President in October 1987, *Newsweek* ran a cover story entitled, "Fighting the Wimp Factor."[51] The label stuck.

Yet, President Bush resolutely presided over one of history's great transitions, the end of the Cold War. As the Soviet Union entered its death throes, Bush urged restraint, knowing that American gloating could slow or even stop Russia's transition to democracy. When much of Europe opposed German reunification, Bush declared the Germans themselves must choose their future. As the Soviet Union was dissolving, Bush signed the Strategic Arms Reduction Treaties, Start I and II, to limit the proliferation of nuclear weapons. When American hardliners urged abandoning the former Soviet Union and its former bloc countries, Bush encouraged American investment and free trade between and with the former Soviet satellites and successor states.

Bush lost his bid for a second term to Bill Clinton in a three-way election complicated by independent Ross Perot, a feisty Texas billionaire. As voters went to the polls in November 1992, the country was still recovering from a stubborn recession. Voters felt Bush had abandoned them, more interested in foreign relations than the economy. They had forgotten Bush's rousing military successes in Panama and Iraq, which, at the time, had brought out American flags all over America. But voters had not forgotten Bush's broken promise: "Read my lips: no new taxes."

★

Before Bush's presidency, only one sitting Vice President had ever been elected President, Martin Van Buren, in 1836. (Eight Vice Presidents had been elevated to the presidency after the death of the President: four by assassination and four naturally.) Both Van Buren and Bush served in the shadows of charismatic, popular Presidents: Andrew Jackson and Ronald Reagan. Both Jackson and Reagan were populists who blamed Washington for many of the nation's problems. Both men handed their successors an economic crisis: the bank panic of 1837 resulted in over 600 bank failures; the savings and loan crisis during the late nineteen-eighties cost taxpayers $130 billion. Both Van Buren and Bush failed to secure reelection, losing to Washington outsiders William Henry Harrison and Bill Clinton.

But history chose to compensate Bush with another historical precedent. Eight years after the first Bush presidency, his son, George W. Bush, was elected President. Only once before had a father and son both served as President: John Adams from 1797 to 1801, and, decades later, his son John Quincy Adams from 1825 to 1829.

William J. Clinton

————— ✦ —————

January 20, 1993 – January 20, 2001

> Profound and powerful forces are shaking and remaking our world, and the urgent question of our time is whether we can make change our friend and not our enemy.... But when most people are working harder for less; when others cannot work at all; when the cost of health care devastates families and threatens to bankrupt many of our enterprises, great and small; when fear of crime robs law-abiding citizens of their freedom; and when millions of poor children cannot even imagine the lives we are calling them to lead, we have not made change our friend.[1]

Our Nation needs a new direction.... Two decades of low productivity, growth, and stagnant wages; persistent unemployment and underemployment; years of huge government deficits and declining investment in our future."[2]

These words are reminiscent of Ronald Reagan's national address on February 5, 1981, when he declared that America was in "the worst economic mess since the Great Depression."[3] But this wasn't Reagan's speech. It was President Bill Clinton's first address to a joint session of Congress on February 17, 1993. After twelve years under Reagan and Bush, was America's economic state as poor as Clinton suggested?

By most measures, yes.

During the three years before Reagan took office, 1978–1980, real GDP grew an average of 2.8 percent annually. Twelve years later, during the three years prior to Clinton taking office, real GDP growth had slowed to 1.8 percent. In addition, average unemployment increased from 6.4 percent to 6.7 percent; poverty rates increased from 12.0 percent to 14.2 percent; average hourly wages decreased from $22.50 to $20.00 (in 2020 dollars); business investment in new factories, equipment and intellectual property decreased from 13.9 percent of GDP to 11.8 percent; real after-tax corporate profits declined from $618 billion to $438 billion; annual budget deficits increased from 2.2 percent of GDP to 4.2 percent; and the national debt as a percentage of GDP nearly doubled from 32 to 58.7 percent.

By nearly every measure, Clinton inherited a far worse economy than Reagan. That was especially true for the decline in personal incomes.

Most Americans saw their inflation-adjusted incomes fall during the Reagan and Bush years. Based on the annual IRS Statistics of Income reports, in 1980 the average middle-class taxpayer (the three middle-income quintiles) had an after-tax income of $38,400 (in 2020 dollars). By 1992, their real income had declined to $37,700. For those at the very bottom of the economic ladder, the hourly minimum wage declined 23 percent in real dollars from $9.74 to $7.51.

But the wealthy flourished. The top 20 percent saw their after-tax incomes increase from $105,300 to $135,600; the top five percent from $163,200 to $256,100; and the top one percent more than doubled their incomes from $293,200 to $613,400.

After 12 years of supply-side economics under Reagan and Bush, no wealth had "trickled down" to the middle- and lower-income classes. Their real after-tax income declined. Only the wealthy had thrived.

It's the Economy, Stupid

Clinton made repairing the economy his top priority. Seven months after taking office Clinton signed the Omnibus Budget Reconciliation Act, which raised the maximum individual tax rate from 31 to 39.6 percent, corporate taxes from 34 to 35 percent, the federal gas tax from 14.1 to 18.4 cents per gallon, as well as making other changes to the tax code to raise revenues.[4]

Clinton's opponents were quick to predict the tax increases would wreck the economy. "We have all too many people..." House Minority Whip Newt Gingrich claimed, "who are talking about bigger government, bigger bureaucracy, more programs, and higher taxes. I believe that that will in fact kill the current recovery and put us back in a recession."[5] Earlier, the National Center for Policy Analysis had concluded that by 1995 the Bush tax increase would, relative to the Congressional Budget Office's baseline forecast, reduce employment by 408,000 jobs and lower GDP by $168.6 billion. "The last thing the U.S. economy needs," the report concluded, "is another round of tax increases—destined to further depress the economy and make the recession deeper and longer than it otherwise would be."[6] The Heritage Foundation was equally pessimistic. "If enacted," a Heritage report concluded on February 18, 1993, "the Clinton tax hike will fuel more federal spending, destroy jobs, undermine America's international competitiveness, reduce economic growth, and increase the budget deficit."[7]

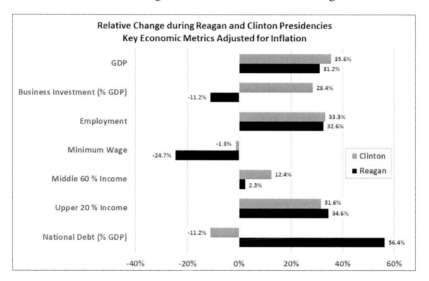

Many economists predicted economic stagnation after Clinton raised taxes in 1993. Instead, the economy boomed, outperforming the Reagan Expansion in many respects.   U.S. BUREAU OF ECONOMIC ANALYSIS

Instead, the economy blossomed. From 1992 through 1995, real GDP growth averaged 3.2 percent, which added 6.4 million jobs to the economy. Pundits who had earlier predicted economic stagnation quickly pivoted, claiming the economy would have done even better if taxes had not been increased. For example, the Heritage Foundation, in a 1995 study, wrote: "The Heritage analysis indicates that, compared with how the economy would have performed without the 1993 tax legislation, Clinton's 1993 tax and budget plan will have: cost the economy $208 billion in output; cut the number of private jobs created by 1.2 million… and cut the value of business investment in durable goods by $42.5 billion."[8]

But even as Heritage doubled down on their gloomy predictions, the economy was on the brink of five more years of continued spectacular growth. From 1996 through 2000, real GDP grew 4.3 percent annually, putting 10.2 million more people to work.

Those new jobs also paid well. America's middle-class thrived under Clinton and enjoyed its largest income gains since the nineteen-sixties. After declining 7.5 percent from 1980 through 1992, real hourly wages increased six percent from 1992 through 2000. Growing wages helped America's middle-class increase their after-tax income from $37,600 in 1992 to $42,300 by 2000 (in 2020 dollars). The poor did better as well. After poverty rates increased from 13 to 14.8 percent from 1980 through 1992, under Clinton, poverty declined to 11.3 percent by 2000. Nor were the wealthy forgotten. During the Clinton years, the top one percent, helped by strong stock market gains, increased their after-tax income from $613,400 to $1,062,000.

Further confounding skeptics, after the Bush and Clinton tax increases, income tax revenues rose from an average of 7.7 percent of GDP between 1983 and 1990 to 8.1 percent between 1993 and 2000. During those periods total federal tax revenues increased from 17.1 to 18.2 percent of GDP.

Rising tax revenues during the nineteen-nineties, after what Clinton's political opponents derided as the largest tax increase in history, forced non-partisan economists to question the routine use of the Laffer Curve to condemn every tax increase.

Also wrong, was Newt Gingrich's prediction that any new tax income would just be spent for "bigger government, bigger bureaucracy [and] more programs." Federal spending from 1993 through 2000 averaged 19.0 percent of GDP, well below the 21.3 percent during the Reagan years when Gingrich came of age politically.

The combination of increased tax revenues and lower spending resulted in President Clinton's signature economic achievement and a truly historic accomplishment, a $559 billion budget surplus. Other Presidents had grown the economy, cut taxes or slashed inflation. But no President since Calvin Coolidge back in the Roaring Twenties had managed to string together four consecutive budget surpluses as Clinton did from 1998 through 2001. Not Eisenhower, not Nixon, and certainly not Reagan or Bush. During his eight years in office, Clinton reduced the gross national debt from 64.1 to 54.7 percent of GDP.

Clinton's economic policies were critical, but Clinton was also lucky. The nineteen-seventies were a perfect storm economically, with high unemployment, high inflation, and two oil shocks, which contributed to years of stagflation. In comparison, Clinton's eight years were a perfect summer day. The Cold War had ended, allowing reductions in defense spending. Baby Boomers, in their peak earning years, were generating large Social Security tax surpluses. A technology boom drove employment, corporate profits, and the stock market to record highs.

Clinton was proud of his historic debt reduction. "Those in the Republican Party," he boasted during a *Meet the Press* interview ten years after leaving office, "believe that they've talked a good game about balancing the budget, but the debt was quadrupled in the twelve years before I became President, and then we paid down the debt for four years, paid down $600 billion on the national debt, and then my budget was abandoned and they doubled the debt again."[9]

The Best Antipoverty Program

Second only to the economy, Clinton made welfare reform a major issue during his 1992 presidential campaign, promising to "end welfare as we have come to know it."[10] Welfare reform was hardly a new issue. Since President Johnson declared the War on Poverty in 1964, federal spending on income security, measured as a percentage of GDP, had steadily increased from 2.5 percent to 3.2 percent by 1992. Although the higher spending had helped reduce poverty rates from 19 to 15 percent during that period, many believed welfare spending to be too high.

Waste and fraud were often blamed. Years earlier, Ronald Reagan made welfare fraud a major issue during his 1976 presidential campaign. Reagan's stump speech included references to working people buying hamburgers while "strapping, young buck[s]" used food stamps to buy T-bone steaks.[11]

Reagan famously singled out one woman, the "Welfare Queen," as representative of the program's failure. "She used eighty names," Reagan told astonished campaign crowds, "thirty addresses, fifteen telephone numbers to collect food stamps, Social Security, veterans' benefits for four nonexistent deceased veteran husbands, as well as welfare. Her tax-free cash income alone has been running $150,000 a year."[12]

Reagan's Welfare Queen, first chronicled by the *Chicago Tribune*, was an actual person whose real name was Linda Taylor. The *Chicago Tribune* had written stories describing how Taylor had outrageously gamed the system, driving a Cadillac to the welfare office and collecting hundreds of thousands of dollars under her many aliases. One of Taylor's other scams was posing as Dr. Connie Walker, an open-heart surgeon driving a new Cadillac with an "Afri-Med" license plate. Taylor finally went to jail in 1978. Welfare fraud was one of her minor crimes. Later investigations suggested that, while posing as a nurse, she had kidnapped the Fronczak baby, an infamous 1964 kidnapping case, and likely murdered several people after bilking them out of thousands of dollars.[13]

Reagan has been accused of using racial dog-whistles (suggestive language to appeal to a particular faction) to win white votes. Many white Southerners, for example, interpreted "strapping young buck" to be a Black man. The accusations weren't unfounded. During both his 1980 and 1984 presidential campaigns, Imperial Wizard Bill Wilkinson of the Ku Klux Klan endorsed Reagan calling his campaign platform "pure Klan."[14]

But Reagan was right about welfare fraud, he was just focused on the wrong culprits. From 1981 through 1983, a federal task force resulted in 1,390 indictments for food stamp fraud.[15] But much of the fraud resulted from organized crime rings which found it easy to churn out counterfeit food stamps by the millions. Once paper food stamps were replaced with electronic vouchers, food stamp fraud declined substantially. By 1993, as Clinton took office, fraud was down to a few percent of the federal program.

The more substantial issue was the concern that welfare programs discouraged work; that benefits were handed out too freely to the chronically unemployed and marginally disabled.

After vetoing two earlier versions, on August 22, 1996 Clinton signed the Personal Responsibility and Work Opportunity Reconciliation Act. "This Act... requires work of welfare recipients," Clinton declared during the signing, "limits the time they can stay on welfare, and provides child-care and health care to help them make the move from welfare to work.... It demands personal responsibility and puts in place tough child support enforcement measures. It promotes family and protects children."[16] The Act placed strong emphasis on getting people off the welfare rolls and back to work. It remains the most comprehensive welfare reform since Johnson's Great Society legislation in 1964.

The Act helped to decrease welfare costs. From 1970 through 1996, an average of 3.2 percent of GDP was spent annually on federal welfare programs, primarily income security for the unemployed and disabled, housing assistance and food stamps. After the Act, from 1997 through 2019, federal welfare spending declined to 2.8 percent.

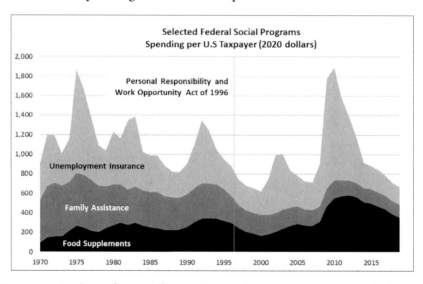

Clinton promised to reform welfare, with mixed success. Spending on family assistance and supplemental nutrition programs initially declined, but soon resumed their upward climb.   CONGRESSIONAL BUDGET OFFICE | U.S. BUREAU OF ECONOMIC ANALYSIS

Unfortunately, poverty remained stubbornly around 13 percent. In 1996, one in seven Americans were living in poverty. That year the poverty threshold for a family of four was $16,036, or about $26,500 in 2020 dollars. Poverty legislation specifically created to encourage personal responsibility and work opportunities, as the Act's name declares, should have drawn millions back into the workplace. It didn't. Starting in the mid nineteen-seventies, labor force participation had increased steadily, largely due to women joining the workforce. By 1996, 67 percent of eligible Americans were in the labor force, a historic high. That trend leveled off after Clinton signed the 1996 Act, and then began to decline starting in 2000. By 2019, labor force participation had declined to 63 percent. Part of the decline was due to Baby Boomers entering early retirement. But much of the decline was due to working-age men with limited educations dropping out of the labor force. According to a 2019 Congressional report, inflation-adjusted wages for men with earnings in the bottom 10 percent of the workforce declined 13.3 percent from 1979 through 2018.[17] For workers at the very bottom of the pay scale, the minimum wage, measured in 2020 dollars, during those years declined from $10.34 to $7.47, a 28 percent wage cut—hardly an incentive to rejoin the workforce.

The reduction in labor force participation has hurt the economy. If the labor force, as a percentage of the population, had remained at its 1996 level, ten million more Americans would have been working by 2019, adding over $1.0 trillion to the economy.[18]

For those who work, poor wages have forced millions of families, the working poor, to turn to government aid to supplement their earnings. A 2015 University of California study found that 56 percent of federal and state welfare spending is paid to working families and individuals and that less than half of total welfare goes to the unemployed and disabled. Welfare payments targeted at children, such as the Children's Health Insurance Program and food supplements, are overwhelmingly spent—83 percent by an Urban Institute estimate[19]—on families that have at least one member working.

For decades, the working poor had been forced to rely on welfare to supplement their low wages.[20] A 2013 University of California study found that 52 percent of all front-line fast-food workers were enrolled in one or more public assistance programs that cost taxpayers $7 billion annually.[21] Another analysis estimated that McDonald's alone cost taxpayers $1.2 billion annually.[22]

This wasn't always the case. In 1968, a family of four with one parent working full-time and the other half-time earned $35,700 measured in 2020 dollars, well above the $26,100 poverty level. But in 2020, our hard-working family with the $7.25 minimum wage earned only $21,800 putting them deeply in poverty. Yet, the United States was a far wealthier country in 2019 than it had been in 1968. Measured in 2020 dollars, per capita GDP increased from $27,100 in 1968 to $66,000 in 2019. How did this happen?

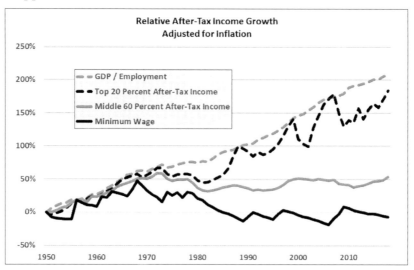

Productivity, measured as GDP divided by employment, has risen steadily. But starting about 1970, the resulting wealth largely flowed upward, leaving lower and middle-class incomes stagnant.   U.S. BUREAU OF ECONOMIC ANALYSIS | IRS STATISTICAL REPORTS OF INCOME | U.S. DEPARTMENT OF LABOR

Credit the Nobel laureate economist Milton Friedman. In 1962, Friedman wrote a landmark book, *Capitalism and Freedom*. In the book, Friedman declared that corporations have no social responsibility beyond increasing profits. Friedman provided corporations a simple, unequivocal yardstick for measuring success:

> There is one and only one social responsibility of business, to use its resources and engage in activities designed to increase its profits so long as it stays within the rules of the game, which is to say, engages in open and free competition without deception or fraud.[23]

Under the Friedman doctrine, the welfare of customers, employees, communities and the environment are secondary to maximizing shareholder returns through stock appreciation and dividends. Friedman propagated his doctrine more broadly in a September 13, 1970, *New York Times Magazine* article aptly entitled: "The Social Responsibility of Business is to Increase its Profits."

Profit maximization became such accepted corporate dogma that by the late nineteen-seventies the CEO of Burroughs, a major computer manufacturer at the time, could famously boast that Burroughs' tight-fisted corporate spending kept their locked-in customers "sullen, but not rebellious."[24] (This was during a period when computer software was proprietary, making it extremely difficult for users to change computer manufacturers.)

The singular focus on corporate profits propelled the upward shift in American wealth. America's middle-class was built in the postwar years from 1946 through 1972 when real, after-tax incomes increased from $25,800 (in 2020 dollars) to $44,400, an average annual increase of 2.2 percent. But after 1972, as Friedman's philosophy of profit maximization was adopted, middle-class incomes began a slow decline, falling to $43,000 by 2018 (the latest IRS data at this writing). The affluent (the top income quintile), on the other hand, thrived and enjoyed an increase in after-tax income from $118,500 in 1972 to $201,600 in 2018. The truly wealthy, the top one percent, did far better, growing their after-tax incomes in those same years from $333,000 to $1,193,000. Much of that new wealth came from stock appreciation and dividends driven by rising corporate profits.

Under the Friedman doctrine, Walmart, for example, had a fiduciary responsibility to pay its employees the lowest possible wage, even if it required that taxpayers supplement the pay of their employees through food and income supplements. But in 2015, Walmart broke with the Friedman doctrine when the company announced that it would raise wages for entry-level employees to $9.00 an hour and then to $10.00 by early 2016. Walmart executives exceeded their promise when the company raised the hourly wage for 1.2 million Walmart workers to $13.38 in January 2016. After decades of a singular focus on profits, Walmart's decision to balance the interests of shareholders and employees was historic.

On August 19, 2019, the Business Roundtable, an association of America's most powerful CEOs, abandoned the Friedman doctrine. That day it announced that 181 members had signed a statement declaring that CEOs should "commit to lead their companies for the benefit of all stakeholders—customers, employees, suppliers, communities and shareholders." Jamie Dimon, CEO of JPMorgan Chase and also Chairman of the Business Roundtable, summarized their decision: "The American dream is alive, but fraying. . . . These modernized principles reflect the business community's unwavering commitment to continue to push for an economy that serves all Americans."[25]

Time will tell. Two years later, an August 18, 2021 *Wall Street Journal* editorial reported: "Companies still have guidelines that explicitly align the interests of directors and stockholders... [sending] a clear signal that shareholder value is the objective that directors are expected to pursue."[26]

International Trade

"If goods don't cross borders, soldiers will," the nineteenth-century economist, Frederic Bastiat, warned.[27] Earlier, Adam Smith had promoted the economic benefits of free trade when he published *The Wealth of Nations* in 1776. "It is the maxim of every prudent master of a family," Smith wrote, "never to attempt to make at home what it will cost him more to make than to buy. . . . If a foreign country can supply us with a commodity cheaper than we ourselves can make it, better buy it of them with some part of the produce of our own industry, employed in a way in which we have some advantage."[28] In short, nations, like people, should focus on producing what they do best while acquiring from other nations the goods that those nations excel in producing. Even the renowned Adam Smith had his skeptics, though. It took two world wars to convince countries to adopt Smith's theory for open trade borders.

After World War I, the great industrial powers erected trade barriers to protect their farmers and industries. These barriers made it difficult for Germany to achieve the level of exports needed to meet its huge reparations burden. Economic and political turmoil resulted, leading to the rise of Nazism in the nineteen-twenties. Then, at the dawn of the Great Depression, the Smoot–Hawley Tariff Act precipitated an international trade war that further increased world tensions. More controversially, American trade embargoes following Japan's invasion of China—particularly of the American oil on which Japan depended—allowed Japan's ultra-nationalist military to justify their war against the United States.

Even before World War II had ended, the United States and Great Britain proposed the establishment of the International Trade Organization (ITO) to promote world trade. The ITO failed to emerge after the war, but in 1947, twenty-three nations signed the General Agreement on Tariffs and Trade (GATT) as a major step towards opening world trade. Ten years later, six nations—Belgium, France, West Germany, Italy, Luxembourg, and the Netherlands—established the European Economic Community (EEC) as the first step to a European Common Market. It was soon clear that a free-trading Europe was growing stronger and represented a rising trade threat to the United States.

If Europe could unite economically, why couldn't North America? Ronald Reagan answered that question during a campaign speech on November 13, 1979. Reagan proposed the establishment of a North American common market, stating: "Within the borders of this North American continent are the food, resources, technology, and undeveloped territory which, properly managed, could dramatically improve the quality of life of all its inhabitants.... A developing closeness among Canada, Mexico, and the United States—a North American accord—would permit achievement of that potential..."[29]

From the beginning, there was strong resistance to a North American trade pact. Canada and Mexico feared the United States would dominate the agreement. American trade unions predicted their jobs would migrate to lower-cost Mexico. Mexican farmers were concerned that subsidized American agricultural products would flood their market and drive them out of business. The "Zapatistas," named after the early twentieth-century Mexican revolutionary Emiliano Zapata, predicted that giant international corporations would appropriate ancestral Indian lands to build large commercial agricultural operations.

Despite widespread opposition, progress towards an agreement was slowly made over the next decade. In 1989, President Bush took a major step when he signed the Canada-U.S. Free Trade Agreement. Bush then opened discussions with Mexico. In 1992, Mexican President Salinas, Canadian Prime Minister Brian Mulroney, and President Bush signed the North American Free Trade Agreement (NAFTA) pending ratification by their respective legislatures. By 1993, as Clinton took office, the United States was anxious to lead the way in opening the world's markets. Clinton's first challenge was to convince Congress to ratify NAFTA. It would prove to be a major political battle.

During the preceding presidential election, Ross Perot, a self-made Texas billionaire, ran as an independent and made NAFTA a major campaign issue. Even then, the loss of American jobs to low-cost countries had become a political issue. In 1992, 41 percent of all goods imported into the United States were manufactured by American firms overseas.[30] In the second presidential debate, Perot argued:

> We have got to stop sending jobs overseas. It's pretty simple: If you're paying twelve, thirteen or fourteen dollars an hour for factory workers and you can move your factory south of the border, pay a dollar an hour for labor... have no health care—that's the most expensive single element in making a car—have no environmental controls, no pollution controls and no retirement, and you don't care about anything but making money, there will be a giant sucking sound going south.[31]

People laughed at Perot's prediction of a "giant sucking sound." Branded as a crackpot, Perot's prediction was mocked on both sides of the aisle. House Minority Leader Robert H. Michel labeled Perot the Groucho Marx of NAFTA.[32] Had Michel been a more informed film buff, he would have known that Groucho's humor was often insightful.

Overall, NAFTA enjoyed wide support from the business community, most economists, and all former Presidents. Former President Gerald Ford warned Congress on September 14, 1993, that "if you defeat NAFTA, you have to share the responsibility for increased immigration to the United States, where they want jobs that are presently being held by Americans. It's that cold-blooded and practical, and members of the House and Senate ought to understand that."[33] Free market economists were naturally confident that NAFTA would bring many benefits. Michael G. Wilson of the Heritage Foundation predicted on November 23, 1993 that "[NAFTA] will offer Americans cheaper goods and increase U.S. exports by making them more affordable for the rest of the world. Moreover, it will create an estimated 200,000 new jobs for Americans, reduce illegal immigration from Mexico, help tackle drug trafficking, strengthen Mexican democracy and human rights, and serve as a model for the rest of the world."[34]

After a year of debate, the NAFTA adherents won out. The bill passed the House, 234 to 200, and the Senate, 61 to 38. President Clinton signed NAFTA into law on December 8, 1993. "When I affix my signature to the NAFTA legislation a few moments from now," Clinton promised, "I do so with this pledge: to the men and women of our country who were afraid of these changes and found in their opposition to NAFTA an expression of that fear... the gains from this agreement will be your gains, too."

At its signing, NAFTA was the world's largest free trade agreement. NAFTA removed nearly all tariffs and most non-tariff barriers between Canada, Mexico, and the United States. Although NAFTA did not provide provisions for managing environmental and labor regulations, side agreements were quickly adopted to promote cooperation in these areas and enforce their provisions.

But as Perot had warned, NAFTA also removed barriers to foreign investment, making it easier for American companies to export factories, and jobs, to Canada and Mexico.

Two months after signing NAFTA, Clinton lifted the trade embargo with Vietnam that had been in place since 1975. Like Gerald Ford's decision to pardon the Vietnam War draft dodgers two decades earlier, many veterans were enraged, viewing Clinton's action as an insult to those who had fought and died in Vietnam. But not Senator John McCain, the war's most famous prisoner-of-war. McCain had traveled to Hanoi in 1985 to visit the infamous "Hanoi Hilton" where he had been imprisoned. For years, McCain advocated for reconciliation between the two countries, believing "war is the best lesson for peace,"[35] as one Vietnamese historian described McCain's advocacy.

Today, Vietnam is a major trading partner and America's closest ally in Southeast Asia. Both countries share a mutual interest in countering China's ambitions in East Asia. Secretary of State Mike Pompeo summarized the relationship in July 2020, declaring, "We've built a friendship on common interests, mutual respect, and bold resolve to overcome the past and look toward the future."[36]

On December 8, 1994, Clinton approved an agreement, known as the Uruguay Round, which established the signatories of the General Agreement on Tariffs and Trade as founding members of the World Trade Organization (WTO) in 1995. The WTO was chartered to negotiate, regulate, and adjudicate international agreements to ensure world trade "flows as smoothly, predictably, and freely as possible."[37] Today, the WTO is the largest international economic organization in the world—and arguably the most controversial. It's been that way almost from its inception. In 1999, an estimated 40,000 protesters nearly shut down the Third WTO Ministerial Conference in Seattle. The demonstrators claimed global trade was moving jobs overseas, trampling workers' rights, damaging the environment, and leading to the takeover of the global economy by rapacious multinational companies. It took two battalions of the National Guard to restore order. The protesters had chained themselves together at major intersections to stop traffic. Today's anti-globalists consider the Seattle protests, remembered today as the "Battle of Seattle," as one of the first major strikes against globalization.[38]

Shortly before leaving office in 2000, Clinton signed the U.S.-China Relations Act. The Act granted China normal trade relations with the United States contingent upon China's acceptance into the World Trade Organization. It was a controversial decision. An October 10, 2000 CNN news report summarized the arguments for and against the deal at the time:

> The ceremony capped years of negotiations with Beijing and an intense debate at home among the Clinton administration, business and labor interests.... U.S. business interests wanted the agreement in order to gain access to China's market of one-billion-plus people. But critics argued that such an agreement would reward a repressive

communist state, undermine the country's labor and environmental protections and cost jobs for U.S. workers.[39]

Concerns over lost U.S. jobs and China's rising power would drive America's trade debate years later and become a major plank of Donald Trump's presidential campaign.

Clinton's trade agreements with NAFTA, the WTO, and China quickly changed American trade, but not as expected. American exports slowed while imports grew. From 1974 through 1994, exports, adjusted for inflation, grew an average of 4.3 percent annually. Then, as the agreements came into effect, from 1995 through 2015, export growth slowed to 3.6 percent. During those same years, annual import growth increased from 3.8 to 4.1 percent. The result: America's trade deficit in goods jumped from $295 billion in 1995 to $832 billion in 2015 (both in 2020 dollars).

American manufacturing was severely affected. For two decades prior to 2000, manufacturing employment had held relatively steady, averaging 17.5 million workers. In 2001, manufacturing employment began a steep decline and hit a low of 11.5 million in 2010.

American companies, coupled with increased manufacturing productivity, are primarily responsible for the job losses. As Canada, Mexico, and China opened their borders, American companies eagerly established foreign operations to gain access to cheap labor and local markets.

Leading this trend was General Electric's CEO, Jack Welch. In 1999, *Fortune* magazine proclaimed Welch "Manager of the Century," after growing GE's profits and stock price to stratospheric levels.[40] A brilliant but ruthless manager, Welch explained his global business strategy to Lou Dobbs on *CNN Moneyline*. "We've never had a better opportunity to source joint ventures around the globe. . . . Ideally, you'd have every plant that you own on a barge to move with currencies and changes in the economy."[41] Little wonder GE employees called Welch "Neutron Jack" for eliminating people while leaving the buildings intact, just as a neutron bomb does.

The American business community embraced Welch's hard-nosed strategy which *Businessweek* summarized as:

GE's U.S. workforce has been shrinking for more than a decade as Welch has cut costs by shifting production and investment to lower-wage countries. Since 1986, the domestic workforce has plunged by nearly 50 percent, to 163,000, while foreign employment has nearly doubled, to 130,000.... GE has made clear its desire that its suppliers [also] move to Mexico.[42]

For globe-straddling, multinational companies, labor had become a mere commodity to be acquired at the lowest possible cost. And why not? One of America's most iconic companies, General Electric, felt no loyalty to American workers. In GE's ideal world, factories would be located on barges to move freely around the globe seeking cheap labor.

Tough on Crime

Violent crime increased sharply in the United States during the twentieth century. In 1900, according to the U.S. Department of Justice, the United States homicide rate was 1.2 murders per 100,000 persons[43], similar to England's 0.96 rate.[44] But England's homicide rate barely changed over the ensuing century, rising to only 1.11 by 1980, while the U.S. rate climbed inexorably to 5.3 in 1950 (after spiking during Prohibition), 8.3 in 1970, and 10.7 in 1980.

(Compared to the American West during the late nineteenth century, today's most violent cities are relatively tranquil. Murder rates per 100,000 persons back then were horrendous: Dodge City, Kansas—165, San Luis Obispo, California—228, Abilene, Texas—317, Deadwood, South Dakota—442, Monterey County, California—609.)[45]

By 1988, as Vice President Bush was running for President, violent crime had become a major national issue. Random shootings, home invasions, and drug wars had made Americans fearful. Every year, over 2,000 people, one every four hours, were murdered in New York City alone.

The Bush campaign capitalized on that fear by painting Bush's opponent, Michael Dukakis, as soft on crime. With Bush running fourteen points behind,[46] Bush's campaign manager Lee Atwater launched a desperate attack against Dukakis. The campaign's first television ad opened with a mug shot of a Black man with an afro and beard. "Dukakis not only opposes the death penalty," Atwater's ad ominously declared, "he allowed first-degree murderers to have weekend passes from prison. One was Willie

Horton, who murdered a boy in a robbery, stabbing him nineteen times. Despite a life sentence, Horton received ten weekend passes from prison, Horton fled, kidnapped a young couple, stabbing the man and repeatedly raping his girlfriend..."[47] For five months, right up to the election, Atwater's campaign relentlessly hammered Dukakis. "By the time we're finished," Atwater had promised, "they're going to wonder whether Willie Horton is Dukakis' running mate."[48]

It worked. Dukakis lost the popular vote to Bush by nearly eight percent. Few today remember Dukakis's actual running mate, Lloyd Bentsen, but they remember Willie Horton.

Lee Atwater died of brain cancer three years later. Before his death, Atwater expressed regret for the Willie Horton campaign in a *Life* magazine article. "In 1988, fighting Dukakis," Atwater admitted, "I said that I 'would strip the bark off the little bastard' and 'make Willie Horton his running mate.' I am sorry for both statements: the first for its naked cruelty, the second because it makes me sound racist, which I am not."[49] During the last weeks of his life, Atwater may have come to regret the cruel campaign he ran against Dukakis. But it worked and ever since, his Willie Horton attack ad has set the standard for negative political campaigning.

Four years later, Bush was running for reelection. Focused on defending his broken promise not to raise taxes, Bush allowed Bill Clinton to seize the tough-on-crime mantle. Clinton grabbed it. Standing on the steps of New York City Hall, Clinton declared, "We cannot take our country back until we take our neighborhoods back. Four years ago, this crime issue was used to divide America. I want to use it to unite America. I want to be tough on crime and good for civil rights. You can't have civil justice without order and safety."[50]

Clinton kept his word. On September 13, 1994, he signed the Violent Crime Control and Law Enforcement Act, which to this day remains the largest crime bill ever enacted. It included more than a dozen major provisions: a ten-year ban on military-style assault weapons; expansion of the federal death penalty; tightened firearm sales; stiffer sentences for gang, drug, and immigration-related crimes; adult prosecution for adolescents thirteen and older for certain violent crimes; stronger laws against sexual offenders; truth-in-sentencing to guarantee offenders would serve at least 85 percent of their sentence; and the "three strikes" law that mandated life imprisonment without parole for federal offenders with three or more serious convictions. The bill also provided federal grants to hire 100,000 community police officers as well as to construct additional prisons.[51]

The bill was sponsored by Senator Joe Biden, who attempted to balance tough-on-crime provisions with prevention and rehabilitation programs. Much of the Senate disagreed, believing that Biden's version of the crime bill wasn't tough enough. Forty-one senators wrote to Senator Robert Dole, the Senate Minority Leader, complaining the bill was too weak. The letter read in part:

> We want to pass a tough crime bill. . . . Unfortunately, in its current form, the [proposed bill] is seriously deficient in several important areas. The [bill], for example, still earmarks billions of dollars for wasteful social programs. It also fails to include a number of important tough-on-crime proposals adopted by the Senate last November. . . . The American people deserve the toughest crime bill possible. We should not lose this opportunity to fix what is wrong. . . and make the crime bill even stronger.[52]

Expectations were low as Clinton signed the bill. *The New York Times* grumbled that Clinton had been too soft on crime. "The $30 billion crime bill signed into law today by President Clinton," the *Times* opined, "responds to the country's rising fear of crime, but law-enforcement experts contend that it is a symbolic swipe that does not go far enough toward stopping the kind of street violence that is increasingly haunting America."[53]

The critics were wrong. Violent crime—murder, rape, robbery, and aggravated assault—began to fall, significantly. Violent crime had soared five-fold over the prior thirty years to 747 violent crimes per 100,000 of the population. Few predicted crime would slow, much less abruptly reverse, but that's what happened. By 2000, six years after Clinton signed the crime bill, violent crime had fallen by a quarter. And kept falling, to 369 by 2018, half its 1993 level and the lowest since 1970.[54]

But even as violent crime rates were dropping, prisons remained full. Americans had demanded a tough crime bill. And they got it. Stiffer sentences, three strikes, and minimum sentencing laws put more criminals in prison for longer, often lifetime, sentences. While crime rates dropped by half from 1993 through 2018, prison incarcerations fell only 18 percent. Blacks bore most of the burden.

Black incarceration rates have historically been higher than for whites. The 1994 crime bill made it worse. In 1993, the year before Clinton signed the crime bill, the ratio of Black to white violent crime was 5.4[55], while their incarceration rate was 6.9 times higher than whites.[56] Blacks, per capita, committed 5.4 more violent crimes than whites, yet their incarceration rates were nearly seven times higher. By 2018, the ratio of Black to white violent crime had fallen to 3.7, yet Black incarceration remained nearly as high as in 1993 at 6.1 times that of whites.

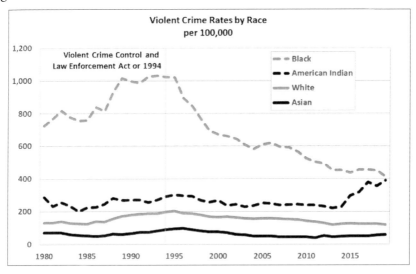

Black violent crime dropped significantly after the 1994 crime bill sponsored by President Clinton and Senator Biden. Criminologists disagree on whether the crime bill or other factors were responsible for the reduction.   U.S. DEPARTMENT OF JUSTICE

Did imprisoning criminals longer, especially Blacks, contribute to the decline in violent crime after 1993? Criminologists disagree. James Wilson, emeritus professor at UCLA, supported tough sentencing. "Putting people in prison," Wilson declared, "is the single most important thing we've done to decrease crime."[57] New York University's Brennan Center for Justice disagreed. "Increased incarceration has had little effect on the drop in violent crime in the past twenty-four years. Instead, new technologies allowing police to better identify crime patterns and target resources has, along with additional police officers, played a role in bringing down crime in cities."[58]

Although violent crime has fallen steeply since its peak in the nineteen-nineties, the United States remains, by far, the most violent nation in the developed world. That's especially true for murder. The intentional homicide rate in 2016 for the United States was 5.35 per 100,000, far surpassing Canada at 1.68, France at 1.35, Germany and the United Kingdom at 1.2, Italy at 0.67, and Japan at 0.28.[59]

Many blame America's high murder rate on the nation's gun culture. There are, after all, 1.2 guns for every man, woman, and child in the United States.[60] Having a gun handy certainly makes impulsive murders easier. Yet 27 percent of all murders are committed without guns, primarily by knives and blunt instruments. Five percent of American murderers manage to kill their victims without a weapon: by strangulation, with their fists, by kicking or pushing their victim down stairs, off buildings, or into moving vehicles.[61] Take away America's guns, and the United States murder rate would still exceed every other developed nation except Canada.

Others blame interracial crime. Politicians, over the years, have stoked interracial fears, from the Black Willie Horton to Hispanic MS-13 gangs. Most murders, though, occur within the same race or ethnic group. [The United States consists of five races: white, Black, American Indian, Asian and Pacific Islander. Hispanics are an ethnic group and may be either white or Black.] Eighty-one percent of whites are killed by other whites, 16 percent by Blacks, and three percent by either American Indians or Asians. Eighty-nine percent of Blacks are killed by other Blacks, eight percent by whites.[62] Recent claims that Hispanics are murderers and rapists are unfounded. Although Hispanics in 2018 constituted 18.3 percent of the U.S. population, they committed just 17.6 percent of all violent crimes.[63]

Twenty-five years ago, violent crime was a major national issue. Politicians on both sides of the aisle were competing to be the toughest on crime. Thirty-eight senators voted against the 1994 crime bill because it wasn't tough enough.[64] Hillary Clinton condemned street hooligans as "super-predators" with "no conscience, no empathy... we have to bring them to heel."[65] Lee Atwater's Willie Horton campaign helped turn Bush's fourteen-point deficit into an eight-point popular vote win.

By 2019, violent crime had fallen to fifty-year lows. With violent crime far down, the focus turned to America's high incarceration rates, especially for Blacks. Many blame Bill Clinton and Joe Biden, the crime bill's primary proponents.[66] They're probably right. In 1994, nearly everyone was calling for tougher prison sentences. But then, do Clinton and Biden also deserve credit for the many thousands of lives saved as violent crime fell to historic lows after the passage of their crime bill?

The Ruby Ridge and Waco Sieges

During the early nineteen-nineties, most Americans wanted the government to get tougher fighting crime. But two events convinced a segment of Americans that a tyrannical government was the greater threat.

In August 1992, hundreds of law enforcement and federal agents converged on the Ruby Ridge, Idaho cabin of Randy Weaver after Weaver had repeatedly failed to appear for trial on illegal weapons charges. Weaver and his family were religious fundamentalists who had been peacefully living in their isolated cabin without electricity or running water since 1984. The siege lasted for eleven days including a firefight during which a U.S. Marshall was killed. Weaver only surrendered after his wife and son were killed by FBI snipers. Tried for murder and conspiracy, Weaver was only convicted for failing to appear for trial on the original weapons charge.[67]

Six months later, a massive federal siege led to far more deaths. On February 28, 1993, federal agents raided the Waco, Texas compound of David Koresh, the founder and leader of the Branch Davidian Christian sect. The charges, like at Ruby Ridge, were federal firearms violations. There were also rumors that Koresh was sexually abusing young girls. Four federal agents and six Davidians were killed in the raid. A fifty-one-day siege ensued, watched on television by millions around the world. Koresh eventually announced he and his followers would surrender once he had transcribed a message he believed God had sent him. But the FBI, impatient after 754 phone calls spent negotiating with Koresh, chose to end the siege on April

19 by driving two armored vehicles into the compound. Fires erupted that soon engulfed the building. As the siege ended, seventy-six Davidians, including twenty-five children, were dead, consumed by fire and self-inflicted gunshots.[68] Most Americans viewed these events as human tragedies, but a few considered them confirmation of the federal government's growing tyranny.

The federal government's siege of the Branch Davidian compound in Waco, Texas resulted in 76 deaths, including 25 children. The siege confirmed, for some Americans, growing government tyranny.   GREGORY SMITH/GETTY

Two years to the day after federal agents stormed the Branch Davidians' Waco compound, on April 19, 1995, Timothy McVeigh detonated a bomb-laden truck in front of the Murrah Federal Building in Oklahoma City. The blast killed 168 people and wounded hundreds more. It remains the greatest act of home-grown terrorism in U.S. history. McVeigh, a decorated veteran of the First Gulf War, had been radicalized by the federal actions at Ruby Ridge and, especially, Waco.

Shortly before his execution, McVeigh sent a letter to Fox News explaining his twisted justification for the bombing. It reads, in part:

> The bombing was a retaliatory strike; a counter-attack, for the cumulative raids (and subsequent violence and damage) that federal agents had participated in over the preceding years (including, but not limited to, Waco.) From the formation of such units as the FBI's "Hostage Rescue" and other assault teams amongst federal agencies during the '80's; culminating in the Waco incident, federal actions grew increasingly militaristic and violent, to the point where

at Waco, our government—like the Chinese—was deploying tanks against its own citizens.[69]

In 1964, based on Gallup polls, 77 percent of Americans trusted their government to do the right thing. That trust began to deteriorate in the nineteen-sixties with the Vietnam War, followed by the Watergate scandal in the nineteen-seventies and the Iran-Contra scandal in the nineteen-eighties. The government sieges of Ruby Ridge and Waco further disillusioned many Americans. By June 1994, public trust in government had fallen to 17 percent, a postwar low. Public trust would never again approach its earlier, far higher levels.[70]

A Lost Opportunity

As President Clinton entered office, Russia was emerging from the once-powerful Union of Soviet Socialist Republics (USSR). A smaller, weaker, and humbled country, Russia renamed itself the Russian Federation. Russia's economy had collapsed, with its GDP declining from $517 billion in 1990 to $196 billion at the end of the decade in 1999,[71] only slightly larger than Indiana's gross state product.[72] Military spending plummeted, falling to $6.5 billion by 1999, just two percent of America's military budget and on a par with the Netherlands.[73]

With the collapse of the Soviet Union and Russia's seeming drift towards irrelevance, there were optimistic expectations of a peace dividend. The cost of fighting the Cold War had been immense. From 1947 through 1991, the United States spent $20.8 trillion on defense measured in 2020 dollars. By comparison, World War II had cost a mere $4.0 trillion.[74]

America had an opportunity to redirect much of its military spending to domestic purposes such as schools, hospitals, and social programs. President Eisenhower had dreamed of this in his *Cross of Iron* speech back in 1953: "Every gun that is made, every warship launched, every rocket fired signifies, in the final sense, a theft from those who hunger and are not fed, those who are cold and are not clothed..."[75]

There was good reason to be hopeful. Five years after World War II, America's real military spending, even while fighting the Korean War, had declined by 80 percent from its 1944 peak. But after forty years fighting the

Cold War, America's military, armaments industry, and lawmakers could not adjust to the new reality that the United States no longer faced an existential foe. As the Cold War ended, America's defense spending, measured in 2020 dollars, declined a mere 14 percent, from $510 billion in 1991 to $438 billion in 1996.[76]

Russian President Boris Yeltsin and President Bill Clinton during Yeltsin's 1995 visit to the United States. Clinton encouraged NATO expansion eastward, threatening Russia's borders, and cooling East-West relations.   ITAR-TASS NEWS AGENCY/ALAMY

Eisenhower had foreseen this. "We must guard against the acquisition of unwarranted influence," Eisenhower warned as he was leaving the presidency, "whether sought or unsought, by the military-industrial complex. The potential for the disastrous rise of misplaced power exists and will persist..."[77] Thirty years after his prophetic warning, a peace dividend on the scale achieved after World War II was impossible. America's military was now composed of volunteer-based professionals, not conscripts anxious to get back to civilian life. Its armaments were manufactured by a $100 billion defense industry that had become the world's largest exporter of weapons. Finally, the United States now viewed itself as the world's peacekeeper with hundreds of military installations around the world. All these factors contributed to a continuation, rather than a de-escalation, of America's Cold War mentality and associated military spending.

With the end of the Cold War, the North American Treaty Organization (NATO) had lost its original mission. But rather than disband or even just reduce its footprint, a 1991 NATO strategy paper concluded that "the changed environment offers new opportunities for the Alliance to frame its strategy within a broad approach to security."[78]

New opportunities. Like all bureaucracies, NATO was seeking not only to justify its existence, but also new opportunities to expand. NATO could have accepted Russia as a member, as it had Germany after World War II. But it did not. Should its erstwhile adversary become a part of NATO, and no serious threats on the horizon, who exactly would NATO be protecting its members from?

The 1991 NATO paper represented the international organization's second missed opportunity to engage the Soviets. The first had occurred forty years earlier. In 1954, the Soviet Union, a World War II ally of the United States, had applied for NATO membership.[79] But NATO rebuffed the Soviet request and instead, a year later, invited West Germany as a member. As part of its membership, West Germany was allowed to rebuild its military, a move Moscow considered highly threatening. The Soviets had hardly forgotten that a little over a decade earlier, Germany's invasion of Russia had resulted in the deaths of an estimated twenty-five million Russians. So, it was little surprise that two weeks after West Germany joined NATO, Russia and its six satellite states signed the Warsaw Pact as the Soviet Union's counterbalance to NATO and the threat of a German resurgence.

NATO's 1954 rebuff of the Soviets was not the first time Western Europe had rejected Soviet overtures. Russia's estrangement with the West can be traced back to April 16, 1939. That day, Soviet Premier Josef Stalin proposed forming a triple alliance that consisted of the USSR, Great Britain, and France to counter Germany's territorial ambitions. Stalin's proposal had a solid historical precedent: the three nations had been allies in World War I against Germany. But Neville Chamberlain, Britain's Prime Minister, wasn't interested. Winston Churchill disagreed and urged Chamberlain to accept Stalin's offer. "Ten or twelve days have already passed since the Russian offer was made..." Churchill warned in a May 4 Parliament speech:

> There is no means of maintaining an eastern front against Nazi aggression without the active aid of Russia. Russian interests are deeply concerned in preventing Herr Hitler's designs on Eastern Europe. It should still be possible to range all the states and peoples from the Baltic to the Black Sea in one solid front against a new outrage of invasion. Such a front, if established in good heart, and with resolute and efficient military arrangements, combined with the strength of the Western Powers, may yet confront Hitler, Goering, Himmler, Ribbentrop, Goebbels and company with forces the German people would be reluctant to challenge.[80]

Chamberlain remained unmoved. After months of failed diplomatic efforts with Britain, the frustrated Soviets signaled to Berlin it was open to a proposal from Germany. Unlike the British, the Germans moved quickly. Three weeks after their first meeting, on August 23, 1939, the Soviet Union and Germany signed a non-aggression pact. With the USSR now aligned with Germany, Hitler invaded Poland a week later, on September 1. World War II had begun.[81]

One of history's great questions is what would have been the outcome if Chamberlain had agreed to Stalin's triple alliance proposal? Declassified Soviet documents released in 2008 document that the Soviets intended to commit "120 infantry divisions (each with some 19,000 troops), 16 cavalry divisions, 5,000 heavy artillery pieces, 9,500 tanks and up to 5,500 fighter aircraft and bombers on Germany's borders in the event of war in the west."[82] Such a huge force on Germany's eastern front may well have deterred Hitler from invading Poland, the spark that led to World War II.

Unfortunately, as happened in 1939 and again in 1954, the West rebuffed Russia as the Cold War ended. Rather than embracing the struggling country, NATO viewed the Soviet Union's collapse as a recruiting opportunity and welcomed the Czech Republic, Hungary and Poland in 1999.

Russia bitterly viewed NATO's recruitment of its former Warsaw Pact partners not only as a threat, but a broken promise made by the United

States and its European allies. As part of the 1990 agreement to the reunification of East and West Germany, declassified documents strongly suggest that Gorbachev was promised NATO would not expand "as much as a thumb's width further to the east" of Germany.[83] Gorbachev claims he was so confident of the personal promises made by President George H.W. Bush, West German Chancellor Helmut Kohl, French President Francois Mitterrand, British Prime Minister Margaret Thatcher, and others, he didn't believe it necessary to include the promise of non-expansion in the reunification agreement.[84]

In 1946, George F. Kennan predicted the Soviet Union's global ambitions leading to the formation of NATO in 1949. In 1997, he urged against NATO recruiting former Soviet bloc countries. His advice was ignored.   AP PHOTO/RIETHAUSEN

President Clinton, though, didn't feel constrained by the promises of the Bush administration, if indeed they were made. A year after taking office, during a speech in Prague, Clinton asserted: "The question is no longer whether NATO will take on new members, but when and how."[85] Clinton was pursuing a dubious dual-prong strategy of promoting a Partnership for Peace program with Russia while courting Russia's former allies with NATO membership.

America's most respected Cold War diplomat, George F. Kennan, was strongly opposed to NATO's eastward expansion. No U.S. diplomat understood the Soviet psyche better than Kennan. In 1946, while stationed in Moscow, Kennan had sent his famous "Long Telegram" to the State Department condemning the Soviet leadership and predicting the Soviet Union's expansion into Eastern Europe. A year later, in *Foreign Affairs*, he published one of the most renowned articles in American diplomatic history, describing the Soviet threat as "a fluid stream which moves constantly, wherever it is permitted to move, toward a given goal [of worldwide communist domination]."[86] The article outlined a strategy of containment that directly led, two years later, to the formation of NATO in 1949.

Now, with the Soviet Union defeated, Kennan argued against NATO expansion to the east, a move he believed would threaten Russia and reignite East-West tensions. Writing in *The New York Times,* Kennan, in a 1997 article as prescient as his *Foreign Affairs* article fifty years earlier, predicted:

> Expanding NATO would be the most fateful error of American policy in the entire post-cold-war era. Such a decision may be expected to inflame the nationalistic, anti-Western and militaristic tendencies in Russian opinion; to have an adverse effect on the development of Russian democracy; to restore the atmosphere of the cold war to East-West relations, and to impel Russian foreign policy in directions decidedly not to our liking... And it is doubly unfortunate considering the total lack of any necessity for this move.[87]

Kennan's advice was ignored. On May 2, 1998, after the Senate had ratified NATO's eastward expansion, the ninety-four-year-old Kennan, in a *New York Times* interview, predicted: "I think it is the beginning of a new cold war. I think the Russians will gradually react quite adversely and it will affect their policies. I think it is a tragic mistake. There was no reason for this whatsoever. No one was threatening anybody else."[88]

Kennan was, unfortunately, just as prophetic as he had been in 1946. As NATO began to absorb Russia's former allies, Russia quickly reversed its ten-year decline in defense spending and began to rebuild its military.

On January 1, 2000, after a decade of domestic turmoil, international humiliation, and as an expansionist NATO threatened Russia, President Boris Yeltsin, resigned, appointing Vladimir Putin as his successor. A former KGB officer, Cold War Warrior, and ardent Russian patriot, Putin shrewdly positioned himself as the Russian version of Ronald Reagan as he set out to restore pride, confidence, and a sense of destiny to his dispirited nation. And to rebuild the military. During his May 7, 2000 inauguration, Putin's honor guard, rich in symbolism, wore uniforms from the Patriotic War of 1812 to remind Russians of their victory over Napoleon's army. During his speech, Putin proclaimed his ambitions for Russia. "We want our Russia," Putin declared, "to be a free, prosperous, flourishing, strong and civilized country, a country that its citizens are proud of and that is respected internationally."[89]

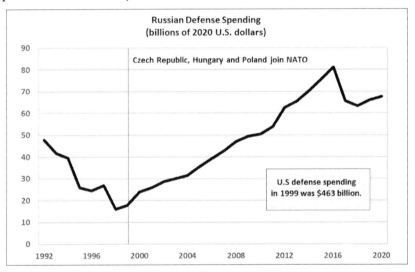

After declining for nearly a decade, Russian defense spending began to increase after three former Soviet Bloc countries joined NATO. Nine months later, Vladimir Putin became the acting Russian President.   STOCKHOLM INTERNATIONAL PEACE RESEARCH INSTITUTE

Years later, Sergei Karaganov, a prominent Russian political scientist, summarized Moscow's view of the "victors' peace" dictated by the West after the collapse of the Soviet Union:

> The West has consistently sought to expand its zone of military, economic and political influence through NATO and the [European Union]. Russian interests and objections were flatly ignored. Russia was treated like a defeated power, though we did not see ourselves as defeated. A softer version of the Treaty of Versailles was imposed on the country.[90]

President Truman's policies after World War II turned Germany and Japan into two of America's greatest allies. President Reagan's diplomacy helped end the Cold War. President Bush had patiently overseen the collapse of the Soviet Bloc and the reunification of Germany. But President Clinton let Russia slip away.

The Clinton Impeachment

The tragic pursuit of an obsession is one of literature's great themes. In Victor Hugo's *Les Misèrables*, Inspector Javert spends twenty years pursuing Jean Valjean, convicted for stealing a loaf of bread. After finally capturing Valjean, Javert drowns himself in the River Seine, disillusioned when he finally realizes Valjean's humanity and his own cruelty. Hermann Melville, in *Moby Dick,* recounts Captain Ahab's maniacal pursuit of a great white whale. After pursuing the whale across the world's oceans, Ahab and every member of his crew, save one, perish. And every movie-goer knows the fate of Captain Quint and his fanatical pursuit of a great white shark.

Bill Clinton had his own obsessive pursuer: Kenneth Starr. Like Inspector Javert, Starr spent years pursuing his quarry.

In 1978, Bill and Hillary Clinton were an up-and-coming couple in Little Rock, Arkansas. Bill was the thirty-two-year-old Arkansas Attorney General and Hillary was the first female associate at the Rose Law Firm, the oldest law firm west of the Mississippi. Together the Clintons were earning $51,000, over $200,000 in 2020 dollars. Relatively affluent, the Clintons partnered with their long-time friends James and Susan McDougal to form the Whitewater Development Corporation. Whitewater intended to develop vacation properties along the White River in the Ozark Mountains.

Later that year, Bill Clinton was elected Governor of Arkansas, the youngest in the nation. Busy with their careers, the Clintons left Whitewater's management to James and Susan McDougal. The venture soon failed due to the development's poor location and the crippling mortgage rates of the late nineteen-seventies. From the beginning, Whitewater's finances were murky. Hillary Clinton could only say they had "lost a bunch of money" on the failed project.[91]

Ten years later, Clinton was running for President. On March 8, 1992, *The New York Times* ran a story questioning the Clintons' business dealings related to Whitewater and Madison Guaranty, a savings and loan association founded by James McDougal after Whitewater's failure.[92] Although the issues raised in the *Times* story never threatened Clinton's presidential campaign, they also never went away.

In June 1993, Vincent Foster was found dead in a Washington D.C. park. Foster, a fellow Arkansan, had been Deputy White House Counsel and the caretaker of the Clintons' Whitewater documents. Although Foster's death was ruled a suicide, rumors soon surfaced that Foster had been murdered to cover up the Clintons' Whitewater dealings.

Clinton asked Attorney General Janet Reno to appoint a special prosecutor to investigate the claims of Whitewater fraud. In January 1994, Reno appointed Robert Fiske, a respected private-practice attorney to investigate Whitewater and Foster's death. On June 30, Fiske released his initial report, which found the Clintons blameless and Foster's death to be a suicide.

Six weeks later, a three-judge panel replaced Fiske with Kenneth Starr, a former federal appeals court judge. The panel was concerned that Fiske, appointed by Clinton's Attorney General, had worked under a conflict of interest.

Over the next four years, Starr's investigation expanded far beyond Whitewater to include the firing of White House travel office employees; the misuse of FBI files; the Clintons' interactions with Madison Guaranty while Bill Clinton was Arkansas Governor; a sexual harassment lawsuit filed by Paula Jones, a former Arkansas state government employee; and, finally, an affair between Clinton and Monica Lewinsky, a White House intern.

Clinton denied having sexual relations with Lewinsky, but Starr threatened the young intern with imprisonment if she didn't testify. In the end, every sordid detail came out regarding the affair between the President and Lewinsky.

On September 9, 1998, Starr issued his long-awaited report. Uploaded to the Internet, twenty million Americans suddenly developed an interest in the arcane dealings of the federal government. The 453-page report dealt almost exclusively with the Lewinsky affair, in great and often salacious detail. Starr's report was as much a bodice-ripping potboiler as it was a legal document mentioning "sex" and related words 590 times.

After five years of investigation, the Starr Report recommended eleven grounds for impeachment. Whitewater was never mentioned. Every charge was based on Clinton's attempts to keep the affair secret—for his political survival but also to spare his wife and young daughter, the humiliation they would surely suffer. An understandable, if unlawful, effort by a husband and father.

The House voted to impeach Clinton on grounds of perjury to a grand jury (228–206) and obstruction of justice (221–212). Clinton was only the second President to be impeached. The first was Andrew Johnson in 1868, who had attempted to remove his Secretary of War without the Congressional consent required at the time. Johnson barely survived; he was acquitted in the Senate by one vote.

On February 12, 1999, the Senate voted on the two articles of impeachment. Both votes fell far short of the two-thirds majority necessary to remove Clinton from office. Shortly afterward, CNN reported that the Starr and four related investigations had cost $79.3 million ($123 million in 2020 dollars).[93] After years of investigation, neither Bill nor Hillary Clinton was ever charged with a Whitewater-related crime.

At the end of *Les Misèrables,* Inspector Javert drowns himself when he realizes his long pursuit had been morally wrong. Clinton's pursuer was hardly that remorseful. But fate turned the tables in an ironic twist. Years later, Kenneth Starr, by then president of Baylor University, was fired by the school's board of trustees after an outside investigation found that "every level of Baylor's administration" had largely ignored accusations by at least seventeen women of sexual assault by the school's football players, including four instances of gang rape.[94]

A Mixed Legacy

Bill Clinton's 1992 presidential campaign had a simple theme: "It's the economy, stupid." Once elected, Clinton remained steadfast in his economic focus. "This is not an ordinary time," President Clinton declared in his February 17, 1993 speech to Congress, "and for all the many tasks that require our attention, I believe tonight one calls on us to focus, to unite, and to act. And that is our economy. For more than anything else, our task tonight as Americans is to make our economy thrive again."[95] Clinton set four major objectives during his speech: shift the economy from consumption to investment; honor work; reduce federal deficits; and cut government spending.

Clinton delivered, with a few qualifiers, on all four promises.

Under Clinton, non-residential business investment climbed from 11.4 percent of GDP in 1992 to 14.6 percent by 2000 at the end of Clinton's term. Under Reagan and Bush, it had fallen from 14.7 percent to 11.4 percent.

President Clinton's Personal Responsibility and Work Opportunity Act of 1996 permanently slashed welfare rolls to encourage work. But labor participation rates later declined and average poverty, measured over decades, remained unchanged hovering around 13 percent.

Clinton did more than reduce federal deficits. His administration ran four years of budget surpluses, the longest sustained period of budget surpluses since Calvin Coolidge was President.

Lastly, Clinton kept a promise few Presidents ever manage. He shrank government. The Executive Branch workforce was reduced from 2.2 million in 1992 to 1.8 million as Clinton was leaving office. Federal spending, as a percent of GDP, averaged two percent below Reagan and Bush, although much of the decline was due to defense cuts.

Clinton's success in hitting his economic objectives evokes Babe Ruth's famous home run during the 1932 World Series. Ruth, raising two fingers, (allegedly) pointed to center field, then hit a long, arcing home run over the fence into the bleachers. Even the opposing Chicago Cubs had to give Ruth credit that day. But there's little sportsmanship in politics. As Clinton was leaving the presidency, Senator Trent Lott declared: "For Bill Clinton to be taking credit for this economic boom we're experiencing is like the rooster taking credit for the sunrise."[96]

While Clinton handed George W. Bush a bright economic outlook, three other developments during Clinton's presidency hinted at a darker future.

On February 26, 1993, a terrorist bomb placed in the underground parking lot of the World Trade Center killed six people and wounded a thousand others. In 1996, nineteen U.S. Air Force personnel were killed during the bombing of the Khobar Towers apartment complex in Dhahran, Saudi Arabia. And in 1998, the American embassies in Kenya and Tanzania were bombed in simultaneous attacks that killed 224. The bombings occurred on August 7, eight years to the day that American troops first entered Saudi Arabia.[97] After living with the threat of nuclear annihilation during the Cold War, these sporadic attacks never garnered America's full attention. That would change on September 11, 2001 after 3,000 innocent people were killed by nineteen radical Islamists less than eight months after Clinton left office.

After the collapse of the Soviet Union, the United States encouraged the expansion of NATO eastward threatening the borders of Russia. After a feckless decade of economic collapse, international humiliation, and NATO expansion, Boris Yeltsin appointed Vladimir Putin the President of Russia. Putin, a former KGB officer and ardent Russian patriot, promised to restore Russia's rightful role in the world.

As Clinton ended his presidency, America's unchallenged military, its booming economy, innovative technology, and influential culture were unmatched in the world. Newly-elected George W. Bush surely believed his presidency would preside over a period of prosperity and peace. Unfortunately, that would not be the case. The worst foreign attack on American soil since Pearl Harbor, the worst economic collapse since the Great Depression and the longest war in America's history awaited.

George W. Bush

✦

January 20, 2001 – January 20, 2009

> I ask you to uphold the values of America and remember why so many have come here. We are in a fight for our principles, and our first responsibility is to live by them. No one should be singled out for unfair treatment or unkind words because of their ethnic background or religious faith.[1]

During the 2000 presidential campaign, both George W. Bush and Al Gore knew that the next President would inherit the strongest economy in decades. GDP was growing nearly four percent annually. Middle-class incomes were growing at an annual rate of three percent after years of stagnation. Higher wages were drawing millions of new workers into the labor force; the labor force participation rate was at an all-time high of 67.1 percent. The S&P 500 stock index had increased 335 percent over the prior decade, its largest ten-year increase ever recorded. And the federal government was running its largest budget surpluses in seventy years.

"Massive surpluses and retirement of Treasury debt are 'baked in the cake' almost no matter what the economy does over the next ten years," is how the normally guarded economists at Credit Suisse First Boston described the economic outlook.[2] Even the dour Congressional Budget Office was feeling cheerful, stating in a January 1, 2000 report: "The budgetary picture is a bright one. Between 2001 and 2010, accumulated surpluses are projected to total $3.2 trillion...."[3]

Like two dogs tugging on a bone, the candidates argued over what to do with the growing budget surpluses that President Clinton had handed them. Gore proposed using part of the surpluses to improve education, healthcare, and environmental protections while devoting the remainder to reducing the federal debt. Bush argued it would be possible to significantly cut taxes, build a national missile defense program and still leave plenty of money to reduce the debt.[4]

Bush won the election by a scant five electoral votes after the Supreme Court ruled in his favor over contested Florida ballots. It was the smallest electoral margin since Rutherford B. Hayes won by a single vote in 1876.[5]

As he entered the White House, Bush surely was feeling lucky. In 1994, in his first political race, he had won the Texas governorship after defeating the popular incumbent, Ann Richards; in 1998, Bush sold his share of the Texas Rangers baseball team for a $14.3 million profit; and then, won the presidency when the Supreme Court ruled in his favor. After an unbroken string of good fortune, Bush never imagined his presidency would begin and end with two historic and tragic crises: the worst attack on American soil since Pearl Harbor and a financial crisis second only to the Great Depression.

The War on Terror

Early on December 7, 1941, hundreds of Japanese fighters launched a surprise attack against the naval base at Pearl Harbor, Hawaii. Over 2,400 American sailors, soldiers and civilians died that day. It was the worst foreign attack on American soil in the nation's history. Hawaii, though, is 2,500 miles off America's continental shores. Isolated by two oceans, bordered by friendly neighbors and protected by the world's strongest military, Americans believed it inconceivable that the United States mainland would ever suffer a similarly devastating attack.

They were wrong. In 1941, it took the mighty Japanese Navy to inflict death and destruction on American soil. Yet on September 11, 2001, nineteen Al-Qaeda terrorists inflicted an even more deadly attack when they hijacked four civilian airliners and crashed them into the World Trade Center, the Pentagon, and the Pennsylvania countryside killing 2,977 innocent people.[6]

President Bush speaking at the collapsed World Trade Center Towers on September 14, 2001. When a worker called out, "I can't hear you," Bush responded, "I can hear you! The rest of the world hears you. . . and the people who knocked these buildings down will hear all of us soon!"   HUM HISTORICAL/ALAMY

That day saw Americans at their best. Two flight attendants relayed information to their headquarters calmly describing the terrorists minutes before their aircraft crashed into the World Trade Center. Passengers on United Airlines Flight 93 rushed the cockpit to selflessly prevent the terrorists from steering their doomed airliner towards Washington D.C. and the White House. Hundreds of firefighters, law enforcement and common citizens rushed into the burning towers to rescue office workers and others trapped on the upper floors.[7]

Within days, American intelligence agencies determined the attacks had been conducted by Al Qaeda terrorists based in Afghanistan. On September 20, President Bush spoke before a joint session of Congress to demand that Afghanistan's Taliban government, "Deliver to United States authorities all the leaders of Al Qaeda who hide in your land.... Close immediately and permanently every terrorist training camp in Afghanistan, and hand over every terrorist, and every person in their support structure, to appropriate authorities."[8]

The Taliban refused. America was ready and resolute. On October 7, 2001, the United States and its NATO allies began a bombing campaign against Afghanistan, followed by a ground assault twelve days later. The Taliban and Al Qaeda fighters were no match for the American military. By mid-December, the Taliban regime had fallen, replaced by a United Nations-sanctioned interim government. But hundreds of Taliban fighters and their leader, Mullah Oman, had slipped into the mountains, while Al-Qaeda's leader, Osama bin Laden, fled to Pakistan on horseback.

On April 17, 2002, President Bush, believing the war nearly over, announced an Afghanistan reconstruction plan patterned after the Marshall Plan that had rebuilt Europe after World War II.

Bolstered by a seemingly easy victory in Afghanistan, the confident Bush Administration turned its focus to Iraq. A decade earlier, Bush's father, George H.W. Bush, had fought the first Iraq War after Saddam Hussein's army invaded Kuwait. That war was won in only 100 hours. But war hawks were dissatisfied and claimed the senior Bush had not finished the job. Hussein had been allowed to remain in power and, purportedly, build an arsenal of chemical, biological, and nuclear weapons.

Many Americans were skeptical of an Iraqi war. The war on Afghanistan, the unapologetic haven for the 9/11 terrorists, was seen as necessary and broadly supported. But there was no evidence Iraq had contributed to the 9/11 terrorist attacks, nor was there reliable evidence that Iraq possessed weapons of mass destruction, only suspicions and unsubstantiated claims.

But the Bush administration insisted that Iraq was an existential threat and conducted a public relations campaign to convince Americans.

Their message was simple. The war was necessary, would be easy to win and would present no burden on taxpayers.

"Intelligence gathered by this and other governments," President Bush told Americans during a March 16, 2003 radio address, "leaves no doubt that the Iraq regime continues to possess and conceal some of the most lethal weapons ever devised.... The security of the world requires disarming Saddam Hussein now."[9] Defense Secretary Donald Rumsfeld assured Americans the war would be over quickly, "I can't tell you," he declared in a CBS interview, "if the use of force in Iraq today would last five days, or five weeks or five months. But it certainly isn't going to last any longer than that."[10] Vice President Dick Cheney was even more optimistic, declaring during an NBC interview that "from the standpoint of the Iraqi people, my belief is we will, in fact, be greeted as liberators."[11]

Bush's administration not only claimed the war would be easily won but would place little burden on taxpayers. "There's a lot of money to pay for [the Iraq war]," Deputy Defense Secretary Paul Wolfowitz testified to Congress. "It doesn't have to be U.S. taxpayer money. We are dealing with a country that can really finance its own reconstruction, and relatively soon... oil revenues of Iraq could bring between $50 and $100 billion over the course of the next two or three years."[12]

"We can go kick their butts, kill them, remake their societies, hopefully have other people pay for it, remake the Middle East, promote democracy, people will be safer, and we're going to give you a tax break!"[13] is how Neta Crawford, a Boston University political scientist, summarized the message coming out of the Bush administration at the time.

A few stood up to the PR onslaught, urging caution. "The United States could certainly defeat the Iraqi military and destroy Saddam's regime," warned Brent Scowcroft, the National Security Adviser under Presidents Gerald Ford and George H.W. Bush, "but it would not be a cakewalk. On the contrary, it undoubtedly would be very expensive—with serious consequences for the U.S. and global economy."[14]

James Webb, Secretary of the Navy under Ronald Reagan, made the most perceptive prediction when he compared the postwar occupation of Japan with his projection of a long and bloody occupation of Iraq in a September 2, 2002 *Washington Post* editorial:

> The Japanese are a homogeneous people who place a high premium on respect, and they fully cooperated with MacArthur's forces after having been ordered to do so by the emperor. The Iraqis are a multiethnic people filled with competing factions who in many cases would view a U.S. occupation as infidels invading the cradle of Islam. Indeed, this very bitterness provided Osama bin Laden the grist for his recruitment efforts in Saudi Arabia when the United States kept bases on Saudi soil after the Gulf War. In Japan, American occupation forces quickly became 50,000 friends. In Iraq, they would quickly become 50,000 terrorist targets.[15]

Bush and his war cabinet ignored those urging caution. Six months after Webb's warning, the United States and a handful of allies launched the second Iraq War on March 16, 2003. Within a month American and allied forces had routed the Iraqi army, occupied most of Iraq and put Saddam Hussein to flight.

By May 2003, victory in Afghanistan and Iraq seemed assured, and with remarkably few deaths; less than 300 American and allied soldiers had died in combat.[16] On May 1, 2003, during a visit to Kabul Secretary of Defense Rumsfeld, declared an end to "major combat [in Afghanistan].... We are at a point where we clearly have moved from major combat activity to a period of stability and stabilization and reconstruction and activities."[17] That same day, President Bush, wearing a Navy flight jacket aboard the aircraft carrier USS *Abraham Lincoln*, triumphantly announced that "major combat operations in Iraq have ended."[18]

Rumsfeld and Bush were tragically mistaken. Their Middle East wars weren't over, they had only just begun. Afghan and Iraqi insurgents had simply melted into the hundreds of caves, mountain strongholds, and remote villages spread across the two rugged countries. Like the Mujahedeen Freedom Fighters who two decades earlier had driven the Soviets out of

Afghanistan, Afghan and Iraqi *Ghazi* (killers of infidels) would soon rise again to wage a guerrilla war against the American infidels.

President Bush aboard the USS *Abraham Lincoln* on May 1, 2003, six weeks after U.S. Army troops invaded Iraq. "Major combat operations in Iraq have ended." Bush declared. "In the battle of Iraq, the United States and our allies have prevailed." Bush's advisors had served him poorly; the war had just begun.   AP PHOTO/J. SCOTT APPLEWHITE

By 2020, the wars in Afghanistan and Iraq had taken the lives of 15,000 American service members and private contractors. The total death toll is far higher, as nearly 500,000 soldiers, unofficial militants and civilians have died in the two wars since 2001.[19] Millions more were displaced, driven from their homes or forced to seek asylum elsewhere. A September 2020 Brown University study concluded that 5.3 million civilians in Afghanistan and 9.2 million in Iraq became displaced persons after being driven from their homes.[20] Many fled northward to Europe resulting in the worst refugee crisis since the end of the Second World War.

An earlier Brown University study concluded that the Afghan and Iraqi Wars will eventually cost $5.9 trillion, far more than even the most pessimistic estimates in 2003. The study included the direct cost of troops and support personnel plus the cost of long-term veterans' care, Homeland Security efforts to counter terrorists spawned by the war and interest payments on the debt resulting from the war. The $716 billion in estimated interest payments alone dwarf the Bush administration's original estimates of the war's cost.[21]

Middle East War Deaths: 2001 - October 2019				
	Afghanistan	Iraq	Syria/ISIS	Total
U.S. Military	2,298	4,572	7	6,877
U.S. DOD Civilians & Contractors	3,820	3,603	18	7,441
National & Allied Forces	65,269	50,660	62,483	178,412
Opposition Forces	42,100	37,344	67,065	146,509
Civilians	43,074	195,769	49,591	288,434
Media, Humanitarian & NGO Workers	491	340	260	1,091
Total	157,052	292,288	179,424	628,764

The Middle East Wars cost nearly 15,000 American lives over two decades. Civilians, as in most wars, paid, by far, the highest price in lives lost.

BROWN UNIVERSITY / WATSON INSTITUTE

The actual costs may be even higher. The last check to a Civil War dependent went out in 2020. Moses Triplett joined the Confederate Army in 1862 at the tender age of sixteen. Moses deserted soon afterward as his unit was headed to the Battle of Gettysburg and, in 1864, switched sides to join the Union Army. Sixty years later, and remarkably vigorous well into his eighties, Moses fathered five children with his second wife, fifty years his junior. A daughter, Irene, was born in 1930. Mentally disabled, Irene spent much of her life in institutions supported by the $73.13 Civil War pension checks mailed by the Veterans Administration. Irene died May 31, 2020 at a nursing home in Wilkesboro, North Carolina, 155 years after the end of the Civil War.[22]

The Experts Get It Wrong, Again

Bush moved quickly after taking office to honor his campaign promise to cut taxes. "Forty years ago," he declared in his first address to Congress, "and then twenty years ago, two Presidents, one Democrat, one Republican, John F. Kennedy and Ronald Reagan, advocated tax cuts to, in President Kennedy's words, 'get this country moving again.' They knew then what we must do now. To create economic growth and opportunity, we must put money back into the hands of the people who buy goods and create jobs."[23]

President Bush's use of Kennedy and Reagan as precedents for cutting taxes was badly flawed. Kennedy and Reagan started with much higher tax rates, 91 and 70 percent, respectively. By the time Bush took office, the top marginal rate had already been cut to 39.6 percent—the lowest rate, except for a brief period a decade earlier, since 1931. Additional tax cuts would do little, if anything, to stimulate the economy.

Bush did not mention President Eisenhower, who, similarly, was pressured to cut taxes. But America still owed a large war debt from World War II. "The objective of tax reduction is an absolutely essential one," Eisenhower declared in 1953, "and must be attained in its proper order. . . . That means, to my mind, that we cannot afford to reduce taxes, reduce [government] income, until we have in sight a program of expenditures that shows that the factors of income and of outgo will be balanced."[24] Bush wasn't faced with a massive war debt, but America's national debt was still draining trillions from the economy: $3.8 trillion (in 2020 dollars) in interest payments during the nineteen-nineties. That's nearly three percent siphoned annually from the national economy, well above the 1.2 percent Eisenhower fretted over during his administration.

But economists were feeling bullish, declaring America could both cut taxes and pay down its debt. In January 2001, the Congressional Budget Office (CBO) issued an economic analysis even more upbeat than its report a year earlier, "The outlook for the federal budget over the next decade continues to be bright. . . . Under current policies, total surpluses would accumulate to an estimated $2.0 trillion over the next five years and $5.6 trillion over the coming decade. Such large surpluses would be sufficient by 2006 to pay off all debt held by the public that will be available for redemption."[25]

Caught up in the excitement was the Heritage Foundation. Heritage, believing the bullish CBO report was too conservative, issued its report on April 27, 2001. The report went beyond the CBO analysis by using dynamic simulation. Unlike the CBO report, which assumed economic growth would be unchanged by tax cuts, the Heritage analysis assumed the tax cuts would stimulate economic growth. From 2001 through 2007, Heritage forecast that real GDP would grow 22 percent, employment nine percent, nominal tax revenues 26 percent, and the publicly-held portion of the federal debt (which excludes debt owed to repay Social Security and other trust funds) would be reduced by 60 percent.[26]

Supported by rosy financial forecasts, Congress quickly approved the Economic Growth and Tax Relief Reconciliation Act, which Bush signed on June 7, 2001, just five months after taking office. Most of the Act's tax cuts were to be phased in over several years. The top bracket was decreased from 39.6 to 35 percent, while the lower percent bracket was reduced from fifteen to 10 percent. Estate taxes were scheduled to be eliminated by 2010.

Three months later, Al Qaeda terrorists launched their September 11 attacks.

For President Bush, that tragic day began peacefully in a Sarasota, Florida classroom reading *The Pet Goat* to second graders.[27] Twelve hours later, President Bush was on national television: "Today," Bush told stunned Americans, "our fellow citizens, way of life, our very freedom came under attack in a series of deliberate and deadly terrorist acts. The victims were in airplanes, or in their offices; secretaries, businessmen and women, military and federal workers; moms and dads, friends and neighbors. Thousands of lives were suddenly ended by evil, despicable acts of terror."[28] Overnight, Bush had become a war-time President faced with the greatest threat to the American homeland since the Japanese attack on Pearl Harbor.

Within a year, defense spending was growing nearly 15 percent annually. The Department of Homeland Security was established with a workforce nearly the size of the French and German armies, combined. And thousands of American troops were fighting in Afghanistan, and soon, Iraq.

By 2003, the $236 billion budget surplus Bush inherited had turned into a $377 billion deficit. Yet Bush approved the second round of tax cuts and even made rate reductions scheduled for 2006 retroactive to the 2003 tax year. Congress contributed to the largesse by approving a prescription drug benefit for Medicare, adding tens of billions in additional annual spending.

The combination of lower tax revenues and higher spending generated large budget deficits. Heritage had projected $1.9 trillion in budget surpluses from 2002 through 2007, which would "effectively pay off the federal debt." Instead, deficits ballooned to $1.7 trillion, a difference of $3.6 trillion. By 2007, the nation's publicly-held debt had grown to $5.1 trillion, nearly $4.0 trillion over Heritage's $1.3 trillion forecast.

The actual debt was even worse. The Bush administration, like others before it, had siphoned off tax revenues intended for the Social Security trust funds. By 2007, the administration had borrowed $1.4 trillion from the trust funds, which pushed the total national debt—the amount owed to the public and future Social Security recipients—to $9.2 trillion.[29]

The Congressional Budget Office, Heritage and others had gotten it wrong. Heritage predicted Bush's tax cuts would supercharge the economy. They didn't. Actually, the economy should have exceeded their forecasts. America was at war, and nothing boosts an economy like war. Real GDP grew 10.6 percent annually during World War II, 5.7 percent during the Korean Conflict and five percent during the peak Vietnam War years. But real GDP grew only 2.8 percent annually from 2002 through 2007, even as defense spending surged 7.5 percent annually during those years.

Opinions, inevitably, vary as to what happened. One factor, certainly, was declining consumer sentiment during the Bush years, from a historic peak of 112 in January 2000 to 76 by December 2007. (Sentiment dropped to 55.3 in 2008 as the financial crisis unfolded.) It is confidence, that elusive intangible economist Adam Smith called "animal spirits," which fuels consumption and investment, the two essential elements of economic growth.

After the booming and relatively peaceful nineteen-nineties, Americans were shaken by the 9/11 Terrorist Attacks, the collapse of the dot-com stock market, and the bankruptcy of Enron and WorldCom after the discovery of massive accounting fraud in both firms.

Personal income declined for 80 percent of Americans during the Bush years, whereas, the lower 80 percent of Americans enjoyed strong income growth under Clinton. From 1993 through 2000, real, after-tax income for the middle-class (the middle three income quintiles) increased 13.7 percent. But from 2000 through 2007, their income fell 1.4 percent. For those struggling at the bottom, the minimum wage dropped from $7.74 to $7.30 (in 2020 dollars). The wealthy did well, though. The top one percent's income jumped 23 percent, from $1.06 million to $1.30 million.

President Kennedy, promoting his tax cut in 1963, declared "a rising tide lifts all boats."[30] But often, that rising tide had favored just the wealthy, leaving others behind.

The Bush tax cuts were not the first-time economists who subscribed to Ronald Reagan's dictum that "lower taxes are always better" (and its corollary, "higher taxes are always worse.") had missed their forecasts, and badly. In the early nineteen-nineties, as Bush and Clinton were raising taxes to cut deficits, supply-side economists predicted sluggish growth or worse. In 2001, they predicted the Bush tax cuts would generate an economic boom. They were wrong on both counts.

Unfortunately, the poor economy during Bush's first six years was but a minor flurry. An economic storm was growing on the horizon.

The Bubble Explodes

For decades, the safest investment most Americans could make was to purchase a home. From 1950 through 1999, the total equity America held in its homes, adjusted for inflation, grew an average of 3.4 percent annually. Not as rapidly as the stock market, but unlike stock markets, the nation's collective home equity never took a nosedive. Home prices might slow, even dip slightly, but they had never crashed. For millions of Americans, homeownership translated to economic security.

That changed, beginning in the nineteen-nineties. After averaging just over seven million new home sales a year for decades, the housing market took off, climbing from eight million home sales in 1995 to 10.6 million in

2000 and 15.3 million in 2005. New home prices nearly doubled, driven by the super-heated market.

For many Americans, the booming real estate market was an economic windfall. A family that bought a new home in 1995 for $150,000 with a $30,000 down-payment saw their home equity increased to over $180,000 by 2005 as home prices rose. For many, their growing home equity became a pot of mad money used to purchase cheap properties to "flip" for a quick profit.

It wasn't just speculators driving the surge in home sales. Starting in the nineteen-eighties, federal legislation promoted broad homeownership through subsidies and loosened regulations. Banks and mortgage brokers lowered their requirements, making it easier for borderline buyers to purchase a home. By 2003, home sales were growing at a rate over 10 percent annually, fueled by easy money. For those worrywarts concerned the nation was entering a housing bubble, the experts offered confident assurances their worries were unwarranted:

> "Housing bubble? What housing bubble? The signs are in place for a further run-up in real estate. Breathe easy, mortgage holders. There's still no place like home."[31]
>
> Jim Cramer, *CNBC Mad Money*
> December 8, 2003

> "All the bond bears have been dead wrong in predicting sky-high mortgage rates. So have all the bubbleheads who expect housing-price crashes in Las Vegas or Naples, Florida, to bring down the consumer, the rest of the economy, and the entire stock market."[32]
>
> Larry Kudlow, *National Review Online*
> June 20, 2005

> "There is no housing bubble in this country. Our strong housing market is a function of myriad factors with real economic underpinnings. . . . What we do have is a serious housing shortage and housing affordability crisis. . . . Anyone waiting for prices to collapse before buying a home is likely to be in for a disappointment."[33]
>
> Neil Barsky, *The Wall Street Journal*
> October 28, 2005

But small business owners, those individuals closest to the real economy, weren't feeling as sanguine. The National Federation of Independent Business (NFIB) Small Business Optimism Index had begun to swing wildly. The index peaked in November 2004 at 107, its highest level since record-keeping began, then fell steeply to 82 by early 2009, its historical low.[34] A potent mixture of low interest rates, lax government regulation, and a voracious finance industry was pushing the nation to the brink of the largest economic collapse since the Great Depression.

The first rumblings of the coming crisis began in 2006 when average home prices, after rising for years, declined from $305,000 to $300,000. Prices quickly recovered, hitting $322,000 by early 2007.[35] The housing market had just peaked. Home prices began to fall to $301,000 in mid-2007, $285,000 in 2008 and then $257,000 in 2009. New home sales plummeted, falling from 15.3 million in 2005 to 5.8 million by 2008, finally bottoming out at 3.7 million in 2011.[36]

For decades, rising home prices had been the cornerstone of the risk models that Wall Street relied on to finance the mortgage industry. Confident that prices would continue to rise, lenders promoted risky loans with little money down, scant documentation, and low interest rates. If the homeowner defaulted, the lender would simply foreclose and then sell the home at a profit. For a few years, it was a sure way to make money, and lots of it.

But once home prices began to decline, that business model collapsed taking industry profits with it. In 2006, ten of the nation's top financial firms—AIG, Bear Stearns, Countrywide, Fannie Mae, Freddie Mac, IndyMac, Lehman Brothers, Merrill Lynch, Wachovia, and Washington Mutual—had net profits of $48 billion. A year later their profits collapsed to under $2 billion.

Like canaries in a coal mine, the smaller firms were the first to fail. Many didn't last through the first months of 2007. By the end of March, two dozen sub-prime lenders had gone out of business, starting with the cheeky-named Own-It Mortgage Solutions.[37] By November, the damage had become so severe that Treasury Secretary Hank Paulson hastily set up a $75 billion superfund to buy distressed mortgage portfolios. No one else would touch them. Paulson was only able to convince Bank of America, Citigroup, and JP Morgan Chase to back the fund by promising the U.S. Treasury would reimburse any losses the banks incurred. This was the federal government's first intervention in the burgeoning crisis. Much more would follow.

Four months later, in March 2008, the Federal Reserve Bank of New York stepped in to loan Bear Stearns $25 billion when other banks refused. It didn't help. A few days later, Bear Stearns was again out of money, which left it little option but to sell itself to JP Morgan Chase for $2.00 a share wiping out shareholders. A year earlier, its stock had traded at $172.[38]

In September, Fannie Mae and Freddie Mac, like prodigal children, were forced into federal conservatorship after decades of private ownership. The two firms had originally been established as government-sponsored enterprises to support the mortgage industry but later spun-off as private companies. Together, the two firms held or guaranteed half the nation's mortgages, worth $5.0 trillion, tens of billions of which were defaulting every month. The U.S. Treasury eventually invested $187 billion in the two companies to assure their survival.[39]

That same month, after suffering $6.7 billion in losses during the first half of 2008, Lehman Brothers ran out of cash. The government refused to step in, believing its failure would have a limited impact on the markets. Failing to find a merger partner, Lehman was forced into bankruptcy on September 15, 2008. With nearly $700 billion in assets, it was the largest American bankruptcy filing ever recorded. Washington, however, had underestimated the impact that Lehman's failure would have on financial markets. Lehman's collapse panicked investors around the world. Little wonder. Lehman was the fourth largest investment bank with a history dating back to 1850. If Lehman could fail, no bank was safe. Banks stopped lending, which turned a financial crisis into the worst banking panic since the Great Depression.

AIG was next. But AIG truly was too big to fail. AIG had insured trillions of Mortgage-Backed Securities for clients spread around the world, all of whom were now looking to AIG for redress as their mortgage-based securities failed. But AIG didn't have the money. Confident in their risk models, AIG had neither set aside reserves nor reinsured the obligations to protect itself. Unwilling to let AIG's failure bring down scores of other firms. the Federal Reserve bought $150 billion in AIG shares, effectively nationalizing the company. By the end of 2008, AIG had recorded $99 billion in losses, the largest ever reported by an American corporation.[40]

On October 3, Wells Fargo announced it would acquire Wachovia in a government-mandated merger. After $9.6 billion in losses during the first half of the year,[41] Wachovia also had run out of money. Nine months earlier the bank had reported $6.3 billion in 2007 net income.[42]

That same day Congress passed the Emergency Economic Stabilization Act, which authorized the U.S. Treasury to spend $700 billion to shore up banks by purchasing their bad assets, especially Mortgage-Backed Securities. Better known as TARP (Troubled Asset Relief Program), the Act was controversial. Twenty-five senators opposed the bail-out. "Maybe I am the only person in America who thinks so," Senator Bernie Sanders declared in a Senate speech, "but I have a hard time understanding why we are giving $700 billion to the Secretary of the Treasury, who is the former C.E.O. of Goldman Sachs, which, along with other financial institutions, actually got us into this problem..."[43]

An alternative proposal had been to revive the Homeowners' Loan Corporation, established during the Great Depression to help homeowners refinance their failing mortgages. Failing mortgages were, after all, the root cause of the 2008 crisis. When a homeowner failed to pay his mortgage, the effect rippled upward through Mortgage-Backed Securities, collateralized debt obligations, credit default swaps, and the other derivatives Wall Street had concocted. Why not funnel money to the source of the problem?

But with the U.S. Treasury largely staffed by former investment bankers, it was the financial industry, not homeowners, who got the bulk of the bail-out money. The U.S. Treasury injected $105 billion in fresh cash into eight banks by purchasing preferred stock. A separate $20 billion went to Citigroup, $386 million went to twenty-three small community banks, and $182 billion to AIG. The U.S. Treasury also invested $80.7 billion in General Motors and Chrysler after their executives warned their companies were on the verge of bankruptcy, putting a million jobs at risk.[44]

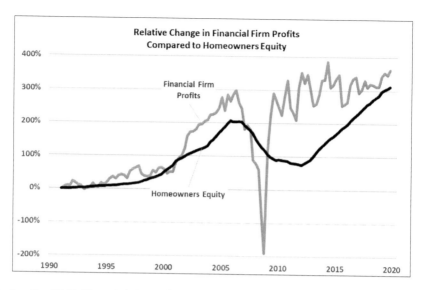

Relative Change in Financial Firm Profits Compared to Homeowners Equity

During the 2008 Financial Crisis, financial firms received $1.7 trillion in federal bail-outs. Homeowners received little, if any, help. As a result, Wall Street recovered quickly while homeowners struggled over ten years to recover their lost home equity.

U.S BUREAU OF ECONOMIC ANALYSIS | FEDERAL RESERVE BOARD OF GOVERNORS

The tens of millions of Americans who lost thousands in home equity, often their life savings, and even their homes, suffered the most. As home prices fell, Americans' total home equity plummeted 54 percent from $13.4 trillion in 2006 down to $6.1 trillion three years later in 2009.[45] The Dow Jones average fell from 14,165 in October 2007 to 6,547 in March 2009. Millions of homeowners were wiped out as their home equity sank deeply underwater. Over ten million homes were foreclosed between 2006 and 2010.[46] From 2007 through 2010, seven million workers lost their jobs.[47] It would be years before the economy fully recovered.

Forbes magazine, the chronicler of American capitalism since 1917, summarized the feeling of millions of Americans in a July 14, 2015 article:

> The operating principles of the big banks is a cesspool of greed, ethics and criminal intent and they give a very bad name to free-market capitalism. During the housing bubble, Wall Street was considered the heart and soul of free-market capitalism, but when they were in danger of total collapse, they fell on their knees as socialists, begging the government and taxpayers to bail them out.[48]

The real estate boom lasted only five years but ended in the worst financial crisis since the Great Depression. How did that happen? How could the legions of government economists, bank experts, mortgage officers, and small-town bank managers get it so wrong?

Like a fire, three factors contributed to the financial melt-down in 2008. Government policies supporting broad homeownership, low interest rates, and deregulation provided the oxygen. An avaricious mortgage industry provided the fuel. The finance industry provided the spark that ignited the flames.

The Oxygen: Government Policies

The federal government's encouragement of homeownership began during the Great Depression. In 1934, to help get the economy moving again, President Roosevelt and Congress established the Federal Housing Administration (FHA), which provided federally-backed insurance to protect FHA-approved lenders against losses. The FHA expanded the housing market by allowing banks to provide mortgages to home buyers they formerly would have declined.[49]

Four years later, the Federal National Mortgage Association, popularly known as Fannie Mae, was established to provide liquidity to the mortgage industry by buying and selling home mortgages. Previously, banks were limited to loaning money acquired through deposits. Fannie Mae changed that. By selling their mortgages to Fannie Mae, a bank could immediately monetize their mortgages rather than waiting decades for the loans to be repaid. The fresh cash could then be used to make more home loans.

Starting with Roosevelt's New Deal programs, Washington has a long history of supporting homeownership. In 1944, the G.I. Bill offered veterans low-cost home mortgages. In 1954, President Eisenhower established a commission to encourage the development of low-income housing.[50] In 1968, the Government National Mortgage Association, or Ginnie Mae, was established to provide liquidity for a new financial instrument, Mortgage-Backed Securities (MBS). In 1970, the Emergency Home Finance Act, or Freddie Mac, was established to reduce interest-rate risks for lending banks. In 1977, Congress passed the Community Reinvestment Act mandating that the Federal Reserve encourage its banking partners to provide credit to low- and medium-income neighborhoods.[51] In 1995, President Clinton announced his National Homeownership Strategy, a presidential initiative to increase homeownership to 67.5 percent of families by 2000. In 2002, President George W. Bush announced his initiative to increase Hispanic and Black homeownership by 5.5 million families.[52] A year later, Bush signed the American Dream Down Payment Act to help first-time home buyers.[53] That year, a few bellwethers began to caution that the declining mortgage standards were dangerous and could lead to a housing collapse. But government-sponsored homeownership had powerful supporters in Congress. Representative Barney Frank was one of the most fervent. "I want to roll the dice a little bit more in this situation toward subsidized housing," Frank declared during a housing debate in the House Financial Services Committee on September 25, 2003.[54]

Falling interest rates spurred the market. During the late nineteen-nineties, the Federal Funds rate hovered just above six percent, but then fell sharply starting in 2001, hitting 0.98 percent by late 2003. That year mortgage rates fell to under six percent, the lowest since the early nineteen-sixties.[55] The combination of government housing programs and historically low mortgage rates enabled millions of low-income families, formerly locked out of the housing market, to purchase a home. From 2000 through 2007, the percentage of home mortgages held by low-income homeowners increased from 2.5 to 14 percent.[56]

Another Washington initiative, deregulation, unleashed Wall Street. The hundreds of banking failures during the Great Depression led to extensive banking regulations, which proved successful. Over the next forty years, few major banks failed.[57] But by the mid nineteen-seventies, memories of the Depression had grown hazy and resulted in calls to reduce federal banking regulations.

Banking regulations had been so successful, Congress was hesitant to meddle with them. One of the nation's top economists and later Federal Reserve Chairman, Alan Greenspan, helped to change that. Greenspan claimed that self-interest made industries self-regulating. "It is critically important to recognize that no market is ever truly unregulated," Greenspan wrote in 1977. "The self-interest of market participants generates private market regulation. Thus, the real question is not whether a market should be regulated. Rather, the real question is whether government intervention strengthens or weakens private regulation."[58]

Alan Greenspan was Chairman of the Federal Reserve from 1987 through 2006. Greenspan's policies supporting low interest rates and financial deregulation contributed to the 2008 Financial Crisis.   FEDERAL RESERVE

Greenspan's contention that markets regulated themselves shifted the political argument from how much Washington should regulate financial institutions to whether they should be regulated at all.

The first test of Greenspan's theory was a failure. Promising to "get America moving again," President Reagan deregulated the savings and loans industry in 1982. The formerly staid industry went on a spending spree, investing wildly in marginal real estate and junk bonds. Four years later, the first banks began to fail. By 1995, over 1,000 savings and loans institutions, nearly a third of the industry, had failed, costing taxpayers $132 billion.[59] But Wall Street was unfazed—those failing savings and loans had been managed by local yokels who got in over their heads. That would never happen to the "Masters of the Universe" as Tom Wolfe christened Wall Street's elite in *The Bonfire of the Vanities*.[60]

In November 1999, Congress passed the Gramm-Leach-Bliley Act, which repealed significant portions of the Glass-Steagall Act of 1933. For sixty-five years, Glass-Steagall had separated commercial and investment banking. Commercial banks provide checking and savings accounts, auto and home loans, and credit card services. Investment banks provide capital for companies, governments, and other organizations by buying and selling stocks, bonds, and other financial instruments, as well as arranging mergers, acquisitions, and other corporate services.[61]

The year before, Citicorp and Travelers Group had merged. Citicorp was an eminent bank that dated back to 1812 and Travelers was a sexy, new conglomeration of insurance and investment banking. The merger formed the world's largest financial-services firm. It also was a monumental act of hubris; for the merger to remain intact, significant portions of Glass-Steagall would need to be repealed.

For years, the financial industry had unsuccessfully lobbied Congress to repeal Glass-Steagall. By 1999, memories of the many banking failures during the Great Depression had faded. After intensive lobbying by the two firms' powerful CEOs, John Reed and Sandy Weill, and with the tacit support of Fed Chairman Alan Greenspan and Treasury Secretary Robert Rubin, Congress and President Clinton, acquiesced.[62]

The partial repeal of Glass-Steagall tore down the wall that protected depositors from speculators. Financial firms were now free to offer commingled banking, investment, and insurance services—as well as trade securities themselves. Profits soared. Before Glass-Steagall's repeal, pre-tax profits of financial firms, adjusted for inflation, grew a healthy 3.9 percent annually from 1980 through 2000. But from 2001 through 2005, profits skyrocketed to nearly 17 percent annually.[63]

Helping fuel the incredible growth was the Commodity Futures Modernization Act of 2000 (CFMA). CFMA, among other provisions, eliminated all trading restrictions, other than fraud, on derivatives, Wall Street's hottest new financial product. Like their support for the repeal of

Glass-Steagall, Greenspan and Rubin supported deregulating derivatives, claiming that even discussing their regulation "might drive the market overseas."[64]

Derivatives are securities based on another security. Consider stocks and stock options, for example. Stock in a company represents a share of the ownership of that company. A stock option gives the holder the right to buy a stock at a guaranteed price in the future. Since the option's value is derived from the underlying stock, it and numerous other derivative financial instruments are naturally called derivatives.

Derivatives aren't new. The Greek philosopher Thales around 600 BCE, expecting a strong olive harvest, paid all the olive-press owners in the region to guarantee him exclusive use of their presses during the harvest. The press owners, unsure of the demand for their olive presses months in the future, were "hedging" against a poor harvest. Thales' prediction of a strong harvest was correct, allowing him to charge a premium to olive growers for the use of his presses. Thales, the world's first hedge fund manager, made a small fortune.[65]

More recently, in 1848, the Chicago Board of Trade institutionalized the trading of farm produce when it began selling corn, rye, and wheat contracts for delivery at a set price in the future. Known logically as "futures," the contracts guaranteed the farmer a price on his produce at a specified future date. On the other side of the trade, a cannery, for example, would be assured a supply of corn at a guaranteed price. Hedging allowed both the farmer and cannery to reduce their risks.[66]

Managed prudently, derivatives play a valuable role in commerce.

The CFMA deregulated derivatives, justified by the arguments of top economists including Treasury Secretaries Robert Rubin and Larry Summers, Fed Chairman Alan Greenspan, and SEC Chairman Arthur Levitt. Since derivatives were traded exclusively among sophisticated investors, these economists claimed the derivatives market was self-regulating.[67]

By the early two-thousands, the zeal to cut regulations was so strong that federal agencies were competing amongst themselves to see who could cut the deepest. A foolish example of this mania was depicted in the Federal Deposit Insurance Corporation's (FDIC) 2003 annual report that featured a photograph of its top administrators and three banking executives—the regulators and the regulated—gleefully slashing a stack of regulations with a chainsaw.[68]

Just a few years later, a humbled FDIC, with new management, paid out $73 billion to reimburse depositors of hundreds of failed banks, including the largest bank failure in FDIC history, Washington Mutual.[69]

The Fuel: The Mortgage Industry

For much of the twentieth century, the mortgage industry was simple. Homebuyers would visit their local bank or savings and loan, complete a loan application, confirm their employment status, and, if approved, obtain a fixed-rate thirty-year mortgage. The bank, to convert the mortgage into ready cash, might then sell the mortgage to Fannie Mae.

That was pretty much the mortgage industry for decades, but starting about 1980, Wall Street began to buy mortgages. Some buyers—pension funds, for example—bought and held the mortgages for their steady earnings and relatively high yields. Wall Street, though, repackaged the mortgages into Mortgage-Backed Securities, segmented by maturity, yield, and risk, and then resold them. The secondary mortgage market was quickly transformed from a sleepy backwater to Wall Street's hottest new money-maker. In 1983, Salomon Brothers alone generated $200 million ($520 million in 2020 dollars) in after-tax profits from mortgage-related securities.[70]

For twenty years, this system worked well. More homeowners were able to obtain mortgages, the banks made more money and the nation benefited through increased homeownership. But a subtle risk was creeping into the system. The incentive for mortgage lenders to carefully evaluate loan applications was slowly eroding. Lenders expected to quickly resell their loans which, crucially, shifted the risk from the mortgage lender to the mortgage buyer.

By 2000, the secondary mortgage market was booming. Financial firms were repackaging mortgages into an alphabet soup of derivatives—ABS, CDO, CMO, MBS—and then selling the packaged derivative to investors worldwide. The mortgage of a homebuyer in Des Moines might be owned by a Wall Street bank, a London hedge fund, or the Qatar Central Bank.[71]

Two other players were feeding the mortgage boom: shadow banks and mortgage brokers.

Firms that invest or lend money but do not accept deposits are considered shadow banks, from pawn shops to investment banks. These firms, since they don't hold deposits, are largely unregulated. Hungry for mortgages to package into derivatives, Wall Street pushed trillions of dollars into shadowy mortgage originators such as Countrywide Home Loans, American Home Mortgage, SunTrust Mortgage, and New Century Mortgage.[72] Thousands of independent mortgage brokers soon sprung up to channel home buyers into these new mortgage lenders. Typically, working from their home, brokers were paid a one or two percent commission on the value of the mortgage. This army of independent brokers drove business to the mortgage lenders, reducing the need for lenders to hire a direct sales force allowing lenders to spend heavily on television and radio promotions.

The drive for quick profits steadily drove down the required minimum down-payments. Putting $50,000 down on a $250,000 home that later appreciated to $300,000 meant a $50,000 profit, a nice doubling. Putting down just $12,500 increased profits five-fold. Of course, if the home depreciated $50,000, the buyer would be deeply underwater, putting both the deposit and the home at risk. That's the bipolar nature of leverage. It's intoxicating when markets are rising but devastating when they are falling.

Few home buyers worried about their mortgages going underwater. For decades, real estate prices had risen reliably. From 2000 through 2007, average home prices increased 58 percent, from $203,000 to $322,000.[73] With home prices soaring, mortgage firms loosened their down-payment requirements even further to attract more business. Before 2004, Countrywide, for example, required a 20 percent down-payment. The firm dropped that long-standing requirement to 10 percent in mid-2004 and five percent in early 2005. A home buyer could purchase a $250,000 home for only $12,500 down.[74] Many did so with borrowed money, often buying secondary homes using equity loans on their primary residences.

An even more perilous incentive to entice buyers was the Adjustable-Rate Mortgage (ARM), and its dangerous mutation, the Option ARM which offered two features: low initial interest rates and optional payment plans. To attract buyers, the ARM's initial rate was set as low as one percent. But after the initial period, typically two years, the interest rate reset to actual market rates, often two, three, and even five times the initial rate. Gullible home buyers took out ARM mortgages, attracted by the low initial rate, and then, when their monthly payments sky-rocketed, couldn't make their mortgage payment and lost their home to foreclosure.

Equally insidious was the option that gave the home buyer the choice of four monthly payments: (1) a minimum payment which did not even cover the interest due; (2) an interest-only payment; (3) a fifteen-year amortizing payment; or (4) a thirty-year amortizing payment. The third and fourth options were typical of regular mortgage payments in which the mortgage is paid off over fifteen or thirty years. Option two paid the monthly interest, but none of the principle, similar to a revolving credit-card account in which the borrower never pays off the balance.

The first option devastated millions of mortgage holders. Believing they could refinance as their home's value increased, or simply not understanding the complicated terms, many borrowers selected the minimum payment option. The unpaid interest due each month was added to the mortgage balance. When the mortgage holder later tried to re-finance, he was shocked to discover that his loan balance was well above the original loan! Even worse, if the loan balance reached 10 to 20 percent above the original loan, the terms of the loan, typically buried in the small print, automatically switched to options two, three or four, increasing monthly payments from a few hundred dollars to well over a thousand.

Option ARM mortgages attracted home buyers for their flexibility and perceived low cost. The mortgage industry marketed them aggressively. By 2007, over $255 billion in Option ARM loans were outstanding. Most borrowers elected to make only the minimum payments: 90 percent for Countrywide and 82 percent for Washington Mutual, the nation's two largest mortgage firms.[75]

As mortgage applications poured in, overwhelmed mortgage lenders found it difficult to keep up with their traditional loan documentation. The industry responded by slashing documentation requirements. Called "Ninja Loans" by brokers to impress prospective clients, the only requirement was an acceptable credit score: no proof of income, job, or assets were required.[76] The home buyer might be unemployed, but who was asking? By 2007, nearly 10 percent of outstanding mortgages were low or no-documentation mortgages.[77]

The mortgage industry had gone mad. Little or no money down. No job verification. Monthly payments so low that they reduced the homeowner's equity. How could they have been so foolish? Market exuberance. Average home prices were growing nearly seven percent annually.[78] A lucky home buyer putting 10 percent down in 2000 on a $200,000 home would have seen her home's equity increase from $20,000 to over $140,000 by 2007.

America was in a housing bubble. Favorable government housing programs, low mortgage rates, deregulation, and a mortgage industry gone mad provided the oxygen and the fuel. All that was needed to set the market ablaze was a spark.

The Spark: Wall Street

Wall Street never had much use for mathematicians. Savvy, street-smart traders drove the business. A few math majors might be working in some backroom, analyzing stock trends, but that was about it.

Derivatives changed that. Constructed of thousands of individual securities, derivatives required an advanced understanding of mathematics, finance, and computer science to analyze. Wall Street was soon paying top dollar to hire the very brightest from the nation's top schools. Employed as quantitative analysts, or "Quants," these seemingly brilliant individuals constructed arcane models to quantify and manage risk. Few, other than the Quants, understood the models. Yet Wall Street wasn't worried. As late as February 2008, the quarterly Survey of Professional Forecasters, comprised of the nation's top economists, estimated that nominal GDP would increase to $15.1 trillion in 2009, up from $13.8 trillion in 2007.[79] Nine months later, the country was in its worst economic crisis in eighty years.

Warren Buffett was one of the few who foresaw the danger. "The derivatives genie [having been deregulated two years prior] is now well out of the bottle," Buffett wrote in his 2002 Berkshire Hathaway annual report, "and these instruments will almost certainly multiply in variety and number until some event makes their toxicity clear.... In our view, however, derivatives are financial weapons of mass destruction, carrying dangers that, while now latent, are potentially lethal."[80]

Warren Buffett's "financial weapons of mass destruction" were the Mortgage-Backed Securities (MBS) that Wall Street had embraced as the engine generating its unprecedented profits. When Buffett issued his warning to shareholders, MBS and their derivatives had already become one of the most toxic financial instruments ever devised by Wall Street. Yet few economists and investors foresaw the danger, save Buffett and a handful of renegades.

How did Wall Street's elite, the so-called Masters of the Universe, convince themselves they had finally conquered risk? That's an intriguing question and worth a digression.

Anatomy of a Mortgage-Backed Security

CMLTI 2006-NC2 (NC2) was Wall Street's designation for a specific Mortgage-Backed Security marketed by Citibank in 2006.[81] Citibank was one of the nation's most revered financial firms, founded in 1812 as the City Bank of New York. The long-established bank hadn't survived 200 years by being reckless.

NC2 consisted of 4,499 mortgages sold earlier that year to home buyers by New Century, a major originator of sub-prime mortgages. New Century sold the mortgages, which had a face value of $947.4 million, to Citigroup for $979 million, making a quick, tidy profit. The sale provided New Century with fresh funds to loan out more mortgages and Citibank with a steady stream of interest payments from borrowers.[82]

Citibank, however, wasn't interested in collecting mortgage payments over the next thirty years. Rather, the bank packaged the mortgages into nineteen segments, or "tranches," and then sold shares of the tranches to dozens of investors around the world. Although NC2 contained mortgages from fifty states and the District of Columbia, 39 percent originated in the four "sand states:" Arizona, California, Florida, and Nevada, all notorious for land speculation.

The tranches were ranked by risk. The riskiest tranches paid the highest interest rates but would also be the last to be paid in the event the underlying mortgages defaulted. Standard & Poor's and Moody's provided credit ratings for each of the nineteen tranches. The two rating agencies, together, charged $343,000 for their ratings.[83]

The safest mortgages were placed into four tranches and given a AAA rating; the credit agencies' highest rating reserved only for the safest investments. The four AAA tranches contained 78 percent of all the mortgages. The remaining mortgages were placed into 15 smaller tranches with consecutively declining credit ratings.

Fannie Mae bought one of the AAA tranches for $155 million. Other buyers included banks and investment funds in China, Italy, France, and Germany as well as Fidelity, Northern Trust, State Street, JP Morgan, and dozens of others.

JP Morgan paid for part of their tranche by using a loan obtained from another bank which used their clients' securities as collateral. If the tranche defaulted, it would be the bank's unsuspecting clients who would be on the hook—precisely the sort of dodgy behavior that Glass-Steagall had formerly forbidden.

The AAA credit rankings suggested the mortgages in the top tranches belonged to homeowners with excellent credit ratings. That was not the case. Over 70 percent of the home buyers had FICO credit scores below 650, classifying them as poor credit risks.[84] Even more worrisome, 56 percent of the mortgages were two-year adjustable-rate mortgages, meaning these low-income homeowners would be pushed into much higher monthly payments in 2008, or default if they couldn't make the higher payments.

Traditionally, Standards & Poor's and Moody's had jealously guarded their AAA rating. In 2006, only six American companies were granted the coveted top rating: Automatic Data Processing, Exxon Mobil, General Electric, Johnson & Johnson, Microsoft, and Pfizer.[85] Yet, the credit agencies deemed 78 percent of the debt held in NC2 worthy of their AAA rating. This wasn't unusual. A 2010 study conducted by the New York

Federal Reserve regarding 3,144 MBS deals found that 87.6 percent were rated AAA. Yet, the underlying mortgages had an average FICO score of 656, which connoted only a fair credit risk. Nearly 50 percent were rated as having "low" documentation, suggesting the loan originators had little understanding of the homeowner's ability to meet mortgage payments.[86]

Why did the two credit-rating agencies grant their safest credit rating to such poor credit risks?

Because their business was based on a flawed business model. Prior to the nineteen-sixties, credit agencies were paid by the users of their ratings—pension fund managers, for example. Users demanded accurate ratings since they bought and sold securities based on the ratings. Later, as the new Xerox copiers proliferated during the nineteen-sixties, users began to share credit reports among themselves, threatening the credit agencies' revenues. This forced the agencies to switch to charging the issuers of securities—a fundamental change in their business model. Unlike their original clients who had demanded accurate ratings, issuers pressured the credit agencies for favorable ratings to make their offerings easier to sell.

Inevitably, issuers began to "shop ratings" by playing the credit agencies off against one another. A former Moody's executive, during Congressional testimony in 2008, explained the game:

> My view is that a large part of the blame can be placed on the inherent conflicts of interest found in the issuer-pays business model and rating shopping by issuers of structured securities. A drive to maintain or expand market share made the rating agencies willing participants in this shopping spree. It was also relatively easy for the major banks to play the agencies off one another because of the opacity of the structured transactions and the high potential fees earned by the winning agency.[87]

The pressure to please MBS issuers was enormous. From 2000 through 2006, Moody's operating income increased from $289 million to $1.3 billion, fed by the booming market for mortgage-backed securities.[88] In its 2006 annual report, Moody's chairman and chief executive officer, Raymond McDaniel, Jr., commented on the company's remarkable growth. "This strong performance," McDaniel explained, "was in large part due to the prevalence of new mortgage products, the persistence of low long-term interest rates and an increase in the percentage of mortgages being securitized."[89]

But the credit agencies, perhaps because it was convenient, had also drunk the same Kool-Aid as their clients, believing that the brilliant Quants and their financial models had mastered risk.[90] That, by aggregating individual, high-risk securities into complex, financial instruments, risk could be understood, managed, and eliminated. The Quants' financial models were so complex, their explanations so arcane, so brilliant, few questioned the premise that aggregating low-quality assets somehow spun straw into gold.

In 2007, Wall Street discovered how wrong the Quants had been. Home prices sputtered and then began to fall. Many adjustable-rate mortgage holders, no longer able to refinance, began to default. With the underlying mortgages defaulting, thousands of Mortgage-Backed Securities failed.

NC2 was typical. By 2010, 52 percent of the NC2 mortgages were in foreclosure or seriously past due in their payments. The four sand states suffered the worst failure rates. By 2010, over 80 percent of the mortgages in Nevada were in foreclosure or serious default. Over 60 percent of the mortgages in Arizona, California, and Florida were distressed.[91]

The mass destruction Warren Buffett had predicted in 2002 was just beginning.

Years earlier, Wall Street, seeking additional products to market, reasoned that if AAA securities could be constructed by aggregating risky loans into Mortgage-Backed Securities, why not aggregate the riskier tranches of MBSs into a new security? These new MBS-based securities, known as Collateralized Debt Obligations (CDO), took off after 2003. By 2006, $520 billion in CDOs were outstanding around the world.[92]

But much like MBSs, CDOs have riskier tranches, so Wall Street bundled these CDO tranches into a new security which the Quants, in an inside joke, dubbed CDO Squared. Just what was a CDO Squared buyer getting? A CDO based on the lower tranches of other CDOs which were based on MBS tranches which were typically based on sub-prime mortgages purchased by high-risk home buyers.

Sound fishy? Think of fish soup. The celebrity chef Anthony Bourdain, in the movie *The Big Short,* described a chef's version of a CDO:

> OK, I'm a chef on a Sunday afternoon, setting the menu at a big restaurant. I ordered my fish on Friday, which is the mortgage bond. . . . But some of the fresh fish doesn't sell. I don't know why. Maybe it just came out halibut has the intelligence of a dolphin. So, what am I going to do? Throw all this unsold fish, which is the BBB level of the bond, in the garbage, and take the loss? No way. Being the crafty and morally onerous chef that I am, whatever crappy levels of the bond I don't sell, I throw into a seafood stew. See, it's not old fish. It's a whole new thing! And the best part is, they're eating three-day-old halibut. That, is a CDO.[93]

Wall Street didn't stop with their version of fish soup. The Street understood that even top-rated securities could occasionally default. This opened a new market for an insurance-like product that would reimburse investors if their MBSs failed. But, rather than real insurance, MBS investors purchased Credit Default Swaps (CDS). These instruments were even more toxic than the CDOs they insured. Their failure would have toppled one of the world's largest insurance companies, American International Group (AIG), absent a massive government bail-out.

A CDS, on the surface, resembles an insurance policy. If an MBS tranche defaults, the CDS reimburses the investor for their loss. The purchaser of the CDS pays a quarterly premium, much like an insurance policy. The riskier the tranche, the higher the premium.

This all sounds like a normal insurance policy, but there were two crucial differences. First, CDS issuers, unlike normal insurance companies, were not required to set aside cash reserves to cover losses. Government regulators, tutored by the redoubtable Alan Greenspan, believed that self-interest would motivate firms to self-regulate. Wall Street had plenty of self-interest, but it, unfortunately, was focused on growing profits rather than managing risks.

Second, unlike most insurance policies, an investor could purchase a CDS for an asset that they did not actually own. Think about buying fire insurance on your neighbor's house. This changed CDS issuers from insurance brokers to a type of gambling parlor, taking side bets.

For a few years, CDSs were a sure-fire way to make lots of money. Weren't Mortgage-Backed Securities solid investments? Didn't the credit agencies rate them AAA? Hadn't Wall Street's smartest investors been buying MBS tranches for years? The CDS market exploded. In 2001, $918 billion in assets were secured by CDSs. By 2007, CDS-backed assets had grown to a phenomenal *$62 trillion*, four times the size of the United States economy.[94]

No firm sold Credit Default Swaps more enthusiastically than AIG, one of the world's top insurance companies dating back to 1919. CDSs, another fish soup that smelled like insurance, were a natural for AIG and, even better, no pesky regulators were poking around. AIG, finally, was self-regulating!

For a few years, selling Credit Default Swaps proved incredibly profitable. AIG's profits ballooned from $4.1 billion in 2001 to $14 billion by 2006.[95]

Few AIG shareholders realized the risk these esoteric derivatives added to the company's balance sheet. In 2006, AIG's annual 10-K report to the SEC briefly mentioned Credit Default Swaps just three times in the 192-page document.[96] A year later, as the real estate market swooned, AIG's 2007 10-K filing included 85 references to the term. Ominously, the first mention was: "In 2007, both revenues and operating income (loss) include an unrealized market valuation loss of $11.5 billion on [AIG Financial Products] super senior credit default swap portfolio..."[97]

A few months later, in July 2008, AIG announced a $13.2 billion loss for the first half of the year.[98] AIG was functionally bankrupt. By mid-September, AIG's bankruptcy was imminent. Abandoned by Wall Street, AIG reached out to the Federal Reserve for a bail-out. On September 16, with AIG minutes away from filing bankruptcy, the Fed stepped in to loan AIG $85 billion in return for a 79.9 percent stake in the company. The Fed bail-out eventually reached $182 billion.

"The failure of AIG," the Federal Reserve concluded, "a company with more than 76 million customers in approximately 140 countries—more than thirty million customers in the United States alone—posed a direct threat to millions of policyholders, state and local government agencies, 401(k) participants, banks and other financial institutions in the United States and abroad, and would have shattered confidence in already fragile financial markets."[99] In short, AIG was too big to be allowed to fail.

The nation's top financial firms—AIG, Bank of America, Citigroup, Goldman Sachs, JPMorgan Chase, Morgan Stanley, PNC, US Bancorp, Wells Fargo—and many others around the world had made huge bets on derivatives. For a few years, the bets paid off hugely. But it was a game of Russian Roulette. A decade before the financial crisis, the prescient Warren Buffet warned against the reckless speculation developing in the financial markets in a speech on October 15, 1998:

> If you hand me a gun with a million chambers with one bullet in a chamber and put it up to your temple and I am paid to pull the trigger, it doesn't matter how much I would be paid. I would not pull the trigger. You can name any sum you want, but it doesn't do anything for me on the upside and I think the downside is fairly clear. Yet people do it financially, very much without thinking.[100]

Could President Bush have foreseen and then averted the coming financial crisis? Almost surely not. The forces leading to the financial collapse were nearly unstoppable. Government agencies, encouraged by Federal Reserve Chairman Alan Greenspan, were competing with each as to who could deregulate the most. The mortgage industry, now deregulated and encouraged by federal policy to broaden homeownership, abandoned decades of prudent management to make buying a home as easy—and deceptive—as purchasing a used automobile. And Wall Street, those Masters of the Universe, believed it had finally conquered risk allowing it to spin straw into gold.

Education and Financial Reforms

As Bush took the oath of office on January 20, 2001, he surely believed he would preside over years of peace and prosperity: peace after the end of the Cold War and prosperity from a booming economy inherited from

President Clinton. Instead, Bush's presidency opened and closed with two historic catastrophes, the 9/11 Terrorist Attacks and the 2008 Financial Crisis—either of which would have challenged any presidency. These two events, and their aftermaths, have overshadowed much of Bush's presidency. But there was more to his tenure than the Middle East Wars and the 2008 Financial Crisis.

On January 8, 2002, Bush signed the No Child Left Behind Act (NCLB). The Act focused on helping struggling students in poorly performing schools. States receiving federal education funding were required to set high educational standards, establish measurable goals, and test annually against those goals. Schools that failed to meet standards for five consecutive years were required to close, replace the school's management, or become a privately-run charter school. The core curriculum placed heavy emphasis on reading, mathematics, and science and little emphasis on the arts or physical education. Annual testing, with serious consequences for failure, incentivized school administrators to teach to the test and occasionally, to cheat.

Although initially well-received, state educators soon chafed under NCLB's strict guidelines. By 2015, Bush's hallmark educational program was deemed a failure. A February 13, 2015 *Washington Post* article stated, "NCLB's failure to even raise scores on other standardized exams should be considered in light of widespread evidence of curriculum narrowing and extensive teaching to the test. Other serious problems, such as pushing low-scorers out of school and widespread cheating scandals, are also part of the steep price paid for NCLB's testing fixation."[101] A related *Post* article headlined, "No Child Left Behind's test-based policies failed" concluded that, "We as a nation have devoted enormous amounts of time and money to the focused goal of increasing test scores, and we have almost nothing to show for it."[102] Others considered NCLB a case of governmental overreach. "The Constitution," the Cato Institute opined, "gives the federal government no authority to control the nation's education system, Washington should work to largely remove itself from elementary and secondary education."[103]

President George W. Bush, like his father before him, had said he wished to be remembered as the "Education President." Bush's No Child Left Behind Act was a laudable effort to improve American education, but America's educational challenges extend beyond better schools. Academic achievement is closely related to family income. Children from families earning $40,000 have average Scholastic Aptitude Test (SAT) scores of 1463 while those from families earning over $200,000 have average scores of 1722. Lower-income families are preoccupied with "unemployment, underemployment, food insecurity, a lack of stable housing and many other obstacles that seriously undermine children's opportunities to learn."[104]

The disparity between lower- and upper-income families has affected educational attainment for decades. According to the IRS Statistics of Income annual reports, the real after-tax income for the lower 80 percent of taxpayers has scarcely increased from $41,600 in 1970 to $42,500 in 2018. During those years, the upper 20 percent enjoyed an income increase from $109,700 to $199,000. These disparities give affluent children a significant educational advantage due to better schools, supportive homes, and broader community resources.

Still, American educators, perhaps with help from NCLB, have made progress. Measured by the Program for International Student Assessment (PISA) scores, the United States has slowly improved while many developed countries have declined. In 2003, the average combined math and reading score for the Organisation for Economic Co-operation and Development (OECD) countries was 994 while the United States trailed at 978. By 2018, the OECD countries had fallen to 976 while the United States climbed to 984.[105] Meager progress, but progress, nonetheless.

Six months into his presidency, *The Wall Street Journal* reported on President Bush's efforts to cut burdensome regulations. "Cheering on Mr. Bush's approach to regulation," the *Journal* reported, "are the corporate executives who financed his presidential bid, helping raise a record-smashing $104 million for his primary campaign and $166 million in unregulated soft money donations..."[106] Within a year, that cheering stopped when Bush signed the "the most far-reaching reforms of American business practices since the time of Franklin D. Roosevelt."[107]

Bush had little choice. Corporate fraud seemed to be rampant everywhere. In 2001, Enron, crowned "America's Most Innovative Company" for six consecutive years by *Fortune* magazine, was caught hiding billions in corporate debt. Shareholders lost $74 billion. In 2002 alone, Wall Street was shaken when: WorldCom filed for bankruptcy after auditors uncovered $3.8 billion in accounting fraud that cost shareholders $180 billion; Tyco's CEO and CFO were indicted for accounting and stock fraud; and Wall Street's top brokerage firms including Citigroup, JPMorgan Chase, Credit Suisse First Boston, and Merrill Lynch were fined $1.4 billion for fraudulent security analysis during the nineteen-nineties dot-com boom.[108]

Congress responded with the Sarbanes-Oxley Act (SOX) which placed tight regulations on companies, security analysts, and accounting firms. Sarbanes-Oxley mandated that corporate executives personally certify financial statements, restricted auditors from performing non-auditing services, established an independent oversight board for monitoring accounting firms, established a code of conduct for security analysts, and delegated additional powers to the Securities and Exchange Commission to monitor and enforce against fraud.

These new regulations were enthusiastically supported by the American public, and Congress. Sarbanes-Oxley passed the House (423–3) and Senate (99–0) with overwhelming margins. President Bush signed the bill on July 30, 2002 wryly commenting: "No more easy money for corporate criminals, just hard time."[109]

Yet within a scant few years, calls for the repeal of Sarbanes-Oxley were proposed. In 2006, a *Baltimore Examiner* editorial, contributed by the Cato Institute, denounced Sarbanes-Oxley as a failure due to its high compliance costs, the personal risk placed on corporate executives and board members, and the steep decline in publicly-listed companies in the United States. Cato claimed that, most importantly, Sarbanes-Oxley had not restored investor confidence since "the price-earnings ratio of the S&P 500 stock index has declined continuously beginning with the second quarter of 2002 when Congress drafted and approved this legislation."[110] The Cato report did not mention that during the first six months of 2002, the S&P 500 price-earnings ratio had surged to a peak average of 43.4, its highest level in, at least, a century. A decline was nearly inevitable.[111]

More recently, after serving six years in prison, former Enron CFO Andrew Fastow has said he doubts Sarbanes-Oxley would stop corporate fraud since, in his view, the legislation is only asking, "Are you following the rules?" Fastow told a 2017 financial conference he never overtly broke the law, just stretched the rules to their limit:

> When I was at Enron, it never even dawned upon me that I might be committing fraud, I thought that what I was doing was the right thing. The way I thought about it was everybody gets the rulebooks. Whoever can best exploit those rules and find the loophole gets an advantage. They called me CFO, but my job title should have been 'chief loophole officer.' That's all I did. Everyday. Looking for ways to get around the intent or purpose of the rules.[112]

But, most importantly, those whom Sarbanes-Oxley was created to protect, investors, believe SOX has been highly beneficial. In a February 23, 2018 letter to *The Wall Street Journal,* the general counsel for the Council of Institutional Investors wrote:

> The benefits of SOX are vast and, in many cases, quantifiable. . . . [Researchers] have found companies that voluntarily comply with [SOX's] Section 404 have fewer financial restatements, as well as a lower cost of capital—and that includes smaller companies. In light of this research, it isn't surprising that a 2017 poll found that 85 percent of CFOs believe the internal-control audit function has helped their companies.[113]

Social Security and Medicare

Bush campaigned on improving Social Security by allowing Americans to invest a portion of their Social Security taxes in voluntary, personal investment accounts. Like Ronald Reagan twenty years earlier, Bush, shortly after taking office, created a bipartisan commission to develop a comprehensive plan for overhauling Social Security.

The commission issued its report in December 2001. "Social Security will be strengthened," the report concluded, "if modernized to include a system of voluntary personal accounts. Personal accounts improve retirement security by facilitating wealth creation and providing participants with assets that they own and that can be inherited, rather than providing only claims to benefits that remain subject to political negotiation."[114]

The notion of privatizing a portion of Social Security was a reasonable proposal. In theory, privatization not only increased returns but reduced the financial burden on the government. From its inception in 1935, Social Security has been a pay-as-you-go system. That works fine when workers paying in and retirees taking out are in balance. But by 2001, with the retirement of the Baby Boomers looming, Social Security benefits were forecast to eventually exceed revenues by trillions of dollars. Something needed to be done.

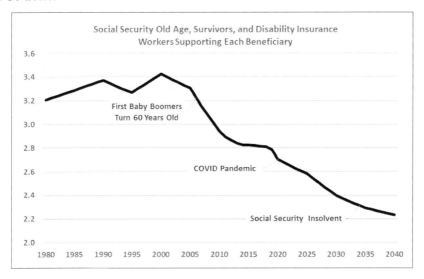

For decades, Baby Boomers paid Social Security taxes resulting in large surpluses. As they began to retire, fewer workers supported each Social Security beneficiary. Social Security is projected to be insolvent by 2034.   SOCIAL SECURITY ADMINISTRATION

The commission's proposal met immediate resistance. In addition to haggling over benefits, taxes, and implementation details, the plan's fiercest opponents claimed that Bush's personal investment accounts were a backdoor stratagem to eliminate government-based Social Security entirely.

Bush failed to build a Congressional coalition to pass his Social Security agenda. Labeled as radical and irresponsible, it wasn't. During Bush's first year in office, Congress had enthusiastically privatized a federal retirement plan even older than Social Security.

During the Great Depression, after scores of railroads had defaulted on their pension plans, Congress established a federal railroad workers retirement plan. This was landmark legislation. Washington promised to guarantee the pensions of the nation's largest labor force, the railroad workers. A year later, in 1935, the railroad plan became the model for Social Security. Seven decades later, while arguing over Bush's Social Security plan, Congress approved the Railroad Retirement and Survivors' Improvement Act of 2001. The Act, among other provisions, "empowered [the trustees] to invest trust assets in non-governmental assets, such as equities and debt, as well as in governmental securities."[115] This allowed trustees of the Railroad Workers Trust Fund to invest in high-yield stocks and bonds.

But Congress failed to adopt the same, or a modified, approach for Social Security. The failure was a lost opportunity for America's retirees. From 2003 through 2018, the Railroad Workers Trust Fund averaged 8.2 percent annual growth.[116] During these same years, Social Security's trust funds (together known as Old Age, Survivors, and Disability Insurance, or OASDI) averaged only 4.4 percent.[117] That may seem like a small difference, but compounded over a lifetime, the increase in wealth is substantial. A $5,000 payroll tax invested annually from 1980 through 2020 would have grown to $550,470 earning 4.4 percent annually, but $1,482,408 when earning 8.8 percent. That's the difference between retiring with a nice nest egg versus retiring with a nice nest egg, plus a small vacation home, plus a fishing boat, plus an annual vacation, plus college education for the grandkids. Quite a difference.

The danger though of total privatization is that markets fluctuate, often wildly. A person who retired after a market implosion such as the 2008 Financial Crisis would find her retirement savings significantly smaller than expected. So, any retirement plan must balance its various assets to assure it's not devastated during a market downturn.

Bush tried again in January 2005 after winning reelection. But the more Bush promoted privatization, the less the public liked it. By June, a Gallup poll registered the public's 64 percent disapproval. In August of that year, Hurricane Katrina took 1,800 lives, devastating New Orleans, and Bush's political capital as well. His Social Security plan quietly died.

Bush failed to reform Social Security. He took a different approach with Medicare. Like Social Security, Medicare is a pay-as-you-go program projected to lose trillions as Baby Boomers retire. But rather than focus on reform, Bush aggravated Medicare's weak financial underpinnings when he signed the Medicare Prescription Drug, Improvement, and Modernization Act on December 8, 2003. The Act added outpatient prescription drug coverage to Medicare Part D. The bill only passed in the House by a single vote after a desperate all-night, arm-twisting session.

The Congressional Budget Office projected the new drug program would cost $550 billion between 2006 and 2013.[118] Their estimate was right on. By 2013 Medicare Part D expenditures had hit $69 billion rising to $100 billion three years later in 2016.[119]

Regrettably, to achieve its passage, the bill's sponsors agreed to forbid Medicare, the nation's largest drug purchaser, from negotiating drug prices. Instead, drug price negotiation was left to a fragmented collection of insurance companies, hospital networks, and pharmacies. But these middle-men, falling between drug manufacturers and their consumers, have little incentive to encourage drug price economy. Health insurance premiums are based on costs. If drug prices fall, insurance premiums will decline, in turn, reducing revenues and profits. So, insurance companies dutifully pass on drug price increases and cut costs elsewhere by reducing coverage and benefits.

A decade after the passage of the Medicare Modernization Act, *The Wall Street Journal* reported on drug prices in Norway, England, and Ontario, Canada. "The U.S. nearly always pays more for branded drugs," the 2015 *Journal* article revealed, "than England, Norway and Ontario [and] the U.S. is responsible for the majority of profits for most large pharmaceutical companies."[120] Norwegians, for example, paid less for thirty-seven of the top forty drugs than Americans. A dose of the common macular degeneration medication Lucentis cost Norwegians $894 while Americans paid $1,936. The second most popular, Eylea, was $919 in Norway and $1,930 in the United States, more than double. For the top ten drugs, Norwegians paid an average of 49.5 percent less.

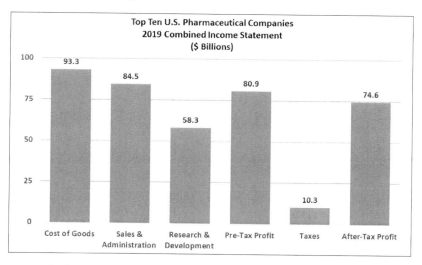

Pharmaceutical companies claim high drug prices are needed to support drug research and development. But most drug firms give priority to marketing and profits. In 2019, the average tax rate for the largest ten firms was only 13 percent.   YCHARTS

The Wall Street Journal findings were reinforced by an August 2016 Harvard Medical School study that concluded:

> In 2013, [U.S.] per capita spending on prescription drugs was $858 compared with an average of $400 for 19 other industrialized nations. . . The most important factor that allows manufacturers to set high drug prices is market exclusivity, protected by monopoly rights awarded upon Food and Drug Administration approval and by patents. . . prescription drugs are priced in the United States primarily on the basis of what the market will bear.[121]

America's pharmaceutical companies claim they need to charge high prices in the United States to finance research for new drugs. But that's misleading. Relative to marketing and profits, drug research is a low priority. In 2019, the top ten American pharmaceutical companies (Johnson & Johnson, Pfizer, Merck, Abbvie, Abbott, Bristol-Myers Squibb, Eli Lilly,

Stryker, Biogen, and Regeneron) spent only 26 percent of their revenues, on average, manufacturing their products. Twenty-five percent went to sales and administration while only 19 percent was spent on research and development. Plenty, 26 percent, was left over for pre-tax profits.[122]

Pharmaceutical companies can charge Americans the world's highest drug prices because money buys votes. From 1999 through 2018, the pharmaceutical and healthcare industry spent an astonishing $4.7 billion on lobbying Congress and campaign contributions, by far the most of any industry.[123] During the 2020 election alone, the industry spent $622 million on campaign contributions and employed an army of 2,908 lobbyists to influence the 535 members of Congress.[124]

Fate Had Other Plans

Few presidencies began with brighter prospects than George W. Bush. As Bush took the oath of office, the United States was the world's unquestioned economic, military, and cultural power. With the Soviet Union vanquished, China still a developing nation and terrorism a distant threat, American military spending measured against GDP had fallen to its lowest point since the nineteen-thirties. Unemployment was at a thirty-year low. The Internet was revolutionizing everything from commerce to people's social lives. Consumer sentiment was near historical highs. And the government was running the largest budget surpluses in seventy years. In his first State of the Union message, Bush confidently predicted:

> Many of you have talked about the need to pay down our national debt. I listened, and I agree. We owe it to our children and grandchildren to act now, and I hope you will join me to pay down $2 trillion in debt during the next ten years. At the end of those ten years, we will have paid down all the debt that is available to retire. That is more debt, repaid more quickly than has ever been repaid by any nation at any time in history.[125]

But fate had other plans. Eight years later America was mired in two Middle East wars; hordes of war refugees were pouring into Europe and beyond as they fled their devastated homelands; millions of Americans had lost their jobs, savings, and homes after the real estate bubble burst; the national debt had doubled to $12 trillion; and the nation was entering the deepest recession since the Great Depression eighty years earlier.

Bush's presidency was, perhaps, the most difficult in modern times. He presided over unpopular wars as had Lyndon Johnson, a historic economic collapse as had Herbert Hoover, and left the presidency with the lowest approval ratings since Richard Nixon. Yet Bush retained a measure of humility, personal integrity, and self-awareness that Americans are growing to increasingly appreciate. In his farewell address, President Bush reflected:

> Like all who have held this office before me, I have experienced setbacks. And there are things I would do differently if given the chance. Yet, I've always acted with the best interests of our country in mind. I have followed my conscience and done what I thought was right.... President Thomas Jefferson once wrote, "I like the dreams of the future better than the history of the past." As I leave the House he occupied two centuries ago, I share that optimism.[126]

Barack Obama

January 20, 2009 – January 20, 2017

> What troubles me is when I hear people say that all of government is
> inherently bad. . . . When our government is spoken of as some menac-
> ing, threatening foreign entity, it ignores the fact that, in our democracy,
> government is us.[1]

Barack Obama and Ronald Reagan had little in common, with one
exception: both assumed the presidency at the height of a national
crisis.

During the years preceding Reagan's presidency, Americans had seen
President Nixon resign in disgrace and Vietnam abandoned in defeat; suffered oil embargoes, persistent unemployment and historic inflation; and
been humiliated after Iranian students stormed the American embassy taking fifty-two hostages. By May 1980, as Reagan was on the campaign trail,
consumer sentiment had fallen to 51.7, its lowest point ever recorded.[2]
Americans were despondent and disillusioned.

If Americans suffered through a national drought in the years preceding
Reagan, they were hit by a financial flash flood as Obama took office. In
2008, the financial markets had collapsed. The ferocity of the crisis caught
America by surprise.

In early 2008, the Federal Reserve issued an optimistic forecast that predicted that unemployment would hold steady and the American economy
would grow real GDP two percent or more annually over the next three
years.[3] The Fed forecast was badly mistaken. By January 20, 2009 as Obama
assumed the presidency, real GDP had fallen 2.1 percent, 4.4 million jobs

had been lost, nearly a million homes foreclosed[4], Lehman Brothers had filed the largest bankruptcy in history, Chrysler and General Motors were teetering on bankruptcy, and the stock market had plunged 41 percent, its worst drop since 1931.[5] By the time the job market hit bottom in February 2010, nearly nine million Americans had lost their jobs.[6]

Reagan and Obama held opposing visions for how to turn the country around. Reagan believed government was the problem. Obama believed government was the solution.

"[My] plan," Reagan declared in his first Congressional address, "is aimed at reducing the growth in government spending and taxing, reforming and eliminating regulations which are unnecessary and unproductive or counterproductive, and encouraging a consistent monetary policy aimed at maintaining the value of the currency."[7]

President Reagan's economy boomed. Following double-dip recessions beginning in 1980 and 1981, real GDP grew 4.5 percent annually from 1983 through 1988. The economy added 15.4 million jobs. The Reagan post-recession expansion remains the strongest since the end of World War II.

President Obama took the opposite approach. "The private sector [is] so weakened by this recession," Obama declared in his first press conference, "the federal government is the only entity left with the resources to jolt our economy back into life. It is only government that can break the vicious cycle where lost jobs lead to people spending less money, which leads to even more layoffs."[8]

Backed by a supportive Congress, Obama moved quickly by signing the American Recovery and Reinvestment Act of 2009 (ARRA) less than a month after taking office. ARRA was a stimulus package intended to jump-start the economy by funneling nearly $800 billion to needy families; investing in infrastructure, alternative energy production, healthcare, education, and technology development; and encouraging business development through tax cuts and other incentives. Obama quickly followed ARRA with a stream of additional government programs that focused on economic recovery, healthcare, and tighter regulation of financial institutions.

Many modern presidents played golf, but few basketball, and none as well as Barack Obama. While president, Obama briefly coached his daughter Sasha's fourth-grade basketball team.   WHITE HOUSE PHOTO/ALAMY

The results were disappointing. Although the recession officially ended shortly after Obama took office, economic growth, adjusted for inflation, was the slowest since the nineteen-thirties—only 2.2 percent annually— well below the preceding nine post-recession expansions between 1954 and 2007, which averaged 4.3 percent.[9] The recovery was so weak that economists even revived a term from the Great Depression to describe it: *secular stagnation.*

Why was the Obama recovery so slow? In June 2009, even the Federal Reserve predicted real GDP would grow between 3.8 to 4.6 percent in 2010.[10] The Fed missed it by a mile. Real GDP grew an anemic 1.6 percent.

Traditional economic theory predicts the economy should have come roaring back. For decades, economists believed the deeper the recession, the stronger the recovery. Nobel Prize-winning economist Milton Friedman, after researching American recessions over 150 years, concluded in 1964 that "a large contraction in output tends to be followed, on the average, by a large business expansion."[11]

Friedman whimsically described his theory as plucking a violin string. A healthy economy is analogous to a tightly stretched violin string. A recession occurs when economic growth is declining, like plucking a violin string downward. The further down the string is pulled, the more quickly, and strongly, it bounces back. But Friedman's violin string theory failed during the 2008 Great Recession. Although Friedman's violin string had been plucked the furthest since the Great Depression eighty years earlier, it hardly sprang back.

Restoring the Economy

By the beginning of the twentieth century, the United States had suffered eight major banking crises since its founding. Over the next 120 years, only three, yet each nearly brought down the nation's entire banking system.

In 1907, two stock speculators, Augustus Heinze and Charles Morse, triggered a banking panic. The two speculators bought millions of shares of United Copper in a scheme to corner the copper market. It didn't work. United Copper's share price plummeted from $60 to $10. The company's collapse drove its bank, State Savings Bank of Butte, Montana, into bankruptcy. Nearly a dozen banks followed, toppling like a row of dominoes. Many more would have fallen except for J.P. Morgan, the nation's richest banker. Morgan and his friends stepped in and used their personal fortunes to bail out banks, the New York Stock Exchange, and even New York City itself. In 1907, Morgan saved the American banking system. Today, most only know J.P. Morgan's caricature as Monopoly's mustached Money Man.[12]

Twenty-three years later, in 1930, President Herbert Hoover took the opposite approach. After the 1929 stock market crash, hundreds of banks failed, wiping out the savings of millions of Americans. Hoover refused to intervene, confident that the government should allow weak banks to fail. Bank failures, Hoover believed, "culls the herd" of the weak resulting in a stronger financial system. "It will purge the rottenness out of the system," Treasury Secretary Andrew Mellon counseled the President.[13] It didn't work. By 1932, the nation had fallen into the Great Depression, putting nearly one in four Americans out of work.

Eighty years later, during the 2008 Financial Crisis, the lessons of 1907 and 1930 had been largely forgotten.

Within days of taking office, President Obama proposed an $800 billion stimulus program to create jobs through tax incentives and investments in education, healthcare, and infrastructure. Four months earlier, President Bush had signed the Troubled Asset Relief Program (TARP), passed with large majorities in both the House and Senate, which allocated $700 billion to purchase troubled financial assets, primarily mortgage-backed-securities that others would not touch.

Obama's stimulus program, the American Recovery and Reinvestment Act of 2009 (ARRA), immediately encountered strong resistance. On January 28, 2009 nearly 250 economists, including three Nobel laureates, signed a full-page advertisement in *The New York Times* stating their disagreement with Obama's proposed plan. In the ad, paid for by the Cato Institute and echoing Herbert Hoover eighty years earlier, the economists suggested that "We the undersigned do not believe that more government spending is a way to improve economic performance.... To improve the economy, policymakers should focus on reforms that remove impediments to work, saving, investment and production. Lower tax rates and a reduction in the burden of government are the best ways of using fiscal policy to boost growth."[14] The Cato ad was an endorsement of supply-side economics, which encourages the production of goods and services rather than consumption by consumers. The voice that spoke to Kevin Costner in the movie *Field of Dreams* was a supply-sider: "If you build it, he will come."[15]

In response, proponents of Obama's stimulus plan, channeling Franklin Roosevelt, sent a letter to Congress on February 8 supporting Obama's plan.[16] The letter was signed by over 200 economists, including six Nobel laureates. "The $825 billion American Recovery and Reinvestment Act of 2009," the letter stated, "is of the scale and breadth necessary to begin tackling the mounting problems faced by our economy. The plan proposes important investments that can start to overcome the nation's damaging loss of jobs by saving or creating millions of jobs and put the United States back onto a sustainable long-term growth path."[17]

Obama's proponents advocated demand-side economics, whose policies encourage consumption by having the government "put people back to work, to let them buy more of the products of farms and factories and start our business at a living rate again," as President Roosevelt explained his New Deal in 1933.[18]

The field of economics began in 1776 with Adam Smith's monumental work, *The Wealth of Nations*. Today, the economics profession is nearly 250 years old. Yet, in 2009, 450 of the nation's top economists, including nine Nobel Prize winners, could not agree on how to pull the nation out of a recession. Congress might as well have replaced all their advice with a coin toss.

There's plenty of money, though, advocating for each side of the coin.

The Cato Institute, for example, was founded by Charles G. Koch in 1977 with the mission to promote government policies that "create free, open, and civil societies founded on libertarian principles."[19]. *Forbes* magazine recently ranked Koch, and his (now deceased) brother, David, as the world's eighth richest individuals with a combined net worth of $120 billion.[20] On the other end of the political spectrum is the Roosevelt Institute which is focused on issues regarding corporate and public power, labor and wages, and the economics of race and gender inequality. The Institute is a partner of the FDR Library and Museum.

Between these two poles lie dozens of privately funded think tanks established to promote specific economic and political philosophies. Up until about 1970, most economists were tenured university professors free to conduct and publish independent research as they chose. But with the development of mission-focused think tanks, funded by wealthy interests, many economists have become salaried employees obliged to advance the special interests of their patrons.

Much of the resistance to Obama's economic programs was political, not economic. Obama's economic programs contained provisions that should have pleased both supply- and demand-side economists.

More than half of the ARRA, 54 percent, was devoted to tax cuts and other tax incentives that should have pleased supply-siders. To put more money in consumers' pockets, the program allocated $166 billion in tax credits that reduced payroll taxes by $400 for individuals and $800 for couples. $70 billion was allocated to a one-time increase in the Alternative Minimum Tax floor. Thirty-six billion dollars were allocated for increased tax credits for children, college and new home purchases. To encourage job growth, companies received $51 billion in tax incentives, making them eligible for tax refunds. State and local governments were allocated $144 billion to continue local health and education services without the need to raise state or local taxes.

The remaining 46 percent was reserved for demand-side programs designed to put people back to work rebuilding the nation's infrastructure. Nearly $49 billion was spent on energy programs, including a $535 million loan guarantee made to Solyndra, a solar panel manufacturer. That investment was lost when Solyndra filed bankruptcy in 2011, resulting in a major political scandal for the Obama administration. (Through 2014, the Department of Energy had loaned $34.2 billion to clean-energy companies with a loss rate of 2.28 percent. Overall, the clean-energy program turned a small profit of $30 million.)[21]

Obama followed the ARRA with a second economic recovery act, the Tax Relief, Unemployment Insurance Reauthorization, and Job Creation Act of 2010. The Act extended President Bush's tax cuts for two years beyond their 2010 expiration. The Act also included an additional $55 billion in tax cuts and incentives to businesses and extended unemployment insurance an additional 13 months.[22]

Finally, on January 2, 2013, Obama signed the American Taxpayer Relief Act of 2012. For individuals earning $400,000 or less, the Act froze taxes on income, capital gains, and dividends at their 2012 levels. For those above the threshold, the top tax rates on income increased from 35 to 39.6

percent; capital gains and dividends taxes increased from 15 to 20 percent; and estate taxes increased from 35 to 40 percent.[23]

The economic recovery programs started under Bush and continued by Obama pumped nearly $2.0 trillion into the economy, an amount unmatched since Roosevelt. Yet, the economic recovery under Obama was the slowest since World War II. The recovery under Ronald Reagan was far better. After the double-dip recessions early in Reagan's presidency, the economy grew a healthy 4.3 percent annually.[24]

Why? Were Reagan's economic policies more effective than Obama's, or were there other contributing factors?

The Reagan and Obama Recoveries

Economists and politicians tend to think they control the levers of the economy through their tax and economic policies. But often, other issues dominate, issues over which governments have little control. This was especially true during the Reagan and Obama economic recoveries.

Employment during the Reagan expansion increased far faster than during the Obama expansion, growing employment 2.4 percent annually from 1983 through 1988; Obama only managed 1.1 percent from 2010 through 2016. But Obama's slow employment growth was not due to poor economic policies. It reflected a larger trend.

President Reagan's economy benefited from the postwar baby boom as millions of Baby Boomers came of age. The population growth of those 25 - 54 years old peaked during the Reagan expansion at 2.3 percent annually, the highest rate in over a century. These young Americans were highly motivated, needing jobs to purchase new homes, goods, and services to support their growing families. From 1981 through 1988, this vital population grew by nearly seventeen million and contributed millions of new workers and consumers providing the locomotive force to drive the Reagan economy forward.[25]

Obama, however, inherited the tail-end of the Baby Boom population surge. As Boomers aged, the population growth of 25 - 54 years old slowed, reached a peak of 126 million in 2007, and then began a slow decline as the population of those 55 and older increased by nearly nineteen million during Obama's presidency. This demographic shift replaced the youthful energy of twenty-five-year-olds with the retirement needs of pensioners.

Population growth, employment, and GDP are tightly interconnected. A growing population increases consumption which increases jobs which increases GDP. A growing GDP increases business investment which further increases jobs, completing the cycle. Thus, the prevailing population demographics, while strongly boosting Reagan's economy, were a heavy drag on Obama's.[26]

But another, more intangible factor distinguished the Great Recession, and its slow recovery, from all other postwar recessions.

An old economist joke goes, "A recession is when your neighbor loses his job. A depression is when you lose yours." During the 1980 presidential campaign, Ronald Reagan added the quip, "And a recovery is when Jimmy Carter loses his."[27] Reagan was adept at memorable humor, in this case to conflate an economic recovery with Carter's departure. But there's an important insight in Reagan's joke beyond scoring a political point. A person's perception of the economy is strongly influenced by the economy's effect on them personally. Those who had parents or grandparents who lived through the Great Depression know their outlook was profoundly changed. Millions lost not only their jobs, but their life savings, homes, or farms. The experience affected the financial habits of a generation of Americans.

This wealth effect is a powerful factor in human behavior. How many of us treat ourselves to a special night out after a healthy raise at work? Or maybe a large screen TV after the stock market hits a new high? It's natural to treat oneself when feeling more affluent. But the reverse also applies. A decline in wealth causes most of us to become cautious, limiting our spending.[28]

Household Net Worth (HNW) is a household's total assets including home equity, automobiles, stocks and bonds, bank and retirement accounts less its liabilities, such as mortgage and credit card balances. Reductions in HNW, understandably, reduce consumer confidence and, consequently, spending.

Personal consumption represents approximately 70 percent of America's economy. When Americans are feeling affluent, they consume more, driving the economy upward. When wealth declines, whether due to a banking, housing, or stock market crisis, people pull back and slow their spending, and thus economic growth slows or even declines. Over the last seventy years, when real HNW was rising, personal consumption increased an average of 4.1 percent annually. But during wealth troughs, when HNW declined, growth fell to a feeble 1.1 percent.

There were seventeen wealth troughs lasting six or more months from 1950 through 2020. The longest trough, by far, was the trough that enveloped the Great Recession. That trough lasted nearly seven years beginning in February 2007 and ending in July 2013, four years after the recession officially ended.[29]

The equity in their homes is the largest component of most Americans' HNW. During the four years preceding Reagan's presidency, 1978 through 1981, the nation's total home equity, measured in 2020 dollars, increased 11 percent, from 5.6 to 6.2 trillion dollars. But from 2006 through 2009 as Obama was taking office, total home equity collapsed, falling from $18.3 to $11.3 trillion, an unprecedented decline of 38 percent.[30] Millions of homeowners had much, if not all, of their life savings wiped out.

Those holding stocks also suffered. The Standard & Poor's Index fell 41 percent in 2008, the year before Obama took office. It was the worst one-year decline since 1931. Shareholders not only suffered losses in their stock portfolio, but also dividend income. Corporate dividends fell 26 percent in 2009, the worst one-year decline since 1938.[31] Reagan was far more fortunate. The year before he took office, the market climbed 24 percent buoying consumer confidence.

For most Americans, nothing affects financial well-being more than holding a regular job. The Great Recession shed jobs faster and deeper than any since the Great Depression. From January 2008 through December 2009, 8.4 million Americans lost their jobs—nearly 16,000 workers every workday for over two years. Reagan, again, was lucky. From 1980 through 1983, employment remained relatively stable; between 99 and 100 million.

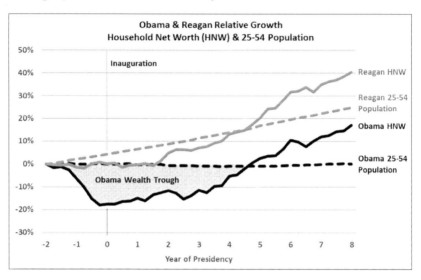

President Reagan had the strongest postwar recession recovery, Obama the weakest. The Obama expansion suffered from flat working-age population growth and the most severe "wealth trough" since the Great Depression eighty years earlier.

U.S. CENSUS BUREAU | FEDERAL RESERVE

The collapse of home values and stock prices coupled with over eight million lost jobs devastated HNW in the years leading up to and shortly after Obama took office. American HNW peaked in July 2007 at $89.1 trillion then fell to $72.8 trillion (both in 2020 dollars) by January 2009 as the housing and stock markets crashed. It was the greatest destruction of national wealth since the Great Depression.[32]

The decline in HNW was worst for those least able to afford it. From 2005 through 2010, HNW for the bottom 20 percent (the lowest quintile) of wage earners declined 43 percent. The second and third quintiles declined 37 and 28 percent, respectively. The top two income quintiles, those most able to weather a financial setback, lost less than 13 percent of their HNW.[33]

No economic crisis since 1938 destroyed more HNW than the Great Recession. These huge losses were a primary contributor to the slow recovery during the Obama years.

Reagan presided over the strongest economic recovery since World War II. Obama oversaw the weakest. Partisan economists and politicians view these different results through their particular ideological lenses. But changes in population and Household Net Worth were primarily responsible for the differences between the Reagan and Obama recoveries, not economic policies.

The Budget Control Act of 2011

In 2001, the economy and the Congressional Budget Office parted ways. That year, the CBO forecast a budget surplus of $2.7 trillion through 2007.[34] "After paying the bills, my plan reduces the national debt, and fast. So fast, in fact, that economists worry that we're going to run out of debt to retire," President George W. Bush declared in February.[35] But rather than huge surpluses, federal deficits totaled $1.5 trillion, a $4.2 trillion miscalculation by the CBO. Then, in January 2008, the CBO, like nearly everyone, failed to foresee the impending financial crisis when it estimated deficits from 2009 through 2010 at $439 billion.[36] Actual deficits exploded to $2.7 trillion.

In February 2010, Obama created a bipartisan commission to propose recommendations for regaining control of the federal budget. The commission consisted of twelve members of Congress and six private citizens. It was headed by Alan Simpson, the former Senator from Wyoming, and Erskine Bowles, Bill Clinton's former White House Chief of Staff.

Simpson and Bowles moved quickly, releasing their report on December 1. The report proposed six steps to lower the deficit from 10 percent to 2.3 percent of GDP by 2015. The report proposed a shared burden of spending cuts, tax increases, and reductions in Medicare and Social Security benefits.[37]

Government agencies would be required to cap future growth at half the inflation rate; cut federal and military retirement programs $70 billion over ten years; institute multiple measures to reduce healthcare spending; increase Social Security taxes and increase the retirement age to sixty-nine; end $1.1 trillion in individual and corporate tax loopholes while lowering taxation rates; and institute various other reforms to control spending, including moving to a balanced budget except during recessions. To help the nation continue its economic recovery, the report recommended delaying spending cuts for two years.[38] It was bitter medicine for a very sick economy.

Simpson and Bowles knew their spending cuts and tax increases would be strongly opposed by many of their colleagues. Joking with reporters, "[Bowles and I]" Simpson said, "will be on the witness-protection list when this is over."[39] Simpson was right. Everyone hated it. The report, titled "The Moment of Truth," proposed dozens of painful changes that were required, but political poison. Even the commission was divided. Requiring fourteen of its eighteen members to approve the report, only eleven did so.

With the federal deficit growing by trillions, if there ever was a time for political courage, this was it. Reagan faced a similar situation in 1983 as the Greenspan Commission was preparing its final report to revamp the Social Security system. At the time, the nation was still recovering from the double-dip recession two years earlier. Like Obama, Reagan's commission members were unable to agree on a proposal. Undeterred, Reagan and House Speaker Tip O'Neill bypassed the commission and assigned a small group of insiders to propose a workable plan that they handed to the deadlocked commission with instructions to approve it. Six months later, after considerable arm twisting, Reagan signed the plan into law.[40] The new law cut Social Security benefits and raised taxes, forcing nearly everyone to compromise. The result was that Social Security was put on a sound financial footing for the next thirty-five years. It was presidential leadership at its best.

But Obama was unable to develop a working relationship with Congress as Reagan had done. From the beginning, Obama was faced with fierce, often personal opposition. Senate Minority Leader Mitch McConnell, in a 2010 interview, declared: "The single most important thing we want to achieve, is for President Obama to be a one-term President." House Speaker John Boehner promised, "We're going to do everything—and I mean everything we can do to kill [the Obama agenda], stop it, slow it down, whatever we can."[41] Years later, in his 2021 book, *On the House*, Boehner's views on Obama had moderated:

> What I also had not anticipated was the extent to which this new crowd hated—and I mean hated—Barack Obama.... He's a secret

Muslim! He hates America! He's a communist! .... All of this crap swirling around was going to make it tough for me to cut any deals with Obama as the new House Speaker. Of course, it has to be said that Obama didn't help himself much either. He could come off as lecturing and haughty. He still wasn't making Republican outreach a priority. But on the other hand—how do you find common cause with people who think you are a secret Kenyan Muslim traitor to America?[42]

After rejecting the Simpson-Bowles Plan, Congress was forced to find a stop-gap approach for managing the swelling deficit. By 2011, thirty-six cents of every federal dollar spent needed to be borrowed.

In early 2011, the U.S. Treasury forecast the federal debt ceiling would be reached by August. If Congress didn't raise the ceiling, the federal government would be unable to pay its creditors, forcing the nation into default. Argentina, Greece, and Russia had recently defaulted on their sovereign debt with little international impact. But the U.S. dollar is the world's reserve currency. Most international transactions are conducted in American dollars and U.S. Treasury securities are considered the world's safest investment. A default on America's financial obligations would trigger an international financial crisis—and make it far more difficult for the U.S. Treasury to finance the nation's habitual deficit spending.

Ordinarily, raising the debt ceiling was routine. Congress had increased the ceiling seventy-four times from 1962 through early 2011.[43] But by July 2011, partisans in Congress had deadlocked negotiations, refusing either to raise taxes or cut spending. Unable to reach agreement legislatively, Congress was reduced to grasping at straws: declare the debt ceiling unconstitutional (it had been uncontested law since 1917); revalue the 8,000 tons of gold held by the Federal Reserve; or, most incredibly, mint a trillion-dollar coin to pay the deficit since there is no federal law prohibiting the denomination of minted coins.[44]

Ultimately, it was the White House that broke the deadlock when it proposed a draconian approach known as sequestration. A sequester (derived from the Latin, to separate) would automatically force deep spending cuts if Congress did not act on its own. Sequestration proposed mandatory budget cuts if Congress was unable to develop a deficit reduction plan. The notion was the cuts would be so onerous, cutting legislators' favorite programs so deeply, that Congress would be forced to act. Bob Woodward in his book, *The Price of Politics*, describes how Gene Sperling, the White House National Economic Director explained his proposal to President Obama: "A trigger [sequester] would lock in our commitment. Even though we disagree on the composition of how to get to the cuts, it would lock us in. The form of the automatic sequester would punish both sides. We'd have to September to avert any sequester."[45] It was said the idea of sequestration came to Sperling while disciplining his children: "Either clean your room or no video games for a week!"

Gridlocked and unable to agree on a solution, Congress approved the Budget Control Act (BCA) of 2011 on August 2. President Obama signed it the same day. The BCA immediately raised the debt ceiling $400 billion and provided for an additional debt increase of up to $1.5 trillion. In return, the BCA required Congress to develop a deficit reduction plan with a minimum of $1.2 trillion in spending cuts over ten years. If unable to do so by December 23, 2011, sequestration would automatically trigger, mandating deep, across-the-board spending cuts starting in 2013.

Watching the entire spectacle was Standard & Poor's, the credit rating agency. Credit agencies assess the risk of financial assets. In doing so, they determine the value of the asset. High-risk assets pay high yields (interest rates) to offset the risk. Consequently, the agencies are under constant pressure to rate assets as low risk.

Three days after the BCA was signed, S&P in a historic act downgraded the nation's credit rating to AA+, one notch below its top AAA rating. As their rationale, S&P provided a clear description of a dysfunctional Congress:

> The political brinksmanship of recent months highlights what we see as America's governance and policymaking becoming less stable, less effective, and less predictable than what we previously believed. The statutory debt ceiling and the threat of default have become political bargaining chips in the debate over fiscal policy.[46]

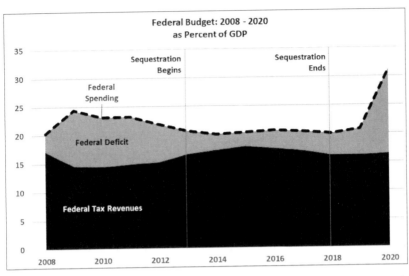

Sequestration was a desperate attempt to slow federal spending after Congress failed to do so. It succeeded for five years but was abandoned in 2018.

WHITE HOUSE OFFICE OF MANAGEMENT AND BUDGET

Eleven countries including diminutive Denmark, Liechtenstein, Luxembourg, Norway, and Switzerland were now a safer credit risk than the great United States.[47] After the downgrade, recriminations ensued with politicians blaming their opponents, and President Obama calling Standard & Poor's down-rating "flawed."[48]

But S&P was right. American governance had, indeed, become "less stable, less effective, and less predictable." On November 21, sequestration was triggered. The Congressional Joint Select Committee on Deficit Reduction had thrown in the towel. "After months of hard work and intense deliberations," the committee co-chairs declared, "we have come to the conclusion today that it will not be possible to make any bipartisan agreement available to the public before the committee's deadline."[49]

Sequestration drastically cut federal spending. From 2000 through 2012, federal spending, after inflation, had increased 3.3 percent annually. After sequestration, from 2013 through 2017, federal spending growth fell to 1.1 percent annually. Reagan had tried to curb federal spending by "starving the beast" of tax revenues, but that failed when Congress continued to spend even as tax revenues fell. Sequestration succeeded by disciplining Congress as an exasperated parent would a spoiled and unruly child.

By 2017, the defense industry was chafing under the spending caps. In a December 1, 2017 letter to Congress, defense CEOs from Boeing, Lockheed Martin, Raytheon, and other defense contractors petitioned Congress to repeal the spending caps. "Without repeal or substantial alteration of the discretionary spending caps introduced by the Budget Control Act of 2011," their letter asserted, "[the BCA] could undermine our collective commitment to strengthening military readiness. We strongly support your efforts to. . . repeal or raise the BCA caps, and keep the promises made to our military and our American workforce."[50]

The defense industry was concerned it was falling behind. In 2010, before sequestration, American defense spending represented 45 percent of the world's defense budget. The United States, with only four percent of the world's population, consumed nearly half the world's appetite for military defense spending. By 2017, the U.S. share had fallen to 38 percent. The United States spent $647 billion that year on defense—billions more than the combined defense spending by China ($228 billion), Saudi Arabia ($70.1 billion), Russia ($66.5 billion), India ($64.6 billion), France ($49.2 billion), United Kingdom ($46.4 billion), Japan ($45.4 billion) and Germany ($42.4 billion).[51]

President Trump supported higher defense spending declaring, "When I took over our military, we did not have ammunition I was told by a top general, maybe the top of them all, 'Sir, I'm sorry sir, we don't have ammunition.'"[52]

After five years of sequestration, and with an advocate of strong defense sitting as President, Congress needed little convincing. The sequestration caps were abolished by 2018, three years before their scheduled expiration. The next year, federal deficits climbed to nearly a trillion dollars.[53]

Still, even after the deep sequestration cuts, the national debt doubled from $10 trillion to $19.6 trillion during Obama's presidency. Obama saw it coming, and in a speech at George Washington University on April 13, 2011 discussed the nation's growing debt:

> Our leaders came together three times during the nineteen-nineties to reduce our nation's deficit. . . . As a result of these bipartisan

efforts, America's finances were in great shape by the year 2000. We went from deficit to surplus. America was actually on track to becoming completely debt free, and we were prepared for the retirement of the Baby Boomers. But after Democrats and Republicans committed to fiscal discipline during the nineteen-nineties, we lost our way in the decade that followed. We increased spending dramatically for two wars and an expensive prescription drug program—but we didn't pay for any of this new spending. Instead, we made the problem worse with trillions of dollars in unpaid-for tax cuts. . . . And so, by the time I took office, we once again found ourselves deeply in debt and unprepared for a Baby Boom retirement that is now starting to take place.[54]

Obama was right. In 1992, President George H.W. Bush handed Clinton a $290 billion annual deficit as he left office. Eight years later Clinton, with the help of Congress and a booming economy, turned the deficit into a $236 billion surplus.

The younger Bush didn't reciprocate. Rather than a surplus, George W. Bush left Obama a $458 billion deficit. Certainly, the Middle East Wars after 9/11 and the 2008 Financial Crisis contributed to the deficit, but Bush, just a year after taking office, had allowed tax revenues to fall well below expenditures, and they continued falling. By 2008, tax revenues were 17.2 percent of GDP while expenditures had climbed to 20.3 percent.

Measured in 2020 dollars, the deficit Bush left Obama was nearly identical to the deficit his father, George H.W. Bush, had left Clinton sixteen years earlier, approximately $542 billion. As the old expression goes: "Like father, like son."

In January 2009, the CBO projected deficits would peak that year at $1.2 trillion then fall rapidly to a total deficit of $3.7 trillion from 2009 through 2016. Obama's actual deficits during those years were far worse: $7.3 trillion. What happened?[55]

Surprisingly, slow economic growth wasn't responsible. The CBO projected total GDP from 2009 through 2016 at $133.5 trillion. The actual total was $132.4 trillion, just $900 billion less than the CBO's forecast and costing, at most, $180 billion in foregone tax revenues. Nor was it overspending. The CBO projected total spending at $29.1 trillion from 2009 through 2016. Actual expenditures, constrained by sequestration, were $465 billion less. That leaves tax revenues. The CBO forecast tax revenues would average 19 percent of GDP. Instead, tax revenues averaged only 16.1 percent. Total tax revenues were $21.3 trillion versus the forecast $25.4 trillion, resulting in $3.9 trillion in foregone tax revenues.

Based on the CBO's 2009 forecast, it wasn't lower GDP growth or higher spending that resulted in the Obama deficits, it was falling tax collections. The CBO report assumed "current laws and policies regarding federal spending and taxation remain the same," including no tax cuts. However, a month after taking office Obama signed the American Recovery and Reinvestment Act, which provided extensive tax cuts and credits.[56] A year later Obama extended the Bush tax cuts and then, in 2013, made the cuts permanent.[57]

The tax cuts were meant to stimulate economic growth by putting more money into the pockets of working Americans. And that's where they kept it, in their pockets. An aging population and the largest loss of Household Net Worth in three generations had made Americans cautious. Personal consumption, which averaged 3.3 percent annual growth from 1980 through 2008, fell to 1.6 percent from 2009 through 2016, while the personal savings rate jumped to an average of 7.1 percent from 2009 through 2016. Americans had chosen to save rather than spend as they rebuilt lost wealth.

While still recovering from the Great Recession, President Obama and a divided Congress passed two significant legislative acts. Both promised to reform industries that together represent nearly 40 percent of the American economy. The Dodd-Frank Wall Street Reform and Consumer Protection Act (Dodd-Frank) had its roots in George W. Bush's administration. The Patient Protection and Affordable Care Act (known both as the ACA and Obamacare) represented a project seventy years in the making, originally taking root with President Harry Truman.

Wall Street Reform and Consumer Protection

After seven years as Goldman Sachs chairman and CEO, Henry "Hank" Paulson represented the pinnacle of American capitalism when he became Treasury Secretary under President Bush in 2006. He hardly suspected that he would soon lead the most sweeping reform to financial regulations since Franklin Roosevelt's New Deal, reforms despised by many of Paulson's industry peers.

By early 2007, as the first banks and mortgage lenders were beginning to fail, Paulson had concluded the nation's financial regulations needed a major overhaul. Within months, Paulson announced a plan to develop a modernized financial regulatory system. "To maintain our capital markets' leadership," Paulson declared on June 27, "we need a modern regulatory structure complemented by market leaders embracing best practices."[58]

Paulson knew the last few years had been rife with corporate fraud. In 2001, Enron was caught hiding billions of debt from the company's balance sheet. Shareholders lost nearly $75 billion. A year later, MCI Worldcom was caught inflating assets by $11 billion, costing shareholders $180 billion. That same year the SEC and the Manhattan District Attorney caught Tyco inflating company income by $150 million. The CEO went to jail. In 2003, the SEC nabbed HealthSouth for inflating earnings by $1.4 billion. The CEO received a seven-year jail sentence for bribing the governor of Alabama. Freddie Mac in 2003 and Freddie Mae in 2004 were caught by the SEC overstating earnings by $5 billion. Management was fired. In 2005, a whistleblower tipped off the SEC that American Insurance Group (AIG) was booking loans as revenue and steered clients to insurers with whom AIG had pay-off agreements. AIG settled with the SEC and damaged parties for nearly $2.5 billion. The iconic Chairman and CEO, Maurice "Hank" Greenberg, was fired.

It was like the Wild West all over again except the bank robbers used accounting tricks rather than guns.

On March 31, 2008, Paulson's Treasury Department released a sweeping 212-page plan, "The Department of the Treasury Blueprint for a Modernized Financial Regulatory Structure."[59] Paulson's plan provided for the regulation of non-depository financial institutions, known as shadow banking institutions, that operated outside of normal banking regulations; additional regulation of mortgage originators; improvements in the regulation of state-chartered banks; the establishment of a federal insurance regulatory structure; improved regulation of the futures and securities industries; and empowerment of the Federal Reserve as a Market Stability Regulator to monitor risks across the entire financial system. The plan also installed a Prudential Regulator with powers to monitor capital adequacy requirements, investment limits, activity limits, and direct on-site risk management supervision, and a Business Conduct Regulator to monitor business conduct across all types of financial firms, including key aspects of consumer protection such as disclosures and business practices.[60]

Congress, oblivious to the coming financial crisis, ignored Paulson and his sweeping plan.

That changed within months when, as the nation plunged into the 2008 Financial Crisis, President Bush urged the adoption of Paulson's plan. "Our twenty-first century global economy," Bush lectured Congress, "remains regulated largely by outdated twentieth century laws.... Earlier this year, Secretary Paulson proposed a blueprint that would modernize our financial regulations. [These are] good ideas, and members of Congress should consider them."[61]

Two years later, Paulson's plan served as the blueprint for the Dodd-Frank Wall Street Reform and Consumer Protection Act of 2010. Signed by President Obama on July 21, 2010, Dodd-Frank, at 848 pages, was the largest overhaul of the nation's financial system since the Glass-Steagall Act of 1933.[62] The Dodd-Frank Act had six major components.[63]

First, Dodd-Frank established tight capital and liquidity rules that institutions accepting deposits must follow. This was to assure these institutions have enough funds to cover demands during financial crises. Before Dodd-Frank, some large financial institutions only held one dollar of cash for every fifty dollars in liabilities, a leverage ratio of fifty to one. After Dodd-Frank leverage ratios moved closer to ten to one.

Second, it regulated the trading of over-the-counter derivatives such as mortgage-backed securities and credit default swaps. Formerly, these securities were traded privately between institutions with little oversight.

These unregulated securities allowed huge amounts of risk to creep into the system.

Third, it required large banks to create detailed plans, similar to a person's living will, specifying how the bank would wind itself down without affecting other institutions as an alternative to bankruptcy. During both the 2008 Financial Crisis and the 1987 Savings and Loan Crisis, the federal government was forced to provide hundreds of billions in costly bailouts to save the financial system from total collapse.

Fourth, it prohibited commercial banks from engaging in proprietary trading, including speculative investments such as hedge funds and private equity funds. Known as the "Volcker Rule" after Paul Volcker, the prescient Federal Reserve Chairman appointed by President Carter, the rule was a step towards restoring the separation between investment and commercial banking that the 1933 Glass-Steagall Act had mandated before its effective repeal in 1999.

Fifth, the Financial Stability Oversight Council was established to identify and then monitor Systemically Important Financial Institutions (SIFIs), which are too big to be allowed to fail. These SIFIs would then be subject to increased capital and regulatory requirements by the Federal Reserve. The largest example of such an institution was AIG, which required a $180 billion bailout after it sold massive numbers of credit default swaps without adequate capital reserves.

Finally, Dodd-Frank established the Consumer Financial Protection Bureau (CFPB) to oversee financial institutions that provide mortgages, consumer and student loans, and credit cards. Deceptive and predatory practices by mortgage lenders had contributed to the high default rates leading up to the 2008 financial crisis. Like Paulson's Business Conduct Regulator, CFPB's mission was to reduce, if not eliminate, these abuses as well as educate the public regarding responsible personal financial management.

As the largest overhaul of financial regulations in eighty years, Dodd-Frank remains controversial. Critics claim Dodd-Frank has driven small banks out of business, failed to slow the growth of mega-banks, and reduced the numbers of small business loans.

"Dodd-Frank was supposedly aimed at Wall Street, but it hit Main Street hard," a July 19, 2015, *Wall Street Journal* editorial proclaimed, "Government figures indicate that the country is losing on average one community bank or credit union a day."[64] The *Journal* editorial was correct but misleading. From 2010 through 2015 the nation indeed lost an average of 4.5 banks per week. What the paper didn't mention was that from 1990 through 2007, the decline was significantly larger: 5.7 banks, on average, every week for 17 years. The decline of small banking in America began well before Dodd-Frank.

Since its passage, there has been pressure to roll back Dodd-Frank (and Sarbanes-Oxley passed earlier during the George W. Bush administration). Similarly, there was pressure to deregulate savings and loans during the early nineteen-eighties and to repeal portions of the Glass-Steagall Act in the late nineteen-nineties. Both times, Congress acquiesced. Both times, major financial crises followed costing hundreds of billions in government bailouts.

The Great American Healthcare Debate

On March 17, 2017, President Donald Trump and German Chancellor Angela Merkel held a White House press conference. The topic was trade and international relations. Yet, the first question wasn't trade-related, but whether President Trump would stand by his campaign promise to provide every American affordable healthcare.[65]

What was Chancellor Merkel thinking as the President struggled to answer? In contrast to the United States, Merkel knew that Germany had resolved its healthcare question in 1883 when Chancellor Otto von Bismarck established the world's first national health insurance system. Merkel also knew that America's per capita healthcare costs were twice Germany's. Yet, Americans lived shorter lives and suffered higher death rates for many diseases including heart disease, lung cancer, diabetes, kidney disease, and even common influenza.[66] (Years later, the United States would suffer a COVID death rate twice that of Germany during the pandemic.) Merkel may have wondered how the United States, so generous to Germany after World War II, had become so divided over its own citizens' healthcare.

Why is this? Ideology. Americans are ensnared in an ideological trap over the role government should play in healthcare. Presidents Truman and Eisenhower framed that debate seven decades ago:

> We are rightly proud of the high standards of medical care we know how to provide in the U.S. The fact is, however, that most of our people cannot afford to pay for the care they need. I have often and strongly urged that this condition demands a national health program. The heart of the program must be a national system of payment for medical care based on well-tried insurance principles. This great nation cannot afford to allow its citizens to suffer needlessly from the lack of proper medical care.[67]
>
> President Harry S. Truman

> I am flatly opposed to the socialization of medicine. The great need for hospital and medical services can best be met by the initiative of private plans. But it is, unfortunately, a fact that medical costs are rising and already impose severe hardships on many families. The Federal Government can do many helpful things and still carefully avoid the socialization of medicine.[68]
>
> President Dwight D. Eisenhower

Seventy years later, Americans still can't agree. Should healthcare be a right, available, in some form, to all citizens as are police and fire protection, or is healthcare simply another commodity like food, clothing, and housing?

America's healthcare debate began November 19, 1945 when President Truman, in a speech to Congress, proposed his Comprehensive Health Program. "The principal reason why people do not receive the care they need," Truman told Congress, "is that they cannot afford to pay for it on an individual basis at the time they need it. This is true not only for needy persons. It is also true for a large proportion of normally self-supporting persons... Sickness not only brings doctor bills; it also cuts off income."[69] Truman found it wrong that honest Americans, after working hard their entire lives, faced financial hardship or even ruin when faced with illness resulting in huge medical bills.

But by the late nineteen-forties America had entered its Red Scare period when communism was feared to be spreading throughout the nation.

It was Truman against the formidable American Medical Association (AMA). In a multi-million-dollar publicity campaign, the AMA condemned Truman's plan as un-American and a step towards socialism, even going so far as to call the White House "followers of the Moscow party line."[70] Congress never allowed Truman's plan to come up for a vote. It was Truman's greatest disappointment as President.

Even President Eisenhower, America's top military commander during World War II and, according to Gallup, the nation's most admired man, got the same Red Scare treatment.[71] In 1955, Eisenhower proposed the federal government subsidize insurance for individuals with pre-existing conditions. But Congress rejected Eisenhower's moderate proposal as a step towards communism. Senator Barry Goldwater, in a 1957 speech, later declared Eisenhower had been lured by the "siren song of socialism" which would result in the "consequent dissipation of the freedom and initiative and genius of our productive people, upon whom the whole structure of our economic system depends for survival."[72] The fringe John Birch Society claimed, outrageously, that Eisenhower was "a conscious agent of the Communist conspiracy."[73]

But by 1965, the Red Scare fever had burned itself out; America was thriving. That year, President Johnson sponsored Medicare and Medicaid legislation, which passed the House and Senate with healthy margins. These programs provide healthcare to the retired, the disabled, and the poor.

After President Johnson signed the Medicare bill, three Presidents attempted to expand federal healthcare over the next fifty years. All failed.

On February 6, 1974, President Nixon, in a special message to Congress, proposed a seven-point national healthcare plan. Echoing President Truman twenty-five years earlier, Nixon told Congress: "For the average family, it is clear that without adequate insurance, even normal care can be a financial burden while a catastrophic illness can mean catastrophic debt.... These gaps in health protection can have tragic consequences. They can cause people to delay seeking medical attention until it is too late. Then a medical crisis ensues, followed by huge medical bills—or worse. Delays in treatment can end in death or lifelong disability."[74] Nixon's healthcare plan died with Nixon's resignation in the wake of the Watergate scandal.

In 1977, President Carter and Senator Edward Kennedy attempted to collaborate on a comprehensive healthcare plan. But Kennedy's plan was ill-timed. It was too ambitious and too expensive for a nation then struggling with high unemployment and runaway inflation. Carter later proposed a more limited plan. But with Carter consumed with the Iran Hostage Crisis and fighting for reelection, the plan quietly died.[75]

The last national healthcare effort prior to Obama was in 1993. That year, President Clinton appointed Hillary Clinton to head a task force to develop a healthcare proposal, a plan quickly dubbed Hillarycare. The plan met a solid wall of resistance. It didn't help that Hillary Clinton was a private citizen who conducted the task force's deliberations in private. Like the healthcare plans presented by Truman, Nixon, and Carter, Hillarycare never came up for a vote in Congress.[76]

Fifteen years later, Barack Obama won a landslide victory against Senator John McCain.[77] Although the nation was just beginning to recover from the worst financial crisis in eighty years, Obama put healthcare at the top of his priority list.

Obama knew it would be a fight. With the Soviet Union defeated, opponents would have a harder time claiming national healthcare was a communist Trojan horse. But that claim was replaced by the argument that overreaching federal programs like national healthcare were unconstitutional, an issue that extended back to President Washington's first term.

Washington, in 1792, promoted the establishment of a national postal system to encourage the education of Americans by "circulating newspapers and political documents that would guard the public from tyrants and demagogues spreading misinformation."[78] But Thomas Jefferson argued a national postal service would be "a massive federal system that would be as oppressive as European monarchies" and that a national postal service, holding all the nation's citizens' names and addresses, might become "a dangerous force, spying on the public... and meddling in politics."[79]

Similarly, Treasury Secretary Alexander Hamilton engaged in a bitter fight in 1791 with Thomas Jefferson and James Madison over the establishment of a national bank. Hamilton believed a national bank was necessary for the United States to meet its financial obligations while Jefferson and Madison argued a federal bank was unconstitutional.

These arguments remain familiar today. From America's inception, the central issue in American politics has been the proper role of the federal government. The debates over a national postal service, federal bank, taxation, slavery, Social Security, civil rights, and healthcare are all deeply rooted in the question of the proper role of the federal government. No other question has been more passionately debated, or more widely interpreted, throughout the history of the United States.

The Patient Protection and Affordable Care Act

Unlike Truman, Nixon, Carter, and Clinton, Obama's healthcare plan succeeded. President Obama signed the Patient Protection and Affordable Care Act on March 23, 2010.

Pejoratively labeled "Obamacare," no legislation since Franklin Roosevelt's New Deal was more despised by its opponents. New Hampshire State Representative Bill O'Brien: "And what is Obamacare? It is a law as destructive to personal and individual liberty as the Fugitive Slave Act of 1850..."[80] Alaska Governor Sarah Palin: "The America I know and love is not one in which my parents or my baby with Down Syndrome will have to stand in front of Obama's 'death panel'.... Such a system is downright evil."[81] Representative Michele Bachmann: "Let's repeal this failure before it literally kills women, kills children, kills senior citizens.... Let's repeal it now while we can."[82] Radio host Glenn Beck: "This is the end of prosperity in America forever, if this passes. This is the end of America as you know it."[83]

A decade later, America had survived Obamacare's alleged death panels, retained its constitutional liberties, and grown its economy by trillions of dollars. But if Obamacare's opponents were overly zealous in their predictions of death, tyranny, and economic collapse, its adherents were too optimistic. President Obama promised "If you like the plan you have, you can keep it. If you like the doctor you have, you can keep your doctor, too. The only change you'll see are falling costs as our reforms take hold."[84]

Obamacare has neither been the scourge its opponents predicted nor the universal remedy its adherents promised.

If the Patient Protection and Affordable Care Act of 2010 had a corporate-style mission statement, it would be to provide comprehensive health-care services to all Americans efficiently and cost-effectively. But Obamacare, born of political compromise, is a complex amalgam of laws, rules, and guidelines fragmented across federal and state governments, employers, the healthcare industry, and insurance companies. That's hardly a model of efficiency.

Yet, Obamacare has successfully delivered the ten essential benefits the legislation promised Americans:

1. Preventive care including regular physicals and screenings such as cancer, diabetes and high cholesterol with no out-of-pocket costs.
2. Maternity and newborn care, also provided without additional cost.
3. Mental health treatment, including alcohol and drug addiction treatment.
4. Rehabilitative services and devices needed for treating both short and long-term disabilities and illnesses.
5. Laboratory tests including those needed to diagnose illnesses that are covered at no additional cost.
6. Pediatric care including dental and vision care.
7. Prescription drugs with out-of-pocket costs charged against deductibles.
8. Outpatient care.
9. Emergency room services including those without prior authorization.
10. Hospital stays.[85]

Obamacare proponents argue that these mandated services make not only medical but economic sense. The preventive care provisions of

Obamacare reduce long-term healthcare costs by identifying illnesses early, allowing less expensive treatments. Preventive care helps to identify and discourage unhealthy lifestyles such as obesity, smoking, and lack of exercise. Treatment for alcoholism, drug abuse, and mental illness reduces crime and suicides. Basic maternity, newborn, and pediatric healthcare is not only moral but also avoids medical problems later in life.

Nearly half of all Americans, 158 million in 2019, receive health insurance through their employer, a system that originated during World War II. During the war, due to wage freezes to control inflation, companies could not raise wages to compete for scarce employees. Instead, companies began to offer health insurance to attract and keep employees. The disadvantage of employer-provided healthcare insurance is that employees lose their coverage upon leaving the company.

For individuals without company-based insurance, Obamacare provides state-based health exchanges and expanded Medicaid.[86]

The healthcare exchanges serve as online shopping malls for medical insurance. Like a shopping mall, the exchanges promote competition by allowing shoppers to compare services and prices. Obamacare mandates that all states provide healthcare exchanges whether directly themselves, through a federal exchange, or a combination of state and federal services.

For those unable to afford insurance, Obamacare provides subsidized healthcare—but only if their state offers expanded Medicare. Many states, for ideological reasons, resisted Obamacare's expansion. Georgia Insurance Commissioner Ralph Hudgens, for example, declared in an August 2013 political rally: "The problem is Obamacare. Let me tell you what we're doing: everything in our power to be an obstructionist. . . . I'm not going to do anything in my power to make this law successful."[87] That year, 26 percent of Georgia's citizens aged nineteen to sixty-four were uninsured, the fourth highest in the nation.[88]

In 2015, twenty-two states refused Obamacare's Medicaid expansion.[89] But states soon began to slowly drop their opposition—especially after the COVID pandemic struck in 2020. By October 2020, only twelve states were still opting out: Alabama, Florida, Georgia, Kansas, Mississippi, North Carolina, South Carolina, South Dakota, Tennessee, Texas, Wisconsin, and

Wyoming.[90] During the pandemic, several of these states suffered some of the highest COVID death rates in the nation.

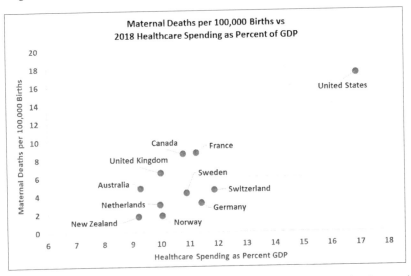

There are few better measures of a nation's healthcare system—and values—than how it cares for its mothers. The United States fares very poorly. U.S. maternal death rates are more than twice those of other developed nations even while spending far more on healthcare.   COMMONWEALTH FUND | STATISTA

Many detested Obamacare. For Americans with access to quality health-care, Obamacare provided little additional benefit and often increased their healthcare costs. Insurance premiums and taxes went up to pay for the broader coverage Obamacare provided. Religious organizations, such as the Little Sisters of the Poor, were forced to provide insurance that covered abortion, a practice the sisters vehemently opposed as a mortal sin against their Fifth Commandment, "Thou shall not kill." People with limited healthcare insurance that did not meet Obamacare's requirements were forced to upgrade their plans, and even change doctors. Others objected to Obamacare as government overreach, concerned that Obamacare would be the "end of America as you know it," as radio pundit Glenn Beck warned his listeners.[91]

But for Americans with pre-existing conditions, or unable to afford health insurance, Obamacare provided real benefits. In 2010, 15.6 percent of Americans had no health insurance. By 2016, as Obama was leaving of-fice, that figure had been cut nearly in half to 8.6 percent. That's nearly twenty million Americans.[92] Before Obamacare, a person with a pre-existing condition could work for a company for thirty years, dutifully paying insurance premiums, be laid off in a recession, and, if lucky enough to find another job, be turned down for health insurance due to a pre-existing condition. Obamacare ended that shameful practice.

Although still polarized, Americans' feelings about Obamacare continue to evolve. In 2014, after a rocky roll-out, a Gallup poll found that only 37 percent approved of Obamacare. Approval rates then began a steady climb and hit a peak approval rate of 55 percent in early 2017 as President Trump was taking office. By late 2019, approval rates had fallen to 50 percent.[93] This is not surprising. Trump consistently promised to repeal and replace Obamacare, declaring: "Obamacare is a disaster. It's too expensive by far... we will have a plan that's far better than Obamacare."[94]

President Trump never replaced Obamacare. But was Trump right? Is Obamacare a disaster? Here's how one study, conducted by the Commonwealth Fund, summarized the state of American healthcare in 2019:

> While the United States spends more on health care than any other country, we are not achieving comparable performance. We have poor health outcomes, including low life expectancy and high suicide rates, compared to our peer nations. A relatively higher chronic disease burden and incidence of obesity contribute to the problem, but the U.S. health care system is also not doing its part. Our analysis shows that the U.S. has the highest rates of avoidable mortality because of people not receiving timely, high-quality care. . . . The U.S. health care system is the most expensive in the world, but Americans continue to live relatively unhealthier and shorter lives than peers in other high-income countries. Efforts to rein in costs, improve affordability and access to needed care, coupled with greater efforts to address risk factors, are required to alleviate the problem.[95]

Since President Truman, ideological debates over healthcare have contributed to uneven healthcare and shorter lives for millions of Americans. Obamacare has helped but is hardly the final answer.

The Arab Spring

For Mohamed Bouazizi, December 17, 2010 opened like any other day. By 8:00 am Bouazizi had set up his street cart in the town square of Sidi Bouzid, a rural village in Tunisia. The twenty-six-year-old Bouazizi supported his mother and siblings by selling fruits and vegetables. Bouazizi had hoped for a better life but was unable to find other work and had been rejected by the army.

Around 10:30, two police officers confronted Bouazizi for selling without a license. Bouazizi had been confronted before and reputedly paid bribes to be left alone. But this time, Bouazizi objected. The officers kicked over his street cart and the senior officer, a woman, slapped him in the face, the ultimate humiliation for an Arab man. Angry and disgraced, Bouazizi went to the local governor's office to protest. The governor refused to see him, even after Bouazizi threatened to set himself on fire.

Minutes later, Bouazizi, outside the government office, struck a match to his gasoline-soaked body. "How do you expect me to make a living?" Bouazizi shouted as the flames engulfed him.[96]

Bouazizi's act of self-immolation set off a firestorm throughout North Africa and the Middle East. On January 14, 2011, Tunisian President Zine el-Abidine Ben Ali fled the country after stepping down. On January 25, Egypt erupted in protest. An estimated 840 protesters were killed by Egyptian security forces before Egyptian President Hosni Mubarak stepped down on February 11.

A week later, Libyans rose up to overthrow Colonel Mu'ammar al-Gaddafi. After months of fighting, Libyan revolutionaries dragged Gaddafi's mutilated body through the streets. On March 15, Syrian protesters were brutally suppressed by government forces, initiating a civil war that, as of this writing in 2021 has killed more than 250,000 people and forced six million from their homes. On March 18, Yemeni security forces killed fifty protesters, thus sowing the seeds of an unending civil war that would erupt in 2014.[97]

History, somehow confused, has named these violent months the Arab Spring.

The mother and two sisters of Mohamed Bouazizi during a 2011 Reuters interview. Bouazizi triggered the Arab Spring when he set himself afire in protest to his poverty and government indifference.   REUTERS/ALAMY

President Obama helped fuel the Arab Spring's revolutionary fire. Two years earlier, in June 2009, Obama, in a wildly popular speech at Cairo University, promised the Arab world, "Americans are ready to join with citizens and governments; community organizations, religious leaders, and businesses in Muslim communities around the world to help our people pursue a better life... a world where governments serve their citizens."[98]

Yet, Obama largely stood by as the Arab world erupted in revolution.

In March 2011, United Nations forces in Libya supported the rebels fighting to overthrow Colonel Gaddafi. The U.N. forces quickly departed after Gaddafi's death, leaving a power vacuum in the shattered country. That power vacuum contributed, on September 11, 2012, to the deaths of four American diplomats when terrorists stormed United States government facilities in Benghazi. Libya, formerly a brutal but stable dictatorship under

Gaddafi, today is a breeding ground for terrorism nurtured by competing geopolitical interests.[99]

Yemen, a wretchedly poor country with a per capita GDP of just four percent that of Saudi Arabia, has suffered immensely since the Arab Spring.[100] After years of political turmoil, the country fell into civil war in 2014. After Yemeni President Abdrabbuh Mansur Hadi fled the country, Saudi Arabia and a coalition of nine countries intervened against Houthi rebels backed by Iran. Yemen had become the battleground for a proxy war between Saudi Arabia and Iran. After six years of fighting, the conflict became so routine it was called "the forgotten war."[101] But not by the Yemenis. By 2019, Amnesty International estimated 233,000 Yemenis had died from the fighting, starvation, and disease.[102]

No country, though, has suffered more than Syria. There, beginning in March 2011, peaceful protests demanding democratic reforms by President Bashar al-Assad were met by lethal force. Two months later, 1,200 Syrians had died. By mid-2012, the death toll reached 16,000 as the fighting broke into a raging civil war. Like in Yemen, outsiders intervened and turned the fighting into a geopolitical conflict. Russia, Iran, and Hezbollah militants based out of Lebanon came to Assad's aid, while Saudi Arabia and the United States supported the Syrian rebels.

President Assad has been brutal in his use of cluster and thermobaric bombs, and poison gas against his own citizens. (Thermobaric bombs spread a large cloud of explosive material before igniting, causing widespread destruction.) In August 2012, when reports arose of Assad's use of poison gas, President Obama told reporters that Syria's use of chemical weapons would cross a "red-line." A year later, on August 21, Assad's forces used Sarin gas—a gas so toxic even Hitler banned its use during World War II—to bomb a Damascus suburb, asphyxiating over 1,000 civilian men, women, and children.[103]

Obama blinked. Rather than immediately ordering a military strike on Syria, Obama dithered. A month later, Russian President Vladimir Putin rescued Obama when he offered to force Russia's ally, Syria, to destroy its chemical weapons cache if Obama promised not to bomb Syria, an offer Obama readily accepted.[104]

Obama was roundly criticized as weak for failing to punish Assad after crossing his red-line. "When it comes to military power, Obama is an agnostic at best. For him, eloquent words are more effective than sharp swords," the *Cairo Review* opined.[105] Less circumspect was Donald Trump who, during the October 9, 2016 presidential debate, called the incident a national "humiliation" as the United States "was laughed at all over the world."[106]

But Obama believed he had made the right decision. "We've ended one war in Iraq," Obama declared in a White House speech ten days after Assad's gas attack. "We're ending another in Afghanistan. And the American people have the good sense to know we cannot resolve the underlying conflict in Syria with our military. In that part of the world, there are ancient sectarian differences, and the hopes of the Arab Spring have unleashed forces of change that are going to take many years to resolve. And that's why we're not contemplating putting our troops in the middle of someone else's war."[107]

Obama and, earlier, President George W. Bush both supported pulling American troops out of the Middle East. In 2008, Bush signed the U.S.–Iraq Status of Forces Agreement that committed the United States to pull American troops out of Iraq by the end of 2011. A month after taking office, Obama reaffirmed Bush's agreement with the Iraqis. By early 2012, as Bush had committed four years earlier, all American troops had left Iraq, leaving a contingent of 8,000 private contractors—paid mercenaries—to support Iraqi defense efforts.[108]

America's withdrawal seemed to be working. From 2012 through 2016, as Obama left office, thirty-four unfortunate American soldiers had died in Iraq, a fraction of the 1,486 deaths in the prior five years.[109] But as American troops departed, Abu Bakr al-Baghdadi, an Iraqi cleric turned terrorist, was quietly merging local terrorist factions in Iraq and Syria into a terrifying new force. That quiet coalescence surfaced on April 8, 2013, when Baghdadi announced the formation of the Islamic State of Iraq and Syria (ISIS), appointing himself as its caliph.[110]

President Obama initially discounted the rise of ISIS, disparaging the terrorist organization as the JV (Junior Varsity) team. He soon regretted his statement after ISIS terrorists shocked the world with their brutality.   RICHARD LEVINE / ALAMY

For the next three years, ISIS seemed unstoppable. By late 2015, ISIS had established a caliphate that spanned northern Syria and western Iraq, occupying a territory the size of Great Britain. The Central Intelligence Agency estimated that ISIS had 31,500 active fighters. Oil revenues, extortion, and taxation brought in as much as $1.0 million a day, putting ISIS, as a religious organization, on par financially with the Vatican.[111] Attracted by its rapid rise, ISIS affiliates spread rapidly from Libya in North Africa through a dozen countries in the Middle East to Asia and the Philippines in the Pacific.[112]

Where ISIS spread, death followed. Civilians in Iraq and Syria suffered the most. From 2012 through 2016, over 68,000 Iraqi civilians died, caught in the crossfire between ISIS and Iraqi security forces.[113] Nearly 88,000 civilians died in Syria over those same years.[114]

To support itself, ISIS taxed its subjects and exported oil on the black market. But its main export was terror. In 2014 and 2015, ISIS and its affiliates posted videos showing the shockingly cruel executions of scores of captives in its caliphate and Libya. Beyond its borders, ISIS inspired a wave of horrific terrorist attacks seldom seen in the modern world.

Over the next five years, thousands of innocent people were brutally murdered in ISIS-related terrorist attacks. In the United States: fourteen healthcare workers were shot down in San Bernardino, California on December 2, 2015; forty-nine revelers murdered at the Pulse Nightclub in Orlando, Florida on June 12, 2016. In Europe: terrorist attacks killed 130 people out for the evening in Paris on November 13, 2015; explosions at Brussels Airport killed thirty-two travelers on March 22, 2016; suicide bombers killed forty-four people at Ataturk Airport in Istanbul, Turkey on June 28, 2016; eighty-four died when a French-Tunisian drove a truck through a crowd celebrating Bastille Day in Nice, France on July 14, 2016. In the Middle East and North Africa: ten people murdered at the Corinth Hotel in Tripoli, Libya on January 27, 2015; car bombs killed twenty-six people in Cairo, Egypt on January 29, 2015; twenty-three murdered while visiting the Bardo Museum in Tunis, Tunisia on March 18, 2015; 137 died in mosque bombings in Sanaa, Yemen on March 20, 2015. And dozens of other terrorist attacks whose videos horrified millions around the world.[115]

Buoyed by the death of Osama Bin Laden at the hands of Navy Seals on May 2, 2011 and the decline of Al Qaeda, Obama initially dismissed the motley terrorist groups emerging in Afghanistan, Iraq, and Syria. In January 2014, David Remnick of the *New Yorker* asked Obama about the rising threat. "The analogy we use around here sometimes," Obama replied, "and I think is accurate, is if a [Junior Varsity] team puts on Lakers uniforms, that doesn't make them Kobe Bryant."[116]

Obama soon regretted that dismissive statement. Six months later ISIS began its terror spree. On June 19, 2015, the State Department, in its annual terrorism report, declared ISIL "the greatest threat globally."[117] (ISIS and ISIL are used interchangeably. ISIS stands for the Islamic State of Iraq and Syria while ISIL stands for the Islamic State of Iraq and the Levant.)

With the United States uninterested in "putting our troops in the middle of someone else's war" as Obama declared in 2012, a disparate collection of forces joined in the fight against ISIS. France, hard-hit internally by terrorist attacks, began bombing ISIS targets in Syria. Russia, an ally of Syria, did the same. Iran sided with Iraq in its fight against ISIS. The United States, though, did support the Kurds, an ancient people descended from the Persians, who were fighting ISIS. Standing somewhat aloof from the fray, Saudi Arabia organized a coalition of thirty-four countries to fight "Muslim extremism."[118] Attacked on all sides and bombed from above, the ISIS caliphate slowly shrank. As Obama left office, the caliphate had lost 40 percent of its territory. By 2019, under President Trump, the caliphate had been reduced to controlling only a few square miles in western Iraq.[119]

Trump rendered ISIS a major blow on October 26, 2019 with Operation Kayla Mueller, named after the twenty-six-year-old humanitarian aid worker who died in the custody of ISIS. That day, U.S. Delta Force commandoes raided the hideout of Abu Bakr al-Baghdadi in northwest Syria. Baghdadi fled into a tunnel with two young children. Trapped, Baghdadi detonated a suicide vest obliterating himself and the two children.

By 2020, ISIS may have been rendered dormant, but hardly defeated. As their caliphate collapsed, ISIS survivors carried away an estimated $400 million in cash and gold. Buried, hidden away in bank accounts, and laundered through legitimate businesses, the stolen money is used today to finance ISIS operations in Iraq and Syria and affiliated terrorists abroad. "ISIS is still very much intact," Masrour Barzani, the Prime Minister of Iraqi Kurdistan declared in a February 14, 2020 interview. "Yes, they have lost much of their leadership. They have lost many of their capable men. But they've also managed to gain more experience and to recruit more people around them. So, they should not be taken lightly."[120]

The Iran Nuclear Deal

Early on the afternoon of January 17, 2016, an Iranian Boeing 737 departed Geneva and turned eastward for Tehran. On-board were wooden pallets stacked with $400 million in Swiss francs.[121]

A few hours later, a beaming President Obama strode into the Cabinet Room for a news conference. Obama was ostensibly there to discuss progress on the Iran Nuclear Agreement signed six months earlier on July 14, 2015. But Obama had other more dramatic news he was anxious to disclose: the announcement that five Americans, held in Iran as hostages, were being released. "Americans unjustly detained by Iran are finally coming home," Obama announced. "Our diplomats at the highest level, including Secretary Kerry, used every meeting to push Iran to release our Americans. I did so myself, in my conversation with President Rouhani."[122]

After years of captivity, the hostages were finally coming home. It was a proud day for America. "The United States and Iran," Obama declared near the end of his speech, "are now settling a longstanding Iranian government claim against the United States government. Iran will be returned its own funds, including appropriate interest. . . . With the nuclear deal done, prisoners released, the time was right to resolve this dispute as well."

Few eyebrows were raised by Obama's brief comment regarding the resolution of a few sundry legal claims. That changed on August 3 when *The Wall Street Journal* published an explosive story: "The Obama administration secretly organized an airlift of $400 million worth of cash to Iran that coincided with the January release of four Americans detained in Tehran. . . . The money represented the first installment of a $1.7 billion settlement the Obama administration reached with Iran."[123] *The Wall Street Journal* story also disclosed that as part of the hostage deal, the United States freed seven imprisoned Iranian citizens and dropped extradition requests for fourteen others.

A political conflagration erupted, fueled by election-year politics. "President Obama's disastrous nuclear deal with Iran was sweetened with an illicit ransom payment and billions of dollars for the world's foremost state sponsor of terrorism," Senator Marco Rubio proclaimed. "Sending the world's leading state sponsor of terror pallets of untraceable cash isn't just terrible policy," Senator Ed Royce declared, "it's incredibly reckless, and it only puts bigger targets on the backs of Americans. . ."[124] "We paid $400 million for the hostages," Donald Trump fumed. "Such a bad precedent was set by Obama. We have two more hostages there, right? What's are we going to pay for them? What we're doing is insane."[125]

Obama's agreement to pay $1.7 billion to Iran was the culmination of thirty-five years of negotiations between the two countries. Before its 1979 revolution, Iran had been one of America's largest weapons buyers under the U.S. Foreign Military Sales (FMS) Program. "As part of the FMS Program, a trust fund was established with Iranian funds to pay U.S. contractors as work progressed on the various contracts."[126] In February 1979, during the Iranian Revolution, the United States froze the $600 million then in the FMS trust fund, agreeing to eventually return the funds to Iran with accrued interest. Eleven years later, President George H.W. Bush quietly returned $200 million to Iran in a partial settlement, leaving a $400 million balance. That balance accrued interest annually for the next twenty-six years. By 2016, the trust fund had swollen to $1.7 billion.

Obama's $1.7 billion payment was political poison but only marginally contributed to Iran's defense spending. After the payment, Iran increased its defense spending 28 percent to an average of $13.1 billion in 2016 and 2017. Still, Iran's defense spending was dwarfed by its Middle Eastern foes whose combined defense spending averaged over $110 billion annually, led by Saudi Arabia ($67 billion) and Israel ($18.5 billion).[127]

The larger issue was the Joint Comprehensive Plan of Action Agreement, or simply the Iran Nuclear Deal, signed the prior year on July 14, 2015 by the United States, Iran, the European Union, France, Germany, the United Kingdom, China, and Russia. "After two years of negotiations," Obama declared at the signing, "the United States, together with our international partners, has achieved something that decades of animosity has not—a comprehensive, long-term deal with Iran that will prevent it from obtaining a nuclear weapon."[128] Obama believed his deal was only a first step to curbing Iranian belligerence. "We share the concerns expressed by many of our friends in the Middle East," Obama declared as he announced the agreement, "including Israel and the Gulf States, about Iran's support for terrorism and its use of proxies to destabilize the region.... We will maintain our own sanctions related to Iran's support for terrorism, its ballistic missile program, and its human rights violations."

Certainly, the Iran Nuclear Deal was incomplete. The agreement expired after fifteen years. Skeptics were concerned Iran would violate the agreement by secretly developing nuclear technology, making it possible to quickly achieve nuclear capability once the agreement expired. The agreement only covered the development of nuclear fuels and allowed Iran to continue the development of other weapons including ballistic missiles. Finally, the deal's opponents believed Iran would channel money freed up from the easing of sanctions into its terrorist efforts throughout the Middle East and North Africa.

President Obama, believing the Nuclear Deal was a first step towards defanging Iran, considered the agreement his signature foreign policy accomplishment.

The Obama Legacy

Jackie Robinson was the first Black ballplayer to play major league baseball in 1947. During Robinson's first year, several of his Dodger teammates threatened to sit out rather than play alongside him. There were rumors the St. Louis Cardinals and other National League teams would strike if Robinson entered the field. The crowd, other players, and even managers yelled racial epithets. "Hey, you black [racial slur], go back to the cotton fields."[129] But Robinson's talent and calm assurance prevailed. He won the National League's Most Valuable Player award in 1949; became the first Black player to be inducted into the Baseball Hall of Fame in 1962; and was posthumously awarded the Congressional Gold Medal and Presidential Medal of Freedom by President Reagan.[130]

Sixty years after Jackie Robinson stepped onto a major league baseball field, Obama's elevation to the United States presidency provoked similar hostility.

From the beginning, Donald Trump questioned Obama's legitimacy as President. "I have people that have been studying [Obama's birth certificate]," Trump repeatedly claimed, "and they cannot believe what they're finding.... If he wasn't born in this country, which is a real possibility...then he has pulled one of the great cons in the history of politics."[131] Just four days after Obama's inauguration, talk show host Rush Limbaugh, when asked by *The Wall Street Journal* to write a 400-word opinion piece on

Obama, told his audience he didn't need 400 words, four were sufficient: "I hope he fails."[132] Similarly, days after Obama's inauguration, then-Representative Mike Pence encouraged his allies to fiercely oppose Obama, using a clip from the film *Patton* that depicts General Patton rallying his troops to battle the Nazis. "We're going to kick the hell out of him all the time!" Patton bellowed. "We're going to go through him like crap through a goose!"[133] Two years later, House Speaker John Boehner promised, "We're going to do everything—and I mean everything we can do—to kill [the Obama agenda], stop it, slow it down, whatever we can."[134]

As America's first Black president, Barack Obama was loved and despised in equal measure. For years, Donald Trump led a conspiracy suggesting Obama was born in Kenya and hence an illegitimate president.   JOHN MOORE/GETTY

Although despised by his political opponents, Obama left office with a 59 percent approval rating, a postwar rating only exceeded by Reagan and Clinton.[135] Obama's ratings were even better internationally. Canada, China, France, Germany, Japan, Mexico, Russia, South Korea, and the United Kingdom collectively rated him an average of 67 percent during his presidency.[136]

Obama's supporters credit him with saving the country from another Great Depression after inheriting the worst recession in eighty years; the

Affordable Care Act, the Dodd-Frank Wall Street Reform Act and the Consumer Protection Acts; the DACA "Dreamers" executive order protecting immigrant children; the Paris Climate Accord, the Iran Nuclear Deal and the Trans-Pacific Partnership Agreement; the execution of Osama Bin Laden; and a scandal-free administration.

Others blame Obama for the slowest economic recovery since World War II, the loss of American prestige overseas, the birth of ISIS, the Affordable Care Act, the swelling of environmental, energy, and economic regulations, and the $10 trillion increase in the national debt.

Blocked in Congress, Obama used executive orders to move his policies forward. Angered at being sidelined, Senator Ted Cruz declared: "The President's taste for unilateral action to circumvent Congress should concern every citizen, regardless of party or ideology." Senator Rand Paul likened Obama to a king. "Someone who wants to bypass the Constitution, bypass Congress, that's someone who wants to act like a king or a monarch."[137] Yet, Obama issued only 276 executive orders, the fewest of any two-term President since Grover Cleveland.[138]

Many believed Obama despised entrepreneurs based on an awkward comment he made during the 2012 presidential campaign:

> If you were successful, somebody along the line gave you some help. There was a great teacher somewhere in your life. Somebody helped to create this unbelievable American system that we have that allowed you to thrive. Somebody invested in roads and bridges. If you've got a business, *you didn't build that*. Somebody else made that happen. The Internet didn't get invented on its own. Government research created the Internet so that all the companies could make money off the Internet (author's emphasis).[139]

Obama's detractors claimed "*you didn't build that*" referred to the entrepreneur's business and not, as Obama claimed, the American system which provided the framework for success. Mitt Romney made the comment a major 2012 presidential campaign issue when he declared: "The idea to say that Steve Jobs didn't build Apple, that Henry Ford didn't build Ford Motor; to say something like that is not just foolishness. It's insulting to every entrepreneur, every innovator in America."[140] It would seem to stretch the imagination to suggest Obama believed Henry Ford didn't build the Ford Motor Company, but after Obama's grammatical gaffe was made a major campaign issue in 2012, many firmly believed Obama hated businessmen.

Obama's sloppy grammar recalls President Coolidge's response when asked what's it like to be President: "You got to be mighty careful."[141]

Many Americans also believed Obama inflamed racial tensions. In July of 2009, after the African-American Harvard professor Henry Louis Gates Jr. was arrested on his doorstep by a Cambridge policeman, Obama opined: "The Cambridge police acted stupidly in arresting somebody when there was already proof that they were in their own home... there's a long history in this country of African Americans and Latinos being stopped by law enforcement disproportionately."[142] In February of 2012, after the unarmed seventeen-year-old Trayvon Martin was fatally shot by community watch-man George Zimmerman, critics accused Obama of playing the "race card" when he remarked, "If I had a son, he'd look like Trayvon."[143]

Obama's comments infuriated millions. More than a year after Obama left office, in a 2018 interview, former presidential candidate Rick Santo-rum summed up their feelings: "Many people saw Barack Obama... doing more to exacerbate racism in this country.... Every time there was a con-troversy where someone in color was involved, he took the side of, many times, against the police—he did it over and over and over again."[144]

Many simply found Obama irritating. "[Obama] doesn't know how to speak in any other rhetorical register than above and beyond the partisan fray," political journalist Damon Linker observed. "He invariably sounds reasonable, his tone fair-minded, objective. He speaks of the grand sweep of American history, renders Solomonic judgments, and looks down on the disputants on the field of battle..."[145]

Americans, today, embrace Jackie Robinson. "Thinking about the things that happened," Robinson teammate, Pee Wee Reese, reminisced. "I don't know any other ballplayers who could have done what he did. To be able to hit with everybody yelling at him. He had to block all that out, block out everything but this ball that is coming in at a hundred miles an hour... to do what he did has got to be the most tremendous thing I've ever seen in sports."[146]

How will history remember Barack Obama? Will future American's agree with Donald Trump that "[Obama] has been a disaster as a President. He will go down as one of the worst Presidents in the history of our country."[147] Or with professional historians, who in 2018 ranked Obama just below Lyndon Johnson and above Andrew Jackson.[148] Or perhaps, simply as a contemporary Jackie Robinson who rose above those determined "to kick the hell out of him," as then-Representative Mike Pence, channeling General Patton, had encouraged.

Donald J. Trump

January 20, 2017 – January 20, 2021

> Together, we will make America strong again. We will make America wealthy again. We will make America proud again. We will make America safe again. And, yes, together, we will make America great again.[1]

By late afternoon on November 8, 2016, the exit polls were clear; Hillary Clinton would be elected as America's forty-fifth President. "It wasn't even close. It looked like she was going to win big," political pollster Frank Luntz later commented. Fox News analysts predicted it would be an early night with Clinton declared the winner by 11:00 pm. Fox (and every other news channel) was ready. News teams were deployed. Narratives were fine-tuned. Graphics were prepared: "Fox News declares Hillary Clinton elected President."[2]

Throngs of jubilant Clinton supporters had begun to assemble at Manhattan's Jacob K. Javits Convention Center to celebrate the election of the nation's first woman President. A few blocks away, the Trump team had rented a dreary ballroom at the Midtown Hilton. Filled by the media, many anxious to see Trump humbled, there was little room for supporters. The Trump team had seen the exit polls. Nearly everyone, including Donald Trump, believed the election was lost.

Then the returns began to trickle in. Trump was running stronger than expected. By 8:05 pm Trump and Clinton were in a virtual tie with 67 to 68 electoral votes, respectively. By 9:39 pm, Trump had gained the lead, 147 to 109. Now ahead, Trump never surrendered his lead. Five hours later, at 2:40 am, a huge on-screen graphic at Fox News proclaimed: "Donald Trump

Elected President."[3] "I remember. . ." Fox Host Chris Wallace recalled, "just looking at that and almost wondering whether this was a dream. Was this really happening? I remember asking myself, being so stunned by the fact."[4]

Donald Trump (center) looking sharp. Trump attended New York Military Academy for five years starting in 1959.   YEARBOOK LIBRARY LLC

Nearly every major poll had predicted a Clinton win. Respected political strategist Karl Rove, when asked by Fox News two weeks before the election if Trump could win, declared: "I don't see it happening. If he plays an inside straight, he could get it, but I doubt that he's going to be able to play it."[5] *Politico* called Trump's election win the "biggest upset in U.S. history."[6] *The New York Times* declared Trump's upset victory "a powerful rejection of the establishment forces that had assembled against him, from the world of business to government, and the consensus they had forged on everything from trade to immigration."[7]

The New York Times was right. No presidential candidate since Andrew Jackson had so successfully tapped into the frustration and anger felt by millions of Americans. Americans whose jobs had left the country, who believed their cultural and religious beliefs to be threatened and who feared and resented the millions of illegal aliens flooding into the country.

After fighting a bruising campaign, Trump gave a gracious victory speech. "Now it is time for America to bind the wounds of division..." Trump declared. "I pledge to every citizen of our land that I will be President for all of Americans.... We're going to get to work immediately for the American people, and we're going to be doing a job that hopefully you will be so proud of your President. You will be so proud."[8]

A Total Political Witch Hunt

Donald Trump never enjoyed the traditional honeymoon period granted most new Presidents. Two months after the election, on January 6, 2017, the Director of National Intelligence released an unclassified summary of an investigation conducted by the Central Intelligence Agency, the National Security Agency and the Federal Bureau of Investigation into Russian interference in the 2016 presidential election. The three agencies concluded:

> We assess with high confidence that Russian President Vladimir Putin ordered an influence campaign in 2016 aimed at the U.S. presidential election, the consistent goals of which were to undermine public faith in the U.S. democratic process, denigrate Secretary Clinton, and harm her electability and potential presidency. We further assess Putin and the Russian Government developed a clear preference for President-elect Trump.... We also assess Putin and the Russian Government aspired to help President-elect Trump's election chances when possible by discrediting Secretary Clinton and publicly contrasting her unfavorably to him.[9]

President-elect Trump was briefed on the report by senior intelligence officials. Hours later, Trump issued a measured and supportive statement declaring, in part:

While Russia, China, other countries, outside groups and people are consistently trying to break through the cyber infrastructure of our governmental institutions, businesses and organizations including the Democrat National Committee, there was absolutely no effect on the outcome of the election.... Whether it is our government, organizations, associations or businesses we need to aggressively combat and stop cyberattacks. I will appoint a team to give me a plan within ninety days of taking office.[10]

Four days later, *BuzzFeed* published an unverified, thirty-five-page report compiled by Christopher Steele, the former head of the Russia Desk with British Intelligence. The astonishing report had been circulating in Washington since October, but no major media outlets would touch it until an aide to Senator John McCain leaked the report to *BuzzFeed*.

The report, dubbed the "Steele Dossier," made the sensational claim that Trump, perhaps because he was being blackmailed, had long colluded with the Russians. "[The] Russian regime has been cultivating, supporting and assisting Trump for at least five years," the report asserted. Trump and "his inner circle have accepted a regular flow of intelligence from the Kremlin." The Steele dossier also stated, rather incredibly, that the FSB (the Russian Federal Security Service) "has compromised Trump through his activities in Moscow sufficiently to be able to blackmail him... [which] included perverted sexual acts which have been arranged/monitored by the FSB."[11]

Steele's report was the outgrowth of a project started in September 2015 when *The Washington Free Beacon*, a political journal backed by billionaire Paul Singer, hired GPS Fusion, a private investigative firm, to do political opposition research on Donald Trump. GPS Fusion then hired Steele, a respected twenty-two-year veteran of British intelligence, to investigate the rumors that Trump had connections with Russia. Months later, Hillary Clinton's presidential campaign took over the project in Spring 2016 after Singer backed out when it became clear that Trump would secure his party's nomination.[12]

Trump was furious. Hours after *BuzzFeed* leaked the report he tweeted, "FAKE NEWS—A TOTAL POLITICAL WITCH HUNT!"[13] Trump's tweet, issued at 8:19 pm on January 10, 2017, was Trump's declaration of war with the Washington establishment. A war that would only escalate over the next four years.

On May 9, 2017, Trump precipitously fired FBI Director James Comey. Comey learned of his dismissal from television reports while visiting FBI offices in Los Angeles. "When I decided to just do it," Trump told NBC's Lester Holt, "I said to myself, I said, you know, this Russia thing with Trump and Russia is a made-up story, it's an excuse by the Democrats for having lost an election that they should've won."[14] Comey's abrupt firing set off a political firestorm. Trump's crude dismissal of Comey was reminiscent of President Nixon's infamous Saturday Night Massacre when Nixon fired Archibald Cox, the special prosecutor investigating the Watergate break-in. In firing Cox, Nixon had tried to shut down the Watergate investigation. Many believed Trump was trying to do the same with the Russia investigation. And with good reason. *The Wall Street Journal*, normally a Trump supporter, reported that Comey's firing came just as "a federal investigation into potential collusion between Trump associates and the Russian government was heating up. . . . Mr. Comey was concerned by information showing possible evidence of collusion. . ."[15]

A week later, on May 17, the Deputy Attorney General, Rod Rosenstein, appointed a Special Counsel to investigate "coordination between the Russian government and individuals associated with the campaign of President Donald Trump."[16] (As a member of Trump's presidential campaign, the Attorney General, Jeff Sessions, had recused himself from the Russian investigation.) Rosenstein appointed Robert Mueller to head the investigation. It was an excellent choice. Mueller was widely respected in Washington as a decorated Vietnam War veteran and former head of the FBI from 2001 through 2013.

The next morning, referencing Mueller's appointment, Trump tweeted, "This is the single greatest witch hunt of a politician in American history!"[17]

Witch Hunt? What choice did Rosenstein have? For months there had been suggestions of, if not direct links, the indirect collaboration between Russia and Trump. In July 2016, during a press conference at his Doral resort, Trump, staring directly at the camera, and in a serious tone, said:

"Russia, if you're listening, I hope you're able to find the 30,000 emails that are missing. I think you will probably be rewarded mightily by our press." Trump's request was shocking at the time. Even were it a joke, asking for Russian interference in an American election was unprecedented. (Trump later falsely claimed he had made the statement at a rally and was joking.)[18] On August 17, 2016, the FBI "briefed and warned" the Trump campaign of Russia's efforts to interfere in the election.[19] In December, the American intelligence community confirmed that Russia had interfered in the election in favor of Trump. The Steele Dossier had correctly disclosed links between the Trump campaign and Russia including a private visit by Carter Page, a Trump campaign aide, with Kremlin officials. Then, on December 29, 2016, U.S. security agents taped a series of secret conversations between Michael Flynn, soon to be appointed Trump's National Security Advisor, and Russian Ambassador Sergey Kislyak. The calls were made the same day President Obama announced economic sanctions on Russia in retaliation for interference in the presidential election. So, when Trump abruptly fired FBI Director Comey on May 9, it wasn't surprising many suspected a Nixonian cover-up.

The Mueller investigation concluded in March 2019. The twenty-two-month investigation "identified numerous links between the Russian government and the Trump Campaign," but "did not establish that members of the Trump Campaign conspired or coordinated with the Russian government in its election interference activities."[20] Although no collusion was established, the investigation resulted in thirty-seven criminal indictments. Included in the indictments were charges against the Russian Internet Research Agency, which "allegedly tricked Americans into following fake social media accounts filled with pro-Trump and anti-Clinton propaganda;" twelve Russian officers accused of stealing files, including Hillary Clinton emails, from the Democratic National Committee; Trump campaign chairman Paul Manafort for hiding payments received from political consulting in Ukraine; Trump confidant Roger Stone for witness tampering and obstructing a congressional investigation; Former National Security Advisor Michael Flynn and former Trump campaign aides Rick Gates and George Papadopoulos for lying to investigators; former Trump personal lawyer

Michael Cohen for tax and bank charges, campaign finance violations and lying to Congress; plus eight other individuals on lesser charges.[21]

For nearly two years, other than the issuance of criminal indictments, the Mueller investigation had been drum-tight. No official pronouncements, no leaks, no media interviews. Yet, the investigation was often at the top of the news, almost entirely due to President Trump. Trump simply could not stop railing against the investigation. From May 2017 through March 2019, the President disparaged the investigation in over 300 tweets and numerous public comments. Every tweet, every public pronouncement of "Witch Hunt," helped to keep the investigation near the top of the news. But Trump's efforts to sway public opinion failed. As Mueller's report was released in March 2019, only 39 percent of Americans approved of Trump's handling of his job as President.[22]

Twenty years earlier, President Clinton had endured a far longer investigation by Special Prosecutor Kenneth Starr. The Starr investigation lasted four years beginning with a real estate probe and ending with a sexual scandal. In contrast to Trump, Clinton's job approval ratings climbed steadily during the investigation, reaching 73 percent shortly after Starr released his report.[23]

The Trump Economy

On September 15, 2016, Trump spoke to the Economic Club of New York, an association founded in 1907 whose "membership is curated from the senior executives and leaders in [the] New York City Metro Area."[24] During his campaign speech, Trump graphically captured his view of America's industrial decline. "It used to be cars were made in Flint," Trump declared, "and you couldn't drink the water in Mexico. Now, the cars are made in Mexico and you can't drink the water in Flint."[25] America's elite, Trump asserted, had abandoned their fellow countrymen. American companies had fled the country seeking cheap labor. Once flourishing American cities had become third-world ghettos. Shamefully, a few powerful Americans—personified by Hillary Clinton—seemed to blame their fellow countrymen for their misfortune by labeling "tens of millions of Americans as deplorable and irredeemable."[26]

Trump promised to "replace the present policy of globalism—which has moved so many jobs and so much wealth out of our country—and replace it with a new policy of Americanism.... Over the next ten years," Trump declared, "the economy will average 3.5 percent growth and create a total of twenty-five million new jobs."

Three years later, on November 12, 2019, President Trump made a triumphal return to the Economic Club: exuberant, confident, boastful. Trump's exuberance was justified. When Trump took office in January 2017, the nation's top economists were dispirited. A January 13, 2017 Heritage Foundation forecast "slow growth, low economic participation, and a high cost of living."[27] A Congressional Budget Office (CBO) report that same month corroborated Heritage's dreary forecast, declaring "economic growth over the next two years would remain close to the modest rate observed since the end of the recession in 2009."[28]

Trump beat those middling forecasts. The CBO projected that real GDP would grow 2.0 percent annually from 2017 through 2019; Trump delivered 2.5 percent. The CBO estimated unemployment would average 4.5 percent in 2019; by December 2019, Trump's economy had pushed unemployment down to 3.5 percent, the lowest since 1969. Impressively, from 2017 through 2019, employment growth averaged 169,000 new jobs per month, far higher than the 89,700 forecasted by CBO.

The forecasters had missed an important factor. American business, especially small businesspeople, were enthusiastic as Trump came into office. The Small Business Optimism Index, measured by the National Federation of Independent Business (NFIB), had spiked upwards of twelve points after Trump's election win. The spike was the largest the NFIB had ever recorded.[29]

Like Ronald Reagan before him, Trump's optimism and confidence were contagious. "We have ended the war on American workers," Trump told his New York audience. "We have stopped the assault on American industry, and we have launched an economic boom the likes of which we have never seen before."[30] Trump's Economic Club audience enthusiastically agreed, disrupting his speech thirty-seven times with applause.

★

Donald Trump's proud boasts were understandable, but had his administration actually "launched an economic boom the likes of which we have never seen before?" No, Trump was merely indulging in "truthful hyperbole" described in his 1987 best-selling book, *The Art of the Deal*, as an "innocent form of exaggeration."[31] "People want to believe that something is the biggest and the greatest and the most spectacular." Trump had practiced truthful hyperbole for decades starting in 1979 when he marketed Trump Tower as the tallest New York high-rise after unabashedly adding ten imaginary floors to his sales pitch. (The nearby former General Motors Building remained 41 feet higher.)[32]

Once President, nearly every announcement by the Trump White House got the same treatment, including the Tax Cuts and Jobs Act passed in December 2017. President Trump pitched the tax cuts as "the biggest tax cuts and reforms in American history," and nothing less than economic "rocket fuel."[33] "We have twenty-one trillion dollars in debt," Trump declared on Sean Hannity's Fox News radio show, "When this really kicks in, we'll start paying off that debt like water."[34]

If Trump's optimism was contagious, so to, it seemed, was his hyperbole. Two days after Trump signed the tax bill, Larry Kudlow, a CNBC commentator at the time, predicted: "[W]e are on the front end of a major business investment boom. And that boom is going to carry economic growth faster, it's going to create more jobs, it's going to create more wages. The deficit is going to be much lower. The [2017 Tax Cuts and Jobs Act] is going to pay for itself inside of a couple of years."[35]

Four months later, President Trump appointed Kudlow as Director of the National Economic Council to replace Gary Cohn. Cohn, formerly the president of Goldman Sachs, had resigned over disagreements with Trump's trade policies. Kudlow must have been pleased with his prestigious new role, no doubt expecting to ride a wave of historic economic growth. Kudlow was disappointed. Annual GDP growth never came close to the 3.5 percent Trump's economic team had projected, much less the "four, five, and maybe even six percent"[36] Trump predicted after signing the tax cuts. GDP growth inched up from 2.4 percent in 2017 to 2.7 percent in 2018 then slid back to 2.3 percent in 2019, hardly rocket-fueled growth. Nor did the tax cuts pay for themselves. During 2018 and 2019, the combined deficit soared to $1.76 trillion, the largest two-year increase since the 2008 Financial Crisis.

Kudlow's promise of a "major investment boom" never happened. Corporate income tax revenues, after averaging 1.7 percent of GDP the five years before the tax cuts, fell to 1.0 percent of GDP in 2018 and 2019, saving companies nearly $100 billion a year. Trump's economic team had predicted the tax savings would fuel a business investment boom. Instead, business investment growth ticked up two percentage points to 5.3 percent in 2018, then plummeted to 1.5 percent in 2019.

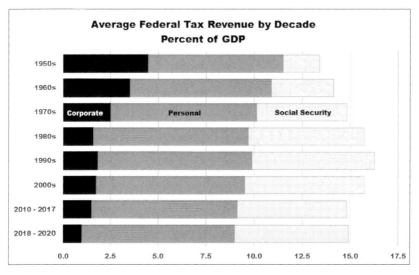

For seventy years, corporate taxes have steadily declined, shifting the burden to individuals. The trend accelerated after the Tax Cuts and Jobs Act of 2017.

TAX FOUNDATION

Rather than funding new business investments, companies used the tax savings to reward shareholders. During 2018 and 2019, public companies distributed $2.5 trillion in stock buybacks and dividends, $600 billion more than the two preceding years. Rather than building new factories and hiring American workers, it was "raining stock buybacks" as *Barron's*, the venerated financial publication, described the shareholder windfall.[37]

The shareholder distributions fueled a stock market boom. During Trump's first three years, the market's total capitalization jumped from $27.4 to $37.7 trillion, a whopping increase of $10.3 trillion.[38] Most Americans, though, benefited little from the market's rise. In 2016 the wealthiest 10 percent of American households owned 84 percent of stocks.[39] These affluent Americans—as most members of the Economic Club certainly were—enjoyed, on average, a $675,000 market gain. Little wonder they applauded Trump so enthusiastically.

Trump may have oversold his economic plan, but he excelled in other important areas. Trump reversed, at least temporarily, the long decline of mining and oil jobs. After falling from 797,000 jobs in 2013 to 600,000 in 2016, by 2019, mining and oil extraction employment jumped to 663,000 workers.[40] Trump also contributed to America's energy independence. During Obama's administration, the annual growth of energy production averaged 1.8 percent annually. Trump changed that. From 2017 through 2019, energy production increased an average of 6.2 percent annually largely due to more natural gas production. By 2019, Trump could boast the United States had reached energy independence, a claim last made by President Eisenhower in 1957.[41]

Trump, though, was standing on the shoulders of President Carter and Texas wildcatter George P. Mitchell. Carter's energy conservation legislation played a pioneering role reducing the nation's per capita energy consumption. Mitchell perfected hydraulic fracturing, "fracking," whose effectiveness revolutionized oil and gas extraction.[42] It was their earlier contributions that made America's energy independence possible. But it was Trump's aggressive energy policies that accelerated America's energy independence by several years.

Working Americans thrived during Trump's first three years. In 2019, average unemployment fell to its lowest level since 1969, 3.7 percent. Black unemployment hit a historic low, 6.1 percent. That same year, household median income after inflation jumped 7.4 percent, the highest single-year increase ever recorded. Poverty rates dropped from 12.7 percent in 2016 to 10.5 percent in 2019, the lowest ever recorded.[43]

Trump's unemployment, median income, and poverty records were historic accomplishments. For decades, Presidents had promised their economic policies would "trickle down" to the middle and lower economic classes. They seldom did. Poverty and income inequality increased after the Reagan and George W. Bush tax cuts. During Clinton's presidency, unemployment stagnated at 5.4 percent even as the dot-com stock market spawned thousands of new millionaires. During Obama's term, after-tax income for the top one percent increased 30 percent while the bottom 20 percent increased less than one percent. For decades, America's wealth had flowed upward. But Trump's economy lifted nearly all American workers: white and Black, professional and laborer, rich and poor.

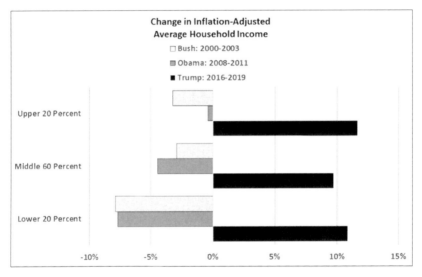

President Trump's economy delivered impressive personal income gains to all levels of workers. Black workers especially thrived benefiting from historically high family incomes and low unemployment rates.   IRS STATISTICS OF INCOME REPORTS

Rebuilding the Military

Trump had other significant accomplishments. He was particularly proud of rebuilding the military, whose decline he blamed on the Obama administration. "When I took over," Trump asserted, "it was a mess.... One of our generals came in to see me and he said, 'Sir, we don't have ammunition.'"[44] The general was apparently misinformed. The American military had hardly been reduced to throwing rocks. In 2017, U.S. defense spending represented 35 percent of the world's defense budget.[45]

Still, defense spending cuts in the years preceding Trump were a sorry instance of Congressional dysfunction. After the 2008 Financial Crisis, federal deficits ballooned as tax revenues fell while stimulus spending increased. Unable to agree on how to reduce the deficits, the deadlocked Congress passed the Budget Control Act of 2011. The Act had an unusual provision: sequestration. If Congress could not agree on spending cuts, the Act's sequestration provision would automatically trigger deep, across-the-board spending cuts. Surely, the threat of sequestration—a Sword of Damocles hanging over their heads—would force Congress to agree on a budget reduction plan.

It didn't work. In 2013, after months of Congressional bickering, the Act's sequestration provision was invoked, automatically triggering deep cuts for the next eight years.[46] By 2016, real military spending had fallen 21 percent from its 2011 levels.

Although the budget cuts were scheduled to continue another three years, President Trump and a friendly Congress quickly abandoned sequestration. By 2019, defense spending had climbed to $732 billion,[47], up $92 billion from 2016. It was "the most significant investment in our Military and our warfighters in modern history!"[48] President Trump boasted.

As Trump was rebuilding the military, he continually scolded NATO's leaders for not spending enough on defense. For years, NATO guidelines suggested its members spend two percent of their GDP on defense, a suggestion most NATO countries ignored. In 2014, after Russia invaded Ukraine, NATO changed the two percent guideline to a firm requirement to be met by 2024. In 2016, aside from the United States, only the United Kingdom, Poland, Greece and Estonia were meeting the requirement.

NATO's stinginess was, perhaps, understandable. Since its formation in 1949, NATO's primary threat had been the Soviet Union. But after the collapse of the powerful Soviet Union, the Soviet threat was replaced by an impoverished Russia. In 2016, Russia's defense spending, measured in U.S. dollars, was a paltry $69.2 billion, a figure dwarfed by NATO's $262 billion European defense spending.[49] Even though few NATO countries had met their two percent defense commitment, NATO, even without the United States, was outspending Russia by nearly four to one.

Over the next three years, NATO moved towards its self-imposed 2024 targets. On December 3, 2019, as the organization celebrated its seventieth anniversary, NATO's Secretary-General Jens Stoltenberg announced: "Since 2016, Canada and European allies have added $130 billion more to the defense budgets, and this number will increase to 400 billion U.S. dollars by 2024."[50] Eight countries, in addition to the United States, were now meeting NATO's two percent standard. Stoltenberg, shrewdly, let Trump take credit for the increase.

Trump made rebuilding the military a top priority. Measured by spending alone, he was highly successful. In 2019, the United States spent $732 billion on defense: $103 billion more than the combined spending by China ($261 billion), Russia ($65 billion) and the twenty-seven European NATO countries ($303 billion).[51]

International Trade as War

President Trump viewed international trade as another form of war. For decades, America had been foolish to allow "foreign countries to subsidize their goods, devalue their currencies, violate their agreements and cheat in every way imaginable.... It does not have to be this way," Trump promised Pennsylvania metal-workers in a 2016 campaign speech. "We can turn it around and we can turn it around fast."[52]

Trump's speech tapped into years of festering anger over the loss of manufacturing jobs in the American heartland. For decades, one in four American workers were employed in manufacturing. That began to change around 1970 as American consumers developed a taste for fuel-efficient cars, innovative electronics, and scores of other imported goods, often of higher quality and less expensive than their American counterparts. For the next thirty years, as American companies lost market share, manufacturing employment flat-lined, averaging 17.5 million jobs. Then, starting in 2000, manufacturing employment plummeted and by 2016, as Trump was campaigning, had fallen to 12.3 million, a loss of five million jobs.[53]

Much of that job loss, as Trump rightly claimed, was due to American jobs moving to Mexico, Canada, and China. The Alliance for American Manufacturing, a trade organization, estimated that 3.7 million jobs were lost to China from 2001 through 2020.[54] Most of the other jobs flowed to Mexico whose own manufacturing employment increased by 2.1 million workers from 2005 through 2019.[55]

Trump had a simple answer for stopping the bleeding of American jobs: use import tariffs to build an economic wall around the country. The tariffs, typically ranging from five to 30 percent, started in January 2018 with solar panels and washing machines, progressed to aluminum and steel in March and, by September, to $250 billion across a diverse range of Chinese goods.[56] By the end of 2018, the United States was in a trade war with Mexico, Canada, the European Union, China, Turkey, India, and Russia, which all imposed their own retaliatory tariffs.[57] China went further, drastically cutting its soybean imports from the United States from $12.2 billion in 2017 to $3.1 billion in 2018, a move aimed at the heart of Trump's midwestern political base.[58] The trade war continued through 2019 as President Trump threatened tariffs on $80 billion in European Union goods, including German automobiles, the heart of the German economy. By the end of 2019, the United States was collecting $79 billion annually in tariffs.[59]

But few Americans benefited. JPMorgan Chase estimated the higher tariffs cost American households as much as $1,000 annually.[60] Nor did the tariffs help taxpayers, either through contributing to lower taxes or reducing the national debt. The Council on Foreign Relations estimated that 92 percent of the tariffs collected on Chinese imports were redirected to American farmers to offset their reduced exports to China.[61] The trade war had turned America's proud farmers into virtual welfare recipients.[62]

While industries that benefited from tariff protection, such as steel foundries, increased their employment, other industries, forced to use more expensive steel, lost workers. American exports stopped growing and then declined from a peak of $144 billion in May 2018 to $138 billion in December 2019.[63] With falling exports, the nation's trade deficit in goods deteriorated, increasing from $771 billion in 2016 to $886 billion in 2019.[64]

Furthermore, the tariffs were hurting the economy. The Tax Foundation estimated the tariffs cost 179,800 American jobs and reduced long-term GDP growth by a quarter percent.[65] An American Action Forum study concluded, "President Trump's tariffs are increasing annual consumer costs by roughly $57 billion annually."[66] The Heritage Foundation declared that "tariffs are a failed policy, and… in fact, they are counterproductive to achieving strong economic growth."[67]

President Trump remained undeterred.

Donald Trump detested multilateral trade agreements as much as he favored tariffs. "[The North American Free Trade Agreement] was the worst trade deal in the history... of this country," Trump told Pennsylvania metal-workers. "The [Trans-Pacific Partnership trade agreement]," Trump declared, "would be the death blow for American manufacturing.... A Trump administration will change our failed trade policies, and I mean quickly."[68]

President Trump confronted German Chancellor Angela Merkel and other world leaders at the 2018 G7 conference. Trump shocked America's allies when he announced steep tariffs on imported steel and aluminum.   HANDOUT / GETTY

Trump kept his promise. Three days after taking office, he signed an executive order withdrawing the United States from the Trans-Pacific Partnership (TPP). The TPP was a twelve-nation economic alliance encircling the Pacific Rim that included the United States, Mexico, Canada, Japan, Australia, New Zealand, Vietnam, Peru, Chile, Malaysia, Singapore, and Brunei.[69]

Reactions were mixed. Teamsters Union President James Hoffa was pleased. "With this decision," Hoffa declared, "the President has taken the first step toward fixing thirty years of bad trade policies that have cost working Americans millions of good-paying jobs." But Senator John McCain feared Trump's decision would "send a troubling signal of American disengagement in the Asia-Pacific region at a time we can least afford it [and] create an opening for China to rewrite the economic rules of the road at the expense of American workers."[70] McCain was echoing President Obama's earlier declaration that TPP would serve as a counterweight to China. "With the TPP," Obama claimed, "we can rewrite the rules of trade to benefit America's middle-class. Because if we don't, competitors who don't share our values, like China, will step in to fill that void."[71]

Three years after leaving the TPP, Trump announced a Phase 1 Trade Agreement with China on January 15, 2020.[72] A gifted speaker, the President was effusive at the signing ceremony, offering words of thanks, compliments, or personal anecdotes for members of his staff, Congress, and the Chinese delegation. "With this signing," Trump stated, "we mark more than just an agreement; we mark a sea change in international trade. At long last, Americans have a government that puts them first at the negotiating table. First in trade. First in every deal, every decision, and every action we take with incredible enforceability."[73]

But the Phase I Trade Agreement was misnamed. It wasn't a formal trade agreement, but simply a memorandum of understanding. The memorandum promised better intellectual property controls, reduction of counterfeit goods, better cooperation in financial services, and increased exports to China. The agreement, though, had no enforcement provisions. A year later, well after China had recovered from the COVID pandemic, China has failed to meet its commitments to buy more American goods.

Instead, on November 15, 2020, fifteen Asian nations, with China as the polestar, signed the Regional Comprehensive Economic Partnership (RCEP). RCEP members represent nearly a third of the world's population and a similar share of the world economy.[74] In a thinly veiled jab at Trump's trade policies, Chinese Premier Li Keqiang declared during the ceremony, "The signing of the RCEP shines light and hope through dark clouds under the current international situation, showing that multilateralism and free trade are the right way forward, and remain the right direction for promoting the growth of the world economy and the progress of humanity."[75]

China's endorsement of the RCEP fulfilled Obama's 2016 prediction: If the United States fails to lead in Asia, "China will step in to fill [the] void."

Two weeks after announcing the Phase I China agreement, on January 31, 2020, Trump signed a revised version of the twenty-six-year-old NAFTA, now renamed the United States-Mexico-Canada-Agreement (USMCA). "The USMCA, which is the biggest trade deal of all time, covers more than $1.3 trillion of commerce [and] is expected to create 80,000 new jobs tied to the auto industry and bring in up to $30 billion of new investment in the sector," *Fox Business News* reported.[76]

The USMCA passed with strong bilateral support in Congress: 385–41 in the House and 89–10 in the Senate.[77] The largest changes to the agreement were expanded access to Canada's dairy market, an increase in the percentage of the North American manufactured component of an automobile from 62.5 to 75 percent to qualify as being "Made in America" and thus receive preferential trade treatment, a requirement that 70 percent of the steel and aluminum used in automobile manufacture be produced in North America, and that 40 percent of car parts must be produced by workers earning $16 or more an hour.[78]

The requirements for North American content minimums and a $16 an hour minimum wage were included to protect American automobile workers. American dairy farmers also benefited. Canada's dairy industry, like American tobacco and light trucks, is a politically favored industry with high tariffs. "Canada will finally provide greater access for American dairy. Canada is opening up," Trump declared during the USMCA press conference.[79]

Canadians must have winced as they watched Trump's jab at their country. During the first three years of Trump's presidency, American dairy farmers enjoyed a $753 million trade surplus with Canada exporting $1.15 billion in dairy products[80] while importing only $397 million.[81] Yet, Trump continually disparaged Canada, America's closest ally for over a century. "In Canada," Trump told rally crowds, "some very unfair things have happened to our dairy farmers.... What's happened to you is very, very unfair. It's another typical one-sided deal against the United States."[82] Trump's claim was simply untrue. The United States, rather than a victim, was the overwhelming beneficiary of the dairy trade with Canada.

Millions of disenfranchised Americans applauded Trump for promising to bring back American jobs. "One by one, the factories shuttered and left our shores," President Trump declared during his inaugural speech, "with not even a thought about the millions upon millions of American workers left behind."[83]

Trump was right. For decades American industry had abandoned American workers as they moved jobs to lower-cost countries. "Ideally, you'd have every plant that you own on a barge to move with currencies and changes in the economy," General Electric's iconic CEO, Jack Welch, had declared in 1998.[84]

But in many industries, automation had destroyed far more American jobs than the move to foreign factories. Technology was making nearly every industry more productive, from semiconductors to steel. In 1980, it took 10.1 man-hours to manufacture one ton of steel. By 2017, only 1.5 hours were required.[85] From 2007 through 2017, U.S.-based semiconductor sales increased 60 percent from approximately $120 to $190 billion,[86] while semiconductor employment remained flat at 200,000 workers.[87] In 2000, General Motors, Ford, and Chrysler manufactured twenty-one vehicles for every employee.[88] By 2019, the Big Three were utilizing automation to produce thirty-two vehicles for every worker, eliminating thousands of middle-class jobs.[89]

The result is that real U.S. manufacturing output rose 43 percent[90] from 1993 to 2016 while the manufacturing workforce shrank by 4.4 million workers.[91] Economists applaud productivity gains because the gains, if passed onto the consumer, reduce consumer prices, encouraging consumption.

But for decades the benefits have largely flowed upward to the elite—educated professionals, executives, and shareholders—leaving the workers behind.[92] That trend had been accelerating for decades. In 1965, an average worker needed to work fifteen weeks to match the weekly earnings of the CEO. By 1989, forty-five weeks were required. And by 2019, the forgotten worker would need to work an incredible 223 weeks—four years and four months—to match a single week of CEO compensation.[93]

Does automation inevitably lead to "rusted-out factories scattered like tombstones across the landscape,"[94] as Trump described the American Rust Belt? Absolutely not. Many high-wage countries have a thriving manufacturing sector and positive trade balances: Germany, the Netherlands, Australia, Taiwan, South Korea, and Switzerland, for example.[95]

Consider tiny Austria. The Austrian iron industry predates Columbus. By the early nineteen-hundreds, Austria was home to Europe's largest steel mill. But Austria didn't grow complacent. Austria has continued to innovate to stay competitive in world markets. One automated steel mill, perhaps the world's most advanced, produces 500,000 tons of steel wire annually with only fourteen workers. In 2018, Austrian steel makers weren't complaining about unfair trade practices. Austria had a favorable steel trade balance of 2.6 million metric tons.[96]

Ronald Reagan, decades earlier, struggled with the loss of American jobs. Japan was flooding the American market with automobiles, consumer goods, and semiconductors. Reagan, grudgingly, imposed trade barriers to hold back the onslaught. Reagan knew they were a short-term solution. "Today protectionism is being used by some American politicians as a cheap form of nationalism...." Reagan warned in 1988. "We should beware of the demagogues who are ready to declare a trade war against our friends—weakening our economy, our national security, and the entire free world—all while cynically waving the American flag."[97]

Ronald Reagan was committed to free and open trade. His 1988 speech predated Donald Trump by thirty-five years. Since then, the world has learned much about the impact of globalization. Trump may have lost his war on trade, but he awakened Americans to the impact unbridled globalization has had on American workers, critical supply chains, and the empowerment of a globally ambitious China.

Build the Wall!

"When Mexico sends its people, they're not sending their best.... They're sending people that have lots of problems, and they're bringing those problems with us [sic]. They're bringing drugs, they're bringing crime, they're rapists, and some, I assume are good people..."[98] For many Americans, these are the words they most remember from Donald Trump's presidential campaign announcement on June 16, 2015.

For the next eighteen months, Trump campaigned relentlessly against America's immigration policies. It was an emotionally charged platform that resonated with millions of Americans. And why shouldn't it? In 2015, an estimated eleven million illegal immigrants—nearly one in thirty residents—were residing in the United States.[99] Although millions were working in seasonal, low-paying jobs most Americans shunned, many Americans believed the immigrants were "...taking our jobs.... They're taking our money. They're killing us," as Trump declared.[100] Far worse, radical Islamic terrorism was rising throughout the world with its horrific executions and terrorist attacks. In 2001, nineteen Islamic terrorists easily entered the country determined to kill as many Americans as possible—which they did on September 11. America, Trump declared, would be stupid to let it happen again.[101]

Trump's claims of hordes of violent Mexicans invading the country were exaggerated. When Trump declared his candidacy in 2015, illegal immigration had been falling for years. America's population of illegal aliens peeked in 2007 at 12.2 million, then began a slow but steady decline to 11 million by 2015. During that period, the number of illegal Mexican migrants fell even faster, from 6.9 million to 5.0 million. Furthermore, most illegal

Mexican immigrants entered the country not by slipping across the border, but legally on temporary visas and then overstaying their mandated departure date.[102] Nor were Mexicans, and Hispanics in general, the violent criminals Trump claimed them to be. In 2015, violent crime among Hispanics was 16.7 per 1,000 persons, lower than whites at 17.4 and far lower than Blacks at 22.6.[103]

Congress understood this. So even as Trump's rally supporters chanted "Build the Wall! Build the Wall!" Congress during Trump's first two years refused to fund the wall.[104] But Trump bypassed Congress, redirecting funds allocated for drug interdiction and military construction to fund the southern border wall.

As Trump left office, 438 miles of the wall had been constructed, 365 miles of which were replacing existing, crumbling border barriers.[105]

President Trump's efforts to ban Muslims were more fruitful. A week after taking office, Trump signed an executive order temporarily prohibiting foreign nationals from seven Muslim countries from entering the United States. A week later, a federal court in Seattle issued an order temporarily blocking Trump's Muslim ban as unconstitutional religious discrimination. Trump persisted and on June 26, 2018, the Supreme Court ruled in favor of Trump's third version of the ban. Chief Justice John Roberts wrote the majority opinion which concluded that the Immigration and Naturalization Act granted the President broad authority to defend the national security of the United States.[106] President Trump kept his promise to slash immigration. That was especially true of refugees fleeing the Middle East. During Trump's last years in office, refugee immigration had fallen to its lowest levels in nearly fifty years.[107]

President Trump's anti-immigration stance was part of a larger, historical cycle that has repeated over much of the nation's history. America resisted Irish immigration in the mid-nineteenth century, Italian immigration at the turn of the twentieth century, Eastern European and Jewish immigration after World War I, and Asian immigration almost entirely until shortly after World War II. Just forty years ago, over 60 percent of Americans disapproved of immigration from Vietnam and Cuba.[108] Today, Vietnamese and Cuban emigrants have proven themselves to be especially hard-working contributors to American society. The same is true of the Chinese, Japanese, Italians, and Irish who earlier had been denied immigration so that "America be kept American" as President Coolidge declared in 1924.[109] Yet, all these nationalities, with their different cultures and religions, have assimilated into America, each providing their distinctive contribution to the great American melting pot.

Iran, North Korea and Afghanistan

In 1513, Nicolo Machiavelli wrote a private manuscript on the application of political power. Later published as *The Prince*, Machiavelli observed that a leader can rule either through love or fear. Of the two, fear is preferable, as "love is preserved by the link of obligation... but fear preserves you by a dread of punishment which never fails."[110]

President Trump tried both: fear with Iran and love with North Korea.

In his 2011 book, *Time to Get Tough*, Trump wrote, "Iran's nuclear program must be stopped–by any and all means necessary. Period."[111] Four years later, when the United States, China, Russia, France, Germany, the United Kingdom, and the European Union signed the Joint Comprehensive Plan of Action (JCPOA), Trump predicted: "You know the Iranians are going to cheat. They're great negotiators and you know they're going to cheat."[112] Trump promised, if elected, to cancel the deal.

Trump kept his word. On May 8, 2018, Trump withdrew the United States from the JCPOA, declaring it to be "one of the worst and most one-sided transactions the United States has ever entered into." Trump imposed strict sanctions on Iran and even threatened those American allies "who fail to wind down [their business] activities with Iran by the end of [the transition] period will risk severe consequences."[113]

Iran was not cheating though. The United Nation's International Atomic Energy Agency had, every ninety days, regularly confirmed Iran remained in compliance with "the implementation by Iran of its nuclear-related commitments under the JCPOA."[114]

But after Trump abandoned the JCPOA, Iran restored its uranium enrichment efforts. By September 2020, the BBC reported Iran had produced ten times the enriched uranium permitted under the deal. "Iran's move," the BBC reported, "came in retaliation against U.S. sanctions reinstated by President Donald Trump when he abandoned the deal."[115]

Trump had been right that the JCPOA was incomplete. It did not limit Iran's development of ballistic missiles or its interventions in Syria, Yemen, and elsewhere. But the original deal was meant as a first step. Rather than attempt to extend the existing agreement, Trump terminated the deal convinced he could force Iran to the negotiating table.

It didn't work. "President Trump has reasonably offered to negotiate with Iran many times," according to John Ullyot, speaking for the White House National Security Council on August 11, 2020.[116] But Iran wasn't interested. "Donald Trump is lost in a daydream when he says Iran will soon come to the negotiating table," Iran Foreign Minister Mohammad Javad Zarif declared in a *Tehran Times* interview.[117]

In July 2017, CIA Director Mike Pompeo, alarmed by North Korea's growing nuclear arsenal, declared the United States needed to find a way to remove North Korean Leader Kim Jong-un. North Korea angrily responded that it would "preemptively annihilate those countries" which imperil North Korea, including launching a nuclear strike "on the heart of the U.S."[118] President Trump responded in kind. "North Korea best not make any more threats to the United States, they will be met with fire and fury like the world has never seen."[119]

That September, during his first speech to the United Nations, Trump again threatened "Rocket Man," his new nickname for Kim Jong-un. "If [the United States] is forced to defend itself or its allies," he declared, "we will have no choice but to totally destroy North Korea."[120] The UN delegates sat in stunned silence. Never had they heard an American President threaten to annihilate an entire nation.

The two leaders' nuclear saber-rattling soon devolved into farce. Shortly after Trump's UN speech, Kim Jong-un, asserting that "a frightened dog barks louder," called Trump "a rogue and a gangster fond of playing with fire," and promising to "surely and definitely tame the mentally deranged U.S. dotard with fire."[121] (Kim's use of 'dotard' sent thousands to their dictionaries seeking its definition: a person in senile decay marked by decline of mental poise and alertness.) But Trump, perhaps because he couldn't top Kim's clever rejoinder, didn't respond in kind. Rather, he humorously tweeted: "Why would Kim Jong-un insult me by calling me 'old,' when I would NEVER call him 'short and fat?'"[122]

The world had never seen diplomacy between two nuclear powers conducted in such a manner, but it seemed to work. By March 2018, the name-calling had been replaced by discussions of a possible summit between the two leaders. On June 12, Trump and Kim Jong-un met in Singapore. The historic meeting was the first-ever between the leaders of North Korea and the United States.[123] The summit ended favorably with a signed agreement committing the two nations to "the building of a lasting and robust peace regime on the Korean Peninsula."[124] It was a promising start. Unfortunately, the Singapore meeting was the high point between Trump and Kim Jong-un.

The two leaders met again, in Hanoi, on February 27–28, 2019. The summit ended abruptly when Trump walked out of the meeting. The two sides disagreed on what happened. In separate news conferences, Trump told reporters, "Sometimes you have to walk." Trump claimed North Korea asked for a lifting of all sanctions in exchange for only a partial dismantling of its nuclear production facilities. North Korean Foreign Minister Ri Yong-ho disagreed, claiming North Korea had offered to "permanently dismantle all its nuclear material production, including plutonium and uranium, around the Yongbyon facility under observation by U.S. experts" in return for only partial relief of sanctions.[125]

Four months later, President Trump, hoping to reconcile, offered to meet Kim Jong-un at the demilitarized zone separating North and South Korea. Kim Jong-un agreed and on June 30, 2019, Trump became the first sitting President to enter North Korea as he stepped across the line demarcating the border between the two Koreas. With smiles all around, the two leaders agreed to resume negotiations.

On October 4–5, North Korean and United States diplomats met in Stockholm for a working session. The talks failed on the second day. "The negotiations have not fulfilled our expectation and finally broke off,"[126] North Korea's chief nuclear negotiator commented afterward. The next month, in a conciliatory gesture, South Korea and the United States canceled a joint military training exercise. That month, Trump again reached out to Kim Jong-un tweeting, "I am the only one who can get you where you have to be. You should act quickly, get the deal done. See you soon!" But North Korea refused to meet, later declaring: "The U.S. is mistaken if it thinks things like negotiations would still work on us," and adding, "we do not feel any need to sit face to face with the U.S., as it does not consider the DPRK-U.S. dialogue as nothing more than a tool for grappling its political crisis."[127]

During their negotiations, Trump and Kim Jong-un exchanged twenty-seven "love letters," as Trump called their overwrought missives. On Christmas 2018, referring to Trump graciously as "Your Excellency," Kim, influenced perhaps by the nineteenth century Victorian romance novels he may have read during his schooling in Switzerland, wrote, "I cannot forget that moment of history when I firmly held Your Excellency's hand at that beautiful and sacred location..." referring to their meeting in Singapore.[128] Six months later, Kim implored: "Like the brief time we had together a year ago in Singapore, every minute we shared 103 days ago in Hanoi was also a moment of glory that remains a precious memory. Such a precious memory that I have in my unwavering respect for you will provide impetus for me to take my steps when we walk toward each other again someday in the future."[129]

Kim Jong-un's fawning letters suggest a man eager to negotiate. North Korea, impoverished, desperately needed relief from America's economic sanctions. Yet the brief opportunity was lost. Trump and Kim never met again. Six days before Trump left office, instead of a peace deal, Kim Jong-un presided over a military parade showcasing "the world's most powerful weapon," a massive submarine-based nuclear missile capable of striking the United States.[130]

Trump's personal negotiations with Kim Jong-un were a lost opportunity potentially on a par with the Reagan and Gorbachev negotiations that helped end the Cold War. Instead, they echo those between President Gerald Ford and Soviet leader Leonid Brezhnev. During their 1974 Vladivostok meeting, Ford and Brezhnev developed a warm friendship opening the possibility of negotiations leading to an end to the Cold War. But Washington hard-liners intervened, killing any chance of a rapprochement between the two powers, even banning the word 'détente' from official communications. Similarly, during Trump's negotiations with Kim Jong-un, hard-liners, including National Security Advisor John Bolton, may have insisted on unrealistic initial terms, such as full denuclearization before any easing of sanctions; terms Kim Jong-un could never accept.[131]

President Trump's withdrawal from the JCPOA and negotiations with Kim Jong-un were regularly in the news, boosted by Trump's expansive tweets. But neither effort led to an agreement. In contrast, on February 29, 2020 the United States and the Afghan Taliban quietly signed an agreement ending America's twenty-year war in Afghanistan. Uncharacteristically, Trump did not put out a single congratulatory tweet. Yet, historians may someday consider his agreement with the Taliban to be the most consequential of the Trump presidency.

The agreement had four provisions. First, a guarantee by the Taliban that "will prevent the use of the soil of Afghanistan by any group or individual against the security of the United States and its allies." Second, "guarantees, enforcement mechanisms, and announcement of a timeline for the withdrawal of all foreign forces from Afghanistan." Third, a commitment by the Taliban to begin peace negotiations with the Afghan government by March 10, 2020. Fourth, a commitment to pursue a permanent and comprehensive ceasefire to be announced "along with the completion and agreement over the future political roadmap of Afghanistan."[132]

The existing Afghan government, headed by President Ashraf Ghani, was not included in the negotiations. Ghani and his government were on their own to deal with the Taliban. That included the release of 5,000 Taliban prisoners which the agreement, in a confidential annex, had stipulated without Ghani's approval. "Freeing Taliban prisoners is not [under] the authority of America but the authority of the Afghan government. There has been no commitment for the release of 5,000 prisoners," Ghani stated on March 1, the day after the agreement was signed.[133] But under pressure from the United States, Ghani soon relented, agreeing to release one-hundred prisoners a day.

The agreement specified that the United States and NATO would withdraw their forces contingent on measures by the Taliban to bring about "a permanent and comprehensive ceasefire." But progress was slow and by October, Trump was becoming impatient. "We should have the small remaining number of our BRAVE Men and Women serving in Afghanistan home by Christmas!" Trump tweeted on October 7.[134] Defense Secretary Mark Esper objected, believing the Taliban had not met their commitments towards establishing a permanent ceasefire. Esper sent Trump a memo stating that "we [should] not reduce below 4,500 troops unless and until conditions were met by the Taliban." Weeks later, Trump fired Esper on November 9.[135]

By January 15, 2021, U.S. military forces were down to 2,500, the lowest level since 2001. That day, Afghan Vice-President Amrullah Saleh told the BBC:

> I am telling them [the U.S.] as a friend and as an ally that trusting the Taliban without putting in a verification mechanism is going to be a fatal mistake. The U.S. delegation came to us and swore on every Holy Scripture that if you release these 5,000 Taliban prisoners there will be no violence. We told them at the highest level that our intelligence indicated otherwise, and if we do this violence will spike. Violence has spiked. You want to negotiate with terrorism, it's your choice. But we are telling you, don't be deceived. Taliban were terrorists. They are terrorists today. They are killing women, activists, civil rights activists. . .[136]

Five days later, Joe Biden was inaugurated as the nation's forty-sixth president. Afghanistan was now his problem.

Whoppers and Censorship

In September 2016, Salena Zito, writing in *Atlantic* magazine, offered an insightful perspective on the politics of Donald Trump: "The press takes [Trump] literally, but not seriously; his supporters take him seriously, but not literally."[137]

Salena Zito's observation was not entirely accurate.

Yes, Trump's supporters understood that Trump made wildly exaggerated claims: During the 2016 presidential campaign Trump claimed the real unemployment rate was forty-two, not five percent; that Ted Cruz's father may have been involved in the Kennedy assassination; that a two-year-old boy "got autism" a week after being vaccinated; that he had seen thousands of Muslims cheering the collapse of the World Trade Center Towers on September 11.

During the early stages of his presidential campaign, Trump's fallacious claims were so outrageous that many were amused rather than concerned. The fact-checking site, FactCheck.org, on December 21, 2015, crowned Trump the "King of Whoppers."[138]

But Trump's supporters soon began to take his wild claims seriously. That Obama was born in Kenya and hence an illegitimate President: "If [Obama] wasn't born in this country, which is a real possibility... then he has pulled one of the great cons in the history of politics."[139] That Hillary Clinton had committed crimes ranging from deleting emails to murder and should be locked up. That he, and not Hillary Clinton, had won the 2016 popular vote: "I won the popular vote if you deduct the millions of people who voted illegally."[140]

Trump's distortions went further than wild exaggeration. It started the day President Trump was inaugurated. Trump called media reports contradicting his claim 1.5 million people attended his inauguration fake news propagated by "the most dishonest human beings on earth."[141] Counselor to the President Kellyanne Conway was more circumspect, describing the Trump administration's version of the inauguration as "alternative facts."[142] Conway's memorable phrase seems borrowed from George Orwell's dystopian novel, *1984*, in which the Party's Doublethink doctrine required "a loyal willingness to say that black is white when Party discipline demands this."[143]

The inane dispute over the size of the inauguration crowd was just the beginning. Trump's accusations quickly grew more sinister. A month into his presidency, Trump accused the established media of being "the enemy of the people," a phrase formerly associated with the Soviet Union, particularly Josef Stalin.[144] It was a claim Trump would repeat over the next four years. Often, on slow news days, Trump would gratuitously tweet, "Fake News is truly the ENEMY OF THE PEOPLE!" By the end of his presidency, Trump had sent 931 tweets, nearly five a week, labeling unfavorable coverage—whether news, polls, or opinions—as fake news.[145]

Trump believed that the so-called mainstream media—typically *The New York Times*, *Washington Post* and CNN—despised him. He was right. Trump had never pandered to the Eastern Establishment and reveled in his bad-boy image. That was never clearer than during a November 24, 2015 political rally when Trump, flailing his arms spastically, mocked the Pulitzer-winning *New York Times* reporter, Serge F. Kovaleski.[146] Kovaleski suffers from arthrogryposis, a congenital condition affecting the joints. It was a cruel, adolescent joke. The establishment despised him for the tasteless mocking but his rally crowd loved it.

Trump enjoyed defiantly ignoring Mark Twain's reputed advice to "Never pick a fight with people who buy ink by the barrel."[147] His crowds cheered when Trump vilified CNN as he pointed to the television cameras at the back of the room. "We are in a rigged system, and a big part of the system are these dishonest people in the media…" Trump told an October 21, 2016 rally crowd. "They don't even want to look at you folks, I think they consider you, like Hillary, they consider you deplorable and irredeemable also."[148]

The establishment attempted to counter Trump's misleading claims with fact-checking. PolitiFact, FactCheck.org, the *Washington Post* and Snopes all tracked misinformation propagated by President Trump.[149] By November 5, 2020, the *Washington Post* claimed Trump had made 29,508 false or misleading claims, about one every waking hour.[150] Although the fact-checks were well documented—and seldom disputed—for many of his supporters, fact-checking was nothing more than censorship by the elites to muzzle Trump. Fox News host Sean Hannity diagnosed the elites as "overpaid, out of touch, lazy leftist ideologues that are suffering from Trump Derangement Syndrome," which Hannity defined as the knee-jerk opposition to everything Trump does.[151]

Hannity may be right about elites suffering from Trump Derangement Syndrome, but why? Trump probably never read Calvin Coolidge's obscure 1929 auto-biography. Few people have. But every President should. Coolidge offered valuable advice to future Presidents:

> The words of the President have an enormous weight and ought not to be used indiscriminately. It would be exceedingly easy to set the country all by the ears and foment hatreds and jealousies, which, by destroying faith and confidence, would help nobody and harm everybody.[152]

2020: Annus Horribilis

Queen Elizabeth II needed the gravitas of Latin to describe the fortieth anniversary of her monarchy. The Queen called the year 1992 her "annus horribilis," or horrible year. That year, the British royalty suffered three divorces, a sex scandal, and a major fire in Windsor Castle.[153]

As 2020 dawned, President Trump could never have known he would suffer his own annus horribilis; a year that would begin with an impeachment trial, suffer the deadliest pandemic in a century, be consumed by the worst race riots in half a century, lose the presidential election, see the United States Capitol attacked for the first time since 1814, and, finally, end with a second impeachment trial.

For most Presidents, a single impeachment would have largely defined his presidency. For Trump, his first impeachment was but a mild precursor to the year's coming events.

On January 15, 2020, the House of Representatives sent two articles of impeachment to the Senate. The first article charged Trump with abuse of power for threatening to withhold military aid to Ukraine unless Ukrainian President Volodymyr Zelensky announced an investigation into presidential candidate Joe Biden and his son, Hunter. Hunter Biden had been accused of corruption while serving on the board of Burisma, a Ukrainian natural gas company, while his father was Vice President. The second article charged Trump with obstruction of Congress. Trump had instructed his White House staff to ignore House subpoenas requesting documents and testimony related to the impeachment investigation.[154]

The Senate trial was political theater. A month earlier, even before the House had sent over the impeachment articles, Senate Majority Leader Mitch McConnell told Sean Hannity of Fox News, "I'm coordinating with the White House counsel. There will be no difference between the President's position and our position as to how to handle this..."[155]. In effect, McConnell, serving as the role of jury foreman, was happy to conspire with the defendant to assure his acquittal. Senate impeachment trials follow the rule of politics, not the rule of law. On February 5, the Senate voted to acquit Trump on both charges. The votes fell along party lines, with one exception: Senator Mitt Romney voted to convict Trump for abuse of power. Romney's vote was the first time in American history a Senator from the same political party as the President had voted to convict during an impeachment trial.

The next day, February 6, 2020, Patricia Dowd of San Jose, California died unexpectedly. Patricia Dowd was the first American to die of a mysterious new illness known as a coronavirus.[156]

The COVID-19 Pandemic

The first serious effort to document the spread of a new virus originating in China wasn't done by the Center for Disease Control (CDC) or the World Health Organization (WHO). That task fell to a seventeen-year-old American high school student working out of his bedroom. Over the 2019 Christmas holidays, Avi Schiffmann had learned of a deadly new virus spreading rapidly in China. Unable to find a website tracking the spread of the virus, Schiffmann built his own, which launched on December 29, 2019.[157] Within weeks, the website, ncov2019.live, was reporting thousands of cases and hundreds of deaths in 23 countries.[158]

By then, the world was awakening to the threat. On January 22, 2020, WHO issued a statement saying there was evidence of human-to-human transmission of a deadly new coronavirus in Wuhan, China.[159]

President Trump quickly moved to slow the spread of the virus starting on January 31 when he banned the entry of foreign citizens traveling from China. Six weeks later, on March 12, Trump announced a travel ban from twenty-six European countries. On March 13, Trump declared a national emergency, authorizing $50 billion to fight the pandemic. By April 1, forty-three states had ordered various degrees of lockdowns that confined millions to their homes and shuttered non-essential businesses, travel, and recreation.[160]

By May 1, 64,000 Americans had died from the coronavirus, now officially named coronavirus disease 2019, or COVID-19.[161] Yet millions of Americans remained skeptical that COVID was a serious threat or even real. For months, the Internet and cable news channels had been awash with misinformation and conspiracy theories. Seemingly, a pandemic capable of killing millions would be immune from politicization, but no natural tragedy in American history has been more divisive.

On January 21, the government epidemiologist Dr. Anthony Fauci inadvertently contributed to months of COVID denial. "Obviously, you need to take [COVID] seriously," Fauci commented on *Newsmax*, "and do the kinds of things that the CDC and the Department of Homeland Security are doing. But this is not a major threat to the people in the United States, and this is not something that the citizens of the United States right now should be worried about."[162] Coronavirus skeptics would quote Fauci's "not a major threat" for months.

On January 30, Fox News' Jesse Watters on "The Five" mocked the coronavirus and a fellow host for "shaking in his shoes," declaring "Do I look nervous? No. I'm not afraid of this coronavirus at all."[163]

On February 17, Dr. Fauci again added to the confusion when he told *USA Today* that the danger from the coronavirus was "just minuscule" and that "The only people who need masks are those who are already infected to keep from exposing others. . . . Now, in the United States, there is absolutely no reason whatsoever to wear a mask."[164] Once again, Fauci's quote lived on for months.

On February 27, Rush Limbaugh opened his radio show with a facetious threat. "The apocalypse is imminent and you're going to all die, all of you in the next forty-eight hours. And it's all President Trump's fault," Limbaugh ranted, "or at least that's what the media mob and the Democratic extreme radical socialist party would like you to think." The next day Limbaugh, reading from the *Western Journal,* a website "Equipping Readers with The Truth,"[165] informed his fifteen million listeners that COVID "appears far less deadly" than the flu, but the government and the media "keep promoting panic."[166]

On March 8, Fox Business host Trish Regan, dramatically flashing a screen declaring "CORONAVIRUS IMPEACHMENT SCAM," told viewers, "The hate is boiling over. Many in the liberal media [are] using—and I mean using—coronavirus in an attempt to demonize and destroy the President."[167]

Fox executives apparently distrusted their own pundits. On March 12—five days before California issued the nation's first stay-at-home order—Fox News CEO Suzanne Scott announced Fox was going into lockdown "reducing the staff footprint at our headquarters in New York and some of our bureaus and will be instituting telecommuting starting Monday." For months, few Fox viewers realized their favorite hosts were in lockdown, broadcasting from their home or other remote studios even as they railed that the pandemic was a hoax.[168]

On April 15, a month after Governor Gretchen Whitmer locked down Michigan, hundreds of protesters, some heavily armed, surrounded the state capitol in Lansing waving American flags and chanting "Open up Michigan" and "Lock her up."

Governor Whitmer's challenge was representative of those handed public officials throughout the nation. Thousands were dying of the coronavirus—in Michigan 1,912 had died by April 15—yet millions of Americans considered the forced lockdowns of their homes, schools, and businesses as government overreach, even unconstitutional. "This arbitrary blanket spread of shutting down businesses, about putting all of these workers out of business, is just a disaster. It's an economic disaster for Michigan, and people are sick and tired of it," Michigan political activist, Meshawn Maddock, declared during the Lansing protest.[169]

President Trump sympathized with the protesters. Two days after the Michigan protests, the President tweeted "LIBERATE MICHIGAN" undercutting the governor and his own CDC. From the beginning of the pandemic, Trump's actions and words often sent a mixed message. He quickly closed the borders, declared a national emergency, expedited the production of critical material, dispatched a hospital ship to New York City, and, most critically, launched Operation Warp Speed. Warp Speed promised drug makers, even while their vaccines were still in clinical trials, that the federal government would purchase 800 million vaccine doses. By reducing the drug makers' financial risk, Warp Speed greatly accelerated the development of the life-saving COVID vaccines.[170] Of all President Trump's decisions during his presidency, Operations Warp Speed may have been the most consequential.

Yet, Trump often downplayed COVID, suggesting there was little to fear. "The fifteen (cases in the U.S.) within a couple of days is going to be down to close to zero," he declared on February 26. "This is going to go away without a vaccine. It is going to go away. We are not going to see it again," on May 8. "And it is dying out. The numbers are starting to get very good," on June 18.[171] Trump's ambivalence was clearly apparent on April 3 when the CDC issued a directive recommending social distancing and the universal use of cloth face coverings to reduce the spread of the disease.[172] (An earlier CDC recommendation had limited cloth face coverings to the symptomatic.) At a news conference announcing the CDC guidelines, Trump told reporters, "I don't think I'm going to be doing it… somehow I don't see it for myself. I just don't…"[173]

Throughout the remainder of their term, except on rare occasions, Trump and Vice President Pence openly flouted the CDC guidelines. On April 28, Pence ignored the Mayo Clinic's policy when he toured the renowned medical facility mask-less, escorted by an entourage of fully masked physicians and scientists.[174] A month later, Trump, seemingly oblivious to the irony, toured Honeywell's mask manufacturing plant—without a mask—while his campaign song, *Live and Let Die*, blared surreally in the background.[175]

By June, after months of restrictions and with summer approaching, most Americans were anxious to resume their normal lives. COVID death rates had declined to 750 a day, a rate unimaginable just a few months earlier, but well below the May peak of 2,200 daily deaths. But the CDC continued to urge caution as new COVID hot spots popped up around the country. "States in the South, West and Southwest," *The New York Times* reported on June 15, "are seeing upticks in their COVID case counts—and in some cases setting records..."[176]

The White House disagreed. The next day, Vice President Pence responded with a blistering rebuttal in *The Wall Street Journal* entitled, "There Isn't a Coronavirus Second Wave." "In recent days," Pence wrote, "the media has taken to sounding the alarm bells over a 'second wave' of COVID infections. Such panic is overblown.... The media has tried to scare the American people every step of the way, and these grim predictions of a second wave are no different. The truth is, whatever the media says, our whole-of-America approach has been a success."[177]

Pence's *Journal* editorial marked the beginning of White House efforts to prioritize re-opening America over containing the spread of the coronavirus. Starting in February, the economy had gone into free-fall as the first wave of lockdowns went into effect. By April, twenty-two million Americans had lost their jobs as businesses across the nation, from coffee shops to automobile factories, closed. So, the Trump Administration's efforts to re-open the economy were understandable, just grossly premature.

Trump soon resumed his signature rallies. By November 2, on the eve of the election, the President had conducted sixty-seven rallies across sixteen states drawing hundreds of thousands of supporters. Those supporters followed his lead. In August, an estimated 366,000 motorcyclists converged on Sturgis, South Dakota for their annual rally.[178] The motorcyclists, many sporting "Screw COVID I Went to Sturgis" t-shirts, celebrated with parades, carousing, and live concerts, nearly always tightly packed and mask-less.[179]

A fault line had divided the nation. States leaning towards Trump in the upcoming election tended to resist CDC guidelines regarding masks, social distancing, and business restrictions considering the federal guidelines and state-based mandates as infringements on their personal freedoms. South Dakota Governor Kristi Noem, for example, condemned an academic study critical of the Sturgis rally as "an attack on those who exercised their personal freedom."[180]

On the other side of the national divide were states led by governors such as Vermont Governor Phil Scott. In a November 17, 2020 press conference,

Scott defended his ban on multi-household gatherings. "In the environment we're in," Scott declared, "we've got to prioritize 'need' over 'want.' [I understand people] can do what they want. But please don't call it patriotic or pretend it's about freedom. Because real patriots serve and sacrifice for all..."[181]

A confrontation in Phoenix, Arizona between an intensive care nurse and protester objecting to the governor's stay-at-home order. The COVID pandemic divided America over the conflict between personal freedom and civic responsibility.
MICHAEL CHOW/THE REPUBLIC VIA IMAGN CONTENT SERVICES, LLC

Some Americans simply didn't believe COVID was real; that the COVID pandemic was a political hoax to discredit President Trump, or a sinister worldwide plot by Bill Gates on the scale of a James Bond movie. Even in death, some refused to believe it was COVID that was killing them. On November 20, 2020, after a heartbreaking day treating COVID patients, a South Dakota emergency room nurse, tweeted:

I have a night off from the hospital. As I'm on my couch with my dog I can't help but think of the Covid patients the last few days. The ones that stick out are those who still don't believe the virus is real. . . . All while gasping for breath on 100% Vapotherm. They tell you there must be another reason they are sick. They call you names and ask why you have to wear all that "stuff" because they don't have COVID because it's not real. Yes. This really happens.[182]

Covid death rates varied tremendously by state. Some states such as Washington, Utah, Maine and Vermont had death rates far below most developed countries, while other states such as New Jersey, Mississippi, Massachusetts and Louisiana were significantly higher. For many states, population density determined death rates, but for others, politics was a contributing factor.

During the first wave ending June 16, 2020, forty-three states went into lockdown, but the densely-populated eastern states, where the virus made its initial inroads, suffered the overwhelming number of COVID deaths. Much of the rest of the nation was relatively untouched. That first wave took 116,000 American lives, more than half in northeast cities alone.

But during the second and third waves, COVID had spread across the nation at a time when the Trump administration was encouraging states to reopen the economy. Many complied; in general, those states which supported Trump (the "Trump States") in the November 3 election. The Trump States generally prioritized economic growth and personal freedoms over COVID mitigation measures. Florida Governor Ron DeSantis, for example, issued an executive order on September 25, 2020 suspending "the collection of fines and penalties associated with COVID-19 [restrictions] enforced upon individuals [by local jurisdictions]."[183]

It didn't seem to matter. Lockdowns hurt the economy, but so did high death rates. From June 30, 2020 through June 30, 2021, the economies of the Trump States grew at virtually the same rate as the other states: an average of 12.0 percent versus 11.8 percent.[184] But COVID death rates in the Trump States, 2,000 per million, were a third higher than the other states whose COVID death rates were 1,500 per million.

No states better represented the two extremes of the COVID political spectrum than South Dakota and Vermont. During the first COVID wave ending in June 2020, the two states had nearly identical death rates:

86 deaths per million for South Dakota versus 88 deaths per million for Vermont.

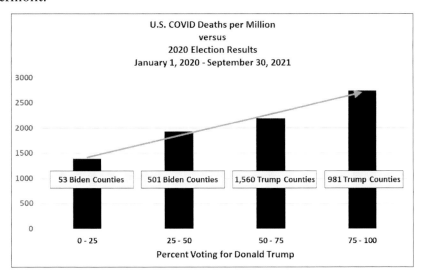

A strong correlation exists between voting patterns and COVID death rates. But factors other than politics such as age, religion or disinformation may be responsible for the higher death rates.   NEW YORK TIMES | MIT ELECTION DATA + SCIENCE LAB

It was during the second and third waves that the two states diverged. "I advised people to take common-sense precautions against this common enemy," Governor Noem wrote in a March 10, 2021 Fox News editorial, "But I did not order South Dakotans to shelter in place. I never mandated masks. And South Dakota was the only state in America to never order a single business or church to close."[185] On the other end of the spectrum, Vermont Governor Scott issued executive orders "limiting Vermonters' travel, shutting down in-person business operations, directing residents to quarantine and issuing a statewide mask mandate."[186]

The result was that Vermont's COVID death rates during the second and third waves, June 16, 2020 through June 16, 2021, were a fraction of South Dakota's: 324 per million for Vermont versus 2,174 per million for South Dakota.[187] But surprisingly, during that same period Vermont's real GDP growth actually exceeded South Dakota's growth even after Vermont's strict COVID mandates: 12.4 percent GDP growth for Vermont versus 11.8 percent for South Dakota.[188]

As Vermont and South Dakota suggest, Governor Noem's emphasis on personal liberties and the economy over public health failed to yield better economic results. Yet the citizens of South Dakota paid a very high price in human suffering and death—the ultimate loss of personal liberty.

Pence's claim that "there isn't a coronavirus second wave" may someday be remembered as one of the greatest political misjudgments in American history—even akin to British Prime Minister Neville Chamberlain's claim that his agreement with Adolf Hitler had bought "peace for our time." By June 16, 2021, a year after Pence's *Wall Street Journal* editorial, 600,000 Americans[189] had died—480,000 of whom died in the year after Pence declared there was no second wave. In a little more than a year, COVID had taken more American lives than World War II and the wars in Korea, Vietnam, and the Middle East combined.[190]

In the past, when tragedy struck the nation—after Pearl Harbor, President Kennedy's assassination, the 9/11 Terrorist Attacks—Americans came together, united. But during the COVID pandemic, politics and disinformation divided the nation, dictating whether Americans chose to wear a face mask, take the vaccine, or even accept the pandemic as real.

Black Lives Matter

"Please, please, I cannot breathe" were the last words George Floyd spoke. He died on May 25, 2020 after Minneapolis police office Derek Chauvin kneeled on Floyd's neck for nearly eight minutes as the dying man begged for his life.[191]

For years, unarmed Blacks had died at the hands of law enforcement. From seventeen-year-old Trayvon Martin, shot to death in 2012 by a neighborhood watch volunteer, to Breonna Taylor, killed in her home during a botched police raid in March 2020. But never had an African-American's death by a police officer been captured so graphically as the video of Floyd's death. The video, taken by a teenage bystander, instantly went viral.

President Trump was appalled. "That's a very shocking sight," Trump told reporters. "I saw it last night and I didn't like it... [it was a] very, very bad thing that I saw." After watching Floyd slowly die on the video, nearly all Americans agreed.

The video of Floyd's death triggered months of protests, riots and pillaging in nearly 150 American cities. Four days after Floyd's death, as protesters rampaged through Minneapolis, Trump tweeted, "These THUGS are dishonoring the memory of George Floyd, and I won't let that happen. Just spoke to Governor Tim Walz and told him that the Military is with him all the way. Any difficulty and we will assume control but, when the looting starts, the shooting starts. Thank you!"[192]

Peaceful protests after the death of George Floyd soon turned violent during summer 2020 resulting in multiple deaths and billions in property damage. Many Americans blamed Black Lives Matter agitators for the violence damaging the cause of all Black Americans.   AP PHOTO/JOHN MINCHILLO

By the end of October, an estimated twenty-five Americans had died, primarily in gunfire between Black Lives Matter (BLM) protesters and counter-protesters.[193] Wanton arson and looting destroyed nearly $2.0

billion in property. Law-abiding Americans watched in disgust as mayhem spread across the nation. It was the worst rioting since the summer of 1968 when the nation reeled from race and anti-war riots.[194]

Trump's tweets, including his inflammatory claim that "when the looting starts, the shooting starts. Thank you!" often fueled rather than reduced racial tensions. But Trump was right. The riots dishonored the memory of George Floyd and, for many Americans, discredited the cause of Black Lives Matter. But George Floyd's family ultimately got a measure of justice. On June 25, 2021, a Minnesota state judge sentenced Officer Derek Chauvin to twenty-two and a half years in prison.

The 2020 Presidential Election

By April 2020, national polls were consistently predicting that former Vice President Joe Biden would win the presidential election.[195] That month, President Trump tweeted his first claim regarding voter fraud. Two-hundred and fifty more would follow before the election.

"Mail in ballots," Trump tweeted on April 11, "substantially increases the risk of crime and VOTER FRAUD!" By August 23, Trump was telling his supporters to expect a stolen election, "The greatest Election Fraud in our history is about to happen."[196] Mail-in voting, though, was hardly new. Trump never mentioned that during his successful 2016 election thirty-three million votes, 24 percent of all votes, were cast by mail with no credible claims of fraud.[197]

Months before the election, Trump knew that he was in trouble. During the summer, Trump fired his top campaign manager, Brad Pascale,[198] after seventy polls conducted by Fox News, CNN, NBC, and others predicted that Joe Biden would win the November 3 election by an average of 8.1 percentage points. For months, not a single poll had predicted a Trump win.[199]

Yet, Trump relentlessly maintained his stolen election drumbeat, telling his supporters at an August 17 rally, for example, that "The only way we are going to lose this election is if the election is rigged. Remember that."[200]

Trump's prediction of a stolen election became a mantra at his rallies. "Trump is telling untold numbers of supporters," a September 15 *Washington Post* story reported, "that they shouldn't accept a losing outcome as legitimate.... Trump has also suggested to his supporters in every which way that they should prepare to resist such an outcome as well."[201]

Two months before the election. Trump's plan to overturn a lost election had become clear. On September 18, Supreme Court Justice Ruth Bader Ginsburg died after a long battle with pancreatic cancer. By then, Trump was publicly acknowledging he would lose the election, an election he claimed was rigged against him. "I think [the election] will end up in the Supreme Court," Trump commented at a September 23 press conference, "and I think it's very important that we have nine justices.... I think it's better if you [confirm a new Supreme Court Justice] before the election, because I think this scam that the Democrats are pulling—it's a scam—the scam will be before the United States Supreme Court."[202] On October 26, eight days before the presidential election, the Senate confirmed Amy Coney Barrett to replace Ruth Bader Ginsburg on the court.

President Trump's prediction he would lose the election was correct. It wasn't even close. He lost by seven million popular votes and 74 electoral votes.

In the weeks following the November 3 election Trump's legal team filed over sixty lawsuits claiming election fraud. All but one were rejected by the courts, which typically declared the evidence presented by Trump's lawyers to be "nothing but speculation and conjecture" and "largely based on anonymous witnesses, hearsay and irrelevant analysis."[203] Many were adjudicated by Trump-appointed judges.[204] Trump's own Department of Justice and the Department of Homeland Security declared no meaningful fraud had occurred. Attorney General William Barr told Trump his legal team was a "clown show" and that their charges of election fraud were "just a joke."[205] Even Trump's chief pollster, Tony Fabrizio, in a detailed analysis, confirmed Trump had lost the election, largely due, Fabrizio concluded, to Trump's divisive behavior and poor management of the COVID pandemic.[206]

The dispute never made it to the Supreme Court. On December 11, the Supreme Court refused to hear a case brought by the Texas Attorney General that challenged election results in Georgia, Pennsylvania, Michigan, and Wisconsin.[207] Trump's three Supreme Court appointees had failed him. "The Supreme Court really let us down. No Wisdom, No Courage!" Trump tweeted.[208]

January 6, 2021

"Remember this day forever," President Trump tweeted on January 6, 2021 after hundreds of his inflamed supporters had stormed the United States Capitol—the first attack on the Capitol since the War of 1812.[209]

Congress was meeting that day to certify the November 3 election results under rules specified by the Constitution in which the states transmit their certified election results "to the Seat of the Government of the United States, directed to the President of the Senate. The President of the Senate shall, in the Presence of the Senate and House of Representatives, open all the Certificates, and the Votes shall then be counted. The Person having the greatest Number of Votes shall be the President."[210]

Trump began the day with sixteen tweets repeating his claim that the 2020 presidential election had been stolen from him. He urged Vice President Mike Pence to reject the Electoral College votes and "send them back to the States." For weeks, Trump and his supporters had planned the "March to Save America." Trump hoped a sea of his MAGA-capped supporters marching on the Capitol would convince Vice President Pence to reject the election results.[211]

The speeches started early that morning at a rally held on the Ellipse overlooking the White House and only blocks from the U.S. Capitol Building. Alabama Representative Mo Brooks, in a combative speech, told Trump supporters why they were there:

> Today, Republican senators and congressmen will either vote to turn America into a godless, amoral, dictatorial, oppressed and socialist nation on the decline, or they will join us and they will fight and vote against voter fraud and election theft and vote for keeping America great. . . . Today is the day American patriots start taking down names and kicking ass. . . . Our ancestors sacrificed their blood, their sweat, their tears, their fortunes and sometimes their lives to give us, their descendants, an America that is the greatest nation in world history. So, I have a question for you. Are you willing to do the same? [crowd cheers] Louder! Are you willing to do what

it takes to fight for America? [crowd cheers] Louder! Will you fight for America?[212]

For any faint-hearted Trump supporters remaining in the crowd, Donald Trump, Jr. had a clear message: "You have an opportunity today: You can be a hero, or you can be a zero. And the choice is yours. But we are all watching. The whole world is watching, folks. Choose wisely."[213]

At noon, an hour before Congress was set to certify the election, President Trump stepped up to the podium. "All Vice President Pence has to do," Trump told his agitated supporters, "is send [the electoral votes] back to the States to recertify, and we become President, and you are the happiest people." And if Pence refuses? "We fight like Hell," Trump exhorted, "and if you don't fight like Hell, you're not going to have a country anymore."[214]

Even as Trump was speaking, a crowd of Trump supporters had made their way to the Capitol where they found additional encouragement from Missouri Senator Josh Hawley. Passing on his way to vote against the election certification, Hawley gave an enthusiastic thumbs-up and fist-pump as the energized crowd cheered.[215] Trump's supporters weren't mere protesters, they were patriots on a mission to Save America. "Today is 1776," a tweet from Colorado Representative Lauren Boebert had declared earlier that morning.[216]

Minutes later, waves of Trump supporters streamed through the hallways, a sea of red MAGA hats and blue Trump flags. A few were dressed in tactical gear. Pounding on doors, the rioters chanted, "Fight for Trump!" "Stop the Steal!" "Hang Mike Pence!" And like a horror film killer stalking his victim, "Nancy, Nancy, we're looking for you. Oh, Naaaaancy, where are you?"[218]

A quick-thinking Capitol police officer, Eugene Goodman, intercepted a scrum of rioters and managed to lure them up a flight of stairs and away from the Senate chambers. Had the rioters arrived only seconds earlier, they would have caught sight of Vice President Pence just feet away as he fled the House chamber. Outside the chambers, rioters pushed and battered the barricaded doors. Inside, Capitol police with guns drawn warned the rioters to back away. The mob persisted. Seconds later, Ashli Babbitt, a fourteen-year Air Force veteran turned fierce Trump supporter, fell to the floor, fatally shot.[219]

The January 6, 2021 Capitol siege was the first attack on the National Capitol since the War of 1812. Led by hundreds of Trump supporters, the attack was both a farce and deadly assault in which five people ultimately died.   SAUL LOEB/GETTY

Minutes later, rioters breached the empty Senate chamber. Dumbfounded to find themselves in the hallowed center of American government, the insurgents seemed unsure how to proceed. Several sat in the Senate President's chair, last defiled by an invader on August 24, 1814 when British Admiral George Cockburn lounged in the chair before setting fire to the Capitol.[220] Others rummaged through Senators' desks, 150-year-old cherished relics.[221] Jake Angeli, the self-described "QAnon Shaman," sported red, white and blue face paint, tattoos of Norse warriors, and a fur headdress topped with prominent horns.[222] Howling like a wolf at the full moon, Angeli's image streamed around the world, an extraordinary image of America gone mad.

For months, Trump had told his supporters that only he could win the election. Any other outcome would be a stolen election. Tens of millions believed him. Trump's political rulebook had worked, a rulebook he had followed for years:

> Never allow the public to cool off; never admit a fault or wrong; never concede that there may be some good in your enemy; never leave room for alternatives; never accept blame; concentrate on one enemy at a time and blame him for everything that goes wrong; people will believe a big lie sooner than a little one; and if you repeat it frequently enough people will sooner or later believe it.[223]

Trump followed these rules masterfully. But they weren't his. These words were written in 1943 by psychoanalyst Walter Langer describing his subject. Langer had been commissioned by the U.S. Office of Strategic Services (OSS), the precursor to the CIA, to conduct a psychological study of Adolf Hitler, the master of the Big Lie.

The Trump Legacy

In January 2021, the international research firm, YouGov, asked Americans who they considered the nation's best and worst Presidents, from George Washington to Donald Trump. The results were depressing, Americans had become so absurdly partisan that they selected the same two men as both the best and worst: Barack Obama and Donald Trump.[224] Those ranking

Obama the best President overwhelmingly ranked Trump the worst; those ranking Trump the best, ranked Obama the worst.

Professional historians take a longer view. The last presidential survey before President Trump left office was conducted in 2018 by the Siena College Research Institute. The Siena historians ranked George Washington America's best President. Trump was ranked third from the bottom, just below Warren G. Harding.[225] Harding (unjustly in the author's opinion) is invariably rated one of America's worst Presidents, "a corrupt, poker-playing womanizer" who "died before he could do great damage,"[226] as James Jay Carafano of the Heritage Foundation described him.

Were historians, right? Was Trump a worse President than the scorned Warren G. Harding? It's too early to say. It takes decades for history to render its judgment. Harry Truman, for example, left office a deeply unpopular President. Today, he's recognized as one of America's best Presidents for guiding the nation after World War II, confronting Soviet aggression, supporting desegregation of the Army, recognizing Israel's independence and, like Trump, for his "Give 'em Hell, Harry" personal style.

History's final judgment of Donald Trump may be years away. But today, we should be able to objectively compare the acknowledged accomplishments of the Harding and Trump presidencies.

The Harding and Trump presidencies, separated by a century, paralleled each other in many respects.

Both were one-term Presidents. Harding died after only two and one-half years in office, while Trump—as certified by Congress—lost reelection.

Both Presidents ran on America First, a campaign slogan popularized by Harding. Americans were disillusioned after the First World War, a war fought over European interests; Harding refused to join the League of Nations. Similarly, believing American interests had been abused, Trump pulled the United States out of the Paris Climate Accord, Human Rights Council, World Health Organization, and Trans-Pacific Partnership.

Harding promised Americans a "Return to Normalcy" after years of unsettling change under Presidents Teddy Roosevelt, William Howard Taft, and Woodrow Wilson. Similarly, Trump promised to "Make America

Great Again" by restoring prosperity and endangered cultural values to the millions of Americans who had been left behind by both political parties.

Both slashed immigration. Harding signed the Emergency Quota Act of 1921, the first immigration legislation to set numerical limits by country, excluding Eastern and Southern Europeans, to preserve American racial homogeneity. Trump slashed immigration, demonized Muslims, condemned Mexicans as murderers and rapists and began the construction of a wall on the southern border.

Both Harding and Trump cut taxes, grew the economy and appointed multiple Supreme Court judges.

In December 2017, Trump cut the maximum personal tax rate from 39.6 to 37.0 percent and cut the corporate rate from 35 to 21 percent in addition to other reforms. Trump claimed his tax cuts were the largest in the nation's history. That was an exaggeration. Harding did far more. Harding's Revenue Act of 1921 cut the maximum personal tax rate from 73 percent to 58 percent and slashed the capital gains rate from 73 percent to 12.5 percent, a one-hundred year low. In 1924, in what would have been Harding's last year, President Coolidge further cut the top personal rate to 46 percent.[227]

President Trump often claimed, "We have the greatest economy in the history of our country."[228] Harding, again, exceeded Trump. Unemployment under Trump fell from 4.9 percent in 2016 to 3.7 percent in 2019, a 24 percent reduction. Harding cut unemployment from 5.2 percent in 1920 to 2.4 percent in 1923, or 52 percent. Similarly, Trump grew real GDP by 2.5 percent annually (excluding the pandemic year 2020). Real GDP under Harding grew 4.7 percent annually. Trump ballooned the national debt, Harding shrank it.

Trump appointed three Supreme Court justices. Harding appointed four.

Harding appointed four exceptional cabinet members whose achievements would be historical. Charles Evans Hughes presided over the world's first disarmament conference and later became Chief Justice of the Supreme Court. Charles Dawes won the Nobel Peace Prize for the "Dawes Plan," which ended the German war reparations crisis. Andrew Mellon, in his book *Taxation*, founded modern supply-side economics. Similarly, Herbert Hoover, in *American Individualism,* established the rugged individual as the foundational basis for American Exceptionalism. The historic contributions of Trump's cabinet members are yet to be determined.

Both Presidents were tainted by sexual and legal scandals.

In 1927, Nan Britton published *The President's Daughter*, claiming that Harding had fathered her daughter when still a Senator from Ohio. DNA tests later confirmed Harding's paternity. In 2018, Trump's personal lawyer, Michael Cohen, pled guilty to making hush-money payments to porn star Stormy Daniels and Playboy model Karen McDougal to keep Trump's alleged affairs quiet. Over twenty other women claimed that Trump had sexually assaulted them ranging from forced kissing to rape. (As Trump left office, none of their claims had been proven.)[229]

After Harding's death, evidence of pervasive corruption within his administration emerged, most famously the Teapot Dome scandal. But Harding, other than reputedly gambling away the White House chinaware during a boozy poker game, was never implicated in any corruption himself.

Trump though was dogged by corruption issues including two impeachments. Early in his presidency, Trump paid $27 million to settle lawsuits regarding corruption at Trump University and the Trump Foundation. Eight of Trump's campaign associates were charged or imprisoned for criminal acts (five received a presidential pardon). As Trump left office, he faced more than two dozen lawsuits and years of civil and, potentially, criminal investigations involving inauguration payments, sexual assault, hush money, tax evasion, insurance and bank fraud, election interference, and insurrection incitement.[230]

Lastly, following Harding's sudden death in 1923, his Vice President, Calvin Coolidge, after winning the presidency himself in a 1924 landslide, largely continued Harding's presidential agenda for the remainder of the decade. Trump lost the 2020 presidential election, an election certified by fifty state election boards and the U.S. Congress on January 6, 2021. Trump rejected the results, praised the insurrectionists who stormed the Capitol that day and later mounted an unprecedented campaign to overturn the election.

By these measures, historians would have little choice but to rank Warren G. Harding a better President than Donald Trump.

These objective comparisons, though, pale relative to the impact the two Presidents, separated by a century, had on the American spirit.

Harding promised to return America to normalcy after the First World War, the Spanish Flu pandemic, and three progressive Presidents. He largely did so. Harding's genial nature calmed and soothed America. Americans' affection for him crossed political boundaries. An estimated nine million Americans came out to honor Harding's funeral train as it traveled across the country. America's 19,134 newspaper boys contributed one copper penny each to be melted down and sculpted into a statue of Laddie Boy, Harding's beloved dog.[231] One million Americans donated $978,000 ($14.8 million in 2020 dollars) to construct his tomb in Marion, Ohio.[232]

Trump inherited a divided, anxious nation. Rather than heal, Trump seemed to enjoy sowing discord. During hundreds of political rallies, impromptu press meetings, and over 26,000 tweets, Trump disparaged nearly every American institution from sports leagues to the Supreme Court. Washington was controlled by the Deep State. News media was the enemy of the people. Science was manipulated by elites. Academia was infested with radicals who hated America. Even the American presidency was not immune. During the 2016 presidential campaign, Trump repeatedly suggested that Barack Obama was born in Kenya and an illegitimate President. Then, four years later, Trump claimed he and his supporters had been "stabbed in the back" after the stolen 2020 election and that he, not Joe Biden, was the legitimate President.

Sadly, Donald Trump could have used his tremendous charisma and communication skills to bring Americans together, as Roosevelt and Reagan had done decades earlier. Instead, Trump's rhetoric and actions divided America. Those who supported Trump were true American Patriots who loved God while those who condemned Trump and his politics were traitors and atheists. "I have learned from President Trump," one well-accomplished individual emailed the author, "to ignore false accusations, defamations and insults by leftists and to proclaim my way, my convictions and my resistance to the socialist/communist satans of this world even more strongly and call out my response wherever possible. God bless America."[233]

As Trump's presidency was ending, political and personal animosities had become so inflamed *Newsweek* declared America was in a Cold Civil War.[234]

Is this Donald Trump's legacy? Will history condemn Trump for leaving Americans the most bitterly divided in modern history? And worse, for undermining Americans' trust in the nation's most essential democratic institution, free and fair elections? Or will history be forgiving and credit Trump as a modern-day Andrew Jackson—a flawed president, but also a champion of common Americans and a bold disruptor who dared to challenge the long complacent establishment?

Regardless of history's final rendering of Donald Trump, every American must never forget how fragile democracy truly is. America's Founders understood this. At the conclusion of the 1787 Constitutional Convention, Benjamin Franklin was asked what form of government America would have. "A republic, if you can keep it,"[235] Franklin replied.

Epilogue

————✴————

On January 6, 2021 Americans watched, dumbfounded, as hundreds of seemingly patriotic, but enraged Americans attacked the nation's Capitol. The sight of flag-waving Americans violently crashing through police lines, beating police officers, bashing in windows and besieging the House and Senate chambers were unnerving. The videos of the attack, and the fiery speeches before the attack, left no question as to who was responsible:

> The President bears responsibility for Wednesday's attack on Congress by mob rioters. He should have immediately denounced the mob when he saw what was unfolding. These facts require immediate action by President Trump to accept his share of responsibility, quell the brewing unrest and ensure President-elect Biden is able to successfully begin his term.[1]
>
> House Minority Leader Kevin McCarthy
> January 13, 2021

The people who stormed this building believed they were acting on the wishes and instructions of their President. And their having that belief was a foreseeable consequence of the growing crescendo of false statements, conspiracy theories, and reckless hyperbole which the defeated President kept shouting into the largest megaphone on planet Earth. The issue is not only the President's intemperate language on January 6th. It is not just his endorsement of remarks in which an associate urged 'trial by combat.' It was also the entire manufactured atmosphere of looming catastrophe; the increasingly wild myths about a reverse landslide election that was being stolen in some secret coup by our now-President.[2]

Senate Minority Leader Mitch McConnell
February 13, 2021

Peggy Noonan, President Reagan's former speechwriter and respected *Wall Street Journal* opinion writer, was unequivocal, writing in a *Journal* editorial the day after the attack: "This was a sin against history. . . . As for the chief instigator, the President of the United States, he should be removed from office by the 25th Amendment or impeachment, whichever is faster."[3]

But denunciations of Trump and his role in the attack on the Capitol quickly faded as politicians heard from their constituents. Millions of Americans weren't buying the Capitol Insurrection, claiming instead that the event was just a non-violent protest over-blown by the media, or perhaps a conspiracy led by Trump-haters "trying to make Trump look bad."[4] Three weeks after the Capitol attack, a contrite House Minority Leader Kevin McCarthy visited Trump at his Mar-a-Lago resort to make peace with the former President. By June, Trump had resumed his signature campaign rallies to huge, adoring crowds.

On July 19, the first person charged with a felony was sentenced for the Capitol attack. The thirty-eight-year-old man was given an eight-month prison term. Videos showed the intruder carrying a red and white "Trump 2020" flag onto the Senate floor while others stood over the abandoned vice-president's chair. Upon passing sentence, U.S. District Judge Randolph D. Moss stated: "He was staking a claim on the floor of the U.S. Senate not with an American flag but declaring his loyalty to a single individual over the nation. In that act, he captured the threat to democracy that we all witnessed that day."[5]

Many more prison sentences will undoubtedly follow. As of late-August, approximately 570 persons of an estimated 800 individuals who entered the Capitol building had been arrested.[6]

Nearly a year after the 2020 presidential election, America remains deeply divided. Nearly a third of Americans hold an unwavering belief that the election was stolen from Donald Trump.[7] Yet to date, not a shred of evidence has come forth that would pass a simple evidentiary hearing. This is despite intense efforts to uncover fraud by Trump's legal team and his most zealous supporters, notably My Pillow CEO Mike Lindell. For months the courts have consistently ruled against claims of election fraud. Federal District Judge Linda V. Parker, for example, on August 25 ordered sanctions against nine members of Trump's legal team, admonishing the lawyers that their lawsuit to overturn election results "was never about fraud. It was about undermining the People's faith in our democracy and debasing the judicial process to do so."[8]

The claim of a stolen national election involving 160 million voters seems wildly implausible. Trump lost by thirty-eight electoral votes. To prove the election was stolen, investigators would need to find irrefutable evidence of fraud in three of the five disputed states: Arizona (11 electoral votes), Georgia (16), Michigan (16), Pennsylvania (20) and Wisconsin (10). Either there was a broad conspiracy secretly coordinated across multiple states, or three states, somehow, just happened to act independently to steal the election. Both scenarios are fantastical.

Today, it seems likely that former Attorney General William Barr's summary of Trump's election fraud investigations will stand as definitive: "My attitude was: It was put-up or shut-up time. If there was evidence of fraud, I had no motive to suppress it. But my suspicion all the way along was that there was nothing there. It was all bullshit."[9]

Yet, Donald Trump continued to double-down on his claim that he is the rightful President. During a July 6 interview with Fox News Host Maria Bartiromo, Trump declared: "We won this election in a landslide. We got twelve million more votes, Maria. . . This was a rigged election. And the people aren't standing for it. So, we will go forward."[10]

On January 20, as President Trump was leaving office, the COVID virus was taking an American life every thirty seconds. Fortunately, effective COVID vaccines had become available, and in record time, largely due to President Trump's Operation Warp Speed. Yet, Trump failed to promote the vaccines. In January, he and First Lady Melania were quietly vaccinated. It wasn't until two months later, in March, that Trump acknowledged they had gotten their shots. Later that month, Trump, during a political conference, tepidly urged the audience to be vaccinated.

Fox News Host Tucker Carlson refused even to disclose whether he had been vaccinated claiming questions concerning his vaccination status were as intrusive as queries regarding his married sex life.[11] Carlson, though, readily discussed the vaccine. After the Centers for Disease Control and Prevention (CDC) recommended that individuals wear a mask after being vaccinated, Carlson speculated in April 2021: "So maybe [the vaccine] doesn't work, and they're simply not telling you that. Well, you'd hate to think that, especially if you've gotten two shots. But what's the other potential explanation? We can't think of one."[12] In July, Carlson told his viewers that the Biden Administration's proposed grassroots campaign to promote the vaccine were an attempt to "force people to take medicine they don't want or need," declaring Biden's initiative "the greatest scandal in my lifetime, by far."[13] That month a Yale School of Public Health study reported that COVID vaccines had saved an estimated 279,000 American lives.[14]

Fox News was hardly alone in their criticism of the vaccine. Newsmax Host Rob Schmitt, for example, declared that "I feel like a vaccination in a weird way is just generally kind of going against nature. . . . Maybe there's just an ebb and flow to life where something's supposed to wipe out a certain amount of people, and that's just kind of the way evolution goes. Vaccines kind of stand in the way of that."[15] Schmitt's Darwinian logic would suggest all modern medicine seems to be "kind of going against nature."

The disinformation inevitably had an effect. Vaccination rates began to slow. In response, the Biden Administration proposed a door-to-door campaign to educate Americans as to the safety and efficacy of the COVID vaccines. Biden was adopting the grassroots campaign taken during the nineteen-fifties to promote the new polio vaccines. That campaign had been hugely successful, helped in part by a beaming Elvis Presley being vaccinated on the popular Ed Sullivan Show.

Yet, in 2021 a political firestorm ensued. "We're here to tell government, we don't want your benefits, we don't want your welfare, don't come knocking on my door with your Fauci ouchie. You leave us the hell alone!" U.S. Representative Lauren Boebert fumed during a political convention on July

10.[16] (Fauci ouchie was a reference both to Dr. Anthony Fauci, the director of the U.S. National Institute of Allergy and Infectious Diseases and to the needle prick of the vaccine shots he advocated.) One-upping Boebert, U.S. Representative Madison Cawthorn, in a media interview, raised the threat of an Orwellian government arising from the vaccine campaign: "And now they're sort of talking about going door-to-door to be able to take vaccines to the people. . . . They could then go door-to-door to take your guns. They could go door-to-door to take your Bibles."[17] Taking a lighter approach, a political action committee associated with Florida Governor Ron DeSantis mocked Dr. Anthony Fauci, the nation's top epidemiologist, with a merchandising campaign selling apparel shouting the message, "Don't Fauci my Florida."[18] Earlier, Governor DeSantis had banned local school districts from mandating masks within schools. DeSantis threatened to fine the districts and cut the pay of school administrators who failed to comply.[19] DeSantis issued his order while COVID cases in Florida were skyrocketing from 1,800 in mid-June to 25,000 two months later—Florida's highest infection rate since the beginning of the pandemic.

Months of anti-vaccine rhetoric had convinced millions of Americans that the vaccines either were ineffective, unsafe, or a sinister government plot. Trump supporters were especially affected. By mid-summer, the ten states with the lowest vaccination rates, an average of only 39 percent, with the exception of Georgia, had all voted for Trump in the 2020 presidential election while the states with the highest rates, averaging 58 percent, were exclusively Biden states.[20]

In contrast, Puerto Rico never allowed COVID to become politicized. Its Spanish language isolated most of the island's citizens from the disinformation promoted by U.S. politicians and media pundits. By October 2021, over 73 percent of Puerto Ricans had been fully vaccinated, far above the U.S. national average of 57 percent and surpassing even Vermont, the nation's most vaccinated state. "[Puerto Rico has] done this largely by not tying vaccines to politics," commented Dr. Ashish Jha, dean of the Brown University School of Public Health. As a result, "there are hundreds of people—if not thousands—right now walking around somewhere in Puerto Rico and they wouldn't be there if it wasn't for these efforts," as Daniel

Colón Ramos, a Yale medical professor advising the Puerto Rican government, declared.[21]

Tragically, the politicization of COVID contributed to hundreds of thousands of unnecessary American deaths. By November 2021, 765,000 Americans had died of COVID—one in every 435 Americans. In Puerto Rico, the death rate was far lower, one in 1,060. In Canada, with 73 percent of Canadians also vaccinated, one in 1,300. Had the United States fought COVID as successfully as its Canadian and Puerto Rican neighbors, nearly 500,000 American lives would have been spared.[22]

On August 15, Taliban fighters entered Kabul, the Afghanistan capital, without a single shot being fired. Fourteen provincial capitals had already fallen during the preceding days after the Taliban promised amnesty to the dispirited Afghan forces. After nearly twenty years, the Taliban were again in power.

In 1975, the American-backed South Vietnamese government survived two years after the last American soldier departed. Two decades later, the Soviet-backed Afghan government lasted three years after the defeated Soviets abandoned the country. But in 2021, the world watched in shock as the Taliban swiftly defeated the American-backed Afghan government, only weeks after American soldiers had begun to depart the country.

Two weeks after the Taliban entered Kabul, on August 30, the last Americans departed Afghanistan in the dark of night. The day before, the remains of thirteen U.S. service members killed by an ISIS-Khorasan suicide bomber had come home to Dover Air Force Base. The Americans had died defending the Kabul airport as 122,000 Americans and Afghan allies were evacuated during the preceding seventeen days in the largest airlift in American history. But it wasn't enough. Left behind were several hundred Americans and thousands of former Afghan allies.

Just a month earlier, there was still hope the Afghan government and military would stand on their own as American and allied soldiers departed the country. On July 12, former Secretary of State Mike Pompeo, in an interview with Fox News Host Maria Bartiromo, stated:

Afghanistan needs to begin to stand up on its own. . . . You have got Afghan leaders with beautiful homes all over the Middle East, in Europe. There's corruption everywhere. It's time for the Afghan people to do the hard work, the heavy lifting, and demand that they push back against the Taliban, not just militarily, but politically, exercise their own rights, secure their own freedom. We have provided all the resources the Afghan National Security Forces could possibly ever have dreamed of and all the training over two decades. . . .[23]

But Pompeo's hopes that Afghanistan's political and military leadership would find the resolve to defend their country were quickly dashed. For two decades, the United States had poured blood and treasure into Afghanistan, only to see the country collapse as U.S. support departed the besieged nation. It was an ignominious end to America's twenty-year struggle to transform ancient, tribal Afghanistan into a modern, democratic society.

Appendices

——————⋆——————

1920–2020

Appendix A
KEY ECONOMIC INDICATORS
See appendices endnotes for definitions and sources

	Real GDP (2020 Billions)	Employment (thousands)	Consumer Price Index	National Debt as % GDP	Productivity (2020 = 100)	S&P 500
	Warren G. Harding & Calvin Coolidge					
1921	850	37,061	17.9	32.9%	16	105.7
1928	1,177	45,123	17.1	18.1%	18	350.4
AGR	4.8%	2.9%	-0.7%	-8.2%	1.9%	18.7%
	Herbert Hoover					
1929	1,260	46,207	17.1	16.2%	19	323.9
1932	941	38,038	13.7	32.7%	17	128.8
AGR	-9.3%	-6.3%	-7.1%	26.4%	-3.2%	-26.5%
	Franklin D. Roosevelt / Depression Years					
1933	928	38,052	13.0	39.4%	17	198.5
1940	1,510	47,520	14.0	41.8%	22	194.7
AGR	7.2%	3.2%	1.1%	0.8%	3.9%	-0.3%
	Franklin D. Roosevelt / War Years					
1941	1,779	50,350	14.7	37.9%	25	154.2
1945	2,646	52,820	18.0	113.5%	35	249.2
AGR	10.4%	1.2%	5.2%	31.6%	9.1%	12.7%
	Harry S. Truman					
1946	2,340	55,250	19.5	118.4%	30	200.8
1952	2,926	60,272	26.5	70.5%	34	254.3
AGR	3.8%	1.5%	5.2%	-8.3%	2.3%	4.0%
	Dwight D. Eisenhower					
1953	3,063	61,206	26.7	68.4%	35	240.7
1960	3,704	65,785	29.6	52.8%	40	496.6
AGR	2.8%	1.0%	1.5%	-3.6%	1.7%	10.9%
	John F. Kennedy & Lyndon B. Johnson					
1961	3,799	65,744	29.9	51.4%	41	620.7
1968	5,446	75,913	34.8	37.0%	51	791.9
AGR	5.3%	2.1%	2.2%	-4.6%	3.1%	3.5%
	Richard M. Nixon & Gerald R. Ford Jr.					
1969	5,615	77,875	36.7	34.8%	51	642.5
1976	6,760	88,753	56.9	33.1%	54	476.1
AGR	2.7%	1.9%	6.5%	-0.7%	0.8%	-4.2%

	Real GDP (2020 Billions)	Employment (thousands)	Consumer Price Index	National Debt as % GDP	Productivity (2020 = 100)	S&P 500
			James E. Carter Jr.			
1977	7,073	92,017	60.6	33.6%	54	400.7
1980	7,679	99,303	82.4	31.8%	55	419.3
AGR	2.8%	2.6%	10.8%	-1.8%	0.2%	1.5%
			Ronald Reagan			
1981	7,874	100,400	90.9	31.1%	55	352.5
1988	10,075	114,974	118.3	49.7%	62	604.9
AGR	3.6%	2.0%	3.8%	6.9%	1.6%	8.0%
			George H.W. Bush			
1989	10,444	117,327	124.0	50.6%	63	727.5
1992	11,004	118,488	140.3	62.3%	66	803.6
AGR	1.8%	0.3%	4.2%	7.2%	1.4%	3.4%
			William J. Clinton			
1993	11,307	120,259	144.5	64.3%	66	834.5
2000	14,920	136,901	172.2	55.3%	77	2,000.3
AGR	4.0%	1.9%	2.5%	-2.1%	2.1%	13.3%
			George W. Bush			
2001	15,068	136,939	177.1	54.9%	78	1,673.2
2008	17,729	145,373	215.3	68.1%	86	1,054.9
AGR	2.4%	0.9%	2.8%	3.1%	1.5%	-6.4%
			Barack Obama			
2009	17,280	139,894	214.5	82.4%	87	1,339.5
2016	20,145	151,436	240.0	104.4%	94	2,422.6
AGR	2.2%	1.1%	1.6%	3.4%	1.1%	8.8%
			Donald J. Trump / Pre-COVID Pandemic			
2017	20,616	153,335	245.1	103.6%	95	2,813.2
2019	21,692	157,536	255.7	106.0%	97	3,218.1
AGR	2.6%	1.4%	2.1%	1.2%	1.2%	7.0%
			Donald J. Trump / COVID Pandemic			
2019	21,692	157,536	255.7	106.0%	97	3,218.1
2020	20,935	147,794	258.8	128.7%	100	3,756.1
AGR	-3.5%	-6.2%	1.2%	21.4%	2.9%	16.7%

Appendix B
PERSONAL INCOME ADJUSTED TO 2020 DOLLARS
FEDERAL INCOME TAX FILINGS
See appendices endnotes for definitions and sources

Income Bracket	Gross Income	Tax Rate	After-Tax Income	Gross Income	Tax Rate	After-Tax Income	Gross Income	Tax Rate	After-Tax Income
				Warren G. Harding & Calvin Coolidge					
		1921			**1928**			**Change**	
Lower 20%	17,302	1%	17,179	22,926	0%	22,903	5,624	-0.6%	5,724
Middle 60%	30,997	1%	30,819	51,908	0%	51,788	20,911	-0.3%	20,970
Upper 20%	102,146	7%	94,998	290,298	7%	269,038	188,152	0.3%	174,040
Top 1%	524,887	19%	425,847	2,282,826	15%	1,951,581	1,757,938	-4.4%	1,525,733
				Herbert Hoover					
		1929			**1932**			**Change**	
Lower 20%	22,596	0%	22,588	20,222	0%	20,136	-2,374	0.4%	-2,452
Middle 60%	52,501	0%	52,456	40,886	1%	40,666	-11,615	0.5%	-11,790
Upper 20%	283,962	7%	265,357	141,062	5%	133,770	-142,900	-1.4%	-131,587
Top 1%	2,270,722	13%	1,964,981	774,802	13%	672,939	-1,495,920	-0.3%	-1,292,042
				Franklin D. Roosevelt / Depression Years					
		1933			**1940**			**Change**	
Lower 20%	20,194	0%	20,127	18,927	0%	18,843	-1,267	0.1%	-1,284
Middle 60%	40,854	0%	40,663	36,361	1%	36,171	-4,492	0.1%	-4,492
Upper 20%	151,542	6%	142,178	101,896	8%	93,427	-49,646	2.1%	-48,751
Top 1%	885,116	15%	748,604	508,578	25%	379,568	-376,538	9.9%	-369,035
				Franklin D. Roosevelt / War Years					
		1941			**1945**			**Change**	
Lower 20%	16,442	1%	16,279	7,041	2%	6,897	-9,401	1.1%	-9,382
Middle 60%	31,722	2%	31,141	28,264	9%	25,743	-3,458	7.1%	-5,398
Upper 20%	88,322	13%	77,194	82,007	21%	65,076	-6,315	8.0%	-12,118
Top 1%	433,814	33%	290,433	395,757	41%	235,328	-38,057	7.5%	-55,105
				Harry S. Truman					
		1946			**1952**			**Change**	
Lower 20%	7,152	2%	7,018	7,815	3%	7,564	663	1.4%	545
Middle 60%	27,416	7%	25,553	31,349	9%	28,617	3,934	1.9%	3,064
Upper 20%	80,074	18%	65,514	86,206	18%	70,269	6,132	0.3%	4,755
Top 1%	392,175	37%	246,811	361,229	35%	235,744	-30,946	-2.3%	-11,066

Income Bracket	Gross Income	Tax Rate	After-Tax Income	Gross Income	Tax Rate	After-Tax Income	Gross Income	Tax Rate	After-Tax Income
Dwight D. Eisenhower									
	1953			**1960**			**Change**		
Lower 20%	7,815	3%	7,569	7,567	3%	7,329	-247	-0.0%	-240
Middle 60%	32,795	9%	29,813	37,881	9%	34,455	5,086	-0.0%	4,642
Upper 20%	87,835	18%	71,992	105,371	17%	87,616	17,536	-1.2%	15,624
Top 1%	344,329	34%	228,778	389,662	30%	272,876	45,333	-3.6%	44,098
John F. Kennedy & Lyndon B. Johnson									
	1961			**1968**			**Change**		
Lower 20%	7,651	3%	7,409	7,516	3%	7,325	-134	-0.6%	-84
Middle 60%	38,750	9%	35,203	46,779	10%	42,146	8,029	0.7%	6,943
Upper 20%	108,905	17%	90,073	137,261	18%	112,145	28,356	1.0%	22,072
Top 1%	399,390	32%	273,499	514,711	32%	347,774	115,320	0.9%	74,275
Richard M. Nixon & Gerald R. Ford Jr.									
	1969			**1976**			**Change**		
Lower 20%	7,475	3%	7,259	8,224	1%	8,169	749	-2.2%	910
Middle 60%	47,373	11%	42,256	46,082	9%	41,811	-1,290	-1.5%	-445
Upper 20%	132,931	19%	108,248	136,607	18%	111,389	3,676	-0.1%	3,141
Top 1%	479,405	32%	323,892	428,839	33%	289,062	-50,566	0.2%	-34,830
James E. Carter Jr.									
	1977			**1980**			**Change**		
Lower 20%	8,183	0%	8,152	7,696	1%	7,615	-487	0.7%	-536
Middle 60%	46,060	9%	41,783	43,038	11%	38,384	-3,023	1.5%	-3,399
Upper 20%	138,703	19%	112,178	133,076	21%	105,251	-5,627	1.8%	-6,928
Top 1%	429,486	33%	286,411	452,454	35%	293,230	22,968	1.9%	6,819
Ronald Reagan									
	1981			**1988**			**Change**		
Lower 20%	7,712	1%	7,600	6,885	2%	6,758	-827	0.4%	-842
Middle 60%	42,123	11%	37,309	43,009	9%	39,261	886	-2.7%	1,952
Upper 20%	130,447	21%	102,600	171,490	17%	141,694	41,043	-4.0%	39,094
Top 1%	433,497	34%	284,557	900,669	24%	681,133	467,172	-10.0%	396,576
George H.W. Bush									
	1989			**1992**			**Change**		
Lower 20%	7,582	2%	7,407	7,560	2%	7,421	-22	-0.5%	14
Middle 60%	42,540	9%	38,736	41,110	8%	37,639	-1,430	-0.5%	-1,097
Upper 20%	167,851	17%	139,147	163,757	17%	135,644	-4,093	0.1%	-3,503
Top 1%	831,082	24%	634,396	822,045	25%	613,445	-9,037	1.7%	-20,951

Income Bracket	Gross Income	Tax Rate	After-Tax Income	Gross Income	Tax Rate	After-Tax Income	Gross Income	Tax Rate	After-Tax Income
William J. Clinton									
	1993			**2000**			**Change**		
Lower 20%	7,431	2%	7,301	7,517	2%	7,387	87	-0.0%	86
Middle 60%	40,591	8%	37,194	46,246	9%	42,302	5,655	0.2%	5,108
Upper 20%	161,751	18%	132,783	223,486	20%	178,486	61,735	2.2%	45,703
Top 1%	788,871	28%	564,808	1,464,476	28%	1,061,688	675,605	-0.9%	496,880
George W. Bush									
	2001			**2008**			**Change**		
Lower 20%	7,453	1%	7,376	7,204	1%	7,155	-249	-0.4%	-221
Middle 60%	45,723	8%	42,017	42,772	6%	40,171	-2,951	-2.0%	-1,846
Upper 20%	201,528	19%	162,911	213,112	17%	177,440	11,584	-2.4%	14,529
Top 1%	1,144,889	28%	829,366	1,333,568	23%	1,020,633	188,679	-4.1%	191,267
Barack Obama									
	2009			**2016**			**Change**		
Lower 20%	7,582	0%	7,549	7,648	1%	7,598	66	0.2%	48
Middle 60%	41,864	5%	39,756	44,258	7%	41,212	2,394	1.8%	1,456
Upper 20%	194,253	16%	163,431	226,485	19%	183,787	32,232	3.0%	20,357
Top 1%	1,040,380	24%	788,037	1,411,765	27%	1,026,542	371,385	3.0%	238,505
Donald J. Trump									
	2017			**2018**			**Change**		
Lower 20%	7,681	1%	7,627	7,858	0%	7,843	177	-0.5%	216
Middle 60%	44,866	7%	41,682	45,823	6%	43,069	956	-1.1%	1,386
Upper 20%	237,858	19%	192,038	244,878	18%	201,587	7,020	-1.6%	9,549
Top 1%	1,582,418	27%	1,150,616	1,607,269	26%	1,192,765	24,851	-1.5%	42,149

Appendix C

U.S. PRESIDENTIAL ELECTION RESULTS: 1920–2020

See appendices endnotes for definitions and sources

Year	President	Popular Vote		Electoral Vote		% Voter Turnout
		Won	% Total	Won	% Total	
1920	Warren G. Harding	16,147,249	60.3	404	76.1	49.2
1924	Calvin Coolidge	15,725,016	54.1	382	71.9	48.9
1928	Herbert Hoover	21,392,190	58.0	444	83.6	56.9
1932	Franklin D. Roosevelt	22,821,857	57.3	472	88.9	56.9
1936	Franklin D. Roosevelt	27,476,673	60.2	523	98.5	61.0
1940	Franklin D. Roosevelt	27,243,466	54.7	449	84.6	62.4
1944	Franklin D. Roosevelt	25,602,505	53.3	432	81.4	55.9
1948	Harry S. Truman	24,105,695	49.4	303	57.1	52.2
1952	Dwight D. Eisenhower	33,778,963	54.9	442	83.2	62.3
1956	Dwight D. Eisenhower	35,581,003	57.4	457	86.1	60.2
1960	John F. Kennedy	34,227,096	49.7	303	56.4	63.8
1964	Lyndon B. Johnson	42,825,463	61.1	486	90.3	62.8
1968	Richard M. Nixon	31,710,470	43.4	301	55.9	62.5
1972	Richard M. Nixon	46,740,323	60.7	520	96.7	56.2
1976	James E. Carter, Jr.	40,825,839	50.0	297	55.2	54.8
1980	Ronald Reagan	43,642,639	50.4	489	90.9	54.2
1984	Ronald Reagan	54,455,075	58.8	525	97.6	55.2
1988	George H.W. Bush	48,886,097	53.4	426	79.2	52.8
1992	William J. Clinton	44,909,889	43.0	370	68.8	58.1
1996	William J. Clinton	47,402,357	49.2	379	70.4	51.7
2000	George W. Bush	50,456,002	47.9	271	50.4	54.2
2004	George W. Bush	62,028,285	50.7	286	53.2	60.1
2008	Barack Obama	69,456,000	52.9	365	67.8	61.6
2012	Barack Obama	65,446,032	50.9	332	61.7	58.6
2016	Donald J. Trump	62,979,636	46.0	304	56.5	60.1
2020	Joseph R. Biden	81,268,924	51.3	306	56.9	66.8

Appendices Endnotes

Appendix A

1. Real GDP: U.S. Gross Domestic Product adjusted for inflation
   Source: U.S. Bureau of Economic Analysis[1]

2. Employment: U.S. Civilian Employment
   Source: U.S. Bureau of Labor Statistics[2] | U.S. Census Bureau[3]

3. Consumer Price Index: Average change over time in the prices paid by urban consumers for a market basket of consumer goods and service
   Source: MeasuringWorth Foundation[4] | U.S. Bureau of Labor Statistics[5]

4. National Debt as % GDP: The federal debt held by the public plus the debt held by federal trust funds and other government accounts measured as a percentage of the U.S. Gross Domestic Product
   Source: U.S. Department of the Treasury[6] | U.S. Bureau of Economic Analysis[7]

5. Productivity: Normalized Real GDP divided by U.S. Civilian Employment
   Source: MeasuringWorth Foundation[8] | U.S. Census Bureau[9]

6. S&P 500: Standard & Poor's 500 stock index adjusted for inflation
   Source: multpl.com[10]

7. AGR: Annual Growth Rate

Appendix B

1. Prior to 1940, the federal income tax applied only to the relatively affluent. In 1928, for example, only 4.1 million returns were filed, about nine percent of the working population. Couples earning $3,500 or less ($52,900 in 2020 dollars) were not required to file a tax return. That changed during World War II. By 1948, due to war-time changes, 51.7 million returns were filed representing 89 percent of those employed.

2. The most recent data prior to publication was for the year 2018.

3. Source: IRS Statistics of Income Reports[11,12,13]

Appendix C

1. Source: Britannica[14] | U.S. Elections Project[15]

2. Percent Voter Turnout: Total Votes Cast / Voter Eligible Population

Acknowledgments

Writing is lonely work. Ernest Hemingway claimed he was reduced to cleaning out the refrigerator before finally forcing himself to sit down and start a new book. Staring at a blank page, you wonder how to begin. When finished, you wonder if the results were worth the effort.

But having a circle of supportive "beta readers" helps. I was fortunate to have many friends and acquaintances who generously offered insightful criticism and suggestions during this book's development. These included Alec Karys, Bob Halliday, Brian Gentile, Bruce Ryan, Charles Bures, Egon Behle, Gary Dunn, Gene Bolton, Howard Handy, Jack Cryan, Jack Falvey, Jim Masciarelli, Mark Stear, Mitch Wolfson, Natylie Baldwin, Nick Penniman, Paul Dickson (who wisely suggested I scrap my first draft), and Waldo Potter. Their constructive perspectives can be found throughout *We the Presidents*.

Professors Andrew Daily and Emily Cura Saunders, with doctorates in history and political science, respectively, provided critical insights, bias checks and high-level editing of the final manuscript draft. Art Lizza, a senior editor working with the Greenleaf Book Group, then provided the final substantive edits. If *We the Presidents* happens to be both informative and engaging, much credit goes to Andrew, Emily and Art.

Roustam Nour painted the striking White House watercolor which Greenleaf's Chase Waterman then used as the basis of the book's cover and interior lay-out. Hilda Champion, a friend and prize-winning photographer, provided the author's photograph after her dogged efforts to cajole a hint of a smile.

Many fine professionals at the Greenleaf Book Group contributed to the book's initial development including Chelsea Richards, Corrin Foster, Daniel Sandoval, Lindsay Bohls, Sally Garland, Sam Ofman and Tiffany Barrientos. They were gracious and patient with a crusty and impatient author.

Constructing the bibliography and index for the book's 600 pages were major projects. Rob Napier, a master programmer, constructed an innovative, on-line bibliography for the book's 1,650 archived references. Similarly, Hesham Gneady, on a tight schedule, worked hard and fast constructing the book's index, later expanded by Sergey Lobachev. Thanks to Rob, Hesham and Sergey for your fine work.

And special thanks to David Wogahn and his hard-working team at AuthorImprints for so smoothly managing the final stages of the book's production and distribution.

Finally, heartfelt thanks to my wife, Nancy. Not only did she suggest I write this book, her encouragement and cheerful willingness to assume most household duties during the four-year project played a large role in the book's ultimate completion.

About the Author

RONALD GRUNER founded, served as chief executive and sold three successful technology firms during his long career: Alliant Computer in 1982, Shareholder.com in 1993 and Sky Analytics in 2009.

Each of Gruner's firms was a pioneer and leader in its industry: Alliant in parallel processing, Shareholder.com in investor relations and Sky in legal analytics. Unlike many technology firms, each company delivered a healthy financial return to its investors. Alliant went public in 1986 while Shareholder.com and Sky Analytics were profitably acquired by major public corporations in 2006 and 2015, respectively.

During his thirty-five years as a chief executive, Gruner faced the challenges of making difficult decisions; balancing the interests of shareholders, customers and employees; and focusing on the long-term even as short-term pressures seemed overwhelming.

Gruner's experience as an accomplished executive has resulted in a different breed of presidential history. Taken from his business experience, *We the Presidents* focuses on effects rather than causes, on results rather than politics; on economics rather than ideology; and on the connections linking presidential administrations rather than isolated presidencies.

Gruner lives with his wife, Nancy, in Naples, Florida where he is a private pilot, amateur radio operator and consistently poor golfer.

Bibliography

Readers may access over 1,600 sources listed in the book using an on-line bibliography at:

https://WeThePresidents.us/bibliography/

For example, to access the source of the quotation in the Dwight D. Eisenhower chapter:

"God help this country," Eisenhower confided to his staff, "when someone sits in this chair who doesn't know the military as well as I do."[17]

Select "Dwight D. Eisenhower" as the chapter, enter "17" as the endnote number and click "Open Document".

Revision History

May 2022

- Added an expanded Index.
- Added a Charts and Tables index
- Made minor wording changes to the Warren G. Harding chapter regarding Harding's use of America First as a campaign slogan.
- Made minor wording changes to the conclusion of the Donald Trump chapter to reflect his post presidency.
- Corrected typographical errors.

Charts and Tables

———⋆———

Index

Herbert Hoover

> My country owes me no debt. It gave me, as it gives every boy and girl, a chance. It gave me schooling, independence of action, opportunity for service and honor. In no other land could a boy from a country village, without inheritance or influential friends, look forward with unbounded hope.[1]

If Herbert Hoover were somehow transported to George W. Bush's Texas ranch today, the two former Presidents would discover much in common. Both started their careers in extraction industries: Hoover in metals and Bush in oil. Both made personal fortunes. Bush was a millionaire many times over after selling his shares of the Texas Rangers baseball franchise. Hoover was a successful mining financier with a net worth of $4.0 million (over $100 million in 2020 dollars). Both were inaugurated halfway through their fifty-fourth year.

As Presidents, both men inherited a booming economy and large budget surpluses from their predecessors. And both were wildly optimistic about the future. In his first address to Congress on February 28, 2001, Bush promised, "[Over the next] ten years, we will have paid down all the debt that is available to retire. That is more debt repaid more quickly than has ever been repaid by any nation at any time in history."[2] Seventy-three years earlier Hoover had claimed, "Given a chance to go forward with the policies of the last eight years…we shall soon with the help of God be in sight of the day when poverty will be banished from this Nation."[3]

President Hoover in 1929. Little wonder he was smiling. Respected worldwide, Hoover expected the presidency would be the capstone of his long, successful career. Fate intervened.   SCIENCE HISTORY IMAGES/ALAMY

Fate, however, had other plans, as each was dealt the worst financial crisis of their era: Bush the 2008 Financial Crisis and Hoover the Great Depression. Both left the presidency deeply unpopular. During his last year as President, two-thirds of Americans disapproved of Bush's job performance.[4] Hoover lost the 1932 presidential election to Franklin Roosevelt by 206 electoral votes, the largest electoral loss until Lyndon Johnson's 1964 rout over Barry Goldwater.[5]

Herbert Hoover was the embodiment of the American Success Story. Orphaned at the age of ten, Hoover amassed a mining fortune by the age of

forty. He then retired to public service where he led America's efforts to provide food to starving Belgians during the First World War, coordinate American food production after the United States entered the war, provide relief to twenty-one countries after the war's end, and feed millions of Russians during the Russian Famine of 1921–22. He became known worldwide as the "Great Humanitarian." During his eight years as Secretary of Commerce under Presidents Harding and Coolidge, Hoover led the nation's efforts to promote business development and encourage new technologies from aviation to radio.[6]

By 1927, Hoover had enjoyed seven years of success earning the admiration of the country. As an engineer he reveled in the details of planning airline routes, setting industrial standards for everything from wood screws to baby bottle nipples, and solving complex problems such as devising a formula for allocating the water rights of the Colorado River. Hoover would have been content to continue that course for another four years. But President Coolidge surprised the nation in August 1927 when he announced his decision not to run for reelection. Andrew Mellon and Herbert Hoover were the natural candidates to replace Coolidge, but Mellon chose not to run.

Hoover was so popular that he adopted what must be the most presumptive campaign slogan ever used, "Who, but Hoover?"[7] He won in a landslide, carrying forty states and winning 444 electoral votes. After thirty-five years of uninterrupted success—as an industrialist, humanitarian, and cabinet member—he could hardly have imagined four years later he would leave the presidency in failure, reviled by millions.

Hoover had been in office only eight months when the stock market crashed on October 24, 1929—"Black Thursday." Radio stocks, the high-tech of the day, lost 40 percent of their value that day alone. Over the next week, thousands of investors were wiped out as billions of dollars of wealth vanished. Stock tickers ran hours behind trying to keep up with the losses. Driven by despair, suicides proliferated. Rather than jumping out of windows, gas was often the preferred medium, endorsed by no less than the president of the Rochester Gas and Electric Company when he put his head in an oven after losing $1.2 million. One ruined man with an unwavering sense of humor shot himself to death, but not before leaving a note directing, "my body should go to science, my soul to Andrew W. Mellon and sympathy to my creditors."[8]

His success as a private businessman and the success of his policies as Secretary of Commerce had convinced Hoover that it was private business and not the government that should pull the nation out of the crisis. Shortly after the crash, Hoover held meetings with the nation's business leaders in which he encouraged them to avoid layoffs and wage cuts. Most were cooperative. Henry Ford agreed to increase workers' wages. Railroad and utility companies volunteered to increase their infrastructure spending. But as successful as Hoover had been throughout his career, his instincts failed him as the nation edged towards the Great Depression. Equally mistaken was his Treasury Secretary, Andrew Mellon, whose earlier successful economic policies resulted in the nineteen-twenties being a decade of growth, prosperity, and budget surpluses. Confident in his economic policies, Mellon rejected the idea that the nation was nearing a financial precipice declaring, "I see nothing in the present situation that is either menacing or warrants pessimism." Echoing Mellon, in June 1930 Hoover told a delegation proposing a public works program to put people back to work, "Gentlemen, you have come sixty days too late. The depression is over."[9]

Hoover and Mellon could not have been more wrong. By late 1930, a year after the stock market crashed, it was clear the economy was not recovering. The first banks began to fail in November when the Bank of Tennessee closed, pulling down its affiliates and then hundreds of other banks as panicked investors attempted to withdraw their funds.[10] Business profits collapsed, falling from $10.7 billion in 1929 to $4.4 billion in 1930.[11] As profits cratered, firms and businesses cut workers and stopped investing. Unemployment nearly tripled to 8.7 percent. Spending on factories, equipment, and residential construction fell by a third.[12]

But Hoover remained steadfast. Confident that American self-reliance would pull the nation out of the economic crisis, he lectured Congress in his 1930 State of the Union address:

> Economic depression cannot be cured by legislative action or executive pronouncement. Economic wounds must be healed by...the

producers and consumers themselves. Recovery can be expedited, and its effects mitigated by cooperative action. That cooperation requires that every individual should sustain faith and courage; that each should maintain his self-reliance; that each and every one should search for methods of improving his business or service.... The best contribution of government lies in encouragement of this voluntary cooperation in the community.[13]

Hoover's words echoed his presidential campaign two years earlier. "We [are] challenged," Hoover declared, "with a peace-time choice between the American system of rugged individualism and a European philosophy of diametrically opposed doctrines—doctrines of paternalism and state socialism."[14] Hoover believed the government's role was to encourage private industry, but not to otherwise interfere.

Private enterprise had served as the nation's economic locomotive during the Roaring Twenties, but it failed as the nation turned fearful after 1929. Congress understood this, disagreed with Hoover's non-interventionist approach and proposed multiple bills to "relieve destitution...create employment by authorizing and expediting public works programs...[and] confer to [certain veterans] the benefits of hospitalization and the privileges of the soldiers' homes."[15] Hoover vetoed these government efforts, even for impoverished war veterans, later commenting, "Prosperity cannot be restored by raids upon the public Treasury."[16]

President Hoover's harsh treatment of his fellow Americans contrasted with his humanitarian efforts during and after the First World War, when he led public and private American efforts to feed millions in war-torn Europe and the Soviet Union. Hoover considered his altruistic efforts in Europe and Russia to have been those of a private citizen. Whereas now, as President, he believed that government intervention, even to feed starving Americans during the worst economic crisis in the nation's history, would mean surrendering to the European philosophy of paternalism and state socialism.

One Congressional bill Hoover did not veto was the Smoot-Hawley Tariff Act of 1930. The Act, which increased import tariffs on thousands of items, has been blamed as a primary cause of the Great Depression. That's likely wrong. Throughout the nineteen-twenties, the United States had some of the highest import tariffs in its history, an average of 41 percent. Surprisingly, these high tariffs had little effect on imports, which rose from $2.6 billion in 1921 to $4.5 billion in 1929.[17] Imported foreign grain hit American farmers especially hard as war-torn European countries, their manufacturing bases crippled, exported agricultural products. New farm technologies, including powerful tractors and reapers, were making farmers more productive but also contributed to overproduction.[18] The result was that American farm incomes declined during the nineteen-twenties. Wheat prices fell from $2.45 per bushel in 1920 to $0.60 a bushel in 1930,[19] corn from $0.91 in 1925 to $0.70 in 1930, and soybeans from $2.92 to $1.73.[20]

Hoover, during his presidential campaign, promised to raise agricultural tariffs to provide farm relief. But, once President, lobbyists from across American industry clamored for broader tariffs. By the time Congress approved the legislation, Smoot-Hawley covered thousands of goods, raising tariffs 15 percent or more above their already high levels.

Most economists were against the Act. As the legislation awaited Hoover's signature, 1,028 economists published an open letter urging the President not to sign the legislation. Henry Ford spent an evening with President Hoover urging him not to sign the bill calling it "an economic stupidity." Thomas W. Lamont, the chief executive of J. P. Morgan, warned the Act would intensify "nationalism all over the world."[21] Undaunted, Hoover signed the Act into law on June 17, 1930, increasing average tariffs on over 20,000 imported goods from 41 to 47 percent.[22] Other countries retaliated and raised their own tariffs. The impact was immediate. By 1932, American exports had fallen from $3.8 billion in 1930 to $1.6 billion, far deeper than the decline in GDP. The effect was worldwide: Britain's exports fell from $2.8 to $1.3 billion, France from $1.7 billion to $800 million, Germany from $2.9 to $1.4 billion, and Japan from $710 million to $370 million.[23]

Smoot-Hawley reduced international trade, but was it responsible for turning a recession into the Great Depression? Almost surely not. If a single word were to describe the cause of the worldwide depression, it would be fear. Fear that ruined thousands of banks as panicked depositors withdrew their funds, fear that slowed and then virtually stopped business investment, and fear that caused consumers to hoard their cash rather than spend it.

Besides reducing international trade, Smoot-Hawley had another negative effect. It heightened international tensions. Years later, the Nobel Laureate economist Paul Samuelson wrote, "Cynics were delighted at the spectacle of [the United States] trying to collect debts from abroad and at the same time shutting out the import goods that could alone have provided the payment for those debts."[24] The high trade tariffs of the nineteen-thirties are also a warning for today's advocates of trade barriers. "When goods don't cross borders," the nineteenth-century economist, Frederic Bastiat, warned, "soldiers will."[25]

After a brief correction in early 1930, the stock market swooned, dropping 86 percent by 1932 from its 1929 high. How would that have felt? Think of the Dow Jones Average peaking at 30,600 in 2020 and then falling to 4,300 by 2023.

The market decline during the Great Depression was so deep that it would not be until 1995 that the market returned to its 1929 inflation-adjusted high.[26] As the markets collapsed and businesses turned fearful, millions found themselves without work as unemployment rocketed from 3.2 percent in 1929 to 24 percent in 1932. Housing prices fell 67 percent.[27] Per Capita GDP, measured in 2020 dollars, fell from $10,377 in 1929 to $7,500 in 1932. Government revenues collapsed, dropping from $4.0 billion in 1929 to $1.9 billion in 1932, which resulted in a massive, at the time, $2.85 billion deficit.

The collapsing economy fed fear, and then panic. Banks stopped lending, consumers stopped spending, and companies stopped investing. A third of all banks failed. In the days before federal bank insurance, depositors lost nearly everything when a bank shut its doors, as 9,000 banks did. Industrial production dropped 46 percent, which pushed unemployment to nearly 25 percent with 12.8 million people out of work.[28] Corporate profits fell from $9.1 billion in 1929 to a net loss of $1.7 billion in 1932.[29]

Nature also proved unsympathetic. In 1930 a ten-year drought began that drove thousands of Dust Bowl farmers from their land.[30]

By 1931 shanty towns, dubbed "Hoovervilles," had sprung up throughout the United States.   WORLD HISTORY ARCHIVE/ALAMY

Hoover's reputation collapsed. The Great Humanitarian, who had saved millions in Europe and Russia after the First World War, had failed to protect his fellow Americans. A popular joke circulated: Hoover asks Treasury Secretary Mellon for a nickel to call a friend. Mellon responds, "Here, take a dime and call all your friends."[31]

Breadlines, shanty towns and hobos hopping freights were everywhere. As popular opinion turned against Hoover shanty towns became known as "Hoovervilles," where hobos wandered aimlessly in "Hoover Leather" shoes with cardboard soles and slept under "Hoover Blankets," newspapers that substituted for blankets. Those no longer able to afford gasoline drove "Hoover Wagons," automobiles pulled by horses.[32]

The 1932 General Motors annual report illustrates, in microcosm, the economic devastation wreaked on American industry. Vehicle production dropped 72 percent from 1,899,267 units in 1929 to 525,727 in 1932. GM employment dropped from 233,286 in 1929 to 116,152 in 1932, throwing

over 100,000 people out of work. Profits vanished, falling from $248 million in 1929 to a minuscule $164,979 in 1932.[33]

Similarly, the Opitz family was typical of the millions of American families brought low during the nineteen-thirties. In 1928, their Nebraska farm had an annual income over $2,500, or about $38,000 today. Raising much of their own food, their lives were comfortable. For Christmas Otto Opitz even bought his family a new radio from the Montgomery Ward catalog for $64.64, nearly $1,000 today. But the depression and drought devastated the Dust-Bowl family. After paying their bills the family struggled to live on a little over a dollar a day. But the Opitz family was lucky. Millions of farm families, unable to pay their mortgage, lost their farms when their bank foreclosed.[34]

President Hoover eventually found it impossible for Washington to remain aloof as the nation's economy collapsed. In 1931 and 1932 he signed legislation that protected union contracts and required federally funded construction projects to pay "the prevailing wage" in an attempt to keep wages from falling even more.[35] He expanded the efforts of the Federal Farm Board to support farmers through government loans and policies to stabilize farm prices, and eventually paid farmers not to grow crops in order to reduce surpluses.[36] He established the Reconstruction Finance Corporation to make loans to state and local governments, and to industry to finance the construction of dams, bridges, railroads, and other infrastructure projects.[37] He revised immigration laws to drastically reduce immigration "to protect American workingmen from...new alien immigration" and exclude those "liable to become public charges." During one five-month period, only 884 visas were granted to natives of Mexico versus 19,336 visas the year prior, a reduction of 95 percent.[38]

Hoover's belated intervention was too small and too late to alter the economy's steep descent. One action, a large tax increase, worsened the decline.

In 1930 and 1931, real GDP fell an average of eight percent annually. By 1931 the federal government was running a budget deficit, its first in over a decade. A far larger deficit was projected for 1932. In May 1932 Hoover called for a drastic reduction in government spending as well as a large tax increase. "The course of unbalanced budgets," he warned Congress, "is the road of ruin."[39] A month later Hoover signed the Revenue Act of 1932, the largest peacetime tax increase in American history. Maximum marginal tax rates increased from 25 to 63 percent. Lower-income brackets increased from five to eight percent. Corporate taxes increased from 12 to 13.75 percent. The Act also added numerous new excise taxes on manufactured goods from chewing gum to trucks.

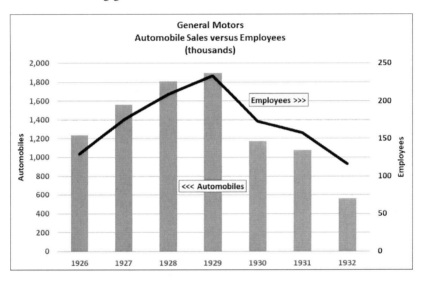

General Motors reflected the overall economy during the Great Depression. As fear spread, automobile sales fell, throwing thousands out of work.

GENERAL MOTORS 1932 ANNUAL REPORT

The next year, 1932, real GDP plummeted 13 percent—the largest decline ever recorded, including during the 2020 pandemic—as the tax increase and spending cuts went into effect. The downturn during an election year cost Hoover the presidency when he lost to Franklin Roosevelt in a historic landslide.

The Hoover administration mishandled the economy as the 1929 stock market crash devolved into the Great Depression. Unfortunately, Hoover had little help from the Federal Reserve.

In 1929, the Federal Reserve was still a sixteen-year-old adolescent. Congress had established the Federal Reserve System (Fed) in 1913, eighty years after President Andrew Jackson abolished the Bank of the United States as a "hydra of corruption."[40] Wary of giving a single central bank too much power, Congress established the new national bank as a network of twelve regional banks loosely governed by a common Federal Reserve Board. Each bank had considerable freedom to set its own monetary policies based on the needs of its region. Furthermore, only about a third of the nation's 24,000 commercial banks were members of the Federal Reserve System and thus subject to its policy directives.

Even more damaging was uncertainty within the inexperienced Fed as to what monetary policy was best for managing a financial crisis. There were three competing doctrines.[41] The Fed, in its desperation, would employ each during the Great Depression.

Liquidationists believed that central banks should allow weak, vulnerable financial institutions to fail during economic crises. Such a policy, proponents argued, "culls the herd" and results in a stronger, healthier financial system. Hoover's Treasury Secretary, Andrew Mellon, was a staunch liquidationist.

The opposing economic policy, Bagehot's Dictum, dates from Walter Bagehot's 1873 book, *Lombard Street*, which recounts the collapse of a major London bank. The dictum advocates fighting a recession by "providing a virtually unlimited source of liquidity to institutions, [which] can avert the fire sales that can lead to decreases in asset values, reductions in wealth, and ultimately to a costly contraction in economic activity."[42]

Lastly, the Real Bills Doctrine, dating to a 1705 treatise by John Law, a Scottish economist, advocates that the singular creation of money be done through loans supporting the creation of real goods and services rather than financial instruments. This theory holds that "money cannot be inflationary if backed by sound productive assets."[43]

For most of the nineteen-twenties, the Fed practiced the Real Bills policy, increasing the money supply to support America's growing industries. Much of this new money, though, eventually found its way into the stock market and helped to drive the Standard & Poor's index from 59 in 1922 to

195 by September 1929. If stocks had been purchased outright, the market downturn would have been a normal correction and not a crash. But much of the speculation during the late nineteen-twenties was financed through margin loans for which the buyer was only required to provide 10 percent of the value of the purchase. The other 90 percent was provided by cash-rich banks. It wasn't until 1928 that the Fed, concerned with the market over-heating, began to restrict monetary growth. But the Fed was too late. When the market turned, banks called in their under-capitalized loans from millions of shareholders, driving many investors into bankruptcy.

The economic shock waves drove the economy into recession. Few expected it to last long. Three earlier contractions in 1920, 1923, and 1926 had lasted an average of just fifteen months. But 1929 was different. Shortly after the stock market crash, the first banks began to fail. In November 1930, the Bank of Tennessee and two of its affiliates closed, followed by the Bank of the United States in December. Within months, hundreds of regional banks had failed. The Fed's reaction to the crisis varied by district. Some districts, such as the sixth, headquartered in Atlanta, actively assisted struggling banks, including non-member banks. Others, like the eighth headquartered in St. Louis, were more hands-off and only supported member banks.

As banks failed, the money supply began to contract. Before the Federal Deposit Insurance Corporation (FDIC) insured bank deposits, when a bank closed, money in depositor accounts simply disappeared as if tapped by a malevolent magic wand. Concerned their own bank might fail, many investors withdrew their deposits literally to stash the cash under a mattress, which effectively removed the funds from the money supply.

The Fed, following the Real Bills doctrine and presented with few "sound productive assets" in which to invest, allowed the money supply to contract. Then, in September 1931, the United Kingdom announced it was leaving the gold standard. Foreigners, worried the United States would follow, began redeeming their dollars for gold. Because the Federal Reserve was lawfully required to guarantee money in circulation with the gold held in its vaults, the Fed was forced to shrink the money supply even further as gold was withdrawn from the Treasury.[44]

From 1929 through 1933 the M1 money supply (money in circulation plus accounts easily converted to cash) fell from $25.9 to $19.3 billion. Years later, the renowned economists Milton Friedman and Anna Schwartz labeled the monetary reduction "the Great Contraction," asserting that the collapse of the money supply turned a recession into the Great Depression. In 1929, an average of $215 in money was circulating for every American which fell to $155 by 1933. People naturally felt poorer. With less money to pay for goods and services, prices declined and pushed the country into a deflationary spiral. In 1931, prices fell nine percent, followed by 10 percent the next year.

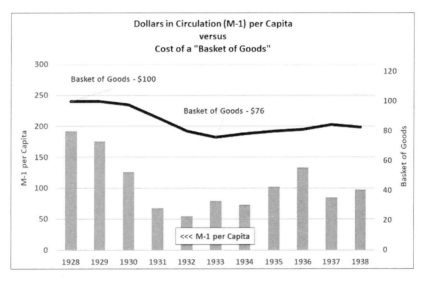

The Great Depression was a period of rare dollar deflation. Money in circulation declined as banks failed and the Federal Reserve failed to intervene. As prices fell, consumers deferred purchases.   U.S. BUREAU OF LABOR STATISTICS | FEDERAL RESERVE

Deflation is deadly to an economy. What board of directors would build a new factory when erecting it a year later would cost 10 percent less? What car buyer would rush to buy a new car if she knew car prices were rapidly dropping? Beyond discouraging consumption and investment, deflation hurts debtors because their loans must be repaid in dollars more valuable than the ones they had borrowed.

President Hoover and Treasury Secretary Mellon were both liquidationists and believed the economy would eventually recover, emerging far
stronger. In his memoirs, Herbert Hoover wrote that Mellon told him the
depression would "liquidate labor, liquidate stocks, liquidate farmers, liquidate real estate. It will purge the rottenness out of the system. High costs
of living and high living will come down. People will work harder, live a
more moral life. Values will be adjusted, and enterprising people will pick
up from less competent people."[45] During the nineteen-twenties, when the
economy was thriving, Mellon's liquidationist policies worked well. But
when the economy reversed, he learned how disastrous they could be during a steep economic downturn.

By early 1932 Hoover and Mellon were forced to concede their policies
had failed and that the nation was in economic free-fall. Unemployment
was 16 percent. GDP had fallen from $105 billion to $77 billion. And the
federal government suffered a $462 million deficit, its first in eleven years.

Overnight, Hoover converted from a liquidationist to a supporter of
Bagehot's Dictum: pump money into a failing economy. In January 1932
Hoover signed the Reconstruction Finance Corporation Act which gave
the Federal Reserve far broader powers to support the banking and monetary systems. The next month Hoover signed the Banking Act of 1932,
which further extended the Federal Reserve's powers including the ability
to make loans secured by a much broader set of assets than allowed in the
original Federal Reserve charter. Within months the Fed, dropping their
long-held Real Bills doctrine and embracing Bagehot's Dictum, injected
over $1.0 billion into the economy. By summer deflation had ceased and
prices were beginning to return to earlier levels. Industrial production was
beginning to recover.

But then, perhaps unaccustomed to playing such an active role and believing the economy was on the way to recovery, the Fed abruptly stopped
its expansionary monetary policies.[46] A little over six months later a national bank panic hit. By March 4, 1933, over 5,000 banks had closed their
doors.[47] Two days later, the new President, Franklin Roosevelt, declared a
"banking holiday" shutting all banks until Congress could pass emergency
legislation to restore trust in the banking system.

During his 1932 presidential nomination speech, President Hoover told his supporters, "We might have done nothing. That would have been utter ruin. Instead, we met the situation with proposals to private business and to the Congress of the most gigantic program of economic defense and counterattack ever evolved in the history of the Republic. We put that program in action."[48] While true, Hoover's actions came too late. Had Hoover acted two years earlier, economists today would likely be discussing the 1930 Recession rather than the Great Depression of the nineteen-thirties.

The Great Depression turned Herbert Hoover and Andrew Mellon into victims of their own prior successes. Both men made personal fortunes before entering government service. Both men believed in laissez-faire capitalism unhindered by an intrusive government. As cabinet members under Harding and Coolidge, their policies contributed to a decade of historic economic growth. But those policies failed during the Great Depression. As the economy collapsed, American industry and banking turned defensive. A new economic philosophy was needed. A British economist, John Maynard Keynes, provided the answer. An answer Franklin Roosevelt embraced. If private enterprise refuses to engage in the fight against economic depression, then the government must.

Rugged Individualism

Not surprisingly, President Hoover lost his bid for a second term in 1932. Relentlessly attacked during the presidential campaign, Hoover refused to burnish his public image. "This is not a showman's job," he declared when asked to visit the unemployed, "I will not step out of character, and you can't make a Teddy Roosevelt out of me."[49] A 1932 newsreel caught the President feeding his dog a T-bone steak in the Rose Garden. The footage played continually in American theaters, casting Hoover as callous and insensitive to the suffering of millions of Americans who could barely afford a hamburger. When 17,000 war veterans and their families marched on Washington D.C. to demand early redemption of their military service bonuses, Hoover ordered the army to clear out the marchers. General Douglas

MacArthur did so, zealously, driving the veterans out and burning their belongings.[50]

Herbert Hoover spent the next thirty years attempting to rehabilitate his image. In 1941, he endowed the Hoover Institution. Eighty years later the Institute remains one of the nation's leading think tanks. In 1947, President Truman asked Hoover to recommend ways to streamline the federal government. More than 70 percent of Hoover's recommendations were accepted. He did the same for Eisenhower in 1953 and, to a lesser extent, Kennedy in 1961.

Hoover died on October 20, 1964. "Mr. Hoover's values," *The New York Times* wrote, "were rooted in uncomplicated Quaker values of thrift, hard work and self-dependence, and he deplored a departure from those values in what he disparagingly termed 'the century of the common man.'" Hoover rejected the notion that the common man was the essence of America, a concept that became popular under Roosevelt. (In 1942 composer Aaron Copeland, inspired by Roosevelt's policies, wrote the popular *Fanfare for the Common Man*.)

Rather, in his 1922 book, *American Individualism*, Hoover had asserted that "[America's success] springs from the one source of human progress that each individual shall be given the chance and stimulation for development of the best with which he has been endowed in heart and mind; it is the sole source of progress; it is American individualism."[51]

Hoover's philosophy rejected government activism. "There are some principles that cannot be compromised," Hoover declared in 1936. "Either we shall have a society based upon ordered liberty and the initiative of the individual, or we shall have a planned society that means dictation no matter what you call it or who does it. There is no halfway ground. They cannot be mixed."[52]

Presidential surveys typically rank Herbert Hoover in the bottom ten of all Presidents, lodged between the forgotten Benjamin Harrison and John Tyler.[53] But unlike Harrison and Tyler, Hoover's legacy remains strong. Hoover's notion of rugged individualism pervades America's self-image, from John Wayne in the classic movie *The Searchers* to John Galt, the personification of rational self-interest in Ayn Rand's novel *Atlas Shrugged*. It's an image Americans proudly embrace.

Hoover's rugged individualism today continues to influence the debate over the role of government in education, healthcare, and social programs. Is individual initiative undermined if the government provides working mothers childcare? Is America a weaker nation if it guarantees healthcare to every American? Does a government mask mandate during a pandemic violate individual liberty? Herbert Hoover would surely answer 'yes' to each of these questions. His successor, Franklin Roosevelt, just the opposite. Today, Americans remain equally divided.

Franklin D. Roosevelt

March 4, 1933 – April 12, 1945

> In my Inaugural, I laid down the simple proposition that nobody is going to starve in this country. It seems to me to be equally plain that no business which depends for existence on paying less than living wages to its workers has any right to continue in this country.[1]

I t was a rainy, wind-swept day when Franklin Roosevelt, his crippled legs buttressed by steel braces, stood before thousands of Americans on the east lawn of the U.S. Capitol. Tens of millions more, from Maine to California, were huddled around radios in their homes, in their cars, in restaurants, any place where a radio might be found.

For three years, America had been captive to a brutal economic depression. Nearly one in four Americans were jobless. Corporate profits had fallen from $10.7 billion to a loss of $1.3 billion.[2] New investments in factories, equipment, and homes had virtually stopped. Thousands of banks had failed and swept away the savings of millions of Americans. Untold numbers were living in shanty towns spread across America. Many were starving. Fear, that evil twin of confidence, had paralyzed the country.

Yet, on this bleak day on March 4, 1933 Americans were hopeful as President Franklin Roosevelt began his inaugural address. Roosevelt opened his speech with words so confident, so heartening, so inspiring, that millions of Americans would remember them for the rest of their lives:

> This great Nation will endure as it has endured, will revive and will prosper. So, first of all, let me assert my firm belief that the only thing we have to fear is fear itself—nameless, unreasoning,

unjustified terror which paralyzes needed efforts to convert retreat into advance.[3]

It's difficult today to appreciate the fear that gripped the country as Roosevelt took the podium. America's private sector had failed to pull the nation out of its economic disaster. Everywhere, capitalism was in question. Communism threatened to replace capitalism with an economic system that promised: "From each according to his ability, to each according to his needs." Fascist regimes had infected Germany, Italy and Japan, offering a "third way" between capitalism and communism. "Today's bourgeoisie is rotten to the core," Germany's Adolf Hitler declared, "it has no ideals anymore; all it wants to do is earn money. . ."[4]

During his inaugural address, Roosevelt was only slightly less strident than Hitler in his condemnation of America's business elite:

> Practices of the unscrupulous money changers stand indicted in the court of public opinion, rejected by the hearts and minds of men. . . . Stripped of the lure of profit by which to induce our people to follow their false leadership, they have resorted to exhortations, pleading tearfully for restored confidence. They know only the rules of a generation of self-seekers. They have no vision, and when there is no vision the people perish.[5]

Most Americans agreed with Roosevelt; America's business elite had failed them. As the nation's economy collapsed, President Hoover and Treasury Secretary Andrew Mellon—both successful, self-made men—implemented policies that emphasized personal responsibility over government intervention.

In his 1922 book, *American Individualism*, Hoover had written, "We build our society upon the attainment of the individual. . .to take that position in the community to which his intelligence, character, ability and ambition entitle him."[6] Other than preserving equality of opportunity, Hoover believed the government had no responsibility to its citizens' welfare. America's strength lay in its "rugged individualism" rather than "[European] doctrines of paternalism and state socialism."[7]

Nobody believed in rugged individualism more than that icon of American entrepreneurship, Henry Ford, who even disapproved of private charity.

"I do not believe in routine charity," Ford declared as unemployment approached 25 percent. "I think it a shameful thing that any man should have to stoop to take it or give it. . . . My quarrel with charity is that it is neither helpful nor human. The charity of our cities is the most barbarous thing in our system. . ."[8]

This was the divided audience Roosevelt was addressing: millions of fearful, unemployed, and often hungry Americans, and an American elite who denied government any role in alleviating human suffering, some even rebuking personal charity as immoral. Roosevelt had a simple plan. If business wasn't hiring, the government would:

> This Nation is asking for action, and action now. . . . Our greatest primary task is to put people to work. This is no unsolvable problem if we face it wisely and courageously. It can be accomplished in part by direct recruiting by the Government itself, treating the task as we would treat the emergency of a war, but at the same time, through this employment, accomplishing greatly needed projects to stimulate and reorganize the use of our great natural resources. . . . These, my friends, are the lines of attack.[9]

Roosevelt's use of government spending to stimulate economic growth was based on the theories advocated by John Maynard Keynes, a British economist. In contrast to Andrew Mellon, who promoted tax policies to stimulate private investment in production, Keynes believed stimulating demand, even if it required the government give jobs to the unemployed, was the more effective approach during economic downturns. The two philosophies are known today as supply-side and demand-side economics.

Roosevelt called his economic program the "New Deal," evocative of distant cousin Teddy Roosevelt's "Square Deal" thirty years earlier. From 1933 through 1935, Roosevelt signed New Deal legislation that increased Americans' purchasing power, established liberating labor regulations, and introduced a social safety net that included unemployment insurance, workmen's compensation, and pension programs.

The New Deal grew the economy at a rate never again repeated during peacetime. From 1933 through 1940, employment increased 25 percent, real GDP 63 percent, and corporate profits 530 percent. Roosevelt's Works

Progress Administration (WPA) put 8.5 million unemployed back to work building 4,000 new schools, 130 hospitals, 150 airfields, 280,000 miles of roads and 29,000 bridges.[10] Roosevelt had become the nation's largest employer.

Roosevelt at his Hyde Park, NY home in 1941 with his caretaker's daughter and dog, Fala. Photos of Roosevelt in a wheelchair were rare; few Americans realized Roosevelt had been paralyzed by polio years earlier.   EVERETT COLLECTION HISTORICAL/ALAMY

The massive new government programs created a backlash. Former President Herbert Hoover, rejecting quiet retirement, condemned the New Deal's activism as a "cold-blooded attempt by starry-eyed boys to infect the American people by a mixture of European ideas, flavored with our native predilection to get something for nothing... lead[ing] over the same grim precipice that is the crippling and possibly the destruction of the freedom of men."[11]

Others branded Roosevelt a socialist and a traitor. "I won't stand for allowing [Roosevelt's brain trust] to march under the banner of Jackson or Cleveland...." former New York Governor Al Smith declared in a speech to business leaders in 1936. "There can be only one capitol. Washington or

Moscow. There can be only one atmosphere of government, the clear, pure, fresh air of free America, or the foul breath of communistic Russia. There can be only one flag, the Stars and Stripes or the flag of the godless Union of the Soviets."[12]

Antipathy for Roosevelt and his policies persists to this day. In 2012, employing its ultimate insult, the Cato Institute declared that "Obama is a Mini-Me version of FDR, which is a lot better (or, to be more accurate, less worse) than the real thing."[13] In 2014 Stephen Moore, then a Visiting Fellow at the Heritage Foundation, lectured that "Almost everything FDR did to jump-start growth, retarded it. . . . [The New Deal] caused more human suffering than any other set of ideas in the past century."[14]

Most Americans during Roosevelt's era would have strongly disagreed with today's FDR critics. In 1936, after four years of the New Deal, Americans reelected Roosevelt in a landslide with 98.5 percent of the electoral college vote, the highest by any President, ever. From 1932 through 1944 voters elected Roosevelt as their President four times with an average of 56.6 percent of the popular vote, the highest of any multi-term President. (Presidents were not restricted to two terms until 1951).[15]

Today's partisan pundits may criticize Roosevelt as a socialist or traitor, but in his time, Americans loved him. Even their movies depicted that affection. In the movie version of John Steinbeck's Pulitzer Prize winning *The Grapes of Wrath*, the kindly camp director who took in the impoverished Joad family clearly evoked President Roosevelt.

The First 100 Days

Two days after his inauguration Roosevelt declared a "banking holiday" that closed banks nationwide. Roosevelt's bold act gave Congress time to pass the Emergency Banking Relief Act. The Act directed the Federal Reserve to issue additional currency to guarantee banks would be able to meet every legitimate demand for withdrawal. The banks reopened four days later. Remarkably, the American public so trusted Roosevelt's plan that when the banks reopened their doors depositors were standing in line to return the cash they had squirreled away at home. Senator Hiram Johnson summed up the mood of the nation when he observed, "The admirable trait in Roosevelt is that he has the guts to try. . . . He does it all with the rarest, good nature.... We have exchanged [Herbert Hoover's] frown in the White House with a smile. Where there were hesitation and vacillation, weighing always the personal political consequences, feebleness, timidity, and duplicity, there are now courage and boldness and real action."[16]

Within weeks depositors returned over half of the cash they had been hoarding. Bank deposits soared. Having declined from $22.7 billion in 1929 to $14.8 billion in 1933, deposits increased to $17.2 billion in 1934 and then $21.2 billion the next year.[17] The banking crisis which had nearly bankrupted the nation was over.

To further boost the nation's spirits, three weeks after taking office Roosevelt signed the Cullen-Harrison Act that ended Prohibition, the noble experiment which had banned the sale of alcohol in 1920 after the passage of the 18th Amendment.

"I think this would be a good time for a beer," Roosevelt famously joked.[18] After twelve years of forced abstinence, Americans quickly regained their taste for a drink, although few enjoyed the new freedom more than Roosevelt. He made it a regular practice to have cocktails with his immediate staff at the end of each day. There were only two rules. Roosevelt would mix the cocktails to assure they were sufficiently strong and no business could be discussed.

Roosevelt's first one hundred days in office were a whirlwind in which fifteen major pieces of legislation were passed, a record that remains unmatched by any President. These included the establishment of the Federal Emergency Relief Administration responsible for training and jobs for the unskilled; the Civilian Conservation Corps that put unemployed men to work on projects such as soil erosion and fighting forest fires; the Agricultural Adjustment Administration whose charter was to help stabilize farms prices; the National Industry Recovery Act which authorized massive government spending on national infrastructure; the Tennessee Valley Authority, which built dams along the Tennessee River to control flooding as well as generate hydro-electric power.[19]

So much legislation was passed so quickly it was said "[Congress] did not so much debate the bills it passed. . .as salute them as they went sailing by."[20]

Falling just outside the first 100 days was the passage of the monumental 1933 Banking Act on June 16, known today as the Glass-Steagall Act. The Act forced the separation of commercial and investment banking.

Commercial banks take deposits and then recycle those deposits into loans for homes and businesses. Think of George Bailey, the local banker in the classic movie *It's a Wonderful Life*. Investment banks aren't banks as most people think of them. Nobody deposits money into an investment bank for safekeeping. Their original purpose was to raise money for business by selling and buying stocks, a much riskier business than making secured loans like commercial banks. Over the years, investment banks took on far riskier clients involved not in building companies but in stock speculation and corporate takeovers. Think of Gordon Gecko ("Greed is good.") from the movie *Wall Street* as the ultimate example of this new breed of banker.

Before the Glass-Steagall Act, banks could provide both commercial and investment banking services. This led to hundreds, and eventually thousands, of banking failures starting in 1929. During the Roaring Twenties, as the stock market climbed, bankers began to tap into their commercial banking deposits, using their depositors' money to speculate in the stock market. When the market crashed, the savings of millions of unsuspecting Americans were wiped out. Bankers became pariahs. Formerly considered celebrities, they became "banksters" after their gun-toting counterparts who also robbed banks.[21]

Glass-Steagall also established the Federal Bank Deposit Insurance Corporation (FDIC), which guaranteed individual bank deposits. After the FDIC was established, depositors could be assured that if their bank failed, they would not lose their savings up to $2,500 initially, about $50,000 in today's dollars. (In 2020 the federal limit was $250,000.)

Banks were also given one year to decide if they wished to remain a commercial bank or an investment bank. During the transition, approximately 4,000 banks failed.[22] Fortunately, most depositors were, by then, protected by FDIC insurance.

Glass-Steagall was remarkably effective in preventing bank failures. After it went into effect, an average of only thirteen banks failed annually from 1934 through 1981. But starting with Ronald Reagan's presidency, that trend began to reverse. In 1982 the savings and loan banks, struggling to compete with other lenders, were deregulated. From 1982 through 1992 2,800 banks failed, an average of 255 a year.[23] In 1999, the section of Glass-Steagall that prohibited the consolidation of commercial and investment banking was effectively repealed. But there were strings attached. Banks that chose to combine commercial and investment banking would be subject to intense government scrutiny. Consequently, most commercial banks chose not to add investment banking to their services. But a few did, notably Citibank, which speculated heavily in subprime mortgages in the years leading up to the 2008 Financial Crisis. As the real estate market imploded, Citibank, a bank considered "too big to fail," was hit hard, which forced the government to step in with a $476 billion bailout, the largest in history.[24]

The Glass-Steagall Act of 1933 was second only to Social Security as one of the most consequential pieces of legislation passed during the Great Depression. For many, though, the Works Progress Administration (WPA) was either the best or the worst of Roosevelt's New Deal. Although unemployment had declined from a high of 25 percent in 1933, it was still 20 percent in 1935. That year Roosevelt established the WPA to put millions of the unemployed back to work. By late 1938, the WPA was the nation's largest employer with 3.3 million workers, or over 10 percent of the nation's non-farm labor force.[25]

Before it was disbanded in 1943, the WPA built monumental structures including La Guardia Airport in New York, Midway Airport in Chicago, the Grand Coulee Dam in Washington, and the Hoover Dam in Nevada. (Hoover Dam was named after President Hoover in 1930. Roosevelt changed the name to Boulder Dam and then spitefully refused to invite Hoover to its completion ceremony in 1935. President Truman changed the name back to Hoover Dam in 1947.) But the WPA also built hundreds of small, local projects which continue to enrich people's lives today: the River Walk in San Antonio, Texas; the French Market in New Orleans; the University of New Mexico Zimmerman Library; the Dock Street Theater in Charleston, South Carolina; the iconic Griffith Observatory in Los Angeles; and 350 public golf courses, including one of the nation's most respected, the Bethpage Black Golf Course in Farmingdale, New York.[26]

The WPA was a huge intrusion of the federal government into the private sector. Many were concerned that projects were assigned based on political considerations; that industry was forced to compete with the government for workers, which raised wage rates; that "make work" jobs were breeding a generation of lazy, low productivity workers; and, of course, that the higher taxes needed to pay this huge new labor force were coming out of the pocket of American industry and its workers.

But the most serious charge was that Roosevelt was abandoning capitalism and the American Way.

Did Roosevelt Save Capitalism?

Today, after decades of growing income inequality, job loss due to foreign competition, healthcare inequities, and concerns over global climate change, there is a growing chorus for massive government intervention to provide universal healthcare, free college education, renewable energy, and even universal income. Many believe these demands are unique to our era. But they are not. Roosevelt faced strident, persistent demands for government intervention far beyond those heard today. They came from many directions: private citizens, the CEO of a major company, a prominent author, a governor, even a Catholic priest.

During Roosevelt's era, many advocates for change believed that capitalism had failed. With a quarter of Americans out of work, millions of whom had lost their homes, farms, and lifetime savings, and with no end to the suffering in sight, it's conceivable that America could have abandoned capitalism. Fortunately, it did not, and Roosevelt deserves a measure of credit for that.

In 1933, Dr. Francis Townsend, a retired physician, was one of the first to propose a federally funded, national pension system. Townsend proposed that all individuals over sixty who were retired and "free from habitual criminality" be paid $200 a month ($3,950 in 2020 dollars). A further requirement was that the recipients must spend the money in the United States within thirty days to stimulate the economy. He proposed paying for the program through a two percent national "transaction" tax, similar to

Europe's value-added tax today. Townsend claimed that one of the major benefits of his plan was that it would encourage older workers to retire and open positions for unemployed younger workers.

It sounds like a harebrained scheme today, but Townsend's proposal hit a chord with Depression-era Americans. By 1935 there were 7,000 Townsend Clubs with over 2.2 million members actively promoting the Townsend Plan. Public opinion surveys indicated that 56 percent of Americans favored the adoption of the plan. In 1936 Dr. Townsend sent a petition to Congress in support of his plan with an estimated ten million signatures.[27]

Hugely popular at the time, but largely forgotten today, the Townsend Plan had a major impact on political thinking during the Great Depression. Years later, Frances Perkins, Roosevelt's Secretary of Labor from 1933 through 1945, wrote in her autobiography:

> One hardly realizes nowadays how strong was the sentiment in favour of the Townsend Plan and other exotic schemes for giving the aged a weekly income. In some districts, the Townsend Plan was the chief political issue, and men supporting it were elected to Congress. The pressure from its advocates was intense.[28]

A year after Dr. Townsend published his plan, Upton Sinclair, the author of the revelatory novel, *The Jungle*, ran for governor of California under his End Poverty in California (EPIC) campaign. Sinclair was already a well-known author whose 1905 book described the horrifying conditions in the meat-packing industry. "Open vats near the level of the floor," Sinclair wrote, "their peculiar trouble was that [workers] fell into the vats; and when they were fished out, there was never enough of them left to be worth exhibiting."[29] The nation was appalled. Within a year President Teddy Roosevelt signed the Pure Food and Drug Act of 1906, which later led to the formation of the U.S. Food and Drug Administration.

Sinclair, an avowed socialist, proposed California take over closed factories, abandoned farms, and even movie studios and operate them to maximize employment rather than profit. The EPIC Plan called for repealing the sales tax while increasing corporate and income taxes on the wealthy to finance the plan. Sinclair promoted his plan in a small book optimistically entitled, *I, Governor and How I Ended Poverty: A True Story of the Future*. Within a year it became the highest-selling book in California's history.[30]

The program was wildly popular with 800 EPIC clubs springing up in California within a year. Its weekly newspaper, *EPIC News*, had a circulation of nearly a million. The California business community, not surprisingly, opposed Sinclair's proposal and fought it with a clever media offensive developed by the world's first political consulting agency aptly named Campaigns, Inc. Poring through Sinclair's novels the firm pulled out damaging quotes and then planted them in California newspapers inferring they came from Sinclair himself, and not his fictional characters.

Sinclair was soundly defeated. Undaunted, he wrote a book about his campaign, *I, Candidate for Governor: And How I Got Licked*, which described modern politics' arsenal of dirty campaign tricks. Campaigns, Inc. employed the same tactics against President Truman's universal healthcare plan 15 years later.[31]

An even more extreme reformer was Huey Long, Louisiana's populist governor and senator, known as "the Kingfish." Huey Long's "Share Our Wealth" proposal called for the government to guarantee every family a generous annual income of $5,000 ($95,000 in 2020 dollars). Writing in his 1932 biography, the Kingfish provided a populist view on the causes of the Great Depression:

> I foresaw the depression in 1929.... The wealth of the land was being tied up in the hands of a very few men. The people were not buying because they had nothing with which to buy. The big business interests were not selling, because there was nobody they could sell to. One percent of the people could not eat any more than any other one percent; they could not wear much more than any other one percent; they could not live in any more houses than any other one percent. So, in 1929, when the fortune-holders of America grew powerful enough that one percent of the people owned nearly everything, ninety-nine percent of the people owned practically nothing, not even enough to pay their debts, a collapse was at hand.[32]

Comments like Huey Long's declaration that "one percent of the people owned nearly everything" continue to be heard today.

Huey Long proposed paying for his program by distributing wealth from the rich to the poor, limiting annual incomes to $1.0 million, inheritances to $5.0 million and family fortunes to $50 million. By 1935, there were more than 27,000 Share Our Wealth clubs in the country with over 7.5 million members. Huey Long regularly received more mail than President Roosevelt. Following one of his radio speeches, the Kingfish received 720,000 letters requiring thirty-two typists working around the clock to answer. He was the third most photographed person in America, surpassed only by President Roosevelt and famed-aviator Charles Lindbergh.[33]

Huey Long had presidential aspirations, and a wry sense of humor. He wrote a book entitled *My First Days in the White House* that detailed his proposed presidential agenda. He even included whimsical cabinet selections, one of which restored Herbert Hoover to his former role as Secretary of Commerce. Roosevelt need not worry if he lost the election; the Kingfish had reserved Secretary of the Navy for him.[34] Huey Long's book was published posthumously. On September 8, 1935, Long was assassinated in the Louisiana State Capitol, shot by the son-in-law of a judge Long had targeted to be removed from office.[35]

Father Charles Coughlin was the first media firebrand to incite and divide America. An anti-Semitist, members of the Nazi-sympathizing German-American Bund cheered his speeches.   EVERETT COLLECTION INC/ALAMY

As popular as Dr. Townsend, Upton Sinclair and Huey Long were, they were eclipsed by the Catholic priest, Father Charles Coughlin. Father Coughlin's radio career began in 1926 broadcasting weekly sermons from a Detroit radio station. By 1932 Coughlin had a massive national audience—his *New York Times* obituary estimated (an improbable) ninety million listeners[36]—and had gone far beyond weekly sermons to proselytize on whatever he considered to be the ills of the nation and the failings of its leaders.

An early Roosevelt supporter, Father Coughlin claimed he spoke for God and told his credulous audience, "God is directing President Roosevelt" and "the New Deal is Christ's Deal."[37] But by 1935 Father Coughlin, feeling that Roosevelt's policies had become too timid, began to support Huey Long's run for President. As he became increasingly disappointed with what he considered Roosevelt's timid approach to social reform, he railed against him in his radio broadcasts, raging in one:

> The great betrayer and liar, Franklin D. Roosevelt, who promised
> to drive the money changers from the temple, had succeeded [only]
> in driving the farmers from their homesteads and the citizens from
> their homes in the cities. . . . I ask you to purge the man who claims
> to be a Democrat, from the Democratic Party, and I mean Franklin
> Double-Crossing Roosevelt. The great betrayer and liar. . . Franklin
> Double-Crossing Roosevelt.[38]

As the decade progressed, Coughlin's condemnations went beyond Roosevelt and the New Deal. He began to blame a worldwide order of Jews for the economic chaos in Europe and the United States. After Kristallnacht on November 8, 1938, when Nazis burned hundreds of Jewish synagogues, looted thousands of Jewish businesses and killed dozens of Jews in Germany, Coughlin argued the acts were justified retaliation for the thousands of Christians the Jews had persecuted.[39] *The New York Times* reported that the mere mention of his name at rallies of the Nazi-sympathizing German-American Bund touched off wild cheering.

Nearly a century later, Father Coughlin remains an unmatched media firebrand. As Coughlin's commentaries became increasingly unhinged, the Catholic Church banned him from all political activity in 1942. A loyal

Catholic, Coughlin quietly returned to Royal Oak, Michigan as a parish priest.

Today though, there's little chance mean-spirited, divisive pundits will be reined in. After the repeal of the Fairness Doctrine in 1987, angry political punditry, regardless of its consequences, has become a multi-billion-dollar industry.

A Lunch Meeting Leads to Social Security

Although Dr. Townsend, Upton Sinclair, Huey Long and Father Coughlin garnered tens of millions of supporters, it was a respected member of the American business community who arguably had the largest influence on Roosevelt's New Deal.

Starting as a dollar-a-day helper at General Electric in 1893, Gerald Swope had risen to become GE's President by 1922, a role he served for twenty years. During the First World War, Swope went into public service to facilitate the war effort and was awarded the Distinguished Service Medal by President Wilson for his contributions. By 1931, Swope was one of the most respected businessmen in the country. That year he proposed a national recovery plan to help pull the nation out of the depression. Swope proposed a network of trade associations whose dual mission was to administer business practices promoting the growth of commerce and the protection of employees. To assure that the public interest was protected, the Swope Plan called for the Federal Trade Commission to oversee the trade associations.

The Swope Plan proposed that all companies with over fifty employees and engaged in interstate commerce provide employees a common set of benefits including disability, unemployment, and life insurance plus a pension plan for retirement at age sixty-five. Swope proposed these programs be administered by the trade associations rather than the companies. The funds collected from employees and companies to finance the programs would be placed in trusts administered by the associations which would then distribute the benefits to employees and their dependents. In no case would the funds remain under the control of an individual company.

Swope knew workers no longer trusted their employers to protect their pension savings. The nation's leading business association, the Chamber of Commerce, supported Swope's Plan as did other business organizations. But President Hoover did not, calling it compulsory, inefficient, and monopolistic.[40]

Lacking Hoover's support, the Swope Plan went nowhere for three years. Then, on March 8, 1934, President Roosevelt and Gerald Swope had lunch at the White House. Roosevelt had invited Swope to discuss labor programs and, in particular, social insurance including unemployment, disability, and old-age pensions. During the meeting, Swope advocated a modified version of his 1931 plan which replaced the original plan's trade associations, each administering their own benefit programs, with a single, government-based social insurance plan.[41]

Roosevelt was intrigued and asked Swope to prepare a memo outlining his plan. Two weeks later Swope delivered a memo that included a detailed statistical analysis for unemployment, disability, and old-age pension programs. Roosevelt's advisors felt many aspects of Swope's plan were too ambitious, especially considering similar plans were being developed by the Industrial Relations Counselors, a business organization funded by the Rockefeller Foundation.

Swope's proposal, both as General Electric's president and chairman of the Business Advisory Council (which today endures as the respected Business Council comprising America's top CEOs)[42], gave Roosevelt confidence to proceed with a less ambitious plan. Three months after meeting with Swope, Roosevelt established the Committee on Economic Security to develop a proposal for a Social Security program. The Committee submitted its plan to Congress in January 1935 and it quickly gained strong support.

Not all agreed. Many claimed Roosevelt's plan was a giant step towards socialism. New York Representative Daniel Reed predicted, "the lash of the dictator will be felt and twenty-five million free Americans will for the first time submit themselves to a fingerprint test." Delaware's Senator Hastings argued that Social Security would "end the progress of a great country and bring its people to the level of the average European."[43]

Senator Hastings' condescending reference to Europeans was not unusual. From its founding, Americans have considered America exceptional to

Europe in its democratic ideals, rugged individualism and unbridled opportunity. A century before Hastings' comments, Alexis de Tocqueville wrote in *Democracy in America* that, "the position of the Americans is therefore quite exceptional, and it may be believed that no democratic people will ever be placed in a similar one."[44] De Tocqueville gave birth to the idea of American Exceptionalism, but it was Herbert Hoover, in his 1922 book, *American Individualism*, who made rugged individualism the cornerstone of American Exceptionalism.

Government-based social programs were hardly new in 1935. Germany instituted the first old-age pension program in 1889 under Chancellor Otto von Bismarck. Britain followed with national insurance for unemployment and sickness in 1911. By the mid nineteen-thirties some twenty countries had instituted some form of federal insurance benefits.[45] The United States resisted this trend, but by the time Swope and Roosevelt met, resistance to a government-based social insurance program had declined. The Great Depression had left millions impoverished after investing for years in private pension programs only to see their retirement savings vanish when thousands of corporations failed taking their pension plans down with them.

Railroad workers were especially hard hit after scores of railroad failures. Workers lobbied for the Railroad Retirement Act, which was enacted in 1934. It was the nation's first federally managed retirement system for non-governmental workers. With the nationalized railroad retirement program paving the way, the House quickly approved the Social Security bill on April 17, 1935, with 372 voting in favor, 33 against and 25 abstaining. The Senate passed the bill with seventy-seven in favor, six against and twelve abstentions. President Roosevelt signed Social Security into law three days later.[46] Although hugely popular with the American public, Social Security inflamed Roosevelt's opponents who believed the President had put the nation on a path to socialism.

A Landslide Reelection

Alf Landon, a former Kansas governor, challenged Roosevelt in the 1936 presidential election. Governor Landon had a national reputation for successfully balancing the Kansas budget, a singular achievement at the time. Roosevelt, though, was a brutal campaigner. During the prior four years, the relationship between Roosevelt and America's business elite had moved from hostile to outright war. Shortly before the election, Roosevelt gave a speech announcing his plans for his second term. It was largely a harangue against his political enemies:

> We know now that Government by organized money is just as dangerous as Government by organized mob. Never before in all our history have these forces been so united against one candidate as they stand today. They are unanimous in their hate for me—and I welcome their hatred.[47]

I welcome their hatred. Those were remarkable words to be uttered by a President. Not until Donald Trump's presidency, was a President more hated by his opponents and more loved by his supporters than Franklin Roosevelt. And like Trump, Roosevelt was unmatched in his skill disparaging political opponents. In his nomination speech, Roosevelt eloquently dispatched the prior Coolidge and Hoover administrations:

> For twelve years this Nation was afflicted with hear-nothing, see-nothing, do-nothing Government. The Nation looked to Government, but the Government looked away. Nine mocking years with the golden calf and three long years of the scourge! Nine crazy years at the ticker and three long years in the breadlines! Nine mad years of mirage and three long years of despair![48]

Landon campaigned against Roosevelt's big-government policies. "National Economic Planning violates the basic ideals of the American system," Landon pronounced, "The price of economic planning is the loss of economic freedom. And economic freedom and personal liberty go hand in hand."[49] On that issue, reasonable people could disagree, but Landon made a prophetic claim that rings true today. "There is every probability that the cash [workers] pay [into Social Security] will be used for current deficits and new extravagances. We are going to have trouble enough to carry out an economy program without having the Treasury flush with money drawn from the workers."[50] Landon was right. Over the ensuing eight decades, Washington has spent every penny of the Social Security taxes it's collected, leaving behind trillions of dollars in federal debt owed to future Americans.

Landon ran a valiant campaign, but Roosevelt's New Deal was overwhelmingly popular with voters. In the 1936 reelection, they gave Roosevelt the largest landslide win since the inception of the modern two-party system in 1824.[51] It was the strongest possible endorsement of Roosevelt and his policies.

The Fight Over Social Security

As early as 1934, lower courts had begun to overturn major parts of the New Deal as unconstitutional. The National Industrial Recovery Act, giving the President power to regulate prices and establish regulations, was declared unconstitutional by the Supreme Court in 1935. In 1936 the Supreme Court found the Agricultural Adjustment Act unconstitutional, ruling the Act was "a matter beyond the powers delegated to the federal government." Emboldened by the court's rulings, Roosevelt's opponents next set their sights on Social Security.

Roosevelt countered with a plan: increase the Supreme Court from nine to fifteen judges. Roosevelt would, by law, nominate the six new judges. Roosevelt's "court packing" scheme was roundly criticized and had little chance of passage by Congress.[52] But a packed court would prove unnecessary to preserve Social Security.

The reserve clause of the Constitution's 10th Amendment, states: "The powers not delegated to the United States by the Constitution, nor prohibited by it to the States, are reserved to the States respectively, or to the people." Certainly, Social Security as a New Deal program was not a delegated power when the Constitution was framed. The authors of the Social Security legislation anticipated this issue but were unsure which of two Constitutional approaches would justify the new federal power: the commerce clause or the right to levy taxes to provide for the general welfare.

The Constitution's commerce clause (Article I, Section 8, Clause 3) gives Congress the power "to regulate Commerce with foreign Nations, and among the several States, and with the Indian Tribes." Over time, the definition of commerce had been expanded by the courts to include not only commerce itself but those activities which affect commerce. Could Roosevelt's Justice Department make a case that Social Security affects interstate commerce and so is protected under the commerce clause?

Or did Social Security provide for the general welfare? The right of the federal government to levy new taxes for the general welfare of its citizens had been a debate going back to the Founders. Article 1, Section 8, Clause 1 states: "The Congress shall have Power To lay and collect Taxes, Duties, Imposts and Excises, to pay the Debts and provide for the common Defence and general Welfare of the United States; but all Duties, Imposts and Excises shall be uniform throughout the United States."

James Madison and Thomas Jefferson interpreted the general welfare clause as applying only to funds specifically identified in the Constitution, an interpretation that came to be known as the strict construction doctrine. Alternatively, Alexander Hamilton believed the clause meant the federal government could undertake new spending and levy new taxes provided those actions improved the general welfare. These were disagreements among the Founders who had written the Constitution. Little wonder that today the Supreme Court still grapples with constitutional issues related to a document written over two centuries ago.

Although the courts had wavered between the two interpretations ever since the Constitution was ratified, by the mid nineteen-thirties Hamilton's interpretation had tended to prevail and was known as the doctrine of implied powers.[53]

Roosevelt's brain trust chose Hamilton's doctrine of implied powers to defend their new legislation against the Supreme Court challenge. Their strategy worked. On May 24, 1937, the Supreme Court ruled in favor of the federal government in three landmark Social Security cases. Justice Benjamin N. Cardozo wrote the majority opinion on two of these cases, stating in part:

> There have been statesman in our history who have stood for other views.... We will not resurrect the contest. It is now settled by decision. The conception of the spending power advocated by Hamilton...has prevailed over that of Madison.... The hope behind this statute is to save men and women from the rigors of the poor house as well as from the haunting fear that such a lot awaits them when journey's end is near.[54]

After winning a second term in a landslide and with the major court challenges behind him, Roosevelt was ready to address the two major criticisms of the original 1935 Social Security Act. The first issue was that the Act did not go far enough to alleviate the financial risks many families continued to face, such as the needs of surviving spouses and children after the death of the family breadwinner. The second, voiced by Alf Landon during his presidential campaign, was that Social Security tax receipts went into the federal government's general account with no assurance they would be repaid to Social Security recipients.

Roosevelt's efforts resulted in amendments to the original Act signed into law on August 11, 1939. These amendments added dependent benefits for the spouse and minor children of a retired worker, and survivor benefits in the event of the premature death of a covered worker. Thus, the Social Security program was transformed from a simple pension program into a family-based economic security program.

To address the concern that Social Security funds would be misused, the 1939 amendments established the Federal Old-Age and Survivors Insurance ("OASI") Trust Fund. The fund was to be invested in federal securities, both marketable securities identical to what the public purchases, and also special obligation bonds reserved exclusively for Social Security funds. In effect, the Social Security program was loaning the federal government money for which it received notes backed by the "full faith and credit of the U.S. government." The federal government was then free to use these borrowed funds as it wished—just as Alf Landon had predicted during the 1936 presidential campaign.

Few U.S. government decisions have caused as much controversy, misunderstanding, and political posturing as the decision to establish the Social Security trust fund whose only asset was federal government-issued securities. Alf Landon's prediction that Social Security payments would be used for "current deficits and new extravagances" would echo for decades. Fifty years after the establishment of the trust fund, Senator Ernest Hollings of South Carolina, in a 1989 Senate speech stated, "the most reprehensible fraud in this great jambalaya of frauds is the systematic and total ransacking of the Social Security trust fund...in the next century...the American people will wake up to the reality that those IOUs in the trust fund vault are a twenty-first century version of Confederate banknotes."[55]

Alf Landon's prediction was right. For decades Social Security ran surpluses taking in more money through payroll taxes than it distributed as pensions. Washington spent those surpluses on other programs and issued IOUs in their place. Social Security taxes paid for much of Ronald Reagan's increased defense spending, Bill Clinton's budget surpluses and George Bush's Middle-East wars. But today, as Baby Boomers retire, Washington is grappling with how to repay those massive loans borrowed from Social Security.

By 1940, the key elements of today's Social Security program had been established. On January 31, 1940, the first Social Security benefit, $22.54, was paid to Ida May Fuller of Ludlow, Vermont. She continued receiving Social Security checks until her death on January 27, 1975.[56]

The Recession of 1938

As Roosevelt gave his second inaugural address on January 20, 1937 (the first inauguration held in January rather than March since the nation's founding), the nation's positive economic progress was so accepted Roosevelt barely mentioned the economy. Feeling no need for even a touch of restrained braggadocio, Roosevelt merely commented, "Our progress out of the depression is obvious."

Roosevelt's quiet confidence seemed justified. His economic programs over the last four years had, with one critical exception, been hugely successful. From 1934 through 1936, real annual GDP growth averaged a blistering 11 percent, a modern record unbroken except during World War II. By 1936, only four years after hitting bottom in 1932, real GDP had recovered to its 1929 level. Net corporate profits increased from a 1.7 billion loss in 1932 to a $5.6 billion profit in 1936. During those years, the S&P 500 stock index more than doubled, as did stock dividends. Employment was also growing rapidly, an average of five percent annually from 1934 through 1936.

Halfway through 1937, a deep recession hit. For thirteen months the "Roosevelt Recession," as his political opponents inevitably christened it, threatened to reverse the gains of the previous four years. Real GDP fell 10 percent; industrial production 32 percent; the stock market 36 percent. Unemployment climbed back to 20 percent. Manufacturers, and their workers, were particularly hard hit. General Motors' production declined 42 percent from 1.9 million vehicles in 1937 to 1.1 million in 1938. That year 72,938 GM workers—one in four—lost their jobs.

The General Motors 1937 annual report[57] documents how America's largest corporation viewed itself, and the nation's economic environment as the recession was taking hold. Clearly and simply written, the report is both erudite yet easy to understand, like Warren Buffett's shareholder letters eighty years later.

GM was pleased to announce the worldwide market for automobiles and trucks in 1937 had recovered to 95.5 percent of the peak year 1929. Sales were $1.61 billion, pre-tax profits $246 million, and taxes $49 million ($29 billion, $4.4 billion and $880 million in 2020 dollars). The company paid a surtax of $5.74 million on undistributed profits. The surtax was unpopular within the business community but had an important economic role, in that it encouraged companies to distribute their profits to shareholders as dividends, which in turn promoted consumption.

GM sales were affected by a six-week strike at the beginning of the year and the onset of the recession near the end. Yet sales increased a healthy 11.6 percent in 1937. Dividends were down, however, to $159.7 million from $202.1 million the year before, earnings having been affected by the strike and increased costs.

The automaker published a section on the Cost of Government, as it had since 1935. The report stated that the 1937 taxes paid by the company were equivalent to $2.45 per common share versus $2.13 in 1936 and $1.47 in 1935, adding that these were only taxes paid by the company and not the entire tax load paid by its customers. With understatement rarely heard today, the report suggested: "Specific consideration is asked of the stockholders with respect to the increasing share that the Government is taking from the business." In other words: we're very unhappy with all these new taxes and you should tell your congressman about it.

After adjustments to wage levels and hours worked during the year, average hourly wages increased two percent relative to 1936. The company noted that "Giving weight to the lower cost of living in 1937, the purchasing power of the General Motors worker's annual earnings was approximately 32 percent greater than in 1929." Although deflation had made each dollar more valuable, GM had generously continued paying its workers at, or above, 1929 levels. The report cautiously suggested that the steep economic decline during the latter part of 1937 was "a growing lack of confidence and a fear as to the future of American business enterprise, due to the attitude of Government toward business and economic policies affecting business."

The annual report discussed GM's emerging management philosophy of separating execution from strategy, or what the company labeled, "administration" and the "formation of policy." This was one of the first efforts by an American company to separate these management functions, a philosophy later made famous by management consultant Peter Drucker in his book *Concept of the Corporation* that documented GM's business practices.

The report proudly emphasized that its vehicles were manufactured from materials from every state. Missouri, for example, provided cadmium, clay, corn, mohair, hogs for upholstery, lead, limestone and wheat straw. Vermont's sole contribution: asbestos.

The executive compensation section is intriguing. The highest-paid executive (unnamed but certainly its prominent chairman, Alfred P. Sloan) earned between $561,161 and $112,500 over seven years based on the company's financial results, equivalent to about $10.1 and $2.0 million in 2020 dollars. Remarkably, only 346 executives, out of 261,977 total employees, earned more than $10,000 ($180,000 in 2020 dollars).

The report provided the impact of executive compensation on the cost of a new car. For a car with a list price of $1,000, executive compensation represented only $3.80 of its manufacturing cost. The report concluded on a positive note. By 1937, American vehicle ownership had climbed to nearly thirty million vehicles, well above the previous peak in 1929.

As the 1938 Recession deepened, Roosevelt renewed his attack on America's wealthy elites, blaming them for the downturn. A 1937 best-selling book, *America's 60 Families*, reinforced Roosevelt's claim. The book claimed that sixty dynastic families—Astor, DuPont, Ford, Mellon, Morgan, Rockefeller and Vanderbilt, among them—controlled the country's mainstream media, economy, and political institutions. Howard Ickes, Roosevelt's Interior Secretary, suggested in a December 1937 speech that the sixty families had engineered the Great Depression for their own selfish purposes.[58]

In recent years, similar claims have been made of shadowy cabals: The Deep State determined to undermine President Trump; a global conspiracy led by Bill Gates to profit from the COVID pandemic; an Antifa revolution to destroy America financed by billionaire George Soros, and, fantastically, the QAnon claim that a secret cabal of Satan worshipers composed of cannibalistic pedophiles exists within the government. Like the unhinged conspiracy theories during the nineteen-thirties, none have been proven to be true.

Roosevelt continued his war against America's elite when he gave a blistering speech to Congress in 1938 attacking income inequality:

> [It's] as if, out of every 300 persons in our population, one person received 78 cents out of every dollar of corporate dividends while the other 299 persons divided up the other 22 cents between them.... Democracy is not safe if the people tolerate the growth of private power to a point where it becomes stronger than their democratic state itself. That, in its essence, is fascism.[59]

It's an interesting historical note that the term, fascism, has a complicated history. By 1938, when Roosevelt used the term to vilify his opponents, fascism described the malevolent form of government with which the word is associated today. But throughout the nineteen-twenties and early nineteen-thirties, fascism merely suggested a centralized government led by a powerful leader.

It's forgotten today, but until the mid nineteen-thirties Benito Musso-lini, the *Il Duce* of Fascist Italy, was an admired leader both in and outside Italy. "[Mussolini] has many points in common," *The New York Times* wrote in 1923, "with that of the men who inspired our own constitution—John Adams, Hamilton and Washington."[60] During a 1927 speech, Church-ill expressed his admiration for Mussolini: "If I had been an Italian, I am sure I should have been whole-heartedly with you from the start to finish in your triumphant struggle against the bestial appetites and passions of Leninism."[61] In 1928, the *Saturday Evening Post* serialized a complimen-tary biography of Mussolini written by the U.S. ambassador to Italy. Cole Porter even included Mussolini in the lyrics for the 1934 musical *Anything Goes*, "You're the top! You're the Great Houdini! You're the top! You are Mussolini!"[62]

Admiration of Mussolini and his efficient government—he famously made the trains run on time—extended into Roosevelt's brain trust. Econ-omist Rexford Tugwell declared Italian Fascism, is "the cleanest, neatest, most efficiently operating piece of social machinery I've ever seen. It makes me envious."[63] Years later, Ronald Reagan accused Roosevelt of being a Mussolini admirer. To an extent, Reagan was right. Fascism during the early nineteen-thirties was regarded as a promising middle-ground between lais-sez-faire capitalism and communism.[64]

But by 1935 Fascist Italy, an American ally in the First World War, had aligned itself with the German Nazis. America's ardor for Mussolini and fascism quickly cooled. Cole Porter removed Mussolini from his lyrics. By 1938 Roosevelt was using fascism as a pejorative, just as Reagan would forty years later.

Roosevelt claimed that America's business elite had engineered the 1938 recession to torpedo his chances for a third term in 1940. An FBI investi-gation found no evidence of a conspiracy. Rather than an elite conspiracy, Roosevelt's own policies contributed to the recession. Roosevelt's attacks on the American business community affected business confidence and in-vestment. His fiscal policies leading up to 1937 may have also contributed. To fund the New Deal, Roosevelt repeatedly raised taxes: income taxes in

1934, a new "wealth tax" in 1935, an undistributed corporate profits tax in 1936, and the closure of tax loopholes in 1937. Also, in 1937 the first Social Security taxes went into effect with workers and their employers each paying one percent.

With the economy recovering and pressured by rising federal debt, Roosevelt cut federal spending from $8.2 billion in 1936 to $7.6 billion in 1937 and then to $6.8 billion in 1938. The spending reductions coupled with rising tax revenues came within one percent of balancing the budget. But Keynesian economists today believe Roosevelt cut stimulus spending too soon, thus helping to trigger the 1938 recession.

The Federal Reserve also played a role. The Fed had grown the money supply by 15 percent annually from 1933 through 1936.[65] Then, concerned over growing inflation, the Fed abruptly reversed its policies and tightened money by increasing reserve requirements on banks. Interest rates then spiked in 1937, slowing business investment.[66]

The international situation was also deteriorating. Japan invaded China in 1937; Spain was plunged into a brutal civil war with Germany and the Soviet Union intervening on opposite sides; Germany reclaimed the French-occupied Rhineland and then annexed Austria. Hitler next demanded that the Sudetenland region of Czechoslovakia be ceded to Germany. Concern that the United States might soon become involved in a major war overseas dampened business confidence at home.

Economists continue to debate the causes of the 1938 recession through their own ideological lens: Monetarists blame reductions in the money supply; Keynesians blame a premature attempt to balance the budget; supply-side economists blame government intervention itself as the root cause.

The recession departed as quickly as it arrived. By early-1939 America had bounced back. After declining steeply in 1938, real GDP climbed 8.2 percent in 1939. The S&P 500, measured in real dollars, rebounded even stronger, up 16 percent from December 1937. General Motors' North American auto production jumped 39 percent.

But unemployment lagged, falling only slightly, from 19 to 17.2 percent.

To assist the recovery, the Federal Reserve cut its reserve rate to allow banks to loan more money. The federal government resumed stimulus spending by providing more government-paid jobs. And it helped to allay war fears when Germany, the United Kingdom, France, and Italy signed the Munich Agreement on September 30, 1938, granting Hitler the Sudetenland region of Czechoslovakia in return for his promise to cease further German expansion. Returning home to a hero's welcome, Britain's Prime Minister Neville Chamberlain declared:

> My good friends, for the second time in our history, a British Prime Minister has returned from Germany bringing peace with honour. I believe it is peace for our time. We thank you from the bottom of our hearts. Go home and get a nice quiet sleep.[67]

Chamberlain's trust in Hitler would prove one of history's greatest diplomatic blunders. Hitler soon broke his promise. (Some historians believe Chamberlain knew war with Germany was inevitable and only signed the pact to give Britain time to prepare for the coming war.[68]) By March 1939 Germany had seized the remainder of Czechoslovakia. Then, less than a year after the Munich Agreement, Germany invaded Poland on September 1, 1939. Roosevelt knew the United States would soon be at war. "When peace has been broken anywhere," he told Americans two days after Hitler attacked Poland, the "peace of all countries everywhere is in danger."[69]

Roosevelt's Economic Record

Asked how long the Great Depression lasted, most informed citizens would answer from the 1929 Stock Market Crash to the start of World War II. They might add that the war "pulled" America out of the depression. But the Great Depression only lasted 43 months, ending March 1933 when GDP growth resumed. For the next eight years nearly every sector of the American economy, with one notable exception, enjoyed a historic boom.

From 1933 through 1940, real GDP grew an average of 6.3 percent annually. Remarkably, the period included two years of deep economic decline, Roosevelt's first year in office and the 1938 Recession. Other than during World War II, Roosevelt's record of GDP growth has never been broken. The Reagan years, 1981 through 1988, averaged 3.5 percent; the

Clinton years, 1993 through 2000, 3.9 percent. Even the go-go years during the Kennedy and Johnson administrations averaged only 4.9 percent.

Employment growth was also spectacular. Non-farm employment grew an average of 4.0 percent annually. No postwar President came close: Kennedy and Johnson, 2.3 percent; Reagan and Clinton, 1.9 percent.

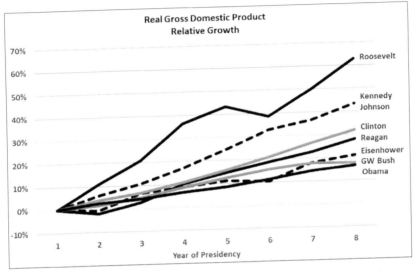

No modern president has matched Roosevelt's peacetime economic growth, even after the sharp downturn during the 1938 recession.   U.S. BUREAU OF ECONOMIC ANALYSIS

Weekly non-farm wages, after inflation, also set records, rising from $18.60 in 1932 to $26.05 (1932 dollars) in 1940, an average annual increase of 4.3 percent.[70] Sears Roebuck, the Amazon of its day, boasted in its 1940 annual report that "the real income of employees in terms of what their wages would buy has been improved upwards of 20 percent" since 1929.[71] In comparison, from 1964 through 2019, average hourly earnings, after inflation, have stagnated, rising less than a quarter percent annually. After-tax corporate profits also grew strongly from $1.3 to $7.3 billion (1932 dollars), or 24 percent annually. Corporate dividends doubled, from two to four billion dollars.

These are spectacular results. Regardless, some pundits today discount Roosevelt's economic record claiming it was due to massive government spending. Federal spending did increase from 3.4 to 6.6 percent of GDP from 1932 through 1940, but during those years state and local spending declined from 11.6 to 8.5 percent offsetting the increase in federal spending.

Bottom line, during Roosevelt's first two terms, before World War II, total government spending remained flat, averaging about 15.5 percent of GDP.

High, stubborn unemployment was the laggard. Unemployment, specifically the percentage of the labor force seeking work but unable to find it, fell from 25.2 to 14.6 percent from 1933 through 1940. Certainly, an economic recovery that ends with nearly 15 percent unemployment can hardly be called a recovery.

Yet reducing unemployment from 25 percent in 1933 to, say, five percent by 1940, would have been nearly impossible.

When Roosevelt took office, unemployment was 24 percent and rising. Only 38 million Americans were working out of a labor force of fifty million. By 1940, the labor force had grown to 55.6 million due to population growth. A five percent unemployment rate that year would have required that 95 percent, 52.8 million, of the labor force be employed. But growing employment from 38.0 million in 1932 to 52.8 million in 1940 would have required 4.2 percent annual employment growth over eight years, a level never even remotely achieved since government record-keeping began. The Roaring Twenties under Harding and Coolidge averaged only 2.8 percent annual employment growth; the Reagan and Clinton administrations a mere 1.8 percent. (Employment growth briefly surged over 10 percent in mid-2020 after the first COVID wave but slowed to an average of 2.2 percent during the first half of 2021.)

Another factor that contributed to high unemployment during the nineteen-thirties was rapidly improving labor productivity. Real GDP per employed worker, expressed in 1929 dollars, climbed from $2,263 in 1929 to $2,638 by 1940, a 17 percent improvement that made nearly one in five workers unnecessary.

General Motors provides a good example. Rapidly improving technology reduced the need for workers. In 1932, GM required 221 employees for every 1,000 vehicles produced. By 1940, the company only needed 123, cutting its workforce requirements nearly in half.[72]

Growing productivity was also reducing farm employment. During Roosevelt's first two terms, farm employment fell from 10.1 to 9.5 million workers. New technologies, from tractors to hybrid seeds, were making farming more productive. A new thirty-five horsepower tractor could plow an acre of land in fifteen minutes versus an hour and a half using a team of horses.[73]

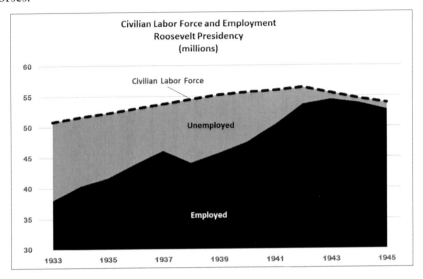

Employment grew an average of 2.9 percent annually during Roosevelt's first two terms, an unmatched record. After 1942, unemployment shrank as soldiers went to war, reducing the civilian labor force and, counter-intuitively, unemployment.

U.S. BUREAU OF LABOR STATISTICS

Dust Bowl Farmers were "tractored-out" as banks foreclosed on family farms. "Pa borrowed money from the bank," John Steinbeck wrote in *The Grapes of Wrath*, "and now the bank wants the land. The land company—that's the bank when it has land —wants tractors, not families on the land... But the tractor does two things—it turns the land and turns us off the land."[74]

Labor productivity made the nation wealthier: real GDP per capita grew 5.5 percent annually—another unbroken record—from 1933 through 1940. However, the same productivity that fueled economic growth eliminated millions of jobs.

It took World War II to reduce unemployment. By the end of the war, unemployment had fallen to 1.9 percent, a decrease from 14.6 percent in 1940. What was responsible for such a huge drop?

Soldiers going to war. From 1940 through 1945, the civilian labor force shrank as nearly 12 million workers left their civilian jobs to join the armed services.[75] It was the smaller labor force during the war that shrank unemployment, not growing employment. Employment growth during the war years actually slowed: from 1940 through 1945 employment growth averaged only 2.1 percent, well below the 2.9 percent growth from 1933 through 1940.

Confused? A worker leaving the labor force—whether to fight a war, retire or just not work—is no longer categorized as unemployed and thus represents the same change in unemployment as a worker getting a job. During the war, the labor force shrank by nearly 1.8 million workers. It was a statistical anomaly, not employment growth, which was responsible for the low unemployment rate during World War II.

Politics has affected our thinking about Roosevelt and the Great Depression. Since Roosevelt's first inaugural address, much of the American business community has despised Roosevelt and his New Deal politics. You can't blame them. From the start, Roosevelt accused "unscrupulous money changers" for the 1929 stock market crash and subsequent Great Depression. Beyond being blamed for the nation's economic collapse, American business resented Roosevelt's high taxes, his regulatory agencies as government intrusions into the private sector, his public works programs as creeping socialism, and Social Security as an erosion of Americans' rugged individualism.

These issues have fueled criticism of Roosevelt and his New Deal for eight decades. In 1940, Herbert Hoover blamed Roosevelt for shifting "the relation of government to free enterprise from that of umpire to controller."[76] In 1976, Ronald Reagan told reporters that "fascism was really the basis of the New Deal."[77] In 1995 Robert Higgs of the Mises Institute wrote, "Roosevelt's interventions meant that the market was never allowed to correct itself. Far from having gotten us out of the depression, FDR prolonged and deepened it, and brought unnecessary suffering to millions."[78] In 2018, the Foundation for Economic Education blamed much of the Great Depression on "the relentless assaults of the Roosevelt administration against business, property, and free enterprise [which] guaranteed that the capital needed to jumpstart the economy was either taxed away or forced into hiding."[79] And, as noted earlier it's hard to top economist Stephen Moore's condemnation that "[The New Deal] caused more human suffering than any other set of ideas in the past century."[80]

What these contemporary critics have forgotten is the political environment during the early nineteen-thirties. As Roosevelt took office the national economy had been in free fall for three years with no indication the economy would correct itself. Even former President Calvin Coolidge—an ardent supporter of minimalist government—had lost hope. "In other periods of depression," Coolidge lamented in 1933, "it has always been possible to see some things which were solid and upon which you could base hope, but as I look about, I now see nothing to give ground to hope."[81]

Millions of Americans had lost faith in capitalism. Radicals including Dr. Francis Townsend, Huey Long, Upton Sinclair, and Father Charles Coughlin clamored for massive government intervention. Even Gerald Swope, President of General Electric and chairman of the Business Advisory Council, promoted a sweeping, national plan to provide life insurance, unemployment benefits, and pensions for workers—a plan too ambitious for even Roosevelt's brain trust to accept.

Roosevelt tread a middle ground between the laissez-faire capitalism of Harding and Coolidge and the massive government programs radicals were advocating. Rather than destroying American Capitalism, Roosevelt may well have saved it.

A Sleeping Giant, Awakened

By 1940 Europe was at war. The Soviet Union had occupied Finland. German U-boats prowled the Atlantic and the German Army was sweeping through the Netherlands, Belgium, Luxembourg, and France. On June 14, German troops marched triumphantly into Paris. A month later, the German Luftwaffe began to bomb England, confident that German airpower would subdue the island nation. But Britain resisted, inspired by Prime Minister Winston Churchill's defiant declaration:

> We shall go on to the end, we shall fight in France, we shall fight
> on the seas and oceans, we shall fight with growing confidence and
> growing strength in the air, we shall defend our Island, whatever the

cost may be, we shall fight on the beaches, we shall fight on the landing grounds, we shall fight in the fields and in the streets, we shall fight in the hills; we shall never surrender.[82]

Across the Atlantic, the United States remained at peace. Real GDP was up nearly 20 percent from its 1938 low. Corporate profits had more than doubled. Unemployment was falling.[83] Disney's *Pinocchio* was playing in the theaters, Americans were dancing to Glenn Miller's "In the Mood," and *The Adventures of Superman* debuted on the radio.

And Franklin Roosevelt ran for an unprecedented third presidential term. After eight years of the New Deal, Americans still loved Roosevelt. A January 1940 Gallup poll gave Roosevelt a 69 percent approval rating.[84]

Roosevelt easily won, capturing 85 percent of the electoral vote. "In Washington's day the task of the people was to create and weld together a nation," Roosevelt declared during his 1941 inaugural address, "In Lincoln's day the task of the people was to preserve that Nation from disruption from within. In this day, the task of the people is to save that Nation and its institutions from disruption from without."[85] After eight years in the presidency, Roosevelt had begun to compare his challenges to those faced by Washington and Lincoln.

Americans, however, disagreed with Roosevelt that the nation was threatened with "disruption from without." Two decades earlier, 117,000 American soldiers had died[86] in the First World War, a war President Woodrow Wilson promised would make the world "safe for democracy."[87] Now Europe was at war again.

In 1940, the America First Committee was founded to discourage American intervention in another European war. The association quickly reached a peak membership of 800,000 and recruited scores of prominent members including future Presidents John F. Kennedy and Gerald Ford; Robert E. Wood, the chairman of Sears Roebuck; the architect Frank Lloyd Wright; automaker Henry Ford (later dropped for his outspoken anti-Semitic views); Robert R. McCormick, the publisher of the Chicago Tribune; and aviator Charles Lindbergh.[88]

Today, Donald Trump is inextricably linked with America First. But even during the nineteen-thirties the slogan was hardly new. President

Woodrow Wilson used the phrase to define his neutrality policy prior to the United States' entry into the First World War. Warren G. Harding later adopted America First as his campaign slogan in 1920.[89] During the nineteen-twenties, the Ku Klux Klan usurped America First as their motto falsely claiming they had copyrighted the slogan.[90]

Charles Lindbergh, immensely popular after his 1927 Atlantic flight, was the America First Committee's leading spokesman. "[America's destiny means] that the future of America will not be tied to these eternal wars in Europe," Lindbergh declared in a 1941 speech. "It means that American boys will not be sent across the ocean to die so that England or Germany or France or Spain may dominate the other nations."[91]

Americans overwhelmingly agreed with Lindbergh. Responding to a December 1940 Gallup poll that asked, "If you were asked to vote on the question of the United States entering the war against Germany and Italy, how would you vote—to go into the war or to stay out of the war," 88 percent answered, "stay out."[92]

Congress, responding to popular sentiment, was intent on keeping the United States out of the war. A series of Neutrality Acts starting in 1935 prohibited the export of American war materials to nations at war. After Hitler's occupation of Czechoslovakia in 1939, Congress relented somewhat and allowed arms sales but on a strict "cash and carry" basis, meaning buyers had to pay in full and transport the arms on non-American ships. But in early 1941, after Hitler had invaded and occupied nearly all Western Europe, Congress accepted that Hitler had to be stopped and approved the Lend-Lease Act that authorized foreign aid, from wheat to warships, for Britain and the Soviet Union.[93]

Yet Congress, though now willing to assist with munitions and aid, refused to be drawn into a fighting war. Roosevelt, though, believed war was inevitable and it would be far more dangerous for the United States if Britain fell to the Germans. Defying Congress, Roosevelt, in an executive action, authorized American destroyers to escort cargo ships carrying Lend-Lease goods. Within weeks, a German U-boat torpedoed the USS *Kearny* on October 17, 1941. The ship survived but eleven sailors were lost. Then, on October 31, the USS *Reuben James* was sunk near Iceland with the loss of ninety-nine American sailors. Yet, Congress still refused to declare war, claiming that Roosevelt, having authorized the Navy escorts, was "personally responsible for whatever lives may have been lost" as Senator George Aiken declared.[94]

Five weeks later, on December 7, 1941, the war came to American shores when Japan launched a surprise attack on the U.S. Naval Base at Pearl Harbor. The next day, the United States declared war on Japan.

Within the week, Adolf Hitler declared war on the United States, a foolish and rash mistake. Germany had no obligation to come to Japan's aid. Their mutual-defense pact was only invoked when an ally was attacked. Japan, of course, had not been attacked. But Hitler was confident his powerful war machine would quickly crush the United States, a nation composed of little more than "beauty queens, millionaires, stupid records and Hollywood," as Hitler had earlier scoffed.[95] The top Japanese brass weren't so confident. "I fear all we have done," Japan's Admiral Yamamoto reputedly said after the Pearl Harbor attack, "is to awaken a sleeping giant and fill him with a terrible resolve."[96]

The Arsenal of Democracy

Admiral Yamamoto was right. Pearl Harbor changed everything. After resisting intervention for years, Americans rushed to join the fight, breaking enlistment records. Within weeks, America began shifting to a wartime economy.

Less than a month after Pearl Harbor, a government war board directed that, effective immediately, automobile companies convert all their capacity to weapons production.[97] Regularly derided as a socialist by his critics, Roosevelt chose not to nationalize American industry, preferring to establish top-down planning boards instead. Defense contracts were issued on a cost-plus basis that provided manufacturers a small profit incentive.

But after years of resisting rearmament after the First World War, how could America catch up to Germany and Japan, whose finely tuned weapons factories had been running at full capacity for years?

Germany was confident America would never match its military might. "[America's] greatest technical accomplishments are refrigerators and radios," Hitler's indefatigable propaganda minister Joseph Goebbels boasted in August 1942. "So far, not a single U.S.A. soldier has set foot on foreign soil, but many have been chased back to U.S. soil in disgrace. . . . We are not impressed by American big talk and orgies of numbers."[98]

Back in the States, the chairman of General Motors, Alfred Sloan, was also skeptical that automobile factories could be converted to war production. "Mass production processes," Sloan warned, "do not lend themselves to rapid change. Very little flexibility exists. Our peacetime industrial plants can be adapted only to a small extent to the needs of national defense."[99] Sloan wasn't alone. Much of the automobile industry believed, understandably, that aircraft were too complex to be manufactured in automobile plants. Aircraft engines require machining tolerances far tighter than automobile engines and aircraft wings and fuselages required hand-assembly. Consequently, military planners assumed entirely new factories would be needed to manufacture the thousands of aircraft that were anticipated for the war effort.

But a clever machinist and labor organizer disagreed with the auto executives. Anticipating the coming war, in late 1940 Walter Reuther published *500 Planes a Day: A Program for the Utilization of the Automobile Industry for Mass Production of Defense Planes.*[100] Reuther and his fellow machinists had analyzed dozens of automobile plants in detail down to the number of stamping presses in each plant. They concluded that the auto industry was operating at only 50 percent capacity and that within six months it would be possible to manufacture 500 fighter aircraft a day even while maintaining much of the current auto production. "Why wait for entirely new plants to be built which cannot go into production until almost two years have passed?" Reuther asked in a radio address. "We believe we can do the job of adapting idle automotive machinery to plane production in six months."[101]

Industry management, not surprisingly, was resentful that a labor organizer would propose how to run their business. "Everyone admits that Reuther is smart," GM President Charles Wilson responded, "but this is none of his business. . . . If Reuther wants to become part of management, GM will be happy to hire him. But so long as he remains vice president of the Union, he has no right to talk as if he were vice president of a company."[102] Wilson's comment that Reuther had "no right to talk" typified the fraught relations between labor and management during the Roosevelt years.

But Reuther was right. Automobile factories quickly converted to defense plants. By 1943, General Motor's annual report was proudly boasting, "Airplanes, airplane engines, subassemblies and equipment now account for more than 40 percent of General Motors war production volume.... In December 1943 only a year after the first Avenger (a carrier-based aircraft) was produced by General Motors, the 1,000th Avenger came off the production line in what had been in peacetime an automobile hardware plant."[103]

America had quickly become the Arsenal of Democracy supplying not only its own needs but those of its allies. The figures are astounding. By 1944 America's military spending exceeded the combined GDP of Germany and Japan.[104] A single American factory, the Detroit Arsenal Tank Plant, built more tanks than were produced in all of Germany during the war.[105] By the war's end, 324,000 aircraft, 2.5 million military vehicles, tanks, and self-propelled guns, 21 fleet aircraft carriers, 206 destroyers, and 120 submarines had been produced by American factories and shipyards.[106]

American industry profited little during the war. General Motor's revenues, for example, more than tripled from 1939 to 1943, but net profit margins declined from thirteen to four percent. Real dividends (1939 dollars) dropped from $3.50 to $1.61 a share.[107] GM wasn't unique. From 1941 through 1945 industry profits, measured in 1939 dollars, fell from $10.2 to $7.2 billion.

Personal incomes fell across the board during the war. The average after-tax income, measured in 2020 dollars, for the top one percent dropped from $518,000 in 1939 to $235,000 in 1945. For the middle 60 percent of taxpayers, incomes dropped from $42,000 to $25,300.

The war changed how Americans were taxed. Since its 1913 inception, the income tax mainly taxed the wealthy. In 1939, only about 14 percent of the civilian labor force filed income taxes. But by 1945, over 90 percent of the labor force was filing returns. Rather than paying taxes with a check once a year, Uncle Sam began deducting taxes from paychecks every week.

Total tax collections ballooned from $6.3 billion in 1939 to $45.2 billion in 1945. Still, taxes covered only about 43 percent of federal spending during the war. The balance was financed through debt, much of which was purchased by working Americans through war bonds. These bonds typically sold for 75 percent of their face value and were redeemable in ten years. By taking money out of the over-heated war economy, war bonds helped reduce inflation and then helped fuel the economic boom of the nineteen-fifties when they injected fresh funds into the economy as they were redeemed.[108]

Promoted heavily by war heroes and movie stars, Americans bought $54 billion ($810 billion in 2020 dollars) of the bonds from 1941 through 1945. One notable campaign, "Stars over America," was promoted by over 300 movie stars and raised $840 million. The New York Yankees, New York Giants, and Brooklyn Dodgers played together in an unusual baseball game where each team came to bat six times during the nine-inning game. The Dodgers won with five runs. Baseball fans around the country bought $56.5 million in war bonds as part of the promotion. Even school children saved their quarters in promotional cardboards with slots and when they had seventy-five, equal to $18.75, turned them in for a $25 savings bond.[109] It was a time when all Americans were happy to pitch in to help the war effort.

Managing the War Economy

During and shortly after the First World War, inflation had exploded, increasing an average of 16 percent annually. By 1920, a 1916 dollar was worth only fifty-four cents. Understandably, many expected inflation to take off again during the Second World War. It didn't happen. Early in 1942, the government instituted wage limits and price controls on thousands of essential items. Administered by hundreds of government panels, it took time for the controls to take effect, which allowed inflation to jump 11 percent in 1942. But from 1943 through 1946, while the controls were in place, average inflation was held to 4.6 percent annually.

With prices controlled by the government, the market could no longer adjust prices to allocate demand. An anxious housewife, rising early, could buy all the bread in a store to assure her family never ran out. So, once price controls were installed, it was necessary to institute rationing to assure everyone got their share. The government issued ration books. To buy a loaf of bread you needed a stamp in your ration book. It was burdensome and complex.

Economists despise price controls and rationing for interfering with the free market. In the ideal market, prices inform suppliers how much to produce. If consumers are willing to pay more for a particular good, suppliers will increase production. If demand falls, suppliers cut prices. That is the theory of an ideal market.

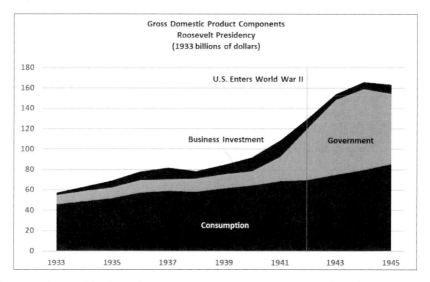

Consumption and business investment, not government expansion, drove economic growth during Roosevelt's first two terms. Government spending dominated the war economy.   U.S. BUREAU OF ECONOMIC ANALYSIS

But what happens when the supply of a critical good, gasoline, for example, is limited? No matter how high prices climb, there is only so much gasoline a wartime economy can produce. Supply cannot rise to meet demand. In that case, wealthy consumers buy all the gasoline while others get none. Hence the need for rationing.

Still, the free-market economists at the time condemned the price controls and rationing as wrong, none more stridently than Ludwig von Mises. Mises was an Austrian-born economist who, naturally, subscribed to the Austrian school of economics, first developed in Vienna in the late nineteenth century. The essence of Austrian economics is unhindered laissez-faire capitalism. Other than the protection of persons and property, Austrian economic theory deems government has no legitimate role. Mises believed government intervention leads inexorably to tyranny as did his fellow Austrian, Friedrich Hayek, who wrote a 1944 book ominously titled *The Road to Serfdom*. That same year, Mises wrote *Omnipotent Government*, warning that:

> If the government, in order to eliminate these inexorable and un-welcome consequences [wage and price controls], pursues its course further and further, it finally transforms the system of capitalism and free enterprise into socialism.... There is no third system between a market economy and socialism. Mankind has to choose between those two systems—unless chaos is considered an alternative.[110]

Claims that Roosevelt's government was inexorably moving the country towards socialism were a consistent theme during his presidency. Opponents of federal public works programs, regulatory agencies, Social Security, and price and wage controls all contributed to this recurring Greek chorus. But by 1944 Roosevelt had shut down the public works programs instituted ten years earlier, including the Public Works Administration and the Civilian Conservation Corps. In 1946, rationing and price controls were terminated. What remained were the regulatory agencies such as the Securities and Exchange Commission (SEC), the Federal Deposit Insurance Corporation (FDIC), the Federal Communications Commissions (FCC) and the Civil Aeronautics Authority, the precursor to today's Federal Aviation Agency (FAA). Today, most Americans believe these federal agencies, rather than being harbingers of socialism, provide a useful purpose. (Ironically, the epitome of American Capitalism, corporate jet owners, have actively fought the privatization of the nation's air traffic control system, a move Canada and Europe made decades ago.)

Roosevelt's policies, as Hayek and Mises had darkly predicted, did not lead to the destruction of freedom in America. In the decades after Roosevelt's death, America's democracy remained intact, the economy flourished and the United States served as a beacon of capitalism and democracy throughout the world.

★

Although America did not succumb to tyranny, the Great Depression and World War II transformed the federal government. Federal spending never returned to its earlier levels. In 1929 federal expenditures were a mere three percent of the nation's GDP. Four years later, Hoover left office after increasing spending to 7.8 percent. Roosevelt ended his second term in 1940 at 9.2 percent of GDP. It was the war that truly transformed federal spending. From 1947 through 1965 federal spending averaged 16.2 percent, nearly twice its 1940 level.

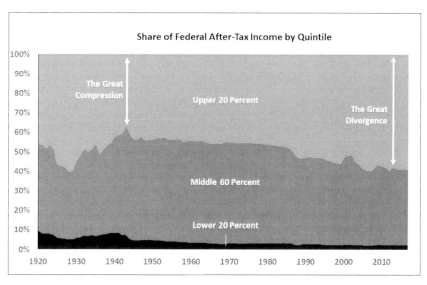

In 1928, wealthy taxpayers took home 60 percent of the nation's federal after-tax income. By 1943 progressive taxation reduced their share to 37 percent. By 2020, wealth distribution again mirrored the late nineteen-twenties. IRS STATISTICS OF INCOME REPORTS

Before the war, Americans were lightly taxed. Individual income tax receipts averaged less than one percent of GDP during Roosevelt's first two terms. During the war, these taxes peaked at nearly nine percent of GDP in 1944. Taxes receded after the war, but never returned close to their pre-war levels. Since 1946, individual income taxes have consistently averaged 7.6 percent of GDP.

It was the wealthy who lost the most under Roosevelt's tax policies, a period economists call "The Great Compression." In 1928, the top 20 percent of taxpayers collected 60.1 percent of total federal after-tax income, the historical high, leaving the lower and middle classes with 40 percent. By

1943 the top 20 percent's share had dropped to 36.8 percent, its historical low. (By 2018, their share had climbed back to 59.5 percent.)

Little wonder so many wealthy Americas despised Roosevelt, considering him a traitor to his privileged class, a class Roosevelt knew well. Roosevelt's earliest American ancestor, Claes Martenzen van Rosenvelt, immigrated to New Amsterdam in 1650.[111] By the time Roosevelt was born, the Roosevelts had become members of the American elite. As a boy, Roosevelt sat on President Grover Cleveland's lap; as an adolescent, he attended the exclusive Groton prep-school; as a young man, he cast his first vote for his distant cousin Teddy Roosevelt; and as an adult, he vacationed at his private estate on Campobello Island. Yet Roosevelt's sympathies were with the common man rather than his wealthy peers. Before Franklin Roosevelt— especially during the Harding, Coolidge, and Hoover years—government was often acquiescent to big business. But Roosevelt reversed that, making business subservient to Washington's regulations and wage and tax policies. Corporate America despised him for it.

Others considered Roosevelt a man without principles, failing to assume the moral high ground when it was not politically expedient. "If he became convinced tomorrow," wrote H. L. Mencken, the renowned Baltimore journalist, "that coming out for cannibalism would get him the votes he so sorely needs, he would begin fattening a missionary in the White House backyard come Wednesday."[112]

When an anti-lynching bill was proposed in the mid-nineteen-thirties, Roosevelt refused to support it. "If I come out for the anti-lynching bill now," Roosevelt told the bill's sponsors, "[Southern Democrats] will block every bill I ask Congress to pass to keep America from collapsing. I just can't take the risk.[113]

In 1939, when the MS *Saint Louis* passenger liner tried to disembark nine-hundred Jews fleeing the Nazis, Roosevelt turned the ship back. A quarter of the passengers were later estimated to have died in Nazi concentration camps.[114]

When pressured by civilian and military leaders after Pearl Harbor, and against the pleas of his wife, Eleanor, Roosevelt issued Executive Order 9066. The order imprisoned 120,000 Japanese-Americans in internment camps, 70,000 of whom were American citizens. There they spent the war living in tar-paper shacks, sharing eating and restroom facilities and having limited social and work opportunities. Evacuated with short notice, thousands of interned Japanese lost their homes, farms, and businesses. Yet, the Japanese remained loyal Americans. The 442d Regimental Combat Team composed of Japanese-Americans was the most decorated combat unit for its size and length of service in the history of the U.S. military.[115]

Eleanor Roosevelt was the longest serving First Lady of the United States. She later served as the U.S. Representative to the United Nation's General Assembly from 1945 through 1952.   PICTURES NOW/ALAMY

Roosevelt's failings are largely forgotten today and is remembered by most Americans as a fighter who won the war and fought for the underprivileged. Historians typically rank Roosevelt as the nation's third-best President, behind only Washington and Lincoln.

Shortly before his death, Roosevelt proposed a "second Bill of Rights under which a new basis of security and prosperity can be established for all—regardless of station, race, or creed."[116] Those rights included the right to a job which pays enough to provide adequate food, clothing, and recreation; the right of every farmer to raise and sell his products at a return that will give his family a decent living; the right of every businessman to trade in an atmosphere of freedom from unfair competition; the right of every family to a decent home, adequate medical care, and protection from the economic fears of old age, sickness, accident, and unemployment; and the right to a good education.

Are these the rights of all Americans or privileges to be earned? The debate continues to this day.

Roosevelt did not live to see the end of the war. He died April 12, 1945, of a massive cerebral hemorrhage at his retreat in Warm Springs, Georgia. Roosevelt had gone to Warm Springs to recover from an exhausting trip two months earlier to Yalta, a resort city in Crimea where he met with Winston Churchill and Josef Stalin.

With the end of the war near, the three leaders had met to plan the division of a postwar Europe. Roosevelt left the Yalta Conference believing Stalin's promise that the countries the Soviet Union captured from the Germans during the war—Bulgaria, Czechoslovakia, Hungary, Poland, and Romania—would be allowed to hold free elections.

Stalin broke his promise. After Germany's surrender, Soviet armies reigned supreme throughout Eastern Europe. Rather than returning to their homeland, the Soviets transformed the countries into communist states, puppets of the Soviet Union. Democratic elections would not be held until the fall of the Soviet Union over 45 years later.[117]

Stalin also deceived Churchill. Hardly a year after their Yalta meeting, Churchill, on March 5, 1946, gave his historical "Iron Curtain" speech. "From Stettin in the Baltic to Trieste in the Adriatic," Churchill proclaimed, "an Iron Curtain has descended across the Continent. Behind that line lie all the capitols of the ancient states of Central and Eastern Europe.... All are subject in one form or another, not only to Soviet influence but to a very high and, in many cases, increasing measure of control from Moscow."[118]

Churchill, Roosevelt and Stalin at the Yalta Conference in February 1945 planning a postwar Europe. Stalin promised free elections in Eastern Europe. He broke his promise after Roosevelt's death, and instead lowered an "Iron Curtain" dividing East and West Europe.   THE HISTORY EMPORIUM/ALAMY

Would Stalin have had the audacity to trample over Eastern Europe had Roosevelt lived? Perhaps not. By the end of the war, U.S. military forces were the strongest in the world. The United States was supreme in the production of aircraft, weaponry, and ships; had total control over the world's oceans; twelve million men and women in uniform; and, most importantly, sole possession of the atomic bomb.

Stalin knew Roosevelt was resolute. He had seen Roosevelt take on America's business elite to transform America's institutions, prepare America for war when most Americans were against intervention, fight and win a two-front war, and finally, develop the most powerful weapon the world had ever known.

Had Roosevelt lived, he surely would have insisted Stalin honor his promise to allow Eastern Europe to determine its own destiny through free elections. Stalin likely would have listened.

Harry S. Truman

April 12, 1945 – January 20, 1953

> Today, America has become one of the most powerful forces for good on earth... We must now learn to live with other nations for our mutual good. We must learn to trade more with other nations so that there may be—for our mutual advantage—increased production, increased employment and better standards of living throughout the world... In that way, America may well lead the world to peace and prosperity.[1]

N o modern President, other than Richard Nixon, left the presidency with a lower job approval rating than Harry Truman. Months before leaving office, President Truman's approval ratings hit a record low of 22 percent—four out of five Americans believed Truman was doing a poor job.[2] Yet today, historians rank Truman, on average, as the nation's sixth-best President, just behind Thomas Jefferson and well above the popular Ronald Reagan and Bill Clinton.[3]

Who was right, the American public, judging Truman in their own time, or historians looking back from the perspective of decades?

Harry Truman had served as Franklin Roosevelt's Vice President for only eighty-two days when Roosevelt died on April 12, 1945 of a massive cerebral hemorrhage. Four hours later Truman was sworn in as President.

Roosevelt didn't think much of Truman. They had met privately only twice after Truman became Vice President. In neither meeting did Roosevelt disclose the greatest military secret of the war, the atomic bomb. "As you know I was Vice President from January 20 to April 12, 1945," Truman later wrote his daughter, Margaret. "I was at Cabinet meetings and saw Roosevelt once or twice in those months. But he never did talk to me confidentially about the war, or about foreign affairs or what he had in mind for the peace after the war."[4] Harry Truman had been given no preparation before he unexpectedly assumed the presidency. Within months, he would face some of the greatest challenges ever asked of an American President.

The Most Terrible Thing

On July 25, after being told of the first successful test of the atomic bomb, Truman confided to his diary, "We have discovered the most terrible bomb in the history of the world. It may be the fire destruction prophesied in the Euphrates Valley Era, after Noah and his fabulous Ark.... It seems to be the most terrible thing ever discovered, but it can be made the most useful." Just three months after assuming the presidency, Truman was faced with the monumental decision of how to end the war: drop the atomic bomb, invade the Japanese mainland, or attempt to negotiate an unconditional surrender.

In June of 1945, Truman's Joint War Plans Committee had estimated an invasion of the Japanese mainland would cost 220,000 Americans killed, wounded, and missing in action, and possibly far more. The Japanese were tenacious fighters. Earlier that year, during the battle for Iwo Jima, a tiny island over 800 miles from Japan, only 126 Japanese were taken prisoner while 18,000 Japanese soldiers fought to the death and 3,000 retreated into a labyrinth of defensive caves to fight on.[5] Over 6,800 American soldiers were killed and 19,000 wounded in the battle to wrest the tiny island from the Japanese. The fight for the Japanese home islands was expected to be far worse.

There were indications that the Japanese were willing to surrender, but only if they could keep their Emperor, whom they considered a god. On May 12, 1945, the Office of Strategic Services (OSS), the precursor to the Central Intelligence Agency (CIA), sent a memorandum to President Truman:

The following information, transmitted by the OSS representative in Bern originates with a German source, an authority on the Far East who is considered anti-Nazi but pro-Japanese: The source, on 11 May, talked with Shunichi Kase, the Japanese Minister to Switzerland. He reports that Kase expressed a wish to help arrange for a cessation of hostilities between the Japanese and the Allies. Kase reportedly considers direct talks with the Americans and the British preferable to negotiations through the USSR because the latter eventually would increase Soviet prestige so much that the whole Far East would become Communist. Kase allegedly believes that one of the few provisions the Japanese would insist upon would be the retention of the Emperor as the only safeguard against Japan's conversion to Communism. Kase feels that Under Secretary of State Grew, whom he considers the best U.S. authority on Japan, shares this opinion.[6]

With no word from the Americans after two months, the Japanese asked the Soviets to broker a Japanese surrender. American intelligence intercepted messages between the Japanese Foreign Minister, Shigenori Tōgō, and Japan's Russian Ambassador in Moscow, Naotake Satō. The Japanese were willing to surrender, but not unconditionally:

July 22: "Special Envoy Konoye's mission will be in obedience to the Imperial Will. He will request assistance in bringing about an end to the war through the good offices of the Soviet Government."

July 25: "It is impossible to accept unconditional surrender under any circumstances, but we should like to communicate to the other party [the United States] through appropriate channels that we have no objection to a peace based on the Atlantic Charter."[7]

The Atlantic Charter, mentioned in Tōgō's July 25 message, was an agreement signed on August 14, 1941 between President Roosevelt and British Prime Minister Churchill that proposed a postwar framework for international cooperation. The Japanese were specifically concerned with Article 3, the right for each country to determine its own form of government, which they believed would allow them to keep their Emperor.[8]

While these messages were being intercepted, Truman, Churchill, and Stalin were meeting in Potsdam, Germany to agree on the establishment of a postwar order. On July 26, the United States, United Kingdom, and China (the Soviet Union was not yet at war with Japan) issued the Potsdam Declaration, which stipulated the terms for a Japanese surrender. Reading the document today, the terms seem remarkably non-vindictive with an emphasis on rebuilding Japan and the restoration of "Freedom of speech, of religion, and of thought, as well as respect for the fundamental human rights…" But Japan's military commanders driven by their samurai warrior ethos found the declaration's last clause too humiliating to accept: "We call upon the government of Japan to proclaim now the unconditional surrender of all Japanese armed forces, and to provide proper and adequate assurances of their good faith in such action. The alternative for Japan is prompt and utter destruction."[9]

Eleven days later, after receiving no response from the Japanese, the B-29 bomber *Enola Gay* dropped the first atomic bomb on Hiroshima on August 6. The Japanese remained silent. Three days later a second bomb was dropped on Nagasaki. Together, an estimated 105,000 were instantly killed,[10] yet the Japanese war cabinet refused to surrender. It was Emperor Hirohito who intervened, directing his ministers to accept the terms of the Potsdam Declaration.

On August 15, Hirohito gave a radio address announcing Japan's surrender. "Should we continue to fight," Hirohito told his fellow countrymen, "not only would it result in an ultimate collapse and obliteration of the Japanese nation, but also it would lead to the total extinction of human civilization…. The hardships and sufferings to which our nation is to be subjected hereafter will be certainly great…. We have resolved to pave the way for a grand peace for all the generations to come by enduring the unendurable and suffering what is insufferable."[11]

On September 2, Japan formally surrendered aboard the United States battleship USS *Missouri*, ending World War II.

Surprisingly, after the war ended, many of America's top military leaders expressed strong disagreement with the atomic bombing of Japan.[12] Major

General Curtis Lemay: "The atomic bomb had nothing to do with the end of the war at all." Fleet Admiral Charles Nimitz: "The atomic bomb played no decisive part from a purely military point of view in the defeat of Japan. The use of atomic bombs at Hiroshima and Nagasaki was of no material assistance in our war against Japan. The Japanese were already defeated and ready to surrender." Brigadier General Carter Clarke: "We didn't need to do it, and we knew we didn't need to do it, and they knew that we didn't need to do it, we used them as an experiment for two atomic bombs." Fleet Admiral William "Bull" Halsey: "The first atomic bomb was an unnecessary experiment.... It was a mistake to ever drop it... [the scientists] had this toy and they wanted to try it out, so they dropped it."

Were America's top military leaders simply chagrined that the Pacific war ended due to a new weapon rather than traditional military victory as had happened in Europe? Likely not. Years later, Dwight D. Eisenhower, the most respected military leader of the twentieth century, also agreed the bombing was unnecessary. He wrote in his memoir, *The White House Years*:

> In 1945 Secretary of War Stimson, visiting my headquarters in Germany, informed me that our government was preparing to drop an atomic bomb on Japan. I was one of those who felt that there were a number of cogent reasons to question the wisdom of such an act. During his recitation of the relevant facts, I had been conscious of a feeling of depression and so I voiced to him my grave misgivings, first on the basis of my belief that Japan was already defeated and that dropping the bomb was completely unnecessary, and secondly because I thought that our country should avoid shocking world opinion by the use of a weapon whose employment was, I thought, no longer mandatory as a measure to save American lives.[13]

Were America's top military leaders right? Were the Japanese willing to surrender even before Hiroshima and Nagasaki were bombed? Or was President Truman justified using a weapon so devastating that Japan would be forced to capitulate?

Truman's Secretary of War, Henry Stimson, tried to answer these questions in February 1947 when he wrote in *Harper's Magazine*:

Had the war continued until the projected invasion on November 1, additional fire raids of B-29s would have been more destructive of life and property than the very limited number of atomic raids which we could have executed in the same period. But the atomic bomb was more than a weapon of terrible destruction; it was a psychological weapon. In March 1945, our Air Force had launched its first great incendiary raid on the Tokyo area. In this raid more damage was done and more casualties were inflicted than was the case at Hiroshima. Hundreds of bombers took part and hundreds of tons of incendiaries were dropped. Similar successive raids burned out a great part of the urban area of Japan, but the Japanese fought on. On August 6, one B-29 dropped a single atomic bomb on Hiroshima. Three days later a second bomb was dropped on Nagasaki and the war was over. So far as the Japanese could know, our ability to execute atomic attacks, if necessary, by many planes at a time, was unlimited. As Dr. Karl Compton has said, "It was not one atomic bomb, or two, which brought surrender; it was the experience of what an atomic bomb will actually do to a community, plus the dread of many more, that was effective."[14]

The debate on whether it was necessary to drop the atomic bomb continues to this day. But two facts are irrefutable. The Japanese had indeed put out peace feelers, but Japan's samurai ethos required an "honorable" peace rather than the unconditional surrender the United States demanded. Then, even after atomic bombs destroyed Hiroshima and Nagasaki, records show the Japanese war cabinet refused to capitulate. Only after Hirohito, their Divine Emperor, intervened did the Japanese military staff agree to surrender.

Truman was faced with two choices. The near certainty that using a weapon so horrible would force the Japanese to surrender, or invading Japan with the possible cost of a million American and Japanese casualties. Given the information he had at the time, Truman chose to end the war quickly and surely.

From War to Peace

With the war over, Truman's immediate challenge was transitioning the nation from war to a peace-time economy. As the war ended, over twelve million men and women were in the armed services, factories were manufacturing war materials, price and wage controls were in place, and many goods were rationed. Somehow, the nation would need to quickly provide jobs for millions of servicemen rejoining the workforce, convert thousands of factories back to civilian production, and eliminate wage and price controls without triggering runaway inflation. That had not happened after the First World War when inflation increased an average of 16 percent annually—$1,000 stashed under a mattress before the war was only worth $545 by 1920. That same year the nation went into an eighteen-month recession that kicked unemployment up to nearly 12 percent.

Those memories were still fresh as the country began to plan for a postwar economy. In 1943, MIT economist Paul Samuelson warned of the consequences of mishandling the transition from war to peace:

> The final conclusion to be drawn from our experience at the end of the last war is inescapable–were the war to end suddenly within the next six months, were we again planning to wind up our war effort in the greatest haste, to demobilize our armed forces, to liquidate price controls, to shift from astronomical deficits to even the large deficits of the thirties—then there would be ushered in the greatest period of unemployment and industrial dislocation which any economy has ever faced.[15]

Samuelson, who later won the Nobel Prize in 1970, was a Keynesian economist who believed government taxation and spending largely controlled the economy. After massive government intervention during the war, he was concerned that premature cuts to government spending would plunge the nation into "the greatest period of unemployment and industrial dislocation which any economy has ever faced."

One American company had a different view. A few months after Samuelson's dire prediction, the General Motors 1943 annual report was downright optimistic about the postwar economy. GM's annual report observed that by the end of 1944 there would be five million fewer cars on the road than at the beginning of the war, and 80 percent of those cars would be over four years old. Furthermore, GM observed that Americans had accumulated a large reservoir of savings and unused installment debt to provide the purchasing power "to maintain our enterprise system, and particularly the automotive and related industries, at a high level of activity for several years."[16]

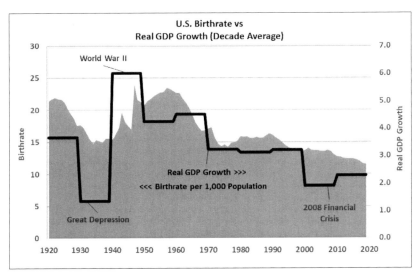

Population growth contributes to economic growth. High postwar birth rates helped drive strong economic growth for decades. As population growth slowed, so did economic growth.   U.S. BUREAU OF ECONOMIC ANALYSIS | U.S. CENSUS BUREAU

GM was right. During the war, Americans were working long hours earning far more, even with wage caps, than they had during the late nineteen-thirties. That included women who joined the workforce as men left for the armed services. At the end of the war, more than a third of American workers were women.[17] From 1940 through 1945 the nation's real personal income increased 72 percent, reaching $137 billion in 1945. With limited consumer goods and services to purchase, personal savings ballooned, averaging 25 percent of income from 1942 through 1944, far above the 3.6 percent average during the nineteen-thirties (and three times the eight percent average from 1950 through 2019). When the war ended, after years of deprivation, Americans had plenty of money to spend—but equally important—the confidence to spend it as the resounding Allied victory had restored a sense of American optimism not seen since the nineteen-twenties.

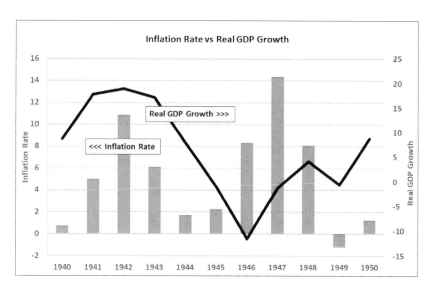

The strong economy during World War II increased inflation leading to wage and price controls. Prices surged after the controls were removed.

U.S. BUREAU OF ECONOMIC ANALYSIS | U.S. BUREAU OF LABOR STATISTICS

Just eighteen months after Japan's surrender, President Truman in his first Economic Report to Congress boasted "at the end of 1946, less than a year and a half after [Victory in Japan]-day, more than ten million demobilized veterans and other millions of war-time workers have found employment in the swiftest and most gigantic change-over that any nation has ever made from war to peace."[18]

Truman had every right to brag. The postwar boom was spectacular. In 1946 the top three automobile brands, Chevrolet, Ford, and Plymouth, sold 1.1 million cars, nearly two-thirds of their entire nineteen-forties production. In 1950 they sold 3.3 million, doubling their pre-war production.[19] Personal consumption from automobiles to washing machines increased from $120 billion in 1945 to $144 billion (1945 dollars) in 1950. During those same years, businesses and homeowners invested heavily in new factories, equipment, and homes, increasing real gross domestic private investment from $12 to $42 billion.

The booming economy made it possible for most returning servicemen to find jobs, helped by women leaving the labor force, often involuntarily, to return to the home. The economy added 5.5 million new jobs from 1945 through 1948, including 2.4 million jobs in 1946 alone.

America had often neglected its war veterans. In 1924, President Coolidge vetoed benefits for First World War veterans as too expensive declaring, "Patriotism which is bought and paid for is not patriotism."[20] Eight years later, President Hoover ordered the forced removal of thousands of impoverished war veterans demanding early payment of their service bonuses. Veterans of the Second World War were treated much better.

The Servicemen's Readjustment Act, or G.I. Bill, assisted the assimilation of veterans into civilian life. Signed by President Roosevelt in 1944, the G.I. Bill provided veterans financial aid for education and homeownership as well as limited unemployment benefits. The bill was very popular. In 1947, half of the new college admissions were veterans, and from 1944 through 1952 alone, nearly 2.4 million veterans acquired homes through the G.I. Bill. The bill not only took pressure off the job market as veterans opted to return to school rather than immediately seek a job but also created new construction jobs as veterans bought new homes under the bill. With a strong job market and the option of returning to school, only 20 percent of veterans applied for unemployment.[21]

Contrary to what Paul Samuelson had warned, the nation achieved these strong economic results while quickly reducing government spending and maintaining tax rates near their high wartime levels. Washington didn't move as quickly, however, to remove wage and price controls. The controls were retained until late 1946 when civilian production had sufficiently recovered to meet most demand. Although imperfect, the controls helped manage inflation during and just after the war. Average annual inflation from 1941 through 1948 was seven percent, far lower than the 16 percent during the First World War.

With the economy strong, President Truman focused on balancing the federal budget and paying down the $270 billion war debt. ($3.9 trillion in 2020 dollars) That debt, even after adjusting for inflation, was nearly ten times the size of the First World War debt. Remarkably, by 1947 the federal government, after years of huge deficits, was running a healthy surplus. On January 7, 1948, during his State of the Union Address to Congress, President Truman summarized his thoughts on taxation:

Certain adjustments should be made within our existing tax structure that will not affect total receipts yet will adjust the tax burden so that those least able to pay will have their burden lessened by the transfer of a portion of it to those best able to pay. Many of our families today are suffering hardship because of the high cost of living. At the same time profits of corporations have reached an all-time record in 1947. Corporate profits total $17 billion after taxes. This compared with $12.5 billion in 1946, the previous high year. Because of this extraordinarily high level of profits, corporations can well afford to carry a larger share of the tax load at this time.[22]

What effect did the high postwar taxes have on the economy? Prior to the nineteen-eighties, Washington considered a balanced budget critical to responsible governance. Americans understood that high taxes were necessary to pay off high government debt, so there was little controversy when Truman increased corporate taxes from 40 percent in 1945 to 42 percent in 1950 and then to 52 percent in 1952. Although no one liked paying higher taxes, Americans of the era considered it their patriotic duty to do so.

From 1947 to 1952 the federal government generated $17.9 billion ($209 billion in 2020 dollars) in budget surpluses. Real GDP grew 3.9 percent annually. With the economy booming and high tax revenues, the national debt fell from 113 percent of GDP in 1945 to 71 percent in 1952. The average American was also prospering. During those years, the after-tax income of the middle 60 percent of taxpayers increased from $24,600 to $28,600 (2020 dollars).

Roosevelt, Truman, and Eisenhower all employed Keynesian economics: run deficits to stimulate a lagging economy or fight a war, then return to surpluses to pay down the debt, even if it requires raising taxes when the economy recovers. From 1933 through 1960, excluding the war years of 1941 through 1945, real GDP grew a robust 3.7 percent annually.

The years from 1961 through 1980 were transitional years economically. Tax rates decreased, but the national debt, which hit a low of 31 percent of GDP in 1974, remained a priority. Real GDP continued its 3.7 percent annual growth.

But after 1980, supply-side economics—cut taxes to encourage business investment—took precedence over managing the national debt. It did not work. Low tax rates have not boosted growth. Real GDP from 1981 through 2019 grew 2.7 percent annually, well below the 3.7 percent from 1933 through 1980 (excluding 1941 through 1945). Furthermore, steep tax cuts ballooned deficits. By 2019, the national debt had climbed to 106 percent of GDP, a level not exceeded since the end of World War II.

Uncle Joe Charms Truman

Russian Premier Josef Stalin had a beguiling personality. Both Roosevelt and Truman were charmed in their early meetings. Roosevelt, who often called Stalin Uncle Joe, declared Stalin a man he "could do business with." When warned by his Russian ambassador that Stalin couldn't be trusted, Roosevelt retorted, "He doesn't want anything but security for his country, and I think if I give him everything I possibly can and ask for nothing in return, noblesse oblige, he won't try to annex anything and will work with me for a world of democracy and peace."[23] Roosevelt even promoted a 1943 war propaganda film, *Mission to Moscow*, which whitewashed Soviet atrocities and portrayed Stalin as a far-sighted, responsible, and honest statesman.

Stalin, Truman and Churchill at the Potsdam Conference in July 1945. "Uncle Joe" Stalin charmed both Roosevelt and Truman. Stalin promised both men free elections in Eastern Europe; a promise soon broken.   PICTORIAL PRESS LTD/ALAMY

Shortly before he died, Roosevelt began to realize his error. At the Yalta Conference in February 1945, Roosevelt, Stalin, and Churchill agreed that in exchange for the Soviet Union's promise to enter the war against Japan, the Soviets would be given responsibility for the postwar reconstruction in the Eastern European countries bordering the Soviet Union. Since the Soviets pledged to allow free elections, Churchill and Roosevelt left the conference believing they had secured, and not sold out, Eastern Europe. But hardly a month after the conference ended the Soviets intervened in Romania, forcing the installation of a Soviet puppet to head the government. The United States and the United Kingdom refused to recognize the new regime. Three weeks before his death Roosevelt told an acquaintance, "We can't do business with Stalin. He has broken every one of the promises he made at Yalta."[24]

Truman fell under the same spell when he met Stalin at the Potsdam Conference in July 1945. "I can deal with Stalin," Truman wrote in his diary. "He is honest—but smart as hell."[25] Truman wrote his wife, Bess, "I like Stalin. He is straightforward, knows what he wants and will compromise when he can't get it."[26] As late as 1948, after the Cold War had begun, Truman didn't blame Stalin. "I got very well acquainted with Joe Stalin, and I like Old Joe!" Truman informed his diary. "He is a decent fellow. But Joe is a prisoner of the Politburo."

In one of history's many ironies, Truman, who liked Old Joe, would soon lead a Cold War against Soviet aggression. That war would include the Truman Doctrine, Marshall Plan, Berlin Airlift, North American Treaty Alliance, and the Korean Conflict.

The Birth of the Cold War

Two events in early 1946 encapsulated the struggle that was developing between the free world and the Soviet Union. On February 22, George F. Kennan, an American diplomat stationed in Moscow, sent a 5,300-word telegram to Washington D.C. warning that the Soviet Union was a threat to world order and must be contained. Famous within diplomatic circles as the "Long Telegram," Kennan's missive opened with a 1927 quote from Stalin:

In course of further development of international revolution there will emerge two centers of world significance: a socialist center, drawing to itself the countries which tend toward socialism, and a capitalist center, drawing to itself the countries that incline toward capitalism. Battle between these two centers for command of world economy will decide fate of capitalism and of communism in entire world.[27]

Two weeks after Kennan's telegram, Winston Churchill gave a historic speech at Westminster College in Fulton, Missouri. "An Iron Curtain," Churchill declared, "has descended across the Continent. Behind that line lie... what I must call the Soviet sphere, and all are subject in one form or another, not only to Soviet influence but to a very high and, in many cases, increasing measure of control from Moscow."[28]

Kennan's Long Telegram and Churchill's Iron Curtain speech framed the beginning of the Cold War. Kennan captured the issues which would drive American foreign policy over the next forty-five years. Churchill dramatically informed the western world that a new adversary had emerged, an adversary intent on world domination.

The challenges that Kennan had written about took substance on March 12, 1947. For 200 years, Great Britain, as the world's superpower, had fought to maintain its view of world order: in North America against the French and American colonists; in Europe against Napoleon; in Crimea against Russia; in China during the Boxer Rebellion; and in Europe during two World Wars. But by 1947, Britain, exhausted and near bankruptcy from the war, was turning inward and shedding much of its empire and international role. That year Britain informed the United States it could no longer provide financial aid to Greece and Turkey which were under threat of communist takeovers supported by the Soviet Union. Before a joint session of Congress on March 12, President Truman requested $400 million in financial aid for the two countries. Within his speech was a proclamation, only slightly more than 100 words, that would steer American foreign policy for seventy years:

At the present moment in world history nearly every nation must choose between alternative ways of life. The choice is too often not a free one. One way of life is based upon the will of the majority, and is distinguished by free institutions, representative government, free elections, guarantees of individual liberty, freedom of speech and religion, and freedom from political oppression. The second way of life is based upon the will of a minority forcibly imposed upon the majority. It relies upon terror and oppression, a controlled press and radio; fixed elections, and the suppression of personal freedoms. I believe that it must be the policy of the United States to support free peoples who are resisting attempted subjugation by armed minorities or by outside pressures.[29]

Truman's declaration that the United States would assume the global role of freedom's safe keeper became known as the Truman Doctrine. Within months, the doctrine would transform America's postwar plans for Germany.

Rebuilding Europe

In 1944, Roosevelt's Secretary of the Treasury, Henry Morgenthau, Jr., had proposed a postwar plan to assure Germany would never again wage war. The plan called for dismantling German industry and "converting Germany into a country primarily agricultural and pastoral in its character."[30] Unfortunately, the plan was widely publicized inside Germany and Germany's Minister of Propaganda, Joseph Goebbels, capitalized on the publicity to spread anger and fear within Germany by claiming the Allies intended to turn a defeated Germany "into a giant potato patch." One American colonel claimed Goebbels's threat was "worth thirty divisions to the Germans." A Swiss newspaper wrote "[the Morgenthau Plan called for] the enslavement of Germany. . . [and] accounts for the fact that the Germans continue to fight. It is not a question of a regime, but of the homeland itself, and to save that, every German is bound to obey the call, whether he be Nazi or member of the opposition."[31]

The Morgenthau Plan was never officially adopted, but its philosophy affected America's immediate postwar strategy. American military commanders occupying Germany in 1945 were instructed that other than providing minimal sustenance to the German population, they should "take no steps (a) looking toward the economic rehabilitation of Germany, or (b) designed to maintain or strengthen the German economy."[32] By early 1946, German steel production was capped at 25 percent of its pre-war level and 1,500 manufacturing plants were closed.

But growing Soviet influence throughout Europe was becoming a greater threat than German rearmament. With surreptitious Soviet backing, communist political parties were growing stronger throughout Europe, especially in Czechoslovakia, France, and Italy. Germany was also susceptible. One American general warned that for a starving German, "there is no choice between being a communist on 1,500 calories a day and a believer in democracy on 1,000 calories."[33]

In January 1947 Truman sent former President Herbert Hoover to Austria and Germany to ascertain postwar conditions in those two countries. Hoover had led America's humanitarian efforts in Europe and Russia after World War I. In March, Hoover reported:

> There is the illusion that the New Germany left after the annexations can be reduced to a pastoral state. It cannot be done unless we exterminate or move 25,000,000 people out of it. . . . The whole economy of Europe is interlinked with the German economy through the exchange of raw materials and manufactured goods. The productivity of Europe cannot be restored without the restoration of Germany as a contributor to that productivity.[34]

The War Department supported Hoover's conclusions, but the State Department, headed by former South Carolina Senator James Byrnes, fiercely opposed German reconstruction, concerned about a resumption of German militancy.

Truman sided with Hoover, as did Truman's newly appointed Secretary of State, George Marshall. Marshall had served as Chief of Staff of the Army from 1939 through 1945 and well understood the issues both surrounding the conduct of war and the maintenance of a successful peace. In July 1947, Marshall reversed the former German suppression policy declaring, "An orderly and prosperous Europe requires the economic contributions of a stable and productive Germany."[35] Germany, rather than being turned into Goebbels' giant potato patch, would be rebuilt into a manufacturing super-power.

On a broader scale, rebuilding Western Europe as a bulwark against the Soviet Union became the first application of the Truman Doctrine. After five years of war, Europe was bankrupt and struggling to finance its reconstruction. Secretary Marshall proposed that the United States help Europe rebuild by providing loans and outright grants. Congress passed the Marshall Plan in early 1948. Over the next four years, the plan distributed $12.7 billion ($136 billion in 2020 dollars) in financial aid to Europe. The United Kingdom, France, and West Germany were the largest benefactors, but even tiny Iceland received $43 million in American aid. Much of the funding quickly returned home to the States as Europeans imported American food, fuel, and industrial goods. The United States also offered aid to the Soviet Union and its Eastern European allies. The Soviets immediately rejected the offer and, fearing American intrusion into their own sphere of influence, pressured their Eastern European allies to do so also. All complied except Yugoslavia, which accepted American aid.

The Marshall Plan helped jump-start the European economies. But no country benefited more than West Germany. From 1948 through 1960 West Germany's real GDP per capita grew an average of 9.2 percent annually, far surpassing its former foes France and the United Kingdom.[36] West German economic growth was so strong the Germans named it *Wirtschaftswunder*, the "economic miracle."

America's role in countering the communist threat didn't stop with the Marshall Plan. Starting in 1948, the United States was challenged by four successive events that together tested the resolve of an American President as few have before or since: the Berlin Blockade, the detonation of a Soviet atomic bomb, the communist take-over of China, and the invasion of South Korea.

The Cold War Heats Up

During the Potsdam Conference in July 1945, the United States, United Kingdom, France, and the Soviet Union agreed to partition Germany into four occupation zones each administered by one of the four powers. The zone held by the Soviets would eventually become East Germany; the other three zones, West Germany. Although Berlin lay deep inside the Soviet zone, it was agreed the city would also be divided into four occupation zones, turning Berlin into a microcosm of the broader Cold War.

By 1948, the Soviets had become concerned that the growing economies of the West German zones would threaten their domination in East Germany. When the United States, Britain, and France unilaterally issued a new currency, the Deutsche Mark, to replace the debased Reichsmark, the Soviets retaliated on June 24, 1948 by closing all water and land connections to Berlin from the west. West Berlin was left with little more than a month's supply of food.

Within days, American and British transport planes were flying in food, fuel, and medicine. The Berlin Airlift was only expected to run for three weeks. It lasted eleven months. By the end of the airlift, over 5,000 tons of supplies were being delivered daily, filling hundreds of aircraft. Ground operations in Berlin were so tightly controlled that flight crews were not allowed to leave their aircraft. Instead, mobile wagons managed by pretty German fraüleins delivered meals and other items to the waiting crews.[37]

Beaten and humiliated, the Soviets agreed to negotiate an end to the blockade on May 12, 1949. In its resistance to a tyrannical adversary, in its logistical success, and in its magnanimity to a defeated enemy, the Berlin Airlift was one of America's finest moments.

The Soviets hoped its blockade of Berlin would weaken the resolve of Western Europe and the United States. It had the opposite effect. Even before the Soviets reopened Berlin, twelve western nations—Belgium, Canada, Denmark, France, Iceland, Italy, Luxembourg, the Netherlands, Norway, Portugal, the United Kingdom, and the United States—signed an agreement that founded the North Atlantic Treaty Organization (NATO). NATO's charter stipulated "an armed attack against one or more [NATO members] in Europe or North America shall be considered an attack against them all."[38] NATO grew out of two earlier European efforts to establish mutual-defense alliances. In 1947, Britain and France signed the Dunkirk Treaty to guard against future German aggression. A year later and just weeks before the Soviets closed Berlin, Belgium, France, the United Kingdom, Luxembourg, and the Netherlands signed the broader Brussels Treaty on

March 17, 1948. The Treaty stipulated that "If any of the [treaty members] should be the object of an armed attack in Europe [the other treaty members] will afford the Party so attacked all the military and other aid and assistance in their power."[39]

The Brussels Treaty implicitly acknowledged that the Soviet Union had replaced Germany as Europe's greatest threat. During the war, the Soviets outright annexed Estonia, Latvia, Lithuania, eastern Finland, Poland, Romania, northeastern Germany, and eastern Czechoslovakia. After the war, the Soviet Union employed political intrigue and the threat of its massive Red Army to turn Albania, Bulgaria, Romania, East Germany, Poland, Hungary, and the remainder of Czechoslovakia into Soviet satellites. By 1948, eighty-seven million non-Russians had fallen under the Soviet Sphere.

The same day the Brussels Treaty was signed, President Truman told Congress, "I am sure that the determination of the free countries of Europe to protect themselves will be matched by an equal determination on our part to help them." Truman understood, as did everyone, that the Europeans alone would never have been able to defend themselves against a Soviet invasion. But, as the French prime minister wryly observed, by the time the United States mustered the political will to intervene, American troops might be doing little more than "liberating a corpse."[40]

By mid-1948, just weeks after the start of the Berlin Blockade, talks were underway between the Brussels Treaty members and the United States and Canada for an alliance that spanned the North Atlantic. Over the next nine months, Denmark, Iceland, Italy, Norway, and Portugal joined the negotiations. Although the Soviet Union tried to block the alliance by claiming, with some justification, it violated the United Nations charter, the twelve countries signed the NATO treaty on April 4, 1949.

By then it was understood the United Nations would be ineffective in countering Soviet expansion. The U.N. charter required a unanimous vote by all five permanent members of the Security Council—China, France, United Kingdom, United States, and the Soviet Union—to authorize U.N. intervention in the cases of aggression of one nation against another. The

Soviets could hardly be expected to vote to deploy U.N. troops against themselves.

As a condition for their support for the original United Nations charter, the Soviets had demanded that a unanimous vote be required to authorize U.N. military intervention. Today, that's seen as a crippling requirement, but in 1944 and 1945 as the charter was being negotiated, the world had been devastated by a war that left over fifty million dead. After the most horrific war in history, why would any Security Council member oppose UN intervention against military aggression? But that optimism quickly faded after the Soviet Union, and to a lesser extent China, began a program of worldwide, communist expansion.

Within months, two new Cold War events stunned the free world.

On September 3, 1949, an Air Force reconnaissance aircraft detected radiation over the North Pacific. U.S. intelligence quickly concluded that the Soviet Union had detonated its first atomic bomb. American intelligence knew the Soviets were developing a nuclear weapon but believed its successful completion was still years in the future. They were stunned that the supposedly backward Soviets had developed a bomb just four years after the United States.[41]

Later it was learned that at least four Soviet spies had infiltrated the Manhattan Project, the secret mission to develop an atomic bomb during the war. One spy, Klaus Fuchs, was convicted of espionage in a British court and spent nine years in prison. He fled to East Germany upon release where he resumed his scientific career and received numerous awards from the East German government. Julius and Ethel Rosenberg were not so fortunate. They were tried, convicted, and sentenced to death in the United States during a controversial trial. Although they could have saved their lives by confessing and naming co-conspirators, they never did, suggesting to many that they were innocent. After personal appeals for clemency by numerous prominent individuals ranging from Albert Einstein to Pablo Picasso, the couple were executed minutes apart in Sing Sing's electric chair on June 19, 1953. (In 1995, decrypted Soviet intelligence documents confirmed Julius and Ethel Rosenberg had been Soviet agents, but their role in connection with revealing atomic secrets remains ambiguous.)

Nine days after President Truman announced the Soviets had developed an atomic bomb, Americans were again shocked when they learned China had fallen to the communists.

The Chinese Nationalists, known as the Republic of China (ROC), had been fighting a relentless communist insurgency for over two decades. The civil war slowed during World War II as the ROC, as American allies, fought the Japanese invaders. But fighting resumed fiercely as the war ended. Although the ROC had American support and financial aid, the communists fought a brilliant war of attrition during which the ROC suffered millions of casualties. Truman tried to broker peace between the two factions, but after years of bitter fighting, it was impossible to reach an agreement. By August 1949, the Truman administration concluded that a communist victory was inevitable. Less than two months later, on October 1, the communist leader, Mao Zedong, proclaimed the founding of the People's Republic of China. Two million ROC soldiers and their leader, Chiang Kai-shek, fled to the island of Taiwan. While Washington knew the defeat of the ROC was inevitable, the American public was shocked. Truman's political opponents capitalized on the loss when they proclaimed that it was Truman's incompetence that was responsible for "losing China" to the communists.[42]

Ironically, it was the Chinese Nationalists' alliance with the United States during the war which contributed to their defeat by the communists. Years later, when Japanese Prime Minister Kakuei apologized to Chairman Mao for Japan's invasion of China, Mao told the prime minister to relax. The Chinese Nationalists, Mao explained, had been depleted fighting the Japanese alongside the Americans during the war, enabling a communist victory when the civil war resumed after 1945.

By late 1949, it was apparent that a fundamental change in the world order had occurred. An Iron Curtain had been drawn dividing communist Eastern and democratic Western Europe, the Soviet Union had become a nuclear power, and the world's most populous country, China, had turned communist. How should America respond?

Secretary of State Dean Acheson would answer that question when he commissioned a study by the National Security Council in early 1950. The resulting top-secret report, the legendary NSC-68, is one of the most influential white papers ever published by American Intelligence. It's a remarkably clear-headed document that opens with a summary of the tremendous change the world had undergone during the first half of the twentieth century:

> Within the past thirty-five years the world has experienced two global wars of tremendous violence. It has witnessed two revolutions—the Russian and the Chinese—of extreme scope and intensity. It has also seen the collapse of five empires—the Ottoman, the Austro-Hungarian, German, Italian and Japanese—and the drastic decline of two major imperial systems, the British and the French. During the span of one generation, the international distribution of power has been fundamentally altered.[43]

Replacing the old order were the United States and the Soviet Union. "The Soviet Union, unlike previous aspirants to hegemony," the report warned, "is animated by a new fanatic faith, antithetical to our own, and seeks to impose its absolute order over the rest of the world."

The report presented four options to address the Soviet threat: (1) the continuation of current policies; (2) a return to isolationism; (3) a deliberate war against the Soviet Union in the near future; or (4) a rapid build-up of political, economic, and military strength in the free world. The committee recommended the fourth option as the only realistic approach "to wrest the initiative from the Soviet Union, confront it with convincing evidence of the determination and ability of the free world to frustrate the Kremlin design of a world dominated by its will [and] is the only means short of war which eventually may force the Kremlin to abandon its current course of action..."

The NSC-68 report took a step beyond the Truman Doctrine. Rather than a passive policy of containment, the United States would now preemptively, through massive political and military power, discourage Soviet aggression around the world. The report acknowledged the strategy would require a substantial increase in military spending funded by tax increases and spending reductions in other areas.

Naturally, there was opposition. America was still recovering from the massive human and financial costs of World War II. Surely, Soviet ambitions could be countered by means other than returning the United States to a wartime economy. A little more than two months after the report was published, events on June 25, 1950 swept away nearly all opposition.

The Forgotten War

Over the centuries China, Russia, and Japan had fought over Korea. Korea bordered China and Russia, vastly larger countries, which coveted the peninsula as a natural extension of their own territory. As a peninsula protruding deep into the Sea of Japan, Japan considered Korea to be "a dagger pointed at the heart of Japan" were it to be occupied by either of its much larger neighbors.[44] After fighting two wars from 1894–1895 with China and 1904–1905 with Russia, by 1910 a triumphant Japan had annexed Korea. A brutal occupier, Japan conscripted hundreds of thousands of Koreans during World War II as soldiers, laborers, and "comfort women" assigned to the Japanese military.

In 1941, to protect its eastern border, Russia signed a neutrality pact with Japan. But on August 8, 1945, two days after the United States dropped the atomic bomb on Hiroshima, an opportunistic Russia tore up the pact and declared war on Japan. Then on August 14, conveniently just one day before Emperor Hirohito declared Japan's surrender, the Soviet Union invaded Japanese-occupied Korea, assuring it would play a role in Korea's postwar fate. Shortly after the war ended, Korea was divided into two occupation zones separated by the thirty-eighth parallel of latitude: the northern zone administered by the Soviet Union and the southern zone by the United States. The division was meant to be temporary until a unified Korean government could be established.[45] But after two years of negotiations the United Nations was unable to unify the country and in 1948 officially split Korea into two countries: North Korea, a communist country supported by China and the Soviet Union, and South Korea, a capitalist country with American support.

Two years later, encouraged by the communist victory in the Chinese Civil War, North Korean troops invaded South Korea on June 25, 1950. Caught by surprise, the South Korean troops were quickly routed. Three days later North Korean troops captured Seoul, the South Korean capital. After United Nations diplomacy failed to stop the fighting, on June 27 President Truman declared that the United States would intervene. The United Nations (with the Soviet Union boycotting the Security Council and China still represented by the friendly government in Taiwan) approved military action against North Korea and named General Douglas MacArthur as commander of the U.N. forces. MacArthur, a World War II hero, was one of America's most popular military leaders.

By September 30, MacArthur had driven the North Koreans back to the North Korean border when China Premier Chou En-lai issued a statement warning that China would intervene if U.N. troops crossed into North Korea. Under MacArthur's orders, U.N. troops ignored China's warning and crossed the border the next day. By October 19, Pyongyang, North Korea's capital, had been captured. MacArthur, confident China would not enter the war, then pushed his troops westward toward the Chinese border.

On November 25 China struck, sending a force of 300,000 troops into North Korea. MacArthur's troops were caught totally by surprise and took heavy losses. China would soon commit over a million troops to the battle. Unless the United States was willing to use nuclear weapons, the war had become unwinnable.

MacArthur had recklessly brought China into the war and then advocated for the use of nuclear weapons to attack North Korean supply lines inside China, actions that surely would have precipitated a major Asian war, perhaps even a third world war. Blocked by Truman, MacArthur attempted an end-run around the President and sent a letter to Congress asking for its support. "[My] views are well known and clearly understood," MacArthur wrote. "as they follow the conventional pattern of meeting force with maximum counterforce, as we have never failed to do in the past."[46]

Truman fired MacArthur on April 11, 1951. Not only had MacArthur's conduct of the war been reckless, MacArthur's political intervention with Congress threatened the President's role as commander in chief.

Years earlier, MacArthur had used "maximum counterforce" in 1932 when he drove impoverished World War I veterans from their Washington camp burning their belongings behind them. The scandal contributed to Herbert Hoover's presidential campaign loss that year. President Roosevelt called MacArthur the most dangerous man in America, telling an aide, "You saw how he strutted down Pennsylvania Avenue.... Did you ever see anyone more self-satisfied? There's a potential Mussolini for you."[47]

In 1951, maximum counterforce meant nuclear weapons, an escalation that President Truman was unwilling to take.

MacArthur returned to a hero's welcome. Truman's popularity plummeted. But never again did the military challenge the President's authority as commander-in-chief.

The Korean Conflict dragged on until July 1953 when President Eisenhower, fulfilling a campaign promise, negotiated an armistice between North Korea, China, and the United States. South Korea, refusing to accept a divided Korea, never signed the armistice. When the war ended, nearly three million people had been killed: 37,000 Americans, 217,000 South Koreans, 406,000 North Koreans, 600,000 Chinese soldiers and 1.6 million civilians.[48]

Falling between World War II and the Vietnam War, historians often call the Korean Conflict the "Forgotten War." But Truman's conduct of the war set three precedents which, to this day, have driven America's approach to war.

First, the United States would no longer pursue unlimited warfare, even if it meant stalemate or defeat. Truman realized that nuclear weapons and the massive armies maintained by China and the Soviet Union had made unlimited war far too dangerous.

Second, by firing MacArthur, Truman reasserted unquestioned civilian control over the military. Although MacArthur was hugely popular—Gallup ranked MacArthur the most admired man in American in 1946 and 1947[49]—Truman fired him with no hesitation. "I fired MacArthur because he wouldn't respect the authority of the President," Truman said. "I didn't fire him because he was a dumb son of a bitch, although he was."[50]

Lastly, Truman, by declaring America's entry into the Korean Conflict a "police action," avoided the need for a Congressional Declaration of War. Article I, Section 8, Clause 11 of the Constitution states: "The Congress shall have power to... provide for the common defence...[and] to raise and support armies."[51] Until the Korean Conflict, it was Congress, not the President, that was responsible for initiating war against the nation's enemies.

In 1951, the Senate Armed Services Committee and the Senate Foreign Relations Committee held a joint inquiry into the conduct of the war. One of the major topics was Constitutional control over the military. Their final report emphasized, "The United States should never again become involved in war without the consent of the Congress."[52]

Unfortunately, Presidents ever since have ignored that directive, a Constitutional breach that Congress has seldom challenged. It was one of Truman's greatest mistakes. Since 1950, over 100,000 American soldiers have died fighting wars that Congress never ratified.

Vietnam: a Lost Opportunity

History largely remembers Harry Truman for his roles in Europe and Korea, but he also made decisions in Southeast Asia and the Middle East whose implications echo yet today.

By the late nineteenth century, France had absorbed Cambodia, Laos, and Vietnam into its colonial empire. Known collectively as French Indochina, the French treated the three countries as *colonies d'exploitation économique,* or "colonies of economic exploitation," to be harvested for their natural resources and cheap labor. Although the French-built railroads, bridges, and roads throughout Indochina, the indigenous population remained impoverished. "France has had the country, thirty million inhabitants, for nearly one hundred years," President Roosevelt declared in 1945, "and the people are worse off than they were at the beginning.... France has milked it for 100 years. The people of Indochina are entitled to something better than that."[53] Roosevelt was strongly anti-colonial. Earlier, during a 1941 meeting, Roosevelt lectured Winston Churchill:

> [Colonialism] takes wealth in raw materials out of a colonial country, but... returns nothing to the people of that country in

consideration.... Twentieth century methods include increasing the wealth of a people by increasing their standard of living, by educating them, by bringing them sanitation, by making sure that they get a return for the raw wealth of their community.... I can't believe that we can fight a war against fascist slavery, and at the same time not work to free people all over the world from a backward colonial policy.[54]

Roosevelt's feelings against European colonialism were well understood and made anti-colonial movements across the globe hopeful. In 1945, Vietnam experienced one of these movements. Tragically, it wasn't successful.

Imperial Japan occupied Vietnam during the war, enjoying Vichy French support. But unlike the compliant French, the Vietnamese patriot Hồ Chí Minh led a guerrilla war against the Japanese with the support of the U.S. Office of Strategic Services (OSS).[55] Hồ Chí Minh considered the United States a friend, having lived in America as a young man where, from 1911 through 1913, he worked at Boston's Parker House Hotel baking Parker House Rolls and Boston Crème Pies.[56]

On September 2, 1945, just weeks after Japan's surrender, Hồ Chí Minh declared Vietnam a free country before a Hanoi crowd of hundreds of thousands. It was an eloquent speech that any American revolutionary would have been proud to have given. Appealing for American support, Hồ Chí Minh opened his speech by quoting the Declaration of Independence:

> "All men are created equal. They are endowed by their Creator with certain inalienable Rights; among these are Life, Liberty, and the pursuit of Happiness." This immortal statement was made in the Declaration of Independence of the United States of America in 1776... We are convinced that the Allies, which at the Teheran and San Francisco Conferences upheld the principle of equality among the nations, cannot fail to recognize the right of the Vietnamese people to independence.[57]

This was the second time Hồ Chí Minh had petitioned an American President to help Vietnam obtain freedom from France. In 1919, Minh sent a letter to President Wilson, at the time attending the Versailles Peace

Conference reordering the world after the First World War, asking for assistance to free Vietnam. Wilson did not respond.

Hồ Chí Minh (standing second from left) was an American ally during World War II fighting alongside the American OSS against the Japanese. After the war, Minh asked Truman to support Vietnam's bid for independence from French colonial rule. His request was ignored.   ARMY CENTER OF MILITARY HISTORY

Neither did Truman, assuming that he was even aware of Minh's speech. Nor did he respond a few weeks later, after Ming sent Truman a personal letter pleading for American support in Vietnam's battle for independence from the French. On February 28, 1946, Minh sent Truman a second letter urging "the American people to interfere urgently in support of our independence... in keeping with the Atlantic and San Francisco Charters."[58] The Atlantic Charter had been jointly issued by Great Britain and the United States in 1941 to define their goals for a postwar world. One of its key provisions was "the right of all peoples to choose the form of government under which they will live."[59]

It's not known whether Truman saw Minh's letters. Whatever the case, the Truman administration was unmoved. On April 10, 1946, Secretary of State James Byrnes wired the French ambassador congratulating him for signing an agreement with the Chinese. The agreement allowed French colonial troops to reoccupy Indochina and complete "the reversion of all Indochina to French control."[60] (Earlier, Byrnes had advocated turning Germany into a pastoral country. In January 1947, Truman replaced Byrnes as Secretary of State with George Marshall.)

Within months it was clear that efforts to assure peace in Southeast Asia had failed. An August 9 State Department memo stated:

> The French are attempting to gain [control of Indochina] by maneuvers designed to confine and weaken Viet Nam. In the event that Viet Nam decides to resist these encroachments, which is by no means unlikely, widespread hostilities may result... The crux of the present situation lies in the apparent intention of the French to settle [the Indochina dispute] to their own advantage and without reference to Viet Nam... [potentially leading to] a long and bitter military operation.[61]

Hồ Chí Minh tried four times but was unable to persuade the United States to back his peaceful efforts to free Vietnam from French colonial rule. Wilson ignored him and Truman was preoccupied with postwar Europe and Japan. The pleas of an obscure Asian country were hardly noticed. Truman's failure to recognize Hồ Chí Minh's plea for independence was one of America's greatest lost opportunities.

China and the Soviet Union, with no allegiance to France, recognized Vietnam as a free country in 1950. China was soon providing Vietnam with military supplies for their war against the French. Hồ Chí Minh was pleased to accept China's aid while his top general, Vo Nguyen Giap, based his military strategy on America's War of Independence: employ guerrilla tactics, avoid major defeats, wear the enemy down, and eventually make it too expensive in blood and treasure for the enemy to continue.

To counter Chinese support, the United States provided the French military aid which soon reached $1.0 billion ($9.6 billion in 2020 dollars) annually. But even with massive American support, by 1954, after an overwhelming defeat at Dien Bien Phu, the French had had enough and withdrew from Indochina. As a condition of their withdrawal, the French stipulated that Vietnam be divided along the 17th parallel, ruled in the north by Hồ Chí Minh's communist government, and in the south by Bảo Đại, the last emperor of Vietnam's Nguyen dynasty, and a Japanese puppet installed during the war.[62]

A year later, North and South Vietnam fell into civil war. With the opposing sides supported by the United States and China, the Vietnam War continued for twenty years. A tragedy of lost opportunity, the war cost 58,000 American and millions of Vietnamese lives. Hồ Chí Minh, the diminutive former baker of Boston Crème Pies and admirer of the United States Constitution, ultimately prevailed over the mighty United States.

The Birth of Israel

President Truman played a critical role in the establishment of Israel. But he didn't do so out of benevolence towards Jews. No, his actions were guided, like so many others during his presidency, by the Cold War. It's a complicated story that began fifty years earlier.

The modern movement for a Jewish homeland arose in 1897 during the First Zionist Congress held in Basel, Switzerland. At its conclusion, the Congress called for "a home for the Jewish people in Palestine secured under public law." The founder of the Zionist movement, Theodor Herzl, knowing a Jewish homeland was still many years in the future, confided to his diary, "At Basel I founded the Jewish State. If I said this out loud today, I would be greeted by universal laughter. In five years perhaps, and certainly in fifty years, everyone will perceive it."[63] Herzl's prediction was remarkably prophetic: fifty-one years after the Basel Congress, the state of Israel was born.

For 400 years Palestine, the ancient Jewish homeland, had been part of the Ottoman Empire, ruled from what is now modern Turkey. At its peak, the Empire spread from the Balkan countries in the north to Persia in the east and then westward into North Africa. But in 1897 the Empire began a steep decline that culminated in 1918 when Germany and its Italian and Ottoman allies lost the First World War.

From 1915 through 1917 Britain, to assure the support of the Arabs and the Jews during the war made each a promise, promises which would sow conflict in the Middle East for a century. In a series of ten letters exchanged during 1915 and 1916, the British promised the rulers of Mecca a permanent Arab country within Syria after the war. A year later, on November 2, 1917, the British Foreign Secretary Arthur Balfour wrote a letter to Lord Rothschild, the leader of the British Jewish community, stating:

> His Majesty's government view with favour the establishment in Palestine of a national home for the Jewish people and will use their best endeavours to facilitate the achievement of this object, it being clearly understood that nothing shall be done which may prejudice the civil and religious rights of existing non-Jewish communities in Palestine, or the rights and political status enjoyed by Jews in any other country.[64]

Balfour's letter, known today as the Balfour Declaration, was the first statement of support for a Jewish state by a major country. But Britain had also made a secret pact, the Sykes-Picot Agreement, with France in 1916 to partition the Ottoman Empire between themselves once it was defeated. Even then, oil was driving Middle Eastern politics. The Anglo-Persian oil refinery in Abadan, Persia was one of the world's largest.

Despite losing the First World War, Germany remained intact. But its ally, the Ottoman Empire, was dismembered in 1922. Turkey became a republic and its former Ottoman territories were divided among Britain, France, Greece, and Russia. The League of Nations, influenced by the Sykes-Picot Agreement, gave Britain a mandate to govern Palestine until 1948. Echoing the Balfour Declaration, the League assigned Britain responsibility for establishing a Jewish homeland while also safeguarding the rights of Palestine's Arab inhabitants. The Arabs, quite understandably, believed the British had betrayed them.

The need for a Jewish homeland became critical in the nineteen-thirties as European Jews fled Nazi persecution. In 1939, the British called a conference to negotiate the establishment of independent Arab and Jewish states within Palestine. The Arabs refused to even meet in the same room as the Jews. Unwilling to share a conference room, there was little possibility they would share a country. The conference ended in failure.[65] Still, Jewish immigration to Palestine continued sporadically throughout World War II, then surged after the war as Holocaust survivors flooded into Palestine despite Britain's effort to stop the Jewish influx.

In 1947, with Britain's Palestinian mandate expiring the next year, the newly-formed United Nations passed a resolution providing detailed terms for dividing Palestine into independent Arab and Jewish states. Although the resolution passed, it was stillborn. Every Arab state vetoed the resolution, making its peaceful implementation impossible.[66] For fifty years the Jewish movement had worked patiently through international channels to establish a Jewish homeland with little success. That would soon change.

On May 14, 1948, the British Mandate in Palestine ended. The same day, David Ben-Gurion, head of the World Zionist Organization, issued the Israeli Declaration of Independence proclaiming Israel an independent state. Minutes later, President Truman announced America's recognition of Ben-Gurion's provisional government as the *de facto* Israeli government.

Less than a week before Ben-Gurion's proclamation the United States was still undecided on the Israel statehood issue. Secretary of State George Marshall was strongly against recognizing an independent Israel until the Arab issues were resolved, believing Israeli independence would only lead to more conflict and threaten Arab oil production. Marshall argued instead for a United Nations compromise to establish a neutral trusteeship in Palestine to oversee the Arab and Jewish regions.[67]

Barely a week before the expiration of the mandate, an eight-page memo issued on May 9, not by the State Department but by the White House legal counsel, framed the pros and cons of recognizing Israel were it to declare independence. The memo recommended the immediate recognition of Israel, concluding:

> The chief advantage resulting from American recognition of the Jewish will be lost if prompt action is not taken by the President. The Soviet Union and its satellites are expected to recognize the state promptly. Once they have already recognized the Jewish state, any similar action on our part will seem begrudging—no matter how well-intentioned. In fact, it would be a diplomatic defeat.[68]

The Truman administration knew the Soviet Union sought to establish strongholds in the Middle East and that Israel would be a natural ally of the Soviets. For centuries, much of the Jewish diaspora had lived in the Russian Empire and later the Soviet Union. Jewish immigrants were also far more socialist than capitalist. Even before Israel was established, Jews had adopted Marxist practices in their collective farms, or Kibbutzim. No private property was allowed; rather, the Kibbutz leadership allocated all property and assigned jobs. Even children were collective property raised by Kibbutz teachers and allowed to see their parents only a few hours a day.[69]

Weighing all this, Truman reluctantly overruled Marshall, a man he greatly admired and trusted. With Europe now divided by the Iron Curtain, Truman believed the United States could not allow the Soviets to gain a foothold in the Middle East. It was imperative that the United States block the Soviets and be the first to embrace Israel.

As a concession to Marshall, the United States on May 14 granted Israel *de facto* recognition rather than *de jure* recognition. Within diplomatic circles *de facto* recognition merely recognizes the reality that a government has control over a territory but connotes no legal authority; *de jure* recognition is full diplomatic and legal recognition of a state. Ironically, the Soviet Union was the first country to announce *de jure* recognition of Israeli on May 17. It wasn't until 1949 after Israel had its first elections that the United States granted the new country *de jure* recognition.[70]

There's an ugly irony to Truman's political support of Israel. If not outright anti-Semitic, Truman seemed to dislike Jews based on his diary entry written the evening of July 21, 1947:

> Had ten minutes conversation with Henry Morgenthau about Jewish ship in Palestine. Told him I would talk to General Marshall about it. He'd no business to call me. The Jews have no sense of proportion nor do they have any judgement on world affairs. Henry brought a thousand Jews to New York on a supposedly temporary basis and they stayed. When the country went backward—and Republican—in the election of 1946 this incident loomed large on the [Displaced Persons] program. The Jews, I find are very selfish. They care not how many Estonians, Latvians, Finns, Poles, Yugoslavs or

Greeks are murdered or mistreated as [Displaced Persons] as long as the Jews get special treatment. Yet when they have power, physical, financial or political neither Hitler nor Stalin has anything on them for cruelty or mistreatment to the underdog. Put an underdog on top and it makes no difference whether his name is Russian, Jewish, Negro, Management, Labor, Mormon, Baptist he goes haywire. I've found very, very few who remember their past condition when prosperity comes. Look at the Congress attitude on [Displaced Persons]—and they all come from [Displaced Persons].[71]

Were Truman's diary comments regarding Jews the frustrated rantings of a tired President after a long day (perhaps after a glass or two of bourbon), or were they his true feelings? Regardless, Israel owes much to Harry Truman.

The Second Bill of Rights

Although President Truman was largely focused on foreign affairs, he made two domestic programs a priority: the expansion of Roosevelt's New Deal policies and universal healthcare.

On September 6, 1945, four days after Japan officially surrendered, Truman presented a Special Message to Congress outlining a twenty-one-point economic and political plan for a postwar America. Embedded in his plan was a reminder to Congress of the so-called second Bill of Rights presented by President Roosevelt in 1944 as his postwar political agenda. Roosevelt's Bill of Rights proposed every American should have the right to a remunerative job, own a decent home, obtain a good education, receive adequate medical care, and be free from economic fears resulting from old age, sickness, accidents, and unemployment.

Many objected to Roosevelt's, and now Truman's concept of the government taking responsibility for its citizens' welfare, believing instead that the American spirit was embodied by what former President Herbert Hoover called Rugged Individualism. Upon being nominated for President, Hoover declared: "My country owes me no debt. It gave me, as it gives every boy and girl, a chance.... In no other land could a boy from a country village, without inheritance or influential friends, look forward with unbounded hope."[72]

Truman's economic agenda was successful, quickly restoring the country to a robust peace-time economy. But his ambitious social agenda had limited success. Congress did pass the Employment Act of 1946 but it had little teeth, simply declaring it was the policy of the federal government to "to foster and promote free competitive enterprise and the general welfare; conditions under which there will be afforded useful employment for those able, willing, and seeking to work; and to promote maximum employment, production, and purchasing power."

In 1947 Truman submitted a ten-point agenda for securing civil rights reform, later saying, "My forebears were Confederates... but my very stomach turned over when I learned that Negro soldiers, just back from overseas, were being dumped out of Army trucks in Mississippi and beaten."[73] African-Americans had greatly contributed to the war effort. The all-Black Tuskegee Airman, for example, flew 15,000 combat missions and earned more than 150 Distinguished Flying Crosses. Yet they returned home to deep racial prejudice. When it was clear Congress would not pass his civil rights legislation, Truman issued executive orders that desegregated the armed forces and ended discrimination within the civil service. Truman's actions were the early rumblings of the modern civil rights movement.

In 1948, Truman won reelection in the greatest election upset in American history. Virtually every pollster had predicted Truman would lose to New York Governor Thomas E. Dewey, as did the *Chicago Daily Tribune*, which famously preprinted its papers with the headline "Dewey Defeats Truman." Truman was resigned to the loss and went to bed early on election night. He awoke at 4:00 am and, after turning on the radio, was astonished to hear he had won. Dressing, Truman dryly commented to his Secret Service agents, "It looks as if we're in for another four years."[74]

Truman didn't just squeak by. He won by a large margin with 303 electoral votes to Dewey's 189 votes. South Carolina Governor Strom Thurmond, a third-party candidate who ran opposing Truman's civil rights agenda, got 39 votes.

Encouraged by his dramatic election win, Truman pursued his domestic agenda, now labeled the "Fair Deal," with renewed energy. In October

1949, Congress increased the minimum wage from $0.40 to $0.75, equivalent to an increase from $4.35 to $8.15 in 2020 dollars. Before the increase, a minimum wage worker worked nearly two hours to buy a pound of butter.[75] Afterward, slightly less than an hour was sufficient.

The 1949 minimum wage increase was the largest percentage increase ever enacted. Opponents of the increase, including major companies such as General Motors and Standard Oil, the U.S. Chamber of Commerce, and most farmers, claimed the increase would raise costs, slow economic growth and increase unemployment. But that didn't happen, even after an estimated 1.3 million minimum wage workers received immediate pay raises.[76] Instead, the economy boomed. The next year, the economy grew by 1.8 million new non-farm jobs, a rate not exceeded until thirty years later as the Baby Boomers entered the workforce. Real GDP increased 8.7 percent. By 1953, unemployment had fallen to a historic low of 2.9 percent.

Workers also benefited from union efforts to increase benefits and wages after the end of wartime controls. In 1950, General Motors and the United Auto Workers (UAW) signed the "Treaty of Detroit," a union agreement that provided GM workers expanded vacation, health and pension benefits, and automatic cost-of-living adjustments. In return, the UAW agreed to a long-term contract that protected GM from strikes. Similar agreements were quickly adopted by Ford and Chrysler. For years the GM-UAW contract served as a model for corporate-labor relations throughout much of American industry.

Truman's minimum wage increase and the Treaty of Detroit signaled the beginning of twenty-five years of rising prosperity for the American middle-class. Measured by income tax filings, the middle three quintiles of taxpayers increased their real, after-tax income (in 2020 dollars) from $28,200 in 1950 to $44,800 in 1973. It was the golden age of the American middle-class. After 1973, real income growth for the middle-class largely stopped. Foreign competition, automation, globalization and a new focus on maximizing corporate profits slowly killed the high-paying jobs that had made the decades after World War II so prosperous for millions of Americans.

Truman had mixed success passing other parts of his Fair Deal. The Housing Act of 1949 funded 800,000 units of low-income housing. In 1950, Social Security was significantly expanded, opening the program, with a few exceptions, to the self-employed, domestic and farmworkers, and certain government employees. Benefits were increased substantially, raising the average monthly benefit from $26 to $46 for current retirees. But other initiatives including civil rights, labor rights, and farm subsidies failed.

Nothing disappointed Truman more than his failure to pass universal healthcare legislation. "I have had some stormy times as President," Truman later wrote in his memoirs. "I have had some bitter disappointment... but the one that has troubled me most, in a personal way, has been the failure to defeat the organized opposition to a national, compulsory, health insurance program."[77]

America's First Healthcare Battle

America's ongoing healthcare battle began seventy-five years ago on November 19, 1945. President Truman, in a special message to Congress[78], proposed his Comprehensive Health Program. His plan addressed five basic problems in the nation's health system.

The first problem was that "the distribution of physicians in the United States has been grossly uneven and unsatisfactory. Some communities have had enough or even too many; others have had too few."

The second problem was "the need for development of public health services and maternal and childcare... Great areas of our country are still without these services."

Third was the need for additional medical research that, when "well directed and continuously supported, can do much to develop ways to reduce those diseases of body and mind which now cause most sickness, disability, and premature death."[79]

The fourth problem Truman identified plagues Americans to this day: the cost of medical care. "The principal reason why people do not receive the care they need is that they cannot afford to pay for it on an individual basis at the time they need it. This is true not only for needy persons. It is also true for a large proportion of normally self-supporting persons...

They may be hit by sickness that calls for many times the average cost, in extreme cases for more than their annual income. When this happens, they may come face to face with economic disaster. Many families, fearful of expense, delay calling the doctor long beyond the time when medical care would do the most good."

Similarly, the fifth problem "has to do with loss of earnings when sickness strikes. Sickness not only brings doctor bills; it also cuts off income." Honest people who may have worked hard their entire lives faced financial hardship, poverty or even bankruptcy when confronted with huge medical bills and no income with which to pay them.

Truman's first three proposals were uncontroversial. Who is going to argue against more rural doctors, better maternal care and more medical research? Major elements of each were quickly adopted, notably the Hospital Survey and Construction Act of 1946.[80] The Act provided for the construction of hospitals and other health facilities assuring that all states would have a minimum of 4.5 hospital beds per 1,000 people. By 2000, nearly 7,000 medical facilities in 4,000 communities had been financed fully or in part by the federal government as a result of Truman's 1946 law.

In addition to funding thousands of hospitals, the 1946 Act introduced concepts that remain in use throughout healthcare. Today, hospitals receiving federal funding are required to provide free or subsidized care to the indigent. Non-profit hospitals must provide demonstrable, community-targeted benefit to retain their tax-free status. All patients must be treated regardless of race, religion, or creed (although, until 1965, "separate but equal" meant segregation by race). Federal grant spending must be matched by state spending, which in 1965 became the basis for Medicaid. All these practices were pioneered by the Hospital Survey and Construction Act of 1946, the foundation of today's healthcare infrastructure.[81]

To address his fourth and fifth objectives, the cost of medical care and lost earnings during sickness, Truman proposed an extension to the existing Social Security system requiring compulsory participation in a national healthcare insurance program. The program would pay medical and dental bills as well as partial income supplements to those with extended illnesses. Truman estimated a four percent increase in Social Security taxes would finance the medical insurance with an additional premium adjustment needed to finance the income supplement. Most importantly, the plan allowed people to choose their doctors and hospitals. Doctors retained the right to accept or reject patients.

Truman knew his proposal would be stamped as socialism, just as Roosevelt's New Deal had been. Anticipating this attack, during his speech to Congress Truman declared:

> The American people are the most insurance-minded people in the world. They will not be frightened off from health insurance because some people have misnamed it socialized medicine. I repeat, what I am recommending is not socialized medicine. Socialized medicine means that all doctors work as employees of government. The American people want no such system. No such system is here proposed. Under the plan I suggest, our people would continue to get medical and hospital services just as they do now, on the basis of their own voluntary decisions and choices. Our doctors and hospitals would continue to deal with disease with the same professional freedom as now. There would, however, be this all-important difference: whether or not patients get the services they need would not depend on how much they can afford to pay at the time.[82]

Although Truman's popularity was at a high during his first term, he was unable to advance his domestic agenda. World events from Berlin to Korea had taken center stage. But Truman never forgot healthcare, and in 1948, after winning a stunning reelection, he redoubled his efforts.

But even after Truman and his allies threw all their efforts into passing healthcare legislation, they were no match for the American Medical Association (AMA). The AMA for decades had opposed any form of government intervention in healthcare.[83] In late 1949, the AMA hired Campaigns, Inc., a powerful public relations firm that had just defeated a California initiative for state-wide universal healthcare, to lead the fight.

Years earlier, Campaigns, Inc. had invented modern political campaign management in 1934.[84] Previously, party leaders ran political campaigns themselves, hiring their own advertising firms, speechwriters, press agents, and other staffers. Campaigns, Inc. made political campaigning a full-time, full-service business. The firm developed the overall political strategy; wrote the speeches, press releases, radio scripts, and newspaper editorials; designed and placed political advertisements; wrote and distributed pamphlets; and organized political events.

Leone Baxter and Clem Whitaker founded the nation's first political public relations firm in 1934. They defeated Truman's national healthcare plan by positioning it as "socialized medicine" and the Truman administration as "followers of the Moscow party line."   CALIFORNIA STATE ARCHIVES

The firm's two founders, Clement Whitaker and Leone Baxter, were smart, shrewd, and ruthless. One of the firm's precepts was, "Never wage a campaign defensively! The only successful defense is a spectacular, hard-hitting, crushing offensive."[85] Whitaker and Baxter employed these tactics in 1934 when they helped defeat Upton Sinclair's bid for California governor by labeling him a communist anxious to plant the red hammer and sickle flag over California.[86] Sinclair's gubernatorial campaign was based on his End Poverty in California (EPIC) plan which proposed giving government jobs to the unemployed.

The AMA financed the campaign against Truman's healthcare program by charging their 140,000 members a substantial $25.00 annual fee ($270 in 2020 dollars) raising the modern equivalent of nearly $40 million annually. To be near the AMA headquarters, Campaigns, Inc. moved their thirty-seven person staff to Chicago. To help assess public sentiment, Whitaker and Baxter persuaded one hundred friendly Congressmen to let them read their constituent mail.

After researching alternatives, Whitaker and Baxter decided on a two-prong campaign strategy: promote voluntary private health insurance as "The American Way" and instill fear by labeling compulsory health insurance "socialized medicine." This was shrewd. Following the loss of China, America had entered a period in which communist infiltration was suspected everywhere. Early in 1950 Senator Joe McCarthy, in a public address to President Truman had claimed, "The State Department harbors a nest of communists and communist sympathizers who are helping to shape our foreign policy... Failure on your part [to cooperate] will label the Democratic Party of being the bedfellow of international communism."[87]

Campaigns, Inc. amplified this fear. An internal document described their core message as: "Basically, the issue is whether we are to remain a Free Nation, in which the individual can work out his own destiny, or whether we are to take one of the final steps toward becoming a Socialist or Communist State."[88] Their rhetoric became so extreme the AMA even began calling the Truman administration "followers of the Moscow party line."[89]

President Truman's healthcare campaign was overwhelmed by the money, skill, and frenetic zeal of its opponents. His proposed legislation never came up for a vote in Congress. Truman's campaign did raise awareness of the deficiencies in American healthcare resulting in more companies offering health insurance to their employees. But part-time employees, retirees, the self-employed, and the unemployed were left out.

For the next seventy years, new healthcare initiatives would routinely be branded as socialism and its supporters as un-American. It is a political strategy that has worked well for the adversaries of universal healthcare. Ironically, America's veterans receive their healthcare through government-run medical facilities provided by the Veterans Administration. Similarly, many of America's most revered institutions—its public libraries, schools, fire departments, and police forces are government-funded and managed.

Whitaker and Baxter's strategy, developed in the early nineteen-thirties of positioning opponents as socialists, has become widespread. Today, no person or institution is immune from the socialist, or even communist, label.

That includes the embodiment of American capitalism itself, *The Wall Street Journal*. On August 8, 2019, a *Journal* editorial titled, "The Navarro Recession," criticized Peter Navarro as the misguided economist behind President Trump's China tariffs. Navarro responded with an insult likening the *Journal* to a communist newspaper. "[*The Wall Street Journal*] doesn't sound a lot different from *The People's Daily* in terms of the news that it puts out,"[90] Navarro told Fox Business News. *The People's Daily* is the official outlet of the Chinese Communist Party.

History and Character

In 1948, Truman ended his first presidential term with a job approval rating of nearly 70 percent. Only Dwight Eisenhower enjoyed higher ratings. Truman's popularity was well-deserved. From 1945 through 1948, he had presided over the victory in World War II, the Marshall Plan, the Berlin Airlift, the recognition of Israel, and the creation of 5.5 million new jobs. America seemed unstoppable, and Truman was leading America.

But Truman's popularity plummeted after 1949. Nine months into his second term, China fell to the communists; Truman's political opponents blamed him for the loss. Truman fired General MacArthur; the grandstanding MacArthur came home to a hero's welcome. Truman proposed universal healthcare; the American Medical Association spent millions labeling his administration as socialists and "followers of the Moscow party line." Truman integrated the military; the segregated South was furious.

Truman's pugnacious, "Give 'em Hell," style didn't help. Truman was ridiculed, for example, when he chastised a music critic who gave his vocalist daughter, Margaret, a scathing review. "I've just read your lousy review of Margaret's concert... Someday I hope to meet you," Truman wrote the critic on White House stationary. "When that happens, you'll need a new nose, a lot of beefsteak for black eyes, and perhaps a supporter below!"[91]

But history soon forgets headlines that fleetingly capture public interest. What distinguished Truman was his resolute leadership during three historic challenges.

After the Allies won World War II, the Truman administration was magnanimous and insightful in its administration of Germany and Japan. Japan was allowed to keep its Emperor while handed a democratic constitution. Similarly, Germany was allowed to keep much of its governing bureaucracy after it had been "de-Nazified." Truman's policies stabilized America's former enemies and allowed them to rebuild and become staunch American allies. Another President could easily have been vindictive. After World War I, the victors forced Germany to pay crippling reparations and after the second Iraqi War, President Bush purged Saddam Hussein's government, leaving a power vacuum. These short-sighted policies contributed to Hitler's rise in Germany and two decades of instability in the Middle East.

Truman's second challenge was the threat of global communism. Truman thwarted communism in Western Europe through the Marshall Plan, confronted Soviet bullying with the Berlin Airlift, provided Europe a defensive umbrella through NATO, and sent American troops into Korea to stop communist aggression. For over forty years, the Truman Doctrine defined America's policy of resisting communist expansion throughout the world.

Finally, Truman faced the spread of nuclear weapons. Truman understood war firsthand. He had distinguished himself during the First World War as an artillery captain. Although he ordered the bombing of Hiroshima and Nagasaki, Truman showed courage under great political and public pressure when he fired General MacArthur for advocating the use of nuclear weapons during the Korean Conflict. Truman's tempered restraint set a precedent that has lasted to this day.

President Truman's approval ratings fell to 32 percent during his last year in office, the lowest Gallup rating ever recorded. Yet presidential historians today, on average, rank Truman as America's sixth-best President.[92]

What made Truman one of the great Presidents? History and character. Few Presidents preside over a major historical transition. Truman led the world through three. A small sign on Truman's desk read, "The Buck Stops Here." Although Truman made mistakes, he governed with resolve and courage. Rather than deflect, he took responsibility. That's character.

Dwight D. Eisenhower

———— ✦ ————

January 20, 1953 – January 20, 1961

> We cannot safely confine government programs to our own domestic progress and our own military power. We could be the wealthiest and the most mighty nation and still lose the battle of the world if we do not help our world neighbors protect their freedom and advance their social and economic progress. It is not the goal of the American people that the United States should be the richest nation in the graveyard of history.[1]

Donald Trump built his presidential campaign around "Make America Great Again" raising the question, to which golden period in America was Trump referring? Was it the nineteen-nineties after America had won the Cold War, banished the Soviet Union, invented the Internet, and was getting rich on the dot-com boom? Probably not. The nineties seem too recent to engender the nostalgic longing Trump's slogan evokes.

The nineteen-eighties? Possibly. President Reagan had reinvigorated America after the disillusionment of Watergate, defeat in Vietnam and the stagflation of the prior decade. Under Reagan the economy boomed, American prestige soared, and American pride was restored. But Reagan's campaign slogan (borrowed from Warren G. Harding and later recycled by Donald Trump), "Let's Make America Great Again,"[2] evoked not a contemporaneous golden period, but nostalgia for the past. Reagan, like Trump, was looking backward in search of American greatness.

Certainly, no American longed for a return to the nineteen-seventies, the decade of Watergate, defeat in Vietnam, stagflation, and oil embargoes.[3]

And Trump surely wasn't referring to the nineteen-sixties with its Bay of Pigs fiasco, Vietnam War, Chicago riots, and the assassinations of President John F. Kennedy, Martin Luther King Jr. and Senator Robert Kennedy.

So, we are left with the nineteen-fifties; the earliest decade Trump and his generation can recall. For Americans today, the hazy fifties decade conjures a vision of peace and prosperity. The United States had won World War II, becoming in the process the leader of the Free World. At home, traditional American families laughed at *I Love Lucy*, admired John Wayne's swagger, saw polio conquered, listened to Dinah Shore sing *See the USA in your Chevrolet* while cruising on America's new interstate highways, shimmied with hula-hoops and danced to rock-n-roll.

The fifties, then, must be the golden age to which Trump wished to restore America. It was the decade presided over by President Dwight D. Eisenhower, known to millions simply as "Ike."

Keeping America Out of War

The nineteen-fifties, though, weren't as happy and tranquil as many might remember it. The decade began with the war in Korea.

American troops had occupied South Korea since the end of World War II, but by 1949 Truman began a withdrawal. He had broad support for the move, including from the Joint Chiefs of Staff, the Secretary of State Dean Acheson, and even General Douglas MacArthur. "Korea is of little strategic value," the Joint Chiefs declared. "A commitment to use military force in Korea would be ill-advised and impracticable."[4]

But a few believed that withdrawal was premature. General Albert Wedemeyer, returning from an East Asian fact-finding mission, warned Congress: "The withdrawal of American military forces from Korea would result in the occupation of South Korea by either Soviet troops or, as seems more likely, by the Korean military units trained under Soviet auspices in North Korea."[5] Wedemeyer was right. On June 25, 1950, North Korean troops crossed the thirty-eighth parallel to invade South Korea.

During the 1952 presidential election, Eisenhower campaigned on ending the war. "[If elected,] I will go to Korea..." Eisenhower promised, "to bring the Korean Conflict to an early and honorable end."[6] Two months after winning a landslide victory over Adlai Stevenson, Eisenhower made a secret trip to Korea. Eisenhower concluded that the war was unwinnable without a massive escalation that would require, perhaps, the use of nuclear weapons to counter the massive Chinese army that was supporting their North Korean allies.

General Eisenhower speaking to American paratroopers on June 5, 1944 before the Normandy Invasion. Eisenhower was the Supreme Commander of the Allied Forces in Europe during World War II.   GL ARCHIVE/ALAMY

Once in office, Eisenhower ended the fighting but failed to end the war. A peace treaty was never signed. Instead, a weak armistice, little more than a temporary ceasefire, was signed on July 27, 1953. During the negotiations, both North and South Korea initially refused to agree to the ceasefire. China and the Soviet Union eventually pressured North Korea to sign, but South Korea refused. A peace conference held in Geneva nine months later failed to reach an honorable peace. Legally, Korea has been frozen in a state of war for nearly seventy years.

A critical provision of the armistice specified that neither side could introduce new weapons into Korea. Both sides quickly accused the other of violating these terms. On June 21, 1957 the United States informed North Korea it was abandoning the armistice's weapons limitation.[7] Six months later, the United States began installing nuclear-tipped Honest John missiles and 280mm atomic cannons aimed at North Korea. These were formidable weapons. The atomic cannon, for example, fired a nuclear projectile with the destructive power of the fifteen-kiloton bomb that destroyed Hiroshima, and could do so repeatedly. Imagine an artillery barrage with each shell packing the destructive power of the Hiroshima bomb.[8] North Korea retaliated by building a massive network of underground artillery bunkers which to this day threaten Seoul just fifty miles south of the armistice line.

In 1991 the United States withdrew its nuclear weapons from South Korea. They were no longer needed as other land and sea-based missiles could provide Korea with a "nuclear umbrella." Twenty-five years later, on October 9, 2006, after decades of effort, North Korea detonated its first nuclear weapon. By 2020, North Korea was estimated to have between fifty and one hundred nuclear weapons along with ballistic missiles that can reach North America.

Eisenhower ended the fighting in Korea, a war that killed more than three million people, the majority of whom were civilians.[9] But no American President since has been able to secure a permanent peace in Korea, the last major remnant of the Cold War.

After signing the Korean Armistice, Eisenhower kept America out of war for the next seven years. A remarkable achievement. These were unsettled years around the world with ample provocations for a belligerent President to commit American troops. But Eisenhower, as the Supreme Allied Commander during World War II, knew war and resisted.

In 1954, as the French faced defeat in Indochina, Eisenhower refused France's urgent request to intercede, declaring "this war would absorb our troops by divisions" and writing prophetically in his diary, "I'm convinced no military victory is possible in that kind of theater."[10]

After the French defeat, a Geneva Conference partitioned French Indochina into two zones, North and South Vietnam. The agreement stipulated that free elections to unify the two Vietnams must be conducted by July 1956. The elections were never held and the country remained bitterly divided.

After the French withdrew from the region, Eisenhower organized the Southeast Asia Treaty Organization (SEATO) comprising the United States, Britain, France, Australia, and New Zealand to counter communist expansion as had earlier happened in Korea and was now feared in Vietnam. The United States was now committed to South Vietnam's defense. By 1960, as Eisenhower was leaving office, the United States had 900 military advisors in South Vietnam training its army.

After ten years of festering conflict after the French departed in 1954, Vietnam exploded into war in 1964. Eisenhower's efforts in both Korea and Vietnam forestalled war, but eventually led, years after Eisenhower left office, to defeat in Vietnam and the dangerous instability in Korea that continues to this day. Yet, faced with the massive armies of China and the nuclear weapons of the Soviet Union, what other choice but forbearance did Eisenhower have?

Twice in 1956 Eisenhower showed that same restraint.

On July 26, Egyptian leader Gamal Abdel Nasser nationalized the Suez Canal. Nasser was frustrated with Britain's military presence in the Suez and with Israeli incursions into Egypt. Angered by Nasser's take-over of the canal, Israel invaded Egypt on October 29. Britain and France quickly followed. Eisenhower condemned the attack even though Israel, Britain, and France were strong American allies. Eisenhower threatened economic sanctions if the three countries did not withdraw. In a humiliating reversal, they promptly complied.

Also in October, when 1,100 Soviet tanks and 31,000 troops crossed into Hungary to crush the Hungarian Revolution, Eisenhower stayed out of the conflict. Short of invading Hungary, Eisenhower knew there was little he could do other than welcome Hungarian refugees who somehow managed to reach America. It must have been difficult for Eisenhower to stand aside. "Support by United States rulers," Soviet Premier Nikita Khrushchev mocked, "is rather in the nature of the support that the rope gives to a hanged man."[11]

But Eisenhower was not easily provoked. Having fought in two World Wars, Eisenhower abhorred war. After the Korean Armistice, only one American died in combat during Eisenhower's presidency, a soldier killed by a Lebanese sniper in 1957. No President since has approached Eisenhower's record of military restraint.

The Cold War

Six weeks after Eisenhower assumed the presidency, Josef Stalin died. Stalin had ruled the Soviet Union for thirty-one years through the early optimism of communism in the nineteen-twenties, the murderous pogroms of the nineteen-thirties, and the iron-fisted repression of Eastern Europe after World War II. Eisenhower saw Stalin's death as an opportunity to send a message to Moscow that America sought peace over war and schools over bombers. He did so in his "Cross of Iron" speech on April 16, 1953:

> Every gun that is made, every warship launched, every rocket fired signifies, in the final sense, a theft from those who hunger and are not fed, those who are cold and are not clothed. This world in arms is not spending money alone. It is spending the sweat of its laborers, the genius of its scientists, the hopes of its children. The cost of one modern heavy bomber is this: a modern brick school in more than thirty cities. It is two electric power plants, each serving a town of 60,000 population. It is two fine, fully equipped hospitals. It is some fifty miles of concrete pavement. We pay for a single fighter with a half-million bushels of wheat. We pay for a single destroyer with new homes that could have housed more than 8,000 people.... This is not a way of life at all, in any true sense. Under the cloud of threatening war, it is humanity hanging from a cross of iron.[12]

With Stalin gone, Eisenhower hoped to reduce tensions between the United States and the Soviet Union. He and Nikita Khrushchev, the Soviet Union's emerging leader, were World War II allies, both having fought against the Germans.

Khrushchev, even more than Eisenhower, had seen first-hand the ravages of total war in Kyiv, Stalingrad, and Kursk. Eisenhower knew that the Soviets were spending 30 percent of their economy on defense, a percentage far greater than that of the United States. And, unlike America, the

Soviets still needed to rebuild their war-ravaged cities. Surely the Soviets would welcome an invitation to reduce tensions, not to mention, the billions being spent for defense.

But the fear of foreign invasion runs deep in the Russian psyche. The German invasion of the Soviet Union during the Second World War cost twenty-five million Soviet lives. Nearly five million Russians died fighting the Germans during the First World War. Britain and its allies fought the Crimean War on Russian soil in the eighteen-fifties (memorialized in Tennyson's poem, *The Charge of the Light Brigade*). In 1812, Napoleon's Grand Army invaded Russia; nearly a million Russians died.

Eisenhower's plea to end the Cold War wasn't successful. After 150 years of fighting wars on Russian soil, the Soviet Union was determined to protect its European border with Soviet-controlled puppet states stretching from Poland to Albania, an army of more than three million soldiers, and a nuclear arsenal powerful enough to destroy any invader.

With the Cold War unabated, an arms race between the United States and the Soviet Union developed that lasted for thirty years. Both countries raced to stay ahead in the quantity and lethality of their nuclear weapons and the missiles, aircraft, and submarines to deliver them. Fueling American anxiety was the belief that the Soviets were catching up with the United States, and for good reason. The Soviets tested their first atomic bomb in 1949, years before American intelligence agencies had predicted. In 1953, the Soviet Union again shocked Americans when it tested its first hydrogen bomb, a mere nine months after the United States. It was undeniable: the Soviets were catching up. Then, in 1957, the Soviet Union launched Sputnik, the world's first satellite. Americans were dumbfounded, and alarmed, as they looked up at the night sky to see the Soviet satellite passing overhead while transmitting an unnerving, steady beep to radios around the world.

The United States was losing the space race. Rushing to match the Soviets, America's first attempt to launch a satellite exploded ignominiously on the launch pad. The world snickered while Khrushchev gleefully goaded the Americans. "Soviet factories are turning out missiles like sausages," Khrushchev boasted. "History is on our side. We will bury you."[13]

The arms race forced Eisenhower to devote an average of 10 percent of GDP to defense spending, equivalent to $2.1 trillion in 2020—nearly four times the $686 billion spent that year.[14] Near the end of his presidency, Eisenhower learned that much of the massive defense expenditures had been unnecessary. A top-secret spy plane, the Lockheed U-2, had begun to regularly overfly the Soviet Union capturing photos that showed the Soviet threat was far less than his military advisors had feared. Eisenhower refused to defend himself against political attacks that he was soft on national defense by divulging the U-2 program which confirmed that the American weapons advantage was massive. Based on top-secret information released years later, when Eisenhower left office, the United States had 18,638 nuclear weapons to the Soviet Union's 1,627.[15]

Three days before leaving office, Eisenhower gave his most memorable speech: one that bookended his "Cross of Iron" speech eight years earlier. Eisenhower warned Americans to guard against the nation's new military-industrial complex:

> Until the latest of our world conflicts, the United States had no armaments industry.... But now we can no longer risk emergency improvisation of national defense; we have been compelled to create a permanent armaments industry of vast proportions.... This conjunction of an immense military establishment and a large arms industry is new in the American experience .... We recognize the imperative need for this development. Yet we must not fail to comprehend its grave implications.... In the councils of government, we must guard against the acquisition of unwarranted influence, whether sought or unsought, by the military/industrial complex. The potential for the disastrous rise of misplaced power exists and will persist.[16]

After forty-five years of military and government service, Eisenhower well understood the shared interests, and the potential for collusion, between the military and the defense industry. "God help this country," Eisenhower confided to his staff, "when someone sits in this chair who doesn't know the military as well as I do."[17]

The United States soon abandoned Eisenhower's policy of limited intervention. Although Congress hasn't formally declared war since 1942, over 65,000 American soldiers have died since Eisenhower left office.[18] The United States fought, and lost, major wars in Vietnam, Iraq, and Afghanistan, and it pursued smaller conflicts in the Dominican Republic, El Salvador, Lebanon, Grenada, Libya, the Persian Gulf, Panama, Iraq, Somalia, Haiti, Bosnia-Herzegovina, and Kosovo.

The McCarthy Era

"I have here in my hand a list of 205—a list of names that were made known to the Secretary of State as being members of the Communist Party and who nevertheless are still working and shaping policy in the State Department." Senator Joseph McCarthy made this claim on February 9, 1950 in a speech in Wheeling, West Virginia.[19] It marked the beginning of the McCarthy Era, a period in which hundreds of Americans in Washington, the armed services, Hollywood, labor unions, and academia were accused of being communist agents, spies, or sympathizers.

Congress had reason to be concerned. In the years after the war, communist spies seemed to be popping up everywhere.

Three days after World War II ended, Igor Gouzenko, a Soviet code specialist stationed in Canada, defected with 109 documents detailing the activities of Soviet spies during the war. The documents described how the Soviets had planted "sleeper agents" in the government, universities and defense companies throughout North America to steal nuclear secrets.[20]

Two months later in November 1945, Elizabeth Bentley confessed to having been a Soviet spy since 1935 while working for a Soviet shipping company as a cover. During her FBI testimony, Bentley identified 150 alleged Soviet spies operating in the United States, including thirty-seven in the federal government.[21]

In 1948, Whittaker Chambers, a prominent *Time* magazine journalist, testified before Congress that he had been a Soviet spy during the nineteen-thirties and implicated Alger Hiss, a senior government official, as a fellow spy. Hiss operated at the highest levels of the federal government, attended the Yalta Conference with President Roosevelt, and helped write the United Nations charter after the war.[22]

In January 1950, a month before McCarthy's Wheeling speech, Klaus Fuchs, a scientist with the Manhattan Project, confessed to having been a Soviet spy and providing the Soviets details on America's atomic bomb. Six months later, Julius and Ethel Rosenberg were arrested for passing nuclear secrets to the Soviets while Julius worked for the U.S. Army Signal Corp at Fort Monmouth, New Jersey. Years later, released Soviet documents revealed the couple had been active recruiters of additional Soviet spies throughout the war.

Senator McCarthy was not the first to raise the alarm. In 1938, the House Committee on Un-American Activities (HUAC) was formed to investigate subversive activities by private citizens and members of the government, trade unions, and other organizations. HUAC's initial focus had been on German sympathizers, but soon turned to communists. Nine years later, HUAC held ten movie producers, directors, and screenwriters in contempt of Congress for refusing to reveal the names of possible communist sympathizers in Hollywood. Eight of the "Hollywood Ten" were sentenced to a year in prison, the other two received six months.[23]

In 1947, President Truman issued Executive Order 9835, which mandated screening federal employees for loyalty to the United States. Over the next ten years, an estimated five million federal employees were screened, which resulted in 2,700 dismissals and 12,000 resignations.[24]

So, there was ample reason to believe that communists had infiltrated American institutions. But Senator McCarthy, assisted by his chief counsel Roy Cohn, turned the search for communists into an inquisition. As chairman of the Senate Committee on Government Operations, McCarthy brought hundreds of Americans before the committee, often with little justification. McCarthy relied on degradation, intimidation, and the threat of imprisonment to extract testimony. Just being brought before the committee resulted in guilt by association, destroying reputations and careers. In Hollywood, an estimated 300 executives and artists were blacklisted, including Charlie Chaplin, Orson Welles, and Dalton Trumbo. Some, such as Charlie Chaplin, fled to Europe, while others like Carl Foreman worked under pseudonyms. A few, like Orson Welles, survived, but most were forced to leave the industry.[25]

During the late nineteen-forties and early fifties Americans became fearful communists had infiltrated America from Hollywood to Washington.

PICTORIAL PRESS LTD/ALAMY

Others chose to cooperate, "not to save their lives, but to save their swimming pools" as Orson Welles dryly commented.[26] Edward G. Robinson admitted he was "a choice number one sucker" for associating with communists during the nineteen-forties. Robinson reluctantly provided names of other suspected communists including Dalton Trumbo, a top Hollywood screenwriter. Trumbo had written screenplays for *Thirty Seconds Over Tokyo* and *Roman Holiday* (and after being blacklisted, secretly penned the screenplays for *Exodus* and *Spartacus*).

During the McCarthy years, concern turned to fear and ultimately paranoia. Radical organizations, such as the Keep America Committee, claimed the fluoridation of public water supplies and the new polio vaccines were communist plots designed to wipe out entire populations.[27] The Indiana Textbook Commission even banned the book *Robin Hood* as communist. Robin Hood, as every schoolchild knows, robbed from the rich and gave to the poor, a concept the Indiana commission considered subversive.[28]

Eisenhower abhorred McCarthy's methods but chose not to challenge him directly—McCarthy enjoyed strong support with much of the American public. Instead, in April 1954, Eisenhower, in a brilliant political gambit, arranged to have McCarthy's investigation of the U.S. Army aired on live television.

Eisenhower knew his man. Millions of Americans soon saw McCarthy badgering and belittling American heroes. When Lt. Colonel Chester T. Brown refused to answer a question, McCarthy responded, "Any man in the uniform of his country who refused to give information to a committee of the Senate which represents the American people, that man is not fit to wear the uniform of his country." Going a step further, McCarthy badgered Brigadier General Ralph Zwicker, a decorated war hero, calling him "a disgrace to the uniform he wore."[29]

McCarthy had finally gone too far. It was one thing to belittle a Hollywood screenwriter, but quite another to bully a decorated war hero. Joseph Welsh, the Army's legal counsel during the hearings, admonished McCarthy, "I think I never really gauged your cruelty or your recklessness. Have you no sense of decency, sir, at long last?"[30]

America had seen enough. McCarthy was not a patriot. He was a common bully. The Senate agreed, and, in December 1954 censured McCarthy for violation of Senate behavioral norms.[31] After the censure, McCarthy fell into obscurity. He died of liver failure in 1957.

During McCarthy's five years as chair of the Senate committee, not one person was sent to prison as a communist agent. Nor did McCarthy ever release the 205 names he claimed on February 9, 1950 were communist conspirators. Today, Senator McCarthy is remembered primarily through a descriptive noun, McCarthyism: the use of unfair and unsubstantiated personal attacks to intimidate or destroy an individual.

The classic 1952 western, *High Noon,* is a political allegory of the McCarthy era. The Oscar-winning movie stars Gary Cooper as Marshal Will Kane and Grace Kelly as his new bride, Amy. While writing the screenplay, Carl Foreman, who had briefly joined the American Communist Party in 1938, was asked by the House Un-American Activities Committee to testify against his Hollywood friends. Foreman had to decide whether to betray his friends or lose his Hollywood career. As he pondered his decision, Foreman changed the movie's script to write himself in as Will Kane, the stoic marshal forced to defend the town alone; the House committee as the murderous gang intent on killing Kane; and the passive townspeople as the Hollywood establishment.

Marshal Will Kane was saved by his pacifist wife in the final gunfight. Nobody, however, stepped in to save Foreman when he ultimately chose not to testify against his Hollywood associates. Blacklisted in Hollywood, Foreman moved to England where he continued to write screenplays under pseudonyms, including Academy Award winners *The Bridge on the River Kwai* and *The Guns of Navarone.*[32]

President Eisenhower loved *High Noon* and screened the film three times at the White House.[33]

Falling Dominoes

In April 1954, Eisenhower gave a speech regarding the imminent defeat of the French in Indochina. Eisenhower cautioned that the French defeat would have a ripple effect, like falling dominoes. "You have a row of dominoes set up," Eisenhower explained. "You knock over the first one, and what will happen to the last one is a certainty that it will go over very quickly."[34] The fear of global communism during the nineteen-fifties was so powerful that Eisenhower, and millions of others, believed that defeat in an obscure Asian country would result in Asia, Japan, Australia and New Zealand falling, like dominoes, to the communists.

After the 1957 Suez Canal crisis, the domino theory led to the adoption of the Eisenhower Doctrine, which promised that any Middle Eastern country threatened by "international communism" could request economic and military aid from the United States. The doctrine had become necessary after France and Britain, forced to retreat by Eisenhower after invading Egypt, abandoned the Middle East, leaving the United States alone to deter Soviet aggression in the region.

Eisenhower's domino theory influenced American foreign policy for decades, leading to questionable wars and clandestine operations around the world. During the Carter and Reagan Administrations, the Eisenhower Doctrine was responsible for America's support of the Afghan mujahedeen after the Soviet invasion of Afghanistan in 1979. Years later, the mujahedeen turned on the United States and provided aid to Osama Bin Laden, the mastermind behind the September 11, 2001 terrorist attacks on America.

But during the early stages of the Cold War, Americans had reason to fear communism. Russia and China aggressively promoted global communism in Eastern Europe, Southeast Asia, and Latin America. Communist leaders were confident that communism would prevail over capitalism. "When we hang the capitalists," Stalin claimed, "they will sell us the rope we use."[35]

Communism never replaced capitalism. Today, Russia and China have embraced market-based economics albeit paired with strong central government control. Nor did any dominoes topple after America's defeat in Vietnam. Instead, the reunited Vietnam became strongly pro-American with growing trade and cultural relations between the two countries.

Covert Operations and Future Wars

There was a dark side to Eisenhower's presidency which didn't become evident for decades. Eisenhower pioneered the use of covert operations to intervene in the affairs of foreign nations. Eisenhower's first covert operation, just months after taking office, led to decades of unrest, wars, and terrorism. It all began with a phone call from Winston Churchill.[36]

In 1951, *Time* magazine named Iran's Prime Minister Mohammad Mosaddegh as Man of the Year, christening him "Iran's George Washington." Two years later, a covert CIA coup removed Mosaddegh from power after he refused to negotiate oil profits.
WORLD HISTORY ARCHIVE/ALAMY

In 1950, the Abadan oil refinery, located in western Iran, was the largest in the world. Oil was first discovered in the Middle East by the British at Abadan in 1908. Six years earlier, the Shah of Iran (the Persian monarch) sold exclusive rights to Iran's oil and gas to the British. The British formed the Anglo-Persian Oil Company to exploit the Iranian oil fields, granting the Iranian government royalties of only 16 percent, royalties that the British company alone calculated. In 1920, the shameless oil company paid Iran £47,000 while making millions. The Iranian venture was so profitable that Winston Churchill, at the time the First Lord of the Admiralty, wrote: "Fortune brought us a prize from fairyland beyond our wildest dreams."[37]

Over the years, Iran slowly negotiated larger royalties, but by 1951 negotiations were at an impasse. Saudi Arabia had recently negotiated a fifty-fifty profit sharing split with the Arabian-American Oil Company (today's Aramco). Iran demanded the same share from the British.[38] The British refused expecting to intimidate the Iranians as they had for the past forty years. But on April 28, 1951 the British lost control of Iranian politics when Mohammad Mosaddegh was appointed prime minister. Mosaddegh was a hugely popular figure in Iran who single-mindedly promoted Persia-for-the-Persians. In January 1952, *Time* magazine honored Mosaddegh as 1951 Man of the Year calling him the Iranian George Washington.[39]

Mosaddegh, finding the British unwilling to negotiate, nationalized the Anglo-Persian Oil Company on May 2, 1952. The British pulled out, bringing production to a near halt. Britain sought redress in the International Court of Justice, which rejected their claim. The British then approached President Truman in late 1952 for help either through military intervention or the overthrow of the Iranian government. Truman refused.

A year later, after Eisenhower assumed the presidency, the British approached Eisenhower through a personal plea from Winston Churchill, Eisenhower's former World War II ally. Eisenhower initially rejected Churchill's pleadings, considering the British-Iranian spat nothing more than a colonial issue. Churchill then shrewdly claimed that oil-rich Iran was leaning towards communism. The threat of communism spreading to the Middle East goaded Eisenhower into action.

But what action to take? As the two men conferred, Eisenhower was working to reduce tensions with the Soviet Union following Stalin's death. An overt American attack to take back the Iranian oil fields and replace Mosaddegh would irreparably damage these peace efforts.

President Eisenhower and former British Prime Minister Winston Churchill in December 1953. Four months earlier the American CIA and British Intelligence had orchestrated a covert coup to overthrow Iran's democratically-elected government.
ASAR STUDIOS/ALAMY

There was another approach. During the war, Eisenhower had successfully used the Office of Strategic Services (OSS) to covertly collect intelligence, sabotage enemy facilities, and generally wreak havoc on the enemy.[40] At the end of the war, Eisenhower credited the OSS and its British counterpart for "[playing] a very considerable part in our complete and final victory."[41] After the war, the OSS was reorganized into the Central Intelligence Agency (CIA). So, not surprisingly, Eisenhower turned to the CIA to conduct a covert operation to replace Mosaddegh. However, in 1953, the United States and Iran were not at war.

That August, CIA and British intelligence operatives working with Iranian insurgents covertly removed Mosaddegh in Operation Ajax and replaced him with the pliable Mohammad Reza, the son of Iran's first Shah. After the coup, the United States dictated the terms under which a new oil consortium was established, which now included five American oil companies with collective ownership of 40 percent. Ironically, the consortium agreed to share profits with Iran on a fifty-fifty basis, Iran's original demand of the British.

For twenty-five years Iran, the ancient home of Shia Islam, masqueraded as a westernized, secular country. Iranian women wore mini-skirts, young couples danced the Tehran Twist and both genders mingled freely at the country's beaches.[42] But at its core, the country was a harsh dictatorship run by the Shah and maintained by SAVAK, the Shah's secret police. In 1979 Iranians, brutalized and fed up with government corruption and secularism, ousted the Shah and replaced him with a fervent Muslim cleric, Ayatollah Khomeini. Khomeini, still angered by America's 1953 overthrow of Iran's legitimate government, branded the United States the "Great Satan."

In 1954, a year after the United States toppled the Iranian government, the CIA engineered a similar coup d'état in Guatemala to remove the left-leaning, but democratically elected, government of Jacobo Árbenz. America's intervention was criticized worldwide, and when CIA Director Allen Dulles declared the coup a victory for democracy, the world scoffed. One diplomat joked that Dulles's comment "might almost be Molotov speaking about ... Czechoslovakia or Hitler speaking about Austria."[43] The American-installed government didn't last. Carlos Castillo, the American puppet, was assassinated three years later, pushing Guatemala into thirty-five years of civil war.

Historically, relations between sovereign countries were limited to diplomacy and war. Covert operations, falling somewhere between the two, provided a seemingly attractive third alternative, inferior to diplomacy but preferable to war.

But with mixed success, at best. After Eisenhower instigated covert operations against Iran, the CIA secretly intervened in, at least, eighteen countries: Afghanistan, Angola, Bolivia, Brazil, Cambodia, Chile, Cuba, the Dominican Republic, Ecuador, El Salvador, Greece, Haiti, Indonesia, Laos, Nicaragua, Panama, Uruguay, and Vietnam. Few interventions resulted in long-term, democratic governments.

African-American Civil Rights

Born in a small Texas town just thirty-five years after the end of the Civil War, Eisenhower might be described as a well-meaning segregationist. Raised in a nearly all-white community, attending West Point among an all-white cadet corps, serving in a segregated Army, and vacationing at the lily-white Augusta National Golf Club, Eisenhower assumed segregation was the natural order of things.

As late as 1948, Eisenhower testified before Congress that he opposed integration below the platoon level where soldiers lived, ate, and fought together as a unit.[44] That year, President Truman, appalled by the treatment of Black soldiers coming home from the war, signed Executive Order 9981 ordering the desegregation of the military.

The Secretary of the Army, Kenneth C. Royall, refused to desegregate the Army and was forced to resign. Little progress was made over the next three years. But eighteen months after taking office, President Eisenhower, who had recommended against the desegregation of the services, abolished all Black-only military units including within military schools, hospitals, and bases.

It was the military, that segment of American society whose very lives depend on the absolute trust among its members, in which the doctrine of "separate but equal" was first repealed. The doctrine originated in 1896 when the Supreme Court, in *Plessy v. Ferguson,* first ruled that segregation was legal if both races were treated equally as required by the 14th Amendment, establishing for the first time the concept of "separate but equal."[45].

Interestingly, the Court's 1896 ruling used the phrase "equal but separate," which tends to emphasize equality. The phrase was later reversed to "separate but equal" during the doctrine's adoption.

However, Black and white facilities were seldom equal. In 1930, African-Americans comprised 42 percent of Florida's population yet Black schools represented just six percent of the state school system's total property value. Only twenty-eight of Florida's sixty-seven counties offered Blacks a high school education. African-American teachers were paid less than half the salaries of whites. During that same period, Alabama spent thirty-seven dollars per white child but only seven dollars per Black child; Georgia thirty-two dollars and seven dollars; Mississippi thirty-one dollars and six dollars, respectively. South Carolina spent ten times more on white students than Black students: fifty-three dollars versus five dollars.[46]

In 1954, after nearly sixty years of undeniable inequality, the Supreme Court reversed its 1896 decision in the landmark case, *Brown v. Board of Education of Topeka,* in which it declared that "separate educational facilities are inherently unequal." A year later, in a second decision, known as *Brown II,* the Court ordered states to desegregate "with all deliberate speed."

Two years after *Brown II,* Little Rock, Arkansas began to integrate its Central High School, starting with nine of the top African-American students in the city, all handpicked by the NAACP (National Association for the Advancement of Colored People). But the governor, Orval Faubus, intervened by dispatching the Arkansas National Guard to stop the Black students from entering the school. The Little Rock School District condemned the governor for interfering in a local matter. Faubus was unmoved, which forced the mayor to make a personal plea to President Eisenhower to send federal troops to enforce integration. Eisenhower responded with soldiers from the elite 101st Airborne Division and federalized the Arkansas National Guard to remove it from Faubus's control. By late September, the nine students were attending Central High.

Fifteen-year-old Elizabeth Eckford was one of the first nine Black students to integrate Little Rock Central High School in 1957. An honor student, she was brutally harassed on the first day.   EVERETT COLLECTION HISTORICAL/ALAMY

President Eisenhower's strong response in Little Rock affirmed that public school integration was the law of the land. Although decades later, many American school systems remain segregated, Eisenhower's resolute action in Little Rock represented the first step towards ending the failed policy of "separate but equal."

Notably, Eisenhower personally believed the nation was moving too quickly to integrate Blacks and whites, especially in schools. He never publicly endorsed the Supreme Court's decision and privately told his staff, "I personally think the [Brown] decision was wrong."[47] Yet Eisenhower resolutely enforced the Court's ruling as a matter of law. On September 24, 1957, the evening he sent federal troops to Little Rock, Eisenhower spoke to Americans in a nationally televised speech:

> As you know, the Supreme Court of the United States has decided that separate public educational facilities for the races are inherently unequal and therefore compulsory school segregation laws are unconstitutional. Our personal opinions about the decision have no bearing on the matter of enforcement.... The very basis of our individual rights and freedoms rests upon the certainty that the President and the Executive Branch of Government will support and insure the carrying out of the decisions of the Federal Courts...[48]

Eisenhower, though, never used the presidency's bully pulpit to provide moral support for the civil rights of African-Americans, nor the full power of the executive branch. He never commented on the 1955–56 Montgomery, Alabama bus boycott triggered by Rosa Park's refusal to give up her all-white seat. The year-long boycott led to the integration of the city's bus system and is considered by many to be the birth of the modern civil rights movement.[49] That same year, when Emmett Till, a fourteen-year-old African-American, was brutally murdered in Mississippi for allegedly whistling at a white woman, Eisenhower failed to condemn the murder. When Till's mother telegraphed the White House asking for support, Eisenhower did not reply, deferring to FBI Director Hoover's claim that the boy's mother was a communist rabble-rouser.[50]

The only African-American on Eisenhower's administrative staff, E. Frederic Morrow, respected Eisenhower but was disappointed by his unwillingness to speak out on behalf of African-Americans. "[President Eisenhower was] a great, gentle and noble man," Morrow later wrote, "but couldn't take that single bold step of courageous pronouncement that would have moved the Blacks another mile towards freedom."[51] Roy Wilkins, the head of the NAACP, held a similar sentiment. "President Eisenhower was a fine general and a good, decent man, but if he had fought World War II the way he fought for civil rights, we would all be speaking German now."[52]

Eisenhower, like many Presidents before and after him, feared a backlash from Southern voters. He knew the American South well and counted many Southerners as good friends. He understood the anger and fear integration stirred throughout the South. A typical letter Eisenhower received was written by a Texan mother:

> I say you do not know how closely you have struck in the homes of the Southern People. You do not know how many tempers you have stirred in the Southern States. . . . I feel disillusion, anger plus emotion; as I am the mother of two small daughters who in three years will be entering school for the first time. . . . Give the negroes freedom of speech, freedom of press, etc., but let there be provided adequate separate schools for them.[53]

Yet, knowing much of the nation would oppose it, Eisenhower proposed the first civil rights legislation since the Reconstruction Era (1865–77) that followed the Civil War. Eisenhower's proposal created a federal authority to investigate civil rights cases and established a civil rights division in the Department of Justice to enforce voting rights.[54] The next year, Congress passed the Civil Rights Act of 1957.[55] It was a first step towards enforcing the 15th Amendment, which in 1870 had guaranteed the right of citizens to vote regardless of "race, color or previous condition of servitude."[56] For decades millions of African-Americans had been denied that right through intimidation, poll taxes, literacy tests, and other discriminatory tactics.

The 1957 Act, the first civil rights legislation signed in nearly a century, paved the way for the broader civil and voting rights acts under President Lyndon Johnson less than a decade later. President Eisenhower may personally have been a segregationist, but no President between Abraham Lincoln and Lyndon Johnson, except for Ulysses S. Grant who enforced Reconstruction and Black voting rights, did more to advance African-American civil rights.

The Interstate Highway System

What has been called "greatest public-works program in the history of the world" was quietly signed into law from a hospital room on June 29, 1956. That day, President Eisenhower, recovering at Walter Reed Army Medical

Center after abdominal surgery, signed the Federal-Aid Highway Act of 1956. The Act authorized a system of superhighways that would extend 41,000 miles, crisscrossing the nation from Maine to California.

Eisenhower must have felt deeply satisfied. His interest in American roads began in 1919. That year, as a young Army officer, Eisenhower participated in a cross-country convoy conducted by the Army Motor Transport Corp to assess America's road system. It was tortuously slow going. After departing Washington, the eighty-two-truck convoy covered just forty-six miles the first day. The pace did not get much better. Over the sixty-day trip, the convoy averaged fifty-two miles a day. "Absence of any effort at maintenance has resulted in roads of such rough nature as to be very difficult of negotiating," Eisenhower dryly reported. "In such cases, it seems evident that a very small amount of money spent at the proper time would have kept the road[s] in good condition."[57] Eisenhower wrote glowingly, though, about the custom-designed $40,000 Militor Tractor Truck which pulled the Army vehicles out of ditches, mud holes, and, occasionally, quicksand.[58]

Years later, in 1945 as American troops entered Germany, Eisenhower was impressed by the German autobahns. German autobahn construction began in the nineteen-twenties, but by 1933, when the Nazis came to power, only a few hundred miles of road had been completed. Hitler quickly embraced the concept as his own and elevated autobahn construction to a top national priority, putting over 100,000 Germans back to work. By 1941, when the war interrupted construction, 2,400 miles had been completed. The German autobahns were unparalleled in the world, featuring four lanes, sweeping curves, broad medians, comfortable rest stops, and limited access. Rather than advertising, notice boards alerted travelers to waiting phone messages.[59]

"The old convoy had started me thinking about good, two-lane highways," Eisenhower later wrote. "But Germany had made me see the wisdom of broader ribbons across the land."[60] A decade after admiring the German autobahns, Eisenhower's presidency would result in an American highway system unsurpassed worldwide.

In 1954, shortly after signing the Korean Armistice, Eisenhower proposed spending $50 billion ($480 billion in 2020 dollars) to construct the Interstate Highway System.[61] The cost was massive. The total federal budget that year was only $71 billion.

Funding wasn't the only issue. Eisenhower's more radical opponents claimed his national highway system was another case of "creeping socialism,"[62] a denunciation heavily used during the Cold War. In 1952, Truman's national healthcare plan was defeated after being labeled "socialized medicine." In 1955, partisan politicians argued against a free polio vaccine available to all children as a "back-door" to socialized medicine.[63] (Polio killed 3,145 children in 1955 and crippled many thousands more.)

Eisenhower, as he had Senator McCarthy, out-smarted the Cold War fear mongers. This time with a simple name change. The highway system would be renamed the National System of Interstate *and Defense* Highways. The new highways would not only provide civilian transportation but would also be essential to evacuate cities and move military convoys during an atomic war.

That left the issue of how to pay for the new highways. Eisenhower insisted that the highway program be "pay-as-you-go" and not contribute to budget deficits. This meant increasing fuel, tire, and other vehicle-related taxes—tax increases the automobile, oil, and trucking industries adamantly opposed.

The highway lobby had, for years, petitioned Congress to eliminate vehicle-related taxes and fund highway construction from general taxation sources, claiming that everybody benefited from better roads.[64] A gasoline tax increase was unthinkable. To make the point, one American Trucking Association campaign parked a tractor-trailer outside the Capitol covered with dollar bills. A large sign on the trailer proclaimed, "Dollars bills both sides of this trailer show federal and state taxes *now* paid on the average vehicle this size and type—total $4,480."[65] That week truckers sent nearly 100,000 telegrams to members of Congress claiming a tax increase would be ruinous to the trucking industry and cost thousands of jobs.

Ultimately, a compromise was reached to increase federal gasoline taxes from two cents to three cents a gallon ($0.285 in 2020 dollars). These taxes would be deposited into a Highway Trust Fund to assure they were spent on highways and not diverted for other purposes.

Once the tax issue was resolved, the legislation flew through Congress. Six weeks later, on August 13, 1956, work began on the first stretch of road near St. Louis, Missouri. When Eisenhower left office four years later, 10,440 miles of Interstate Highway had been completed at a cost of approximately $10 billion—nearly $1.0 million a mile.[66] The final segment of the original highway plan wasn't completed until 1992 when I-70 opened through Glenwood Canyon, Colorado.[67]

The Interstate Highway System changed America. Contrary to the highway lobby's grim predictions, the automobile, trucking, and oil industries thrived after the Highway Act was passed. Rather than the trucking industry being driven out of business, the new superhighways fueled explosive growth: fifteen-fold from 1956 through 2006.[68]

Unlike 1956, the American Trucking Association today supports higher fuel taxes. "Higher federal fuel taxes are the best way to fund repairs of crumbling roads and bridges that cost the trucking industry billions of dollars a year in lost productivity," according to Chris Spear, chief executive of the American Trucking Association.[69]

Eisenhower and the "Old Guard"

Eisenhower had never held elected office before his presidency. Consequently, with one exception, his original cabinet was staffed with successful businessmen rather than politicians. The exception was the Secretary of Labor, Martin Durkin, formerly President of the Plumbers and Steamfitter's Union. One pundit described Eisenhower's cabinet as "nine millionaires and a plumber." They must have liked working for Eisenhower; seven of his original ten cabinet members stayed four years or more.

With little interest in politics, Eisenhower refused to join a political party before his run for President. Once elected, he was amused by what he called the "Old Guard"; politicians who despised Franklin Roosevelt and his New Deal programs. Writing to his brother in 1954, Eisenhower was clear in his feelings for what he considered regressive politicians and their rich backers:

Should any political party attempt to abolish social security, unemployment insurance, and eliminate labor laws and farm programs, you would not hear of that party again in our political history. There is a tiny splinter group, of course, that believes you can do these things. Among them are H. L. Hunt (you possibly know his background), a few other Texas oil millionaires, and an occasional politician or businessman from other areas. Their number is negligible and they are stupid.[70]

Caught between his party's Old Guard and his own beliefs, Eisenhower strived to find "a middle way between untrammeled freedom of the individual and the demands for the welfare of the whole Nation"[71] as he described his governing approach in his first State of the Union Message to Congress. In this, Eisenhower was echoing Abraham Lincoln who, a century earlier, had written, "Why, then, should we have government? Why not each individual take to himself the whole fruit of his labor, without having any of it taxed away. . . . The legitimate object of government is to do for the people what needs to be done, but which they cannot, by individual effort, do at all, or do so well, for themselves."[72]

So rather than appease party ideologues by cutting Roosevelt's New Deal programs, Eisenhower extended the programs he considered beneficial. Two weeks after taking office, Eisenhower moved to expand Social Security. "The provisions of the old-age and survivors insurance law," Eisenhower advised Congress, "should promptly be extended to cover millions of citizens who have been left out of the social security system."[73] Eisenhower increased Social Security coverage and benefits for millions of the self-employed, for farmers and domestic workers as well as dependents of existing beneficiaries, groups not covered by the original law. All of this was expensive. Human resource spending increased significantly under Eisenhower, from 3.3 percent of GDP in 1952 to 4.9 percent in 1960.[74]

To manage the nation's growing social programs, Eisenhower established the Department of Health, Education, and Welfare (HEW), the first new cabinet-level department since the Department of Labor was established in 1913. HEW grew quickly, so quickly that the department became a symbol for bloated, over-reaching government. President Nixon would later disband the department in 1979, replacing it with two separate departments:

The Department of Health and Human Services and the Department of Education.

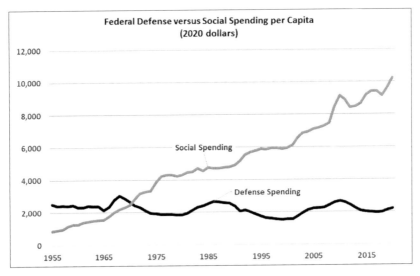

Federal Defense versus Social Spending per Capita (2020 dollars)

Defense spending per capita has remained flat since the mid-nineteen-fifties. Today, social spending dominates the federal budget.

WHITE HOUSE OFFICE OF MANAGEMENT AND BUDGET

In 1956, Eisenhower once again defied the Old Guard when he raised the minimum wage from $0.75 to $1.00, increased the number of establishments subject to the minimum wage, and added 300 additional investigators to enforce the law. An estimated 2.1 million workers benefited from the wage and coverage increases. The National Association of Manufacturers, the U.S. Chamber of Commerce, and other business organizations resisted the minimum wage increase, claiming it would increase unemployment and inflation.[75] They were wrong. Employment growth remained unchanged during the five years after the increase. Inflation, rather than rising as predicted, fell to 2.0 percent after averaging 2.2 percent during the preceding years.[76]

But Eisenhower's domestic policies could be harsh at times. In 1954, Eisenhower instituted "Operation Wetback" ("Wetback" was a disparaging term for Mexicans who entered the United States illegally by swimming across the Rio Grande River.). The operation used military tactics to round up and deport an estimated 1.3 million Mexicans. These people were largely workers who had been invited into the United States as part of the Bracero

(Spanish for "laborer") program established during World War II. Mexico, not wishing to enter the war, provided the United States temporary laborers rather than military support. American farmers quickly became dependent on the hard-working, and low-wage, men and women from south of the border. After the war, Washington turned a blind eye to the illegal workers who failed to return to Mexico. By the early nineteen-fifties, however, Mexico was suffering from its own labor shortages and demanded the laborers be returned. Eisenhower complied, but the deportation was considered a failure. Although over a million Mexicans were deported to Mexico, many soon returned to the United States.[77]

Was Eisenhower's America Great?

Were the nineteen-fifties the golden age that many Americans consider that decade to have been? The decade was exceptional in many ways. After fighting wars in Europe, the Pacific and Korea, Americans relished the peaceful years during Eisenhower's administration. No President since has presided over a longer period of peace. The United States was respected worldwide: for the magnanimity it showed Germany and Japan, its industrial and technological leadership, its appealing culture, and its worldwide commitment to freedom. The decade also saw the admission of two new states into the Union: Alaska and Hawaii.

America prospered during the fifties. A postwar boom fueled pent-up demand for consumer goods and housing. From 1950 through 1959, real GDP grew 4.3 percent, a postwar decade only exceeded, and then only slightly, by the nineteen-sixties. The stock market boomed. The Standard & Poor's 500 stock index more than tripled, from 16.8 in 1950 to 58.1 by 1959. Much of America's growing prosperity flowed to the middle-class. The middle 60 percent of taxpayers saw their after-tax income, after inflation, increase 23 percent from $2,603 to $3,209 (1950 dollars) from 1950 through 1959. Those extra dollars went a long way when a McDonald's hamburger cost $0.15 and a Chicago steak dinner with all the trimmings was only $3.00.[78]

During the decade, automation and better-educated workers made America more productive. By 1956, eight million war veterans had taken advantage of the G.I. Bill to further their educations. Educated workers are productive workers. In 1950, one civilian worker produced $5,088 of GDP, which by 1959 had increased to $6,440, both measured in 1950 dollars. That represented a 27 percent increase, a level never again matched.

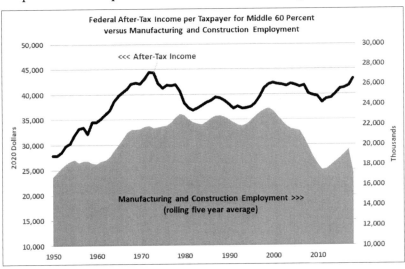

The middle-class enjoyed strong income growth for two decades after World War II. Starting after 1970, middle-class income has stagnated, partially due to the decline of well-paying, blue-collar jobs.

IRS STATISTICS OF INCOME REPORTS | U.S. BUREAU OF LABOR STATISTICS

But growing productivity had a downside. It decreased the need for workers. Consequently, employment growth during the decade averaged a mediocre 1.2 percent. Automation especially impacted agriculture, making farming more productive but reducing the need for farmworkers. Farm employment declined by 1.6 million workers during the decade.

Automation also affected factory workers as one well-known exchange recounts. Union leader Walter Reuther and Henry Ford II were touring a new state-of-the-art automobile engine factory when Ford, proudly pointing to a row of his newly installed machines, chided the labor union leader, "Walter, how are you going to get these robots to pay union dues?" Laughing, Reuther replied, "Henry, how are you going to get them to buy cars?"[79]

There was another aspect of the nineteen-fifties that made them great, at least by historical standards. America achieved these strong financial results while reducing the national debt. The debt, measured as a percentage of GDP, declined from 86 to 55 percent during the decade. For a family, a

$5,000 credit card debt is easier to repay if the family's income is $50,000 rather than $25,000. The same applies to nations.

During his first press conference, Eisenhower presented his presidential priorities.[80] He touched on farm prices, the Korean conflict, and the Soviet Union's recent hydrogen bomb test. But economists most remember his comments regarding taxes. Eisenhower acknowledged that high taxes confiscate wealth but noted that budget deficits lead to inflation that erodes wealth over time just as surely as taxes.

Roosevelt and Truman before him were from the same school regarding debt. To finance World War II, Roosevelt increased tax rates to phenomenal levels. By 1945 the maximum tax bracket was 94 percent for those earning $200,000 ($2.9 million in 2020 dollars) or more.[81] Truman kept taxes high to pay off the war debt. By 1952, the maximum marginal tax rate had declined only slightly to 91 percent.

Many hoped that Eisenhower would cut taxes upon taking office. They were disappointed. During the press conference, Eisenhower declared that reducing the debt took priority over cutting taxes:

> The objective of tax reduction is an absolutely essential one and must be attained in its proper order.... So, whether we are ready to face the job this minute or any other time, the fact is there must be balanced budgets before we are again on a safe and sound system in our economy. That means, to my mind, that we cannot afford to reduce taxes, reduce income, until we have in sight a program of expenditures that shows that the factors of income and of outgo will be balanced. Now that is just to my mind sheer necessity.... I have as much reason as anyone else to deplore high taxes. I certainly am going to work with every bit of energy I have towards their reduction.... But I merely want to point out that unless we go at it in the proper sequence, I do not believe that taxes will be lowered.[82]

We cannot afford to reduce taxes. Imagine a President today leveling with the public as Eisenhower did. High taxes didn't hurt economic growth during and after the Eisenhower years. From 1950 through 1979, a period when the highest marginal tax rate was 70 percent or higher, real GDP growth averaged four percent. From 1980 through 2019, when tax rates were much lower, real GDP growth slowed to 2.6 percent annually.

The combination of low taxes and high spending has badly damaged the nation's balance sheet. From 1950 through 1979, America's national debt fell from 86 percent of GDP to 32 percent. After 1980, the combination of low taxes and high spending caused the debt to climb to 107 percent of GDP, its highest level since 1946.

There's another measure of American greatness beyond peace and prosperity. That's the respect Americans hold for their government and its leaders.

"In the 29 months since Dwight Eisenhower moved into the White House," *Time* magazine reported on July 4, 1955, "a remarkable change has come over the nation. Blood pressure and temperature have gone down; nerve endings have healed over. The new tone could be described in a word: confidence."[83]

Americans trusted Eisenhower. He refused to cut taxes, used federal troops to enforce desegregation and told Israel, Britain, and France to get out of the Suez—all courageous policies unpopular with much of the American public. Yet no postwar President, except John Kennedy during his tragically short term, enjoyed higher job approval ratings than Eisenhower's 65 percent.[84]

During the 1956 election, the esteemed *New York Times* columnist Tom Wicker, at the time a young newspaper writer in North Carolina, intended to vote for Adlai Stevenson. After being chided by the publisher's wife, Mrs. Bill Hoyt, for not supporting Eisenhower, Wicker replied, "But Mrs. Hoyt, don't you realize that Eisenhower has had a heart attack?" Mrs. Wicker, taking a deep breath, drew herself up. "Young man," she said, "I would vote for Eisenhower if he were *dead!*"[85]

Historians, though, didn't initially think particularly well of Eisenhower. For years they considered Eisenhower an affable but bumbling caretaker who spent much of his presidency golfing and fishing, an impression reinforced by Eisenhower's vibrant successor, John Kennedy, with his young family and eloquent, inspiring speeches.

Eisenhower's greatest quality was his quiet self-assurance. In 1982, after gaining access to Eisenhower's private presidential papers, Fred Greenstein wrote *The Hidden Hand Presidency*. The book described how Eisenhower intentionally avoided the spotlight, steering policy quietly through his staff. Eisenhower's definition of leadership was simple: "Leadership consists of nothing but taking responsibility for everything that goes wrong and giving your subordinates credit for everything that goes well."[86]

John F. Kennedy

January 20, 1961 – November 22, 1963

> We choose to go to the moon. We choose to go to the moon in this decade and do the other things, not because they are easy, but because they are hard, because that goal will serve to organize and measure the best of our energies and skills.... To be sure, we are behind, and will be behind for some time in manned flight. But we do not intend to stay behind, and in this decade, we shall make up and move ahead.[1]

On October 27, 1962, Vasili Arkhipov saved millions of lives. Arkhipov was second-in-command on the Soviet submarine B-59. The sub's mission was to escort transport ships carrying nuclear missiles to Cuba. While en route, the sub was detected by a taskforce of American destroyers which forced it to submerge to evade its pursuers. B-59 was an old-style diesel submarine that could only stay submerged, at most, for seventy-two hours. By October 27, the sub had been submerged over two days and oxygen was running low. Late in the afternoon, the USS *Cony* dropped harmless practice depth charges to warn the sub to surface. What the captain of the *Cony* didn't know was that B-59 carried a fifteen-kiloton nuclear torpedo with the explosive power of the Hiroshima bomb.[2]

Exhausted and deprived of oxygen, the sub's captain believed his vessel was under attack. Unable to contact Moscow by radio, believing war had broken out, and suffering from oxygen deprivation, the captain became manic. "We're going to blast them now!" the rattled captain exclaimed. "We will die, but we will sink them all!"[3] The captain ordered the nuclear torpedo readied. Firing the torpedo would destroy not only the USS *Cony* but also the surrounding destroyers and likely B-59 itself. The attack, in the ensuing confusion, would almost certainly have triggered a nuclear response from either the United States or the Soviet Union. Once a nuclear missile struck an American or Soviet city, the military doctrine of Mutually Assured Destruction, or MAD, would almost certainly have triggered an all-out nuclear war killing millions.

Vasili Arkhipov likely saved the world from a nuclear holocaust during the Cuban Missile Crisis. Arkhipov persuaded the captain of Soviet submarine B-59 not to fire a nuclear torpedo, an action that surely would have triggered a nuclear response.
OLGA ARKHIPOVA

But B-59 never fired the horrific torpedo. Soviet Navy protocol required a unanimous vote by the captain, the political officer, and the second-in-command to launch a nuclear weapon. The captain and political officer voted to fire the torpedo, but the cool-headed second-in-command,

Vasili Arkhipov, voted against the launch. Arkhipov convinced the captain to surface. Only then did the crew realize that war had not broken out. Although surrounded by American destroyers, none had attacked. On one destroyer, a jazz band was playing an evening concert on deck.[4]

The B-59 incident remained unknown until 2002 when Soviet documents chronicling the event were declassified. During a conference discussing the incident, Arthur M. Schlesinger Jr., a member of President Kennedy's administration at the time, commented, "[The B-59 incident] was not only the most dangerous moment of the Cold War. It was the most dangerous moment in human history."[5]

The Cuban Missile Crisis

President John F. Kennedy had only been in office for eighteen months when he was challenged with the most dangerous situation faced by any President during the Cold War. On October 14, 1962, two weeks before the B-59 incident, an American U-2 spy plane had taken photos of ballistic missile sites being constructed in Cuba. For months, the CIA had been receiving intelligence from Cuban sources that indicated the Soviets were installing nuclear missiles on the Caribbean island aimed at the United States. Trucks were seen passing through Cuban villages in the dark of night, their long, cylindrical loads covered in canvas. The U-2 photos now confirmed the threat. Unless their deployment was stopped, Soviet missiles launched from Cuba would be able to reach cities on the Eastern Seaboard, from Miami to Boston, within minutes.

Kennedy must have asked himself if he was up to this new challenge. He had already failed twice confronting America's adversaries, once in Cuba and a few months later in Vienna.

Two weeks before Kennedy's inauguration, President Eisenhower had broken off diplomatic relations with Cuba. For months, the CIA had been preparing a covert plan, Operation Zapata, to invade Cuba and replace Fidel Castro with an American-friendly puppet. Two years earlier, Castro had overthrown Fulgencio Batista, Cuba's corrupt president, and was steadily moving against American interests on the island.

Zapata was one of many covert activities the CIA had proposed to undermine the new Castro regime. Operation Dirty Trick would blame Cuba for transmitting electronic interference if John Glenn's mission to orbit the earth failed. Operation Bingo created a fake attack on the U.S. Naval Base at Guantanamo Bay to justify a military invasion of Cuba. Another plan, attempted repeatedly, employed Mafia hitmen to assassinate Castro. Others were even more hare-brained, such as distributing fake photos of an obese Castro cavorting in palace-like settings with prostitutes.[6]

Kennedy had his doubts about the risky Operation Zapata, but three months after his inauguration he authorized the plan to invade Cuba after assurances from his senior generals.

The operation began on April 15, 1961 when American B-26 bombers, disguised with Cuban Air Force markings, attacked Cuban airfields. Two days later, 1,400 paramilitaries, largely composed of American-trained Cuban exiles, came ashore at the Bay of Pigs. The Cubans quickly repelled the attackers, stopping their advance at the beach. When Kennedy, attempting to conceal America's role, refused to provide further air support to the beleaguered fighters, the invasion collapsed. Castro summarily executed hundreds of the invaders. Later that year 1,100 prisoners were exchanged for $53 million ($450 million in 2020 dollars) in food and medical supplies.

It was a humiliating defeat, made worse by the clumsy effort to conceal America's role in the debacle. Kennedy took full responsibility, "There's an old saying that victory has 100 fathers and defeat is an orphan," Kennedy told Americans, "Further statements, detailed discussions, are not to conceal responsibility because I'm the responsible officer of the government..."[7] Privately, he told Ben Bradlee of the *Washington Post*, "The first advice I'm going to give my successor is to watch the generals and to avoid feeling that because they were military men their opinions on military matters were worth a damn. Those sons of bitches with all the fruit salad just sat there, nodding, saying it would work."[8]

Watching from Moscow was the Soviet Premier, Nikita Khrushchev. He and Kennedy would be attending their first summit together in less than two months. Khrushchev must have felt confident. In his mind, he and Kennedy were hardly of the same caliber. He had played a key role during

World War II in the defeat of the Nazis at Stalingrad, the turning point in the war. Kennedy had commanded a small PT boat that was sunk by a Japanese destroyer. He had won a fierce political battle to become Premier after Stalin's death. Kennedy had barely won the presidential election, even with his rich father's help. Kennedy's actions during the Bay of Pigs debacle only reinforced Khrushchev's belief that Kennedy was a young, inexperienced man who was in over his head as President.

The Vienna Summit, held June 3–4, 1961, was a disaster for Kennedy. Believing he could win over Khrushchev with his signature Kennedy charisma, Kennedy had come unprepared, then ignored his staff's warnings not to engage Khrushchev, a sixty-seven year-old committed communist, in an ideological debate. After hours were wasted debating Marxism versus Capitalism, little was accomplished. Kennedy knew he had failed. "[Khrushchev] thought that anyone who was so young and inexperienced as to get into [the Bay of Pigs mess] could be taken," Kennedy confided to James Reston of *The New York Times*. "And anyone who got into it and didn't see it through had no guts. So, he just beat the hell out of me."[9] Khrushchev had quickly sized up his opponent. "This man is very inexperienced, even immature," he told aides leaving the meeting. Two months later an emboldened Khrushchev approved the construction of the Berlin Wall.[10]

After failing in Cuba and Vienna, Kennedy now faced a far more perilous test. The U-2 photos were unmistakable proof the Soviets had become a nuclear threat in the Western Hemisphere. How could he end that threat without triggering a nuclear war?

On October 22, 1962, President Kennedy spoke on national television to inform Americans that the Soviet Union had installed nuclear missiles in Cuba "capable of striking most of the major cities in the Western Hemisphere." To stop the flow of offensive weapons, Kennedy announced that "a strict quarantine on all offensive military equipment under shipment to Cuba is being initiated. All ships of any kind bound for Cuba from whatever nation or port will, if found to contain cargoes of offensive weapons, be turned back." Finally, and most ominously, Kennedy declared the United States would "regard any nuclear missile launched from Cuba against any nation in the Western Hemisphere as an attack by the Soviet Union on the United States, requiring a full retaliatory response upon the Soviet Union."[11]

Surprisingly, Khrushchev didn't play hardball with Kennedy. Four days after Kennedy's speech, Khrushchev responded with a series of personal letters to Kennedy offering to withdraw the Soviet missiles if the United States would first, guarantee not to invade or support an invasion of Cuba and, second, withdraw missiles that the United States had installed in Turkey earlier that year. In a conciliatory gesture, Khrushchev agreed not to disclose the withdrawal of the American missiles in Turkey. "I do understand the delicacy involved for you in an open consideration of the issue of eliminating the U.S. missile bases in Turkey," Khrushchev wrote. "I take into account the complexity of this issue and I believe you are right about not wishing to publicly discuss it."[12]

Although diplomatic negotiations had begun, tensions were rapidly building and reached their peak on October 27. Early that morning, the CIA reported that all the Cuban missiles had been prepared for launch. The Air Force finalized its plan for preemptive airstrikes on the missile sites. Late that morning, the Cubans shot down an American U-2 spy plane, killing its pilot. Kennedy's staff debated whether to retaliate but chose to refrain while negotiations continued. Adding to the tension, a flotilla of Soviet transport ships was approaching the naval blockade, making a confrontation imminent. Accompanying the ships were nuclear-armed Soviet submarines. Any escalation, accidental or intentional, could trigger a response with the potential for a nuclear conflagration.

In Moscow, Khrushchev pondered a letter sent by Castro, known today as the Armageddon Letter, which urged the Soviet Union to launch a preemptive nuclear strike against the United States if Cuba was invaded. "The imperialists' aggressiveness makes them extremely dangerous," Castro wrote. "And... if they manage to carry out an invasion of Cuba... that would be the moment to eliminate this danger forever, in an act of the most legitimate self-defense. However harsh and terrible the solution..."[13]

But Khrushchev didn't intend to start a nuclear war over a small Caribbean island. Khrushchev was ready to make a deal. That night emissaries for Kennedy and Khrushchev met at, of all places, Washington's popular Yenching Palace Chinese restaurant to negotiate the final terms of an agreement.[14] For professional diplomats, apparently, even a nuclear missile agreement can be hammered out over General Tso's Chicken and rice wine.

The next day, October 28, Kennedy announced an agreement had been reached. Publicly, Kennedy agreed the United States would not invade or support an invasion of Cuba. Kennedy did not make public the secret deal to withdraw U.S. missiles from Turkey (And possibly Italy; the terms remain unclear.). Then, in a huge triumph for President Kennedy, Khrushchev announced he had ordered the withdrawal of all Soviet missiles from Cuba.[15] A day later, Khrushchev, again taking the initiative, sent Kennedy a remarkable letter:

> We have now conditions ripe for finalizing the agreement on signing a treaty on cessation of tests of thermonuclear weapons. We fully agree with regard to three types of tests or, so to say, tests in three environments. This is banning of tests in atmosphere, in outer space and under water. In this respect, we are of the same opinion and we are ready to sign an agreement.[16]

The Soviet Union and the United States had been negotiating a nuclear test ban treaty since the mid nineteen-fifties, but progress waxed and waned with Cold War tensions. The missile crisis had shown how easily the world could fall into the abyss of nuclear war and it was Khrushchev's letter that was the catalyst that restarted the treaty negotiations. Ten months later, on August 5, 1963, the Soviet Union, United Kingdom, and the United States signed the Limited Nuclear Test Ban Treaty. Within months, over 100 countries had signed the treaty.

Khrushchev must have been deeply shaken by the possibility of the missile crisis triggering a nuclear war. His letter, going well beyond proposing a test ban treaty, also proposed the United States and the Soviet Union close all military bases outside their own territories and disband the North Atlantic Treaty Organization (NATO) and the Warsaw Pact, mutual-defense pacts established by the two superpowers.

Khrushchev's proposal at détente failed, blocked by hardliners in both the Soviet Union and United States. Today, the United States maintains hundreds of military bases overseas. Russia maintains nine bases, almost all in former Soviet republics. The Warsaw Pact was disbanded in 1991, but NATO has expanded from fifteen countries in 1963 to thirty by 2020.

Kennedy's successful resolution of the Cuban Missile Crisis was his presidency's greatest success, yet from the beginning, it was Khrushchev who had taken the initiative. But as Americans saw it, President Kennedy had gone eye to eye with Khrushchev, and Khrushchev blinked. That's also how the Soviet Politburo saw it. They believed that the Soviet Union had been humiliated by the United States, especially since Khrushchev had agreed to keep secret the withdrawal of American missiles from Turkey. It was, after all, their initial installation which had provoked the Soviets to install missiles in Cuba.

Khrushchev knew Soviet elites would blame him for appearing weak. As the crisis was ending, he wrote Kennedy, "To our mutual satisfaction we maybe even sacrificed self-esteem. Apparently, there will be such scribblers who will engage in hair-splitting over our agreement, will be digging as to who made greater concessions to whom."[17]

After being humiliated by the Bay of Pigs and the Vienna Summit debacles, the Cuban Missile Crisis elevated Kennedy to the status of a world statesman. Khrushchev—who had quietly proposed the terms Kennedy eventually accepted—fared poorly. Two years later he was ousted from power by Politburo hardliners. Khrushchev left proudly, knowing his transition would be peaceful. "Could anyone have dreamed of telling Stalin," he told a colleague, "that he didn't suit us anymore and suggesting he retire? Not even a wet spot would have remained where we had been standing. Now everything is different. The fear is gone, and we can talk as equals. That's my contribution."[18]

The Rise of Fidel Castro

During the fifteen years preceding the Cuban Missile Crisis, the United States had fought communist expansionism around the world from Berlin to Vietnam. Yet, by 1962, only ninety miles off American shores, Cuba had become communist, embraced the Soviet Union, and declared the United States the "Monster of the North." How had this happened? The United

States had gone to war in 1898 to liberate Cuba from Spain. How could the United States have evolved from Cuba's liberator to its mortal enemy?

The United States temporarily acquired Cuba (and permanently Puerto Rico, Guam and, indirectly, Hawaii) during the Spanish-American War of 1898—a "splendid little war" as then Secretary of State John Hay described the conflict. As a condition for declaring war on Spain, Congress passed the Teller Amendment stipulating that the United States could not retain possession of Cuba after the war. Congress was concerned that if Cuba were to become a U.S territory, it would compete against American sugar companies since Cuban sugar would no longer be subject to high import tariffs.

The United States granted Cuba its independence on May 20, 1902, with one condition: the U.S. Senate demanded that Cuba incorporate an amendment—the Platt Amendment—into its new constitution that affirmed the right of the United States to intervene in Cuban affairs when necessary "for the preservation of Cuban independence, the maintenance of a government adequate for the protection of life, property, and individual liberty..."[19] The United States invoked that right multiple times between 1906 and 1933 when it sent in troops to quell insurrections, mediate contested presidential elections, and protect American property. America's regular interventions into their country's internal affairs fostered resentment among Cubans. For many, Cuba had traded Spanish rule for subservience to American private interests, including the American Mafia.

The most influential meeting of American mobsters since 1929 convened at Havana's Hotel Nacional on December 20, 1946. Attending were more than twenty of America's top mob bosses including Charlie "Lucky" Luciano, Meyer "Little Man" Lansky, and Vito "Don Vito" Genovese.[20] The mobsters were there to organize an international criminal empire beyond the reach of U.S. law enforcement. Cuba was ideal. Close to America, Cuba was an efficient trans-shipment point for drugs before their final delivery to mob-friendly ports in the United States and Canada. Havana's warm weather, expansive beaches and fun-loving Caribbean culture made it the perfect location for a string of mob-controlled hotels and casinos, offering world-class entertainment but also easy, and profitable, gambling, drugs and sex.

It was a productive meeting. The mobsters discussed the next *capo di tutti capi*, or boss of all bosses; divided up the Havana casino business; organized their worldwide drug trade; and dealt with the Benjamin "Bugsy" Siegel issue. Although prominently on the agenda, Siegel was not invited. Six months later he was shot dead after the mobsters voted to have him assassinated for embezzling mob money. The conference concluded Christmas Day with a massive gala featuring Frank Sinatra, who flew to Havana for the occasion along with Al Capone's cousins, Charlie, Joseph, and Rocco Fischetti.[21]

Over the next thirteen years the Mafia turned Havana into "a mistress of pleasure, the lush and opulent goddess of delights," as one travel magazine described the city.[22] Celebrities added glamour. George Raft, star of the 1933 film *Scarface*, greeted guests at the Hotel Capri. Ernest Hemingway spent afternoons drinking mojitos at the Floridita Bar. Marlon Brando hung out at the Sans Souci and the Shanghai, infamous for its live-sex acts. Decades before Las Vegas, what happened in Havana stayed in Havana— but not always. Years after it occurred, the mobster Santo Trafficante revealed how he had set-up Senators John Kennedy and George Smathers in a tryst with three young Cuban prostitutes. What the Senators didn't know was that they were being watched through a one-way mirror. Photos, if they ever existed, have never surfaced.[23]

Taking a generous cut of the Mafia's Cuban business was President Fulgencio Batista. Batista was as corrupt as his Mafia cronies. Finding himself far behind in the 1952 presidential election, Batista, with the support of the military, stopped the race and appointed himself President. Two weeks after the coup the United States recognized the illegal government. Batista had been an American sycophant for years. President Franklin Roosevelt reportedly described Batista as "a son of a bitch, but he's our son of a bitch." The U.S. diplomatic corps was more circumspect. America's Ambassador to Cuba, Arthur Gardner, reported to Washington that, "Batista had always leaned toward the United States. I don't think we ever had a better friend. It was regrettable, like all South Americans, that he was known, although I had no absolute knowledge of it, to be getting a cut... But, on the other hand, he was doing an amazing job."[24]

For the seven years Batista was in power, the United States invested heavily in Cuba. "At the beginning of 1959, American companies owned about 40 percent of the Cuban sugar land, almost all the cattle ranches, 90 percent of the mines and mineral concessions, 80 percent of the utilities, practically all the oil industry, and supplied two-thirds of Cuba's imports."[25] Economically and politically, Cuba had become an American colony. For many, that worked well. Cuba's upper and middle-classes thrived, becoming one of the most prosperous in Latin America. Havana residents enjoyed per capita incomes rivaling any in Latin America. They owned automobiles and televisions and loved American movies, music, and baseball. But a third of Cubans lived in deep, unrelenting poverty. The fortunate found back-breaking work a few months a year "on the knife," swinging a machete harvesting sugarcane. Others were often forced into the underworld of Mafia drug-dealing and prostitution. It was from these marginalized peasants that Fidel Castro would draw his earliest followers.[26]

Cuba's President Fulgencio Batista shaking hands with U.S. Under Secretary of State Sumner Welles. "He's a son of a bitch," President Roosevelt said, "but our son of a bitch." Over the years, Batista became as corrupt as his Mafia cronies.

WORLD HISTORY ARCHIVE/ALAMY

Years earlier, Castro had been an obscure young lawyer running for the Cuban Congress in 1952; the year that Batista, fearing he would lose, canceled the national elections. That day, March 10, 1952, a brash and idealistic reformer became a revolutionary.

Eighteen months later, Castro stood before a panel of Cuban judges after he and a small band of survivors had been captured during an ill-conceived raid on one of Batista's military garrisons. Castro was not pleading for clemency; he knew he faced years in prison—if not a firing squad. His four-hour plea before the patient judges could be summarized in a few words, "[Many are] now asking themselves what need the Armed Forces had to assume the tremendous historical responsibility of destroying our Constitution merely to put a group of immoral men in power, men of bad reputation, corrupt, politically degenerate beyond redemption.... How can Batista's presence in power be justified when he gained it against the will of the people and by violating the laws of the Republic through the use of treachery and force?"[27]

Castro received a fifteen-year prison sentence. In 1955, Batista, in a mistake he would forever regret, released Castro and his fellow revolutionaries, believing they were no longer a threat. He was wrong. A year later Castro, now partnered with the Argentinian revolutionary Che Guevara, resumed his guerrilla war against Batista's government. Over the next two years, the revolutionaries slowly prevailed over Batista's 30,000 troops, all supplied with the latest American military equipment. Batista was ruthless, torturing and killing thousands of civilians suspected of harboring the guerrillas. But by late 1958, with Castro's revolutionaries approaching Havana, Batista had lost the support of the Cuban people—and the United States. He and his top cronies fled Havana on New Year's Eve 1958, taking an estimated $300 million with them.[28]

For a brief period, Castro was hailed as a hero by Americans. Within days the United States recognized the new government.[29] *Time* and *Life* magazines put Castro on their covers, depicting "The Liberator's Triumphal March through an Ecstatic Island." Errol Flynn released *Cuban Rebel Girls*, shot the year before with Fidel Castro's help. Flynn played an American war correspondent reporting on Castro's revolution to overturn the corrupt Batista regime.[30] Even the taciturn television host Ed Sullivan had lauded Castro as being "in the real American tradition of George Washington" during an earlier interview in the Cuban jungle.[31]

In April 1959 Castro visited the United States on a goodwill tour where he was well received, including by a captivated crowd of 30,000 in New York's Central Park. After a standing ovation at a meeting of the American Society of Newspaper Editors, *The New York Times* reported Castro's effect was "out of another century—the century of Sam Adams and Patrick Henry and Tom Paine and Thomas Jefferson—Fidel had stirred memories, long dimmed, of a revolutionary past."[32]

But Fidel Castro was no Thomas Jefferson or George Washington—men who returned peacefully to private life after the American Revolution. Castro never restored Cuba's democratic constitution he defended so eloquently in 1953. Hundreds of Batista's supporters were executed—as were many rival revolutionaries. By mid-summer, the new regime began appropriating land from wealthy landowners to hand over to peasants. To reduce Cuba's dependency on American trade, Castro and Soviet Premier Khrushchev agreed to trade sugar for oil. When Esso and Shell refused to process Russian oil, Castro nationalized their refineries. When the United States government asked that the landowners and oil companies be provided compensation, Castro refused.[33]

The United States retaliated with increasing economic sanctions that culminated in a full trade embargo, excepting food and medicine, on October 19, 1960. By late 1960, the State Department had concluded that "breaking relations with the Cuban Government would on balance appear to be in the U. S. interest.... The Cuban Government is no longer representative of the Cuban people or of Cuban national interests, but rather of the Sino-Soviet bloc.... [Breaking diplomatic relations would] further the U. S. objective of securing a change in the Cuban Government."[34] On January 3, 1961, Eisenhower broke off diplomatic relations with Cuba. A little over three months later, on April 17, President Kennedy launched the disastrous Bay of Pigs invasion.

Nine months after the failed invasion, Castro broadcast a speech declaring Cuba a socialist state: "I am a Marxist-Leninist," Castro professed, "and I shall be a Marxist-Leninist to the end of my life.... [Our] Party must always be above individuals because the Party is going to embody, not the value of one mind, but the value of tens of thousands and hundreds of thousands of minds.... This is what the United Party of the Cuban Socialist Revolution must be!"[35]

After years of fighting communists in Europe and Asia, the United States had let one of its closest neighbors slip into communism. Over the course of sixty years, the United States had evolved from liberator to colonial overseer to an enabler of the corrupt Batista regime and, after the Bay of Pigs invasion, to a mortal enemy.

Was another outcome possible? Probably not. Since his university days, Castro had socialist leanings and, after years of fighting Batista's U.S.-backed forces, had developed a strong anti-American bias as well. Still, it was the United States, not the Soviet Union, that Castro visited on his 1959 goodwill trip. Americans embraced him and his revolution on that visit. Back in Cuba, he and Ernest Hemingway laughed together while competing in a friendly fishing competition.[36] For a few months, there was a small window where perhaps Castro's revolution and America's interests could have aligned.

But Castro made powerful enemies when he nationalized, without compensation, the landholdings, companies, and casinos owned by the Cuban elite, American businesses and the Mafia. The United States retaliated by imposing trade embargoes, breaking diplomatic relations, and finally, attempting to invade Cuba. The window had closed.

Castro fought a revolution to overthrow a corrupt regime. Even Kennedy, humiliated by Castro, believed the Cuban Revolution was justified. Shortly before his death, Kennedy told *The New Republic*:

> I believe that there is no country in the world including any and all the countries under colonial domination, where economic colonization, humiliation and exploitation were worse than in Cuba, in part owing to my country's policies during the Batista regime. I approved the proclamation which Fidel Castro made in the Sierra Maestra, when he justifiably called for justice and especially yearned

to rid Cuba of corruption. I will even go further: to some extent it is as though Batista was the incarnation of a number of sins on the part of the United States. Now we shall have to pay for those sins.[37]

For sixty years, the stubborn policies of Cuba and the United States have failed both countries. The Cuban economy under communism stagnated. Cuba's per capita income, once one of the highest in Latin America, has fallen far below other Latin American countries. American boycotts have also failed. Cuba, just miles off American shores, remains defiantly communist.

The Minimum Wage Debate

One of President Kennedy's legislative priorities was an increase in the minimum wage. Kennedy started his minimum wage campaign while still a senator when he introduced the legislation in August 1960. He used a hypothetical family of four working in the New York garment district to illustrate the plight of the working poor, showing how a father working full-time and the mother half-time would only earn $60.00 a week at the $1.00 per hour minimum wage. That put the family well under the $74.00 weekly income the New York City Department of Welfare regarded as the poverty level for a family of four.[38]

How all the countervailing effects ultimately impact the overall economy has been debated since Roosevelt introduced the first minimum wage in 1938 as part of the Fair Labor Standards Act. The Act established forty hours as the standard workweek, abolished child labor and set the first federal minimum wage at twenty-five cents per hour. In a 1937 speech, "A Fair Day's Pay for a Fair Day's Work," Roosevelt declared he intended the minimum wage to "mean more than a bare subsistence level. I mean the wages of a decent living."[39]

But the issue is complicated. A small employer in a competitive market—a garment manufacturer, for example—may have difficulty raising wage rates. That could lead to firing entry-level workers, or even the company's failure. A larger employer with more market power could raise wages but at the cost of lower profits or higher prices. So, not surprisingly, businesses, both small and large, are often opposed to raising the minimum wage. (But not always. Businesses that provide automation to replace work-ers like high wages. It helps sell the products they make to replace workers. Otis Elevator, for example, was hardly altruistic during the nineteen-six-ties when it promoted higher minimum wages as it began replacing white-gloved elevator operators with automated elevators.[40])

Kennedy cited a Department of Labor study that analysed President Ei-senhower's 1955 minimum wage increase and concluded that:

> The Department found that the increase from 75 cents to $1.00 an hour did not substantially affect any of the standard statistical se-ries measuring trends in hours of work, employment, or consumer prices. The impact was too small to be discernible in relation to over-all economic activity.... In short, the Labor Department's study fully supports the conclusion that the 1955 minimum wage increase did not result in any substantial changes for the Nation in either price levels or employment.[41]

From 1963 through 1965, Kennedy's legislation increased the minimum wage from $1.00 to $1.25. The increase did not result in layoffs among low-er-income workers as many predicted. Based on income tax filings during those years, jobs for workers making less than $1,000 a year ($8,500 in 2020 dollars), rather than falling, increased from 6.9 million to 7.4 mil-lion, a growth rate exceeding that of the overall workforce. Nor did the wage increases hurt business. Pre-tax corporate profits climbed from $60.3 to $78.4 million during those same years.

Still, there is evidence that increases in the minimum wage may have a short-term economic impact. From 1938 through 2009 the minimum wage increased twenty-two times. During those years, civilian employment growth averaged 1.2 percent versus 1.8 percent during the years of no wage increase Similarly, real GDP growth averaged 2.3 percent during the years the wage increased versus 3.3 percent otherwise. Are increases in the min-imum wage responsible for these reductions? And if they are, how should their impact be weighed against the benefit of higher wages for Ameri-ca's lowest-paid workers? Questions economists have debated for nearly a century.

A Reluctant Civil Rights Warrior

From his first day in office, President Kennedy focused on fighting global communism: in Cuba, in Berlin, Laos, and Vietnam. Fighting the threat of communism was a cause all patriotic Americans could support. What American could disagree with Kennedy's noble promise during his inauguration to "let every nation know, whether it wishes us well or ill, that we shall pay any price, bear any burden, meet any hardship, support any friend, oppose any foe to assure the survival and the success of liberty?"[42]

Yet in his inaugural address, Kennedy never mentioned a cause for personal liberty much closer to home: African-American civil rights. That would change. By 1961 civil rights was quickly becoming the nation's foremost domestic issue.

Although the civil-rights movement had been simmering for years, it was Rosa Parks' refusal to give up her bus seat to white riders on December 1, 1955 that ignited the modern civil rights movement. Two years later, President Eisenhower desegregated Little Rock Central High School when he sent in federal troops to instill order. By 1961 African-Americans were protesting not only the slow desegregation of schools, but also the continued segregation of lunch counters, theaters, swimming pools, and other public facilities.

For over two years, Kennedy was cautious in his public support for African-American rights. While sympathetic to the plight of African-Americans, he also knew that outright support would cost him politically in the South. Kennedy had been elected with a tiny popular vote margin and needed the support of Southern senators to pass legislation, as well as Southern voters if he expected to be reelected in 1964. So, Kennedy, rather than speaking out forcefully and proposing new civil rights legislation, took a restrained approach, enforcing existing laws, retaining a few Black officials in his administration, submitting amicus court briefs supporting civil rights, and appointing Thurgood Marshall, the plaintiff attorney in the landmark *Brown v. Board of Education* Supreme Court case, to a federal judgeship. In 1967, President Johnson appointed Marshall to the Supreme Court, the court's first African-American justice.

Kennedy would eventually find it impossible to continue his low-key approach to civil rights. Racial unrest was becoming undeniable, both domestically and internationally. In 1961, "Freedom Riders," protesting the continued illegal segregation of interstate buses were attacked by violent mobs. Images of burning buses and battered and bleeding Freedom Riders spread across the world. In 1962, thousands protested when James Meredith, an eight-year Air Force veteran, entered the University of Mississippi as the school's first African-American student. Hundreds were injured and a French journalist, Paul Guihard, was killed in the crossfire after Kennedy sent in 5,000 federal troops to restore order. On April 16, 1963, Dr. Martin Luther King was arrested in Birmingham, Alabama, a city King called the most segregated in America. While King was in jail, eight white clergymen wrote a newspaper editorial entitled "A Call for Unity,"[43] condemning protests "directed and led in part by outsiders." King responded with his "Letter from a Birmingham City Jail." King's letter became the manifesto of the non-violent civil rights movement. King argued that non-violent civil disobedience to unjust laws was justified:

> There are just and there are unjust laws. . . . Any law that uplifts human personality is just. Any law that degrades human personality is unjust. All segregation statutes are unjust because segregation distorts the soul and damages the personality. It gives the segregator a false sense of superiority, and the segregated a false sense of inferiority. . . . I submit that an individual who breaks a law that conscience tells him is unjust, and willingly accepts the penalty by staying in jail to arouse the conscience of the community over its injustice, is in reality expressing the very highest respect for law.[44]

Dr. King's strategy of non-violent civil disobedience mirrored Mahatma Gandhi's non-violent campaign against British rule in India. That campaign was instrumental in achieving India's independence in 1947.[45] But King's followers found it difficult at times to turn the other cheek. On May 11, 1963, bombs almost certainly planted by the Ku Klux Klan exploded in the Birmingham motel where King had been staying and also at the Baptist parsonage of King's brother, A.D. King. Riots erupted with African-Americans burning businesses and attacking the police. The next month on June

11, Alabama Governor George Wallace, who had promised "segregation now, segregation tomorrow and segregation forever,"[46] blocked the entrance of the first two African-American students to the University of Alabama. President Kennedy called in the National Guard to assure their safe admittance.

That night Kennedy addressed the nation on television. He had little choice. Racial unrest had become too toxic politically to ignore. Domestically, the injustice of segregation and the specter of race riots divided the nation. Internationally, photos and newsreels flashed around the world depicting Americans being violently subdued by mounted police, armored cars, snarling dogs, and fire-hoses. It was the height of the Cold War and American racial turmoil had handed the Soviet Union a public relations windfall. A June 1963 State Department memo stated that "Soviet broadcasting on the current U.S. racial crisis has recently attained a level seven times that of the Mississippi crisis last autumn. Recurrent themes in the Soviet treatment have been: that racism is inevitable in the capitalist system [due to the need for cheap labor]; that the federal government is actually supporting the racists by its general inertia...; that the hypocrisy of U.S. claims to leadership of the free world is laid bare."[47]

President Kennedy's speech the evening of June 11 had been written hastily that day, amid the stand-off with Governor Wallace. With little time for revision, it was heartfelt, compelling, and one of Kennedy's best:

> Every American ought to have the right to be treated as he would wish to be treated, as one would wish his children to be treated. . . . if, in short, he cannot enjoy the full and free life which all of us want, then who among us would be content to have the color of his skin changed and stand in his place? Who among us would then be content with the counsels of patience and delay?[48]

Kennedy's speech was eloquent, but also shrewd. Knowing many Southerners would oppose civil rights legislation, Kennedy declared that addressing America's racial injustices was necessary in the fight against global communism:

> We preach freedom around the world, and we mean it, and we cherish our freedom here at home, but are we to say to the world, and

much more importantly, to each other that this is the land of the free except for the Negroes?[49]

It was a compelling argument. How could the United States credibly claim the Soviet Union was unjust when newsreels around the world showed America's discrimination and brutalization against Blacks, their fellow Americans?

Many African-Americans were ecstatic over Kennedy's speech. Dr. Martin Luther King's response was typical. After watching the speech on television with fellow pastor Walter Fauntroy, King jumped up exclaiming: "Walter, can you believe that white man not only stepped up to the plate, he hit it over the fence!" That evening King sent a telegram to the White House congratulating the President and declaring his speech "one of the most eloquent, profound and unequivocal pleas for justice and freedom of all men ever made by any President."[50]

Dr. Martin Luther King's speech, "I Have a Dream," was one of the most powerful speeches of the twentieth century. Like Kennedy, King died from an assassin's bullet.
EVERETT COLLECTION HISTORICAL/ALAMY

Four hours after Kennedy's speech Medgar Evers, a NAACP civil rights activist, was shot in his driveway. Rushed to the Jackson, Mississippi hospital, Evers was initially refused entry to the all-white facility. With Evers near death, the hospital relented and admitted him, where he died shortly afterward. But through his death, Evers played a small, yet tragically ironic role in the march of Black emancipation: Evers was the first African-American to be admitted to an all-white hospital in Mississippi.

Other murders would soon follow. On September 15, four African-American girls, aged eleven to fourteen years, died when a powerful bomb exploded in their Birmingham, Alabama church. Hours later, two Black teenagers were killed in the resulting tumult, one by the Birmingham police, the other by white teenagers. *The New York Times* reported the murders simply fulfilled the wish of Governor George Wallace, who a few days earlier proclaimed "a few first-class funerals" were needed to settle the racial conflict.[51]

Even in the face of these violent crimes, African-American leaders seldom wavered from their advocacy of non-violent protest. During the funeral of Carole Robertson, one of the young church bombing victims, the Reverend C.E. Thomas told the mourners, "The greatest tribute you can pay to Carole is to be calm, be loving, be kind, be innocent."[52]

A month earlier, Dr. King had given a televised speech before nearly a quarter-million people on the Washington Mall. "I have a dream," he told Americans, "that my four little children will one day live in a nation where they will not be judged by the color of their skin but by the content of their character." He urged non-violence and that people "not seek to satisfy our thirst for freedom by drinking from the cup of bitterness and hatred. We must forever conduct our struggle on the high plane of dignity and discipline. We must not allow our creative protest to degenerate into physical violence."[53]

Kennedy sent his civil rights bill to Congress shortly after his June 11, 1963 speech. In 1954 the Supreme Court had ruled racial segregation in schools was unconstitutional. Kennedy's bill went much further, banning segregation on the grounds of race, religion, or national origin at all places of public accommodation, including courthouses, parks, restaurants, theaters, sports arenas, and hotels. No longer could Blacks and other minorities be denied service based on their skin color. The act also barred race, religion, national origin and gender discrimination by employers and labor unions.[54] The bill immediately stalled in Congress. It would take another year and all the persuasive legislative skills of President Johnson after Kennedy's assassination to achieve its passage. One of the winning votes was cast by Senator Clair Engle. Engle, paralyzed by brain cancer and too ill even to speak, overruled his doctors and demanded to be brought to the Senate floor. When the clerk read his name, "Mr. Engle, Aye or Nay?" Engle raised his hand to his eye, thereby casting a vote for "aye."[55]

A Drugged and Fitful Sleep

During his 1960 campaign, Kennedy promised to "get America moving again." This wasn't an empty campaign slogan. For most of the nineteen-fifties the economy had boomed. From 1950 through 1957, middle-class income after taxes and inflation grew a robust three percent annually. By 1957, a middle-class American had 20 percent more take-home pay than in 1950. But the country fell into recession in 1957, recovered briefly, only to fall back into recession in early 1960. The American economy, Kennedy claimed, had been in "years of drugged and fitful sleep."[56]

Kennedy, like Roosevelt thirty years earlier, believed government had a vital role to play in managing economic cycles. To stimulate economic growth during recessions, he believed Washington should cut taxes and increase spending, increasing deficits. During periods of strong growth, Washington should raise taxes and decrease spending, generating surpluses. Ideally, the surpluses and deficits would balance over time. That's the essence of Keynesian economics.

Real GDP grew a healthy three percent annually during Eisenhower's presidency. It could have grown faster, but Eisenhower insisted on paying down the massive debt from World War II by keeping taxes high. It was a reasonable trade-off. The national debt declined from 71 percent of GDP in 1952 to 53 percent when Eisenhower left office in 1960.

To arouse the nation from its "drugged and fitful sleep," Kennedy immediately increased federal spending from $92.2 billion during Eisenhower's last year to $97.7 billion in 1961, then $106.8 in 1962, and $111.3 billion in 1963. Deficits soared, averaging $5.1 billion annually, but so did the economy. During Kennedy's three years, real GDP grew an average of 4.4 percent annually, up from 2.9 percent during Eisenhower's final three years in office. In 1962, real GDP growth hit a record 6.1 percent, raising concerns that the overheated economy would kick off a wage-price inflation spiral. When business is booming, workers demand higher pay. Companies then raise prices to compensate for the higher wages, which results in renewed demand for even higher wages.

When the United Steelworkers threatened to strike for increased pay, Kennedy invited David McDonald, the union president, and Roger Blough, the CEO of US Steel, to the Oval Office. Kennedy proposed the union limit its wage demands to three percent or less, an increase consistent with productivity gains, and hence non-inflationary. Kennedy then proposed that US Steel need not increase its prices since the wage increase was limited to productivity gains and hence would not affect its profits. Blough agreed.[57] After polling their members, the United Steelworkers agreed to a nominal 2.5 percent increase, all to be paid in higher benefits rather than wages. But a week later, US Steel raised its steel price by six dollars per ton. Seven major steel producers did the same the next day. Kennedy was furious. "My father always told me that all businessmen were sons of bitches," Kennedy fumed upon hearing the news.[58]

Calling a press conference, Kennedy accused the steel companies of acting in "wholly unjustifiable and irresponsible defiance of the public interest," pursuing only "private power and profit" while ignoring the "interests of 185 million Americans... in ruthless disregard of their public responsibilities."[59]

Within days the steel companies capitulated and rolled back their price increases. Kennedy had won a Pyrrhic victory. Popular with the public, Kennedy's humbling of US Steel cost him goodwill within the business community. Nor did the stock market like Kennedy's tough-on-business stance. After climbing 20 percent since Kennedy's inauguration, the Standard and Poor's 500 stock index fell steeply, losing its prior gains within weeks.[60] And for naught. Over the next eighteen months, US Steel quietly increased prices. Kennedy said nothing.

Kennedy's relations with the business community improved on December 14, 1962 when he spoke to the Economic Club of New York. During his speech, Kennedy confirmed his plans for a major tax cut in the coming year. Echoing Treasury Secretary Andrew Mellon's plea to Congress forty years earlier, Kennedy lectured:

> It is a paradoxical truth that tax rates are too high today and tax revenues are too low and the soundest way to raise the revenues in the long run is to cut the rates now.... Only full employment can balance the budget, and tax reduction can pave the way to that employment. The purpose of cutting taxes now is not to incur a budget deficit, but to achieve the more prosperous, expanding economy which can bring a budget surplus.[61]

Kennedy saw tax cuts as a means for achieving full employment, and full employment as the only means of balancing the budget. His stimulus spending had spurred the economy, with real GDP growth exceeding six percent in 1962, but at the cost of the largest deficits since World War II. A month later, during his State of the Union address to Congress, Kennedy made tax cuts his administration's top priority:

> The mere absence of recession is not growth.... Our obsolete tax system exerts too heavy a drag on private purchasing power, profits, and employment.... It invites recurrent recessions, depresses our federal revenues, and causes chronic budget deficits.... I am convinced that the enactment this year of tax reduction and tax reform overshadows all other domestic problems in this Congress.[62]

Congress was skeptical. Would cutting taxes actually increase tax revenues? The debate was still ongoing when Kennedy was assassinated on November 22, 1963. Riding a wave of sympathy for the fallen President, Congress approved a version of Kennedy's tax plan in early 1964, three months after his assassination.[63] Through the remainder of the decade, the economy grew an average of five percent annually, a postwar record.

The Kennedy Legacy

It was on a bright, sunny day in Dallas, Texas, November 22, 1963, when President Kennedy became the fourth American President to die by assassination. Three had preceded him: Abraham Lincoln in 1865, shot by a Confederate sympathizer; John Garfield in 1881, shot by an unbalanced assassin; and William McKinley in 1901, shot by a political anarchist.[64]

The motivations of Kennedy's assassin, Lee Harvey Oswald, were never determined. Scores of conspiracy theories circulated over the years. The Mafia, the CIA, Castro, even Vice President Johnson, have all been blamed. But no credible evidence has ever emerged suggesting that the assassin was anyone other than the lone Oswald.

It was a beautiful late autumn day in Dallas, Texas when President Kennedy was assassinated on November 22, 1963 by a sniper's bullet while riding in a presidential motorcade.   WALT CISCO / DALLAS MORNING NEWS

Kennedy was immensely popular during his short presidency, enjoying the highest average approval ratings, 70.1 percent, of the fourteen presidents Gallup has ranked since 1938. Only Dwight Eisenhower came close at 65 percent. Recent presidents hardly compare: George H.W. Bush at

60.9 percent, Clinton at 55.1 percent, Reagan at 52.8 percent, George W. Bush at 49.4 percent, Obama at 47.9 percent and Trump at 41.1 percent.[65]

WANTED

FOR

TREASON

THIS MAN is wanted for treasonous activities against the United States:

1. Betraying the Constitution (which he swore to uphold):
He is turning the sovereignty of the U.S. over to the communist controlled United Nations.
He is betraying our friends (Cuba, Katanga, Portugal) and befriending our enemies (Russia, Yugoslavia, Poland).

2. He has been WRONG on innumerable issues affecting the security of the U.S. (United Nations-Berlin wall-Missle removal-Cuba-Wheat deals-Test Ban Treaty, etc.)

3. He has been lax in enforcing Communist Registration laws.

4. He has given support and encouragement to the Communist inspired racial riots.

5. He has illegally invaded a sovereign State with federal troops.

6. He has consistantly appointed Anti-Christians to Federal office.
Upholds the Supreme Court in its Anti-Christian rulings.
Aliens and known Communists abound in Federal offices.

7. He has been caught in fantastic LIES to the American people (including personal ones like his previous marraige and divorce).

A handbill circulated by supporters of the John Birch Society shortly before President Kennedy's November 22, 1963 visit to Dallas accused Kennedy of being soft on communism among other offenses.   WIKIMEDIA COMMONS

But President Kennedy was also hated: by Cuban exiles for the failed Bay of Pigs invasion, by Protestant religious zealots for Kennedy's Catholicism, and by racial bigots for Kennedy's support of civil rights. Just days before his fatal visit to Dallas, thousands of fliers were circulated in the city with the headline, "Wanted for Treason." The flier accused Kennedy of "Betraying the Constitution [by] turning sovereignty of the U.S. over to the communist-controlled United Nations... [giving] support and encouragement to the Communist-inspired racial riots... illegally [invading] a sovereign state with federal troops."[66]

Sadly, a small minority of Americans hated Kennedy far more than did America's enemies. Kennedy and Khrushchev grew to respect and even like each other. The two exchanged 120 personal communications which grew increasingly warm and cordial over time.[67] Both men strived for mutual understanding and peace. Diplomatic communications are highly nuanced but reading the dispatches it's hard not to be struck by the warmth, personal courtesy, and humility the two world leaders showed each other.

Shortly before Kennedy's death, Khrushchev wrote Kennedy suggesting the possibility of ending the Cold War:

> The Soviet Government considered that things had recently taken a turn for the better in the international situation and in relations between the Soviet Union and the United States. With the signing of the Test Ban Treaty and the exchange of views with Secretary Rusk, there had developed a relaxation of tension and the prerequisite for the settlement of other questions had been established. This could lead to a real turning point and the end of the Cold War.[68]

After Kennedy's death, it would be another twenty years before Cold War tensions began to thaw, warmed by the personal relationship between President Reagan and Soviet Premier Mikhail Gorbachev. Had Kennedy lived, he and Khrushchev might have ended the Cold War much sooner.

Like President Warren G. Harding who was beloved while in office, Kennedy's legacy was marred when his sexual affairs while in the White House became public. In 1977, Judith Exner claimed she had an abortion after becoming pregnant with Kennedy's child. Ben Bradlee, the executive editor of the *Washington Post,* disclosed his sister-in-law, Mary Pinchot Meyer, had confided to her diary her affair with Kennedy. White House interns Mimi Alford, Jill Cowan, and Priscilla Wear were all said to have cavorted with the President. And Marilyn Monroe, who surely sang the sultriest *Happy Birthday* ever rendered in the White House after she and the President had allegedly spent a weekend tucked away in Bing Crosby's Palm Springs home.[69]

John Kennedy led a charmed, but, ultimately, tragic life. Scion of a wealthy Boston family, war hero, U.S. Senator, Pulitzer Prize winning author, and America's youngest elected President, Kennedy was America's fourth president to be assassinated.

PICTORIAL PRESS LTD/ALAMY

Today, President Kennedy is often remembered for his youthful good looks, his glamorous wife, charming children, and wry humor. Few Presidents better deflated their political opponent than Kennedy when, during the 1960 election, Kennedy claimed to read a telegram from his father: "Don't buy a single vote more than necessary. I'll be damned if I'm going to pay for a landslide."[70]

Kennedy had character. He accepted responsibility after the Bay of Pigs fiasco, kept a cool head during the Cuban Missile Crisis, and defied the

Soviets in Berlin when he declared "Ich bin ein Berliner." (Poor German for I am a Berliner.)

Kennedy's soaring rhetoric stirred patriotism when he implored during his inauguration, "Ask not what your country can do for you, ask what you can do for your country."[71]

Few Presidents better challenged Americans to greatness than Kennedy when he declared, "We choose to go to the moon. We choose to go to the moon in this decade and do the other things, not because they are easy, but because they are hard."[72]

And no President better suggested Americans explore their conscience when Kennedy asked:

> If an American, because his skin is dark... cannot enjoy the full and free life which all of us want, then who among us would be content to have the color of his skin changed and stand in his place? Who among us would then be content with the counsels of patience and delay?[73]

Made in United States
North Haven, CT
03 July 2023

38534723R00388